WEBER'S BIG BOOK OF GRILLING™

BY JAMIE PURVIANCE
AND SANDRA S. McRAE

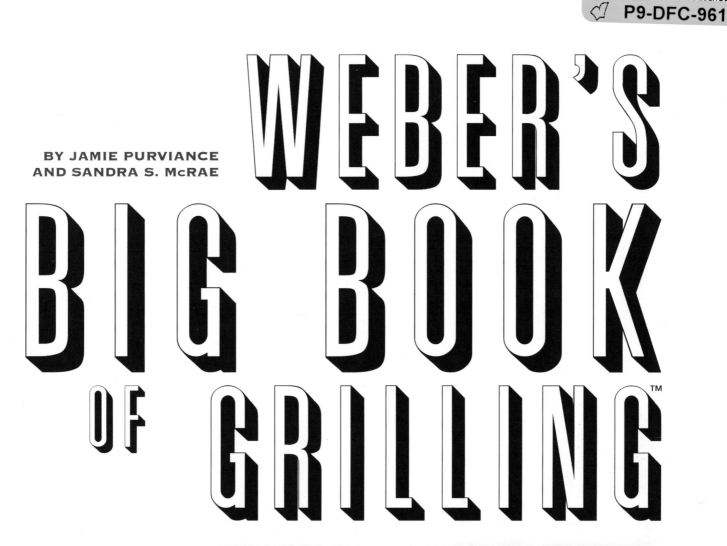

PHOTOGRAPHS BY TIM TURNER   FOREWORD BY AL ROKER

CHRONICLE BOOKS

SAN FRANCISCO

EDITORIAL TEAM

EDITORS: MARSHA CAPEN, CHRISTINA SCHROEDER
WRITERS: JAMIE PURVIANCE, SANDRA S. MCRAE
PHOTOGRAPHER: TIM TURNER
FOOD STYLIST: LYNN GAGNÉ
ASSISTANT FOOD STYLIST: CINDY MELIN
BOOK DESIGN CONCEPT: & WOJDYLA
PROP STYLIST: RENÉE MILLER
PHOTO ASSISTANTS: ROD LAFLEUR, BART WITOWSKI, JOSH SEARS
COVER DESIGN: BOB AUFULDISH
CONTRIBUTORS: JOHN CARROLL; RUSSELL CRONKHITE; HEIDI CUSICK;
   MATT DELANEY; RON DESANTIS; EDWINA GADSBY; LYNN GAGNÉ;
   LINDA GASSENHEIMER; MIKE KEMPSTER SR.; BRUCE J.A. KERR, M.D.;
   AL ROKER; MARIE SIMMONS; FRITZ SONNENSCHMIDT; TIM TURNER;
   MARYANA VOLLSTEDT; RANDY WAIDNER; KEN WINCHESTER
RECIPE TESTERS: CATHERINE ALIOTO, EDNA SCHLOSSER,
   BOB AND COLEEN SIMMONS

WEBER-STEPHEN PRODUCTS CO.
MIKE KEMPSTER SR. — EXECUTIVE VICE PRESIDENT, SALES & MARKETING
CHRISTINA SCHROEDER — VICE PRESIDENT OF MARKETING
MARSHA CAPEN — DIRECTOR OF EDITORIAL DEVELOPMENT

THIS BOOK WAS PRODUCED BY ST. REMY MEDIA

PRESIDENT: PIERRE LÉVEILLÉ
VICE PRESIDENT, FINANCE: NATALIE WATANABE
MANAGING EDITOR: CAROLYN JACKSON
MANAGING ART DIRECTOR: DIANE DENONCOURT
PRODUCTION MANAGER: MICHELLE TURBIDE
DIRECTOR, BUSINESS DEVELOPMENT: CHRISTOPHER JACKSON
PROJECT EDITOR: ELIZABETH LEWIS
ART DIRECTOR: SOLANGE LABERGE
ILLUSTRATOR: MARIE JOSÉE MOREAU
PRODUCTION EDITOR: BRIAN PARSONS
INDEXER: JANE BRODERICK
PREPRESS PRODUCTION: MARTIN FRANCOEUR, JEAN ANGRIGNON SIROIS
SYSTEMS DIRECTOR: EDWARD RENAUD

PRINTED IN CANADA

COPYRIGHT © 2001 WEBER-STEPHEN PRODUCTS CO. ALL RIGHTS RESERVED.
NO PART OF THIS BOOK MAY BE REPRODUCED IN ANY FORM WITHOUT WRITTEN PERMISSION
FROM THE PUBLISHER.

LIBRARY OF CONGRESS CATALOGING-IN-PUBLICATION DATA:
PURVIANCE, JAMIE.
WEBER'S BIG BOOK OF GRILLING / BY JAMIE PURVIANCE AND SANDRA S. MCRAE.
P. CM.
ISBN 0-8118-3197-3 (PBK.)
1. BARBECUE COOKERY. I. TITLE: BIG BOOK OF GRILLING. II. MCRAE, SANDRA S.
III. WEBER (FIRM) IV. TITLE.
TX840.B3 P88 2001
641.5'784—DC21
                    00-050943

CHRONICLE BOOKS LLC
85 SECOND STREET
SAN FRANCISCO, CA 94105
10 9 8 7 6

DISTRIBUTED IN CANADA BY RAINCOAST BOOKS
9050 SHAUGHNESSY STREET
VANCOUVER, BRITISH COLUMBIA
V6P 6E5

WWW.WEBER.COM
WWW.CHRONICLEBOOKS.COM
WWW.STREMY.COM

IN MEMORY OF GEORGE STEPHEN,
WHOSE QUEST FOR THE PERFECT BARBECUE GRILL
SPARKED A PASSION FOR GRILLING
IN BACKYARD HEROES AROUND THE WORLD

CON

TENTS

I feel really manly. It's about 25°F outside and snowing, and I just came in from the cold with a platter of grilled meat in my hand. Anybody can grill when it's sunny and 80°F in the shade, but it takes a real man to brave the elements to heed the yearning for my favorite steak prepared on my Weber® kettle grill. Rib-eye. Two inches thick. Crunchy on the outside, tender and pink on the inside. When the muse beckons, I must heed her call. I must grill.

I grill on a regular basis, but when the entire Roker family began showing up to partake of my grilling skills, I suddenly needed two kettles. After a few family cookouts, I discovered I needed even

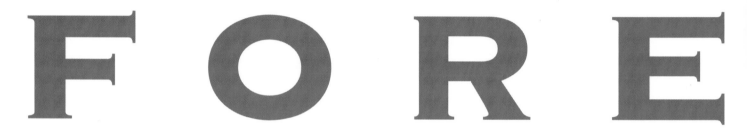

more cooking surface—I wanted to do pork shoulders and authentic slow-cooked ribs. What to do? The answer came to me at the Memphis In May barbecue championship, at the Weber booth. There it was...calling my name with its sweet siren song...THE RANCH™ KETTLE! It's 3 feet in diameter— finally, a grill to match my grilling ambition!

Even though I'm a crossover griller (I own both charcoal and gas grills), I have to admit that I particularly love the ritual of charcoal grilling and barbecuing. I imagine my ancestors cooking not much differently than this: over an open flame, without a lot of fuss, using the freshest ingredients, and not flipping the meat over and over until it's overcooked and dry. Although my ancestors probably used more primitive fuel, I love the challenge of seeing how fast you can start the fire with just a couple of pieces of newspaper wadded up

As the weatherman of "The Today Show," Al Roker has the undivided attention of the nation every weekday morning as America prepares for work. He focuses the same rapt attention on his pork ribs, which he likes to slow-cook over a smoky hickory fire. See page 52 for Al's own rub recipe and see if it doesn't wake up your taste buds with a burst of sunshine!

beneath your chimney starter, a pile of charcoal, and a match. I like playing with different types of wood chunks to impart various flavors, too.

But then I appreciate the oh-so-easy gas grill approach, too. I also own a Weber Summit® built-in gas grill, with 75,000 BTUs, and it is a beauty. I have three Weber charcoal grills at our country weekend home, but I decided to put a Summit grill in our weekday Manhattan home, a recently renovated brownstone. Why irritate the neighbors with all that charcoal smoke? But I'm keeping my chimney starter around for old times' sake. There's something about the charcoal smudges on your shirt and

pieces of charcoal in your shoes that gives you certain bragging rights. After all, life isn't about easy. (Hey, I'm a weatherman, I know about life not being easy. Try predicting sunshine for a big weekend festival and then having 2 inches of "sunny" rain out the event.)

But whether it's gas or charcoal, grilling and barbecuing are great family activities. That's what I love most. Family and food go hand in hand. In fact, the only way to get rid of my family is to run out of food!

And while not everybody is as manic as I am about grilling in all kinds of weather (no grilling during thunderstorms, though, unless Weber comes out with a rubber grill), we all associate a backyard barbecue with sunshine, cold drinks, and good times. But you don't have to be a fair-weather griller. Follow my lead and grill come rain, sleet, snow, or shine. But mostly, have yourself a grand ole grilling time! Enjoy!

Al Roker

Al Roker

A funny thing happens when you tell people you're writing a grilling cookbook. Suddenly the conversation picks up an obvious enthusiasm. Everyone within earshot jumps in with their own grilling story—something like how they mastered a recipe "so unbelievably good" that their guests beg for the recipe, or how they happily trudged through snowdrifts in January to cook on their beloved grill.

We understand. For us, grilling is much more than a cooking method. It's a sport, a hobby, a passion—dare we say, a way of life. And sharing it with fellow grillers is half the fun. We know what the first cave dwellers knew: The flame is a bonding thing.

INTROD

Putting this book together, we let the universal hunger for great grilling lead us. Whatever choices we made, from recipe development to writing, our first question was: Does it help the reader succeed? We wanted to create a world of grilling where the novice develops confidence and grows, the occasional griller is enlightened, the expert is challenged, and—most importantly—everyone leaves the table satisfied.

To make this book work for you, start by searching out the recipes that suit your taste and comfort level. We've loaded you up with ideas from every corner of the world—including all the great standards. Along the way, we explore American grilling culture so you can learn where all the fun began and see how it has evolved (maybe you'll even find a niche where you can leave your mark—go for it!).

Jamie Purviance, accomplished chef and food writer, always looks forward to his recurring dream involving grilled salmon and a glass of red wine. Sandra S. McRae, grilling nut and writer, is wild about barbecued pork ribs and has a shameless addiction to grill-roasted red peppers.

As you work your way through the recipes, remember that attitude is as important to the experience as technique. This is not like platform diving, where the slightest error can make a terrible splash. It's more like surfing or skiing, where you definitely need a certain amount of technique but there's still a lot of room for individuality. The cooking times and temperatures are fully tested for reliability, but as you gain experience, trust your own sense of when something looks ready to turn or when the fire needs some more coals. And please, don't feel confined. If you find a certain sauce or marinade that you like, play with it. Make it your own. Owning a great recipe is almost as much fun as eating it.

To help you navigate the road to great grilling, we've put up a few signposts. Special features will walk you through what you need to know to master the basic burger, prime rib roast, grilled vegetables, and much more. We pride ourselves on showing you techniques that take recipes from mediocre to magnificent. We dispel a few myths along the way, too, so check it out. And let us know about your grilling successes. Weber always enjoys a little chat over the backyard fence with fellow grillers.

We've seasoned the book with a few sidebars on some of our favorite ingredients, too, for a little food history, culture, and inspiration. Forgive us if we wax poetic about fundamentals such as grilled garlic, but some of the humblest things in life deserve hero status. Once you've cooked from this book, we think you'll be a hero in your own right, too. A backyard hero. The person who can turn an ordinary day into a fun culinary romp through the Flavor Zone. So grab the tongs and apron, and let's go!

Jamie Purviance
Chef/Writer

Sandra S. McRae
Writer

ABOUT THE RECIPES

All good cooks have a few secrets they like to keep to themselves. Not us—we like to share them! We think the keys to our success should be yours as well. Here's the inside scoop to help you get the best results from the recipes in this book:

KOSHER SALT: We only use kosher salt in this book for a couple of reasons. First, it's particularly well suited for grilling because of its size. Unlike fine-grained table salt, kosher salt consists of big flakes that sit on the surface of the food. As the flame draws juices to the surface of the food, they melt these coarser flakes, resulting in great surface flavor. We also like the complex flavor of kosher salt, which comes from the other minerals in it. Because kosher salt is less concentrated, if you need to substitute table salt, reduce the quantity by about one third.

FRESHLY GROUND BLACK PEPPER: Our recipes get their flavor balance from the more potent grindings of a pepper mill. The oils that give the black peppercorn its flavor and kick deteriorate quickly when exposed to air. Premilled pepper is thus less flavorful and only holds its power for about 4 months, compared to 1 year for whole peppercorns. Invest in a good pepper mill and you won't regret it.

EXTRA-VIRGIN OLIVE OIL: We prefer extra-virgin, the highest grade of olive oil, for its flavor and purity. It just tastes better. Where we want a more neutral-flavored oil to preserve an already delicate balance, however, we specify vegetable oil. Otherwise, treat yourself to the good stuff.

OTHER INGREDIENTS: The griller's pantry should also include staples such as ketchup, Worcestershire sauce, a variety of mustards, plenty of garlic, and a well-rounded spice rack. Specialty ingredients add variety. Our favorites include fish sauce (a.k.a. *nuoc nam* or *nam pla*), fresh lemongrass, chili oil, sriracha (hot chili-garlic sauce), and chipotles in adobo sauce. If your grocer doesn't carry these, look in international food markets or gourmet shops or on the Internet.

Oh no, we've grown up to be our parents!
Not so bad a deal, as it turns out. Although the fashions have evolved, the lure of the grill and the easy luxury of a sturdy lawn chair are still all the rage.

GRILLING TEMPERATURES: At the top of each recipe, we indicate the requisite cooking method (*Direct* or *Indirect*) and temperature level (*High*, *Medium*, or *Low*). Charcoal grillers especially need this information since arranging coals is a bit more involved that turning dials on a gas grill. Note that a grill set up for Indirect cooking can accommodate both methods (just move the food directly over the fire for Direct cooking). Where searing is particularly important to the texture or flavor, we note that as well (e.g., *Sear: High, Cook: Indirect/Medium*). To achieve a certain effect or accommodate a variety of ingredients, a few recipes include more than one cooking temperature. The bell peppers in Lamb Chops with Grilled Peppers, for instance, are

cooked over Medium heat while the lamb rib chops are grilled over High heat. We have therefore italicized all cooking methods and temperatures in the instructions of each recipe (e.g., *Direct Medium*) to help you set up your grill for success. See "Mastering the Fire," pages 22 to 31, for more details.

KEEP THE LID DOWN! Without a doubt, the most important grilling rule. Lifting the lid allows heat to escape, increasing your grilling time. A closed lid also reduces the chance of flare-ups (and closing the lid extinguishes them quickly). Open the grill only to turn foods as indicated in the recipes. More poking and flipping won't make it taste better, trust us.

IS IT DONE YET?
A WORD OR TWO ABOUT DONENESS

A key to great grilled meat is knowing when to pull it off the grill. That moment, however, is the subject of some debate, with everyone from professional chefs to federal agencies weighing in. If you've been grilling or eating meats for some time, you probably have definite preferences. We all do. But nothing takes the luster off a great grilled meal like a bellyache, so in the interest of promoting healthy barbecues across the land, we adhere to United States Department of Agriculture (USDA) temperatures for doneness in all of our recipes.

There is little debate in the right doneness temperatures for poultry and pork. But it's a different story for lamb, beef, and venison. We recommend the USDA temperatures for medium rare for all of our beef, lamb, and game meats, except burgers. Because ground meats contain so much surface area, where most bacteria take hold, it is very important to cook ground meat to 160°F for medium. For many meat eaters, the USDA temperatures for doneness seem rather high, but we believe these temperatures allow you to safely enjoy a delicious cut of meat without sacrificing flavor. Ultimately, the meat doneness choice is yours to make. If you prefer your meat cooked to a lower doneness temperature, you will need to adjust your grilling times down from those listed in each recipe. We suggest you invest in a good meat thermometer and let it be your guide.

One note on grilling beef: For beef roasts, we instruct you to remove the meat from the grill before it reaches the doneness temperature since the temperature of larger cuts will continue to rise as the meat rests. (The temperature of thick steaks will also increase slightly.) These resting times are important to give the juices a chance to redistribute themselves evenly throughout the meat. We suggest you use your trusty meat thermometer to check doneness at the end of the resting period.

Our recipes for small game birds give you visual doneness clues because getting an accurate thermometer reading on them is harder to do. Note that game bird juices will run a little pink even when safely cooked.

We've also included a "Grilling Guide" in the Appendix on pages 400 to 403. It will give you an idea of how long it will take to reach the USDA's recommended temperature for different degrees of doneness. Note that all times are approximate and your actual cooking times may vary according to weather conditions, type and brand of grill, as well as other factors. Ultimately, your best defense against an undercooked or overcooked feast is a good meat thermometer. Use it in good health!

In the Beginning, there was Fire. And it was good. Then Meat hit the Fire. And it was better. Then Barbecue Sauce was invented and lo, there was much rejoicing among the People, as the food was much improved. And the heavens did smile upon the gathering and the sauce did coat every finger and smite every trace of boredom and sorrow.

Since then, things have only gotten more interesting. If you are among the Enlightened, you know what we're talking about. There's something about grilling that draws us back to Paradise and sets the world right again. It's more than a cooking method, it's a belief system. For some, it's a calling. And yet

THE GRILLING GOSPEL

grilling doesn't require us to take any leaps of faith or make any sacrifices. A hedonist religion? Well, only in that it indulges the senses. But grilling is more than that. It's a way to gather family and friends for two things that really matter: fellowship and nourishment. The fringe benefits aren't bad, either.

There's the smell of the smoke, a sensory trigger that awakens a certain Promethean pride in us. The sound of the sizzle satisfies and intensifies our anticipation at the same time. And the hypnotic appeal of the fire stirs the hearth-builder within.

When all these elements come together—especially on a warm summer evening with the background sounds of sprinklers going, children laughing, and dogs barking—it's like a slice of salvation. The tensions of life seem to melt off your shoulders. Who cares about the dry patches in the lawn or the bills in the mail? The hassle and headache of everyday demands just...disappear.

Some folks get a taste of grilling and are instant converts. We're the ones who don't think twice about shoveling a way through the snow to the grill. From big to small, we grill it all. Prime rib? No problem. Rotisserie-grilled chicken? We can do that. From Mediterranean lamb to

Hawaiian pork, our kabobs *rule*. Our faith is a torch that flares with enthusiasm every time we come across the next great grilling recipe. We're not afraid to take on a challenge—and spend hours concocting sauces to slather on it.

Other folks are slow to answer the call. We're the ones who've only enjoyed a casual brush with the grill at barbecues or on camping trips. We mean to get our act together and start following The Path. But other things get in the way. There are reports to turn in, soccer games to ref, and garages to paint....

Then, one day, a revelation. Food tastes better when it's grilled! Why have we been denying ourselves

ACCORDING TO WEBER

this simple Truth? Timid at first, we make weekend attempts at the easy stuff such as burgers and chicken. Emboldened by early success, we trying grilling on a weeknight. We start to experiment with recipes. A passion is born. Suddenly we find ourselves sizing everything up to see if it's grillable. The stovetop gathers dust. We count our successes as blessings: a perfectly seared steak here, a moist and delicious pork chop there. Triumph! The neighbors go crazy from the tempting smells of dinner at our house. Our redemption is at hand.

If you have seen the Light, follow us through this wondrous and rewarding maze of flavors and textures. If you've been moved by the spirit of grilling but are unsure of how to proceed, read on. We can show you a better way. When you see how simple and fun grilling can be—and how much your quality of life can be improved by doing homage to the flame—you may have steamed your last asparagus spear, baked your last pork roast forever. If you're skeptical, there are plenty of small steps to take along the way to build your faith. If you want the full, glorious taste-bud rapture, give in to the grill. You won't be sorry. You may be saved.

THE BIRTH OF AMERICAN GRILLING

After World War II, our heroes of the Free World came home asking very little in return for their bravery: a bungalow with a small backyard to call their own, and some peace and quiet. In response to their modest wishes, the suburbs were spawned, and the backyard soon became sacred ground. As outdoor entertaining became a slice of the Good Life, simpler, freestanding metal braziers replaced traditional barbecue pits and the focus shifted from slow-cooked techniques to grilling—cooking meat over high heat. Smoke drifting over fences became part of the American landscape.

But by 1951 these cookout rigs were still woefully under-engineered. No one was more aware of their shortcomings than George Stephen, a welder from Chicago. As the father of a growing family, George was used to personal sacrifice, but heck, a decent grilled steak would be nice once in a while! He had struggled with his flat, open brazier with frustrating results. If you didn't end up getting rained out, the slightest wind could blow ashes onto your hard-fought prize.

Well, if necessity is the mother of invention, then hunger must be its godparent. At the time, George worked at Weber Brothers Metal Works outside Chicago, welding large metal spheres together to make buoys for the Coast Guard. It was in these very spheres that his idea took shape. He knew a rounded cooking bowl with a lid was the key to success. He added three legs to the bottom, a handle to the top, and took the oddity home.

The neighbors called it "Sputnik" and had a good laugh—and a taste of delicious grilled steak. Suddenly George's "folly" was in such hot demand he couldn't make them fast enough. So he branched out on his own and went into full-time production. Some years later, George the legend met a young man from Kansas City, Missouri, who would help make Weber the grill of choice.

Mike Kempster was an enthusiastic salesman in the Lawn & Garden department of the Montgomery Ward store that was Weber's top seller. One snowy Saturday, George dropped by the store unannounced, hoping to discover the secret to their success. What he found was chaos. The store was running a

special on 8¢ guppies that day and the department was short-handed. For some reason, all of Chicago was suddenly mad for cheap guppies. Feigning interest in a riding lawn mower, George approached Mike. Besieged by guppy lovers and feeling badly that he couldn't give this customer the attention he deserved, Mike jotted down George's name and address and promised to personally conduct a proper demonstration at George's house. Impressed, George left, then quickly forgot about it. Clearly such an outrageous offer was merely borne of guppy fever.

Imagine George's surprise when weeks later, as soon as the snow had melted, Mike drove up with a large riding mower in tow. Mike was puzzled by the sight of George's patio, which was wreathed with several Weber kettle grills and prototypes. *Man, this guy is into grilling!* he thought, then got down to demonstrating the finer points of this mean mowing machine.

George, for his part, was floored by Mike's dedication. Was this guy for real? He decided to find out and offered Mike a sales position with Weber-Stephen Products Co. right then and there. So that explained the grills! *Why not*, Mike thought, and shook on it. Thus began an inventive and productive career as "Weber's chief grill peddler" as Mike, now Executive Vice President, modestly calls himself.

The round kettle shape so familiar to us today was relatively unknown until Mike and the rest of Weber's sales force spread the Grilling Gospel According to Weber, one live cooking demonstration at a time. Sadly, George is no longer with us, but his legacy lives on every time folks gather for a great grilled meal. Mike's story, it turns out, is a typical one of a sales guy working for a family-owned business with an entrepreneurial spirit that focused on doing one thing right: in this case, helping Americans fall in love with grilling. That's why we've included some of his wilder antics in here for you. Besides being entertaining, we think they embody the spirit of grilling that moves us all—and show how the quest for grilling success can inspire us to take some chances and succeed.

In reality, all that Mike and the entire Weber team ever did was provide the equipment and fan the flames. The true passion of grilling is in anyone who enjoys a good meal, great times with family and friends, and has an aversion to wasting those precious moments scrubbing pots and pans. If you love the texture and flavor of grilled food, if the smell of the smoke makes you a little crazy with desire, then this book is *your* book.

The prototype that launched a national pastime.
No frontier is ever braved without a few bumps and turns. According to company folklore, George Stephen's original kettle grill, which became an icon of the American backyard, failed at first. It wouldn't stay lit! A neighbor peering over the fence offered George a little advice: "Poke some holes in that thing so the fire gets some oxygen!" Whoops.

CHOOSING A GRILL

Okay, you've got the fever. But do you have the right grill? Remember, your results are only going to be as good as your grill, so make sure a one-time bargain doesn't turn into a long-term disappointment. Invest in a good grill and you can focus on dinner, not your toolbox.

Your first decision, charcoal or gas, is really a lifestyle choice. Are you convinced there's nothing like the taste and smell of food grilled over hot coals? Do you pride yourself on your ability to build a good fire and keep it properly tended? Do you need that hands-on primal experience?

Or do you want a perfect fire at the push of a button? Do you demand precise temperature control? Perhaps you'd rather trade the charcoal setup and post-cookout ashes for some serious one-on-one with the cooking grate.

Since taste tests indicate no significant flavor difference either way, the choice is strictly personal. Consider how you plan to use your grill: Will you grill every night or just on special occasions? Will that change over time? Is cost an issue? While gas grills are initially more expensive, they generally cost less to operate in the long run. Both are great choices—pick the one that's right for you! Then, look for three things.

1. Choose a grill with preassembled and/or welded parts. It will be much more stable and less likely to rust. Look for easy-to-follow instructions and precision cast and die-cut parts for easy, accurate assembly. Even if the store assembles the grill for you, you want the least number of parts to fiddle with over the grill's life.

2. Choose a grill with a long warranty period. The best manufacturers can afford to stand behind their products. For charcoal grills, the warranty should be at least a 5-year limited warranty; for gas grills a 10-year limited warranty.

3. Choose a well-known company with a reputation for quality. It will save you lots of trouble right off the bat. Look for one with a history of great customer service—a company you can easily reach later if you need accessories, service, and (eventually) replacement parts. Look for a customer service phone number and a web site address.

WHAT TO LOOK FOR IN A CHARCOAL GRILL

• **CONSTRUCTION:** Choose a grill made of high-grade U.S. steel with a durable porcelain-enamel finish that's baked on, rather than a paint finish that's been sprayed on, to prevent rusting, peeling, and fading. Leg couplings and grate supports should be welded on for added strength and stability. Look for heavy-duty plastic wheels that won't crack in extreme temperatures.

• **BASIC FEATURES:** Look for stainless steel or nickel-plated cooking and charcoal grates—they clean up easily and resist rust. Look for stay-cool plastic or wooden handles. Be sure the grill allows you to cook by both the Direct and the Indirect methods *(see pages 22 to 25)*. Charcoal rails or fuel baskets are a bonus that make Indirect grilling a breeze.

• **ADDED CONVENIENCES:** A hinged cooking grate makes it easier to add briquets. Some grills feature a cleaning system that sweeps out the ashes for you and makes cleanup a snap. Models that include a thermometer make it easier to regulate the internal temperature of the grill.

WHAT TO LOOK FOR IN A GAS GRILL

• **CONSTRUCTION:** Choose a grill made of high-grade U.S. steel. The cart should have welded legs for strength and stability. Also opt for a baked-on, porcelain-enamel finish that won't rust, fade, or peel.

• **BASIC FEATURES:** Look for burners that cook food evenly, with no hot spots. Cooking grates should be stainless steel or coated with durable porcelain enamel for easy cleanup and rust resistance. Most importantly, pay attention to the cooking system. Be sure the burner design will allow you to cook by both the Direct and the Indirect methods *(see pages 22 to 25)*. Look for angled steel bars below the cooking grate. Avoid lava rocks; they tend to collect grease, which causes flash fires. Flavorizer® metal bars virtually eliminate flare-ups because as juices slide down the bars, they vaporize, creating the smoke that gives food that great grilled taste.

• **ADDED CONVENIENCES:** Optional side burners are great for cooking sauces and other dishes. Side tables and condiment holders give you extra space for food preparation. Locking casters keep your grill in place for safer grilling.

• **WHAT ABOUT BTUS?** BTUs are NOT a measure of cooking power. They indicate the volume of gas a grill can burn. Tightly engineered grills use fewer BTUs and cook food more efficiently.

THE GRILLER'S TOOLBOX

If you love the sport, you gotta have the right equipment. Here's a checklist of the basics and a few handy add-ons you might want, too:

CLEANING TIP: *Wash tools with hardwood handles by hand to preserve the wood finish.*

CLEANING TIP: *Wash natural-bristle basting brushes by hand. Use plenty of hot, soapy water to wash oils out and rinse well. Smooth the bristles and allow to air-dry completely.*

ESSENTIALS

WIDE SPATULA: Burgers, chicken pieces, steaks and veggies take a turn for the better with a wide metal spatula.

GRILL TONGS: For turning sausages and franks, but also scallops, shrimp, tortillas/pitas.

MEAT FORK: For lifting large roasts and whole birds once they're done cooking. Also helps with carving.

GRILL BRUSH: Brass bristles resist rust and won't scratch porcelain enamel. Steel brushes are better for cast-iron grates.

BASTING BRUSH: We recommend natural boar bristles (nylon bristles will melt if they touch the cooking grate) and a long handle. Always wear a mitt when basting, in case of flare-ups.

BARBECUE MITTS: Long-sleeve, flame-resistant mitts protect your hands and forearms. Use two when lifting roasts.

MEAT THERMOMETER: Invest in a quality one. Most are a probe you stick into the center of the meat for a quick read and cannot be left in the meat. Others can be left in—the probe is attached to a wire that runs outside the grill. These usually have an alarm that sounds when the food reaches the desired temperature. We prefer the latter type—it saves on guess work (and money) when you want to get dinner right.

NICE ADDITIONS

- A super-wide spatula designed for turning whole fish.
- Skewers make turning small foods quick and easy. Soak wooden/bamboo ones for 30 minutes before loading them.
- A vegetable wok/grill topper makes grilling small and delicate vegetables easy.

BE CAREFUL OUT THERE
GRILLING AND FOOD SAFETY

Don't run with scissors, cross with the light, and read these common-sense guidelines so your backyard gatherings are as safe as they are delicious.

GRILLING SAFETY

- Grills radiate a lot of heat, so always keep the grill at least 10 feet from any combustible materials, including the house, garage, deck rails, etc. Never use a grill indoors or under a covered patio.
- Never add lighter fluid to a lit fire.
- Never use a grill that wobbles, leans, or is otherwise unstable.
- Always use heat-resistant barbecue mitts and long-handled tools to tend the fire and food.
- Never spray or brush oil on a hot cooking grate. Oil the food instead.
- Don't wear loose or highly flammable clothing when grilling.
- Never use water to extinguish a flare-up. Closing the lid will reduce the oxygen and eliminate the flare-up.
- Keep a fire extinguisher handy in case of a mishap. Never pour water on a grease fire. Instead, cover charcoal grills and close all vents; turn off gas grills at the source.
- Never store propane tanks or spares indoors (that means the garage, too).
- Keep children and pets away from hot grills at all times.
- When you're finished grilling on a charcoal grill, close the lid and all vents; on a gas grill, turn off the burners and the LP tank or source.

FOOD SAFETY

- Wash your hands thoroughly with warm, soapy water before starting any meal preparation and after handling fresh meat, fish, or poultry.
- Defrost meat, fish, and poultry only in the refrigerator, never at room temperature.
- When resting meats at room temperature before grilling, note that room temperature is 65°F to 70°F. Do not place raw food in direct sunlight or near any heat source.
- If a sauce will be brushed on meat during grilling, divide the sauce, using one part for brushing and the other for serving at the table. Vigorously boil marinades that were used for raw meats, fish, or poultry for 1 full minute before using as a baste or sauce.
- Never place cooked food on the same platter that the raw food was on.
- Wash all platters, cooking utensils, grilling tools, and countertops that have come into contact with raw meats or fish with hot, soapy water.
- Always grill ground meats to at least 160°F (170°F for poultry), the temperature for medium (well-done) doneness.

LESSON LEARNED
HOT PANTS ARE OUT

Our friend Mike was hip to the styles of the time when he launched his career with Weber, but he learned a valuable lesson about confusing fashion sense with common sense.

I've always been a fan of Chinese food, so I was thrilled when Weber came out with a grilltop wok in the mid-1970s. I was so eager to teach America how to cook fried rice on the grill that I begged my favorite Chinese restaurant chef to teach me the ins and outs of this wonderful dish. I figured I could easily translate the technique to the grill.

The moment of truth arrived at a grilling demonstration in Milwaukee. We had a great feast planned, with Peking duck, sweet and sour pork, and other delicacies being cooked to perfection on Weber charcoal grills. The scene was truly a culinary symphony, with the sound of the spatulas hitting the woks, the steam and aromas from the sauces and meats, and the happy chatter of the

hungry observers. I could hardly contain my joy as I "conducted" the fried-rice portion of the feast. I was in my element. I was having fun. I was...on fire! Literally! Fortunately, the smell of singed polyester reached my nose before the melting fibers of my pants reached the skin on my leg.

Luckily the demonstration was in the parking lot of a shopping center, so I ducked into a men's store and bought a pair of cotton pants.

I learned a potentially painful lesson about grilling attire: Before you fire up the grill, ditch the synthetics and any loose-flowing garments in favor of more close-fitting, natural, and less volatile ones. And never let your zealous love of the grill draw you too close to the fire.

DIRECT COOKING

Want sumptuous steaks and scrumptious veggies? Want sausages that sizzle, pork chops that tantalize? The most important thing to know about grilling is which cooking method to use for a specific food, Direct or Indirect. The difference is simple: Place the food directly over the fire, or arrange the fire on either side of the food. Using the right method is the shortest route to great results—and the best way to ensure doneness safety.

If you've ever had grilled food that was charred outside and undercooked inside, chances are the chef used the wrong grilling method. Direct and Indirect cooking are the two ways to grill food properly. Getting there is as simple as setting up your grill for the right method.

The Direct Method, similar to broiling, means the food is cooked directly over the heat source. For even cooking, food should be turned once halfway through the grilling time.

Use the Direct method *for foods that take less than 25 minutes to cook:* steaks, chops, kabobs, sausages, vegetables, and the like. Direct cooking is also necessary to sear meats. Searing creates that wonderful crisp, caramelized texture where the food hits the grate. It also adds nice grill marks and flavor to the entire surface. Steaks, chops, chicken pieces, and larger cuts of meat all benefit from searing.

To sear meats, place them over Direct heat for 2 to 5 minutes per side. Smaller pieces require less searing time (see recipes for specific times for each cut). Usually after searing, you finish cooking the food at a lower temperature. You can continue to cook fast-cooking foods by the Direct method; or use the Indirect method to finish off longer-cooking foods. Again, each recipe in this book will instruct you on times and temperatures to follow.

Grilling Ponderable:
Why does the smoke always follow you, no matter where you stand?

Direct cooking on a charcoal grill: *To set up a charcoal grill for Direct cooking, spread prepared coals evenly across the charcoal grate. Set the cooking grate over the coals and place food on the cooking grate. Place the lid on the grill and lift it only to turn food or to test for doneness at the end of the recommended cooking time.*

Note: If you are cooking fattier foods that might generate a brief flare-up, leave a small section of the charcoal grate that is not covered in coals. That way you can move the food over Indirect heat (see pages 24 to 25) for a few seconds until the flames subside. Remember, shaking off excess marinade and oil before placing the food on the cooking grate and keeping the lid on the grill are the best ways to minimize flare-ups.

Direct cooking on a gas grill: *To set up a gas grill for Direct cooking, preheat the grill with all burners on High. Place the food on the cooking grate, then adjust all burners to the temperature noted in the recipe. Close the lid of the grill and lift it only to turn food or to test for doneness at the end of the recommended cooking time.*

CHARCOAL BRIQUET GUIDE FOR THE DIRECT METHOD

DIAMETER OF GRILL IN INCHES	BRIQUETS NEEDED
14 1/2	30
18 1/2	40
22 1/2	50
37 1/2	150

In grilling,
as in friendship,
sometimes it's wisest
to be direct.

The most common mistake unseasoned grillers make is to cook everything, regardless of size or dimension, directly over the heat source. If you've ever had overcooked ribs or chicken, you know what we mean. The greatest "eureka!" beginning grillers experience is discovering the Indirect method: arranging the fire on either side of the food to roast it instead of broiling it. Logical, easy, and a sure ticket to grilling success.

The Indirect Method is similar to roasting, but with the added benefits of that grilled texture, flavor, and appearance you can't get from an oven. Heat rises, reflects off the lid and inside surfaces of the grill, and circulates to slowly cook the food evenly on all sides, much like a convection oven, so there's no need to turn the food over.

Use the Indirect method for *foods that require 25 minutes or more of grilling time or for foods that are so delicate that direct exposure to the heat source would dry them out or scorch them.* Examples include roasts, ribs, whole chickens, turkeys, and other large cuts of meat, as well as delicate fish fillets.

To set up for Indirect cooking, charcoal briquets are set on either side of the food; gas burners are lit on either side of the food but not directly beneath it.

The best grills are designed to give you ultimate control of your heat source so you can use the Indirect method. This flexibility is intrinsic to the design of most charcoal grills. As long as you can separate the coals so that food in the middle of the cooking grate isn't sitting directly over the heat, you're set.

Gas grills, on the other hand, are a little more complex. You have to have a burner configuration that allows you to use only the burners on either side of the food. We suggest you look for a grill with at least three burners in order to facilitate Indirect cooking.

Humorless salesmen need not apply.
Early Weber salesmen would stop at nothing to draw a crowd and sell some grills. They also had some wacky fun in the process!

Indirect cooking on a charcoal grill: *To set up a charcoal grill for Indirect cooking, arrange hot coals evenly on either side of the grate. Charcoal/fuel baskets or rails are handy accessories to keep the coals in place. A drip pan placed in the center of the charcoal grate between the coals is useful to collect drippings that can be used for gravies and sauces. It also helps prevent flare-ups when cooking fattier foods such as goose, duck, or fatty roasts. For longer cooking times, add water to the drip pan to keep drippings from burning. Place the cooking grate over the coals and place the food on the cooking grate, centered over the drip pan or empty space. Place the lid on the grill and lift it only to baste or check for doneness at the end of the suggested cooking time.*

Indirect cooking on a gas grill: *To set up a gas grill for Indirect cooking, preheat the grill with all burners on High. Then adjust the burners on each side of the food to the temperature noted in the recipe and turn off the burner(s) directly below the food. For best results, place roasts, poultry, or large cuts of meat on a roasting rack set inside a disposable heavy-gauge foil pan. For longer cooking times, add water to the drip pan to keep drippings from burning.*

HOW MUCH CHARCOAL?

Turkeys and other longer-cooking foods require just a little more vigilance on your part, so use a timer (those holiday football games can get pretty interesting). First set up the grill for Indirect cooking, then replenish the coals every hour as suggested below. Hint: If you haven't already, this is a good reason to get a hinged cooking grate.

DIAMETER OF GRILL IN INCHES	BRIQUETS FOR THE FIRST HOUR	BRIQUETS TO ADD EACH ADDITIONAL HOUR
14 1/2	15 per side	6 per side
18 1/2	20 per side	7 per side
22 1/2	25 per side	8 per side
37 1/2	75 per side	22 per side

If you've ever watched an accomplished grillmeister at work and thought, "Wow, I'd give my right barbecue mitt to be able to grill like that," these two pages are for you. The art of charcoal grilling requires a full understanding of the fire because it's much more involved than adjusting knobs on a gas grill. Maybe that's why charcoal grillers have a strong sense of pride. To join this illustrious pack, read on.

FIRE BUILDING 101. Sounds obvious, but you need to start with the right fuel: *solid hardwood charcoal briquets* are best. Cheaper briquets contain fillers, so they don't burn as hot or as long. Use good lighter fuel, too. *Nontoxic lighter cubes* light as easily as a birthday candle and burn steadily, even when wet, without the chemical taste that liquid fuels give off. (If you use liquid fuel, *never* spray it onto a lit fire since the flame could travel upstream to the container with disastrous results). *A chimney starter,* an aluminum cylinder with a handle and an elevated floor, is great for a quick light. Fill the canister with briquets, place it over fuel cubes or several sheets of wadded-up newspaper, and light them. (Alternatively, build a pyramid of coals over the fuel and light the fuel.) The coals are ready when they have a light coating of gray ash, after about 25 minutes.

ARRANGE THE COALS WISELY. A well-designed grill has space on either side of the cooking grate for adding briquets for longer cooking times (*see chart, page 25*). Fancier models have hinged cooking grates that make this job even easier. Just be sure to place the cooking grate so that these openings are over the coals. Also place the coals on the charcoal grate directly above the vents so you get maximum oxygen to feed the fire. Adjust these vents (wear mitts, they get hot!) to control the speed of the burn and intensity of the heat—the wider the vent opening, the hotter the fire. Place the lid so that the top vent is positioned for maximum air draw and keep the top vent open at all times.

KNOW HOW TO QUIT. Extinguishing the coals is as easy as closing all the vents and putting the lid back on. Before you shut down, however, remove the food from the cooking grate and replace the lid. Allow the grill to continue heating the cooking grate until any smoking stops, 10 to 15 minutes, to burn off any cooking residues. Give the grate a good brushing with a brass grill brush to knock off any charred bits, then extinguish the fire. Once the ashes are completely cooled (best to wait until the next morning), remove them so they don't attract moisture and encourage rust. Some grills are equipped with blades that sweep the ashes into a disposal pan or canister. Dispose of ashes properly in a fireproof container. Always remove all ashes before storing a charcoal grill.

IF YOU CAN'T STAND THE HEAT.... Exactly what do we mean by Low, Medium, and High temperatures and how do you know when you're there? The best way to gauge the temperature is to use an oven thermometer set on the cooking grate. Low is about 300°F, Medium is about 350°F, and High is 500°F to 550°F.

Face it, some of us didn't take Mom seriously when she said don't play with fire. Part of the challenge of cooking on a charcoal grill is learning how to control the temperature. Once you master that, the fun part becomes gaining dexterity at grilling an entire menu or cooking foods that are done by different cooking methods and different grilling temperatures. If you are a dyed-in-the-wool charcoal enthusiast, the challenge of mastering the fire is definitely the reward as well.

When hot dogs and hamburgers were standard grilled fare, a simple direct fire was about all you needed. But as America's tastes have evolved, so has grilling. More advanced recipes (like some of those presented in this book) might have you searing on Direct High and finishing up over Direct Medium. Simple enough on a gas grill, where you just turn a knob or two, but what do you do on a charcoal grill? Hop onto to the barbecue wagon and you'll find chefs and cookbook authors building creative coal configurations they swear give the ultimate control over a charcoal fire. So is there a secret to stacking and stoking the coals that we haven't divulged here?

Many charcoal enthusiasts think the best way to set up your charcoal grill is to "load the deck," so to speak. According to some experts, the solution is as easy as setting up different cooking temperatures, or heat zones, by making two different-sized piles of prepared coals or by sloping the entire bed of coals. They place one-third of the prepared coals in a single layer on one side of the grate and two-thirds in a double layer on the other side. This, they argue, gives them a Medium and a High temperature zone, and better heat control.

So, what's the verdict? Hey, it's your party and you can grill the way you want to, but we think setting up different heat zones is more work than it needs to be. Why? Because you can pretty much control the heat of your charcoal grill by simply adding or subtracting the number of coals you add to the fire. To get a hotter fire, simply add more coals to your initial settings. To achieve a lower temperature, simply use fewer coals. This may require some experimentation on your part to obtain the desired results.

*If the recipe calls for **searing over Direct heat and finishing over Indirect**, set up your grill for an Indirect fire. Sear the food directly over the coals, then move your food over Indirect heat. If the instruction is to **sear over Direct High heat and to finish over Indirect Medium heat**, before you start the fire you can simply add five to ten coals to the side where you'll be searing. Easier still, sear over Medium heat, but extend the searing time by a minute or two.*

*For recipes that require one cooking method (Direct or Indirect) but a change in temperature, here's what you do: For **moving from High to Medium heat**, you can simply adjust the cooking method to grill over Medium heat for the entire time and slightly increase your cooking time. In rare cases when a recipe instructs **moving from Medium heat to High heat**, we think you're better off strictly over Medium heat. Again, you will need to adjust your grilling times. Anytime you have to adjust cooking times, it's wise to use a meat thermometer to ensure the proper doneness temperature is reached.*

What it all boils down to is minor adjustments in timing or charcoal set-up to get you to the desired results. Just remember to always grill with the lid on. With a little practice you'll be shuffling briquets like a pro, or getting very familiar with your trusty timer. Either way, a great meal will be your reward!

GAS GRILLING

Cooking on a gas grill? It's been said that "it's all in the wrists." To some extent, this is true: Turn a knob and you can pretty much control your results, if not your dining destiny. But while you might save a little effort in setting the fire, you can still finesse the flame.

The basic underpinnings of a gas grill are really quite simple: First come burners to create heat. Above them you'll typically find some type of system to disperse the heat (Flavorizer® bars—on Weber grills—or lava rocks, ceramic briquets, etc.). Above those you'll find the cooking grates. Now, while the heat dispersal system and the cooking grates are crucial elements, the burners are the heart and soul of that system. Not only do they do the job of conducting the fire, they also put control of outdoor cooking in your primordial grip.

Most people quickly master the basic Direct and Indirect cooking methods on a gas grill *(see pages 22 to 25)*. But what defines quality in a gas grill is the ability to artfully orchestrate the heat settings. The most functional gas grills have at least three burners, and four- to six-burner models are becoming more common. Why is this important? Well, in a nutshell, more burners equals more options. With multiple burners you can use all or part of the cooking grate as needed. Say you are roasting a whole chicken over an Indirect fire. With multiple burners, you can set up a series of heat zones and use them to simultaneously grill foods that require different cooking methods. So while the chicken is roasting, you can be grilling up some tender asparagus or zucchini, or baking piping-hot twice-baked potatoes over a Direct fire. With a six-burner model you can really show off and grill a prime rib roast and a turkey at the same time, over two Indirect fires. In essence, a large number of burners and a roomy cooking grate allow you to set up your grill like two grills side by side. Impressive and versatile!

Each recipe in this book tells you the cooking method and ideal temperature to use for normal weather conditions (i.e., no wind). But let's say you want to perfect your own recipe or technique. Once you master the heat zones, you can further refine your options and begin regulating the grill temperature by carefully selecting heat settings for each burner. This skill is handy when weather conditions are less than ideal or you have a particular food you want to master. For instance, when grilling pork ribs, you might find that keeping the outermost burners on Medium-Low and the burners closer to the food on Extra-Low gives you the most tenderizing results. (Note: Not all gas grills have Medium-Low or Extra-Low settings, and some have infinite temperature control. Check your owner's manual.) The point is, if you've got the burners, don't be afraid to use them. Experiment with varying heat settings to get the grill temperature you think is ideal for what you are grilling. Whatever you do, always cook with the lid closed!

Whether you stick to the basics or venture out on your own, always start by preheating your gas grill with all burners on High. This allows your grill to thoroughly warm up to maximum grilling temperature and will burn off any residue that might have been left from your last cookout. Give the cooking grate a good swipe with a grill brush before you start grilling. But remember, as easy as gas grills are to operate, they still require proper care and feeding. Be sure to regularly clean the funneled bottom tray (if your grill has one) and empty the grease catch-pan so you don't get flare-ups, grease fires, or uninvited wildlife stopping by for midnight snacks. After you're finished grilling, turn off all the burners and the tank at the source. If you keep your grill protected with a vinyl cover, you'll save yourself some time cleaning the grill's exterior (work tables can get dusty, for example) and reduce the natural wear and tear from the elements.

And if you really love your grill, you might be tempted to baby it. But whatever you do, don't roll it into the garage with the gas tank attached. Liquid propane should never be stored in an enclosed space, so detach the gas tank and leave it outdoors, away from any traffic.

CHECK YOUR CHAR-O-SCOPE

Ever wonder if you're using the right grill for you? Take our quiz to discover your Inner Griller. It's based on play-ful conjecture and loads of research (yeah, right). Choose the answer that most closely reflects your reality.

1. Your favorite meat:
a) any
b) poultry
c) fish
d) beef, beef, beef

2. Your job:
a) blue collar
b) white collar
c) no collar

3. Your wheels:
a) foreign
b) domestic
c) two

4. Your lifestyle:
a) laid back
b) hurry hurry
c) balanced

5. When offered dessert, you:
a) partake.
b) refuse.
c) ask for the recipe.

6. When eating grilled food, you:
a) grab a cold one.
b) pour the wine.
c) make iced tea.

7. Great grilled food _____ .
a) takes time
b) makes any day worthwhile
c) is like oxygen—utterly necessary to sustain life

8. When entertaining, you:
a) invite your friends over, then check what's in the freezer.
b) make a menu, call your friends, hit the store.
c) keep the guest list short so you can go all out.

For scoring method and insights into your Inner Griller, see page 416.

GRILLERS IN THE MIST

GRILLING IN THE ELEMENTS

Even if you're not a die-hard griller ready to brave rain, snow, and gloom of night, occasionally Mother Nature ambushes you. While you should never grill in a lightning storm or a torrential downpour, you can conquer the elements.

Cold weather: *Cold-weather grilling presents some special challenges, so you will need to be more flexible in your cooking and serving schedule. If it's been snowing, remove the snow from the entire grill before preheating. For the Direct method, it may be necessary to add a couple minutes of cooking time per side and use a food thermometer to ensure doneness. Most important is to keep the lid down as heat will escape very quickly and it can take a long time to get back to cooking temperature. Foods cooked by the Indirect method are great because you don't need to lift the lid and turn them, but on very cold days you may have to increase the heat to maintain a roasting temperature. Position the grill near a window so you can monitor its temperature from inside (but keep hot grills at least 10 feet from your house or any other combustible). Make sure your bulky winter clothing doesn't come into contact with the hot grill.*

Wind: *Wind affects gas and charcoal grills more than anything else. When it is windy, it may be helpful to angle a gas grill so the wind is perpendicular to the flow of the gas through the burner tubes. Check through the match-light hole—which avoids any lid lifting—to ensure the flames haven't gone out. If the burners should go out while in operation, turn all gas valves off. Open the lid and wait 5 minutes before attempting to relight the grill. For charcoal grills it may be necessary to add charcoal more often to maintain a consistent temperature when it is windy. Always keep the vents open. Lift the lid slowly and to the side to prevent ashes from blowing up on the food. For safety, avoid using your charcoal grill in high wind.*

High altitudes: *At higher elevations you need to increase most cooking times, especially when you're using the Indirect method (fast-cooking foods over Direct heat don't need much more time). Also adjust for cold and windy weather as above when needed.*

SMOKE COOKING ON THE GRILL

Smoke cooking is truly an art unto itself, with several fine cookbooks—and cooks!—devoted to the subject. The best way to get there, of course, is with a traditional smoker or barbecue pit. Still, you can add a delicious touch of smoke flavor to grilled food on your gas or charcoal grill. Here are some guidelines.

GETTING STARTED

- **WOODS:** Start by soaking wood chunks in water for at least 1 hour, chips (including wine barrel chips) and aromatic twigs (grape vines or fruit wood twigs) for 30 minutes. Shake all excess water off woods before adding them to your fire or smoker box. (See chart, page 31, for tips on matching woods with foods.) You can find smoking woods in hardware stores and home centers—or if you're lucky, in your own backyard! Wine barrel chips are available at specialty food stores and some hardware stores, or search for them online.

- **WATER:** Water adds moisture to the smoking process so meats come out flavorful and tender. If you're using a traditional smoker with a water pan, try adding barbecue sauce, marinades, wine, beer, fruit juices, or herbs and spices to the water for additional flavor. Be sure to keep the water pan full. For large roasts and turkeys, you may have to replenish water whenever you add charcoal—a watering can makes this easy. (Note: When smoking cheese, add ice to the water pan so the cheese above it doesn't melt.) For grills, a water pan is a good idea for longer cooking times (see "Preparing Your Grill or Smoker," right.)

- **FOOD:** Remember that smoke and heat escape each time you lift the lid to turn food; if you are using low temperatures, add several minutes to cooking time for each time you lift the lid (more if you are smoking in cold or wind or at high altitudes). Boneless meats, such as beef brisket and pork shoulder, will shrink considerably during smoke cooking, unless they have a heavy layering of fat. Simply cut the fat off the meat before serving. (Note: Consider grilling your menu a day before serving. The smoke flavor becomes richer after a day or two in the refrigerator. That's why smoked foods make great leftovers.)

PREPARING YOUR GRILL OR SMOKER

- **CHARCOAL GRILL:** If you're smoking foods over Direct heat, simply throw the soaked wood chips or chunks on the prepared coals a few minutes before you start cooking. For Indirect cooking (*see pages 24 to 25*), use a water pan. Place a heavy-gauge aluminum foil pan between the piles of briquets; add 2 cups hot water and any desired flavorings. Add soaked wood chips or chunks to prepared coals, place the food on the cooking grate over the water pan, and cover the grill. Every hour, add briquets to each side and replenish water and seasonings as needed.

- **GAS GRILL:** Many gas grills can be equipped with a smoker box attachment. You can also improvise with a foil pan with holes punched in the bottom with a skewer. Before preheating your grill, simply fill the water pan on the smoker attachment with hot tap water. Place presoaked wood chunks or chips/twigs in the other compartment, or in the prepared foil pan set directly on the Flavorizer® bars or burner tents over the lit burners. (Use a separate pan for water if using a foil pan for the wood.) Begin cooking after preheating and when the grill is fully smoking.

- **SMOKER:** If you have a traditional smoker, follow the manufacturer's instructions for using it. Always position the smoker on a level, heat-proof surface away from buildings and out of traffic patterns. It's best to find a place away from the house since smoke aromas can linger for hours. Replenish water and fuel as instructed.

GETTING STARTED
TIPS FOR BEGINNERS

Aside from noting that your clothes and hair may need a good washing once you're done, here's what you need to know to start learning the art of smoke cooking.

Use a meat thermometer to make sure smoke-cooked foods are done but not overcooked. Smoke-cooked foods look different than other grilled or oven-prepared foods. They may be pink or red when completely cooked (for example, apple wood will make chicken look red).

Use tongs and barbecue mitts to add charcoal, turn meats, refill the water pan, or adjust vents.

Do not use charcoal infused with starter fluid—it can add an unpleasant taste to your smoked foods.

Experiment with different woods and meats until you find the right combination for your tastes.

Start with a small amount of wood to see how you like the flavor, then add more for a more intense smoky taste. (Just don't over-do it; too much wood smoke over long periods can make the food taste bitter.)

Try combining woods: As you gain experience you can achieve unique and flavorful results.

WHERE THERE'S SMOKE, THERE'S FLAVOR
SMOKING WOODS

WOOD TYPE	CHARACTERISTICS	PAIR WITH
Hickory	Pungent, smoky, baconlike flavor	Pork, chicken, beef, wild game, cheeses
Pecan	Rich and more subtle than hickory, but similar in taste; burns cool, so ideal for very low heat smoking	Pork, chicken, lamb, fish, cheeses
Mesquite	Sweeter, more delicate flavor than hickory; tends to burn hot, so use carefully	Most meats (especially beef), most vegetables
Alder	Delicate flavor that enhances lighter meats	Salmon, swordfish, sturgeon, other fish; also good with chicken and pork
Oak	Forthright but pleasant flavor; blends well with variety of textures and flavors	Beef (particularly brisket), poultry, pork
Maple	Mildly smoky, somewhat sweet flavor; try mixing with corncobs for ham or bacon	Poultry, vegetables, ham
Cherry	Slightly sweet, fruity smoke flavor	Poultry, game birds, pork
Apple	Slightly sweet but denser, fruity smoke flavor	Beef, poultry, game birds, pork (particularly ham)
Peach or pear	Slightly sweet, woodsy flavor	Poultry, game birds, pork
Grape vines	Aromatic, similar to fruit woods	Turkey, chicken, beef
Wine barrel chips	Wine and oak flavors; a flavorful novelty that smells wonderful, too	Beef, turkey, chicken, cheeses
Seaweed	Tangy and smoky flavors (wash and dry in sun before use)	Lobster, crab, shrimp, mussels, clams
Herbs and spices (e.g., bay leaves, rosemary, garlic, mint, orange or lemon peels, whole nutmeg, cinnamon sticks)	Vary from spicy (bay leaves and garlic) to sweet (fruit peels and cinnamon sticks) and delicate to mild—generally, herbs and spices with higher oil content will provide stronger flavoring; soak branches and stems in water before adding to fire—they burn quickly, so you may need to replenish often	Vegetables, cheeses, variety of small pieces of meat (lighter, thin-cut meats; fish steaks or fillets; kabobs)

RECIPES FOR ROOKIES

Getting the basics down pat is the first step in learning to grill. If you're new to the sport or still getting the knack of it, these recipes will help you grill the most standard backyard fare. Once you've got these down, you'll be primed for the recipes ahead.

BASIC
BURGERS

DIRECT/MEDIUM

1 1/2 POUNDS GROUND CHUCK (80% LEAN)
    KOSHER SALT
    FRESHLY GROUND BLACK PEPPER
4 HAMBURGER BUNS
    KETCHUP (OPTIONAL)
    MUSTARD (OPTIONAL)

Gently shape the ground chuck into four burgers of equal size and thickness (about 3/4 inch thick). Season with salt and pepper. Grill the burgers over *Direct Medium* heat until the internal temperature reaches 160°F for medium, 8 to 10 minutes, turning once halfway through grilling time. During the last 30 seconds, grill the buns over *Direct Medium* heat until lightly toasted.

Serve the burgers hot on the buns with ketchup and mustard, if desired.

MAKES 4 SERVINGS

SIMPLE
STEAKS

DIRECT/MEDIUM

4 NEW YORK STRIP, TENDERLOIN, T-BONE, SIRLOIN, *OR* RIB-EYE BEEF STEAKS, ABOUT 3/4 POUND EACH AND 1 INCH THICK
    KOSHER SALT
    FRESHLY GROUND PEPPER
    EXTRA-VIRGIN OLIVE OIL

Allow the steaks to stand at room temperature for 20 to 30 minutes before grilling. Season both sides of the steaks with salt and pepper, pressing the spices into the meat. Lightly spray or brush both sides of the steaks with olive oil.

Grill the steaks over *Direct Medium* heat until the internal temperature reaches 145°F for medium rare, 8 to 10 minutes, turning once halfway through grilling time. Remove from the grill and allow to rest for 3 to 5 minutes. Serve warm.

MAKES 4 SERVINGS

CLASSIC BONELESS
PORK CHOPS

DIRECT/MEDIUM

4 BONELESS PORK LOIN CHOPS, ABOUT 1 INCH THICK
    KOSHER SALT
    FRESHLY GROUND BLACK PEPPER
    EXTRA-VIRGIN OLIVE OIL

Season the pork chops with salt and pepper and lightly brush or spray both sides with olive oil. Allow to stand at room temperature for about 20 minutes before grilling.

Grill the chops over *Direct Medium* heat until the juices run clear, 10 to 12 minutes, turning once halfway through grilling time. Serve warm.

MAKES 4 SERVINGS

CLASSIC BONE-IN
PORK CHOPS

DIRECT/MEDIUM

4 BONE-IN RIB PORK CHOPS, ABOUT 1 INCH THICK
    KOSHER SALT
    FRESHLY GROUND BLACK PEPPER
    EXTRA-VIRGIN OLIVE OIL

Season the pork chops with salt and pepper and lightly brush or spray both sides with olive oil. Allow to stand at room temperature for about 20 minutes before grilling.

Grill the chops over *Direct Medium* heat for 12 to 15 minutes, turning once halfway through grilling time. Serve warm.

MAKES 4 SERVINGS

CLASSIC BONELESS
CHICKEN BREASTS

DIRECT/MEDIUM

4 BONELESS, SKINLESS CHICKEN BREAST HALVES,
   ABOUT 6 OUNCES EACH
   KOSHER SALT
   FRESHLY GROUND BLACK PEPPER
   EXTRA-VIRGIN OLIVE OIL

Rinse the chicken breasts under cold water and pat dry with paper towels. Season the breasts with salt and pepper and lightly brush or spray both sides with olive oil. Grill the chicken over *Direct Medium* heat until the juices run clear and the meat is no longer pink in the center, 8 to 10 minutes, turning once halfway through grilling time. Serve warm.

MAKES 4 SERVINGS

CLASSIC BONE-IN
CHICKEN BREASTS

INDIRECT/MEDIUM

4 CHICKEN BREAST HALVES (WITH BONE AND
   SKIN), 10 TO 12 OUNCES EACH
   KOSHER SALT
   FRESHLY GROUND BLACK PEPPER
   EXTRA-VIRGIN OLIVE OIL

Rinse the chicken breasts under cold water and pat dry with paper towels. Season the breasts with salt and pepper and lightly brush or spray both sides with olive oil. Grill the chicken, skin side up, over *Indirect Medium* heat until the juices run clear and the meat is no longer pink at the bone, 30 to 40 minutes. For crispier skin, grill the breasts, skin side down, over *Direct Medium* heat during the last 5 minutes of grilling time. Serve warm.

MAKES 4 SERVINGS

FABULOUS
FISH FILLETS

DIRECT/HIGH

4 SWORDFISH, HALIBUT, *OR* SALMON FILLETS,
   ABOUT 6 TO 8 OUNCES EACH AND 1 INCH THICK
   KOSHER SALT
   FRESHLY GROUND BLACK PEPPER
   EXTRA-VIRGIN OLIVE OIL

   LEMON WEDGES (OPTIONAL)

Season the fish fillets with salt and pepper and lightly brush or spray both sides with olive oil. Grill the fillets over *Direct High* heat until opaque in the center, 8 to 10 minutes, turning once halfway through grilling time (exception: grilling salmon fillets, see page 285). Serve warm with lemon wedges, if desired.

MAKES 4 SERVINGS

TENDER
WHOLE TROUT

INDIRECT/MEDIUM

4 WHOLE BROOK TROUT, GUTTED AND CLEANED,
   10 TO 12 OUNCES EACH
   KOSHER SALT
   FRESHLY GROUND BLACK PEPPER
   EXTRA-VIRGIN OLIVE OIL

   LEMON WEDGES (OPTIONAL)

Season the interior cavity of the trout with salt and pepper. Lightly brush or spray both sides of the exterior with olive oil. Grill the fish over *Indirect Medium* heat until opaque in the center, about 15 minutes. Serve warm with lemon wedges, if desired.

MAKES 4 SERVINGS

A MATCH MADE IN HEAVEN
BEER AND A BARBECUE

For most beer drinkers, the question of what to pour with dinner is a no-brainer. As long as it's cold and foamy, it's good enough! This is especially true at the grill, where beer's quenching qualities are even more in demand. But before you exhaust your favorite brew—and to accommodate any guests' preferences—throw some of these in your cooler. You might discover a new love.

LAGERS: A broad category, we know, but let us point out a few qualities besides their amazing compatibility with a hammock. Generally lighter and drier than ales, lagers refresh and quench wonderfully. They're great with spicy Mexican food. Go ahead and add the lime—it's not a trend, it actually improves the match. Pilsners, highly hopped, are the driest of the lagers and best with grilled meats without heavy sauces. Most Japanese and Chinese beers are pilsners because they complement the clean, crisp flavors of the cuisines so well. Likewise, Jamaican lagers are a natural match for the fiery native cuisine.

ALES: An even larger category, but no need to worry about the finer distinctions; just focus on ales that are best with grilled fare. Red/amber and pale ales are musts for the griller. Reds and ambers (the distinction is often regional) are great with grilled meats because their sweeter flavor plays off the caramelized sweetness of the meat's surface. The redder the meat, the redder the ale is our rule of thumb. With their full body, they can stand up to the beefiest porterhouse. Pale ales, with their crisp, dry profile, are great with spicier dishes such as grilled curries, pita sandwiches, and kabobs.

STOUTS: The tonic properties of a good Irish stout have been touted in folklore and advertising campaigns alike, but don't overlook New World versions. Dark and heavy, stouts run from sweet (sweet and oatmeal stouts) to dry (dry, extra, and imperial). Stout is virtually the only beer that goes with chocolate, if you're so inclined to try such a combo. We like it in our gingerbread (*see page 390*).

WHEAT BEERS: Wheat beers (also called by their German names, *Weisse*, *Weissbeir*, and *Weizen*) are sparkling, light, and refreshing brews that are great with lighter meals or just for summertime sipping. Regular (*Kristall*) wheat beers are clear, crisp, and anything but fussy. *Hefe-Weizen* (yeast wheat) is cloudy with an abundance of live yeasts, which generate a distinct aroma reminiscent of ripe bananas. You can almost feel the B vitamins racing through your veins as you sip this elixir. Slip a lemon slice in there like the Bavarians and Austrians do. Dark (*Dunkel*) wheat beers are sweeter and heavier, and make a great quaffable "sauce" for grilled sausages and meats.

SMOKE BEERS: *Rauchbier*, another German invention, is an acquired taste, but great with smoked meats and sausages. It's made by kilning the malt over a smoky beechwood fire. If you like Scotch, give this one a try.

FRUIT-FLAVORED BEERS: Whether they're infused with real fruit or enhanced with syrups, fruit beers offer an interesting twist. For an apéritif or a post—yard work cool down, try a light raspberry wheat beer or an apricot ale. For dessert, a heavier beer body or bolder fruit flavor will add a special note. Think cherry or raspberry lambic or even a cranberry ale. For a fall feast, try pumpkin ale. Chile beers add to the fire of a spicy meal.

Of course the possibilities for mixing and matching beer with grilled food are endless. As far as we're concerned, that's the fun of it!

PERFECT
MARGARITAS

Need a cure for the lawn-mower blues? Or just a refreshing break in the shade? When wine won't do it and beer is off the mark, try America's next favorite drink, a classic margarita. All the best-dressed summer patios sport a pitcher or two of these when unexpected guests drop by or a party is about to break out.

JAMIE'S MARGARITA

This bright, tangy refresher is right at home with the bold flavors of spicy grilled food. If you've been using that bottled sweet-and-sour mix, step up to the real deal, which is all about fresh lime juice, Triple Sec, and the best tequila in town. Easy to multiply by the number of guests.

- **1** CUT LIME (OPTIONAL)
  KOSHER SALT (OPTIONAL)

- **5** TO 6 ICE CUBES
- **¼** CUP TEQUILA
- **2** TABLESPOONS TRIPLE SEC
- **2** TABLESPOONS FRESH LIME JUICE

If desired, rub the rim of a margarita glass with cut lime and dip the rim into a bowl with a shallow layer of salt.

Thoroughly mix the remaining ingredients in a glass. Serve cold.

MAKES 1 MARGARITA

SIPPIN' IN THE SHADE
SUMMERTIME
LEMONADE

Beer isn't the only sip just made for the hammock. Don't underestimate the thirst-quenching, restorative powers of a tall, icy, homemade lemonade. Here's a quick recipe to get you back to basics. Kids will love you for this—especially if you let them help make it. Pick smooth, bright yellow lemons that are plump and heavy for their size.

CLASSIC LEMONADE

Good lemonade starts with a homemade syrup and ends with freshly squeezed juice. Suit yourself by playing with the proportion of sugar to juice.

- **8** CUPS COLD WATER
- **2** CUPS GRANULATED SUGAR
- **1¼** CUPS FRESH LEMON JUICE
- **½** TEASPOON KOSHER SALT
  ICE CUBES
  FRESH MINT SPRIGS

In a large saucepan over high heat, bring the water and sugar to a boil for 2 minutes. Allow the syrup to cool to room temperature. Add the lemon juice and salt. Fill each glass with ice cubes and a sprig of mint. Pour the lemonade over the ice and serve cold.

MAKES ABOUT 8 SERVINGS

DRINK WHAT YOU LIKE

Let's say you've decided what to cook for dinner—perhaps a dry-rubbed steak and grilled corn on the cob—and now you are standing in the market or liquor store staring at a wall of wine. How do you possibly decide which bottle will make a seamless, spectacular match with your meal?

Well, the standard rules start running through your mind. For a steak dinner, you must forget about all white wines because you *have* to serve red wine with red meat, right? And avoid all sweet wines such as white Zinfandel because they are unsophisticated. Hmmm. But what if you like white wines better than reds, or what if you think white Zinfandel is delicious? What if the sales clerk suggests an expensive red wine that the back label describes as "having a tightly focused core of tobacco and black cherry with a long finish of silky tannins." Excuse me, what was that? The likely conclusion is that many of us abandon our own good sense or good taste for fear of making a "mistake," and we decide to play it safe and bring home some cold beer.

It doesn't have to be like that. The truth is wine tastes good with grilled food. Period. In fact, our friend Tim Hanni, a Master of Wine (nice title, huh?) from Napa Valley, California, explains that the whole concept of "matching" food and wine is a relatively new custom. Hundreds of years ago, folks in France and Italy didn't get caught up in the innumerable rules we are expected to memorize today. Even the gourmands typically drank the same wine, whatever was produced in their region, with whatever they were eating. Easy and delicious. For us, it's grown considerably more complicated because we have so many styles of wine to choose from. So, your biggest challenge as you stare at that wall of wine is just to pick the kind of wine you like, regardless of the food. If you are entertaining a group, the considerate thing to do is to pick a few different styles of wine—red and white, dry and sweet—and let your guests find their favorites. That's the gist of it.

That said, Tim offers two sensible principles to finesse your wine-and-food combinations.

- **SWEET FOODS WILL MAKE WINE TASTE STRONGER.** That is, the wine (no matter what kind of wine) will taste more acidic and possibly more bitter when you drink it with sweet food. Some people like this, some don't. For example, a sweet barbecue sauce may make a red wine taste just too strong for some folks, while others will relish the newfound gusto in the wine. For those who find the wine too acidic, there is an easy solution. Squeeze a few drops of lemon juice or sprinkle just a tiny pinch of salt on your food. The acidity or saltiness will balance with the sweetness of the sauce and make the wine taste milder, which brings us to the second principle....

- **ACIDIC OR SALTY FOODS WILL MAKE WINE TASTE MILDER.** No matter what kind of wine you are drinking, if the food is acidic or salty, the wine will taste less acidic and less bitter. This is great news if you are sipping a wine that seems too strong for your taste. Drink the wine with whatever you like (chicken, fish, meat, etc.), but serve the food with a tangy salsa or a soy-based sauce, for example. You'll be amazed how that salsa's lime juice or the soy's saltiness tames the wildness of wine. On the other hand, if the wine seems a little underwhelming, give the food some sweetness by brushing on a glaze or adding a pinch of sugar to the sauce. The wine will perk up right away.

These are useful principles but the real key here is that if the food you are grilling is balanced—that is, if it is not particularly sweet or acidic or salty—it will not significantly change the character of any wine. Just about all of the recipes in this book are balanced in this way, so simply find the wines you like and drink up. You can enjoy your favorites and your guest can enjoy theirs—all with the same food.

THE FIFTH TASTE
UMAMI

The principles of flavor-balancing revolve around the four basic tastes: sweetness, acidity, saltiness, and bitterness. As long as these tastes are relatively balanced, grilled food is almost always delicious with wine. However, there is a lesser-known fifth taste that also affects our perception of wines. Neuroscientists at the University of Miami have identified certain receptors on our tongues that pick up a taste called umami (pronounced "oo-MOM-my"). This taste is found in many high-protein foods such as meat, seafood, and some vegetables. A 20th-century Japanese food scientist described it as "savoriness," which you taste in foods such as dry-aged steak and shiitake mushrooms. It is a satisfying, mouth-filling taste, but for the purposes of enjoying wine, keep in mind that **foods high in umami make wines taste stronger**. In other words, they work just like sweet foods do. Aged cheeses such as Parmigiano-Reggiano and Roquefort and shell-fish such as fresh crab, scallops, and oysters are classic examples of umami-rich foods. If you are grilling with significant amounts of these and you want to enjoy wine with your meal, you may want to consider using some acidity or salt to balance them. But you be the judge. Remember, it's your taste.

"I drank WHAT?"

— SOCRATES

WITH LEMON, PLEASE
CLASSIC ICED TEA

Is it an alternative beverage or the original? Depends on who you ask, but one thing we all agree on: It's as much a part of summer as suntan lotion and Frisbees ™. Drink up!

BASIC ICED TEA

The strength of this worldwide favorite depends on the type of tea leaves and the length of brewing, and sweetness is of course a matter of preference. If you want a sweet batch, add about 3 tablespoons of sugar to the boiling water in this recipe (if you're from the South, pour it on until it feels right). Otherwise, allow guests to add their own.

- **8 CUPS COLD WATER**
- **12 TEA BAGS OR 1/4 CUP LOOSE TEA**
- **ICE CUBES**
- **LEMON SLICES**
- **FRESH MINT**
- **GRANULATED SUGAR (OPTIONAL)**

In a large saucepan over high heat, bring the water to a boil. Add the tea, stir, and let steep for 3 to 5 minutes. Remove the tea bags or strain the tea. Allow to cool to room temperature. Fill each glass with ice cubes, a slice of lemon, and a sprig of mint. Pour the tea over the ice and serve cold and sweetened with sugar if desired.

MAKES 6 TO 8 SERVINGS

LIFE'S A PARTY
WHAT TO SERVE

Which comes first, the invitations or the menu? Doesn't matter! Whether you insist on planning ahead or the guests are already on their way over, we've gathered some great ideas for you. Go by cuisine or theme—just leave enough room for dessert!

STEAK LOVER'S FEAST

SWEET PEPPER AND EGGPLANT BRUSCHETTA

DRY-RUBBED PORTERHOUSE WITH BARBECUE STEAK SAUCE

NEW POTATO SALAD

ICE CREAM SANDWICHES

SOMETHING ITALIAN, PLEASE

GRILLED POLENTA WITH MUSHROOM RAGOUT

BISTECCA ALLA FIORENTINA

GRILLED GARLIC BREAD

STRAWBERRIES BALSAMICO

VEGETABLES IN ALL THEIR GLORY

EGGPLANT ROLL-UPS

WARM BEET AND ONION SALAD

ARUGULA PIZZA

APPLES GRILLED IN PARCHMENT PAPER

MEXICAN FLAVORS

CHORIZO QUESADILLAS

RED SNAPPER FAJITAS WITH BLACK BEAN SALSA

CITRUS-AVOCADO CHICKEN BREASTS

PARADISE GRILLED

SEAFOOD SPECTACULAR

SMOKEY JOE'S CRAB CAKES

SEARED AHI WITH THAI DIPPING SAUCE

CUCUMBER SALAD WITH TOASTED SESAME SEEDS

PEACHES WITH RASPBERRY SAUCE AND LEMON CREAM

A WINTER FEAST

**MINI GRILLED
BLUE CHEESE BITES**

**BUFFALO STRIP STEAKS
WITH LUSTY RED WINE SAUCE**

**MASHED SWEET POTATOES
WITH GRILLED ONIONS**

**BREAD PUDDING
WITH DRIED CHERRIES**

THE BOSS COMES FOR DINNER

**PROSCIUTTO SCALLOPS
WITH BALSAMIC GLAZE**

**RACK OF LAMB WITH
ORANGE-CRANBERRY CHUTNEY**

**BLUE CHEESE, APPLE,
AND HONEYED WALNUT SALAD**

BLUEBERRY TART

TRADITIONAL SOUTHERN BARBECUE

**PULLED PORK BARBECUE
WITH HOT PEPPER
VINEGAR SAUCE**

SPICY MAPLE BAKED BEANS

**OLD-FASHIONED
CREAMY COLESLAW**

**BUTTERMILK SPICE CAKE
WITH COCONUT-RAISIN FROSTING**

A PACIFIC RIM JOURNEY

SHRIMP SATAY

**PLUM-GLAZED
BABY BACK RIBS**

**LONG NOODLE AND
BEAN SPROUT SALAD**

TROPICAL FRUIT CRISP

EASY SUMMER ENTERTAINING

EGGPLANT-TOMATO DIP

CLASSIC BACON CHEESEBURGER

**MACARONI SALAD
WITH A HORSERADISH KICK**

FROZEN FRUIT POPS

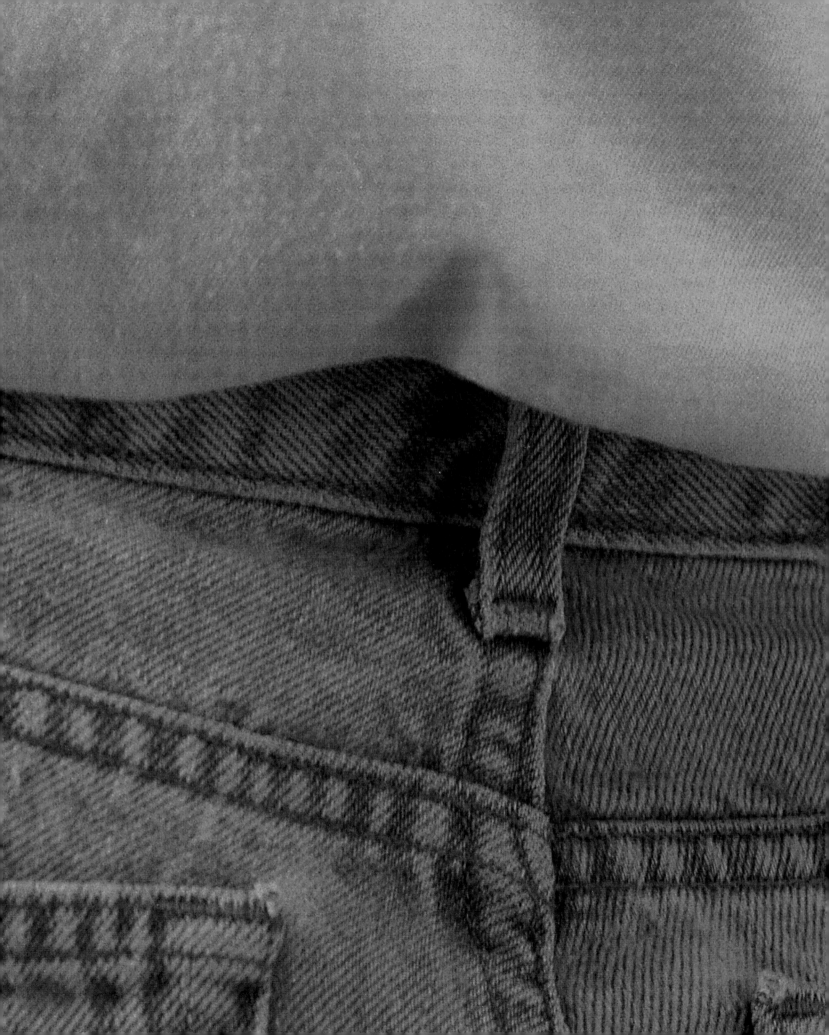

Barbecue sauce. If you are among the grilling faithful, these two words can bring a tear to your eye and a jolt to your taste buds as you imagine your favorite sauce. Many a life has been dedicated to the quest for the Ultimate Concoction: the one that fulfills that desire for hot food cooked over a fire and slathered with the perfect balance of spice, acidity, sweetness, smoke, and even fire. Barbecue sauce!

But alas, there are those among us who have yet to see the light and whose immediate thought is of a ubiquitous, squat glass bottle with a bright red label. Reader, we say unto thee, if thou hast not yet discovered the Joy of Making Sauce from Scratch, read this chapter and be healed!

SAUCES,

Making your own barbecue sauce is not only easy, it's one of the most rewarding experiences the kitchen has to offer. Soufflés may fall and custards may curdle, but once you've discovered your favorite barbecue sauce recipe—or better yet, perfected your very own recipe ("borrowing" from others is not only okay, it's encouraged)—you've created a happy, balanced world. One that you can revisit whenever you want by merely brandishing a basting brush. Best of all, you can have more than one favorite: one for pork, one for beef, and so on.

Another good reason to make your own barbecue sauce is that it allows you to skip the high-fructose corn syrup that's found in a lot of the national brands. Maybe it's not the worst culinary sin, but not everyone needs or wants all that super-concentrated sweetness.

That is not to say, however, that there's a nasty genie in every bottle. In fact, there are countless great handcrafted sauces out there, usually available at specialty shops, by mail-order, or on the Internet. These wondrous sauces are often award-winning recipes straight off the barbecue circuit, now lovingly prepared for an adoring public with natural ingredients.

Their usually creative names might belie the contents, if not the creator's passion for barbecue.
We think they're worth their boutique prices. You know how some people collect T-shirts from all the
cities they visit? We pick up barbecue sauce instead.

Barbecue sauce isn't the only way to add flavor at the grill, however. Marinades add flavor while
tenderizing; rubs add a nice texture along with a big boost of flavor. We've got lots of those in here for
you, too. And talk about time-savers! You probably already have most of the ingredients we use—such as
mustard, ketchup, Worcestershire sauce, soy sauce, Tabasco—in your kitchen already. You can whisk up

MARINADES, & RUBS

a marinade in the morning and come home to a delicious, moist dinner at night. Rubs often require
even less time to work their magic, so sometimes you can be grilling within an hour or two of applying
them. With sauces, marinades, and rubs, the hardest part is deciding what to fix. And of course, waiting
for that delicious-smelling dinner to cook.

One more thing: Sauces, marinades, and rubs can carry a whole dish and make picking side dishes
a breeze. Match a flavor or theme (orange or Italian, for example) and your menu is done. And since
we cover all the basics on how they work in this chapter, you can improvise and experiment on your
own with results you can be proud of.

Some of these recipes are so good they make cameo appearances in later chapters, so if you find one
you really like, look it up in the Index to find another creative and tasty use for it. After reading around,
you might try pairing a marinade or rub with a sauce of the same theme, such as Asian or classic barbecue flavor. Usually the richer, more flavorful cuts of meat—such as ribs or shoulder roasts—are good to
start with. They can take the one-two punch and come out tender and triumphant. Who knows, you may
just devise a trademark dish that makes you famous (at least at home). Remember, the road to Grilling
Heaven is paved with near-misses.

Fritz's Favorite Barbecue Sauce

FRITZ'S FAVORITE
BARBECUE SAUCE

This recipe comes to us from our good friend Chef Fritz Sonnenschmidt of the Culinary Institute of America. Slather it on all kinds of ribs, chicken, and kabobs.

- 1/4 CUP EXTRA-VIRGIN OLIVE OIL
- 1/2 CUP FINELY CHOPPED RED ONION
- 2 TEASPOONS MINCED GARLIC
- 1 CUP LOW-SODIUM CHICKEN BROTH
- 3/4 CUP KETCHUP
- 1/2 CUP ORANGE JUICE CONCENTRATE
- 1/2 CUP STEAK SAUCE
- 2 TABLESPOONS WORCESTERSHIRE SAUCE
- 1 TABLESPOON WHITE WINE VINEGAR
- 1 TABLESPOON GROUND COFFEE
- 2 TEASPOONS DRIED CHERVIL
- 1/2 TEASPOON CELERY SEEDS
- 1/2 TEASPOON FRESHLY GROUND BLACK PEPPER

In a medium saucepan over medium-high heat, warm the olive oil. Add the onion and garlic and cook for 2 to 3 minutes, stirring occasionally. Add the remaining ingredients and whisk to combine. Simmer for 30 minutes, stirring occasionally.

Transfer to a bowl, cover with plastic wrap, and refrigerate until ready to use.

MAKES ABOUT 2 CUPS

CHILI
BARBECUE SAUCE

This one is sweet and spicy. Works well as a dipping sauce for grilled steak.

- 1/2 CUP KETCHUP
- 1 TABLESPOON WORCESTERSHIRE SAUCE
- 1 TABLESPOON RED WINE VINEGAR
- 1 TABLESPOON DARK BROWN SUGAR
- 1 TEASPOON CHILI POWDER
- 1 TEASPOON GRANULATED ONION
- 1/4 TEASPOON FRESHLY GROUND BLACK PEPPER

In a small saucepan whisk together the ingredients with 1/4 cup water. Simmer over low heat for about 10 minutes, allowing the sugar to fully dissolve and all of the flavors to blend, stirring occasionally. Allow to cool to room temperature.

MAKES ABOUT 3/4 CUP

"There is no sauce in the world like hunger."

— MIGUEL CERVANTES,
Don Quixote

SAUCES, MARINADES, AND RUBS

Good cooking relies on good seasoning. At the grill, there are four basic ways to get more flavor out of (or into) your food. The first is good old salt and pepper. A nice layer of each on the surface will turn those escaping juices into a customized "sauce" of the most primitive (and rewarding) type. And then there are sauces, marinades, and rubs—tools that turn on the flavor. Here's how they work:

SAUCES: Barbecue sauce is a many splendored thing indeed. It can be a finishing sauce that's brushed on in the last 10 to 20 minutes (best bet for ones with lots of sugar, which can burn quickly). It can be a baste or mop, a thinner solution that's "mopped" on with a basting brush or special cotton moplike tool for added flavor. And of course, there are dipping sauces, among them steak sauce, which are usually drizzled on, but the effect is the same: a big kick of flavor in which to bathe your grilled prize.

Most barbecue sauces are tomato-based. When ketchup is included in the base, it brings in sugar and vinegar, two other key sauce ingredients. But then there are regions in the U.S. that use nothing but mustard-based sauces. Vinegar alone makes a wonderful base as well. Smoke flavor and chile fire are options that add intrigue and even a competitive edge at barbecue cook-offs. Get the smoke and heat levels just right and you could walk away with a ribbon. And renegade ingredients such as cola, coffee, and bourbon have been known to turn a head or two.

MARINADES: A marinade is an acidic solution that improves the texture and flavor of the food that is soaked in it. The acid in the solution tenderizes the surface; wine, vinegar, and fruit juice (especially citrus) are some of the more common acids used in marinades. Most marinades also contain oil, which leaves a moisturizing coating for cooking. Other ingredients are there for flavor: garlic, spices, herbs, etc. Salt is a common ingredient, but too much draws moisture out of food, so monitor the quantity and the marinating time.

Because of the acid, the container you marinate in must be nonreactive, plastic or glass, for instance. Definitely avoid aluminum, which will discolor and possibly leave a metallic taste.

The key to a good marinade (or sauce or rub, for that matter) is a balance of the four primary flavors: salty, sweet, bitter, and sour. When developing your own marinades, don't be afraid to add a little of each flavor type, but one should dominate. From there you can add other elements such as fruity, herbal, or smoky flavors.

Some marinades can be used again to baste the food while it's cooking. If you use a marinade that came into contact with any raw meat or fish, you MUST first boil the marinade for 1 full minute to kill any harmful bacteria before brushing the liquid on cooked food. Marinades with a high sugar or oil content should be wiped off the food before they're placed on the cooking grate, as sugar burns quickly and excess oil can cause unwanted flare-ups.

Because the acids in marinades break down the fibers of the meat or fish, excessive marinating can lead to mushy food. Veggies need just a brief dip to pick up flavor and oil; mushrooms are particularly thirsty, so 15 minutes is plenty for them. Fish is very susceptible to high-acid marinade overkill. In general, fish should only marinate up to an hour; thin cuts only need 15 to 30 minutes, but thicker cuts and whole fillets can take 30 to 60 minutes. Tougher and bigger beef and pork cuts, such as flank or skirt steak or large roasts, need much longer—4 to 8 hours, or even overnight. Beef and pork ribs can marinate 8 to 12 hours and sometimes even longer without getting mushy. Pork chops and chicken parts are usually ready in 1 to 4 hours. Marinating times for whole and halved chickens and game hens vary by the acid levels of the marinade. Since marinades only penetrate about 1/2 inch below the surface, consider butterflying (splitting) or pounding larger or tougher cuts, as we have.

RUBS: Dry rubs are blends of dried or fresh herbs and spices, salt, pepper, and sometimes sugar. Rubs with a little oil or other liquid blended in are called pastes (or "wet rubs" on the barbecue circuit). Rubs sit on the surface of the food, their flavors seasoning the meat, especially when left to "marinate" in the refrigerator for an hour or more. On the grill, they form a flavorful crust. They are quick and easy to make, and can be infinitely adjusted to hit the spot.

COMBOS: Barbecue enthusiasts long ago discovered an amazing trick: Use more than one of the preceding seasoning methods in the same dish and you could hit the flavor jackpot. A marinade or rub prepares the meat and lays a flavor foundation. A baste or sauce added after that can take it over the top. When blending methods, try to include ingredients common to all the seasoning steps and make sure your sugar content doesn't get too high or the food could burn. Ribs are a good cut to try this on. A nice spice rub followed by a mop and/or finishing sauce have put many a rib joint on the map.

WEBER'S TANGY
BARBECUE SAUCE

A Weber classic that's been around the block-party a few times. Great on Kansas City–style pork ribs, chicken, and beef. Brush it on during the last 20 minutes of grilling.

    2 TABLESPOONS UNSALTED BUTTER
    ½ CUP FINELY CHOPPED CELERY
    3 TABLESPOONS FINELY CHOPPED YELLOW ONION
    1 CUP KETCHUP
    2 TABLESPOONS FRESH LEMON JUICE
    2 TABLESPOONS GRANULATED SUGAR
    2 TABLESPOONS CIDER VINEGAR
    1 TABLESPOON WORCESTERSHIRE SAUCE
    1 TEASPOON DRY MUSTARD
       FRESHLY GROUND BLACK PEPPER

In a medium saucepan over medium-high heat, melt the butter. Add the celery and onion and cook for 2 to 3 minutes, stirring occasionally. Add the remaining ingredients and whisk together. Bring to a boil, reduce heat, cover, and simmer for 15 minutes, stirring occasionally.

Transfer to a bowl, cover with plastic wrap, and refrigerate until ready to use.

MAKES ABOUT 1⅓ CUPS

STRICTLY A MATTER OF TASTE

Did you ever notice how the best grillers in the neighborhood will tell you bits and pieces of their methods, like where they buy their fish, or what kind of wood chips they use, or how they make the skin of their chicken so crispy—but they'll skip over what really makes their food taste good—the marinade. "Oh, I just threw in some oil and herbs," the proud but protective cook is likely to say.

Well, in the spirit of full disclosure, we're here to tell you that there is a little more to it than a splash of this and a handful of that. Good marinades depend on a triad of components: acids, oils, and other flavors.

To get started on your own, create a basic vinaigrette, which is usually about one part acid to three parts oil. Season it to taste with salt and pepper and whisk. Mmm...tastes pretty good already. If you're looking at a steak that already has good taste but you want to take it in a Mediterranean direction, choose a fruity olive oil and a red wine vinegar. For a lean pork chop or chicken breast that needs a kick in the pants, try a strong chile oil and a dip into the mustard jar for the acidity. Fish with subtle flavors work well with mild oils such as canola, and lemon juice gives them a tangy brightness.

But you're not finished yet. To make a marinade truly your own, add some other flavors that reflect your particular style. If you like your food to burn the back of your throat a bit, whisk in some chili powder, red curry paste, or hot pepper sauce. For something on the sweeter side, think about honey, molasses, or ketchup. For some reason minced garlic and fresh herbs almost always seem to help, so if you have 'em, use 'em.

Note to those who want to beat all expectations: Sometimes a marinade can be a shining example of the principles above, but there is still something missing. No problem. There are certain condiments that fill those flavor gaps beautifully and provide a deliciousness that's hard to replicate without them. These condiments are concentrated, often fermented products with extraordinary depth. Good examples: Worcestershire sauce, fish sauce, and balsamic vinegar. Use them judiciously for fantastic results.

Finally, understand that a good marinade does not necessarily taste good. That is, a marinade can be so pungent or spicy on its own that you wouldn't dare pour it on your tongue, but when it works its way into the food and cooks over a hot fire, it becomes that tasty little secret that some cooks don't like to share.

AMERICA'S MAIN SQUEEZE
IN PRAISE OF KETCHUP

Why are the lines that divide our highways mustard yellow and not ketchup red? After all, hasn't every memorable road trip been marked, for better or for worse, with ribbons of ketchup squeezed from little packets? Is ketchup not the condiment of choice for those who dare to dine behind the wheel? While some view it as an accomplice to the "crime" of fast food, let's admit it: We've all indulged, juggling the steering wheel, a burger, and a French fry....

So is ketchup a frivolous habit or a culinary necessity? For the enlightened, it's both. While food snobs and chutney freaks might snub it, consider a world without ketchup. Forget what its absence would do to French fries—Europeans insist a good mustard or (urp!) mayonnaise can pick up the slack. Forget the wasteland of a ketchup-less burger. Ketchup is not only the reason addicts get out of bed in the morning (scrambled eggs and Heinz®, anyone?). Ketchup is the backbone of some of the best barbecue sauces ever brewed. And life without red barbecue sauce would be tragic indeed.

As prepared foods go, ketchup's the one even holistic hardliners can forgive, for it giveth not only great color, but great flavor, too. True, this proud tomato-based descendant of China's "kêtsiap" began life as a fish sauce, but who are we, who rose from the primordial mud one cell division at a time, to point fingers? The fact is, ketchup is good. Ketchup is king. And ketchup is sweeter than most people you'll meet on a daily basis.

Imagine our horror, then, when a certain top-selling brand came out with a green version of our beloved elixir, openly—shamelessly—targeted to young children. It is our express opinion that this is market research gone dangerously too far. Mislead an entire generation of future ketchup connoisseurs? We shudder at the implications.

Purists, don't be lead astray. It's spelled k-e-t-c-h-u-p, not catsup. It's red, it's thick, and it means business. No self-respecting refrigerator would be caught dead without it. Defend your right to enjoy it—and give it a reassuring squeeze!

SIREN
STEAK SAUCE

Pairing this seductive steak sauce with a juicy well-marbled T-bone will send your senses a flutter.

- **1/2 CUP DRY RED WINE**
- **1/2 CUP KETCHUP**
- **1/4 CUP DARK MOLASSES**
- **2 TABLESPOONS RED WINE VINEGAR**
- **1 TABLESPOON DIJON MUSTARD**
- **1 TABLESPOON WORCESTERSHIRE SAUCE**
- **1/2 TEASPOON CHILI POWDER**
- **1/2 TEASPOON CELERY SEEDS**
- **1/2 TEASPOON KOSHER SALT**
- **1/4 TEASPOON CURRY POWDER**
- **1/4 TEASPOON GROUND CUMIN**

In a medium saucepan combine the ingredients with 1/2 cup water. Mix well. Bring to a simmer over medium heat and cook, uncovered, stirring occasionally, until about 2/3 cup remains, about 30 minutes. Allow to cool to room temperature.

MAKES ABOUT 2/3 CUP

HOT PEPPER
VINEGAR SAUCE

This is a classic sauce for pulled pork but it also works well with grilled and shredded chicken, beef, or lamb. Shredded meat is really what it takes to soak up this thin wonder. Pucker up!

- **1 1/2 CUPS CIDER VINEGAR**
- **2 TABLESPOONS GRANULATED SUGAR**
- **1 TEASPOON TABASCO SAUCE**
- **1/2 TEASPOON CRUSHED RED PEPPER FLAKES**
- **KOSHER SALT**
- **FRESHLY GROUND BLACK PEPPER**

In a medium saucepan combine the ingredients, including salt and pepper to taste, and bring to a boil. Reduce heat to low and simmer for about 10 minutes. Allow to cool to room temperature. Sprinkle on the meat just before serving.

MAKES ABOUT 1 1/2 CUPS

LOCO-MOTION
SAUCE

This sauce, with its decisively Kansas City character, really gets your taste buds moving. Terrific paired with a whole grilled chicken.

- ¼ CUP ORANGE JUICE CONCENTRATE
- ¼ CUP MILD CHILI SAUCE
- 2 TABLESPOONS DARK MOLASSES
- 1 TABLESPOON SOY SAUCE
- 1 TABLESPOON WHITE WINE VINEGAR
- 2 TEASPOONS WHOLE-GRAIN MUSTARD
- 1 TEASPOON WORCESTERSHIRE SAUCE
- ½ TEASPOON TABASCO SAUCE
- ½ TEASPOON KOSHER SAUCE

In a small saucepan combine the ingredients. Bring to a boil, then simmer for about 5 minutes. Remove from the heat and allow to cool to room temperature.

MAKES ABOUT 3/4 CUP

CRAZY COLA
BARBECUE SAUCE

Taste for yourself how sweet it is when you simmer this celebrated soft drink with a tangy blend of other pantry staples. Brush it on during the last 10 minutes of grilling and leave a little for a dipping sauce.

- 2 CUPS COLA
- 1 CUP KETCHUP
- ¼ CUP MILD CHILI SAUCE
- ¼ CUP WORCESTERSHIRE SAUCE
- 3 TABLESPOONS CIDER VINEGAR
- 2 TEASPOONS MINCED GARLIC
- ½ TEASPOON FRESHLY GROUND BLACK PEPPER

In a small saucepan whisk together the ingredients. Bring to a boil, then reduce heat to low and simmer for 20 to 30 minutes. Allow to cool to room temperature.

MAKES ABOUT 1 1/2 CUPS

TAPENADE

The mainstay of any tapenade is black olives, although the name comes from "tapéno," the Provençal term for capers, another key ingredient. Spread it on grilled bread, meat, or poultry for a salty flavor boost.

- ¾ CUP PITTED BLACK OLIVES SUCH AS KALAMATA *OR* OTHER IMPORTED OLIVES
- 2 ANCHOVY FILLETS (OIL-PACKED), DRAINED
- 2 TABLESPOONS COARSELY CHOPPED SHALLOTS
- 2 TABLESPOONS EXTRA-VIRGIN OLIVE OIL
- 1 TABLESPOON FRESH LEMON JUICE
- 1 TABLESPOON CAPERS, DRAINED
- 1 TEASPOON MINCED GARLIC
- ¼ TEASPOON FRESHLY GROUND BLACK PEPPER

In a food processor combine the ingredients and process to make a spreadable paste. Cover and refrigerate for up to 1 week.

MAKES ABOUT 1/2 CUP

FRESH TOMATO
SALSA

Simple and straightforward. Spoon it over grilled fish. Add it to a taco. Or sit it next to a steak. Just make sure the tomatoes are ripe! Place the chopped onion in a colander and rinse it under cold water to crisp it up and mellow the flavor.

- 1½ CUPS FINELY CHOPPED RIPE TOMATOES
- ½ CUP FINELY CHOPPED WHITE ONION, RINSED UNDER COLD WATER AND FULLY DRAINED
- ¼ CUP FINELY CHOPPED GREEN BELL PEPPER
- 2 TABLESPOONS FINELY CHOPPED FRESH CILANTRO
- 1 TABLESPOON FRESH LIME JUICE
- 1 TO 2 TEASPOONS MINCED JALAPEÑO PEPPER, WITH SEEDS
- ¼ TEASPOON GROUND CUMIN
- ¼ TEASPOON KOSHER SALT
- ¼ TEASPOON FRESHLY GROUND BLACK PEPPER

In a small bowl combine the ingredients and mix well. Allow to stand for 10 minutes so all of the flavors can blend. It is best served fresh and at room temperature.

MAKES ABOUT 2 CUPS

ROASTED GARLIC
BUTTER

This stuff is so heady you might be tempted to dab a little behind your ears. But save it to spoon over a sizzling steak or smear on grilled bread.

INDIRECT/MEDIUM

- 1   LARGE HEAD GARLIC
- 1   TEASPOON EXTRA-VIRGIN OLIVE OIL

- 2   TABLESPOONS UNSALTED BUTTER, SOFTENED
- 2   TEASPOONS DIJON MUSTARD
- 1   TEASPOON WORCESTERSHIRE SAUCE
- 1/2 TEASPOON KOSHER SALT

Remove the loose, papery outer skin from the head of garlic. Cut about 1/2 inch off the top to expose the cloves. Place on an 8-inch square of heavy-duty aluminum foil and drizzle the olive oil over the top of the cloves. Fold up the foil sides and seal to make a packet, leaving a little room for the expansion of steam. Grill over *Indirect Medium* heat until the cloves are soft, 30 to 45 minutes. Remove from the grill and allow to cool.

When cool enough to handle, squeeze the garlic from the individual cloves into a small bowl. Using the back of a fork, mash the roasted garlic together with the remaining ingredients. Refrigerate until ready to serve.

MAKES ABOUT 1/4 CUP

PACIFIC RIM
MARINADE

Here's an excellent way to bring Chinese flavors to pork, beef, or chicken.

- 1/4 CUP KETCHUP
- 1/4 CUP HOISIN SAUCE
- 2   TABLESPOONS RICE VINEGAR
- 2   TABLESPOONS SOY SAUCE
- 4   TEASPOONS CURRY POWDER
- 4   TEASPOONS ASIAN SESAME OIL
- 1/4 TEASPOON TABASCO SAUCE

In a small bowl whisk together the ingredients. See page 46 for suggested marinating times.

MAKES ABOUT 1 CUP

SWEET SOY
MARINADE

When you crave the sweet-salty character of the Japanese grill, turn to this well-balanced marinade. Excellent on chicken, pork, and beef, but also tasty on thick fish steaks and fillets. Just be careful not to overmarinate.

- 3/4 CUP SOY SAUCE
- 1/2 CUP MIRIN (SWEET RICE WINE)
- 1/4 CUP KETCHUP
- 2   TABLESPOONS RICE VINEGAR
- 2   TEASPOONS MINCED GARLIC
- 1   TEASPOON ASIAN SESAME OIL

In a small bowl whisk together the ingredients. See page 46 for suggested marinating times.

MAKES ABOUT 1 1/2 CUPS

TEQUILA ORANGE
MARINADE

Here's a Mexican cocktail of flavors that makes great things happen with chicken, pork, or beef.

- 1/2 CUP TIGHTLY PACKED FRESH MINT LEAVES
- 1/2 CUP TIGHTLY PACKED FRESH ITALIAN PARSLEY, WITH SOME STEMS
- 1/2 CUP FRESH ORANGE JUICE
- 2   TABLESPOONS TEQUILA
- 2   TABLESPOONS EXTRA-VIRGIN OLIVE OIL
- 2   MEDIUM GARLIC CLOVES, CRUSHED
- 2   TEASPOONS MINCED JALAPEÑO PEPPERS, WITHOUT SEEDS
- 1 1/2 TEASPOONS KOSHER SALT
- 1/2 TEASPOON GROUND CUMIN
- 1/2 TEASPOON CHILI POWDER
- 1/4 TEASPOON FRESHLY GROUND BLACK PEPPER

In a food processor combine the ingredients and process until smooth. See page 46 for suggested marinating times.

MAKES ABOUT 1 CUP

BUTTERMILK HERB
MARINADE

Buttermilk has a tangy kick and it works well as a tenderizer. This recipe has a nice, homey American flavor that suits both chicken and pork.

- 1 CUP BUTTERMILK
- 1 TABLESPOON DIJON MUSTARD
- 1 TABLESPOON HONEY
- 1 TABLESPOON FINELY CHOPPED FRESH ROSEMARY
- 1/2 TEASPOON DRIED THYME
- 1/2 TEASPOON DRIED SAGE
- 1/2 TEASPOON DRIED MARJORAM
- 1 TEASPOON KOSHER SALT
- 1/2 TEASPOON FRESHLY GROUND BLACK PEPPER

In a medium bowl whisk together the ingredients. See page 46 for suggested marinating times.

MAKES ABOUT 1 CUP

MAGICAL MEDITERRANEAN
MARINADE

Inspired by the southern shores of Italy, this marinade makes just about everything better, even (especially) grilled vegetables.

- 2 TABLESPOONS EXTRA-VIRGIN OLIVE OIL
- 2 TABLESPOONS CHOPPED FRESH ROSEMARY
- 1 TABLESPOON CHOPPED FRESH THYME
- 1 TABLESPOON MINCED SHALLOTS
- 1 TABLESPOON BALSAMIC VINEGAR
- 1 TABLESPOON WHOLE-GRAIN MUSTARD
- 1 TEASPOON MINCED GARLIC
- 1 TEASPOON KOSHER SALT
- 1 TEASPOON FRESHLY GROUND BLACK PEPPER

In a small bowl whisk together the ingredients. See page 46 for suggested marinating times.

MAKES ABOUT 1/2 CUP

CONDIMENT EXTRAORDINAIRE
THE GLORY OF MUSTARD

Ever had your heart broken? That first sting of disappointment is like the zap of a good mustard. But while the bad news brings pain, the sinus-inflaming bite of mustard brings mental clarity and an endorphin-like rush. You want more.

Mustard's trademark zing can be delivered many ways. Prepared mustard adds flavor alone or in sauces. Whole mustard seeds can be used in a rub or paste. Mustard powder can be sprinkled wherever you need a boost. But wait. There's more.

With mustard's soul mate, ketchup, you can pick a brand and live happily ever after. But mustard is a condiment of many personalities. You can match it to your mood as well as your food. For hot dogs and lazy lunches, there's the bright yellow stuff in a squeeze tub. For other foods—burgers to pork roasts—there's a range of specialties you can fine-tune to the entrée. Dijon mustard, with or without wine, isn't just fodder for silly TV commercials. Dijon, France, is the holy city of mustard. With its smooth flavor, Dijon mustard spiffs up anything from chicken to cheeses.

In a sporting mood? There's nothing better for bratwurst than beer mustard, a.k.a. sweet mustard. It's coarser grained and has a mild kick that rides shotgun to the sweetness. Wanna start a fire? Super-hot Chinese mustard can sear an egg roll into more than your memory. Feeling mellow? For homemade vinaigrettes, reach for "old style" or coarse-grain mustard ("moutarde à l'ancienne," if you're going French). Its milder flavor is not only great on your favorite meats, but the crushed mustard seeds that give it its character are simply delightful perched on mixed greens.

For the adventurous, there are flavored mustards such as raspberry and jalapeño. Laid-back honey-mustard is often found lounging in sports bars, trolling for a winsome pretzel. Not a bad one to keep in the fridge for a midnight fling with a carbo-packing snack.

When you consider the power of this potent little seed, it's no wonder its praises have been sung since biblical times. If you don't have several different jars in your fridge, what are you waiting for? Life is short. Grab a knife and reach for the mighty yellow.

NORTH AFRICAN
MARINADE

This flavorful Moroccan marinade is excellent for any white fish, shrimp, or scallops. It's also nice on chicken.

- **1/2 CUP FRESH ITALIAN PARSLEY LEAVES**
- **1/4 CUP FRESH MINT LEAVES**
- **1/4 CUP EXTRA-VIRGIN OLIVE OIL**
- **2 TABLESPOONS SHERRY VINEGAR**
- **2 LARGE CLOVES GARLIC, CRUSHED**
- **1 TEASPOON PAPRIKA**
- **1/2 TEASPOON KOSHER SALT**
- **1/4 TEASPOON FRESHLY GROUND BLACK PEPPER**
- **1 TO 2 DASHES TABASCO SAUCE**

In a food processor combine the ingredients and process until smooth. See page 46 for suggested marinating times.

MAKES ABOUT 1/2 CUP

MANGO
MARINADE

In this saucy little number, mango juice does a tango with other tropical flavors to produce something not too sweet, not too sour, and not too hot. You can substitute apricot or orange juice for the mango juice. Perfectly matched with poultry or pork.

- **1 CUP MANGO JUICE**
- **1/4 CUP RICE VINEGAR**
- **3 TABLESPOONS EXTRA-VIRGIN OLIVE OIL**
- **2 TABLESPOONS SOY SAUCE**
- **2 TABLESPOONS MINCED SHALLOTS**
- **2 TEASPOONS MINCED GARLIC**
- **2 TEASPOONS SRIRACHA (HOT CHILI-GARLIC SAUCE)**
- **1 TEASPOON KOSHER SALT**
- **1/2 TEASPOON GROUND CUMIN**
- **1/2 TEASPOON FRESHLY GROUND BLACK PEPPER**

In a medium bowl whisk together the ingredients. See page 46 for suggested marinating times.

MAKES ABOUT 1 1/2 CUPS

NORTH INDIAN
MARINADE

Here's a simple marinade that mingles exotic flavors in a yogurt base. Beef, chicken, and fish are all improved when bathed in this beauty.

- **1 CUP PLAIN YOGURT**
- **3 TABLESPOONS FRESH LEMON JUICE**
- **1 TABLESPOON PAPRIKA**
- **2 TEASPOONS MINCED GARLIC**
- **2 TEASPOONS MINCED JALAPEÑO PEPPER, WITH SEEDS**
- **1 TEASPOON GROUND CUMIN**
- **1 TEASPOON CURRY POWDER**
- **1 TEASPOON KOSHER SALT**
- **1/2 TEASPOON GROUND GINGER**
- **1/2 TEASPOON GROUND CORIANDER**

In a medium bowl whisk together the ingredients. See page 46 for suggested marinating times.

MAKES ABOUT 1 1/2 CUPS

AL ROKER'S
RUB

The rub behind the man behind the legend. Use on pork shoulder or ribs.

- **1/4 CUP DARK BROWN SUGAR**
- **2 TABLESPOONS KOSHER SALT**
- **2 TABLESPOONS FRESHLY GROUND BLACK PEPPER**
- **2 TABLESPOONS ADOBO SAUCE**
- **1 TABLESPOON PAPRIKA**
- **1 TABLESPOON CHILI POWDER**
- **2 TEASPOONS CINNAMON**
- **2 TEASPOONS ALLSPICE**

In a small bowl combine the ingredients. Press the rub into all sides of the meat. And remember…low and slow.

MAKES ABOUT 1 CUP

TYPE-A
RUB

This rub is the overachiever of the family: It's good on virtually everything. Multiply the recipe, store it in a tightly sealed jar, and massage it into whatever needs a quick pick-me-up before it hits the grill.

- **1 TEASPOON DRY MUSTARD**
- **1 TEASPOON GRANULATED ONION**
- **1 TEASPOON PAPRIKA**
- **1 TEASPOON KOSHER SALT**
- **1/2 TEASPOON GRANULATED GARLIC**
- **1/2 TEASPOON GROUND CORIANDER**
- **1/2 TEASPOON GROUND CUMIN**
- **1/2 TEASPOON FRESHLY GROUND BLACK PEPPER**

In a small bowl combine the ingredients. Press the rub into all sides of the meat or fish and refrigerate for 1 hour prior to grilling to intensify flavors.

MAKES 2 TABLESPOONS

ASIAN
RUB

When looking to the Far East for flavor, look no further than this beguiling mixture. It carries chicken and beef thousands of culinary miles in a matter of minutes.

- **1 TEASPOON GRANULATED GARLIC**
- **1 TEASPOON GRANULATED ONION**
- **1 TEASPOON PAPRIKA**
- **1/2 TEASPOON CUMIN**
- **1/2 TEASPOON DRIED LEMONGRASS**
- **1/2 TEASPOON DRIED BASIL**
- **1/2 TEASPOON DRIED THYME**
- **1/2 TEASPOON KOSHER SALT**
- **1/4 TEASPOON FRESHLY GROUND BLACK PEPPER**
- **1/8 TEASPOON CAYENNE**

In a small bowl combine the ingredients. Press the rub into all sides of the meat and refrigerate for 1 hour prior to grilling to intensify flavors.

MAKES 2 TABLESPOONS

SEASONED SALTS

Bet you didn't know you've been using the most basic rub in the world since you first started cooking. It's been the standard since ancient times: salt and black pepper. Yep, common and unglamorous as these seasonings are today, the quests for salt and pepper once led to the development of entire trade routes. Salt and pepper often served as wages in early civilizations and were even used as currency for paying tolls, ransoms, and more.

Add some spices or an herb or two to salt and pepper, and you have a perked-up seasoning for just about anything you can grill—including vegetables—for mere pennies. Below are a few additions to the standard 2:1 proportion of salt to pepper. Use these combos to taste.

To make your own seasoned salts, improvise by adding your favorite dried herbs (such as tarragon or rosemary) or blends (such as herbes de Provence or chili powder) one part at a time until you find the proportion that suits your needs. Store unused seasoned salts in a tightly covered jar, away from light and moisture, for up to one year.

GARLIC SALT
- **2 PARTS KOSHER SALT**
- **1 PART GRANULATED GARLIC**
- **1 PART FRESHLY GROUND BLACK PEPPER**

In a small bowl combine the ingredients.

SZECHWAN PEPPER SALT
- **3 PARTS KOSHER SALT**
- **2 PARTS FRESHLY GROUND SZECHWAN PEPPER**
- **1 PART GRANULATED GARLIC**
- **1 PART FRESHLY GROUND BLACK PEPPER**
- **1 PART GROUND CUMIN**

In a small bowl combine the ingredients.

LEMON PEPPER SALT
- **2 WHOLE LEMONS**
- **4 TEASPOONS KOSHER SALT**
- **2 TEASPOONS FRESHLY GROUND BLACK PEPPER**

Preheat oven to 200°F.

Using a vegetable peeler, cut strips of zest from the lemons, leaving the white, bitter pith still attached. Place the lemon zest on a baking sheet and roast in the oven until dry and golden, 30 to 45 minutes. Allow to cool.

In a spice grinder, pulverize the dried lemon zest. Transfer to a small bowl and mix together with the salt and pepper. Use immediately or store in a tightly covered jar for up to 3 to 4 weeks.

MAKES 2 TABLESPOONS

SOUTHWESTERN
RUB

Good on steak or pork. Even better on chicken. Stellar on fish. An all-purpose rub with gusto.

- 1 TEASPOON CHILI POWDER
- 1 TEASPOON GRANULATED GARLIC
- 1 TEASPOON DRY MUSTARD
- 1/2 TEASPOON PAPRIKA
- 1/2 TEASPOON GROUND CORIANDER
- 1/2 TEASPOON GROUND CUMIN

In a small bowl combine the ingredients. Press the rub into both sides of the meat or fish and refrigerate for 1 hour or more prior to grilling to intensify flavors.

MAKES 1 1/2 TABLESPOONS

MUSTARD SEED
DRY RUB

Mustard seed has a nutty character that plays well with the other members of this rub. Terrific on pork, seafood, and chicken. Heads up: This one has a bit of a kick to it.

- 1 TEASPOON MUSTARD SEEDS
- 1 TEASPOON CELERY SEEDS
- 1 TEASPOON DRIED THYME
- 1/2 TEASPOON KOSHER SALT
- 1/4 TEASPOON FRESHLY GROUND BLACK PEPPER
- 1/4 TEASPOON CAYENNE

In a small bowl combine the ingredients. Press the rub into both sides of the meat or seafood and refrigerate for 1 hour prior to grilling to intensify flavors.

MAKES 1 1/3 TABLESPOONS

TEXAS
DRY RUB

Paprika and chili powder play key roles in any good Texas dry rub. This version, a particularly good one for beef, is no exception.

- 2 TABLESPOONS PAPRIKA
- 2 TABLESPOONS LIGHT BROWN SUGAR
- 1 TABLESPOON CHILI POWDER
- 1 TABLESPOON KOSHER SALT
- 1 TABLESPOON CRACKED BLACK PEPPER
- 2 TEASPOONS GRANULATED GARLIC
- 2 TEASPOONS GRANULATED ONION
- 1 TEASPOON GROUND CUMIN

In a small bowl combine the ingredients. Press the rub into both sides of the meat and refrigerate for 1 hour prior to grilling to intensify flavors.

MAKES ABOUT 1/2 CUP

PICK-ME-UP
PEPPER RUB

People who really like pepper prefer it freshly cracked and not too finely ground. This rub's for them. Start with whole peppercorns, add a team of like-minded spices, and you've got a killer beef or pork rub.

- 1 TEASPOON WHOLE BLACK PEPPERCORNS
- 1 TEASPOON MUSTARD SEEDS
- 1 TEASPOON PAPRIKA
- 1/2 TEASPOON GRANULATED GARLIC
- 1/2 TEASPOON KOSHER SALT
- 1/2 TEASPOON LIGHT BROWN SUGAR
- 1/8 TEASPOON CAYENNE

Using a spice grinder or mortar and pestle, crush the black peppercorns and mustard seeds. Transfer to a small bowl and combine with the remaining ingredients. Press the rub into both sides of the meat and refrigerate for 1 hour or more prior to grilling to intensify flavors.

MAKES 1 1/2 TABLESPOONS

CAJUN
RUB

This sweet and spicy rub was born in the Bayous of Louisiana. Rub it on anything that needs a little fire lit under it.

- 1 TABLESPOON LIGHT BROWN SUGAR
- 1 TABLESPOON GRANULATED GARLIC
- 1 TABLESPOON GRANULATED ONION
- 1 TABLESPOON PAPRIKA
- 2 TEASPOONS DRIED THYME
- 2 TEASPOONS DRIED OREGANO
- 2 TEASPOONS KOSHER SALT
- 2 TEASPOONS COARSELY GROUND BLACK PEPPER

In a small bowl combine the ingredients. Press the rub into both sides of the meat and refrigerate for 1 hour prior to grilling to intensify flavors.

MAKES ABOUT 7 TABLESPOONS

Lemon Pepper Salt

Mustard Seed Dry Rub

Szechwan Pepper Salt

Type-A Rub

Asian Rub

Southwestern Rub

Pick-Me-Up Pepper Rub

Cajun Rub

Texas Dry Rub

The first course of a meal is sort of like a first date. The air is filled with anticipation and promise. This could be the beginning of a beautiful thing! On the other hand, if things don't work out, there are no hard feelings. You simply move on in your quest for fulfillment. And then there are those special morsels that, despite the brevity of your encounter, you'll still remember with a certain wistfulness in years to come. Especially late at night as you pace before the pantry, filled with a certain longing.

We love a meal that starts with a little special something. This first course can be a sneak peek at what's to come, a great way to show off your culinary wizardry, or just a clever ploy to buy you more time while

START

dinner cooks. In some cultures, the serving of small, bite-sized treats has been raised to an art form. Consider the Cantonese ritual of *dim sum* (literally "heart's delight"—now who wouldn't get excited about such a prospect?). An assortment of dumplings, pastries, and other treasures, *dim sum* is enjoyed as breakfast or lunch. When the French, who gave us the word "hors d'œuvres," attend cocktail parties, they fill up on "amuse-bouches," roughly translated as "fun for your mouth." The Spanish tradition of *tapas*, an array of appetizers often served with sherry, can be a forerunner to dinner or dinner itself. The options range from the simple (baked olives) to the sublime (grilled meats). In Greece, they enjoy *meze*—a wonderful kaleidoscope of nibbles that can include such gems as spanikopita, grilled lamb chops, fried zucchini and calamari, and dolmades. The Italians, on the other hand, will woo you with antipasti—a selection of cured meats, aged cheeses, grilled and marinated vegetables, and more—often served with bruschetta.

In North America this first course can go by many names; the connotation is the thing. As "hors d'œuvres," it has a more formal ring; the term conjures silver platters laden with one-bite delicacies. These carefully made bites are then either arranged on a buffet table or brought to you by servers so you don't have to interrupt a witty repartee in order to eat. (This kind of scene figures largely in our personal vision of heaven.) Your only challenge is to gracefully juggle the drink, the napkin, the hors d'oeuvre itself, and any technical equipment such as skewers or toothpicks.

The term "appetizers," on the other hand, can mean two things. In restaurants, of course, they're

a great enhancement to the meal (if not the size of the check). But they may also be presented in a more casual setting, where you might set them out on a table and let your guests serve themselves. This approach to the first course can serve you equally well at a holiday open house, at a summer barbecue, or even on Super Bowl Sunday.

"Starters," meanwhile, covers a variety of interpretations, be it a casual foray into snack foods or a more elaborate offering placed before each guest once seated at the table. In other words, the "starter" can run the gamut from…well, soup to nuts. We chose the term for this chapter because of its versatility. And yes, you'll find both soup and nuts here—all prepared on the grill.

The grill? That's right. Whatever you choose to call your mini works of art, one thing's for sure. The grill adds a special dimension that can't be duplicated, whether adding smoky tones to a classic onion dip or crisping up a delicate crab cake. Of course, there's always the big impression factor—how deft you look pulling course after course off the cooking grate—but that's not why we like our starters grilled. We like the textures and flavors you get. Something as simple as a stuffed mushroom is elevated a notch or two. And let's face it, a boiled shrimp is no match for a grilled one. Duck wraps, anyone? Yee-ow.

MAJORLY TASTY
DRUMETTES

The drumstick part of the chicken wing, sometimes called the drumette, is perfect finger food, but few people know how good it is grilled. Now the secret is out.

DIRECT/MEDIUM

FOR THE MARINADE:

3 TABLESPOONS SOY SAUCE

2 TABLESPOONS FRESH LEMON JUICE

1 TABLESPOON HONEY

1 TABLESPOON ASIAN SESAME OIL

1 1/2 TEASPOONS MINCED GARLIC

1 TEASPOON GRATED FRESH GINGER

1/4 TEASPOON CRUSHED RED PEPPER FLAKES

24 CHICKEN DRUMETTES

To make the marinade: In a small bowl whisk together the marinade ingredients.

Rinse the chicken drumettes under cold water and pat dry with paper towels. Place in a large, resealable plastic bag and pour in the marinade. Press the air out of the bag and seal tightly. Turn the bag to distribute the marinade, place in a bowl, and refrigerate for 4 to 6 hours, turning occasionally.

Remove the drumettes from the bag and discard the marinade. Grill over *Direct Medium* heat until the meat is no longer pink at the bone, 10 to 12 minutes, turning twice during grilling time so they don't burn. Serve warm or at room temperature.

MAKES 6 SERVINGS

HOT, SWEET, AND STICKY
CHICKEN WINGS

The perfect snack to whet that picnic appetite, this one covers all the taste bud zones.

SEAR: MEDIUM, COOK: INDIRECT/MEDIUM

FOR THE MARINADE:

1/2 CUP KETCHUP

1/4 CUP BALSAMIC VINEGAR

2 TABLESPOONS DARK BROWN SUGAR

4 TEASPOONS GRANULATED GARLIC

4 TEASPOONS WORCESTERSHIRE SAUCE

3 TEASPOONS TABASCO SAUCE

2 TEASPOONS DIJON MUSTARD

2 TEASPOONS PAPRIKA

2 TEASPOONS CHILI POWDER

20 CHICKEN WINGS, WING TIPS REMOVED
EXTRA-VIRGIN OLIVE OIL

To make the marinade: In a medium bowl whisk together the marinade ingredients.

Rinse the chicken wings under cold water and pat dry with paper towels. Place in a large, resealable plastic bag and pour in the marinade. Press the air out of the bag and seal tightly. Turn the bag to distribute the marinade, place in a bowl, and refrigerate for 4 to 6 hours, turning occasionally.

Remove the wings from the bag and discard the marinade. Lightly brush or spray the wings with olive oil. Sear over *Direct Medium* heat until well marked, 4 to 6 minutes, turning once halfway through searing time. Continue grilling over *Indirect Medium* heat until the meat is no longer pink at the bone, 8 to 10 minutes. Serve warm.

MAKES 6 TO 8 SERVINGS

**THEIR NAME
SAYS IT ALL.
EAT THEM
HOT OFF THE
GRILL OR
AT ROOM
TEMPERA-
TURE.**

Hot, Sweet, and Sticky Chicken Wings

CHINESE CHICKEN
NOODLE SOUP

This marinade works first on the chicken, giving the thighs a wonderful depth of flavor, then it becomes a base for the soup. These are the kind of tastes and textures you find in many Hong Kong restaurants, a light preamble to the main event.

DIRECT/MEDIUM

FOR THE MARINADE:

2 TABLESPOONS MIRIN (SWEET RICE WINE)

2 TABLESPOONS MINCED FRESH LEMONGRASS

1 TABLESPOON SOY SAUCE

1 TABLESPOON FISH SAUCE

2 TEASPOONS ASIAN SESAME OIL

2 TEASPOONS FRESH LIME JUICE

1/4 TEASPOON CRUSHED RED PEPPER FLAKES

4 BONELESS, SKINLESS CHICKEN THIGHS, ABOUT 4 OUNCES EACH

PEANUT OIL

4 CUPS LOW-SODIUM CHICKEN BROTH

3 TO 4 OUNCES DRIED CHINESE NOODLES (MEIN)

1 CUP BEAN SPROUTS

1 MEDIUM CARROT, CUT INTO 1/4-INCH DICE

1/3 CUP COARSELY CHOPPED FRESH CILANTRO

To make the marinade: In a small bowl whisk together the marinade ingredients.

Rinse the chicken thighs under cold water and pat dry with paper towels. Place in a large, resealable plastic bag and pour in the marinade. Press the air out of the bag and seal tightly. Turn the bag to distribute the marinade, place in a bowl, and refrigerate for 2 to 4 hours, turning occasionally.

Remove the thighs from the bag, reserving the marinade. Pour the marinade into a large saucepan.

Brush or spray the thighs with peanut oil. Grill over *Direct Medium* heat until the juices run clear, 8 to 10 minutes, turning once halfway through grilling time. Remove from the grill and allow to rest for 1 to 2 minutes before cutting into 1/4-inch strips.

Add the chicken broth to the saucepan with the reserved marinade. Bring to a boil over high heat and boil for 1 full minute. Add the noodles and cook until tender, 2 to 3 minutes, then reduce heat to a simmer. Add the chicken strips, bean sprouts, diced carrot, and cilantro. Stir to combine. Serve immediately.

MAKES 4 SERVINGS

JAMAICAN CHICKEN PATTIES
WITH MANGO CHUTNEY

Eat these hot off the grill and topped with a dollop of the cooling chutney.

DIRECT/MEDIUM

FOR THE CHUTNEY:

1 TABLESPOON CANOLA OIL

1/2 CUP FINELY CHOPPED YELLOW ONION

1/2 TEASPOON TURMERIC

1/4 TEASPOON KOSHER SALT

1/4 TEASPOON ALLSPICE

1 MANGO, PEELED AND FINELY DICED (ABOUT 1 1/2 CUPS)

2 TABLESPOONS CHOPPED CRYSTALLIZED GINGER

2 TABLESPOONS FRESH LIME JUICE

1 TEASPOON MINCED JALAPEÑO PEPPER, WITH SEEDS

1 TEASPOON DARK BROWN SUGAR

FOR THE CHICKEN PATTIES:

2 POUNDS FRESHLY GROUND CHICKEN

6 GREEN ONIONS (WHITE PART ONLY), FINELY CHOPPED

2/3 CUP FINE DRY BREAD CRUMBS

1/2 CUP FINELY CHOPPED FRESH CILANTRO

1/4 CUP CANOLA OIL

2 TABLESPOONS FRESH LEMON JUICE

2 TEASPOONS MINCED GARLIC

2 TEASPOONS DRIED THYME

1 TEASPOON KOSHER SALT

1 TEASPOON GROUND ALLSPICE

1/2 TEASPOON CAYENNE

CANOLA OIL

To make the chutney: In a medium saucepan over medium heat, warm the canola oil and cook the onion, stirring occasionally, until soft, about 10 minutes. Add the turmeric, salt, and allspice and cook for 1 minute more, stirring occasionally. Add the remaining chutney ingredients along with 1/2 cup water. Bring to a boil. Reduce heat and simmer until the mango is very soft and the chutney thickens, 15 to 20 minutes. Transfer to a food processor and process until smooth. Place in a small bowl, cover with plastic wrap, and refrigerate until cool. Bring to room temperature before serving.

To make the chicken patties: In a medium bowl combine the chicken patty ingredients and mix well. Moisten your hands slightly with water and shape the mixture into patties, about 2 inches in diameter and 1/3 inch thick. Place on an oiled plate, cover with plastic wrap, and refrigerate for about 2 hours. Just before grilling, generously brush the tops of the patties with canola oil.

Grill the patties over *Direct Medium* heat until the internal temperature reaches 165°F, 8 to 10 minutes, turning once halfway through grilling time. Serve with the chutney.

MAKES 6 TO 8 SERVINGS

DUCK WRAPS
WITH ASIAN SLAW

A crisp cabbage and apple salad wrapped in warm tortillas along with thin slices of succulent grilled duck. Delicious.

DIRECT/HIGH

FOR THE DUCK MARINADE:

1 TABLESPOON SOY SAUCE

1 TABLESPOON RICE VINEGAR

1 TEASPOON ASIAN SESAME OIL

1 TEASPOON MINCED GARLIC

1 TEASPOON GRATED FRESH GINGER

2 BONELESS, SKINLESS DUCK BREAST HALVES, 5 TO 6 OUNCES EACH

FOR THE SLAW:

2 CUPS FINELY CHOPPED OR SHREDDED NAPA CABBAGE

1/2 CUP SHREDDED CARROT

1/2 CUP SHREDDED GOLDEN DELICIOUS APPLE

1/4 CUP COARSELY CHOPPED FRESH CILANTRO

1 TABLESPOON ASIAN SESAME OIL

1 TABLESPOON HOISIN SAUCE

1 TEASPOON RICE VINEGAR

1/2 TEASPOON FRESHLY GROUND BLACK PEPPER

1 TABLESPOON SESAME SEEDS

FOR THE DIPPING SAUCE:

1/4 CUP HOISIN SAUCE

1 TABLESPOON SOY SAUCE

1 TABLESPOON RICE VINEGAR

1/4 TEASPOON HOT MUSTARD POWDER

4 FLOUR TORTILLAS (6 INCHES)

CILANTRO SPRIGS FOR GARNISH

To make the marinade: In a small bowl whisk together the marinade ingredients.

Place the duck breasts in a small, resealable plastic bag and pour in the marinade. Press the air out of the bag and seal tightly. Turn the bag to distribute the marinade, place in a bowl, and refrigerate for 1 to 3 hours, turning occasionally.

To make the slaw: In a medium bowl combine the slaw ingredients. Cover and refrigerate until ready to serve.

In a small sauté pan over medium heat, toast the sesame seeds, stirring occasionally, until golden brown, about 5 minutes. Set aside.

To make the dipping sauce: In a small bowl stir together the dipping sauce ingredients.

Remove the breasts from the bag and discard the marinade. Grill over *Direct High* heat until the internal temperature reaches 160°F, about 6 minutes, turning once halfway through grilling time. Remove from the grill and allow to rest for 3 to 5 minutes before slicing.

Meanwhile, wrap the tortillas in a foil packet and grill over *Direct High* heat until warm, 20 to 30 seconds, turning once halfway through grilling time.

Slice the breasts in half lengthwise, then cut the halves into thin slices. Add the toasted sesame seeds to the slaw. To make a wrap, roll up a portion of duck slices and a portion of slaw in a warm tortilla. Cut each wrap into thirds or fourths and arrange the pieces on a platter with the dipping sauce. Garnish with cilantro sprigs. Serve warm or at room temperature.

MAKES 4 TO 6 SERVINGS

"When you come to a fork in the road, take it."

— YOGI BERRA

CHICKEN-CASHEW
SALAD

Crunchy, tender, salty, sweet—this starter has it all. Plum sauce is a dipping/cooking sauce used in Chinese cuisine. Look for it in the Asian section of your grocery store.

DIRECT/MEDIUM

FOR THE MARINADE:

- 2 TABLESPOONS PINEAPPLE JUICE, RESERVED FROM THE CANNED CRUSHED PINEAPPLE
- 1 TABLESPOON ASIAN SESAME OIL
- 1 TABLESPOON PLUM SAUCE
- 1 TABLESPOON SOY SAUCE
- 2 TEASPOONS GRATED FRESH GINGER
- 1 TEASPOON MINCED GARLIC
- 1/2 TEASPOON GROUND CORIANDER
- 1/4 TEASPOON CRUSHED RED PEPPER FLAKES

- 2 BONELESS, SKINLESS CHICKEN BREAST HALVES, 5 TO 6 OUNCES EACH

FOR THE VINAIGRETTE:

- 1/4 CUP DRAINED CANNED CRUSHED PINEAPPLE
- 2 TABLESPOONS PEANUT OIL
- 2 TABLESPOONS RICE VINEGAR
- 1 TABLESPOON ASIAN SESAME OIL
- 1 TABLESPOON PLUM SAUCE
- 1 TABLESPOON FINELY CHOPPED FRESH CILANTRO
- 2 TEASPOONS SOY SAUCE
- 1 TEASPOON GRATED FRESH GINGER
- 1 TEASPOON MINCED GARLIC

FOR THE SALAD:

- 2 CUPS THINLY SHREDDED NAPA CABBAGE
- 1 CUP BEAN SPROUTS
- 1 CUP THINLY SLICED STRIPS SNOW PEAS
- 1 CUP THINLY SLICED STRIPS BABY CARROTS
- 3/4 CUP ROASTED CASHEWS

To make the marinade: In a medium bowl whisk together the marinade ingredients.

Rinse the chicken breasts under cold water and pat dry with paper towels. Place in a large, resealable plastic bag and pour in the marinade. Press the air out of the bag and seal tightly. Turn the bag to distribute the marinade, place in a bowl, and refrigerate for 3 to 6 hours, turning occasionally.

To make the vinaigrette: In a small bowl whisk together the vinaigrette ingredients.

To make the salad: In a large bowl combine the salad ingredients and toss together.

Remove the breasts from the bag and discard the marinade. Grill over *Direct Medium* heat until the juices run clear and the meat is no longer pink in the center, 8 to 12 minutes, turning once halfway through grilling time. Remove from the grill and allow to rest for I to 2 minutes before slicing into thin strips. Add the chicken and vinaigrette to the salad and toss lightly. Serve at room temperature.

MAKES 4 SERVINGS

MINI GRILLED BLUE CHEESE
BITES

This one packs a lot of intense flavor for very little effort. A great one to round out a smorgasbord.

DIRECT/MEDIUM

- 1 SMALL RED ONION
- 1 TABLESPOON RED WINE VINEGAR
- 1 TABLESPOON FINELY CHOPPED FRESH ITALIAN PARSLEY
- 1/4 TEASPOON FRESHLY GROUND BLACK PEPPER

- 8 SLICES RYE BREAD, ABOUT 1/3 INCH THICK EACH
- 4 TABLESPOONS UNSALTED BUTTER, MELTED
- 6 OUNCES CRUMBLED BLUE CHEESE (ABOUT 1 1/3 CUPS)

Cut the onion in half through the stem, then cut into thin half circles. In a small bowl, mix the onion, vinegar, parsley, and pepper.

Lightly brush one side of each slice of bread with the melted butter. Place four of the slices, buttered side down, on a work surface and evenly distribute the seasoned onions on top. Sprinkle the cheese on top, pressing the cheese down so it doesn't fall off the bread. Top with the four remaining bread slices, buttered side up.

Grill the sandwiches over *Direct Medium* heat until toasted, about 4 minutes, turning with a wide spatula once halfway through grilling time. Transfer the sandwiches to a cutting board. Using a long sharp knife, cut each sandwich into four pieces. Serve warm.

MAKES 4 TO 6 SERVINGS

POBLANO AND WHITE BEAN
QUESADILLAS

This is your basic Southwestern appetizer boosted with the smoky flavor of grilled poblanos and the nutty taste of sesame seeds.

DIRECT/MEDIUM

FOR THE FILLING:

- 2 POBLANO CHILES, ABOUT 2 OUNCES EACH
- 2 TABLESPOONS SESAME SEEDS
- 1 CAN (15 OUNCES) CANNELLINI OR NAVY BEANS, RINSED AND DRAINED
- 3/4 CUP TIGHTLY PACKED FRESH CILANTRO
- 1/4 CUP FINELY CHOPPED RED ONION
- 1/4 CUP EXTRA-VIRGIN OLIVE OIL
- 2 TABLESPOONS HONEY
- 2 TABLESPOONS MINCED JALAPEÑO PEPPER, WITH SEEDS
- 2 TABLESPOONS FRESH LIME JUICE
- 2 MEDIUM GARLIC CLOVES, CRUSHED AND PEELED
- 2 TEASPOONS CHILI POWDER
- 1 TEASPOON GROUND CUMIN
- 1 TEASPOON DRIED OREGANO
- 1/2 TEASPOON KOSHER SALT
- 1/4 TEASPOON FRESHLY GROUND BLACK PEPPER

- 8 FLOUR TORTILLAS (10 INCHES)
- 3 CUPS GRATED MONTEREY JACK CHEESE

To make the filling: Grill the poblano chiles over *Direct Medium* heat until evenly charred on all sides, 7 to 9 minutes, turning as needed. Remove the chiles from the grill and place in a paper bag; close tightly. Let stand 10 to 15 minutes to steam off the skins. Remove the chiles from the bag and peel away the charred skins. Cut off the tops and remove the seeds. Place the chiles in a food processor.

In a small sauté pan over medium heat, toast the sesame seeds, stirring occasionally, until golden brown, about 5 minutes. Add the sesame seeds to the food processor along with the remaining filling ingredients. Process until smooth.

Place four of the tortillas on a work surface. Spread about 1/2 cup of the filling evenly to within 1 inch of the edge of each tortilla. Sprinkle the cheese over the filling and top with the remaining tortillas.

Carefully transfer the quesadillas to the cooking grate and grill over *Direct Medium* heat until the tortillas are well marked and the cheese has melted, about 2 minutes, carefully turning with a wide spatula once halfway through grilling time. Remove from the grill and allow to cool for a couple of minutes. Cut each quesadilla into eight wedges. Serve warm.

MAKES 8 TO 12 SERVINGS

CHORIZO
QUESADILLAS

Mexican chorizo is a spicy sausage made from fresh pork and chili powder; it's usually cooked without its casing. Grill the quesadillas just long enough to toast the tortillas to a crispy texture and melt the cheese inside.

DIRECT/MEDIUM

FOR THE FILLING:

- 2 TABLESPOONS EXTRA-VIRGIN OLIVE OIL
- 5 GREEN ONIONS (WHITE PART ONLY), FINELY CHOPPED
- 1/2 POUND CREMINI MUSHROOMS (STEMS REMOVED), FINELY CHOPPED
- 1/4 TEASPOON KOSHER SALT
- 1/4 TEASPOON FRESHLY GROUND BLACK PEPPER
- 1/2 POUND CHORIZO, CASING REMOVED
- 1 TEASPOON MINCED GARLIC
- 1 TEASPOON FINELY CHOPPED JALAPEÑO PEPPER, WITH SEEDS

- 4 FLOUR TORTILLAS (10 INCHES)
- 1 CUP GRATED MONTEREY JACK CHEESE
- 1/4 CUP COARSELY CHOPPED FRESH CILANTRO

To make the filling: In a medium sauté pan over medium-high heat, warm the olive oil and cook the green onions and mushrooms with the salt and pepper, stirring occasionally, until the mushrooms are tender and the pan is dry, about 5 minutes. Transfer to a medium bowl.

Put the chorizo, garlic, and jalapeño in the sauté pan and cook over medium-high heat, stirring occasionally, until the chorizo is browned, about 3 minutes. Add to the mushroom mixture and stir to evenly distribute the ingredients.

Place two of the tortillas on a work surface. Divide the filling between them, spreading it evenly to within 1 inch of the edges. Spread the cheese and cilantro over the filling and top with the remaining tortillas.

Carefully transfer the quesadillas to the cooking grate and grill over *Direct Medium* heat until well marked and the cheese has melted, about 2 minutes, carefully turning with a wide spatula once halfway through grilling time. Remove from the grill and allow to cool for a couple of minutes. Cut each quesadilla into eight wedges. Serve warm.

MAKES 4 TO 6 SERVINGS

STUFFED PORTABELLOS

These are great served as part of an elaborate antipasto course or set on a salad of lightly dressed mixed greens.

INDIRECT/HIGH

2 SLICES BACON

4 LARGE PORTABELLO MUSHROOMS, ABOUT 4 INCHES IN DIAMETER EACH
EXTRA-VIRGIN OLIVE OIL

FOR THE STUFFING
1/2 CUP FINELY CHOPPED YELLOW ONION
1/2 CUP FINELY CHOPPED RED BELL PEPPER
1 TEASPOON MINCED GARLIC
1/2 CUP DRIED BREAD CRUMBS
2 TABLESPOONS FINELY CHOPPED FRESH ITALIAN PARSLEY
1/4 TEASPOON KOSHER SALT
1/4 TEASPOON FRESHLY GROUND BLACK PEPPER
1/2 CUP FRESHLY GRATED PARMIGIANO-REGGIANO CHEESE

In a large sauté pan over medium heat, cook the bacon until crisp, 10 to 12 minutes, turning occasionally; drain on a paper towel. When cool, finely chop and set aside. Reserve the bacon fat in the pan.

Remove and discard the stems from the portabellos. With a small spoon, gently scrape out the black gills and discard. Wipe the caps clean with a damp towel. Generously brush or spray both sides of the caps with olive oil. Set the mushrooms, top side down, on a platter.

To make the stuffing: In the same large sauté pan used to cook the bacon, warm the bacon fat over medium heat. Add the onion and red pepper and cook, stirring occasionally, until tender, 6 to 8 minutes. Add the garlic and cook for 1 minute more, stirring occasionally. Add the bread crumbs, parsley, salt, and pepper and stir to blend. Remove from the heat. Add the reserved bacon and the cheese and mix well.

Divide the stuffing evenly among the mushroom caps. Grill over *Indirect High* heat until the caps are soft and the tops are lightly browned, 8 to 10 minutes. Carefully remove from the grill with a wide spatula. Serve warm.

MAKES 4 SERVINGS

CHEESY ONION QUICHE

This one is super rich, so follow it with a light entrée, such as grilled fish or a vegetable pasta. Note: The quiche is grilled over Direct Medium heat to start and finished up over Direct Low heat.

DIRECT/MEDIUM

FOR THE SAUCE:
1 LARGE RED BELL PEPPER
1/4 CUP MAYONNAISE
3 TABLESPOONS CRUSHED WALNUTS
2 TEASPOONS TOMATO PASTE
1 TEASPOON MINCED GARLIC
1/4 TEASPOON KOSHER SALT
1/4 TEASPOON FRESHLY GROUND BLACK PEPPER

FOR THE FILLING:
4 TABLESPOONS UNSALTED BUTTER, CUT INTO FOUR PIECES
1 CUP FINELY CHOPPED RED ONION
3 LARGE EGGS
3/4 CUP HEAVY CREAM
1 1/2 CUPS GRATED JARLSBERG, SWISS, OR GRUYÈRE CHEESE
3 TABLESPOONS FINELY CHOPPED FRESH CHIVES
1/4 TEASPOON TABASCO SAUCE
1/4 TEASPOON KOSHER SALT
1/4 TEASPOON FRESHLY GROUND BLACK PEPPER

1 UNCOOKED PIE CRUST (9 INCHES)

To make the sauce: Grill the bell pepper over *Direct Medium* heat until the skin is evenly charred on all sides, 10 to 12 minutes, turning every 3 to 5 minutes. Remove the pepper from the grill and place in a paper bag; close tightly. Let stand 10 to 15 minutes to steam off the skin. Remove the pepper from the bag and peel away the charred skin. Cut off the top and remove the seeds. Coarsely chop the pepper and put in a food processor. Add the remaining sauce ingredients and process until smooth. Pour into a small serving bowl, cover, and refrigerate until ready to serve.

To make the filling: In a medium sauté pan over medium heat, melt the butter. Add the red onion and cook, stirring occasionally, until translucent, 3 to 5 minutes. Transfer to a medium bowl and allow to cool for a few minutes. In a small bowl whisk the eggs and cream together and add to the butter-onion mixture. Add the remaining filling ingredients and mix thoroughly.

Line a 9-inch metal pie tin with the crust. Pour the filling into the crust. Grill over *Direct Medium* heat until the edges of the crust and the filling begin to turn golden brown, about 15 minutes, then continue cooking over *Direct Low* heat until the filling is no longer wet in the center, about 15 minutes more. Remove from the grill and allow to cool for 10 to 15 minutes. Serve with the sauce.

MAKES 6 TO 8 SERVINGS

HERE'S A DELICIOUS STARTER THAT'S ALSO GREAT PARTNERED WITH A TOSSED GREEN SALAD FOR LUNCH.

Cheesy Onion Quiche

HAM AND SWISS
ON A TOOTHPICK

This little retro number makes a great game-time snack. It's warm, sweet, and salty with a kick of spice…and you can eat it in one bite. Score!

DIRECT/MEDIUM

12 BUTTON MUSHROOMS, CAPS ABOUT 1 1/2 INCHES IN DIAMETER EACH

3 OUNCES GRUYÈRE CHEESE, IN A BLOCK

3 OUNCES SMOKED HAM, IN A BLOCK

6 FRESH *OR* CANNED PINEAPPLE CHUNKS, ABOUT 1 INCH EACH

EXTRA-VIRGIN OLIVE OIL

3/4 TEASPOON CHILI POWDER

1/4 TEASPOON KOSHER SALT

Trim the mushroom stems. Cut off enough of the top of the caps so that each mushroom is about 1/2 inch thick. Cut the cheese and ham into twelve 1-inch-square chunks (about 1/4 inch thick). Cut each pineapple chunk in half horizontally.

Place the mushrooms, flat side down, on a work surface. Top with a chunk of cheese, then a chunk of ham, and finally a piece of pineapple. Push a toothpick down through the center of the stack to hold the ingredients together. Brush or spray the flat side of the mushrooms with olive oil and season the entire stack with the chili powder and salt.

Grill the stacks, standing straight up (with only the mushrooms touching the grate), over *Direct Medium* heat until the cheese is melting and the mushrooms are well marked, about 3 minutes. Remove from the grill and serve immediately.

MAKES 12 SERVINGS

PROSCIUTTO SCALLOPS
WITH BALSAMIC GLAZE

Ever heard of simple elegance? This is it. Brace yourself for the rave reviews.

DIRECT/HIGH

1 CUP BALSAMIC VINEGAR

9 PAPER-THIN SLICES PROSCIUTTO

18 LARGE SCALLOPS, ABOUT 1 OUNCE EACH

EXTRA-VIRGIN OLIVE OIL

FRESHLY GROUND BLACK PEPPER

In a small saucepan bring the balsamic vinegar to a boil. Lower the heat and simmer until the vinegar is reduced to about 3 tablespoons; you'll notice a glaze on the bottom of the pan when you tilt it. Do not simmer for too long or the vinegar will burn. Allow to cool at room temperature.

Cut the prosciutto slices in half lengthwise. Wash the scallops and remove and discard the small, tough side muscle (*see page 316*). Wrap a strip of prosciutto around the width of each scallop; don't overlap it by more than an inch. Trim any excess bits of prosciutto. Brush or spray the top and bottom of each scallop with olive oil and season with pepper.

Place the scallops, exposed side down, on the grate 1 to 2 inches apart. Grill over *Direct High* heat until opaque in the center, 4 to 6 minutes, turning once halfway through grilling time. Remove from the grill. Place three scallops on each appetizer plate. Drizzle a spoonful of the balsamic glaze in a thin stream over and around the scallops. Serve immediately.

MAKES 6 SERVINGS

"God is in the details."

— LUDWIG MIES VAN DER ROHE

QUAIL
NIBBLERS

Quail are often sold "semi-boneless," that is, with bones just in the wings and legs—great for eating with your hands. One quail per person works well as an appetizer. Serve over mixed greens tossed with an Asian vinaigrette: 1 part Asian sesame oil, 1 part soy sauce, 2 parts peanut oil, 3 parts rice vinegar, plus salt and pepper.

DIRECT/MEDIUM

FOR THE MARINADE:

1/2 CUP PINEAPPLE JUICE

1/4 CUP SOY SAUCE

2 TABLESPOONS FRESH LEMON JUICE

2 TEASPOONS MINCED GARLIC

2 TEASPOONS MINCED FRESH LEMONGRASS

1 TEASPOON ASIAN SESAME OIL

1/2 TEASPOON CRUSHED RED PEPPER FLAKES

6 SEMI-BONELESS QUAIL, ABOUT 4 OUNCES EACH

To make the marinade: In a small bowl whisk together the marinade ingredients.

Rinse the quail under cold water. Place the quail in a large, resealable plastic bag and pour in the marinade. Press the air out of the bag and seal tightly. Turn the bag to distribute the marinade, place in a bowl, and refrigerate for 4 to 6 hours, turning occasionally.

Remove the quail from the bag and discard the marinade. Grill, breast side down, over *Direct Medium* heat until the juices are slightly pink and the quail are browned all over, 7 to 10 minutes, turning once halfway through grilling time. Serve warm.

MAKES 6 SERVINGS

LAMB CHOPS
WITH GRILLED PEPPERS

A simple Greek marinade makes a delectable snack out of these tiny-but-mighty chops. The peppers can be made several hours ahead and stored in the refrigerator; just bring them to room temperature before serving. Colorful and tasty! Note: The peppers are grilled over Direct Medium heat and the lamb chops over Direct High heat.

DIRECT/MEDIUM

FOR THE MARINADE:

3 TABLESPOONS EXTRA-VIRGIN OLIVE OIL

1 1/2 TABLESPOONS FRESH LEMON JUICE

1 TABLESPOON FINELY CHOPPED FRESH OREGANO

2 TEASPOONS MINCED GARLIC

1/4 TEASPOON KOSHER SALT

1/4 TEASPOON FRESHLY GROUND BLACK PEPPER

8 LAMB RIB CHOPS, ABOUT 2 OUNCES EACH AND 3/4 INCH THICK

1 LARGE RED BELL PEPPER

1 LARGE YELLOW BELL PEPPER

1 TABLESPOON EXTRA-VIRGIN OLIVE OIL

KOSHER SALT

FRESHLY GROUND BLACK PEPPER

To make the marinade: In a small bowl whisk together the marinade ingredients.

Trim the lamb chops of excess fat. Place the chops on a platter and coat both sides with the marinade. Cover with plastic wrap and refrigerate for 3 to 5 hours.

Grill the bell peppers over *Direct Medium* heat until the skins are black and blistered, 10 to 12 minutes, turning every 3 to 5 minutes. Remove from the grill and place in a paper bag; close tightly. Let stand 10 to 15 minutes to steam off the skins. Remove the peppers from the bag and peel away the charred skins. Cut off the tops and remove the seeds. Slice into 1/4-inch strips and toss in a small bowl with the olive oil. Season with salt and pepper.

Grill the chops over *Direct High* heat until medium rare, 3 to 5 minutes, turning once halfway through grilling time. Divide the peppers among four appetizer plates. Place two warm chops on each plate. Serve immediately.

MAKES 4 SERVINGS

Spicy Seafood Bowl

SPICY SEAFOOD BOWL

Try this first-rate first course—light and spicy, to get the taste buds working.

DIRECT/HIGH

FOR THE SAUCE:

- 1 TABLESPOON EXTRA-VIRGIN OLIVE OIL
- 1/4 CUP FINELY CHOPPED YELLOW ONION
- 2 TEASPOONS MINCED GARLIC
- 1/4 TEASPOON CRUSHED RED PEPPER FLAKES
- 1 CAN (14 1/2 OUNCES) CHOPPED TOMATOES WITH JUICE
- 1/4 CUP DRY WHITE WINE
- 1 TABLESPOON TOMATO PASTE
- 1 TABLESPOON FINELY CHOPPED FRESH ITALIAN PARSLEY
- 1 TEASPOON GRANULATED SUGAR
- 1/2 TEASPOON DRIED THYME
- 1/2 TEASPOON DRIED OREGANO LEAVES
- 1/4 TEASPOON KOSHER SALT
- 1/4 TEASPOON FRESHLY GROUND BLACK PEPPER

- 8 SMALL CLAMS
- 8 LARGE SCALLOPS
- 8 LARGE SHRIMP

- 1/2 POUND ROCK COD *OR* OTHER FIRM-FLESH FISH, ABOUT 1/2 INCH THICK
  EXTRA-VIRGIN OLIVE OIL
  KOSHER SALT
  FRESHLY GROUND BLACK PEPPER

To make the sauce: In a medium sauté pan over medium heat, warm the olive oil. Add the onion and cook, stirring occasionally, until soft and translucent, 4 to 5 minutes. Add the garlic and red pepper flakes and cook for 1 minute more, stirring occasionally. Stir in the remaining sauce ingredients, bring to a boil, then reduce heat and simmer until the mixture reaches a saucelike consistency, 10 to 15 minutes. Break up any large tomato pieces with a spoon. Set aside.

Scrub the clams. Rinse the scallops under cold water and remove and discard the small, tough side muscle (*see page 316*). Peel and devein the shrimp.

Brush or spray the scallops, shrimp, and rock cod on all sides with olive oil and season with salt and pepper. Grill the scallops, shrimp, and rock cod over *Direct High* heat until just cooked, turning once halfway through grilling time. The scallops and the rock cod will take 4 to 6 minutes. The shrimp will take 2 to 4 minutes.

Meanwhile, bring the sauce to a boil, add the clams, and cook, covered, for 3 to 4 minutes or until the clams open.

Discard any unopened clams. Cut the rock cod into 1-inch chunks and add to the sauce. Then, add the scallops and shrimp. Warm the fish and shellfish briefly in the sauce, stirring occasionally.

Divide the fish and shellfish among four small soup bowls. Spoon some warm sauce on top and serve immediately.

MAKES 4 SERVINGS

OYSTERS
WITH SRIRACHA

Placing oysters on a hot grill for a few minutes makes them easier to open. They can then be eaten immediately with a little lemon and Tabasco sauce, or topped with a spoonful of this spicy sauce and put back on the grill for a few seconds more. You can find the hot chili-garlic sauce known as sriracha in Asian food stores or the international foods section of many supermarkets.

DIRECT/HIGH

FOR THE SAUCE:

- 3 TABLESPOONS UNSALTED BUTTER, MELTED
- 1 TABLESPOON FINELY CHOPPED SHALLOTS
- 1 TABLESPOON SHERRY WINE VINEGAR
- 1 TEASPOON SRIRACHA (HOT CHILI-GARLIC SAUCE)
  PINCH KOSHER SALT

- 1 DOZEN FRESH OYSTERS, IN THE SHELL

To make the sauce: In a small bowl whisk together the sauce ingredients. Set aside.

Wash the oysters under cold running water. Grill, flat side up, over *Direct High* heat until the oysters sizzle and start to open, 3 to 5 minutes. Using tongs, carefully move the oysters to a work surface without spilling the liquid inside. Discard any unopened oysters. Using an oyster knife or bottle opener, remove the top flat shell and discard. Run an oyster knife or paring knife under the body of each oyster, detaching (but not removing) the oyster from its shell. Top each oyster with a teaspoon of the sauce and carefully return the shells to the cooking grate. Grill over *Direct High* heat until the edges of the oysters begin to curl, 30 to 45 seconds more. Serve immediately.

MAKES 4 SERVINGS

OKAY, PUT DOWN THE CHEESE BALL AND NO ONE WILL GET HURT
STARTERS ON THE GRILL

Why do we only think of serving starters when we're entertaining? And then, after figuring out the rest of the menu, our choices are often a panic-driven search for something to tide everyone over until the entrée. ("Quick, grab a cheese ball!") Hang on there! Planning a starter course is easier—and more rewarding—than you might think. In fact, you might even start serving starters on weeknights, too. Just imagine....

PLAN YOUR TIMING. Ever notice how time flies when you're surrounded by friends and family? What a drag to get back to the grill to start your entrée and find the first round of coals dying out—or the gas tank empty. So make sure you have plenty of fuel to keep you going through all the courses you're preparing. It takes any newly added coals about 25 minutes to get up to cooking temperature, so add charcoal every hour. Don't worry about lag time for them to catch up, just add them on schedule and you'll be fine.

ALIGN YOUR COOKING METHODS. If you're grilling with charcoal, you might not want to reconfigure your coals between courses, so pick a starter that's cooked over the same kind of heat (Direct or Indirect) as your entrée. And pay attention to the temperature. Take steaks, for example. You'll want a Direct fire for steaks, and you may want to sear them over High heat. Grilled shrimp and oysters are great choices for a first course. They can go over Direct High heat, and will be consumed quickly so you can get back to preparing the steaks before the coals burn down.

GET YOUR DIRECTIONS STRAIGHT. If your entrée is a long-cooking one, pick a starter that's meant to be grilled over Direct heat. That way you

can simply slip the starter in over Direct heat alongside your entrée, which will already be set over Indirect heat. Also, pick a starter recipe that won't require you to lift the grill lid too much (forget anything basted), and remember to add grilling time to your entrée to accommodate the heat lost from lifting the lid to tend to the starters.

FIRE IT UP TWICE! If you have a second grill and don't want to worry about timing, by all means, pull it out and use it for your starters. (Who knows, you might be inspired to try a grilled dessert on there after you pull off the starters.) If you have a six-burner grill, try setting it up like two side-by-side grills—but don't forget to adjust cooking times for excessive lid-lifting.

TAKE THE EASY WAY OUT. Another great way to use your grill is to prepare as many make-ahead ingredients as you can the night before. For the early arrivers, we like to put out a few dips and munchy-type snacks made with grilled ingredients prepared earlier, then fire up the grill for the hot and snazzy starters that demonstrate our grilling prowess.

MATCHING STARTERS
WITH ENTRÉES

Which comes first, the starter or the entrée? Well, when you're planning a menu, there's no set rule on which way to pick them. But to give you a hint, here's a little chart that matches some of our favorite starters in this chapter with three entrées from elsewhere in the book. The starter complements the entrée choices because of its textures, relative "lightness" or "heaviness," or flavors. Here each entrée will work equally well with the starter on its left. Still can't decide? Close your eyes and point. Works for us!

• **Lamb Chops with Grilled Peppers**	Game Hens with Sage-Rice Stuffing *(page 263)*
	Swordfish Steaks with Puttanesca Sauce *(page 287)*
	Portabello Burgers with Roasted Peppers *(page 329)*
• **Shrimp Satay**	Korean Short Ribs *(page 126)*
	Plum-Glazed Baby Back Ribs *(page 159)*
	Five-Spice Grilled Quail *(page 210)*
• **Smokey Joe's Crab Cakes**	The Ultimate Bacon-Mushroom Cheeseburger *(page 90)*
	Kansas City–Style Baby Back Ribs *(page 159)*
	The Ultimate Summer Sandwich *(page 248)*
• **Prosciutto Scallops with Balsamic Glaze**	Bistecca alla Fiorentina *(page 104)*
	Pollo Diablo *(page 244)*
	Spring Vegetable Platter *(page 347)*
• **Guacamole with Fire-Roasted Vegetables**	Southwest Sirloin with Corn Salad *(page 112)*
	Tequila-Orange Chicken Breasts *(page 250)*
	Poblano Rellenos *(page 344)*
• **Poblano and White Bean Quesadillas**	Mexican Flank Steak with Jicama-Orange Salad *(page 119)*
	Sonora-Style Green Chile Pork Burritos *(page 170)*
	Citrus-Avocado Chicken Breasts *(page 247)*
• **Grilled Figs with Arugula**	New York Strips with Roasted Garlic Butter *(page 100)*
	Pesto-Stuffed Loin Chops *(page 197)*
	Fabulous Fish Cakes with Lemon Aïoli *(page 285)*
• **Southwest Onion Dip**	Texas Rib-Eye Steaks with Chili Barbecue Sauce *(page 111)*
	Pulled Pork Sandwiches with West Carolina Barbecue Sauce *(page 169)*
	Beer Can Chicken *(page 227)*

*Appetite comes
with eating.*

— FRENCH PROVERB

Zesty Garlic Shrimp

ZESTY GARLIC
SHRIMP

Set a bunch of marinated jumbo shrimp on the grill and your guests will love you. Tah dah!

DIRECT/MEDIUM

FOR THE MARINADE:

- 1/4 CUP EXTRA-VIRGIN OLIVE OIL
- 2 TABLESPOONS FRESH LEMON JUICE
- 2 TABLESPOONS FINELY CHOPPED ITALIAN PARSLEY
- 2 TEASPOONS DRIED OREGANO
- 1 1/2 TEASPOONS MINCED GARLIC
- 1 TEASPOON GRATED LEMON ZEST
- 1/2 TEASPOON KOSHER SALT
- 1/4 TEASPOON FRESHLY GROUND BLACK PEPPER
- 1/4 TEASPOON CRUSHED RED PEPPER FLAKES

- 20 JUMBO SHRIMP (ABOUT 1 1/4 POUNDS), PEELED AND DEVEINED
- 1 TABLESPOON FINE DRIED BREAD CRUMBS

To make the marinade: In a medium bowl whisk together the marinade ingredients.

Place the shrimp in a large, resealable plastic bag and pour in the marinade. Press the air out of the bag and seal tightly. Turn the bag to distribute the marinade, place in a bowl, and refrigerate for 30 minutes to 1 hour.

Remove the shrimp from the bag and discard the marinade. Thread the shrimp onto skewers, either one per skewer as an hors d'oeuvre or five per skewer as an appetizer. Sprinkle the bread crumbs evenly over the shrimp. Grill over *Direct Medium* heat until just opaque in the center and firm to the touch, 4 to 6 minutes, turning the skewers once halfway through grilling time. Serve warm.

MAKES 4 TO 20 SERVINGS

SHRIMP
SATAY

The grill's favorite shellfish on a stick. With an Indonesian twist you can't resist.

DIRECT/HIGH

FOR THE SAUCE:

- 3 TABLESPOONS SMOOTH PEANUT BUTTER
- 2 TABLESPOONS SOY SAUCE
- 2 TABLESPOONS RICE VINEGAR
- 1 TABLESPOON GRANULATED SUGAR
- 1/2 TEASPOON GRANULATED GARLIC
- 1/2 TEASPOON ASIAN SESAME OIL
- 1/4 TEASPOON TABASCO SAUCE

FOR THE SHRIMP:

- 1/2 TEASPOON GROUND CUMIN
- 1/2 TEASPOON KOSHER SALT
- 1/4 TEASPOON GROUND GINGER
- 1/4 TEASPOON CURRY POWDER
- 20 LARGE SHRIMP (ABOUT 1 POUND), PEELED AND DEVEINED
- 2 TABLESPOONS PEANUT OIL

To make the sauce: In a small saucepan whisk together the sauce ingredients with 1/4 cup water. Bring to a simmer over medium heat and cook for 1 to 2 minutes to thicken. Set aside at room temperature.

To prepare the shrimp: In a small bowl mix together the cumin, salt, ginger, and curry powder. Place the shrimp in a medium bowl, drizzle with the peanut oil, and toss. Sprinkle with the spices and toss again. Cover with plastic wrap and refrigerate for 20 to 30 minutes.

Thread the shrimp onto skewers, either one per skewer as an hors d'oeuvre or five per skewer as an appetizer. Grill over *Direct High* heat until just opaque in the center and firm to the touch, 2 to 4 minutes, turning the skewers once halfway through grilling time. Serve warm with the sauce.

MAKES 4 TO 20 SERVINGS

GRILLED
SCALLOP COCKTAIL

Similar to seviche (a Latin American dish in which raw seafood is marinated in citrus juice), this scallop dish is a refreshing start to a summer lunch. We grilled the scallops to add another layer of flavor. Chill everything well before assembling the "cocktail" in something fun like an oversized martini glasses chilled in the freezer.

DIRECT/HIGH

- **2 CUPS SUGAR SNAP PEAS**
- **1 CUP 1/2-INCH DICE PEELED SEEDLESS CUCUMBER**
- **1 CUP 1/2-INCH DICE RIPE TOMATOES**

- **2 TABLESPOONS EXTRA-VIRGIN OLIVE OIL**
- **1 TABLESPOON MILD CHILI SAUCE**
- **1 TABLESPOON FINELY CHOPPED FRESH MINT**
- **1/2 TEASPOON KOSHER SALT**
- **1/4 TEASPOON FRESHLY GROUND BLACK PEPPER**

FOR THE SCALLOPS:

- **10 TO 12 LARGE SCALLOPS, ABOUT 1 1/2 OUNCES EACH**
- **EXTRA-VIRGIN OLIVE OIL**
- **KOSHER SALT**
- **FRESHLY GROUND BLACK PEPPER**
- **1/4 CUP FRESH LIME JUICE**
- **2 TABLESPOONS FINELY CHOPPED FRESH MINT**

In a large pot of boiling salted water, cook the snap peas until barely tender, 4 to 5 minutes. Drain the peas and rinse under cold water to stop the cooking process. Cut the peas into 1/2-inch pieces and combine in a medium bowl with the diced cucumbers and tomatoes.

In a small bowl whisk together the olive oil, chili sauce, mint, salt, and pepper. Pour over the vegetables and stir to evenly distribute. Cover with plastic wrap and refrigerate until ready to serve.

To prepare the scallops: Wash the scallops and remove and discard the small, tough side muscle *(see page 316).* Brush or spray the scallops with olive oil and season with salt and pepper. Grill over *Direct High* heat until barely opaque in the center, 3 to 4 minutes, turning once halfway through grilling time. Remove from the grill and cut into 1/2-inch pieces. Put in a medium bowl and add the lime juice and mint. Stir to combine, cover with plastic wrap, and refrigerate for 1 hour, stirring two to three times.

Transfer the scallops to the bowl with the vegetables, leaving most of the lime juice behind. Stir to evenly distribute. Taste and adjust the seasoning, if necessary. Serve cold.

MAKES 4 TO 6 SERVINGS

SMOKEY JOE'S
CRAB CAKES

Now your favorite crab shack can be in your own backyard (beach optional). Fresh crab tastes best, but frozen or good-quality canned lump crabmeat also works well. Turn the cakes gently with a spatula so they hold together.

DIRECT/HIGH

FOR THE CRAB CAKES:

- **12 OUNCES FRESH, FROZEN, OR CANNED COOKED LUMP CRABMEAT**
- **3/4 CUP PLAIN BREAD CRUMBS**
- **1/2 CUP FINELY DICED RED BELL PEPPER**
- **4 GREEN ONIONS (WHITE PART ONLY), FINELY CHOPPED**
- **3 TABLESPOONS MAYONNAISE**
- **2 TEASPOONS DIJON MUSTARD**
- **1/4 TEASPOON HOT PEPPER SAUCE**
- **1/4 TEASPOON KOSHER SALT**
- **1/8 TEASPOON FRESHLY GROUND BLACK PEPPER**

FOR THE DRESSING:

- **2 TABLESPOONS EXTRA-VIRGIN OLIVE OIL**
- **2 TEASPOONS WHITE WINE VINEGAR**
- **1/2 TEASPOON DIJON MUSTARD**
- **KOSHER SALT**
- **FRESHLY GROUND BLACK PEPPER**

- **4 HANDFULS MIXED SALAD GREENS (ABOUT 4 OUNCES)**

- **VEGETABLE OIL**
- **4 LEMON WEDGES**

To make the crab cakes: In a colander drain the crabmeat (if frozen, allow to defrost) and pat dry with paper towels. In a medium bowl flake the crabmeat with a fork and discard any shell or cartilage. Add the remaining crab cake ingredients and mix gently but thoroughly. Shape into eight small cakes, about 3 inches in diameter and 3/4 inch thick. Place the cakes on a plate, cover with plastic wrap, and refrigerate for 30 minutes to 2 hours so they hold together on the grill.

To make the dressing: In a medium bowl whisk together the salad dressing ingredients, including salt and pepper to taste. Just before serving, toss the salad greens with the dressing and arrange on four plates.

Lightly brush or spray both sides of the crab cakes with vegetable oil. Grill over *Direct High* heat until the bread crumbs are toasted, 6 to 8 minutes, carefully turning with a wide spatula once halfway through grilling time. Place two warm crab cakes on each plate and serve with a lemon wedge.

MAKES 4 SERVINGS

Smokey Joe's Crab Cakes

Sweet and Spicy Grilled Nuts

SWEET AND SPICY
GRILLED NUTS

Tired of dips and chips? These creative munchies make a dynamic duo. Nibblers never had it so good.

INDIRECT/LOW

FOR THE SWEET NUT CRUNCH:

- 1 **CUP RAW UNSHELLED PUMPKIN SEEDS**
- 1 **CUP WHOLE ALMONDS**
- 2 **TABLESPOONS UNSALTED BUTTER, MELTED**
- 1 **TABLESPOON HONEY**
- 1 **TABLESPOON BROWN SUGAR**
- 1 **TEASPOON CINNAMON**
- 1 **TEASPOON KOSHER SALT**
- 1/2 **TEASPOON CAYENNE**
- 1/4 **TEASPOON GROUND NUTMEG**

FOR THE SPICY NUTS:

- 1 **CUP RAW UNSHELLED PUMPKIN SEEDS**
- 1 **CUP WHOLE ALMONDS**
- 1 **CUP ROASTED SPANISH PEANUTS**
- 2 **TEASPOONS HOT CHILI OIL**
- 1 **TEASPOON EXTRA-VIRGIN OLIVE OIL**
- 1 **TEASPOON KOSHER SALT**
- 1 **TEASPOON PAPRIKA**
- 1 **TEASPOON WORCESTERSHIRE SAUCE**
- 1/2 **TEASPOON CAYENNE**

To make the sweet nut crunch: Spread the pumpkin seeds and almonds evenly in a 9- by 9-inch heavy-gauge foil pan. Grill over *Indirect Low* heat, stirring occasionally, until the nuts are fragrant and lightly toasted, about 15 minutes. Remove the pan from the grill.

In a small bowl combine the remaining sweet nut crunch ingredients and mix well. Drizzle the mixture over the nuts and toss to coat evenly. Return the pan to the grill and grill over *Indirect Low* heat for 20 to 25 minutes more, stirring occasionally. Remove from the grill. Allow the nuts to cool in the pan for 1 hour. Break into bite-sized pieces. If not serving immediately, store in an airtight container.

To make the spicy nuts: Spread the pumpkin seeds and almonds evenly in a 9- by 13-inch foil pan. Grill over *Indirect Low* heat, stirring occasionally, until the nuts are fragrant and lightly toasted, about 15 minutes. Remove the pan from the grill and add the peanuts.

In a small bowl whisk together the remaining spicy nut ingredients. Drizzle the mixture over the nuts and toss to coat evenly. Return the pan to the grill and grill over *Indirect Low* heat for 5 to 7 minutes more, stirring once or twice. Remove from the grill and spoon the nuts onto paper towels. Allow to cool. If not serving immediately, store in an airtight container. Serve the nut mixtures in separate bowls.

MAKES 20 SERVINGS

GRILLED FIGS
WITH ARUGULA

This is the kind of salad that catches your eye on a good restaurant menu. For the cheese use aged Asiago or Dry Jack, if available. In a pinch, try curls of Parmigiano-Reggiano or a Dutch cheese called Parrano.

DIRECT/HIGH

FOR THE DRESSING:

- 3 **TABLESPOONS EXTRA-VIRGIN OLIVE OIL**
- 2 **TABLESPOON HONEY, DIVIDED**
- 2 **TABLESPOON CHAMPAGNE VINEGAR, DIVIDED**
- 1/4 **TEASPOON KOSHER SALT**
- 1/4 **TEASPOON FRESHLY GROUND BLACK PEPPER**

- 8 **LARGE *OR* 12 SMALL FRESH FIGS**

- 5 **TO 6 CUPS LOOSELY PACKED BABY ARUGULA**
- 2 **TO 3 OUNCES AGED ASIAGO *OR* DRY JACK CHEESE**

To make the dressing: In a small bowl whisk together the olive oil, 1 tablespoon of the honey, 1 tablespoon of the vinegar, and the salt and pepper.

Trim the stems of the figs and halve lengthwise. Arrange the figs, cut side up, on a platter. In a small bowl whisk together the remaining 1 tablespoon of honey and remaining 1 tablespoon of vinegar until completely blended. Lightly brush the cut side of the figs with the mixture.

Grill the figs, cut side down, over *Direct High* heat until warm and lightly caramelized, about 2 minutes, turning with a spatula once halfway through grilling time. Set aside.

Place the arugula in a large bowl. Whisk the dressing one more time and lightly dress the greens (you may not need to use all of the dressing). Divide the arugula among four plates. Arrange the warm grilled figs, cut side up, around the edges of the salad, dividing them evenly. Curl the cheese with a cheese plane or vegetable peeler. Garnish each salad with curls of cheese. Serve immediately.

MAKES 4 SERVINGS

SOUTHWEST
ONION DIP

One taste of this and you'll toss out the onion soup mix for good. You can't get this kind of sweet smokiness out of a paper envelope. The Southwest seasonings make it that much better.

DIRECT/LOW

FOR THE DIP:

4 SLICES YELLOW ONION, ABOUT 1/2 INCH EACH
   EXTRA-VIRGIN OLIVE OIL

1/2 CUP LOOSELY PACKED FRESH CILANTRO LEAVES,
   WITH SOME STEMS

1/2 CUP SOUR CREAM

1/4 CUP PINE NUTS

1/4 CUP CREAM CHEESE

2 TEASPOONS FRESH LIME JUICE

1 TEASPOON KOSHER SALT

1 TEASPOON GRANULATED ONION

1 TEASPOON CHILI POWDER

1 TEASPOON GRANULATED GARLIC

1/4 TEASPOON GROUND CUMIN

1/4 TEASPOON FRESHLY GROUND BLACK PEPPER

2 FLOUR TORTILLAS (10 INCHES)

To make the dip: Brush or spray both sides of the onion slices with olive oil. Grill the onion slices over *Direct Low* heat until marked and very tender, about 15 minutes, turning once halfway through grilling time. Put the onion slices in a food processor, add the remaining dip ingredients, and pulse into a smooth purée, scraping down the sides of the bowl occasionally. Transfer to a serving bowl.

Grill the tortillas over *Direct Low* heat until crisp and browned in spots, 3 to 5 minutes, turning once halfway through grilling time. Remove from the grill and cut each tortilla into eight wedges. Serve the dip with the tortilla chips.

MAKES ABOUT 1 1/2 CUPS

WHITE BEAN
BRUSCHETTA

The term bruschetta comes from the Italian "bruschare," meaning to roast over coals. In the traditional recipe, toasted bread is rubbed with garlic, drizzled with olive oil, and topped with chopped tomatoes or whatnot—such as white beans and sage, as we've done here.

DIRECT/MEDIUM

FOR THE TOPPING:

2 TABLESPOONS EXTRA-VIRGIN OLIVE OIL

1/4 CUP FINELY CHOPPED YELLOW ONION

1/4 TEASPOON CRUSHED RED PEPPER FLAKES

2 TEASPOONS MINCED GARLIC

2 TEASPOONS FINELY CHOPPED FRESH SAGE

1 CAN (15 OUNCES) CANNELLINI *OR*
   NAVY BEANS, DRAINED

2 TEASPOONS RED WINE VINEGAR
   KOSHER SALT
   FRESHLY GROUND BLACK PEPPER

1 LOAF RUSTIC ITALIAN BREAD, CUT INTO
   1/2-INCH SLICES

2 TABLESPOONS FINELY CHOPPED FRESH
   ITALIAN PARSLEY

To make the topping: In a medium sauté pan over medium heat, warm the olive oil. Add the onion and red pepper flakes, and cook, stirring occasionally, until the onion is tender, 4 to 5 minutes. Add the garlic and sage and cook for 1 minute more, stirring occasionally. Add the beans and vinegar and cook until the mixture comes to a simmer. Transfer to a food processor and process until smooth. Season with salt and pepper.

Grill the bread slices over *Direct Medium* heat until toasted, 2 to 3 minutes, turning once halfway through grilling time. Transfer to a platter. Spread some of the warm bean mixture on each piece of toast and sprinkle with a bit of parsley. Serve immediately.

MAKES 4 TO 6 SERVINGS

SWEET PEPPER AND EGGPLANT
BRUSCHETTA

To make a basil "chiffonade" (herbs or vegetables cut into thin strips), roll up basil leaves like a cigar and thinly slice them crosswise in ribbons. Both the eggplant and the roasted peppers can be prepared ahead. Grill the bread just before serving.

DIRECT/MEDIUM

FOR THE TOPPING:

- **2   LARGE RED BELL PEPPERS**
- **2   MEDIUM JAPANESE EGGPLANTS, TRIMMED, CUT LENGTHWISE INTO 1/3-INCH SLICES**
- **EXTRA-VIRGIN OLIVE OIL**
- **1/4   CUP BASIL CHIFFONADE**
- **2   TABLESPOONS CAPERS, DRAINED**
- **2   TEASPOONS BALSAMIC VINEGAR**
- **2   TEASPOONS EXTRA-VIRGIN OLIVE OIL**
- **1/4   TEASPOON GRANULATED GARLIC**
- **KOSHER SALT**
- **FRESHLY GROUND BLACK PEPPER**

- **1   LOAF RUSTIC ITALIAN BREAD, CUT INTO 1/2-INCH SLICES**
- **8   OUNCES FRESH GOAT CHEESE**

To make the topping: Grill the bell peppers over *Direct Medium* heat until the skins are evenly charred on all sides, 10 to 12 minutes, turning every 3 to 5 minutes. Remove from the grill and place in a paper bag; close tightly. Let stand 10 to 15 minutes to steam off the skins. Remove the peppers from the bag and peel away the charred skins. Cut off the tops and remove the seeds. Cut each pepper into 1/4-inch dice and transfer to a medium bowl.

Brush both sides of the eggplant slices with olive oil and grill over *Direct Medium* heat until soft and browned, 6 to 8 minutes, turning and basting with the oil once halfway through grilling time. Transfer to a cutting board and cut into 1/4-inch dice. Add to the peppers along with the remaining topping ingredients, including salt and pepper to taste. Mix well and set aside.

Grill the bread slices over *Direct Medium* heat until toasted, 2 to 3 minutes, turning once halfway through grilling time. Remove from the grill. Spread a layer of goat cheese on each slice and spoon the vegetable mixture on top. Serve warm or at room temperature.

MAKES 4 TO 6 SERVINGS

DON'T BE BITTER
EGGPLANT
ON THE GRILL

If your only encounters with this purple wonder have been in eggplant parmesan or the creamy dip baba ghanoush, consider expanding your culinary horizons. Eggplant is perfect for the the grill because it absorbs other flavors so easily, including smoky notes from the fire.

There are many types of eggplant, but in this book we stick to two widely available types: Japanese and globe. Japanese eggplant is also called Asian or Oriental eggplant, depending on where you find it. Smaller and more cylindrical, its color ranges from lavender to deep purple. Japanese eggplant is mild, even sweet—to use it, simply grill it in halves or slices.

Globe eggplant is big, dark purple, and shaped like a butternut squash. It grills up best when cut into 1/2-inch slices (crosswise or through the stem), and it may need a salting first.

Why salt it? Globe eggplant can sometimes be slightly bitter. Salting the flesh draws out the bitter juices. How do you know if your purple pal is harboring any ill will? Older flesh and an abundance of seeds are indicators. Select fresh, firm, and glossy eggplants with no bruises or blemishes. Late summer (August to September) is peak season. If you're growing your own, pick them at about two-thirds their full size. Don't refrigerate eggplant. If you have to keep it overnight, place it in a cool part of the kitchen.

Cut soft or seedy eggplant into slices and generously salt each side with kosher salt. You need a good even coating here, so don't hold back. Place the slices on a rack set over a baking sheet for 30 minutes or so. Rinse them well under running water, pat them dry with a paper towel, and proceed with your recipe. Brush eggplant slices well with oil before placing them on the grill over Direct Medium heat, then baste them again when you turn them halfway through the grilling time. Your dish will be magnifico.

EGGPLANT-TOMATO
DIP

Think baba ghanoush with an Italian perspective.

DIRECT/HIGH

FOR THE DIP:

1 GLOBE EGGPLANT, ABOUT 12 OUNCES

1/2 CUP TIGHTLY PACKED FRESH ITALIAN PARSLEY

1/3 CUP TIGHTLY PACKED FRESH BASIL LEAVES

1/4 CUP SUN-DRIED TOMATOES (OIL-PACKED)

1/4 CUP SOUR CREAM

2 TEASPOONS BALSAMIC VINEGAR

1 TEASPOON MINCED GARLIC

1 TEASPOON KOSHER SALT

1/2 TEASPOON FRESHLY GROUND BLACK PEPPER

6 PITA POCKETS

To make the dip: Grill the eggplant over *Direct High* heat until all sides are evenly blistered and blackened and the eggplant has started to collapse, about 15 minutes, turning occasionally. Allow to cool on a cutting board. When the eggplant is cool enough to handle, scoop out the soft flesh from the skin with a large spoon and transfer to a food processor. Add the remaining dip ingredients and process until the mixture is smooth. Transfer to a shallow serving bowl.

Using kitchen scissors or a knife, cut through the folded edges of each of the six pita pockets to make twelve disks. Grill the disks in batches over *Direct High* heat until toasted, 30 to 60 seconds, turning once halfway through grilling time. Transfer the disks to a large tray to cool. Break each disk into four or five pieces. Serve with the dip.

MAKES ABOUT 2 CUPS

EGGPLANT
ROLL-UPS

What to do at the peak of summer when the garden is multiplying eggplants, tomatoes, and herbs? A dish of grilled eggplant slices rolled around goat cheese and surrounded by fresh tomatoes bursting with all their glory makes a knockout, seasonal appetizer.

DIRECT/MEDIUM

4 SLICES JAPANESE EGGPLANT, ABOUT 1/4 INCH THICK EACH AND 6 TO 7 INCHES LONG, CUT IN HALF CROSSWISE *(SEE PAGE 81)*

EXTRA-VIRGIN OLIVE OIL

1 TEASPOON KOSHER SALT

1 TEASPOON FRESHLY GROUND BLACK PEPPER

1 TEASPOON FINELY CHOPPED FRESH ITALIAN PARSLEY

4 OUNCES SOFT GOAT CHEESE

2 CUPS COARSELY CHOPPED RIPE TOMATOES

FOR THE DRESSING:

3 TABLESPOONS EXTRA-VIRGIN OLIVE OIL

2 TEASPOONS FRESH LEMON JUICE

1 TEASPOON BALSAMIC VINEGAR

1/2 TEASPOON MINCED FRESH THYME

1/4 TEASPOON KOSHER SALT

1/4 TEASPOON FRESHLY GROUND BLACK PEPPER

1/4 CUP FINELY CHOPPED FRESH BASIL

Brush or spray both sides of the eggplant slices with olive oil and season with the salt and pepper. Grill over *Direct Medium* heat until tender, 5 to 7 minutes, turning and basting with oil once halfway through grilling time. Remove from the grill and allow to cool.

Mix together the parsley and goat cheese. Spread 1 tablespoon evenly over one side of each eggplant slice. Starting at one end, roll up the eggplant. Arrange the roll-ups on a platter or individual plates. Surround with the tomatoes.

To make the dressing: In a small bowl whisk together the dressing ingredients.

Drizzle the dressing over the eggplant roll-ups (you may not need to use all of it). Garnish with the basil. Serve at room temperature.

MAKES 4 SERVINGS

Eggplant Roll-Ups

Grilled Polenta with Mushroom Ragout

GRILLED POLENTA
WITH MUSHROOM RAGOUT

Polenta, a simple cake of yellow cornmeal, is fantastic grilled. Top it with savory mushrooms and you've got one full-flavored appetizer. Note: The mushrooms are grilled over Direct Medium heat and the polenta over Direct High heat.

DIRECT/MEDIUM

FOR THE POLENTA:

2 CUPS WHOLE MILK

1 CUP POLENTA *OR* COARSE-GROUND YELLOW CORNMEAL

1 TEASPOON KOSHER SALT

1/2 TEASPOON DRIED THYME

FOR THE RAGOUT:

8 OUNCES MIXED WILD MUSHROOMS (PORTABELLO, SHIITAKE, BROWN, AND BUTTON)

2 TABLESPOONS EXTRA-VIRGIN OLIVE OIL, PLUS MORE FOR THE MUSHROOMS AND POLENTA

2 CUPS THINLY SLICED RED ONION

1 TABLESPOON TOMATO PASTE

1/2 CUP CHICKEN BROTH

1/4 CUP DRY VERMOUTH

1 1/2 TEASPOONS FINELY CHOPPED FRESH ROSEMARY

1 TEASPOON FINELY CHOPPED FRESH THYME

KOSHER SALT

FRESHLY GROUND BLACK PEPPER

1/2 CUP FRESHLY GRATED PARMIGIANO-REGGIANO CHEESE (OPTIONAL)

To make the polenta: Line an 8- by 8-inch baking pan with plastic wrap so that the wrap spills over two opposite sides by about 4 inches. In a large heavy saucepan combine the polenta ingredients with 1 cup water and whisk until smooth. Bring the mixture to a boil over high heat, whisking frequently. Reduce heat to low and cook the polenta until tender, about 20 minutes, stirring every 5 minutes or so with a wooden spoon to avoid scorching. Transfer the polenta to the baking pan and smooth the surface with a spatula dipped in water. The polenta should be about 1/2 inch thick. Allow to cool to room temperature. Fold the long ends of the plastic wrap over the top and refrigerate until the polenta is firm, 4 to 24 hours.

To make the ragout: Remove and discard the stems from the mushrooms. With a spoon, scrape the black gills from the portabello mushrooms and discard. Wipe all the mushroom caps clean with a damp towel. Generously brush or spray both sides of the caps with olive oil. Grill the mushrooms, cap side up, over *Direct Medium* heat until tender, turning once and basting with more oil, if necessary, halfway through grilling time. The portabello mushrooms will take 12 to 15 minutes and the shiitake, brown, and button mushrooms will take 8 to 10 minutes. Remove from the grill and cut into 1-inch chunks.

In a large sauté pan over medium heat, warm the 2 tablespoons of olive oil. Add the onion and cook, stirring occasionally, until soft and translucent, about 8 minutes. Add the mushrooms and continue to cook for 2 minutes more. In a small bowl whisk together the tomato paste, chicken broth, and vermouth. Add to the onion and mushroom mixture. Sprinkle with the rosemary and thyme and simmer for 5 minutes, stirring occasionally. Season with salt and pepper. Set aside while you grill the polenta.

Remove the polenta from the baking pan and plastic wrap. Cut into squares or other desired shapes. Brush or spray both sides of the cakes with oil. Grill over *Direct High* heat until warm and marked on both sides, 8 to 10 minutes, turning once halfway through grilling time.

To serve, gently reheat the ragout and spoon it over the polenta cakes, then sprinkle each serving with some of the cheese, if desired. Serve warm.

MAKES 4 TO 6 SERVINGS

GUACAMOLE
WITH FIRE-ROASTED VEGETABLES

This recipe turns everyone's favorite dip into a smoky summit of flavors.

DIRECT/MEDIUM

FOR THE GUACAMOLE:

2 SLICES WHITE ONION, ABOUT 1/2 INCH THICK EACH

1 MEDIUM JALAPEÑO PEPPER, STEM REMOVED

2 GREEN ONIONS (WHITE PART ONLY)

EXTRA-VIRGIN OLIVE OIL

2 AVOCADOS, PEELED, PITTED, AND COARSELY CHOPPED

1 CUP FINELY CHOPPED RIPE TOMATOES

3 TABLESPOONS FINELY CHOPPED FRESH CILANTRO

1 TABLESPOON FRESH LIME JUICE

1/2 TEASPOON KOSHER SALT

1/4 TEASPOON GRANULATED GARLIC

TORTILLA CHIPS

To make the guacamole: Brush or spray the onion slices, jalapeño, and green onions all over with olive oil. Grill over *Direct Medium* heat until well marked and tender, turning once halfway through grilling time. The onion slices will take 10 to 12 minutes, the jalapeño 4 to 6 minutes, and the green onions 3 to 4 minutes.

Finely chop the grilled vegetables and place in a medium bowl. Add the remaining guacamole ingredients and stir with the back of a fork until thoroughly combined. Serve at room temperature with tortilla chips.

MAKES ABOUT 3 CUPS

Most food cravings live short but intense lives. If the real thing isn't available, you can usually be placated with a reasonable facsimile or a close-enough relative. But when you're struck by the deep, maddening yearning for juicy grilled beef, you just gotta have the real thing. Nothing else will do.

If beef is your passion, these moments can border on crisis. Details such as texture, the degree of doneness, and seasonings are sacrosanct. This desired beef serving must not merely *be*. It must be *just so*.

No wonder so many beef lovers turn to the grill for true satisfaction. Whether you're preparing steaks, filets, burgers, or a roast, the grill is the best—some would say only—way to sear the outside quickly,

BEEF

giving it a wonderfully caramelized surface that yields to the tenderness within. But that's only half the story. Without a doubt, beef reaches its fullest flavor when steeped in the smoke that rises up when fat and juices drip onto the flames below. This is the stuff that cowboy dreams are made of.

Then, of course, there is beef's appeal to the chef: versatility. Bovine topography is vast and varied, with a range of textures and flavors that's impossible to replicate. From the tender valleys of the short loin to the massive peaks of the chuck, there's a lot of territory to work with here. This affords the chef the luxury of choosing not only the cut, but the preparation method as well. Let's say you're craving a rich, tender helping. How about a filet mignon, a tenderloin roast, or a sizzling rib-eye? Easy, fast, delicious. Or let's say it's Saturday and you want to treat yourself after a busy day of errands and chores. Just slip a flank or skirt steak into a tenderizing marinade when you wake up and dine on thin slices of beef dripping with

seasoned flavor that evening. And who doesn't appreciate the simplicity of the burger, which you can dress up or down depending on your mood. Fine-tuned to your craving-of-the-moment, the burger can be bliss.

Got more time on your hands? Spend some of it rubbing or stuffing a roast or marinating some beef ribs. You won't regret a minute invested. And wouldn't a savory sauce—say, a velvety blend of red wine, mushrooms, and butter—be worth the effort to create? We think so!

There are even choices today about the quality of beef you start with. We're not talking about the grade and cut, but rather the purity of the cattle's feed and water, whether or not the cattle ever receive growth hormones, how they're treated for illness, and how they're handled over the course of their entire lives. Marketed under the label of "natural" beef, there is a variety of products to choose from. Each producer has specific standards and definitions, however, so read the labels carefully or ask your butcher about them. These products usually cost more, but you may very well find a line of beef products that you'll want at your dinner table every time.

Whatever you decide to season, slice, and devour, look for cuts with the most generous marbling. Trim off the excess outer fat. And ditch the guilt trip. We promise to put the fun back into a menu choice that has been met with a raised eyebrow in the past several years. Beef is about enjoyment. If you've ever wondered how to get there, we've got the inside scoop on how to shop for the good stuff, how to trim it up, and how to grill it to meet your expectations. From the homestead of the classic mouth-watering T-bone to the Elysian fields of garlic- and herb-crusted prime rib, there's something here for every beef lover. But don't take our word for it. Indulge!

THE ULTIMATE BACON-MUSHROOM
CHEESEBURGER

The secret to making the mushrooms that top this burger so succulent is bacon fat. Yes, we shamelessly baste them with it, along with a little olive oil to keep them moist.

DIRECT/MEDIUM

4 SLICES THICK-CUT BACON

1/4 CUP EXTRA-VIRGIN OLIVE OIL

4 MEDIUM PORTABELLO MUSHROOMS, ABOUT 4 INCHES IN DIAMETER EACH
FRESHLY GROUND BLACK PEPPER

1 1/2 POUNDS GROUND CHUCK (80% LEAN)
KOSHER SALT

4 THIN SLICES HAVARTI CHEESE

4 HAMBURGER BUNS

4 TABLESPOONS DIJON MUSTARD

4 CRISP LETTUCE LEAVES

In a large sauté pan over medium heat, cook the bacon until crisp, 10 to 12 minutes, turning occasionally. Remove the bacon and set aside on paper towels to drain. Reserve the bacon fat in the pan and add the olive oil.

Remove and discard the mushroom stems. Clean the caps with a moist paper towel and, using a small spoon, scrape out the black gills from inside the caps. Generously brush both sides of the mushrooms with the bacon fat and oil mixture. Season with pepper.

Gently shape the ground chuck into four burgers of equal size and thickness (about 3/4 inch thick), and season both sides with salt and pepper.

Grill the mushrooms and burgers over *Direct Medium* heat until the mushrooms are tender and juicy and the burgers reach an internal temperature of 160°F for medium, 8 to 10 minutes, turning once halfway through grilling time. Top each burger with a slice of the cheese during the last minute or two of grilling time and allow the cheese to melt. During the last 30 seconds, grill the buns over *Direct Medium* heat until lightly toasted. Spread the mustard on the toasted buns.

Serve the cheeseburgers hot on the buns, topped with a slice of bacon, a mushroom cap, and a lettuce leaf.

MAKES 4 SERVINGS

CLASSIC BACON
CHEESEBURGER

Grab a bun and get in line!

DIRECT/MEDIUM

6 SLICES BACON

2 POUNDS GROUND CHUCK (80% LEAN)
KOSHER SALT
FRESHLY GROUND BLACK PEPPER

6 THIN SLICES EXTRA-SHARP CHEDDAR CHEESE

6 HAMBURGER BUNS

6 CRISP LETTUCE LEAVES

6 SLICES RIPE TOMATO
KETCHUP (OPTIONAL)
MUSTARD (OPTIONAL)

In a large sauté pan over medium heat, cook the bacon until crisp, 10 to 12 minutes, turning occasionally. Remove the bacon and set aside on paper towels to drain. Remove the pan from the heat.

Gently shape the ground chuck into six burgers of equal size and thickness (about 3/4 inch thick). Season both sides of the burgers with salt and pepper.

Grill over *Direct Medium* heat until the internal temperature reaches 160°F for medium, 8 to 10 minutes, turning once halfway through grilling time. Top each burger with a slice of the cheese during the last minute or two of grilling time and allow the cheese to melt. During the last 30 seconds, grill the buns over *Direct Medium* heat until lightly toasted.

Serve the cheeseburgers hot on the toasted buns with a lettuce leaf and a slice of tomato, topped with a slice of the bacon. Serve with ketchup and mustard on the side, if desired.

MAKES 6 SERVINGS

Classic Bacon Cheeseburger

BURGERS ON THE GRILL

The basic beef burger is so beloved, we worry that it has become a victim of its own popularity. It's served up by the millions at virtually every drive-thru, restaurant, and backyard gathering, often with little regard to its composition, condition, and overall appeal. We think it deserves better, so why not vow to reestablish some standards for this national favorite?

FIRST THINGS FIRST. We submit that a burger must meet three criteria to be considered worthy of eating: It must taste of the flame. It must be juicy. And it must be served hot.

HOW TO GET THAT FLAME-BROILED FLAVOR: Are you still using lighter fluid? Say it ain't so. Lighter fluid can impart a chemical taste to foods. If you have a gas grill, you're fine. If you're grilling over charcoal, trust us, breaking the lighter fluid habit will carry you farther down the road to burger greatness than anything else. Try odorless, tasteless, nontoxic fuel cubes to start the fire. They're made out of paraffin so they are safe and won't leave an unpleasant taste on your food. Or try a charcoal chimney. With this cylindrical device you simply put fuel cubes or a few sheets of wadded-up newspaper on the bottom and the coals on top. You'll be grilling as soon as the coals ash over. Almost as easy as a gas grill.

Next, make sure the grate is very hot before you place any burgers on it. Gas grillers, preheat with all burners on High until the grill reaches 500°F, place the burgers on the grate, then reduce the heat to Direct Medium. Charcoal grillers, start with enough briquets for Direct Medium heat. Wait until the coals are lightly ashed over, then spread them evenly across the charcoal grate (leaving a small section without coals in case of flare-ups), place the cooking grate on the grill, close the lid, and wait 5 minutes more to heat the cooking grate. The burgers should sizzle when they hit the grate. After that, it's a matter of letting the grill do the work. Some folks worry about flare-ups, but in a well-designed grill they'll be short-lived at best. If they don't quickly subside, move the burgers over Indirect Medium heat for a moment, then continue grilling over Direct Medium heat.

HOW TO MAKE IT JUICY: This is so easy you won't believe it. Start with 80% lean ground chuck. Yes, that means you're going to use beef that is 20% fat. If the numbers make you uncomfortable, hear us out first. The fact that you're grilling over an open cooking grate and not frying the burgers in a pan means they won't be stewing in their fat—which is as healthy as it sounds. Instead, a great deal of the fat will drip out onto the flames, leaving flavor in its wake and adding even more smoky flavor as it sizzles away on the fire. The intense heat of the grill is going to release all those beefy juices, too, in a way that a pan or griddle just can't. See, already we're making progress.

Another key to juicy burgers is to not overwork the meat as you blend in seasonings and shape it into patties. Rinse your hands in very cold water before you begin and work quickly to gently shape the beef into 3/4-inch-thick patties. Place them on a plate or baking sheet and refrigerate them for at least 15 minutes before placing them on a hot grill. Once they're on the cooking grate, close the lid of the grill. Then, please don't play with your food. Turn the burgers only once, halfway through grilling time. If you flip and flop them, you might as well wring out all the juice. For safety, always grill burgers until the internal temperature reaches 160°F for medium doneness. This will take 8 to 10 minutes, depending on weather and other variables. And never press down on a burger with your spatula. It just squeezes out all that juicy flavor you're striving for.

HOW TO SERVE IT HOT: Don't fall for the trap of sliding your works of art onto a platter and letting everyone fend for themselves. Why let an errant breeze mar the perfection? Rather than leave burger-bliss to chance, serve directly from the grill to the hamburger bun. This may require you to holler like a drill sergeant to get everyone to fall in at the chow line at 18:08 hours, but hey, an Expert must have Standards.

THE REST IS JUST GRAVY. Once you've mastered the patty, anything you add to it (grape jelly aside) can only enhance its regal stature. So layer on the toppings and create the perfect burger just the way you like it. After all, isn't that what makes us American?

WHAT YOUR BURGER TOPPINGS
SAY ABOUT YOU

The burger's simplicity is one of its greatest charms. With no carving or pageantry to slow you down, you can get it from the grill to your mouth while it's still sizzling hot. This approachable profile makes wolfing one down practically a sport. But let's not under-estimate the self-expression factor: How you top it is a show of your good taste.

We have a friend named Paul "Q-Man" Watson who believes you can tell a lot about people by what they put on their burger. His assessment:

Ketchup only: *"My life is complicated enough. Let's just keep this simple and sweet."*

Mustard only: *"Beneath this serious exterior is a wild party animal just waiting to pounce."*

Cheese, lettuce, tomato, mustard, ketchup, pickles: *"I'm an incurable romantic. Where's the beer?"*

Bacon and cheese: *"Life's too short to count cholesterol."*

Grilled mushrooms and onions: *"I've never met a condiment I didn't like."*

Bacon and guacamole: *"Layer it on, but promise not to tell my (wife/boyfriend/doctor) about this."*

Pesto or mushroom stuffing inside: *"I'm in touch with my creative side."*

Mayonnaise and pickle relish: *"You be Ozzie, I'll be Harriet."*

*"I like mine
with lettuce and tomato,
Heinz 57 and French fried potatoes,
Big kosher pickle and a cold draft beer,
Well, good God Almighty,
which way do I steer...?!"*

— JIMMY BUFFET,
Cheeseburger in Paradise

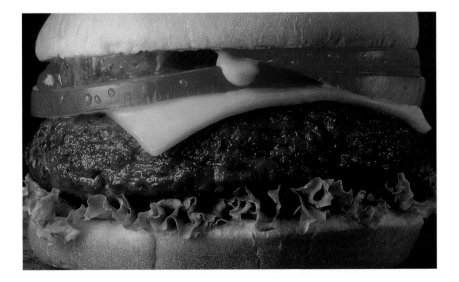

GUACAMOLE CHEESEBURGERS

A fun derivative of the basic cheeseburger. We used jalapeños here, but don't hesitate to try a hotter pepper if you're up to the challenge.

DIRECT/MEDIUM

FOR THE GUACAMOLE:

- 1 LARGE RIPE AVOCADO, PITTED AND SKIN REMOVED
- 1 CUP FINELY CHOPPED RIPE TOMATO
- 2 GREEN ONIONS (WHITE PART ONLY), MINCED
- 1 TABLESPOON FINELY CHOPPED FRESH CILANTRO
- 1 TABLESPOON FRESH LIME JUICE
- 1 TEASPOON MINCED JALAPEÑO PEPPER, WITH SEEDS
  KOSHER SALT
  FRESHLY GROUND BLACK PEPPER

FOR THE BURGERS:

- 2 POUNDS GROUND CHUCK (80% LEAN)
- 2 TABLESPOONS EXTRA-VIRGIN OLIVE OIL
- 3 GREEN ONIONS (WHITE PART ONLY), MINCED
- 2 TEASPOONS GROUND CUMIN
- 2 TEASPOONS CHILE POWDER
- 2 TEASPOONS DRIED OREGANO
- 2 TEASPOONS MINCED JALAPEÑO PEPPER, WITH SEEDS
- 2 TEASPOONS MINCED GARLIC
- 1 TEASPOON KOSHER SALT
- 1/2 TEASPOON FRESHLY GROUND BLACK PEPPER

- 6 THIN SLICES MONTEREY JACK CHEESE

- 6 HAMBURGER BUNS

To make the guacamole: In a medium bowl mash the avocado with the back of a fork, leaving a few lumps. Add the remaining guacamole ingredients, including salt and pepper to taste, and mix well.

To make the burgers: In a large bowl gently mix together the burger ingredients with your hands. Shape the meat into six patties of equal size and thickness (about 3/4 inch thick).

Grill over *Direct Medium* heat until the internal temperature reaches 160°F for medium, 8 to 10 minutes, turning once halfway through grilling time. Top each burger with a slice of the cheese during the last minute or two of grilling time and allow the cheese to melt. During the last 30 seconds, grill the buns over *Direct Medium* heat until lightly toasted.

Serve the cheeseburgers hot on the toasted buns, topped with the guacamole.

MAKES 6 SERVINGS

BLACK THAI BURGERS
WITH GINGERED SHIITAKES

You owe it to yourself to try this one. Exotically seasoned burgers mounded with shiitake mushrooms sautéed in ginger butter—yowza!

DIRECT/MEDIUM

FOR THE BURGERS:

- 1 1/2 POUNDS GROUND CHUCK (80% LEAN)
- 2 TABLESPOONS FINELY CHOPPED FRESH CILANTRO
- 2 TABLESPOONS FINELY CHOPPED FRESH MINT
- 1 TABLESPOON FRESH LIME JUICE
- 2 TEASPOONS FISH SAUCE
- 2 TEASPOONS MINCED JALAPEÑO PEPPER, WITH SEEDS
- 2 TEASPOONS MINCED GARLIC
- 1 TEASPOON GRATED LIME ZEST
- 1 TEASPOON GRATED FRESH GINGER
- 1/2 TEASPOON FRESHLY GROUND BLACK PEPPER

FOR THE MUSHROOMS:

- 3 TABLESPOONS UNSALTED BUTTER
- 2 TABLESPOONS PEANUT OIL
- 2 TEASPOONS GRATED FRESH GINGER
- 8 OUNCES FRESH SHIITAKE MUSHROOMS, STEMS REMOVED AND CUT INTO 1/4-INCH SLICES
- 1/4 TEASPOON KOSHER SALT
- 1/4 TEASPOON FRESHLY GROUND BLACK PEPPER

  PEANUT OIL
- 4 HAMBURGER BUNS

To prepare the burgers: In a large bowl gently mix together the burger ingredients with your hands. Shape the meat into four patties of equal size and thickness (about 3/4 inch thick).

To prepare the mushrooms: In a medium sauté pan over medium-high heat, melt the butter with the peanut oil and add the ginger. Add the mushrooms and cook, stirring occasionally, until tender, 4 to 6 minutes. Season with the salt and pepper. Set aside and keep warm.

Brush both sides of the patties with the oil and grill over *Direct Medium* heat until the internal temperature reaches 160°F for medium, 8 to 10 minutes, turning once halfway through grilling time. During the last 30 seconds, grill the buns over *Direct Medium* heat until lightly toasted.

Serve the burgers hot on the toasted buns, topped with the mushrooms.

MAKES 4 SERVINGS

Black Thai Burgers with Gingered Shiitakes

BLUE-CHEESE BURGERS
WITH SPICY CELERY SLAW

The surprise in these beef burgers is a knob of tangy blue-veined cheese just slightly melted from the grill. A little cheese goes a long way to flavor the burger so you only need a piece about the size of a regular marble. Delicious!

DIRECT/MEDIUM

FOR THE BURGERS:

1 1/2 POUNDS GROUND CHUCK (80% LEAN)

  2 TEASPOONS GORGONZOLA, ROQUEFORT, *OR* OTHER BLUE-VEINED CHEESE

    FRESHLY GROUND BLACK PEPPER

FOR THE SLAW:

  2 TABLESPOONS EXTRA-VIRGIN OLIVE OIL

  1 TABLESPOON CIDER VINEGAR

  1 TEASPOON MINCED JALAPEÑO PEPPER, WITH SEEDS

  1 TEASPOON GRANULATED SUGAR

1/2 TEASPOON KOSHER SALT

1/4 TEASPOON FRESHLY GROUND BLACK PEPPER

  2 CUPS VERY THINLY SLICED CELERY

  1 CUP VERY THINLY SLICED RED ONION

  4 HAMBURGER BUNS

To prepare the burgers: Shape the meat into four equal-sized balls. Divide the cheese into four equal-sized pieces. With your forefinger, make a dimple into the center of each ball of meat and insert a piece of cheese. Close the meat over the cheese. Gently press the meat into patties of equal size and thickness (about 3/4 inch thick). Season both sides of the patties with pepper. Place the patties on a platter, cover with plastic wrap, and refrigerate until ready to grill.

To make the slaw: In a medium bowl whisk together the olive oil, vinegar, jalapeño, sugar, salt, and pepper. Add the celery and onion; toss to coat. Cover with plastic wrap and refrigerate until ready to serve.

Grill the patties over *Direct Medium* heat until the internal temperature reaches 160°F for medium, 8 to 10 minutes, turning once halfway through grilling time. During the last 30 seconds, grill the buns over *Direct Medium* heat until lightly toasted.

Serve the burgers hot on the toasted buns. Pile the slaw on top of the burgers or serve on the side.

MAKES 4 SERVINGS

BACON-MUSHROOM
BEEF ROLLS

These sausage-shaped beef rolls look like a distant cousin to "kefta," a central European patty of chopped, spiced meat. The bacon and mushrooms make these distinctly more American. Roll them into a large lettuce leaf with the sauce and eat them with your hands.

DIRECT/HIGH

FOR THE BEEF ROLLS:

  4 SLICES BACON, CUT INTO 1/2-INCH SQUARES

1/3 CUP FINELY CHOPPED YELLOW ONION

1/4 POUND BUTTON MUSHROOMS, FINELY CHOPPED

  1 TEASPOON MINCED GARLIC

1 1/2 POUNDS GROUND CHUCK (80% LEAN)

1/4 CUP FINELY CHOPPED FRESH ITALIAN PARSLEY

  1 TEASPOON KOSHER SALT

  1 TEASPOON WORCESTERSHIRE SAUCE

1/2 TEASPOON FRESHLY GROUND BLACK PEPPER

1/2 TEASPOON CUMIN

1/2 TEASPOON DRY MUSTARD

FOR THE TOMATO SAUCE:

  1 TABLESPOON EXTRA-VIRGIN OLIVE OIL

1/2 CUP FINELY CHOPPED YELLOW ONIONS

  1 TEASPOON MINCED GARLIC

1/2 CUP DRY RED WINE

  2 TABLESPOONS RED WINE VINEGAR

  1 CAN (8 OUNCES) TOMATO SAUCE

  2 TABLESPOONS TOMATO PASTE

  1 TEASPOON PAPRIKA

  1 TEASPOON LIGHT BROWN SUGAR

    TABASCO SAUCE

    EXTRA-VIRGIN OLIVE OIL

  8 LARGE LETTUCE LEAVES

To prepare the beef rolls: In a medium sauté pan over medium-low heat, cook the bacon, stirring occasionally, until the fat is rendered and the pieces are cooked but not crisp, 6 to 8 minutes. Remove the bacon and set aside on paper towels to drain. Add the onion to the pan and cook over medium-low heat, stirring occasionally, until soft, 6 to 8 minutes. Increase heat to medium, add the mushrooms and cook for 5 to 6 minutes, stirring occasionally. Add the garlic and cook for 1 minute more, stirring occasionally. Remove from the heat and allow the mixture to cool for about 10 minutes.

Place the mixture in a large bowl, add the bacon and the remaining beef roll ingredients, and gently mix with your fingers. Divide into eight equal-sized portions, about 3 1/2 ounces each. Form into small sausage-shaped rolls 3 1/2 to 4 inches long. Place the rolls on a platter, cover with plastic wrap, and refrigerate for 1 to 2 hours.

To make the tomato sauce: In a small, heavy-bottom saucepan over medium-high heat, warm the olive oil and cook the onions, stirring occasionally, until soft and translucent but not brown, 4 to 5 minutes. Add the garlic and cook for 1 minute more, stirring occasionally. Add the wine and vinegar, bring to a boil, and cook over high heat for another 2 minutes. Add the tomato sauce, tomato paste, paprika, and sugar. Reduce heat to low and simmer, stirring frequently, until the mixture thickens to a ketchup consistency, 12 to 15 minutes. Add the Tabasco sauce to taste. Spoon the tomato sauce into a serving bowl and set aside.

Lightly brush the beef rolls with the olive oil and grill over *Direct High* heat until the internal temperature reaches 160°F for medium, 6 to 8 minutes, turning a quarter-turn about every 2 minutes.

Place each hot, grilled beef roll on a lettuce leaf, top with tomato sauce, and wrap it up. Serve immediately.

MAKES 4 SERVINGS

about 5 minutes. Add the garlic and cook for 1 minute more, stirring occasionally. Add the curry and ginger and cook for another minute, stirring occasionally. Remove from the heat and allow to cool to room temperature. Add the cooled sautéed onion mixture and the rest of the steak ingredients to the soaked bread crumbs. Gently mix until the ingredients are well blended.

With wet hands, shape the meat into four patties of equal size and thickness (about 4 inches in diameter and 1 inch thick). Place the steaks on a platter, cover with plastic wrap, and refrigerate for at least 30 minutes before grilling.

Lightly brush or spray both sides of the steaks with olive oil and grill over *Direct Medium* heat until the internal temperature reaches 160°F for medium, 8 to 10 minutes, turning once halfway through grilling time. After turning, glaze the top of each steak with 1 tablespoon of the ketchup and allow it to cook into the meat. Serve hot.

MAKES 4 SERVINGS

CHOPPED "STEAKS"
WITH KETCHUP GLAZE

If you like meat loaf, you'll feel right at home with these. They're a fun spin on Mom's Wednesday Night Special.

DIRECT/MEDIUM

FOR THE STEAKS:

1/2 CUP WHOLE MILK

1/4 CUP FINE DRY BREAD CRUMBS

1 TABLESPOON EXTRA-VIRGIN OLIVE OIL

1/2 CUP FINELY CHOPPED YELLOW ONION

1 TEASPOON MINCED GARLIC

1 TEASPOON CURRY POWDER

1/4 TEASPOON GROUND GINGER

1 1/4 POUNDS GROUND CHUCK (80% LEAN)

1 CUP COARSELY SHREDDED CARROTS

1 LARGE EGG, LIGHTLY BEATEN

1 TEASPOON DIJON MUSTARD

1/2 TEASPOON KOSHER SALT

1/2 TEASPOON FRESHLY GROUND BLACK PEPPER

EXTRA-VIRGIN OLIVE OIL

4 TABLESPOONS KETCHUP

To prepare the steaks: In a large bowl combine the milk and bread crumbs; allow to stand for 10 minutes. In a medium sauté pan over medium heat, warm the olive oil; add the onion and cook, stirring occasionally, until soft and golden,

"What is patriotism but the love of the good things we ate in our childhood?"

— LIN YUTANG

We've come a long way from the humble chuck wagon of the prairie to the glitzy steak houses of Chicago, New York, and other metro meccas. But aside from the atmosphere and the prices, not much has changed. Beef still tastes good over an open fire and everyone still has a personal definition of what makes it excellent. Some universal rules apply, too. Here are the ones to follow to manifest your beefy destiny:

GET GOOD GRADES. The United States Department of Agriculture (USDA) inspects and grades US beef. The inspection is to ensure food safety standards are upheld, but the grading is voluntary—producers don't have to participate. These grades, however, are the best indication of what you can expect in terms of tenderness, juiciness, and flavor. Grades are based on the animal's age (younger is better) as well as the amount and distribution of marbling, the tiny flecks of fat throughout the muscle tissue (more is better). There are eight grades for beef, but you'll probably only encounter three or four of them:

- **Prime** beef is the best—only 2% of US cattle earn this title for their "slightly abundant" marbling. You can see the fine, evenly distributed flecks throughout the meat. Most prime grade beef goes to upscale restaurants and hotels, but why should they have all the fun? Inquire at your local butcher shop or make friends with a rancher and see how the other half lives.
- **Certified Angus Beef™**, while not a USDA grade, is a trademarked designation reserved for only 7 out of 100 cattle, which must meet strict standards for texture, firmness, and marbling. Fans attest to its intense flavor and richness. Try it for yourself if you haven't already done so.
- **Choice** is the second best USDA grade and the most widely available. Choice beef has moderate or small amounts of marbling and the cattle are fairly young. Some say the difference between Prime and Choice is less significant than the difference between Choice and Select. For grilling, buy Choice when possible.
- **Select** beef is the leanest, least expensive grade and the flavor within this grade can vary widely. It has only "slight" amounts of marbling and tenderness. Not the best grade for grilling. Don't hesitate to marinate it first to boost its texture and flavor.

TRY AGED BEEF. There is another beef distinction that makes a big difference in tenderness and flavor, and that is aging. During aging, enzymes in the muscle fibers break down and bingo, you've got yourself a tender morsel. Dry-aged beef is exposed to air for 3 to 6 weeks and kept very cold. During this tenderizing process, the beef can lose up to 10% of its weight through moisture loss—which results in a more concentrated beef flavor. Aficionados swoon for this stuff. If you can find dry-aged beef, pounce on it! Wet-aged beef is sealed in Cryovac® bags for the tenderizing process, so there's no moisture loss. In the end, you have more meat with a "fresher" taste. Try each aging process if you're lucky enough to find samples and you may just have a new, pricey addiction.

CHOOSE YOUR STORE. Today we have many options for purchasing beef. You probably have a grocery store you trust for everyday purchases. For prime grade, special cuts, or special attention, visit a good butcher shop. There's no match for the expertise you can tap over the counter. And if you haven't already, check out the warehouse clubs in your town. You might be surprised at the quality of the meat, and because these stores deal in volume, they often have great deals on Choice cuts.

DON'T FORGET THE ROASTS. If your culinary daring ends at steaks and burgers, we've got good news. Many beef roasts are wonderful on the grill, especially those from the loin, short loin, and rib sections. Grilled roasts not only add a nice dimension to your repertoire, they can feed a crowd (or make someone very happy in the leftover department). Not every roast is made for high-heat cooking like grilling, however. Cuts from the foreshank and round sections fare best in moist heat, i.e., braised or in stews. The chuck has some cuts suited for the grill—we handpicked a couple and included recipes for them in this chapter—and ground up, it does make the best burgers. Take a look at the beef chart in our Grilling Guide (*see page 398*) to find all these cuts.

KNOW WHEN TO QUIT. Doneness is the cornerstone of your beef enjoyment and thus a matter of personal taste. In our recipes we offer the approximate cooking times to reach the USDA's definition of medium rare, with the exception of ground beef, which should always be cooked to 160°F, or medium doneness, to avoid risk of any food-borne illnesses. We use the USDA's definition of medium rare for beef, i.e., an internal temperature of 145°F—some beef eaters will find this a bit high. We think you can enjoy beef that's plenty juicy at a safe 145°F, but if you like your meat rare, enjoy at your own risk (except of course for burgers—sorry, but some aspects of modern living are tough on us all). In order to reach 145°F as your finished temperature, the recipes for large cuts prompt you to remove the beef from the grill when it reaches 135°F; thick steak recipes have you remove them at 140°F. Stopping short allows for carry-over cooking, which means the temperature continues to rise up to 10°F as the meat rests (the larger the cut, the higher it will rise). Thinner steaks can be removed at 145°F.

GO AGAINST THE GRAIN. Beef muscle is made of longer, often tougher fibers than most other four-legged creatures. Cutting across these fibers when you slice the meat will produce more tender bites. This is especially important with tougher cuts such as flank and skirt steak, London broil, and bottom sirloin.

AND A WORD ON SEARING. Many folks think searing locks in juices. But the fact is (and it's been proven in lab tests, so who are we to go against the pros?) searing merely caramelizes the surface of your food, adding nice texture, color, and flavor. Don't get us wrong; this is no trivial matter. Caramelization is a critical quality of masterfully grilled beef, but you can overdo it. Keep in mind that as long as you are searing the beef, or even cooking it at all, you are tightening the proteins and squeezing out juices. If you want juicy meat beyond that beautifully seared surface, just don't overcook it!

AND THE
GOOD NEWS IS...

Beef today has been through some trying times. It used to be you could saunter up to the meat counter, order a nice beef cut with a generous amount of fat in it, and walk away without blinking.

Then America became health-conscious. Suddenly red meat was a borderline if not definite no-no. Beef fat became something to be shunned, a guilty pleasure to be enjoyed in moderation only.

Okay, a little lesson in healthful eating is fair enough. Who has anything against moderation? Ranchers responded to consumer demand in good faith by breeding leaner cattle, but often at the expense of flavor and tenderness. Fortunately, today ranchers are as eager to find a better solution and are striving to develop tastier lean breeds. They also want to elevate grading standards. And now you can find "natural" and organic beef at many meat counters. These products cost more, but their producers insist their quality and flavor is unmatched. Check them out and see for yourself.

In the meantime, you can start out on the right hoof by buying the best Choice cut you can find—look for the one that stands out for its marbling. Season it with a marinade or rub, if desired. Allow the meat to stand at room temperature before you throw it on the grill and don't salt it too soon (see page 133). Then use the grill's heat to sear the outside. Allow it to rest after grilling. Add a sauce if the recipe or your taste dictates. Eat it hot. And don't look back!

FLATIRON STEAKS
WITH STEAKHOUSE SAUCE

A flatiron is a top blade chuck steak, quite tender and delicious. Shaped like an old-fashioned iron, this cut is usually sliced thin for optimum flavor and texture. Cook these steaks quickly over High heat, slice them up, and add the sauce.

DIRECT/HIGH

FOR THE SAUCE:

- 1/2 CUP KETCHUP
- 1 TABLESPOON LIGHT BROWN SUGAR
- 2 TEASPOONS WORCESTERSHIRE SAUCE
- 2 TEASPOONS RED WINE VINEGAR
- 1/2 TEASPOON GRANULATED ONION
- 1/2 TEASPOON GRANULATED GARLIC
- 1/2 TEASPOON DRY MUSTARD
- 1/4 TEASPOON TABASCO SAUCE

- 2 FLATIRON STEAKS, ABOUT 1 POUND EACH AND 1/2 INCH THICK
  EXTRA-VIRGIN OLIVE OIL
- 1 TEASPOON KOSHER SALT
- 1/2 TEASPOON FRESHLY GROUND BLACK PEPPER

To make the sauce: In a small saucepan whisk together the sauce ingredients with 1/4 cup water. Bring to a boil over high heat, then lower the heat to a simmer. Cook for about 10 minutes, stirring occasionally. Set aside.

Brush or spray both sides of the steaks with olive oil. Season with the salt and pepper. Grill over *Direct High* heat for 3 to 5 minutes, turning once halfway through grilling time. Remove from the grill and allow to rest for 2 to 3 minutes. Cut across the grain into 1/4-inch slices and serve warm with the sauce.

MAKES 4 SERVINGS

NEW YORK STRIPS
WITH ROASTED GARLIC BUTTER

Sweet garlic butter sliding across a sizzling slab of peppered steak? Decadent. Outrageous. And 100% legal. Note: You will be moving from Indirect Medium to Direct High in this recipe.

INDIRECT/MEDIUM

FOR THE GARLIC BUTTER:

- 1 LARGE HEAD GARLIC
- 1 TEASPOON EXTRA-VIRGIN OLIVE OIL
- 2 TABLESPOONS UNSALTED BUTTER, SOFTENED
- 1 TEASPOON DIJON MUSTARD
- 1 TEASPOON WORCESTERSHIRE SAUCE
- 1/2 TEASPOON KOSHER SALT

- 4 NEW YORK STRIP STEAKS, ABOUT 3/4 POUND EACH AND 1 INCH THICK
- 1 1/2 TEASPOONS KOSHER SALT
- 1 TABLESPOON WHOLE BLACK PEPPERCORNS, COARSELY GROUND
  EXTRA-VIRGIN OLIVE OIL

To make the garlic butter: Remove the loose, papery outer skin from the garlic head and cut about 1/2 inch off the top to expose the cloves. Place the garlic head on an 8-inch square of aluminum foil and drizzle the olive oil over the top of the cloves. Fold up the foil sides and seal to make a packet, leaving a little room for the expansion of steam. Grill over *Indirect Medium* heat until the cloves are soft, 30 to 45 minutes. Remove from the grill and allow to cool. Squeeze the contents of the cloves into a small bowl. Using the back of a fork, mash the garlic together with the rest of the garlic butter ingredients. Refrigerate until ready to serve.

Allow the steaks to stand at room temperature for 20 to 30 minutes before grilling. Season both sides of the steaks with the salt and pepper, pressing the spices into the meat. Lightly spray or brush both sides of the steaks with the oil. Grill over *Direct High* heat until the internal temperature reaches 145°F for medium rare, 8 to 10 minutes, turning once halfway through grilling time. Remove the steaks from the grill and allow to rest for 2 to 3 minutes. Cut the garlic butter into four equal-sized pieces. Serve the steaks warm with the butter on top.

MAKES 4 SERVINGS

New York Strips with Roasted Garlic Butter

THE OVER-ACHIEVER OF THE STEAK FAMILY, THE PORTERHOUSE IS TWO STEAKS IN ONE: ONE SIDE OF THE T-SHAPED BONE IS THE TENDERLOIN AND THE OTHER IS THE STRIP STEAK. SO, WHEN YOU CAN'T DECIDE BETWEEN A STRIP STEAK OR A FILET, GO FOR THE PORTERHOUSE.

Dry-Rubbed Porterhouse with Barbecue Steak Sauce

DRY-RUBBED PORTERHOUSE
WITH BARBECUE STEAK SAUCE

Nothing hits the grill with force like a hefty porterhouse. Just to up the ante, we added a zesty rub and a homemade sauce that's to die for. And you thought you knew steak!

SEAR: HIGH, COOK: INDIRECT/MEDIUM

FOR THE RUB:

- 2 TEASPOONS BLACK PEPPERCORNS
- 2 TEASPOONS MUSTARD SEEDS
- 2 TEASPOONS PAPRIKA
- 1 TEASPOON GRANULATED GARLIC
- 1 TEASPOON KOSHER SALT
- 1 TEASPOON LIGHT BROWN SUGAR
- 1/4 TEASPOON CAYENNE

- 2 PORTERHOUSE STEAKS, ABOUT 2 1/2 POUNDS EACH AND 1 1/2 INCHES THICK
  EXTRA-VIRGIN OLIVE OIL

FOR THE SAUCE:

- 1/2 CUP KETCHUP
- 2 TABLESPOONS STEAK SAUCE
- 2 TABLESPOONS MOLASSES
- 2 TEASPOONS WORCESTERSHIRE SAUCE
- 2 TEASPOONS DIJON MUSTARD
- 1 TEASPOON GRANULATED GARLIC
- 1/2 TEASPOON FRESHLY GROUND BLACK PEPPER

To make the rub: Using a spice grinder or mortar and pestle, crush the black peppercorns and mustard seeds. In a small bowl mix thoroughly with the remaining rub ingredients.

Trim the steaks of any excess fat. Press the rub into both sides of the steaks and lightly brush or spray with the olive oil. Allow to stand at room temperature for 20 to 30 minutes before grilling.

To make the sauce: In a small saucepan whisk together the sauce ingredients with 1/2 cup water. Simmer over low heat for about 5 minutes. Set aside.

Sear the steaks over *Direct High* heat for 10 minutes, turning once halfway through searing time. Continue grilling over *Indirect Medium* heat until the internal temperature reaches 135°F for medium rare, 3 to 5 minutes, turning once halfway through grilling time.

Remove the steaks from the grill and allow to rest for 5 to 10 minutes. Cut the steaks across the grain into 1/4-inch slices and serve warm with the sauce.

MAKES 4 SERVINGS

SIZZLING T-BONES
WITH MUSTARD BUTTER

The kind of steak that makes beef lovers growl.

DIRECT/HIGH

FOR THE MUSTARD BUTTER:

- 6 TABLESPOONS UNSALTED BUTTER, CUT INTO 6 PIECES, SOFTENED
- 2 TABLESPOONS DIJON MUSTARD
- 1/4 TEASPOON FRESHLY GROUND BLACK PEPPER

FOR THE PASTE:

- 1/4 CUP WORCESTERSHIRE SAUCE
- 1/4 CUP EXTRA-VIRGIN OLIVE OIL
- 4 TEASPOONS MINCED GARLIC
- 4 TEASPOONS PAPRIKA
- 2 TEASPOONS LIGHT BROWN SUGAR
- 2 TEASPOONS KOSHER SALT
- 2 TEASPOONS FRESHLY GROUND BLACK PEPPER

- 4 T-BONE STEAKS, ABOUT 1 POUND EACH AND 1 INCH THICK

To make the mustard butter: In a small bowl combine the mustard butter ingredients. Using the back of a fork, mash the ingredients together, distributing them evenly. Scoop the mixture out of the bowl and transfer to a sheet of plastic wrap. Loosely shape the mixture into a log about 1 inch in diameter. Roll the log in the wrap and twist the ends in opposite directions to form an even cylinder. Refrigerate until ready to serve (this can be made days ahead).

To make the paste: In a small bowl mix the paste ingredients.

Trim the steaks of any excess fat. Spread the paste on both sides of the steaks, cover with plastic wrap and refrigerate for 4 to 8 hours.

Allow the steaks to stand at room temperature for 20 to 30 minutes before grilling. Grill over *Direct High* heat until the internal temperature reaches 145°F for medium rare, 8 to 12 minutes, turning once halfway through grilling time. Remove the steaks from the grill and allow to rest for 3 to 5 minutes. Unwrap the cylinder of butter and slice crosswise into 1/3-inch coins. Serve the steaks warm with a slice of butter on top.

MAKES 4 SERVINGS

BISTECCA
ALLA FIORENTINA

If you can get dry-aged porterhouse steaks for this Tuscan recipe, go for it. But even if you have to settle for whatever your market's offering (including T-bones), be sure to use the best cold-pressed extra-virgin olive oil available and only kosher salt, please. Finish with a squeeze of lemon juice and you'll have traveled to Florence in less than half an hour.

DIRECT/HIGH

- **2 PORTERHOUSE *OR* T-BONE STEAKS, ABOUT 1 1/3 POUNDS EACH AND 1 INCH THICK**
- **1/4 CUP EXTRA-VIRGIN OLIVE OIL, DIVIDED**
- **1 1/2 TEASPOONS KOSHER SALT**
- **1 1/2 TEASPOONS FRESHLY GROUND BLACK PEPPER**

- **2 LEMON WEDGES**

Trim the steaks of any excess fat. Allow to stand at room temperature for 20 to 30 minutes before grilling.

Brush or spray both sides of the steaks with 2 tablespoons of the olive oil. Season with the salt and pepper. Grill the steaks over *Direct High* heat until the internal temperature reaches 145°F for medium rare, 8 to 10 minutes, turning once halfway through grilling time. Remove from the grill, squeeze the lemon wedges over the top, and drizzle with the remaining olive oil. Allow to rest for about 5 minutes before slicing and serving.

MAKES 4 SERVINGS

*I complained
that I had no steak
until I met a man
who had no grill....*

FILETS AND CRAB
WITH BÉARNAISE SAUCE

Even if you've never made béarnaise sauce before, our recipe will walk you through it with grace. The trick is to thicken the egg yolks in the reduced vinegar mixture over very low heat so that they don't scramble and add the butter slowly—in a thin stream—so it has a chance to emulsify with the yolks.

SEAR: HIGH, COOK: INDIRECT/MEDIUM

- **1/2 POUND ASPARAGUS, TOUGH ENDS REMOVED**
- **2 TEASPOONS EXTRA-VIRGIN OLIVE OIL**
- **1/8 TEASPOON KOSHER SALT**
- **1/8 TEASPOON FRESHLY GROUND BLACK PEPPER**

- **1 TEASPOON KOSHER SALT**
- **1 TEASPOON FRESHLY GROUND PINK PEPPERCORNS**
- **1 TEASPOON FRESHLY GROUND BLACK PEPPER**
  EXTRA-VIRGIN OLIVE OIL
- **4 FILETS MIGNONS, ABOUT 6 OUNCES EACH AND 2 INCHES THICK**

FOR THE SAUCE:
- **1/3 CUP WHITE WINE VINEGAR**
- **1 TABLESPOON FINELY CHOPPED SHALLOTS**
- **1 TABLESPOON FINELY CHOPPED FRESH TARRAGON**
- **1/4 TEASPOON KOSHER SALT**
- **1/8 TEASPOON FRESHLY GROUND BLACK PEPPER**
- **2 EGG YOLKS**
- **1 STICK UNSALTED BUTTER, MELTED**

- **2 KING CRAB LEGS, PRECOOKED (THAWED, IF FROZEN)**

Put the asparagus on a plate or platter. Drizzle the olive oil over the asparagus and season with the salt and pepper.

In a small bowl mix together the salt with the pink peppercorns and black pepper. Lightly brush or spray both sides of the filets with the olive oil. Season with the salt and pepper mixture. Allow the filets to stand at room temperature for 20 to 30 minutes before grilling.

Meanwhile, make the sauce: In a small saucepan combine the vinegar, shallots, tarragon, salt, and pepper along with 1 tablespoon water. Bring to a simmer over medium heat and continue cooking until the mixture is reduced to 3 tablespoons. Remove from the heat and allow to cool for a few minutes.

In a small bowl whisk together the egg yolks. Whisk 1 tablespoon of the vinegar mixture into the eggs. Pour the egg mixture into the saucepan with the vinegar mixture and whisk until smooth. Place the pan over low heat and whisk the mixture constantly until it thickens to the consistency of mustard. Then, immediately start drizzling the melted butter in a thin stream into the pan, whisking constantly, until the mixture reaches the consistency of thin mayonnaise. If at any time the sauce looks like it is separating, remove the pan from the heat and continue whisking to cool it down. Set the sauce aside at room temperature.

Sear the filets over *Direct High* heat for 10 minutes, turning once halfway through grilling time. Continue grilling over *Indirect Medium* heat until the internal temperature reaches 135°F for medium rare, 5 to 8 minutes. Grill the asparagus, and crab legs over *Direct Medium* heat, for 6 to 8 minutes, turning once halfway through grilling time.

Remove the filets from the grill and allow to rest for 2 to 3 minutes. Remove the asparagus and the crab legs from the grill. Cut the asparagus into 2-inch lengths and keep warm. Crack open the crab legs with a mallet or cut them open with kitchen shears and remove the meat.

To serve, place one filet on each plate and top with some of the asparagus and crab meat. Drizzle béarnaise sauce over each plate.

MAKES 4 SERVINGS

FILET MIGNON
WITH CREMINI-WINE SAUCE

Talk about sexy. We season velvety filets with fancy herbs, sear them, then drizzle on a heady mushroom-wine sauce. Swoon!

DIRECT/HIGH

FOR THE RUB:

1 TABLESPOON HERBS DE PROVENCE

1 TEASPOON KOSHER SALT

1 TEASPOON FRESHLY GROUND BLACK PEPPER

4 FILETS MIGNONS, ABOUT 1/2 POUND EACH AND 1 1/4 INCHES THICK

FOR THE SAUCE:

1/2 POUND CREMINI MUSHROOMS

3 TABLESPOONS COLD UNSALTED BUTTER, DIVIDED

1 SMALL LEEK (WHITE PART ONLY), TRIMMED, WASHED, AND FINELY CHOPPED

1/2 MEDIUM CARROT, THINLY SLICED CROSSWISE

1 MEDIUM GARLIC CLOVE, CRUSHED

1/2 CUP DRY RED WINE

1 CAN (14 1/2 OUNCES) REDUCED-SODIUM *OR* HOMEMADE BEEF BROTH

1 TABLESPOON FINELY CHOPPED FRESH ITALIAN PARSLEY

EXTRA-VIRGIN OLIVE OIL

To make the rub: In a small bowl combine the rub ingredients. Reserve 1/2 teaspoon of the rub for the sauce. Sprinkle the remaining rub on both sides of the filets, pressing it into the meat. Place the filets on a platter, cover with plastic wrap, and refrigerate until ready to grill.

To make the sauce: Remove and finely chop the mushroom stems. Set the caps aside. In a medium saucepan over medium heat, melt 1 tablespoon of the butter. Add the chopped mushroom stems, leek, carrot, garlic, and reserved 1/2 teaspoon of the rub. Cook, stirring occasionally, until the vegetables are soft, 6 to 8 minutes. Add the wine and cook over high heat until the liquid is reduced to a thin syrup, 3 to 4 minutes. Add the broth and simmer until about 1/2 cup of liquid remains. Set a strainer over a bowl and strain the sauce, pressing down on the solids to extract the juices. Discard the solids. Transfer the sauce to a clean saucepan. Add the parsley and keep warm over low heat.

Generously brush or spray the mushroom caps with the olive oil. Grill over *Direct High* heat until tender, 5 to 7 minutes, turning once halfway through grilling time. Remove from the grill and roughly chop, then add to the warm sauce.

Allow the filets to stand at room temperature for 20 to 30 minutes before grilling. Lightly brush or spray both sides with the oil and sear over *Direct High* heat for 10 minutes, turning once halfway through grilling time. Continue grilling over *Indirect Medium* heat until the internal temperature reaches 135°F for medium rare, 3 to 5 minutes.

Just before serving, remove the sauce from the heat and add the remaining 2 tablespoons butter, swirling the pan until melted. Spoon the sauce over the filets. Serve immediately.

MAKES 4 SERVINGS

STEAK ON THE GRILL

We've all been there. You crave a thick, juicy steak and absolutely no substitute will do. Steaks deserve only the purest flame, the hottest steel. Add an indulgent slab of flavored butter to the finished product and you could come close to tears. Or nirvana. A few pointers to make your fantasy steak a reality:

BUY THE BEST. No, we don't mean filet mignon every night. Just follow your appetite (sirloin tonight?), then scrutinize the cuts before you. You can't go wrong with prime, but chances are you're going to be choosing between Choice and Select at the average grocery store. Go for Choice. (If the steak grades aren't on the packages, ask the folks behind the counter.) Look for bright red meat and hunt down the ones with the finest flecks/streaks of fat. But don't assume that cheaper or leaner cuts can't deliver on flavor. Flank and skirt steaks, once considered culinary stepchildren, are now very popular—just take that extra tenderizing step and you've got a fine meal.

TIDY UP AND DRESS UP. Trimming steaks is easy because the fat is usually around the outer edge. Leave about 1/4 inch of fat for flavor—more will just invite flare-ups. If you're not using a recipe, a light coating of the best extra-virgin olive oil you can afford and a generous sprinkle of kosher salt and freshly ground black pepper is all the seasoning you need for a tasty beef experience.

GET HOT, NOT BOTHERED. Get that cooking grate searing hot! Charcoal grillers, be sure to place the cooking grate on the grill and close the lid for several minutes before you place the steaks on it. You want those steaks to sizzle when they hit the metal. Sear steaks over Direct High heat for a few minutes on each side to get great grill marks (for tips on how to make perfect grill marks, see the sidebar on page 107). Depending on your preferred doneness, you can finish your steak over Direct High or Medium heat (Medium is better for marinade-coated steaks).

KNOW WHEN TO TURN THEM. If you're used to the old "cut and peek" method of checking doneness (we can't think of a surer way to mar a lovely steak), here's a great trick. When meat heats up on the grill, the juices inside rise to the surface. You can tell a steak's doneness by the color of the juices on top of it. For rare steaks, turn while the juices are red. For medium steaks, turn when they're pink. And for well done, wait until they're clear. Note the time they've been cooking. After you turn them, wait the same number of minutes to pull them off the grill. Voilà. You are a steak-grilling genius! If you're grilling steaks to different doneness levels, keep the finished ones warm under foil on individual plates. Be sure to drizzle any escaped juices back over the respective steaks when you serve them.

AND FINALLY, a word about steak sauce. We used to be against this stuff. Somehow, pouring bottled anything onto your grilled masterpiece just seemed wrong. So we started experimenting in the kitchen and guess what? Making your own just adds to the pleasure, not to mention the flavor! While virgin grilled beef will always be near and dear to us, we have experienced some breathless moments with the artful drizzle. Check out our recipes—crafted to match the marinades and rubs we've developed—and see if they don't heighten the flavor.

HOW TO GET GREAT GRILL MARKS

The best steak houses feed all the senses, serving up perfectly seared steaks with even crisscrossed grill marks gracing their surface. Here's how to achieve them at home.

SEAR

Preheat the grill and set it up for Direct High heat (charcoal grills can be set up with Medium heat on one side and High heat on the other; see "Mastering the Fire," page 26). Place the steak over Direct High heat. Allow the meat to sear for 1 to 2 minutes, depending on the thickness.

TURN 90°

With a wide spatula, lift the steak but don't flip it. Give it a quarter turn (90°). Allow the meat to sear for 1 to 2 minutes.

FLIP

Lift the steak with the spatula and flip it. You can already see half your reward on the cooked side! Allow the meat to sear for 1 to 2 minutes.

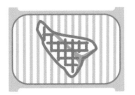

TURN ANOTHER 90°

Lift the steak and, without flipping, turn it 90° again. For this last turn, place the steak over Direct Medium heat if your total cooking time is more than 8 to 10 minutes and finish cooking the steak there. If your total cooking time is 8 minutes or less, finish over Direct High. Depending on the steak's thickness and your desired doneness, the steak may be finished after 1 to 2 minutes. Admire your grill marks—surely your guests will—and allow the meat to rest a few minutes before serving so the juices can ease back to the center.

A GRILLER'S STEAK GLOSSARY

Porterhouse: This hulky cut, taken from the large end of the short loin, can weigh up to 2½ pounds. Be prepared to shell out some bucks for this one. Fortunately, you can feed more than one person with it—if you can convince folks to share.

T-Bone: A smaller version of the porterhouse, cut from the narrow end of the short loin. Prized for its tastiness, which many believe comes in part from the bone.

Strip Steak: Favored by many steak lovers, strip steaks are cut from the center of the top loin and sometimes have a long slice of bone along one side (actually the long bone of the T-bone). These steaks are known by different names in different regions. Aliases include: New York strip, Kansas City strip, shell, Delmonico, Ambassador, hotel cut, sirloin club, and top loin. Delicious by any name!

Rib-Eye: Exceedingly tender and richly flavored, rib-eye is cut from the muscle behind the ribs. If it has a bone attached it's called rib steak. Give it a good sear and maybe a splash of homemade steak sauce. Don't forget the ranch-style pinto beans on the side.

Filet Mignon: Pure, trimmed tenderloin, filets mignons (add an "s" to each word to make the plural) are meaty cylindrical pieces cut up to 2 inches thick. Grilling over High heat is the best way to prepare these fork-tender beauties.

London Broil: Usually a flank steak but also a catchall name for any cut of meat that is broiled or grilled over Direct heat and then sliced across the grain.

Sirloin: The term "sirloin steak" covers a lot of turf. The sirloin (which is also cut into roasts) is the section between the tender short loin and the tougher round. Steaks can be cut from the top or bottom portions of this section. Top sirloin steaks are more tender than bottom sirloin steaks, but a good marinating session for the latter can even out the difference. Go for top sirloin when you can afford it.

Tri-Tip: This lesser-known gem is a thick, lean, triangular cut from the bottom sirloin. Some call it a roast. If you can find it, treasure it. Tri-tip is terrific grilled medium rare and sliced thin like a London broil—an outstanding choice for steak salads and sandwiches. Aliases include tip roast and sirloin bottom butt; also found cut into tip steaks.

Flank Steak: Cut from the lean flank and with virtually no marbling, the relatively inexpensive flank steak is best when pounded or tenderized by a high-acid marinade. Lime juice and red wine are popular ingredients. For some reason, this rather pedestrian cut often gets jazzed up in pinwheel-like beef rolls, perhaps evidence that cooks on a budget can still be pretty creative.

Skirt Steak: Also cut from the flank, the thin and flat skirt steak is what makes beef fajitas so good. Grill it quickly over High heat to tenderize it and coax out its flavor. A marinade is good for it, too. Treat it right and this lean, inexpensive cut will reward you handsomely.

SMOKED SANTA MARIA
TRI-TIP

This style of grilled beef originated about 100 years ago during California's rancho days. Still very popular on Santa Maria restaurant menus, it's also available on weekends from traveling wagons set up in local parking lots for takeout. This is the authentic way to grill and eat it. Macaroni and cheese or cooked small pink beans are traditional sides.

SEAR: MEDIUM, COOK: INDIRECT/MEDIUM

FOR THE SALSA:

- 2 CUPS DICED RIPE TOMATOES
- 1 CAN (7 OUNCES) DICED GREEN CHILES
- 8 GREEN ONIONS (WHITE PART ONLY), THINLY SLICED
- 2 TABLESPOONS FINELY CHOPPED FRESH CILANTRO
- 2 TEASPOONS MINCED GARLIC
- 2 TEASPOONS RED WINE VINEGAR
- 1/2 TEASPOON PREPARED HORSERADISH
- 1/2 TEASPOON WORCESTERSHIRE SAUCE
- 1/2 TEASPOON KOSHER SALT
- 1/4 TEASPOON TABASCO SAUCE

FOR THE RUB:

- 2 TEASPOONS GRANULATED GARLIC
- 1 TEASPOON KOSHER SALT
- 1 TEASPOON FRESHLY GROUND BLACK PEPPER
- 1/2 TEASPOON CELERY SEED
- 1/4 TEASPOON CAYENNE

- 1 TRI-TIP ROAST, 1 1/2 TO 2 POUNDS AND ABOUT 1 1/2 INCHES THICK
  EXTRA-VIRGIN OLIVE OIL

  KOSHER SALT

  OAK OR HICKORY CHIPS SOAKED IN WATER FOR AT LEAST 30 MINUTES

- 1 BAGUETTE (OPTIONAL)
- 1 STICK UNSALTED BUTTER, SOFTENED (OPTIONAL)

To make the salsa: In a medium bowl mix together the salsa ingredients. Cover and set aside until ready to serve.

To make the rub: In a small bowl thoroughly mix together the rub ingredients. Press the rub into the roast. Allow to stand at room temperature for 20 to 30 minutes before grilling.

Follow the grill's instructions for using wood chips. Lightly brush or spray the roast with olive oil and season with salt. Sear over *Direct Medium* heat for about 10 minutes, turning once halfway through searing time. Continue grilling over *Indirect Medium* heat until the internal temperature reaches 135°F for medium rare, 20 to 30 minutes more. Remove from the grill and allow to rest for about 5 minutes.

Cut the roast across the grain into very thin slices and arrange on a platter. Serve with the salsa and baguette, sliced and buttered, so your guests can make their own sandwiches or serve fanned on plates with the salsa spooned on top.

MAKES 6 TO 8 SERVINGS

ROSEMARY
TRI-TIP

A great weekday entrée. For an extra boost of rosemary flavor, toss a few fresh branches on the fire. Serve the meat on warm plates or pile it on grilled French bread with lettuce and tomatoes, if desired.

SEAR: MEDIUM, COOK: INDIRECT/MEDIUM

FOR THE MARINADE:

- 2 TABLESPOONS WHOLE-GRAIN MUSTARD
- 2 TABLESPOONS STEAK SAUCE
- 2 TABLESPOONS EXTRA-VIRGIN OLIVE OIL
- 1 TABLESPOON BALSAMIC VINEGAR
- 1 TABLESPOON FINELY CHOPPED FRESH ROSEMARY

- 1 TRI-TIP ROAST, 1 1/2 TO 2 POUNDS AND ABOUT 1 1/2 INCHES THICK

  KOSHER SALT

To make the marinade: In a small bowl whisk together the marinade ingredients.

Spread the marinade on the roast, cover with plastic wrap, and refrigerate for 4 to 12 hours.

Allow the roast to stand at room temperature for 20 to 30 minutes before grilling. Lightly season both sides of the roast with salt. Sear over *Direct Medium* heat for about 10 minutes, turning once halfway through searing time. Continue grilling over *Indirect Medium* heat until the internal temperature reaches 135°F for medium rare, 20 to 30 minutes more. Remove from the grill and allow to rest for about 5 minutes. Cut across the grain into thin slices. Serve warm.

MAKES 4 TO 6 SERVINGS

Rosemary Tri-Tip

COMBINE A LITTLE WHOLE-GRAIN MUSTARD WITH STEAK SAUCE AND BALSAMIC VINEGAR AND YOU'VE MADE A TOP-RATE MARINADE. ADD FRESH ROSEMARY AND YOU'VE REALLY GOT SOMETHING TO WRITE HOME ABOUT.

Spicy Rib–Eye Steaks with Tomato Chutney

SPICY RIB-EYE STEAKS
WITH TOMATO CHUTNEY

Great barbecue flavor sprinkled on the griller's ultimate steak. For maximum effect, make the chutney—sort of a kicked-up ketchup—a couple days ahead and let it mellow in the refrigerator. Smooooth.

DIRECT/HIGH

FOR THE RUB:

- 2 TEASPOONS PAPRIKA
- 2 TEASPOONS CHILI POWDER
- 1 TEASPOON DRIED THYME
- 1 TEASPOON LIGHT BROWN SUGAR
- 1 TEASPOON KOSHER SALT
- 1 TEASPOON FRESHLY GROUND BLACK PEPPER
- 1/8 TEASPOON CAYENNE

- 4 RIB-EYE STEAKS, ABOUT 3/4 POUND EACH AND 1 INCH THICK

FOR THE CHUTNEY:

- 1 TABLESPOON EXTRA-VIRGIN OLIVE OIL
- 1/4 CUP FINELY CHOPPED YELLOW ONION
- 1/2 TEASPOON MINCED GARLIC
- 1 CAN (14 OUNCES) DICED TOMATOES, WITH JUICE
- 3 SUN-DRIED TOMATO HALVES (OIL-PACKED), CUT INTO SMALL PIECES
- 2 TEASPOONS LIGHT BROWN SUGAR
- 1 TEASPOON WORCESTERSHIRE SAUCE
- 1 TEASPOON BALSAMIC VINEGAR
- 1/4 TEASPOON KOSHER SALT

To make the rub: In a small bowl thoroughly mix the rub ingredients. Reserve 1 tablespoon for the chutney. Coat both sides of the steaks with the remaining rub. Cover with plastic wrap and refrigerate for 1 to 2 hours.

To make the chutney: In a small saucepan over medium heat, warm the olive oil. Add the onion and cook, stirring occasionally, until golden, 4 to 5 minutes. Add the garlic and cook for 1 minute more, stirring occasionally. Add the reserved 1 tablespoon of the rub and stir to blend. Add the canned tomatoes, sun-dried tomatoes, and brown sugar. Stir and bring to a boil over high heat, breaking up the tomatoes with the side of a spoon. Reduce heat and simmer until almost all of the liquid has evaporated, 20 to 30 minutes. Add the remaining chutney ingredients; stir and simmer until most of the liquid has evaporated, about 5 minutes more. Allow the mixture to cool slightly, then purée in a food processor. Transfer to a small serving bowl, cover with plastic wrap, and refrigerate. Allow the chutney to come to room temperature before serving.

Allow the steaks to stand at room temperature for 20 to 30 minutes before grilling. Grill over *Direct High* heat until the internal temperature reaches 145°F for medium rare, 8 to 10 minutes, turning once halfway through grilling time. Remove from the grill and allow to rest for about 5 minutes. Serve warm with the chutney on the side.

MAKES 4 SERVINGS

TEXAS RIB-EYE STEAKS
WITH CHILI BARBECUE SAUCE

If these steaks could walk, they'd have a definite swagger. One of our fiery favorites.

DIRECT/HIGH

FOR THE RUB:

- 1 TABLESPOON MIXED PEPPERCORNS (BLACK, WHITE, PINK, GREEN)
- 1 TEASPOON CHILI POWDER
- 1 TEASPOON KOSHER SALT
- 1 TEASPOON LIGHT BROWN SUGAR
- 1/4 TEASPOON GRANULATED GARLIC
- 1/4 TEASPOON GRANULATED ONION

FOR THE SAUCE:

- 1/2 CUP KETCHUP
- 1 TABLESPOON WORCESTERSHIRE SAUCE
- 1 TABLESPOON RED WINE VINEGAR
- 1 TABLESPOON DARK BROWN SUGAR
- 1 TEASPOON CHILI POWDER
- 1 TEASPOON GRANULATED ONION
- 1/4 TEASPOON FRESHLY GROUND BLACK PEPPER

- 4 RIB-EYE STEAKS, ABOUT 3/4 POUND EACH AND 1 TO 1 1/4 INCHES THICK
- EXTRA-VIRGIN OLIVE OIL

To make the rub: Using a spice grinder or mortar and pestle, crush the peppercorns. Place in a small bowl and thoroughly mix with the rest of the rub ingredients.

To make the sauce: In a small saucepan whisk together all the sauce ingredients with 1/4 cup water. Simmer over low heat for about 10 minutes, stirring occasionally, to allow the sugar to fully dissolve and all of the flavors to blend. Set aside while you grill the steaks.

Allow the steaks to stand at room temperature for 20 to 30 minutes before grilling. Press the rub into both sides of the steaks. Lightly brush or spray both sides of the steaks with the olive oil. Grill over *Direct High* heat until the internal temperature reaches 145°F for medium rare, 8 to 10 minutes, turning once halfway through grilling time. Remove from the grill and allow to rest for about 5 minutes. Serve warm with the sauce on the side.

MAKES 4 SERVINGS

SOUTHWEST SIRLOIN
WITH CORN SALAD

Serve a mighty fine salad and a hot slab of spicy beef and watch the table get very quiet. It's too good for talking.

DIRECT/MEDIUM

FOR THE SALAD:

- 2 CUPS FRESHLY COOKED CORN KERNELS (FROM ABOUT 3 MEDIUM EARS)
- 1/4 CUP FINELY DICED RED BELL PEPPER
- 1/4 CUP FINELY DICED RED ONION
- 1 TEASPOON MINCED JALAPEÑO PEPPER, WITH SEEDS
- 3 TABLESPOONS VEGETABLE OIL
- 1 TABLESPOON DIJON MUSTARD
- 1 TABLESPOON WHITE WINE VINEGAR
- 1 TABLESPOON GRANULATED SUGAR
- 1 TABLESPOON FINELY CHOPPED FRESH DILL
- 1/4 TEASPOON KOSHER SALT

FOR THE RUB:

- 2 TEASPOONS WHOLE BLACK PEPPERCORNS
- 1 1/2 TEASPOONS CUMIN SEEDS
- 1 1/2 TEASPOONS CHILI POWDER
- 1 1/2 TEASPOONS BROWN SUGAR
- 1 1/2 TEASPOONS KOSHER SALT
- 1 TEASPOON DRIED OREGANO
- 1/2 TEASPOON GRANULATED GARLIC

- 1 SIRLOIN STEAK, 1 1/2 TO 2 POUNDS AND ABOUT 1 1/4 INCHES THICK
- EXTRA-VIRGIN OLIVE OIL

To make the salad: In a large bowl combine the corn, bell pepper, onion, and jalapeño.

In a small saucepan whisk together the vegetable oil, mustard, vinegar, sugar, dill, and salt. Bring to a simmer over medium-high heat and pour the warm vinaigrette over the corn mixture, toss well, and allow to stand at room temperature until ready to serve.

To make the rub: Using a spice grinder or mortar and pestle, coarsely grind the peppercorns and cumin seeds. Place in a small bowl and combine with the remaining rub ingredients.

Trim the steak of any excess fat. Press the rub into both sides of the steak and allow to stand at room temperature for 20 to 30 minutes before grilling.

Lightly brush or spray both sides of the steak with olive oil. Grill over *Direct Medium* heat until the internal temperature reaches 145°F for medium rare, 10 to 12 minutes, turning once halfway through grilling time. Remove from the grill and allow to rest for about 5 minutes before slicing thinly across the grain. Serve warm with the salad.

MAKES 4 SERVINGS

MOLTO BENE
SIRLOIN STEAK

Here's a super-easy, authentic Italian recipe that makes good use of one of the grill's favorite beef cuts. This marinade makes it "molto bene" (very good). Use top sirloin for the most tender results. Serve with grilled red peppers and grilled artichokes, if desired.

DIRECT/MEDIUM

FOR THE MARINADE:

- 6 TABLESPOONS EXTRA-VIRGIN OLIVE OIL
- 3 TABLESPOONS RED WINE VINEGAR
- 1 TABLESPOON BALSAMIC VINEGAR
- 1 TEASPOON FINELY CHOPPED FRESH ROSEMARY
- 1 TEASPOON MINCED GARLIC
- 1 TEASPOON KOSHER SALT
- 1/2 TEASPOON FRESHLY GROUND BLACK PEPPER

- 1 TOP SIRLOIN STEAK, 1 1/2 TO 2 POUNDS AND ABOUT 1 1/2 INCHES THICK

To make the marinade: In a medium bowl whisk together the marinade ingredients.

Trim the steak of any excess fat. Place the steak in a large, resealable plastic bag and pour in the marinade. Press the air out of the bag and seal tightly. Turn the bag to distribute the marinade, place on a plate, and refrigerate for 6 to 8 hours, turning occasionally.

Remove the steak from the bag and discard the marinade. Allow the steak to stand at room temperature for 20 to 30 minutes before grilling.

Grill the steak over *Direct Medium* heat until the internal temperature reaches 140°F for medium rare, 15 to 20 minutes, turning once halfway through the grilling time. Remove from the grill and allow to rest for about 5 minutes. Cut across the grain into thin slices and serve warm.

MAKES 4 SERVINGS

Molto Bene Sirloin Steak

Szechwan Sirloin Steak with Green Bean Salad

SZECHWAN SIRLOIN STEAK
WITH GREEN BEAN SALAD

The green bean salad brings both balance and contrast to this spicy-hot steak. Serve warm or at room temperature.

DIRECT/MEDIUM

FOR THE MARINADE:

- 1/4 CUP BLACK BEAN SAUCE WITH GARLIC
- 1/4 CUP FRESH ORANGE JUICE
- 2 TABLESPOONS HOT CHILI PASTE
- 2 TABLESPOONS SOY SAUCE
- 1 TABLESPOON GRATED ORANGE ZEST
- 1 TABLESPOON GRATED FRESH GINGER
- 2 TEASPOONS MINCED GARLIC

- 1 SIRLOIN STEAK, 1 1/2 TO 2 POUNDS AND ABOUT 1 1/4 INCHES THICK

FOR THE VINAIGRETTE:

- 2 TABLESPOONS BLACK BEAN SAUCE WITH GARLIC
- 2 TABLESPOONS RICE VINEGAR
- 1 TABLESPOON ASIAN SESAME OIL
- 1 TABLESPOON PEANUT OIL
- 1 TABLESPOON GRANULATED SUGAR
- 1 TEASPOON SOY SAUCE
- 1/4 TEASPOON GRATED FRESH GINGER

- 1 POUND GREEN BEANS *OR* CHINESE LONG BEANS, STEMS REMOVED

- ASIAN SESAME OIL
- 1 1/2 TABLESPOONS SZECHWAN PEPPERCORNS, CRUSHED
- KOSHER SALT

To make the marinade: In a small bowl whisk together the marinade ingredients.

Trim the steak of any excess fat. Place the steak in a large, resealable plastic bag and pour in the marinade. Press the air out of the bag and seal tightly. Turn the bag to distribute the marinade, place on a plate, and refrigerate for 6 to 8 hours, turning occasionally.

To make the vinaigrette: In a small bowl whisk together the vinaigrette ingredients.

Toss the beans in the vinaigrette to coat them evenly. Remove the beans from the bowl, reserving the vinaigrette, and grill over *Direct Medium* heat until crisp-tender, 8 to 10 minutes. Remove from the grill, transfer to a medium bowl, and pour in the reserved vinaigrette. Gently toss to combine and set aside until ready to serve.

Remove the steak from the bag and discard the marinade. Wipe most of the marinade off the steak with a paper towel. Allow to stand at room temperature for 20 to 30 minutes before grilling.

Lightly brush or spray both sides of the steak with the sesame oil. Season with the Szechwan peppercorns and salt. Grill over *Direct Medium* heat until the internal temperature reaches 145°F for medium rare, 10 to 12 minutes, turning once halfway through grilling time. Remove from the grill and allow to rest for about 5 minutes before thinly slicing on the bias. Serve warm with the salad.

MAKES 4 SERVINGS

SPIRAL STEAKS
WITH PESTO, OLIVES, AND TOMATOES

Select flank steaks of equal thickness for these party-loving pinwheels.

DIRECT/MEDIUM

FOR THE PESTO:

- 1 CUP LOOSELY PACKED FRESH BASIL LEAVES
- 1 SMALL GARLIC CLOVE, CRUSHED
- 1 TABLESPOONS PINE NUTS
- 1/4 TEASPOON KOSHER SALT
- 1/4 TEASPOON FRESHLY GROUND BLACK PEPPER
- 1/4 CUP EXTRA-VIRGIN OLIVE OIL

FOR THE FILLING:

- 1/2 CUP BLACK OLIVES, PITTED
- 1/2 CUP SUN-DRIED TOMATOES (OIL-PACKED)

- 2 FLANK STEAKS, ABOUT 1 1/2 POUNDS EACH

- KOSHER SALT

To make the pesto: In a food processor finely chop the basil, garlic, pine nuts, salt, and pepper. Transfer the mixture to a small bowl and whisk in the olive oil.

To make the filling: In a food processor combine the olives and sun-dried tomatoes and process until smooth.

Trim the flank steaks of any excess fat and trim the edges to form a rectangle. Using a meat mallet or the flat side of a sauté pan, pound the steaks to an even thickness, about 7 inches by 9 inches each.

Coat both sides of the steaks with the pesto. Spread half the filling on each steak and roll up the long sides over the filling like a jelly roll. Cut each roll into four equal-sized spirals, securing each with a toothpick. Place on a platter, cover with plastic wrap, and refrigerate for 2 to 6 hours.

Allow the spirals to stand at room temperature for 20 to 30 minutes before grilling. Season with salt and grill, smooth curved side down, over *Direct Medium* heat until nicely browned on all smooth sides, 12 to 15 minutes, turning occasionally. Remove the toothpicks and serve immediately.

MAKES 8 SERVINGS

PEANUT-CURRY
FLANK STEAK

Don't know what to do with that flank steak in the freezer? Try a little East meets West.

DIRECT/MEDIUM

FOR THE MARINADE:

2 TABLESPOONS PEANUT OIL

2 TABLESPOONS ASIAN SESAME OIL

2 TABLESPOONS DRY SHERRY

2 TABLESPOONS SOY SAUCE

2 TABLESPOONS CREAMY PEANUT BUTTER

2 TABLESPOONS HOISIN SAUCE

2 TABLESPOONS RICE VINEGAR

2 TEASPOONS CURRY POWDER

1/2 TEASPOON GROUND GINGER

1/2 TEASPOON CRUSHED RED PEPPER FLAKES

1 FLANK STEAK, 1 1/2 TO 2 POUNDS AND
   ABOUT 3/4 INCH THICK

To make the marinade: In a small bowl whisk together the marinade ingredients.

Trim the steak of any surface fat. Place the steak in a large, resealable plastic bag and pour in the marinade. Press the air out of the bag and seal tightly. Turn the bag to distribute the marinade, place on a plate, and refrigerate for 6 to 8 hours, turning occasionally.

Remove the steak from the bag and discard the marinade. Allow the steak to stand at room temperature for 20 to 30 minutes before grilling.

Grill the steak over *Direct Medium* heat until the internal temperature reaches 145°F for medium rare, 8 to 10 minutes, turning once halfway through grilling time. Remove from the grill and allow to rest for 3 to 5 minutes. Cut across the grain into thin diagonal slices. Serve warm.

MAKES 4 SERVINGS

"Nothing takes the taste out of peanut butter quite like unrequited love."

— CHARLIE BROWN

GREEK
PITA POCKETS

Inspired by the gyro, this fun and simple meal is just made for the backyard.

DIRECT/MEDIUM

FOR THE MARINADE:

1/4 CUP FRESH LEMON JUICE

1/4 CUP EXTRA-VIRGIN OLIVE OIL

1/4 CUP COARSELY CHOPPED FRESH OREGANO

4 MEDIUM CLOVES GARLIC, CRUSHED

1 TABLESPOON COARSELY GROUND BLACK PEPPER

1 TEASPOON CRUSHED RED PEPPER FLAKES

1 FLANK STEAK, 1 1/2 TO 2 POUNDS AND ABOUT
   3/4 INCH THICK

FOR THE SALAD:

2 CUPS COARSELY SHREDDED ROMAINE LETTUCE

1 CUP COARSELY CHOPPED RIPE TOMATOES

1/2 CUP THINLY SLICED SWEET ONION

4 OUNCES FETA CHEESE, CRUMBLED

1/4 CUP FINELY CHOPPED PICKLED PEPPERS
   OR PEPPERONCINI

EXTRA-VIRGIN OLIVE OIL

KOSHER SALT

4 PITA POCKETS, CUT IN HALF

To make the marinade: In a medium bowl whisk together the marinade ingredients.

Trim the steak of any surface fat. Place the steak in a large, resealable plastic bag and pour in the marinade. Press the air out of the bag and seal tightly. Turn the bag to distribute the marinade, place on a plate, and refrigerate for 6 to 8 hours, turning occasionally.

To make the salad: In a medium bowl thoroughly mix the salad ingredients. Set aside until ready to serve.

Remove the steak from the bag and discard the marinade. Allow the steak to stand at room temperature for 20 to 30 minutes before grilling.

Brush or spray both sides of the steak with olive oil. Season with salt. Grill over *Direct Medium* heat until the internal temperature reaches 145°F for medium rare, 8 to 10 minutes, turning once halfway through grilling time. Remove from the grill and allow to rest for 3 to 5 minutes. Cut the steak across the grain into thin diagonal slices, then cut in the opposite direction to create bite-sized pieces. Fill each pita half with the meat, then the salad. Serve warm.

MAKES 4 SERVINGS

FLANK STEAK
WITH SALSA VERDE

In Mexico, a salsa verde can mean almost any green sauce, but it's quite traditional to use tomatillos, which look like small green tomatoes with a papery husk. Grilling makes them more delicious and soft enough to purée. Try this great salsa on pork and chicken, too.

DIRECT/MEDIUM

FOR THE MARINADE:

1/4 CUP FRESH LIME JUICE

1/4 CUP FRESH ORANGE JUICE

1/4 CUP EXTRA-VIRGIN OLIVE OIL

1 TABLESPOON COARSELY CHOPPED FRESH OREGANO

1 TABLESPOON COARSELY CHOPPED FRESH CILANTRO

1 TABLESPOON GROUND CUMIN

1 TABLESPOON COARSELY GROUND BLACK PEPPER

2 TEASPOONS COARSELY CHOPPED GARLIC

1 FLANK STEAK, 1 1/2 TO 2 POUNDS AND ABOUT 3/4 INCH THICK

FOR THE SALSA:

1 SMALL YELLOW ONION, CUT INTO 1/2-INCH SLICES

EXTRA-VIRGIN OLIVE OIL

3/4 POUND TOMATILLOS

1 JALAPEÑO PEPPER, STEM REMOVED

2 MEDIUM CLOVES GARLIC

1/2 CUP LOOSELY PACKED FRESH CILANTRO

2 TEASPOONS FRESH LIME JUICE

1 TABLESPOON LIGHT BROWN SUGAR

1/2 TEASPOON KOSHER SALT

1/2 TEASPOON FRESHLY GROUND BLACK PEPPER

KOSHER SALT

To make the marinade: In a small bowl whisk together the marinade ingredients.

Trim the steak of any surface fat. Place the steak in a large, resealable plastic bag and pour in the marinade. Press the air out of the bag and seal tightly. Turn the bag to distribute the marinade, place on a plate, and refrigerate for 2 to 4 hours, turning occasionally.

To make the salsa: Brush or spray both sides of the onion slices with olive oil. Remove and discard the tomatillo husks and stems; rinse the tomatillos under water. Grill the onion slices, tomatillos, and jalapeño over *Direct Medium* heat until well marked and tender, turning once halfway through grilling time. The onion slices will take 8 to 10 minutes, the tomatillos 6 to 8 minutes, the jalapeño 5 to 6 minutes. Place the vegetables and the remaining salsa ingredients in a food processor and pulse several times just until you have a chunky salsa.

Remove the steak from the bag and discard the marinade. Allow the steak to stand at room temperature for 20 to 30 minutes before grilling.

Season the steak with salt and grill over *Direct Medium* heat until the internal temperature reaches 145°F for medium rare, 8 to 10 minutes, turning once halfway through grilling time. Remove from the grill and allow to rest for 3 to 5 minutes. Cut across the grain into thin diagonal slices. Serve warm with the salsa.

MAKES 4 TO 6 SERVINGS

STEAK TACOS

Isn't it about time you outgrew the ground-beef version?

DIRECT/MEDIUM

FOR THE PASTE:

3 TABLESPOONS EXTRA-VIRGIN OLIVE OIL

1 TABLESPOON CHILI POWDER

1 TABLESPOON GROUND CUMIN

2 TEASPOONS CRACKED BLACK PEPPERCORNS

1 TEASPOON GRANULATED GARLIC

1 TEASPOON DRIED OREGANO

1 FLANK STEAK, 1 1/2 TO 2 POUNDS AND ABOUT 3/4 INCH THICK

KOSHER SALT

8 FLOUR TORTILLAS (8 INCHES)

2 CUPS GRATED CHEDDAR *OR* MONTEREY JACK CHEESE

4 CUPS SHREDDED ROMAINE LETTUCE

2 CUPS PREPARED CHUNKY SALSA

1 CUP SOUR CREAM (OPTIONAL)

To make the paste: In a small bowl whisk together the paste ingredients.

Trim the steak of any surface fat. Coat both sides of the steak with the paste. Place the steak in a large, resealable plastic bag, press the air out of the bag, and seal tightly. Set the bag on a plate and refrigerate for 4 to 6 hours.

Remove the steak from the bag and allow to stand at room temperature for 20 to 30 minutes before grilling. Season with salt. Grill over *Direct Medium* heat until the internal temperature reaches 145°F for medium rare, 8 to 10 minutes, turning once halfway through grilling time. Remove from the grill and allow to rest for 3 to 5 minutes. Cut across the grain into thin strips.

Divide the tortillas and wrap in two foil packets. Grill the packets over *Direct Medium* heat until warm, about 2 minutes, turning once halfway through grilling time. Place the steak strips in the center of the tortillas. Add the cheese, lettuce, and salsa, top with the sour cream, if desired. Fold up the sides and eat with your hands.

MAKES 8 SERVINGS

A NICE
CONTRAST
OF SPICY
AND SWEET,
TENDER AND
CRUNCHY,
MEATY AND
FRUITY.

Mexican Flank Steak with Jicama–Orange Salad

MEXICAN FLANK STEAK
WITH JICAMA-ORANGE SALAD

What a way to dress up this simple cut!

DIRECT/MEDIUM

FOR THE RUB:

- **1 TEASPOON CHILI POWDER**
- **1 TEASPOON GRANULATED GARLIC**
- **1 TEASPOON DRY MUSTARD**
- **1/2 TEASPOON PAPRIKA**
- **1/2 TEASPOON GROUND CORIANDER**
- **1/2 TEASPOON GROUND CUMIN**

- **1 FLANK STEAK, 1 1/2 TO 2 POUNDS AND ABOUT 3/4 INCH THICK**

FOR THE DRESSING:

- **2 TABLESPOONS FINELY CHOPPED FRESH CILANTRO**
- **1 TABLESPOON WHITE WINE VINEGAR**
- **1 TABLESPOON EXTRA-VIRGIN OLIVE OIL**
- **1 TABLESPOON GRANULATED SUGAR**
- **1 TEASPOON MINCED SERRANO CHILE, WITH SEEDS**

- **1 SMALL RED ONION, CUT CROSSWISE INTO 1/2-INCH SLICES**
- **EXTRA-VIRGIN OLIVE OIL**
- **2 CUPS JICAMA CUT INTO MATCHSTICKS**
- **4 ORANGES, PEELED AND SECTIONED (SEE SIDEBAR, RIGHT)**
- **KOSHER SALT**
- **FRESHLY GROUND BLACK PEPPER**

To make the rub: In a small bowl combine the rub ingredients.

Trim the steak of any surface fat. Press the rub into both sides of the steak. Cover the steak with plastic wrap and refrigerate for 3 to 6 hours.

To make the dressing: In a small bowl whisk together the dressing ingredients.

Lightly brush or spray the onion slices with olive oil. Grill over *Direct Medium* heat until well marked and tender, 8 to 10 minutes, turning once halfway through grilling time. Remove from the grill and chop into 1/2-inch pieces. Place the onion in a medium bowl and add the jicama and orange segments. Pour in the dressing, toss with two forks, and season with salt and pepper. Cover with plastic wrap and refrigerate for up to 4 hours. Serve at room temperature.

Allow the steak to stand at room temperature for 20 to 30 minutes before grilling. Brush or spray both sides of the steak with oil and season with salt. Grill over *Direct Medium* heat until the internal temperature reaches 145°F for medium rare, 8 to 10 minutes, turning once halfway through grilling time. Remove from the grill and allow to rest for 3 to 5 minutes. Cut across the grain into thin diagonal slices. Serve warm with the salad.

MAKES 4 SERVINGS

SECTIONING CITRUS FRUITS

Here's an easy and indispensable technique for cutting sections of oranges, grapefruits, or other citrus so all you get is sweet, juicy pulp and none of the stringy or bitter stuff.

SLICE OFF THE ENDS

Slice off the top and bottom of the fruit just down to the juicy pulp. You should see a small pinwheel of fruit.

REMOVE THE RIND AND PITH

Stand the fruit on one flat end and, using a sharp paring knife, slice off the rind and all the whitish pith in curved, vertical strips. Cut just to where the juice and the pith meet. Turn the fruit as you go, following its curve as you slice downward.

CUT OUT THE SEGMENTS

Proceed with the following cuts over a bowl to catch the juice and segments: Slice along the length of one side of a membrane dividing two sections just to the tapered inner edge. Repeat on the other side of the segment, separating the fruit from the membrane. Give the knife a slight twist to pop out the clean section. Repeat with all remaining sections. It gets tricky on the last one, but you can always forego the last cut and just peel the section away from the membrane. Cut the sections into smaller pieces or leave whole. Give the remaining membrane network a good squeeze—there's always a little juice left in there.

CHILI ON THE GRILL

For incredible chili, use pure chile powder—not the "chili powder" (a blend of ground chiles, garlic, oregano and other spices) that you find in most spice racks. The pure stuff is simply ground ancho chiles (dried poblanos).

DIRECT/MEDIUM

- 3 POUNDS PLUM TOMATOES, CORES REMOVED

- 3 STALKS CELERY
- 2 MEDIUM YELLOW ONIONS, CUT CROSSWISE INTO 1/2-INCH SLICES
  EXTRA-VIRGIN OLIVE OIL
- 1 MEDIUM JALAPEÑO PEPPER, STEM REMOVED

- 2 TABLESPOONS PURE CHILE POWDER, DIVIDED
- 2 TEASPOONS KOSHER SALT, DIVIDED
- 1/2 TEASPOON FRESHLY GROUND BLACK PEPPER
- 1 POUND TOP SIRLOIN STEAK, ABOUT 3/4 INCH THICK
- 3 BONELESS PORK LOIN CHOPS, ABOUT 5 OUNCES EACH AND 3/4 INCH THICK

- 2 TEASPOONS GROUND CUMIN
- 2 TEASPOONS DRIED OREGANO
- 2 TEASPOONS MINCED GARLIC
- 1/4 TEASPOON CAYENNE
- 1 BOTTLE (12 OUNCES) ALE
- 1 CUP BEEF BROTH
- 1 CAN (14 OUNCES) PINTO BEANS

- 1 CUP GRATED SHARP CHEDDAR CHEESE
- 1 CUP SOUR CREAM

Grill the tomatoes over *Direct Medium* heat until the skins are lightly charred on all sides, 8 to 10 minutes, turning as needed. Transfer the tomatoes to a food processor and purée (in batches, if necessary), then pour into a large saucepan.

Brush or spray the celery and onion slices with the olive oil. Grill the celery, onions, and jalapeño over *Direct Medium* heat until well marked, 8 to 10 minutes, turning once halfway through grilling time. Transfer the vegetables to a cutting board. Chop the celery and onions into 1/4-inch pieces. Mince the jalapeño. Add the vegetables to the tomato purée.

In a small bowl combine 1 tablespoon of the chile powder, 1 teaspoon of the salt, and the pepper. Season both sides of the steak and the chops with the spices. Brush or spray the meat with the oil and grill over *Direct Medium* heat for about 8 minutes, turning once halfway through grilling time. Remove from the grill and cut into 3/4-inch cubes, then add to the tomato mixture.

Add the remaining 1 tablespoon chile powder, remaining 1 teaspoon salt, cumin, oregano, garlic, cayenne, ale, and broth to the meat mixture. Bring to a boil over high heat.

Reduce the heat and simmer, stirring occasionally, until the meat cubes are very tender, 1 to 1 1/2 hours. Add the pinto beans and simmer for 15 minutes more.

Serve warm in individual bowls and top with the cheese and sour cream.

MAKES 6 TO 8 SERVINGS

TÍA MARIA SKIRT STEAK

Skirt steaks are great quickly grilled over High heat. Here we soak them in coffee liqueur, then season them with a bold chili-cinnamon rub for a wild and wonderful departure from the mundane. A gratifying alternative for the griller looking to break new ground.

DIRECT/HIGH

FOR THE MARINADE:
- 1/2 CUP TÍA MARIA OR COFFEE LIQUEUR
- 1 TABLESPOON WORCESTERSHIRE SAUCE

- 2 SKIRT STEAKS, ABOUT 3/4 POUND EACH AND 1/2 INCH THICK

FOR THE RUB:
- 2 TEASPOONS BLACK PEPPERCORNS
- 2 TEASPOONS COFFEE BEANS
- 2 TEASPOONS FENNEL SEEDS
- 1 TEASPOON CHILI POWDER
- 1/2 TEASPOON GROUND CINNAMON
- 1/2 TEASPOON KOSHER SALT

EXTRA-VIRGIN OLIVE OIL

To make the marinade: In a small bowl whisk together the Tía Maria and Worcestershire sauce.

Trim the steaks of any excess fat and cut each steak in half. Place the steaks in a large, resealable plastic bag and pour in the marinade. Press the air out of the bag and seal tightly. Turn the bag to distribute the marinade, place on a plate, and refrigerate for 2 to 4 hours, turning occasionally.

To make the rub: Using a spice grinder or mortar and pestle, crush the peppercorns with the coffee beans and fennel seeds. Place in a small bowl and mix with the remaining rub ingredients.

Remove the steaks from the bag and discard the marinade. Pat the steaks dry with paper towels. Coat both sides of the steaks with the rub. Allow to stand at room temperature for 20 to 30 minutes before grilling.

Brush or spray both sides of the steaks with olive oil. Grill over *Direct High* heat for 3 to 5 minutes, turning once halfway through grilling time. Remove from the grill and allow to rest for 2 to 3 minutes. Serve warm, whole or thinly sliced.

MAKES 4 SERVINGS

SPICY SKIRT-STEAK
FAJITAS

Serve with any of the traditional accompaniments: grilled onions, peppers, guacamole, refried beans, or sour cream.

DIRECT/HIGH

FOR THE MARINADE:

- 1 TEASPOON WHOLE CUMIN SEEDS
- 1/4 CUP FRESH LIME JUICE
- 2 TABLESPOONS CANOLA OIL
- 2 TABLESPOONS FINELY CHOPPED FRESH CILANTRO
- 1 TABLESPOON KETCHUP
- 2 TEASPOONS LIGHT BROWN SUGAR
- 1 TEASPOON MINCED GARLIC
- 1 TEASPOON MINCED JALAPEÑO PEPPER, WITH SEEDS
- 1/2 TEASPOON KOSHER SALT

- 2 SKIRT STEAKS, ABOUT 1 POUND EACH AND 1/2 INCH THICK

FOR THE SALSA:

- 1 1/2 CUPS COARSELY CHOPPED RIPE TOMATOES
- 1 LARGE RIPE AVOCADO, FINELY DICED
- 3 TO 4 GREEN ONIONS (WHITE PART ONLY), FINELY CHOPPED
- 2 TABLESPOONS FINELY CHOPPED FRESH CILANTRO
- 2 TEASPOONS MINCED JALAPEÑO PEPPER, WITH SEEDS
- 2 TEASPOONS FRESH LIME JUICE
  KOSHER SALT
  FRESHLY GROUND BLACK PEPPER

- 8 FLOUR TORTILLAS (10 INCHES)

To make the marinade: In a small sauté pan over low heat, warm the cumin seeds just until they release their fragrance, 2 to 3 minutes. Place in a small bowl and mix with the remaining marinade ingredients.

Trim the steaks of any excess fat. Place the steaks in a large, resealable plastic bag and pour in the marinade. Press the air out of the bag and seal tightly. Turn the bag to distribute the marinade, place on a plate, and refrigerate for 8 to 12 hours, turning occasionally.

To make the salsa: In a medium bowl combine the salsa ingredients, including salt and pepper to taste.

Remove the steaks from the bag and discard the marinade. Allow the steaks to stand at room temperature for 20 to 30 minutes before grilling.

Grill the steaks over *Direct High* heat for 3 to 5 minutes, turning once halfway through grilling time. Remove from the grill and allow to rest for 2 to 3 minutes.

Divide the tortillas and wrap in two foil packets. Grill the packets over *Direct High* heat until warm, about 2 minutes, turning once halfway through grilling time.

Cut the steaks into thin diagonal slices. Serve warm on a platter with the warm tortillas and salsa on separate dishes so your guests can assemble their own fajitas.

MAKES 6 TO 8 SERVINGS

THAI
STEAK SALAD

Loaded with classic Thai ingredients, this one's light on the palate but incredibly filling.

SEAR: MEDIUM, COOK: INDIRECT/MEDIUM

FOR THE MARINADE:

- 2 TABLESPOONS PEANUT OIL
- 2 TABLESPOONS KETCHUP
- 1 TABLESPOON SOY SAUCE

- 1 TRI-TIP ROAST, 1 1/2 TO 2 POUNDS AND ABOUT 1 1/2 INCHES THICK

FOR THE DRESSING:

- 2 TABLESPOONS PEANUT OIL
- 2 TABLESPOONS FRESH LIME JUICE
- 2 TEASPOONS FISH SAUCE
- 1/2 TEASPOON GRANULATED SUGAR
- 1/2 TEASPOON GRATED FRESH GINGER
- 1/4 TEASPOON MINCED SERRANO CHILE, WITH SEEDS
- 1/4 TEASPOON MINCED GARLIC
- 1/4 TEASPOON KOSHER SALT

FOR THE SALAD:

- 4 CUPS LIGHTLY PACKED CURLY LEAF LETTUCE, TORN
- 1 CUP LIGHTLY PACKED MINT LEAVES, COARSELY CHOPPED
- 1/2 CUP LIGHTLY PACKED CILANTRO LEAVES, COARSELY CHOPPED
- 4 GREEN ONIONS, TRIMMED, CUT INTO THIN DIAGONAL SLICES
- 2 MEDIUM TOMATOES, CUT INTO THIN WEDGES

To make the marinade: In a small bowl whisk together the marinade ingredients.

Spread the marinade on the roast. Allow to stand at room temperature for 20 to 30 minutes.

To make the dressing: In a small bowl whisk together the dressing ingredients.

To make the salad: In a large bowl combine the salad ingredients. Cover with plastic wrap and refrigerate until ready to serve.

Sear the roast over *Direct Medium* heat for 10 minutes, turning once halfway through searing time. Continue grilling over *Indirect Medium* heat until the internal temperature reaches 135°F for medium rare, 20 to 30 minutes more. Remove from the grill and allow to rest for about 5 minutes. Cut across the grain into 1/4-inch slices and add to the salad. Whisk the dressing and pour over the top. Toss and serve.

MAKES 4 SERVINGS

Beer-Bathed Brisket

BEER-BATHED
BRISKET

Brisket braised slowly in a stout-based braising liquid. The result? A dripping mouthful of saucy heaven.

SEAR: HIGH, COOK: INDIRECT/LOW

FOR THE RUB:

- 1 TABLESPOON PAPRIKA
- 1 TEASPOON GARLIC POWDER
- 1 TEASPOON DRIED OREGANO
- 1 TEASPOON DRIED THYME
- 1 TEASPOON GRANULATED ONION
- 1 TEASPOON KOSHER SALT
- 1/4 TEASPOON CAYENNE

- 1 BEEF BRISKET, ABOUT 3 POUNDS
  EXTRA-VIRGIN OLIVE OIL

FOR THE SAUCE:

- 1 TABLESPOON UNSALTED BUTTER
- 1 TABLESPOON EXTRA-VIRGIN OLIVE OIL
- 1 MEDIUM YELLOW ONION, MINCED
- 1 TABLESPOON MINCED GARLIC
- 1 TEASPOON CARAWAY SEEDS
- 1/2 CUP KETCHUP
- 1 CUP BEEF BROTH
- 2 CUPS (1 PINT) GUINNESS® EXTRA STOUT
- 3 TABLESPOONS BALSAMIC VINEGAR

  KOSHER SALT
  FRESHLY GROUND BLACK PEPPER

- 6 HAMBURGER BUNS

To make the rub: In a small bowl combine the rub ingredients.

Press the rub into the brisket, cover with plastic wrap, and refrigerate for 2 to 4 hours.

Allow the brisket to stand at room temperature for 20 to 30 minutes before grilling. Generously brush or spray the brisket with olive oil. Sear over *Direct High* heat until well browned, about 6 minutes, turning once halfway through searing time. Transfer to a braising pan, such as a 9- by 13-inch heavy-gauge aluminum pan.

To make the sauce: In a medium saucepan over medium heat, melt the butter with the olive oil. Add the onion, garlic, and caraway seeds and cook for 5 to 6 minutes, stirring occasionally. Add the ketchup and broth, whisk, and bring to a simmer. Add the Extra Stout and balsamic vinegar. Return to a simmer, then pour the liquid over the brisket so it comes one-half to two-thirds of the way up the sides; don't overfill the pan. Cover with foil and grill over *Indirect Low* heat until fork tender, 3 to 4 hours, turning twice during grilling time.

Remove the brisket from the grill. Cut across the grain into thin, diagonal slices. Season the sauce with salt and pepper. Serve the meat warm on a bun with the sauce.

MAKES 4 TO 6 SERVINGS

PINEAPPLE-HOISIN
BEEF RIBS

Beef ribs usually come in racks of seven bones. Look for meaty, lean racks. This recipe only makes two (generous) servings because only two racks will fit on a regular-sized grill set up for Indirect heat. Sambal oelek is a ground fresh chili paste made with vinegar and salt. Look for it in Asian grocery stores.

SEAR: MEDIUM, COOK: INDIRECT/MEDIUM

FOR THE MARINADE:

- 2 TABLESPOONS SAMBAL OELEK
- 2 TABLESPOONS SOY SAUCE
- 2 TABLESPOONS ASIAN SESAME OIL

- 2 BEEF BACK RIB RACKS, ABOUT 2 POUNDS EACH

FOR THE SAUCE:

- 1/2 CUP PINEAPPLE JUICE
- 1/4 CUP HOISIN SAUCE
- 1/4 CUP KETCHUP
- 1 TEASPOON HOT CHILI OIL
- 1 TEASPOON RICE VINEGAR
- 1 TEASPOON GRATED FRESH GINGER

To make the marinade: In a small bowl whisk together the marinade ingredients.

Trim the ribs of any excess fat. Rub each rack thoroughly with the marinade. Place the racks on a plate, cover with plastic wrap, and refrigerate for 6 to 8 hours.

To make the sauce: In a small heavy-bottomed saucepan whisk together the sauce ingredients. Bring to a boil over high heat, then reduce heat and simmer for 5 to 10 minutes, stirring frequently. Set aside.

Allow the ribs to stand at room temperature for 20 to 30 minutes before grilling. Sear the ribs, meat side down, over *Direct Medium* heat until lightly browned, about 5 minutes. Turn the ribs meat side up and continue grilling over *Indirect Medium* heat until tender and the meat has pulled away from the ends of the bones, 1 1/2 to 2 hours. Baste the ribs liberally with the sauce during the last 10 to 20 minutes of grilling time. Cut the racks into individual ribs. Serve immediately.

MAKES 2 SERVINGS

MOLASSES SHORT RIBS
WITH ONION MARMALADE

Cut from the chuck, short ribs are nicely marbled and meaty—excellent candidates for slow cooking. The onion marmalade adds a down-home sweetness that's really hard to beat. Note: The onions are grilled on Direct High, the ribs on Indirect Low.

DIRECT/HIGH

FOR THE MARINADE:

1 CUP DRY RED WINE

1/4 CUP MOLASSES

2 TABLESPOONS WORCESTERSHIRE SAUCE

2 TABLESPOONS DIJON MUSTARD

1 TABLESPOON MINCED GARLIC

8 BEEF SHORT RIBS, 4 TO 5 POUNDS TOTAL

FOR THE MARMALADE:

2 LARGE RED ONIONS, CUT CROSSWISE INTO 1-INCH SLICES

EXTRA-VIRGIN OLIVE OIL

1/4 CUP APPLE JUICE

3 TABLESPOONS CIDER VINEGAR

1 1/2 TABLESPOONS GRANULATED SUGAR

KOSHER SALT

FRESHLY GROUND BLACK PEPPER

BARBECUE SAUCE

To make the marinade: In a medium bowl whisk together the marinade ingredients.

Trim the ribs of any excess fat. Place the ribs in a large, resealable plastic bag and pour in the marinade. Press the air out of the bag and seal tightly. Turn the bag to distribute the marinade, place in a bowl, and refrigerate for 12 to 24 hours, turning occasionally.

To make the marmalade: Brush both sides of the onion slices with olive oil. Grill over *Direct High* heat until well marked, 8 to 10 minutes, turning once halfway through grilling time. In a medium heavy-bottomed saucepan combine the onions with the apple juice, vinegar, and sugar. Simmer over low heat, covered, until the liquid is gone, 20 to 30 minutes. If necessary, remove the lid and cook over medium-high heat for 3 to 5 minutes more. Transfer to a food processor and pulse into a chunky marmalade. Season with salt to taste.

Remove the ribs from the bag and discard the marinade. Pat the ribs dry with paper towels. Allow to stand at room temperature for 20 to 30 minutes before grilling.

Brush or spray the ribs with oil and generously season with salt and pepper. Grill over *Indirect Low* heat, keeping the grill's temperature between 300°F and 325°F, until fully cooked and tender, 1 1/2 to 2 hours, turning occasionally. Serve warm with the marmalade and barbecue sauce.

MAKES 4 SERVINGS

BEEF RIBS
WITH CABERNET SAUCE

Beef and wine are natural partners, and this recipe shows the tenderizing power of the grape. Beef ribs never had it so good!

SEAR: MEDIUM, COOK: INDIRECT/MEDIUM

FOR THE RUB:

2 TEASPOONS DRIED MARJORAM

2 TEASPOONS PAPRIKA

1 TEASPOON GRANULATED GARLIC

1 TEASPOON LIGHT BROWN SUGAR

1 TEASPOON KOSHER SALT

1 TEASPOON FRESHLY GROUND BLACK PEPPER

2 BEEF RIB RACKS, ABOUT 5 POUNDS

FOR THE SAUCE:

1 1/2 CUPS BARBECUE SAUCE

1 CUP CABERNET SAUVIGNON

KOSHER SALT

FRESHLY GROUND PEPPER

To make the rub: In a small bowl combine the rub ingredients.

Trim the ribs of any excess fat. Press the rub into the meat, cover with plastic wrap, and refrigerate for 8 to 12 hours.

Allow the ribs to stand at room temperature for 20 to 30 minutes before grilling. Sear over *Direct Medium* heat until evenly browned, about 10 minutes, turning once halfway through searing time. Transfer to a heavy-gauge aluminum pan large enough to hold the ribs in one layer. If necessary, cut the ribs into smaller sections.

To make the sauce: In a medium saucepan whisk together the sauce ingredients. Bring to a boil over high heat. Pour the sauce over the ribs and tightly cover with aluminum foil.

Grill the ribs over *Indirect Medium* heat until very tender, 1 1/2 to 2 hours, turning once halfway through grilling time.

Remove the ribs from the pan and cut into one- or two-rib pieces. Skim off any fat from the sauce and season with salt and pepper. Serve the ribs hot with the sauce on the side.

MAKES 4 SERVINGS

SEARED ON THE GRILL, THEN SIMMERED IN A RICH WINE-BASED BARBECUE SAUCE, THESE RIBS ARE DESTINED TO BECOME A FAMILY FAVORITE.

Beef Ribs with Cabernet Sauce

SPECIAL TECHNIQUE
BUTTERFLYING BEEF SHORT RIBS

Here's one that's well worth the effort. By unfolding the ribs, you expose a lot more surface to the marinade and the grill. Ask your butcher to cut the short ribs crosswise into 2-inch lengths.

MAKE THE FIRST CUT

Cut the rib from the rack and place it on a cutting board, with the bone on the bottom and the meaty section on the top. Using a small, sharp knife and moving from right to left, make a horizontal cut just above the bone. Continue the cut across the top of the bone, but stop just before you reach the left side of the rib to keep the meat attached to the bone.

MAKE THE SECOND CUT

Unfold the meat so that you have the bone section on the right and the meaty section on the left. Once again, moving from right to left, make a second horizontal cut two-thirds of the way down the meaty section. Cut almost to the left edge, but stop before cutting all the way through. Unfold the meat.

MAKE THE THIRD CUT

Make a third and final cut horizontally through the last meaty section, again cutting almost through but stopping before the end. Unfold the meat. You should end up with a thin strip of meat 4 to 5 inches long and 2 inches wide with the bone attached at the right end.

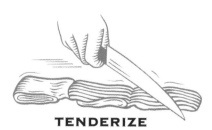

TENDERIZE

To tenderize the meat, use the back of a heavy knife and pound firmly all over the surface of the meat on the diagonal. Then, alter the direction of the diagonal and repeat.

KOREAN
SHORT RIBS

This popular restaurant dish can be served as an appetizer or main course. These are spectacular—with a salty-sweet crust. Don't overlook the meat around the bone; it's the best part.

DIRECT/HIGH

3 POUNDS SHORT RIBS, CUT INTO 2-INCH LENGTHS

FOR THE MARINADE:
- **1/3 CUP SOY SAUCE**
- **3 TABLESPOONS LIGHT BROWN SUGAR**
- **2 TABLESPOONS RICE VINEGAR**
- **2 GREEN ONIONS, MINCED**
- **2 TEASPOONS MINCED GARLIC**
- **2 TEASPOONS ASIAN SESAME OIL**
- **2 TEASPOONS GRATED FRESH GINGER**
- **1/2 TEASPOON TABASCO SAUCE**
- **1/2 TEASPOON FRESHLY GROUND BLACK PEPPER**
- **1/2 TEASPOON KOSHER SALT**

Butterfly the beef short ribs *(see sidebar, left)* and trim off any excess fat.

To make the marinade: In a medium bowl whisk together the marinade ingredients.

Place the ribs in a large, resealable plastic bag and pour in the marinade. Press the air out of the bag and seal tightly. Turn the bag to distribute the marinade, place in a bowl, and refrigerate for 8 to 12 hours, turning occasionally.

Remove the ribs from the bag and discard the marinade. Pat the ribs dry with paper towels. Allow to stand at room temperature for 10 to 15 minutes before grilling.

Grill the ribs, unfolded in strips, over *Direct High* heat until the meat is nicely browned, 5 to 7 minutes, turning once halfway through grilling time. Remove from the grill and serve immediately.

MAKES 4 SERVINGS

TOO-GOOD-TO-BE-TRUE
SLOPPY JOES

If the Sloppy Joes you grew up with were ground beef mixed with a sauce from a packet or a can, this homemade recipe will right a wrong. Kids scarf 'em down and grown-ups get the sandwich they've always deserved. For the absolute best flavor, make the meat a day ahead and gently reheat. Top with lettuce, onion, or dill pickles.

SEAR: MEDIUM, COOK: INDIRECT/MEDIUM

FOR THE RUB:

1 TABLESPOON PAPRIKA

1 TABLESPOON LIGHT BROWN SUGAR

2 TEASPOONS GRANULATED GARLIC

2 TEASPOONS COARSELY GROUND BLACK PEPPER

2 TEASPOONS KOSHER SALT

1 TEASPOON CHILI POWDER

1 BONELESS BEEF CHUCK ROAST, ABOUT 3 POUNDS
EXTRA-VIRGIN OLIVE OIL

FOR THE SAUCE:

2 TABLESPOONS EXTRA-VIRGIN OLIVE OIL

1 CUP FINELY DICED RED ONION

1 CUP FINELY DICED RED BELL PEPPER

2 TEASPOONS MINCED GARLIC

1 TABLESPOON ALL-PURPOSE FLOUR

1 TABLESPOON CHILI POWDER

1 CAN (14$1/2$ OUNCES) BEEF BROTH

1 CAN (14$1/2$ OUNCES) DICED TOMATOES
WITH JUICE

$1/2$ CUP BARBECUE SAUCE

KOSHER SALT
FRESHLY GROUND BLACK PEPPER

8 TO 10 HAMBURGER BUNS

To make the rub: In a small bowl combine the rub ingredients.

Press the rub into the roast and allow to stand at room temperature for 20 to 30 minutes before grilling.

Lightly brush or spray the roast with olive oil. Sear over *Direct Medium* heat for 15 minutes, turning once halfway through searing time. Continue grilling over *Indirect Medium* heat until the internal temperature reaches 160°F, 1 to 1$1/2$ hours. Remove from the grill and allow to rest for 15 to 20 minutes.

To make the sauce: In a large heavy saucepan over medium-high heat, warm the oil. Add the onion and bell pepper and cook, stirring occasionally, until the onion is soft and lightly browned, 8 to 10 minutes. Add the garlic and cook for 1 minute more, stirring occasionally. Sprinkle in the flour and chili powder and stir to distribute evenly. Add the beef broth and bring to a boil over high heat, whisking occasionally. Add the tomatoes and barbecue sauce. Stir to combine. Lower the

heat and simmer, stirring occasionally, until the mixture is the consistency of gravy, about 30 minutes.

Using a sharp knife, chop the meat into $1/4$-inch pieces or matchstick-sized strips. Add to the sauce and simmer for 10 to 15 minutes to allow the flavors to fully incorporate. Season with salt and pepper. If the sauce seems too thick, thin with $1/4$ cup water.

Grill the buns over *Direct Medium* heat until lightly toasted, about 30 seconds. Spoon the beef mixture onto the buns and serve immediately.

MAKES 8 TO 10 SERVINGS

"My mother's menu consisted of two choices: Take it or leave it."

— BUDDY HACKETT

PRIME RIB ON THE GRILL

Ah, succulent, rosy prime rib! Many fine restaurants have built their entire reputation—and patronage—on it. For many beef lovers it's the top pick for a special occasion. If you've never tried it at home, you'll be glad to know that this fab feast is much easier to prepare than you might think. And grilling is the best way to prepare an excellent prime rib roast. A few pointers to get you there:

KNOW THE CODE. First, you need to know what you're shopping for. (Actually, selecting the roast is the hardest part.) The term "prime rib" is somewhat misleading because very few rib roasts are actually of **Prime** grade, and those that are usually are allocated to restaurants, hotels, and specialty butchers. Don't worry, though, because this cut is still quite tender and delicious in the **Choice** grade. (Avoid rib roasts graded "Good.") Still, many stores label the meat "prime rib" rather than by its true name, **beef rib roast**, probably because that's the roast name shoppers are thinking of when they're in the market for one. With the bones attached, the cut's true name is **standing rib roast** and it comes in different sizes: 3-, 5-, and 7-bone. The boneless version is usually called simply a **boneless rib roast**. To confuse you even more, you'll sometimes see labels that say "Choice prime rib." Say what?

Just how did this confusion start? The term "prime rib" was actually first used by a restaurateur who served rib roast on his menu but wanted his patrons to know the grade of the meat he featured. Evidently quite proud of his purveying skills, this chef was also a consummate marketer. The name caught on and now, unless you're sure it's prime, you could just be paying for the dish, not necessarily the grade in the name.

So, now that you know you're really looking for a **Choice standing rib roast** (or **Choice rib roast**), where do you find it? If you've got a good butcher in town, start there. You might pay a premium, but it's the kind of cut that justifies a splurge. If you're on a budget, you can actually fare quite well at a warehouse club or your supermarket. Look for rich red meat and creamy white fat. Yellow or grayish fat indicates a cut past its prime (pardon the pun) or that may not have been handled properly. *Properly* aged beef, on the other hand, is more tender and better tasting than "fresh" beef. But don't worry about sorting through another label mystery. Aged beef is clearly labeled and is easily distinguished by its higher price.

Another important thing to check out is the way the roast has been trimmed. Many butchers pride themselves in shaving the fat off the meat, which allows any rub or seasoning to directly contact the meat. But leaving the "fat cap"—that is, a rind of creamy fat about $1/2$ inch thick—on the top of the roast is also quite nice. That fat cap serves two purposes: to flavor the meat as it cooks and to make a nice pocket for seasonings. See the sidebar on page 129 to learn how to prepare a roast with a fat cap. The prime rib recipes in this chapter are for closely trimmed roasts.

NOW, JUST GRILL IT. For a gas grill, place the roast on a roasting rack set inside a heavy-gauge drip pan and set the pan over Indirect Medium heat. For a charcoal grill, place a drip pan between the coals and center the roast on the cooking grate above the pan. Add some water to the drip pan to keep the drippings from burning.

Grill the meat to 135°F at the roast's center (an accurate instant-read thermometer is a must here—even better is one with a probe you can leave in the meat so you don't overcook your investment). Remove the roast from the grill, remove any strings, and loosely cover the roast with foil to rest for about 30 minutes. During resting, the roast's internal temperature will continue to rise 5°F to 10°F (to 145°F, the USDA's definition of medium-rare beef) and the juices will redistribute themselves evenly throughout. It's impossible to cook a large rib roast to one doneness—the ends will be more fully cooked than the center—but when you're feeding a crowd it's nice to have a range of offerings.

Note: Some folks feel the USDA's assessment of 145°F for medium-rare prime rib is too high; if you're in this camp, you may opt to remove the roast at 130°F.

MEANWHILE, MAKE THE AU JUS. Au jus is a thin sauce made from the natural juices of a beef roast. One cup of au jus is enough for six to eight servings. First, skim the fat off the pan drippings. Heat the drip pan on the grill or stovetop and add enough beef broth (or equal amounts of beef broth and red wine) to make an adequate amount of au jus once reduced. Simmer the liquid until reduced by up to one half, carefully scraping the browned bits off the bottom of the pan. Remove any remaining fat from the surface with a ladle or absorbent paper towel. Season with salt and pepper to taste. Strain the au jus, if desired.

CARVE IT UP. This is where you'll be glad: 1.) you own an electric knife, and 2.) you cut the bones off. If the bones are detached, carefully slide them out from underneath the roast, cut them into individual ribs, and add to the serving platter or reserve for some of the best beef stock you'll ever make. If the ribs are still attached, slice the roast into $1/2$- to 1-inch slabs, making an additional cut to free the slice from where it is attached to the ribs. Serve the meat from the carving board or place it on a platter and drizzle with some au jus. Pass the remaining au jus with the meat.

PREPARING A RIB ROAST

Since it's best not to freeze a rib roast and because it takes up so much refrigerator space, you probably don't want to buy yours more than a day or two ahead of time. Refrigerate it until you're ready to prepare it, then take it out of the wrapping and, if the roast is tied, untie it. Then proceed:

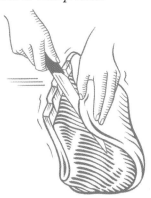

SLICE THE FAT CAP

With a long, sharp knife, carefully slice along the fat cap where the fat meets the meat. Starting on one long side, cut across the top of the roast, following the curve, but don't cut all the way through at the other long side. Leave the cap attached by a nice hinge. Your goal is to create a flap under which you can place a handful or two of seasonings. If you have a boneless roast, skip the next step.

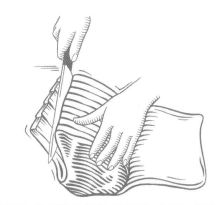

SLICE ACROSS THE RIB BONES

Next, for a bone-in roast, lay the roast on its backbone side and very carefully slice across the top of the rib bones along the length of the roast. You can cut the bones all the way off or leave them attached by a hinge. If you cut them off, reserve the bones. Cutting the bones off partially or completely isn't necessary, but it does make carving easier.

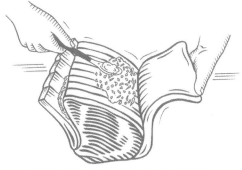

SEASON THE ROAST

Slather a generous layer of minced garlic, an herb-garlic blend, or your favorite seasonings between the bones and the meat and under the fat cap. Spread a handful or two (depending on the roast's size) of coarsely chopped onions in each cavity as well. Season the meat all over the outside with kosher salt, freshly ground black pepper, and any other seasonings. (If you're using a recipe with a rub, simply distribute the rub as described above, but consider adding in the onions and garlic, too.)

TIE THE ROAST

Lay the roast bone side down (or the reserved slab of rib bones) across three to five parallel 2-foot lengths of cotton string. If you cut the rib bones off, lay the roast back on top of them. Pull the strings up over the roast and tie them tightly at the top of the roast, being sure to keep the seasonings tucked under the fat cap. Refrigerate the roast until 30 minutes before you are ready to grill; allow it to stand at room temperature during that half hour.

Serving: A seven-bone roast will make 12 to 15 servings when carved into slices 3/4 to 1 inch thick. Carved into $1/2$-inch-thick slices, it will make 20 to 24 servings.

Garlic and Herb–Crusted Slow–Smoked Prime Rib

GARLIC AND HERB-CRUSTED
SLOW-SMOKED PRIME RIB

This prized melt-in-your-mouth cut gets extra flavor from smoldering hickory and grilled fresh herbs. Great for a buffet or a fancy sit-down dinner.

INDIRECT/LOW

FOR THE PASTE:

- 1/4 CUP CHOPPED FRESH BASIL
- 1/4 CUP CHOPPED FRESH OREGANO
- 1/4 CUP CHOPPED FRESH PARSLEY
- 1/4 CUP CHOPPED FRESH ROSEMARY
- 3 TABLESPOONS EXTRA-VIRGIN OLIVE OIL
- 1 TABLESPOON FRESHLY GROUND BLACK PEPPER
- 1 TABLESPOON KOSHER SALT

- 1 SEVEN-BONE PRIME RIB ROAST, 12 TO 14 POUNDS
- 1/4 CUP FINELY CHOPPED GARLIC

HICKORY WOOD CHIPS *OR* CHUNKS SOAKED IN WATER FOR AT LEAST **30 MINUTES**

To make the paste: In a small bowl combine the paste ingredients and mix well.

Trim the roast of any excess fat. Press the chopped garlic into the top and sides of the roast. Spread the paste over the top and sides of the roast, then wrap with a layer of cheesecloth to hold the paste to the meat surface. Allow to stand at room temperature for 30 to 40 minutes before grilling.

Follow the grill's instructions for using wood chips. Grill the roast over *Indirect Low* heat until the internal temperature reaches 135°F for medium rare, 3 1/2 to 4 hours. Keep the grill's temperature between 275°F and 300°F, replenishing smoking chips as needed.

Remove the roast from the grill, loosely cover with aluminum foil, and allow to rest for 20 to 30 minutes. The internal temperature will rise 5°F to 10°F during this time.

Carefully remove the cheesecloth before carving. Using a sharp knife, remove the bones from the roast and cut the meat into 3/4-inch slices. Serve warm.

MAKES ABOUT 12 TO 15 SERVINGS

MUSTARD PRIME RIB
WITH HORSERADISH CREAM

Prepare prime rib on the grill and you'll impress even the most spoiled taste buds. Try it with this peppery horseradish cream, which sustains mouth-watering anticipation to the very last morsel.

INDIRECT/MEDIUM

FOR THE PASTE:

- 2 TABLESPOONS BLACK PEPPERCORNS
- 2 TABLESPOONS MUSTARD SEEDS
- 1/2 CUP COUNTRY-STYLE WHOLE GRAIN MUSTARD
- 2 TABLESPOONS WORCESTERSHIRE SAUCE
- 2 TABLESPOONS FRESH CHOPPED ROSEMARY

- 1 SEVEN-BONE PRIME RIB ROAST, 12 TO 14 POUNDS

FOR THE HORSERADISH CREAM:

- 1 CUP SOUR CREAM
- 2 TABLESPOONS PREPARED HORSERADISH
- 1 TABLESPOON DRIED GREEN PEPPERCORNS, CRUSHED
- 1 TABLESPOON WORCESTERSHIRE SAUCE

- 2 TABLESPOONS KOSHER SALT

To make the paste: Using a spice grinder or mortar and pestle, crush the peppercorns and mustard seeds. Transfer to a small bowl and combine with the remaining paste ingredients. Mix well.

Spread the paste evenly over the roast, cover with plastic wrap, and refrigerate for 12 to 24 hours.

To make the horseradish cream: In a small bowl whisk together the horseradish cream ingredients. Refrigerate until ready to serve.

Allow the roast to stand at room temperature for 30 to 40 minutes before grilling. Season with the salt and grill over *Indirect Medium* heat, keeping the grill's temperature between 350°F and 375°F, until the internal temperature reaches 135°F for medium rare, about 2 to 2 1/2 hours.

Remove the roast from the grill, loosely cover with aluminum foil, and allow to rest for 20 to 30 minutes before slicing. The internal temperature will rise 5°F to 10°F during this time.

Using a sharp knife, remove the bones from the roast and cut the meat into 3/4-inch slices. Serve warm with the horseradish cream sauce on the side.

MAKES ABOUT 12 TO 15 SERVINGS

KANSAS CITY
BONELESS RIB ROAST

Since the cattle-drive days of the 1800s, Kansas City has been famous for dry-aged and marbled meats. This juicy and full-flavored roast will take you back to those days of thick, hearty cuts and leisurely dining. Go for the gusto and buy the best grade you can find, preferably prime.

INDIRECT/MEDIUM

FOR THE RUB:

2 TABLESPOONS BLACK PEPPERCORNS

1 TABLESPOON MUSTARD SEEDS

3 TABLESPOONS PAPRIKA

2 TABLESPOONS LIGHT BROWN SUGAR

2 TABLESPOONS KOSHER SALT

1 TABLESPOON GRANULATED GARLIC

1 TEASPOON CAYENNE

1 BONELESS RIB ROAST, 10 TO 12 POUNDS

1/4 CUP WORCESTERSHIRE SAUCE

To make the rub: Using a spice grinder or mortar and pestle, crush the black peppercorns and mustard seeds. Transfer to a small bowl and blend with the remaining rub ingredients.

Trim the roast of any excess fat. Brush the meat with the Worcestershire sauce and coat evenly with the rub. Cover with plastic wrap and refrigerate for 8 to 12 hours.

Allow the roast to stand at room temperature for 30 to 40 minutes before grilling. Grill the roast over *Indirect Medium* heat, keeping the grill's temperature between 350°F and 375°F, until the internal temperature reaches 135°F for medium rare, about 2 hours.

Remove the roast from the grill, loosely cover with aluminum foil, and allow to rest for 20 to 30 minutes. The internal temperature will rise 5°F to 10°F during this time. Cut into 1/2-inch slices. Serve warm.

MAKES 20 TO 24 SERVINGS

HICKORY-SMOKED
BONELESS RIB ROAST

First, we expose this refined boneless cut to lots of smoke for great hickory flavor. Then, we glaze it with mustard and wrap it in bread crumbs for a truly tempting dinner.

INDIRECT/MEDIUM

FOR THE BREAD CRUMBS:

2 SLICES FIRM, WHITE COUNTRY-STYLE BREAD

2 TABLESPOONS FINELY CHOPPED FRESH ITALIAN PARSLEY

1/2 TEASPOON KOSHER SALT

1/8 TEASPOON CAYENNE

2 TABLESPOONS EXTRA-VIRGIN OLIVE OIL

1 BONELESS RIB ROAST, ABOUT 5 1/2 POUNDS

1 TABLESPOON KOSHER SALT

1 TEASPOON FRESHLY GROUND BLACK PEPPER

3 TABLESPOONS DIJON MUSTARD

HICKORY CHIPS OR CHUNKS SOAKED IN WATER FOR AT LEAST 30 MINUTES

To make the bread crumbs: Tear the bread into 1-inch pieces and place in a food processor. Process into fine soft crumbs and transfer to a medium bowl. Add the parsley, salt, and cayenne; toss to blend. Drizzle with the olive oil and blend with your fingertips.

Cut and remove any string or mesh wrapping. Allow the roast to stand at room temperature for 30 to 40 minutes before grilling. Trim the roast of any excess fat and wipe with a dampened paper towel. In a small bowl mix the salt and pepper and rub into the roast.

Follow the grill's instructions for using wood chips. Grill the roast over *Indirect Medium* heat, keeping the grill's temperature between 350°F and 375°F, for about 1 hour.

Remove the roast from the grill. Spread the mustard over the top of the roast and sprinkle on the bread crumbs, pressing them into the meat. Return the roast to the grill and continue grilling over *Indirect Medium* heat until the crumbs are browned and the internal temperature reaches 135°F for medium rare, 15 to 30 minutes.

Remove the roast from the grill, loosely cover with aluminum foil, and allow to rest for 10 minutes. The internal temperature will rise 5°F to 10°F during this time. Carve the roast into 1/2-inch slices, reserving the juices. Arrange the meat on a platter; reheat the juices and pour over the meat. Serve warm.

MAKES 10 TO 12 SERVINGS

Let's face it, grilled beef is generous—it gladly rewards you for any attention you pay it. And yet without even knowing it, we sometimes fail to treat it right. If you've ever pulled a roast from the fridge and thrown it on the grill in a beef-craving frenzy, you've short-changed yourself. Same goes for a close encounter with the salt shaker at the wrong time. Here are a few things you need to know to coax out that delicious, rich flavor.

Provide plenty of beauty rest. One of the best things you can do for beef is give it a rest at room temperature before and after grilling. There are many reasons why. First, placing an ice-cold piece of meat on the grill quickly reduces the temperature of the cooking grate surface, thus minimizing the great searing benefit of caramelization (when sugars in the food are cooked quickly on the surface, creating an appealing texture and taste).

Second, a large piece of meat that has been properly refrigerated will be very cold in the middle, where fats and juices will "gel up" or thicken. Trust us, you'd rather have those precious resources flowing evenly throughout the meat, bringing flavor to every bite.

Third, allowing the temperature to even out means you won't end up with a cut that's too rare in the middle and overcooked on the outside. This is especially important for roasts and other thick cuts on the grill, where the outside can dry out "waiting" for the middle to reach the desired temperature. Thinner cuts are an exception, as is "black and blue" steak, where the outside is seared and the middle is still rare and chilled.

Fourth, because cold constricts beef fibers into a tougher texture, you'll get more tender results grilling a warmed up and "relaxed" cut. Who wants beef that's all "verklemmt"?

Finally, for maximum flavor and juiciness, allow grilled beef to rest after you remove it from the grill. Sometimes this is critical to reach a proper doneness temperature, especially on large roasts where "carryover cooking" occurs (the internal temperature continues to rise without risk of the meat drying out). In this case you remove the meat just before the desired temperature is achieved, and cover it with foil for several minutes. But in all cuts, especially steaks, resting allows those delicious juices that were driven by heat to the meat's surface to ease back into the center, where you can enjoy them bite by bite.

Be accurate. "Room temperature" means 65°F to 70°F, so if your house is warmer, shorten the resting time accordingly. And never, ever leave meat in the sun or near a heat source (such as your grill), which can encourage the growth of harmful bacteria. An indoor countertop away from windows, stoves, and heaters is ideal. And heed the resting times suggested in the recipes. Too much of a warm-up before grilling can cause your meat to "bleed out" on the plate or lose juices too quickly when it hits the hot grill, leaving you with dry disappointment.

Obviously, the smaller the cut, the less time it takes to bring the meat's temperature down from its icebox state. The resting times in our recipes are based on true room temperature, so follow them accordingly. Steaks don't need much of a warm-up, especially since they're relatively thin and their size allows you to easily place them on a new hot section of the cooking grate every time you move or turn them for grill marks or cooking (see sidebar, page 107). Super-thin cutlets such as paillards should go straight from the fridge to the grill. But give that big roast enough time to even out its temperature, usually 20 to 30 minutes.

Finally, know when to salt. It's best to salt beef just a few minutes before grilling. That's enough time for the salt to penetrate the meat a little, so the inside gets seasoned a bit as well as the outside. If you salt beef before refrigerating it, the salt absorbs moisture from the refrigerator and the "wet" meat tends to "steam" rather than "sear" to a nicely brown crust. Also, the salt draws some of the moisture out of the meat, which makes it drier overall. So, you could say the best way to achieve grilled beef perfection is to give it a rest and save your moves with the salt for the right moment. Now you know.

EXTREME GRILLING

When it comes to beef, there's nothing like prime rib grilled over a smoky hickory fire. If you've never tried it, you'll be glad to know it's really quite easy. It just seems there's a lot at stake when expectations are high. Consider the time our friend Mike had the future of Weber grills riding on a very important prime rib dinner—and Mother Nature pulled a fast one.

Back in the mid-1970s Weber set out to achieve national distribution. We had a strong foothold in the Midwest, thanks in part to our relationship with Sears. But we had yet to convince Sears that they could sell our grills just as well in the South, East, and West.

One day I learned all Sears' regional vice presidents were coming to Chicago, Weber's hometown, for a January meeting. I volunteered to grill them a special dinner of aged prime rib roast beef. A lowly grill peddler cooking for their top brass was a brash proposal, but I knew if I could wow them with a grilled dinner, I could convince them to carry our grills in their stores across the nation. It took a little persistence, but they agreed to let us entertain them at the Lake Point Towers on the shores of Lake Michigan in mid-January.

Once the rush of my initial success wore off, I began to worry. Chicago's cold in January! We decided to set up on the rooftop of the towers just outside the dining room, where floor-to-ceiling windows provided a panoramic view of the Chicago skyline... including the newly erected Sears Tower. The perfect vantage point for them to watch us grilling dinner on Weber charcoal kettles.

The executive chef, an enthusiastic griller and proud Weber grill owner, helped me with the menu: a hickory-smoked shrimp appetizer followed by a grilled lobster salad, then the prime rib, stuffed with garlic and walnuts and crowned with a garlicky horseradish aïoli. It was ambitious, but I was confident that Mother Nature would provide a crisp, clear windless night.

She sent a major storm instead. Freezing rain, then 10 inches of blowing snow.

The next morning, when the temperature dropped below zero and the wind howled down Lake Michigan, I took my grilling team to a local ski shop to load up on expedition-grade parkas rated to -50°F. We loaded up our vans and made the slippery drive in horrible conditions. On the roof we were nearly blown over by the wind gusts. Bundled like mountaineers, we shoveled, de-iced, and set our grills as close as we could to the restaurant's windows. The temperature continued to drop.

In good conditions, a whole prime rib roast will take 2 to 4 hours to cook, so I added another hour to the cooking time. The wind actually helped start the charcoal and keep it blazing. When we placed two beautiful prime rib roasts on our largest kettle grills at 3:00 P.M., the chef told us the temperature had dropped to -10°F, with a wind-chill of -30°F.

Promptly at 6:00 P.M. the VPs and their staff arrived in their pristine dark suits, starched white shirts, red ties, and—despite the weather—not a windblown lock of hair. They were greeted by the sight of six crazy masked men in parkas and chef aprons grilling shrimp and lobsters in a cloud of steam and smoke driven by a fierce wind against the lights of Chicago's frigid skyline. They were stunned, to say the least, but at least they had their conversation starter.

The smoked shrimp was a hit, and the group marveled at the grilled lobster salad. I checked the prime rib at 7:00 P.M. My meat thermometer registered 135°F. After resting, the roasts would come up to a perfect medium-rare temperature. At the same time the air temperature was -15°F and the wind-chill at ground level was -40°F.

The VPs left their tables and gathered at the window as we lifted the roasts off the grills and carried them into the room on cutting boards. I'm sure they will never forget the image of our grill team in expedition clothing and grilling aprons as we triumphantly placed the steaming prime rib roasts on silver carving carts.

Needless to say, dinner was a success and Sears started offering our grills in all their sales territories the next spring. I still have my expedition parka rated to -50°F. This past winter I dusted it off and cooked a dinner of roasted duck for some friends during an outrageous winter storm. Like the Sears brass, they gathered at my patio door and watched me add charcoal to the fire as the wind blew sparks sideways. I couldn't help but remember that night so many years ago and the fact that a Weber grill has never let me down, no matter what the weather.

WALNUT AND GARLIC STUFFED
PRIME RIB

For an impressive presentation, slice between the embedded walnut and garlic halves, leaving them as little gems seated in the "eye" of the roast.

INDIRECT/MEDIUM

FOR THE RUB:
- 1 TABLESPOON GRANULATED GARLIC
- 1 TABLESPOON KOSHER SALT
- 2 TEASPOONS DRY MUSTARD
- 2 TEASPOONS CHILI POWDER
- 1 TEASPOON PAPRIKA
- 1 TEASPOON GROUND CUMIN
- 1 TEASPOON GROUND CORIANDER

- 1 SEVEN-BONE PRIME RIB ROAST, 12 TO 14 POUNDS
- 20 WALNUT HALVES
- 20 GARLIC CLOVE HALVES

FOR THE AÏOLI:
- 4 MEDIUM GARLIC CLOVES
- 1 CUP TIGHTLY PACKED FRESH ITALIAN PARSLEY LEAVES
- 1 1/2 CUPS MAYONNAISE
- 2 TABLESPOONS WHITE WINE VINEGAR
- 2 TEASPOONS PREPARED HORSERADISH

To make the rub: In a small bowl mix the rub ingredients.

Trim the roast of any excess fat. Using a thin, sharp knife, make 20 cuts evenly spaced across the length of the roast, each 2 to 3 inches deep into the thickest part. Using your forefinger, stuff a walnut half into each cut. Follow with a garlic clove half. Spread the rub over the top and sides of the roast. Allow to stand at room temperature for 30 to 40 minutes before grilling.

Grill the roast over *Indirect Medium* heat, keeping the grill's temperature between 350°F and 375°F, until the internal temperature reaches 135°F for medium-rare, about 2 to 2 1/2 hours. Remove from the grill, loosely cover with aluminum foil, and allow to rest for 20 to 30 minutes. The internal temperature will rise 5°F to 10°F during this time.

Meanwhile, make the aïoli: In a food processor finely chop the garlic cloves. Add the remaining aïoli ingredients and process until smooth. Cover and refrigerate until ready to serve.

Using a sharp knife, remove the bones from the roast and cut the meat into 3/4- to 1-inch slices. Serve warm with the aïoli.

MAKES ABOUT 20 SERVINGS

Stuffed Herbed Tenderloin

STUFFED HERBED
TENDERLOIN

For this one, get out the white tablecloth and candlesticks.

SEAR: MEDIUM, COOK: INDIRECT/MEDIUM

FOR THE STUFFING:

- 1 TABLESPOON UNSALTED BUTTER, DIVIDED
- 1 1/2 TEASPOONS EXTRA-VIRGIN OLIVE OIL
- 1 LARGE LEEK (WHITE PART ONLY), THINLY SLICED
- 1/2 POUND BUTTON MUSHROOMS, THINLY SLICED
- 1 1/2 TEASPOONS MINCED GARLIC
- 1 1/2 TEASPOONS FINELY CHOPPED FRESH THYME
- 1/2 TEASPOON FINELY CHOPPED FRESH ROSEMARY
- 1 TABLESPOON DRY WHITE WINE
- 1/4 TEASPOON KOSHER SALT
- 1/4 TEASPOON FRESHLY GROUND BLACK PEPPER

FOR THE PASTE:

- 2 TABLESPOONS FINELY CHOPPED FRESH THYME
- 2 TABLESPOONS FINELY CHOPPED FRESH ROSEMARY
- 2 TABLESPOONS MINCED SHALLOTS
- 2 TABLESPOONS DIJON MUSTARD
- 2 TABLESPOONS EXTRA-VIRGIN OLIVE OIL
- 1 TABLESPOON FINELY CHOPPED FRESH SAGE
- 1 TABLESPOON MINCED GARLIC

- 1 CENTER-CUT BEEF TENDERLOIN, 2 1/2 TO 3 POUNDS
  KOSHER SALT
  FRESHLY GROUND BLACK PEPPER

To make the stuffing: In a large sauté pan over medium heat, melt 1/2 tablespoon of the butter with the olive oil. Add the leek and cook, stirring occasionally, until soft but not brown, 6 to 8 minutes. Raise the heat to medium-high. Add the remaining 1/2 tablespoon of butter, mushrooms, garlic, thyme, and rosemary. Cook, stirring occasionally, until the mushrooms are tender, 4 to 6 minutes. Add the wine, salt, and pepper. Cook for 1 minute, scraping off any bits clinging to the pan. Remove from the heat. Allow to cool.

To make the paste: In a small bowl mix the paste ingredients.

Trim the tenderloin of any excess fat and silver skin. Cut a large pocket along one side to within 1/2 inch of each end and the opposite side. Fill the pocket with the stuffing and close with toothpicks. Coat the tenderloin with the paste, cover with plastic wrap, and refrigerate for 6 to 8 hours.

Allow the tenderloin to stand at room temperature for 20 to 30 minutes before grilling. Season with salt and pepper. Sear over *Direct Medium* heat until well marked, about 20 minutes, turning a quarter turn every 5 minutes. Continue grilling over *Indirect Medium* heat until the internal temperature reaches 135°F for medium rare, 10 to 15 minutes. Remove from the grill and allow to rest for 5 to 10 minutes. The temperature will rise 5°F to 10°F during this time. Cut into 3/4- to 1-inch slices and serve warm.

MAKES 6 SERVINGS

BOURBON-GLAZED CAJUN
TENDERLOIN

A blend of smooth bourbon and sweet molasses is crossed with a fiery Cajun rub. A match made in New Orleans.

SEAR: MEDIUM, COOK: INDIRECT/MEDIUM

FOR THE MARINADE:

- 1/4 CUP WORCESTERSHIRE SAUCE
- 2 TABLESPOONS MOLASSES
- 2 TABLESPOONS DIJON MUSTARD

- 1 CENTER-CUT BEEF TENDERLOIN, 2 1/2 TO 3 POUNDS

FOR THE RUB:

- 1 TABLESPOON CRACKED BLACK PEPPER
- 1 TABLESPOON GRANULATED GARLIC
- 1 TABLESPOON PAPRIKA
- 2 TEASPOONS KOSHER SALT
- 1/2 TEASPOON CAYENNE

FOR THE GLAZE:

- 1/4 CUP BOURBON
- 1/4 CUP DIJON MUSTARD
- 1/4 CUP FIRMLY PACKED LIGHT BROWN SUGAR

  EXTRA-VIRGIN OLIVE OIL

To make the marinade: In a small bowl whisk together the marinade ingredients.

Trim the tenderloin of any excess fat and silver skin. Place the tenderloin in a large, resealable plastic bag and pour in the marinade. Press the air out of the bag and seal tightly. Turn the bag to distribute the marinade, place on a plate, and refrigerate for 8 to 24 hours.

To make the rub: In a small bowl combine the rub ingredients.

To make the glaze: In a small bowl whisk together the glaze ingredients until the sugar is dissolved.

Remove the tenderloin from the bag and discard the marinade. Wipe excess marinade off the tenderloin with paper towels. Press the rub into the tenderloin and allow to stand at room temperature for 20 to 30 minutes before grilling.

Lightly brush or spray the tenderloin with olive oil. Sear over *Direct Medium* heat until well marked, about 20 minutes, turning a quarter turn every 5 minutes. Continue grilling over *Indirect Medium* heat until the internal temperature reaches 135°F for medium rare, 10 to 20 minutes. During the last 10 minutes of grilling time, turn and baste with the glaze.

Remove the tenderloin from the grill and allow to rest for 5 to 10 minutes. The temperature will rise 5°F to 10°F during this time. Cut into 3/4- to 1-inch slices and serve warm.

MAKES 6 TO 8 SERVINGS

GRILLED BEEF TENDERLOIN
WITH HOISIN-PLUM MOP

A fruity and fulfilling complement to a favorite roast.

SEAR: MEDIUM, COOK: INDIRECT/MEDIUM

FOR THE MARINADE:
- 1/4 CUP FRESH ORANGE JUICE
- 2 TABLESPOONS SOY SAUCE
- 1 TABLESPOON ASIAN SESAME OIL
- 1 TABLESPOON FRESHLY GRATED ORANGE ZEST
- 1 TABLESPOON GRATED FRESH GINGER
- 2 TEASPOONS MINCED SERRANO CHILES, WITH SEEDS
- 2 TEASPOONS MINCED GARLIC

- 1 BEEF TENDERLOIN, 3 1/2 TO 4 POUNDS

FOR THE MOP:
- 4 PLUMS, PITTED AND QUARTERED
- 1 CUP PINEAPPLE JUICE
- 1/4 CUP HOISIN SAUCE
- 1/4 CUP DRY SHERRY
- 1/4 CUP FIRMLY PACKED DARK BROWN SUGAR
- 2 TABLESPOONS RED WINE VINEGAR
- 2 TABLESPOONS SOY SAUCE
- 1 TEASPOON MUSTARD POWDER

  ASIAN SESAME OIL
  KOSHER SALT

To make the marinade: In a medium bowl whisk together the marinade ingredients.

Trim the tenderloin of any excess fat and silver skin. Place the tenderloin in a large, resealable plastic bag and pour in the marinade. Press the air out of the bag and seal tightly. Turn the bag to distribute the marinade, set on a plate, and refrigerate for 8 to 24 hours.

To make the mop: In a medium heavy-bottomed saucepan combine the mop ingredients. Bring to a boil over high heat, stir, and reduce heat to a simmer. Cook, stirring occasionally, until the plums are falling apart and the liquid thickens, about 45 minutes. Using a rubber spatula, press the mop through a sieve to remove the plum skins. Return the mop to the saucepan and simmer until about 1 cup of liquid is left.

Remove the tenderloin from the bag and discard the marinade. Wipe excess marinade off the tenderloin with paper towels. Allow to stand at room temperature for 20 to 30 minutes before grilling.

Brush the tenderloin with sesame oil and season with salt. Sear over *Direct Medium* heat until well marked, about 20 minutes, turning a quarter turn every 5 minutes. Continue grilling over *Indirect Medium* heat until the internal temperature reaches 135°F for medium rare, 15 to 25 minutes, turning and basting occasionally with the mop.

Remove the tenderloin from the grill and allow to rest for 5 to 10 minutes. The temperature will rise 5°F to 10°F during this time. Cut into 3/4- to 1-inch slices and serve warm.

If desired, bring the remaining mop to a boil over high heat and boil for 1 full minute, then serve as a sauce.

MAKES 8 TO 10 SERVINGS

HOLIDAY BEEF TENDERLOIN

Wrap a tender beef roast in garlic, rosemary, and pink peppercorns and you've got a dinner party. Hint: You can roast the garlic a day or two ahead of time while you are grilling something else.

INDIRECT/MEDIUM

FOR THE PASTE:
- 1 WHOLE HEAD OF GARLIC
- 3 TABLESPOONS PLUS 1 TEASPOON EXTRA-VIRGIN OLIVE OIL, DIVIDED

- 1 BEEF TENDERLOIN, 3 1/2 TO 4 POUNDS

- 3 TABLESPOONS WHOLE PINK PEPPERCORNS
- 2 TABLESPOONS CHOPPED FRESH ROSEMARY
- 2 TEASPOONS KOSHER SALT
- 1/2 TEASPOON FRESHLY GROUND BLACK PEPPER

To make the paste: Remove the loose, papery outer skin from the head of garlic. Cut about 1/2 inch off the top to expose the cloves. Place the garlic head on an 8-inch square of aluminum foil and drizzle 1 teaspoon of the olive oil over the cloves. Fold up the foil sides and seal to make a packet, leaving a little room for the expansion of steam. Grill over *Indirect Medium* heat until the cloves are soft, 30 to 45 minutes. Remove from the grill and allow to cool. Squeeze the garlic from the individual cloves into a small bowl. Add the remaining 3 tablespoons of olive oil and mash the garlic and oil together with a fork to form a paste.

Trim the tenderloin of any excess fat and silver skin. Spread the paste on the tenderloin, rubbing it into the meat.

In a small bowl combine the peppercorns, rosemary, salt, and pepper. Mix well and press into the paste on the top and sides of the tenderloin.

Allow the tenderloin to stand at room temperature for 20 to 30 minutes before grilling. Grill over *Indirect Medium* heat until the internal temperature reaches 135°F for medium rare, 30 to 40 minutes.

Remove from the grill and allow to rest for 5 to 10 minutes. The temperature will rise 5°F to 10°F during this time. Cut into 3/4- to 1-inch slices and serve warm.

MAKES 8 TO 10 SERVINGS

Holiday Beef Tenderloin

Hoisin Beef Kabobs with Tomato Salad

HOISIN BEEF KABOBS
WITH TOMATO SALAD

You might not put hoisin and tomato together in your culinary imagination, but tasting is believing here. Easy and quick.

DIRECT/MEDIUM

FOR THE MARINADE:
- 1/3 CUP HOISIN SAUCE
- 1 TABLESPOON DRY SHERRY
- 1 TABLESPOON SOY SAUCE
- 1 TEASPOON ASIAN SESAME OIL
- 1/2 TEASPOON SRIRACHA (HOT CHILI-GARLIC SAUCE)

- 1 SIRLOIN STEAK, ABOUT 1 1/2 POUNDS

FOR THE SALAD:
- 6 PLUM TOMATOES
  EXTRA-VIRGIN OLIVE OIL
- 1/2 CUP VERY THINLY SLICED WHITE ONION
- 1/4 CUP COARSELY CHOPPED FRESH CILANTRO
- 2 TEASPOONS MINCED JALAPEÑO PEPPER, WITH SEEDS
- 1/2 TEASPOON MINCED GARLIC

FOR THE DRESSING:
- 2 TABLESPOONS VEGETABLE OIL
- 1 TABLESPOON RICE VINEGAR
- 1 TEASPOON ASIAN SESAME OIL
- 1 TEASPOON SOY SAUCE
- 1/2 TEASPOON KOSHER SALT

To make the marinade: In a small bowl whisk together the marinade ingredients.

Trim the steak of any excess fat and cut into 1 1/4-inch cubes. Place the cubes in a large, resealable plastic bag and pour in the marinade. Press the air out of the bag and seal tightly. Turn the bag to distribute the marinade, place in a bowl, and refrigerate for 30 minutes to 1 hour, turning occasionally.

Remove the meat from the bag and discard the marinade. Thread the meat onto skewers. Allow to stand at room temperature for 20 to 30 minutes before grilling.

To make the salad: Lightly brush or spray the tomatoes with the olive oil. Grill over *Direct High* heat until the skins are lightly charred and starting to slip off, 5 to 8 minutes, turning once halfway through grilling time. Transfer to a cutting board and carefully remove and discard the skins. Coarsely chop the tomatoes and place in a medium bowl. Add the remaining salad ingredients and stir to combine.

To make the dressing: In a small bowl whisk together the dressing ingredients. Pour the dressing over the salad and gently mix until blended.

Generously brush or spray the beef kabobs with the olive oil and grill over *Direct Medium* heat until the meat is medium rare, 8 to 10 minutes, turning once halfway through grilling time.

Spoon some of the salad onto each plate. Slide the meat onto the salad and serve warm.

MAKES 4 SERVINGS

HANOI BEEF KABOBS

In Hanoi, street vendors offer a great variety of foods. Among them are savory grilled meats bathed in a great marinade like this one.

DIRECT/MEDIUM

FOR THE MARINADE:
- 1/4 CUP FRESH LIME JUICE
- 2 TABLESPOONS SOY SAUCE
- 2 TABLESPOONS ASIAN SESAME OIL
- 2 TABLESPOONS FINELY CHOPPED FRESH BASIL
- 2 TABLESPOONS FINELY CHOPPED FRESH CILANTRO
- 1 TABLESPOON FINELY CHOPPED FRESH MINT
- 1 TABLESPOON FISH SAUCE
- 1 TABLESPOON GRATED FRESH GINGER
- 1 TABLESPOON GRANULATED SUGAR
- 2 TEASPOONS MINCED GARLIC
- 1 TEASPOON MINCED SERRANO CHILE, WITH SEEDS

- 2 POUNDS TOP SIRLOIN STEAK

- 2 BUNCHES GREEN ONIONS (WHITE PART ONLY), CUT INTO 1 1/2-INCH PIECES

To make the marinade: In a small bowl whisk together the marinade ingredients.

Cut the sirloin into 1 1/4-inch cubes. Place the cubes in a large, resealable plastic bag and pour in the marinade. Press the air out of the bag and seal tightly. Turn the bag to distribute the marinade, place in a bowl, and refrigerate for 1 to 2 hours, turning occasionally.

Remove the meat from the bag and discard the marinade. Skewer the meat alternately with the onions, threading the onions crosswise. Allow the kabobs to stand at room temperature for 20 to 30 minutes before grilling.

Grill the kabobs over *Direct Medium* heat until the meat is medium rare, 8 to 10 minutes, turning once halfway through grilling time. Serve warm.

MAKES 6 SERVINGS

LEMON-HERB BEEF KABOBS
WITH COUSCOUS SALAD

Try something new. Tasty kabobs topping an easy salad make a quick weekday meal that everyone will like.

DIRECT/MEDIUM

FOR THE MARINADE:

- ¼ CUP EXTRA-VIRGIN OLIVE OIL
- 2 TABLESPOONS FRESH LEMON JUICE
- 2 TABLESPOONS COARSELY CHOPPED FRESH OREGANO
- 2 TABLESPOONS COARSELY CHOPPED FRESH MINT
- 2 TEASPOONS MINCED GARLIC
- 1 TEASPOON WORCESTERSHIRE SAUCE
- ¼ TEASPOON CRUSHED RED PEPPER FLAKES

- 1½ POUNDS BEEF TENDERLOIN *OR* SIRLOIN

FOR THE SALAD:

- 1½ CUPS QUICK-COOKING COUSCOUS
- ⅓ CUP RAISINS
- 2 CUPS CHICKEN BROTH
- ¼ CUP THINLY SLICED GREEN ONIONS (WHITE PART ONLY)
- 3 TABLESPOONS FINELY CHOPPED FRESH ITALIAN PARSLEY
- 2 TABLESPOONS FINELY CHOPPED FRESH MINT
- 2 TABLESPOONS EXTRA-VIRGIN OLIVE OIL
- 2 TABLESPOONS FRESH LEMON JUICE
- ½ TEASPOON KOSHER SALT
- ¼ TEASPOON FRESHLY GROUND BLACK PEPPER

- 2 MEDIUM RED BELL PEPPERS, CUT INTO 1-INCH PIECES
- 1 MEDIUM YELLOW ONION, CUT INTO 1-INCH PIECES, LEAVES SEPARATED
  EXTRA-VIRGIN OLIVE OIL
  KOSHER SALT

To make the marinade: In a small bowl whisk together the marinade ingredients.

Cut the beef into 1¼-inch cubes. Place the cubes in a large, resealable plastic bag and pour in the marinade. Press the air out of the bag and seal tightly. Turn the bag to distribute the marinade, place in a bowl, and refrigerate for 2 to 4 hours, turning occasionally.

To make the salad: In a large bowl combine the couscous and raisins. In a small saucepan over high heat, bring the broth to a boil and pour over the couscous. Stir to mix, cover, and allow to stand for about 10 minutes.

In a small bowl whisk together the rest of the salad ingredients. Add to the couscous. Stir gently with a fork to combine and to fluff the salad.

Remove the beef cubes from the bag and discard the marinade. Skewer the beef cubes alternately with the bell peppers and onions. Allow the meat to stand at room temperature for 20 to 30 minutes before grilling.

Brush or spray the kabobs with olive oil and season with salt. Grill over *Direct Medium* heat until the meat is medium rare, 8 to 10 minutes, turning once halfway through grilling time. Serve warm with the salad.

MAKES 4 SERVINGS

BEEF SATAY

An inspired use for peanut butter.

DIRECT/HIGH

FOR THE MARINADE:

- 1 GREEN ONION, FINELY CHOPPED
- ⅓ CUP KETCHUP
- ¼ CUP LIGHT SOY SAUCE
- 3 TABLESPOONS DARK BROWN SUGAR
- 3 TABLESPOONS FRESH LIME JUICE
- 1 TABLESPOON PEANUT OIL
- 1 TEASPOON GRATED FRESH GINGER
- 1 TEASPOON MINCED GARLIC
- ¼ TEASPOON CRUSHED RED PEPPER FLAKES

- 1½ POUNDS TOP ROUND *OR* BEEF TENDERLOIN

- ¼ CUP CREAMY PEANUT BUTTER

To make the marinade: In a small bowl whisk together the marinade ingredients with ¼ cup water.

Cut the beef into 3/4-inch cubes. Place the cubes in a large, resealable plastic bag and pour in the marinade. Press the air out of the bag and seal tightly. Turn the bag to distribute the marinade, place in a bowl, and refrigerate for 1 to 2 hours.

Remove the meat from the bag, reserving the marinade. Thread the meat onto skewers, leaving space between the cubes. Allow to stand at room temperature for 20 to 30 minutes before grilling.

Grill the beef cubes over *Direct High* heat until medium rare, 3 to 5 minutes, turning once halfway through grilling time.

Pour the reserved marinade into a small saucepan, bring to a boil over high heat, and boil for 1 full minute. Add the peanut butter, return to a boil, and whisk until the sauce thickens. Serve warm with the beef skewers.

MAKES 4 SERVINGS

HERE A LIME-BASED MARINADE IS TRANSFORMED INTO A SMOOTHLY DELICIOUS PEANUT SAUCE AND SERVED WITH TENDER MORSELS OF GRILLED BEEF.

Beef Satay

TANDOORI BEEF
WITH LENTIL SALAD

These tender beef kabobs are inspired by the unique cooking style from northern India's Punjab region. A touch of curry perks up the lentils.

DIRECT/HIGH

FOR THE MARINADE:

1 CUP PLAIN YOGURT

3 TABLESPOONS FRESH LEMON JUICE

1 TABLESPOON PAPRIKA

2 TEASPOONS MINCED GARLIC

2 TEASPOONS MINCED JALAPEÑO PEPPER, WITH SEEDS

1 TEASPOON CUMIN

1 TEASPOON CURRY POWDER

1 TEASPOON KOSHER SALT

1/2 TEASPOON GROUND GINGER

1/2 TEASPOON GROUND CORIANDER

1 1/2 POUNDS BEEF TENDERLOIN *OR* TOP SIRLOIN STEAK

FOR THE SALAD:

3 TABLESPOONS EXTRA-VIRGIN OLIVE OIL

1/4 CUP FINELY CHOPPED RED ONIONS

1 TABLESPOON MINCED GARLIC

1 TABLESPOON CURRY POWDER

1 CUP DRIED LENTILS

2 1/2 CUPS REDUCED-SODIUM *OR* HOMEMADE CHICKEN BROTH

1 TABLESPOON BALSAMIC VINEGAR

KOSHER SALT

FRESHLY GROUND BLACK PEPPER

2 MEDIUM RED ONIONS, CUT INTO 1-INCH PIECES, LEAVES SEPARATED

EXTRA-VIRGIN OLIVE OIL

To make the marinade: In a small bowl whisk together the marinade ingredients.

Cut the beef into 1-inch cubes. Place the beef cubes in a large, resealable plastic bag and pour in the marinade. Press the air out of the bag and seal tightly. Turn the bag to distribute the marinade, place in a bowl, and refrigerate for 3 to 4 hours.

To make the salad: In a medium heavy saucepan over medium-high heat, warm the olive oil. Add the onion and cook, stirring occasionally, until translucent, 4 to 5 minutes. Add the garlic and curry powder and cook for 1 minute more, stirring occasionally. Mix in the lentils and cook for 2 minutes more, stirring occasionally. Add the broth and vinegar. Bring the mixture to a boil over high heat, then lower the heat to a simmer. Cover and cook until the liquid

is absorbed and the lentils are tender, 30 to 45 minutes. Season with salt and pepper. (The salad can be served warm or at room temperature.)

Remove the beef cubes from the bag and discard the marinade. Skewer the beef cubes alternately with the onion leaves. Allow the meat to stand at room temperature for 20 to 30 minutes before grilling.

Lightly brush or spray the kabobs with olive oil and season with salt. Grill over *Direct High* heat until the meat is nicely seared and medium rare, 6 to 8 minutes, turning once halfway through grilling time. Serve warm with the salad.

MAKES 4 SERVINGS

CORNED BEEF AND SWISS
ON RYE

Having friends over for the big game? You'll score with this salute to a classic sandwich. The homemade dressing beats anything from a bottle and the grill adds a winning edge to the meat. Pile it high!

DIRECT/MEDIUM

FOR THE DRESSING:

1/4 CUP KETCHUP

1/4 CUP MAYONNAISE

2 TABLESPOONS FRESH LEMON JUICE

1 TABLESPOON GRANULATED SUGAR

1 TABLESPOON WORCESTERSHIRE SAUCE

1 TEASPOON CELERY SEEDS

1/2 TEASPOON PAPRIKA

1/4 TEASPOON CAYENNE

FOR THE COLESLAW:

3 CUPS SHREDDED CABBAGE, ABOUT 1 POUND

1/3 CUP FINELY CHOPPED YELLOW ONION

1/4 CUP MAYONNAISE

2 TEASPOONS WHITE WINE VINEGAR

1 TABLESPOON GRANULATED SUGAR

1/8 TEASPOON KOSHER SALT

1 1/2 POUNDS LEAN CORNED BEEF, THINLY SLICED

1/2 CUP UNSALTED BUTTER, SOFTENED

12 SLICES DELI-STYLE DARK RYE BREAD

6 SLICES SWISS CHEESE

To make the dressing: In a small bowl whisk together the dressing ingredients.

To make the slaw: In a large bowl mix together the cabbage and onion. In a small bowl whisk together the mayonnaise, vinegar, sugar, and salt. Pour the mixture over the vegetables, mix thoroughly, and set aside until the sandwiches are ready.

Grill the corned beef over *Direct Medium* heat just long enough to warm, about 30 seconds. Transfer to a platter and cover to keep warm while you prepare the rest of the sandwiches.

Butter one side of each slice of rye bread and spread the dressing on the other side. On six of the bread slices, place one slice of cheese on the side with the dressing.

Grill the bread slices, butter side down, over *Direct Medium* heat until lightly toasted and the cheese begins to melt, 30 to 60 seconds. Remove from the grill.

Pile the corned beef on the bread slices with the melted cheese, then spoon equal portions of the cole slaw on top. Cover each sandwich with the second slice of bread, toasted side up. Cut the sandwiches in half and serve immediately.

MAKES 6 SERVINGS

in opposite directions to form an even cylinder. Refrigerate the cylinder until ready to serve.

To make the paste: In a small bowl whisk together the paste ingredients.

Place the chops on a platter. Rub the paste into both sides of the chops, cover with plastic wrap, and refrigerate for 1 to 2 hours.

Allow the chops to stand at room temperature for 20 to 30 minutes before grilling. Grill over *Direct High* heat until the internal temperature reaches 145°F, 6 to 10 minutes, turning once halfway through grilling time.

Remove the chops from the grill and allow to rest for 3 to 5 minutes. Cut the butter into $1/4$-inch slices and place on top of the chops. Serve immediately.

MAKES 4 SERVINGS

CHILI-RUBBED VEAL LOIN CHOPS
WITH GREEN CHILE BUTTER

Loin chops are the porterhouse steaks of veal cuts. Milk-fed and juicy, these bone-in chops sizzle with spicy flavor. You can prepare the butter days ahead.

DIRECT/HIGH

FOR THE BUTTER:
1 POBLANO CHILE PEPPER
1 SMALL CLOVE GARLIC
1 TABLESPOON FRESH LIME JUICE
$1/4$ CUP UNSALTED BUTTER, SOFTENED
$1/8$ TEASPOON KOSHER SALT

FOR THE PASTE:
3 TABLESPOONS EXTRA-VIRGIN OLIVE OIL
2 TABLESPOONS FINELY CHOPPED FRESH OREGANO
1 TABLESPOON CHILI POWDER
1 TABLESPOON KOSHER SALT
2 TEASPOONS MINCED SHALLOTS
1 TEASPOON MINCED GARLIC
1 TEASPOON GROUND CUMIN
1 TEASPOON FRESHLY GROUND BLACK PEPPER

4 VEAL LOIN CHOPS, ABOUT $3/4$ POUND EACH AND 1 INCH THICK

To make the butter: Grill the poblano chile over *Direct High* heat until the skin is blistered in spots, 5 to 7 minutes, turning occasionally. When the chile is cool enough to handle, peel off the loosened skin. Discard the stem and seeds. In a food processor purée the chile and garlic with the lime juice. Add the butter and pulse until just blended, then add the salt. Scoop the butter mixture out of the bowl and transfer to a sheet of plastic wrap. Loosely shape into a log about 1 inch in diameter. Roll up the log in the wrap and twist the two ends

A smiling face is half the meal.

— LATVIAN PROVERB

Herbed Veal Loin

HERBED VEAL LOIN

This elegant dish is succulent and richly flavored. Have the butcher trim the chine (backbone), then crack it so you can easily cut the roast into individual chops. Try them with grill-roasted potatoes and grilled green beans, if desired.

INDIRECT/MEDIUM

FOR THE RUB:

2 TABLESPOONS WHOLE-GRAIN MUSTARD

2 TABLESPOONS FINELY CHOPPED FRESH THYME

2 TABLESPOONS FINELY CHOPPED FRESH ROSEMARY

2 TABLESPOONS FINELY CHOPPED FRESH SAGE

2 TABLESPOONS CRACKED WHITE PEPPERCORNS

2 TABLESPOONS EXTRA-VIRGIN OLIVE OIL

1 TABLESPOON MINCED GARLIC

1/2 TEASPOON PAPRIKA

1 VEAL LOIN ROAST, 5 TO 6 POUNDS, FRENCHED

KOSHER SALT

To make the rub: In a small bowl combine the rub ingredients.

Place the roast on a tray or in a pan, backbone side down. Coat the veal with the rub, cover with plastic wrap, and refrigerate for 8 to 24 hours.

Allow the roast to stand at room temperature for 30 to 45 minutes before grilling. Season with salt. Grill, backbone side down, over *Indirect Medium* heat until the internal temperature reaches 135°F for medium rare, 45 minutes to 1 hour.

Remove the roast from the grill and allow to rest for 5 to 10 minutes. The temperature will rise 5°F to 10°F during this time. Slice between each bone to separate the roast into individual chops. Serve warm.

MAKES 6 TO 8 SERVINGS

VEAL PAILLARDS
WITH LEMON BUTTER

An easy way to impress VIPs or just indulge yourself. These delicate steaks grill up lightning fast, so don't blink. Because they're so thin and can cool quickly, we recommend you warm the serving plates.

DIRECT/HIGH

FOR THE LEMON BUTTER:

4 TABLESPOONS UNSALTED BUTTER, SOFTENED

1 TABLESPOON FINELY CHOPPED FRESH ITALIAN PARSLEY

2 TEASPOONS CAPERS, DRAINED AND MINCED

1 1/2 TEASPOONS FRESH LEMON JUICE

1/2 TEASPOON FINELY GRATED LEMON ZEST

1 PINCH KOSHER SALT

4 THINLY SLICED VEAL TOP ROUND STEAKS, 4 TO 5 OUNCES EACH

EXTRA-VIRGIN OLIVE OIL

1/2 TEASPOON KOSHER SALT

1/8 TEASPOON FRESHLY GROUND BLACK PEPPER

To make the lemon butter: In a small bowl combine the lemon butter ingredients. Using the back of a fork, mix the butter well until smooth and creamy. Set aside at room temperature so the butter stays soft.

Place the steaks between two large pieces of plastic wrap. Then, using the flat side of a wooden mallet, pound the steaks to an even thickness of about 1/4 inch.

Brush or spray the steaks with olive oil and season with the salt and pepper. Grill over *Direct High* heat for 1 to 2 minutes, turning once halfway through grilling time. Transfer to warm plates and spoon the butter over the top. Serve immediately.

MAKES 4 SERVINGS

VEAL RIB-EYES
WITH TOMATO-PEPPER JAM

The vegetables for this wild and tasty jam are grilled on Direct Medium heat. The steaks get seared on Direct High and then are finished on Indirect Medium heat.

COOK: DIRECT/MEDIUM

FOR THE JAM:

- 1 SMALL ONION, CUT CROSSWISE INTO 1/2-INCH SLICES
  EXTRA-VIRGIN OLIVE OIL
- 4 RIPE TOMATOES, CORES REMOVED
- 1 LARGE RED BELL PEPPER
- 2/3 CUP TOMATO JUICE
- 1 TABLESPOON CIDER VINEGAR
- 1 TABLESPOON GRANULATED SUGAR
- 1 TEASPOON DRIED THYME
- 1 TEASPOON MINCED GARLIC

  KOSHER SALT
  FRESHLY GROUND BLACK PEPPER

FOR THE MARINADE:

- 1/4 CUP MINCED SHALLOTS
- 1/4 CUP EXTRA-VIRGIN OLIVE OIL
- 1/4 CUP FINELY CHOPPED FRESH BASIL
- 1/2 TEASPOON FRESHLY GROUND BLACK PEPPER

- 6 VEAL LOIN RIB-EYE STEAKS, ABOUT 1/2 POUND EACH AND 1 1/2 TO 2 INCHES THICK

To make the jam: Brush or spray the onion slices with olive oil. Grill the onion, tomatoes, and bell pepper over *Direct Medium* heat until the onion slices are well marked and the skin of the tomatoes and bell pepper is blistered. The onion and bell pepper will take 10 to 12 minutes, the tomatoes 8 to 10 minutes. Turn the onion once halfway through grilling time; turn the tomatoes and pepper until charred evenly.

Transfer the onion slices and tomatoes to a medium saucepan. Place the bell pepper in a paper bag; close tightly. Let stand 10 to 15 minutes to steam off the skin. Remove the pepper from the bag; peel away the charred skin. Cut off the top and remove the seeds. Coarsely chop the bell pepper and add to the onion and tomatoes along with the remaining jam ingredients. Bring to a boil, then reduce heat and simmer until the consistency of jam, 45 minutes to 1 hour. Allow to cool for about 10 minutes, then pour into a food processor and pulse to blend, leaving some small chunks of vegetables. Cover and store in the refrigerator. When ready to serve, reheat the jam and season with salt and pepper to taste.

To make the marinade: In a small bowl mix together the marinade ingredients.

Place the steaks in a large, resealable plastic bag and pour in the marinade. Press the air out of the bag and seal tightly, place in a bowl, and refrigerate for 2 to 6 hours.

Remove the steaks from the bag and discard the marinade.

Allow to stand at room temperature for 20 to 30 minutes before grilling.

Season the steaks with salt. Sear over *Direct High* heat for 10 minutes, turning once halfway through grilling time. Continue grilling over *Indirect Medium* heat until the internal temperature reaches 135°F for medium rare, 3 to 5 minutes. Remove from the grill and allow to rest for 3 to 5 minutes. The temperature will rise 5°F to 10°F during this time. Serve warm with the reheated jam.

MAKES 6 SERVINGS

SPINACH-STUFFED
VEAL CHOPS

The luscious stuffing keeps these chops juicy. To save time, ask the butcher to cut the pockets for you.

DIRECT/MEDIUM

FOR THE STUFFING:

- 1 TABLESPOON EXTRA-VIRGIN OLIVE OIL
- 1/2 CUP FINELY CHOPPED YELLOW ONION
- 2 TEASPOONS MINCED GARLIC
- 2 PLUM TOMATOES, CORED, SEEDED, AND CHOPPED
- 1 PACKAGE (10 OUNCES) FROZEN CHOPPED SPINACH, DEFROSTED AND SQUEEZED VERY DRY
- 3 SLICES PROSCIUTTO (ABOUT 2 OUNCES), FINELY CHOPPED
- 1/2 CUP COARSELY GRATED FONTINA CHEESE
- 1/2 TEASPOON KOSHER SALT
- 1/4 TEASPOON FRESHLY GROUND BLACK PEPPER

FOR THE RUB:

- 2 TEASPOONS FINELY CHOPPED FRESH ROSEMARY
- 1/2 TEASPOON KOSHER SALT
- 1/2 TEASPOON FRESHLY GROUND BLACK PEPPER

- 4 VEAL LOIN CHOPS, ABOUT 3/4 POUND EACH AND 1 1/4 TO 1 1/2 INCHES THICK
  EXTRA-VIRGIN OLIVE OIL

To make the stuffing: In a large sauté pan over medium heat, warm the olive oil and cook the onion until soft, 5 to 6 minutes. Add the garlic and cook for 1 minute more. Add the tomatoes and cook for 3 minutes, then add the spinach and cook for 2 minutes. Remove from the heat and allow to cool for 3 or 4 minutes, then add the remaining stuffing ingredients. Divide the stuffing into four portions.

To make the rub: In a small bowl combine the rub ingredients.

Trim the chops of any excess fat and cut a pocket in the side of each chop. Push the stuffing into the pockets and close with toothpicks. Lightly brush or spray the chops with oil and season with the rub. Allow to stand at room temperature for 20 to 30 minutes before grilling.

Grill over *Direct Medium* heat until medium rare, 15 to 20 minutes, turning once halfway through grilling time. Remove from the grill and allow to rest for 3 to 5 minutes. Serve warm.

MAKES 4 SERVINGS

Spinach-Stuffed Veal Chops

It's one of life's little ironies that the meat most likely to inspire people to eat like pigs is…well, grilled pig. When it's good, it's incredible. And when it's just okay, you can always add a sauce.

So you might be surprised to learn that *Multus porcinus* was one of the last species to be domesticated. That's because—according to James Trager's *The Food Chronology*—pigs don't eat readily available foods such as grass and leaves, and their diet of grains and nuts also figures largely on the human menu. But sometime around 2200 B.C., the Chinese discovered that porcine eating habits are what make pork taste so sweet—and they wasted no time expanding their animal husbandry repertoire.

PORK

When swine were first introduced to the Americas in the early 1500s by Spanish explorers (Ponce de Leon, de Soto, and Coronado have each been given primary credit), they were gladly welcomed into the food chain. Coronado took pigs to the Pueblo tribes of the American Southwest and spawned an entire industry. The wondrously spicy cuisine that evolved with it has grown in popularity since then.

Meanwhile, de Soto's pigs were happily proliferating from Florida up to the Carolinas, where they freely roamed the wilds, munching an endless supply of hickory nuts (one hickory species is even called "pignut"). By the 1700s, resourceful inhabitants of the southern colonies had put two and two together: nut-fed pigs + smoke of nut-bearing trees = yum. George Washington himself was a huge fan of the region's whole hog roast. In the South today, seldom is heard the inquisitive words "What's for dinner?" It's more like, "Eeny, meeny, miney, pork." In fact, pork is so popular, it's a wonder the hallowed hog doesn't appear on any of the state flags. But while Southerners have found myriad ways to make even the most negligible bit of pork delectable, most often pork is cooked "slow and low" over a hickory fire. Hours are spent cultivating flavor and texture that is typically devoured in mere minutes. And if you know your barbecue styles, you don't need a map to tell you when you've crossed a state line—or even into the next town.

Barbecue has found its way into Southern politics, too. In the 1960s Lyndon Johnson sponsored Texas-style "campaigning" barbecues. And more recently, House Bill 1737 was introduced in Florida to create the position of "State Secretary of Barbecue"—a strictly ceremonial position, but one of much perceived import as it would "promote the diversity of barbecue created by the many cultures represented in the state's diverse citizenry." While Floridians sometimes find themselves divided over issues of international magnitude, they do agree on the sovereignty of the almighty pig.

In the Midwest, corn-fed pork reigns supreme at the fire. Entire barbecuing societies have grown almost as fast as a profitable 245-pound porker. Here smoke and sizzle inspire more than just appetites. Countless cook-off team names—Squeal of Approval or Smokers Wild, for example—have succumbed to the hokey appeal of the pit where pure emotion unleashes a hankering for puns. Beyond the barbecue circuit, you'll find a strong German influence, manifest in a passion for bratwurst and countless variations on the classic "pork chops with applesauce."

Throughout the rest of the country, pork is prized by home cooks of all abilities for its capacity to absorb other flavors. In New Mexico, they might whip up a spicy ham-steak breakfast to start the day with a kick of chile. In New Orleans, you can find pork aflame with Cajun seasonings. But it would be a sad mistake to limit your grilled pork repertoire to a few regional specialties of the United States. This chapter also features a great variety of seasonings and preparation methods to introduce you to some of the finest pork dishes from around the world. Sample jerk pork with chutney, spicy pork green chile, hearty pork roast with white beans, Chinese-style ribs, or pork laced with tropical fruits. Follow our guidelines for great grilled pork and you can't go wrong. What we can't help you with, however, is the issue of self-control. You've been warned!

SWEET 'N SASSY
CHINESE RIBS

A short list of easy-to-find ingredients adds up to some of the best ribs you'll ever taste.

INDIRECT/MEDIUM

FOR THE MARINADE:

3/4 CUP GRANULATED SUGAR

1/2 CUP SOY SAUCE

3 TABLESPOONS HOISIN SAUCE

2 TABLESPOONS DRY SHERRY

1 TABLESPOON MINCED FRESH GINGER

2 TEASPOONS MINCED GARLIC

2 TO 3 SLABS BABY BACK PORK RIBS, ABOUT 4 POUNDS

To make the marinade: In a medium bowl whisk together the marinade ingredients.

Place the ribs in a single layer in a large roasting pan. Pour the marinade over the ribs. Turn the ribs to coat them evenly. Cover with plastic wrap and refrigerate for 4 to 6 hours, turning the ribs occasionally.

Allow the ribs to stand at room temperature for 20 to 30 minutes before grilling. Drain the ribs and reserve the marinade. Pour the marinade into a small saucepan, bring to a boil, and boil for 1 full minute. Set aside.

Grill the ribs, rib side down, over *Indirect Medium* heat until the meat is very tender and has pulled back from the ends of the bones, 1 1/2 to 2 hours. During the last 20 minutes of grilling time, baste generously with the marinade. Remove from the grill and allow to rest for 5 to 10 minutes before slicing into individual ribs. Serve warm.

MAKES 4 SERVINGS

BABY BACK RIBS
WITH SPICED APPLE-CIDER MOP

If you like your ribs a little crispy on the outside, grill them, meat side down, over Direct Medium heat for 10 to 15 minutes before finishing them over Indirect Medium heat. Don't expect leftovers.

INDIRECT/MEDIUM

FOR THE MOP:

2 CUPS APPLE CIDER

1/4 CUP MINCED SHALLOTS

1 TABLESPOON MINCED JALAPEÑO PEPPER, SEEDS REMOVED

1/4 CUP KETCHUP

2 TABLESPOONS WHITE WINE VINEGAR

2 TABLESPOONS TOMATO PASTE

1 TABLESPOON DARK BROWN SUGAR

1/4 TEASPOON KOSHER SALT

1/4 TEASPOON FRESHLY GROUND BLACK PEPPER

2 TO 3 SLABS BABY BACK PORK RIBS, ABOUT 4 POUNDS

KOSHER SALT

FRESHLY GROUND BLACK PEPPER

To make the mop: In a small saucepan combine the apple cider, shallots, and jalapeño. Bring to a boil and cook over medium-high heat until about 1 cup of the liquid remains, 15 to 20 minutes. Add the remaining mop ingredients, bring to a boil, and remove from the heat. (The mop may be made ahead and refrigerated until ready to use.)

Allow the ribs to stand at room temperature for 20 to 30 minutes before grilling. Season with salt and pepper. Grill, rib side down, over *Indirect Medium* heat until the meat is very tender and has pulled back from the ends of the bones, 1 1/2 to 2 hours. Baste the ribs frequently with the mop throughout grilling time, but stop basting during the last 10 minutes. Remove from the grill and allow to rest for 5 to 10 minutes before slicing into individual ribs. Serve warm.

MAKES 4 SERVINGS

APPLE CIDER, JALAPEÑO, AND VINEGAR CONSPIRE TO MAKE A TENDERIZING MOP FOR IRRESISTIBLE BABY BACKS.

Baby Back Ribs with Spiced Apple–Cider Mop

PORK RIBS ON THE GRILL

The world of barbecue is filled with closely guarded secrets, good-natured rivalry, and superlatives galore—especially when it comes to grilling ribs. The decorated veteran of the pits and the backyard dabbler alike will tell you the "right" way to do them (at the same time refusing to divulge any secret ingredients, of course). Well, we have a few iron-clad tenets in our personal Rib Creed, which we're more than happy to share with you.

REMOVE THE MEMBRANE. Before you even season the meat, remove the membrane from the back of the slab of ribs *(see sidebar, page 157)*.

NEVER PARBOIL RIBS. We know some folks will dispute this, but we'll go tongs to tongs with them over this one. The Truth is, when you boil ribs, you cook out the flavor along with the fat. Then those too-lean ribs turn dry and chewy over the flame. Leave the poor things alone. If you remove the membrane and cook them properly, the fat will still exit, but slowly, leaving flavor and tenderness in its wake.

CHOOSE YOUR COOKING STYLE. If you like your ribs so tender they fall off the bone, cook 'em slow and low (purists insist this is the only way a meat earns the esteemed title of "barbecue"). Steady, low heat—250° to 275°F— and patience are key. But because patience is not the natural twin of today's busy lifestyle, the recipes in this book use Indirect Medium heat. Keep the lid on and hang in there—another trip to the kitchen for appetizers might help you wait it out. The ribs are done when the meat is very tender and has pulled away from the ends of the bone. Worth the wait? We think so.

KNOW YOUR SAUCE. Sugar burns quickly, so if your sauce contains any (that includes maple syrup, honey, ketchup, and the like), don't brush it on until the last 10 to 20 minutes of grilling time. Mops, on the other hand, can be brushed on throughout the grilling time because they're high in acids (vinegar is the most common basic ingredient). But because bacteria can be passed from the uncooked meat to your bowl of mop, we recommend you finish "mopping" a full 10 minutes before you pull the meat from the grill and discard any remaining mop.

A WORD OR TWO ABOUT SMOKE. Some folks wouldn't dream of making ribs without adding cooking woods to the fire. We think smoke flavor is fabulous, but it doesn't work with every recipe or for every palate. Asian-style ribs, for example, feature distinct flavors such as hoisin sauce and chili paste—ingredients that aren't compatible with hickory or other wood flavors. More traditional American rib recipes, however, cry out for wood smoke. When you do want to use cooking woods, follow our smoking guidelines on pages 30 to 31. Be sure to use a water pan, and remember, smoked meats often have a pink or reddish hue, even when they are fully cooked.

FRESH BACON

ARNOLD'S
MEAT MARKET

700 EDINBOROUGH LANE · ATLANTA, GEORGIA

REMOVING THE MEMBRANE
FROM PORK RIBS

Three good reasons for removing the thick, tough membrane that covers the interior side of the rack (if your butcher hasn't already): 1.) Even salt can't penetrate this barrier—if you leave it on, half the rib meat will remain unseasoned. 2.) Removing the membrane allows the fat beneath it to slowly drip away, replacing calories with flavorful smoke. 3.) Cooking turns the membrane papery, chewy, and almost impossible to separate from the meat. Anything but appetizing. Get rid of it this way:

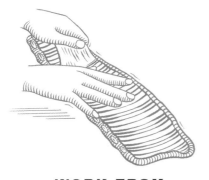

FIRST KNIFE,
THEN FINGERS

To loosen the membrane, carefully slide the tip of a paring knife (the wider blade is more useful here than a boning knife) underneath the membrane at the first or second bone at the widest end of the slab (above). For baby backs, start at the second bone from either end. Gently rock the knife back and forth until you've made a space big enough to slide your finger in, then pull up the membrane carefully until you can get two fingers in.

WORK FROM
BONE TO BONE

Slowly peel back the membrane at an angle. If the membrane tears, just slide your knife tip under the next bone and work your way along the rack. After two or three bones, it should be easy to pull the membrane off in a single sheet, as long as you keep your fingers close to where it connects to the rack (above). Don't get discouraged if you have to start over—one bite of those tender cooked ribs and you'll be glad you took the time.

A GRILLER'S
PORK RIB GLOSSARY

Baby back ribs: These are cut from the top end of the rib bone—flavorful, meaty, and small. Some butchers offer them with the backbone still attached; check that the price per pound drops accordingly.

Spareribs: Sometimes called St. Louis ribs, these longer bones offer more gnawing pleasure. You've had them sauced, but have you tried them with a dry rub, marinade, or mop and then sauce? Yow!

Country-style spareribs (a.k.a. split or butterflied blade chops): Big and meaty, these "ribs" are really individual, thick chops cut from the shoulder end of the loin. If you see a bone, it's actually a shoulder blade, not a rib. Who cares? They taste great and are easy on the budget. Plus, there's no membrane to remove, just trim the fat.

Serving: Count on 1 pound of raw weight per serving. Some folks like more (especially when the sauce is homemade).

FRESH
PINEAPPLE
JUICE TWICE
BLESSES
THESE RIBS:
FIRST IN A
MARINADE,
THEN IN
A SWEET
AND SOUR
GLAZE.

Plum-Glazed Baby Back Ribs

PLUM-GLAZED
BABY BACK RIBS

If you like 'em sliding off the bone, these are the ribs for you. An enzyme found in the pineapple juice doubles as a natural meat tenderizer in the marinade. Brush those ribs with the plum glaze, and you're in Polynesian paradise.

INDIRECT/MEDIUM

FOR THE MARINADE:

- 1 CUP FRESH PINEAPPLE JUICE
- 1/2 CUP FINELY CHOPPED YELLOW ONION
- 1/3 CUP HONEY
- 2 TABLESPOONS RICE VINEGAR
- 2 TABLESPOONS THINLY SLICED FRESH GINGER
- 2 TEASPOONS MINCED GARLIC

- 2 TO 3 SLABS BABY BACK PORK RIBS, ABOUT 4 POUNDS

FOR THE GLAZE:

- 2/3 CUP FIRMLY PACKED DARK BROWN SUGAR
- 1/4 CUP DRY SHERRY
- 2 TABLESPOONS RED WINE VINEGAR
- 2 TABLESPOONS SOY SAUCE
- 1 TEASPOON HOT MUSTARD POWDER
- 4 LARGE PLUMS (ABOUT 1 POUND), PITTED AND QUARTERED

- ASIAN SESAME OIL
- KOSHER SALT

To make the marinade: In a medium saucepan combine the marinade ingredients and bring to a boil. Remove from the heat and allow to cool.

Place the ribs in a large, resealable plastic bag and pour in the marinade. Press the air out of the bag and seal tightly. Turn the bag to distribute the marinade, place in a bowl, and refrigerate for 8 to 12 hours, turning occasionally.

Remove the ribs from the bag. Strain the marinade and reserve 1 cup for use in the glaze.

To make the glaze: In a large saucepan combine the reserved marinade with the glaze ingredients. Bring to a boil and simmer over medium heat, stirring occasionally, until the plums are falling apart and the liquid has thickened, about 40 minutes. Remove from the heat. Strain the glaze, pressing it through a sieve. Reserve 1/2 cup of the strained glaze to serve with the ribs; use the rest for basting the ribs.

Allow the ribs to stand at room temperature for 20 to 30 minutes before grilling. Lightly brush with sesame oil and season with salt. Grill, rib side down, over *Indirect Medium* heat until the meat is very tender and has pulled back from the ends of the bones, 1 1/2 to 2 hours. During the last 20 minutes of grilling time, baste with the glaze. Remove from the grill and allow to rest for 5 to 10 minutes before slicing into portions. Serve warm with the reserved glaze.

MAKES 4 SERVINGS

KANSAS CITY–STYLE
BABY BACK RIBS

We couldn't write a grilling cookbook without paying homage to the illustrious epicenter of great ribs. If you've ever wondered what makes KC ribs legendary, sink your teeth into these and find out.

INDIRECT/MEDIUM

FOR THE SAUCE:

- 1 TABLESPOON VEGETABLE OIL
- 1/4 CUP FINELY CHOPPED YELLOW ONION
- 1 TEASPOON MINCED GARLIC
- 3/4 CUP KETCHUP
- 1/2 CUP CIDER VINEGAR
- 1/4 CUP FIRMLY PACKED LIGHT BROWN SUGAR
- 3 TABLESPOONS WORCESTERSHIRE SAUCE
- 1 1/2 TABLESPOONS YELLOW MUSTARD
- 2 TEASPOONS SOY SAUCE
- 1/2 TEASPOON CHILI POWDER
- TABASCO SAUCE

FOR THE RIBS:

- 2 TO 3 SLABS BABY BACK PORK RIBS, ABOUT 4 POUNDS
- KOSHER SALT
- FRESHLY GROUND BLACK PEPPER

- HICKORY CHUNKS *OR* CHIPS SOAKED IN WATER FOR AT LEAST 30 MINUTES

To make the sauce: In a medium saucepan over medium-high heat, warm the vegetable oil. Add the onion and cook, stirring occasionally, until translucent, 4 to 5 minutes. Add the garlic and cook for 1 minute more. Add the remaining sauce ingredients, including Tabasco sauce to taste, and bring to a boil. Reduce heat and simmer for about 15 minutes. Set aside. Pour some of the sauce in a small bowl to use for basting the ribs.

Allow the ribs to stand at room temperature for 20 to 30 minutes before grilling. Season with salt and pepper. Follow the grill's instructions for using wood chunks. Grill the ribs, rib side down, over *Indirect Medium* heat until the meat is very tender and has pulled back from the ends of the bones, 1 1/2 to 2 hours. During the last 20 minutes of grilling time, baste generously with the small bowl of sauce. Serve warm with the remaining sauce on the side.

MAKES 4 SERVINGS

A FIRST-CLASS LUAU

When the Hawaiian Islands became a state in 1959, Americans flipped. How enamored we were with the swaying palms, the lazy music, and the fru-fru drinks. And how happy we were to discover the Polynesian art of outdoor cooking—backyard grills on the mainland sprouted pineapple kabobs overnight. Our friend Mike tells a story about how Weber jumped on the Hawaii bandwagon—and almost fell off the other side.

As part of Weber's contribution to the national brouhaha over Hawaii's entrance into the Union, we decided to hold luaus at our key retail outlets, featuring grill-roasted whole pigs and Hawaiian hula dancers. My colleagues and I donned Hawaiian shirts and shorts and generally looked completely out of place roasting pigs on giant Weber Ranch® kettles in store parking lots. For live talent, we tried to recruit real hula dancers but, not surprisingly, there weren't many hanging around Chicago's suburbs. So we ended up hiring local dance students willing to debut their careers at the local Montgomery Ward.

Believe it or not, the promotions were a big hit. Shoppers were drawn to the camera flashes as proud parents photographed their daughters. The melodic strains of the greatest ukulele hit of all time, *Tiny Bubbles*, and the aroma of roasting pork lured them even closer, where they'd see the crazy Weber folks dressed like Don Ho and handing out free eats. What a way to make a living! But retailers loved those luaus. They drew customers and racked up sales of Weber grills and Hawaiian clothes. By the early 1970s, we were hosting hundreds of luaus around the country.

For me, the most memorable luau took place in St. Louis at a Famous Barr store in 1971; but I wasn't even supposed to be there. It all started when a fellow Weberhead called me at home late one Friday night. In a sheepish, somewhat inebriated voice, he explained that he and his co-worker were pigless. You see, it's not easy to fly into a town and find a butcher shop that just happens to have a whole pig on hand. So Weber had hired Meeske's Meat Shop in Mount Prospect, Illinois, to prepare and box whole pigs for us. Our grill teams would pick them up on their way to the airport and check them with their luggage to their luau destination.

Turns out this time that each of the Weber pig roasters thought the other had picked up the pig. The airline was serving free booze all the way to St. Louis, so it wasn't until they happily landed (and I do mean happily) that they discovered neither of them had the pig. Frantic, they had called all over St. Louis and, to their dismay, were unable to find a pig. The big luau was scheduled to start the next day at 11:00 A.M. We quickly hatched the following plan. I would pick up their pig, head to O'Hare, buy a ticket, check the pig, but not actually get on the flight. They would then retrieve the pig from baggage claim in St. Louis and race to the luau.

Our mission was all the more critical because the president of the Famous Barr stores was to be there. He had said that if he liked what he saw, he would place our products in his entire chain of stores.

The only problem was that, among all the airlines, there was only one seat left—in first class. It departed Chicago at 9:00 A.M. on Saturday, arriving in St. Louis at 9:50 A.M. It was cutting it close, but we could still have the pig on the grill before the first notes of *Tiny Bubbles* were played.

When Saturday dawned, I was already camped out at Meeske's. Unfortunately, the night before had been Grandpa and Grandma Meeske's 50th anniversary party and the family was running 15 minutes late. I wasn't out of there with my boxed pig until 8:20 A.M., and now I had a 20-minute ride to O'Hare.

Several red lights and a slow-moving freight train later, I realized it was too close to departure time to check my luggage, so I had to go to plan B. Fortunately, I had a good-sized duffle bag in the trunk of my car.

Luckily, I found a parking spot close to the terminal. People looked at me strangely as I removed a plastic-wrapped, semi-frozen pig from a box and stuffed it into a duffle bag, but anything can happen at O'Hare, so they just walked past another crazy.

I raced to the ticket counter, lugging my pig. The agent told me I'd have to run to make the flight. Let me tell you, a pig gets mighty heavy when you're sprinting with it through an airport. Still, I made it just as the door was closing and found that the seat next to mine was a no-show. What a relief. I stuffed my duffled companion below the two seats in front of me. As I caught my breath and the plane gained altitude, I contemplated asking the flight attendant for one of those little wing pins for my pig, but I decided not to press my luck.

The good news is that the pig did beat the president to the luau. When the latter arrived, he was very pleased with the size of the crowd, and complimented us on the food. "Well," I told him, as my hung-over colleagues choked back their laughter, "at Weber we like to do everything in a first-class manner."

ALOHA
GRILL-ROASTED PIG

This island-style method for a pig roast has been updated for the backyard grill. Order the dressed-out pig from your butcher several days ahead. Serve with island drinks and grilled pineapple.

INDIRECT/LOW

1 OVEN-READY SUCKLING PIG, 12 TO 15 POUNDS

FOR THE MARINADE:
1/2 CUP SOY SAUCE
1/3 CUP VEGETABLE OIL
1/4 CUP DRY SHERRY
1/4 CUP FIRMLY PACKED LIGHT BROWN SUGAR
1 1/2 TEASPOONS KOSHER SALT
1/2 TEASPOON FRESHLY GROUND BLACK PEPPER
1 LARGE CLOVE GARLIC, CRUSHED

BREAD STUFFING FOR PORK (SEE PAGE 268)
VEGETABLE OIL
1 FRESH LIME
TI OR GALAX LEAVES, WASHED AND DRIED
FRESH IN-SEASON FRUITS

Wash the pig under cold running water. Pat dry, inside and out, with paper towels.

To make the marinade: In a large bowl combine the marinade ingredients and allow to stand at room temperature for about 1/2 hour.

Brush the pig cavity with the marinade. Refrigerate the pig and remaining marinade until ready to stuff and roast.

To prepare the pig: Brush the cavity with the marinade again. Loosely fill with the bread stuffing for pork. Skewer the cavity shut and lace the skewers together with heavy white cotton cord. Stuff a small block of wood in the mouth to keep it open during grilling. Cover the ears, tail, and snout with aluminum foil. Skewer the back feet under the pig. Prick the skin with a large needle in several places behind the head.

Generously brush the underside of the pig with vegetable oil. Place a heavy metal drip pan filled with 2 cups water on the charcoal grate or on the Flavorizer® bars below where the pig will cook. Place the pig belly side down, front feet forward, on the grate over *Indirect Low* heat. Brush the pig with the marinade. Grill until the internal temperature of the thigh reaches 170°F and the juices run clear, about 25 minutes per pound. Remove the foil 1 hour before the end of grilling time. Allow the pig to rest about 30 minutes before carving.

Remove the skewers and string. Transfer the stuffing to a serving bowl. Substitute the block of wood with the fresh lime. Place the pig on a board lined with ti leaves, garnish with fruits, and serve.

MAKES 8 TO 10 SERVINGS

Everybody's Favorite "Dry" Ribs (top) and Kansas City–Style Spareribs (bottom)

EVERYBODY'S FAVORITE
"DRY" RIBS

In Memphis, Tennessee, they often serve ribs dry—cooked with a spicy rub but no sauce. Taste this memorable spice blend and you'll see how they manage to live without the wet stuff. As the natural juices of the meat are released during cooking, they mingle with a full-flavored rub like this one for a taste some have labeled "killer."

INDIRECT/MEDIUM

FOR THE RUB:

- 3 TABLESPOONS KOSHER SALT
- 3 TABLESPOONS WHOLE BLACK PEPPERCORNS
- 2 TABLESPOONS GRANULATED SUGAR
- 1 1/2 TABLESPOONS WHOLE MUSTARD SEEDS
- 1 1/2 TABLESPOONS SWEET PAPRIKA
- 2 TEASPOONS DRIED OREGANO
- 1 1/2 TEASPOONS WHOLE CUMIN SEEDS
- 1 1/2 TEASPOONS WHOLE FENNEL SEEDS
- 1 1/2 TEASPOONS CELERY SEEDS
- 1 1/2 TEASPOONS CRUSHED RED PEPPER FLAKES
- 1 TEASPOON DRIED THYME

- 2 TO 3 SLABS MEATY PORK SPARERIBS, 6 TO 7 POUNDS, TRIMMED OF EXCESS FAT

HICKORY CHUNKS *OR* CHIPS SOAKED IN WATER FOR AT LEAST 30 MINUTES

To make the rub: In a spice grinder or blender pulse the rub ingredients for a few seconds until the seeds are coarsely ground. Do in two batches, if necessary. The rub should have a slightly coarse texture.

Spread the rub generously on all sides of the ribs and allow to stand at room temperature for 20 to 30 minutes before grilling.

Follow the grill's instructions for using wood chunks. Grill the ribs, rib side down, over *Indirect Medium* heat until the meat is very tender and has pulled back from the ends of the bones, 1 1/2 to 2 hours. Remove from the grill and allow to rest for 5 to 10 minutes before slicing into individual ribs.

MAKES 6 SERVINGS

KANSAS CITY–STYLE
SPARERIBS

Torn between a sauce and a rub? Do like most serious rib fans and use both for unmistakable barbecue flavor. These classic concoctions have been Weber favorites for years.

INDIRECT/MEDIUM

FOR THE RUB:

- 2 TABLESPOONS KOSHER SALT
- 2 TABLESPOONS MILD *OR* HOT HUNGARIAN PAPRIKA
- 1 1/2 TABLESPOONS CUMIN
- 1 TABLESPOON DRIED OREGANO
- 2 TEASPOONS ONION POWDER
- 1 TEASPOON GARLIC POWDER
- 1 TEASPOON FRESHLY GROUND BLACK PEPPER
- 1/2 TEASPOON GROUND ALLSPICE
- 1/2 TEASPOON GROUND CINNAMON

- 2 TO 3 SLABS MEATY PORK SPARERIBS, 6 TO 7 POUNDS, TRIMMED OF EXCESS FAT

FOR THE SAUCE:

- 2 TABLESPOONS UNSALTED BUTTER
- 1/2 CUP FINELY CHOPPED CELERY
- 3 TABLESPOONS FINELY CHOPPED YELLOW ONION
- 1 CUP KETCHUP
- 2 TABLESPOONS FRESH LEMON JUICE
- 2 TABLESPOONS GRANULATED SUGAR
- 2 TABLESPOONS CIDER VINEGAR
- 1 TABLESPOON WORCESTERSHIRE SAUCE
- 1 TEASPOON DRY MUSTARD
- FRESHLY GROUND BLACK PEPPER

To make the rub: In a small bowl combine the rub ingredients and mix well.

Coat the ribs with the rub and place in a large, resealable plastic bag. Press the air out of the bag and seal tightly, place in a bowl, and refrigerate for 2 to 8 hours.

To make the sauce: In a medium saucepan over low heat, melt the butter and sauté the celery and onion until tender, about 10 minutes. Add the remaining sauce ingredients, including pepper to taste, and bring to a boil. Reduce the heat, cover, and simmer for 15 minutes. Set aside. Pour some of the sauce in a small bowl to use for basting the ribs.

Allow the ribs to stand at room temperature for 20 to 30 minutes before grilling. Grill, rib side down, over *Indirect Medium* heat until the meat is very tender and has pulled back from the ends of the bones, 1 1/2 to 2 hours. During the last 20 minutes of grilling time, baste frequently with the small bowl of sauce. Remove from the grill and allow to rest for 5 to 10 minutes before slicing into individual ribs. Reheat the remaining sauce and serve on the side with the ribs.

MAKES 6 SERVINGS

EASY SOUTHERN-STYLE
SPARERIBS

The bourbon and mustard influences here are Southern fo' shore. Serve with cornbread, baked beans, and a big glass of sweet tea.

INDIRECT/MEDIUM

FOR THE MARINADE:
1/2 CUP BOURBON
1/4 CUP MOLASSES
1/4 CUP CIDER VINEGAR
1 TEASPOON CAYENNE
1/2 TEASPOON KOSHER SALT

3 TO 4 SLABS MEATY PORK SPARERIBS, 6 TO 7 POUNDS, TRIMMED OF EXCESS FAT

FOR THE SAUCE:
1/2 CUP YELLOW MUSTARD
1 1/2 CUPS BARBECUE SAUCE

To make the marinade: In a medium bowl combine the marinade ingredients with 1/2 cup water.

Brush the marinade on the ribs, cover with plastic wrap, and refrigerate for 3 to 4 hours.

To make the sauce: In a small saucepan combine the mustard and barbecue sauce. Bring to a boil, stirring, then lower the heat and simmer for 3 to 5 minutes. Remove from the heat. Pour some of the sauce in a small bowl to use for basting the ribs.

Allow the ribs to stand at room temperature for 20 to 30 minutes before grilling. Grill, rib side down, over *Indirect Medium* heat until the meat is very tender and has pulled back from the ends of the bones, 1 1/2 to 2 hours. During the last 20 minutes of grilling time, baste generously with the small bowl of sauce. Remove from the grill and allow to rest for 5 to 10 minutes before slicing into individual ribs. Serve warm with the remaining sauce on the side.

MAKES 6 SERVINGS

COUNTRY-STYLE
PORK RIBS
WITH SOFT PARMESAN POLENTA

Italian-seasoned, juicy grilled ribs simmered in a simple tomato sauce, then ladled over a pool of steaming hot, creamy Parmesan polenta. When's dinner?

INDIRECT/MEDIUM

FOR THE PASTE:
2 TABLESPOONS RED WINE VINEGAR
2 TEASPOONS MINCED GARLIC
1 1/4 TEASPOON FRESHLY GROUND BLACK PEPPER
1 TEASPOON DRIED ROSEMARY
1 TEASPOON DRIED OREGANO
1/2 TEASPOON DRIED THYME
1/2 TEASPOON ANISE SEEDS
1/2 TEASPOON KOSHER SALT

4 TO 5 BONELESS COUNTRY-STYLE PORK RIBS, ABOUT 2 POUNDS, TRIMMED OF EXCESS FAT

FOR THE POLENTA:
3 TABLESPOONS UNSALTED BUTTER
1 CUP YELLOW CORNMEAL
4 CUPS WATER *OR* 2 CUPS WATER AND 2 CUPS CHICKEN BROTH
1 TEASPOON KOSHER SALT
1/2 CUP OR MORE FRESHLY GRATED PARMIGIANO-REGGIANO CHEESE

FOR THE SAUCE:
1 CUP FINELY CHOPPED YELLOW ONION
2 TABLESPOONS EXTRA-VIRGIN OLIVE OIL
1 TEASPOON MINCED GARLIC
1/4 TEASPOON CRUSHED RED PEPPER FLAKES
1 CAN (28 OUNCES) CHOPPED TOMATOES WITH JUICE
1 TEASPOON KOSHER SALT
FRESHLY GROUND BLACK PEPPER

EXTRA-VIRGIN OLIVE OIL

To make the paste: In a small bowl combine the paste ingredients and mix well.

Spread the paste on all sides of the ribs, cover with plastic wrap, and refrigerate for 8 to 12 hours.

To make the polenta: In the top of a double boiler set directly over medium heat, melt the butter. Add the cornmeal and stir until blended, about 3 minutes. Gradually stir in the water and salt; heat to boiling, stirring constantly, about 10 minutes. When the polenta has thickened, place the top of the double boiler over the bottom half that is one-quarter full of boiling water. Reduce heat to low and cook over the simmering water, stirring occasionally, until the polenta is creamy, about 30 minutes. Stir in the cheese during the last 10 minutes.

To make the sauce: In a large, deep saucepan over medium heat, sauté the onion in the olive oil, stirring, until golden, about 8 minutes. Add the garlic and red pepper flakes and cook 1 minute more. Add the tomatoes and bring to a boil. Reduce heat and simmer, uncovered, until thickened, about 20 minutes. Add the salt and season with pepper. Remove from the heat.

Allow the ribs to stand at room temperature for 20 to 30 minutes before grilling. Lightly brush or spray with olive oil. Grill over *Indirect Medium* heat for about 1 hour, turning once halfway through grilling time. Cut the ribs into 1-inch slices and add to the sauce. Cook over low heat, covered, for about 30 minutes. To serve, spoon the polenta onto a large, deep platter and top with the ribs. Serve with the sauce on the side along with more cheese, if desired.

MAKES 4 SERVINGS

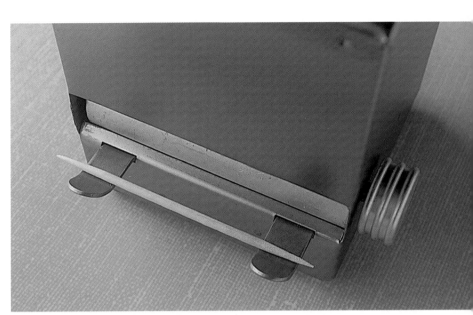

COUNTRY-STYLE PORK RIBS
WITH RED WINE VINEGAR SAUCE

Are they saucy or sassy? Pull up a plate of these meaty, basted ribs and you decide.

INDIRECT/MEDIUM

FOR THE SAUCE:
- 1/2 CUP RED WINE VINEGAR
- 1/4 CUP KETCHUP
- 3 TABLESPOONS SOY SAUCE
- 2 TABLESPOONS HONEY
- 1 TEASPOON MINCED GARLIC
- 1/2 TEASPOON DRIED THYME
- 1/2 TEASPOON TABASCO SAUCE
- 1/4 TEASPOON FRESHLY GROUND BLACK PEPPER
- 1/4 TEASPOON CHILI POWDER

- 8 COUNTRY-STYLE PORK RIBS, ABOUT 4 POUNDS, TRIMMED OF EXCESS FAT
  KOSHER SALT
  FRESHLY GROUND BLACK PEPPER

  HICKORY CHUNKS *OR* CHIPS SOAKED IN WATER FOR AT LEAST 30 MINUTES

To make the sauce: In a medium saucepan combine the sauce ingredients and bring to a boil. Reduce heat and simmer for about 15 minutes, stirring occasionally. Remove from the heat and allow to cool to room temperature. Pour some of the sauce into a small bowl to use for basting the ribs.

Allow the ribs to stand at room temperature for 20 to 30 minutes before grilling. Season with salt and pepper. Follow the grill's instructions for using wood chunks. Grill over *Indirect Medium* heat until the meat is very tender, 1 to 1¼ hours, turning once halfway through grilling time. During the last 20 minutes of grilling time, baste with the small bowl of sauce. Serve warm with the remaining sauce on the side.

MAKES 4 SERVINGS

THE PROPER WAY TO EAT BARBECUED PORK RIBS

At fussy garden parties and formal dinners, you might approach the challenge of a saucy rib course in the following manner: If they are not already separated, use your knife and fork to surgically divide the rack into individual ribs of equal width. Carefully hold a single rib between your forefinger and thumb and raise it to your mouth. Keep your dinner napkin at the ready in your other hand. Pull your lips back from your teeth in a quasi-smile so as not to get sauce on your lips. Carefully nibble the meat from the bone, avoiding any gristle or excess fat. Wipe your mouth frequently. Repeat as often as is socially acceptable.

You will find that the above methodology will spare you a hefty dry cleaning bill, but, based on no scientific research whatsoever, we assert that it will not satisfy you one bit. The proper way to eat pork ribs is to approach the plate (paper will do) with the lust and fervor of a teenager under a full moon. Begin with as much verbal preamble (e.g., "Woooooo-ee, them ribs look good!") as you see fit. Do not hold back. Instead, hold the first rib in one hand and rip it from the rack—when properly prepared, the ribs should tear as easily as a wet paper towel. (Note: Some rib racks are so tender and yielding that, when pulled, an entire bone will just slide right out with no meat attached, leaving the next bone laden with twice as much succulent meat. This situation should be greeted with the same enthusiasm as a bonus round on a game show.)

Grasp each end of the bone and peel the meat off with your teeth. Lick your lips. Savor every delicious bite. Feel the velvety sauce coat your chin, your cheeks, your fingers. (Napkins? What napkins?) Repeat as often as necessary until you can no longer speak, let alone move. Lick your fingers clean. Sigh contentedly as you lean back in your chair. Think about toothpicks.

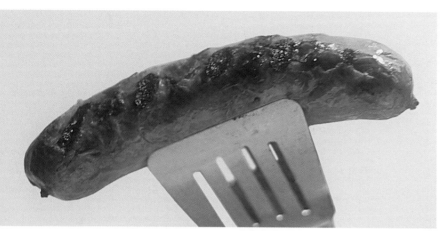

BRATWURST
BROUHAHA

Grilled fresh bratwurst has inspired several great dishes, and even more lively discussions on the best way to prepare them. Nowhere does the brat debate rage hotter than on the hallowed grounds of Lambeau Field, home of the Green Bay Packers. Packers fans are some of the most enthusiastic—and opinionated—brat eaters in the world. As the parking lot fills with smoking grills on game day, you'll hear some spirited exchanges: Which comes first, the simmering beer bath or the grill marks? Onions or sauerkraut or both? Which brand of mustard? Did you say ketchup? Utter heresy! And the beer of choice to wash it all down? Don't even go there.

Far be it from us to put forth the "definitive" method for grilling bratwurst (we'd lose friends either way). But for you beginners, here's a simple recipe to start with that won't leave you cold.

MISS BETTY'S
BEST-EVER BRATWURST

This recipe comes from Betty Hughes, Weber's very own grilling guru. Betty swears this one will at least secure you a first down. You can experiment as you go, or stick with this if it works for you.

INDIRECT/MEDIUM

1   CAN (12 OUNCES) BEER
5   FRESH BRATWURST
5   HOT DOG BUNS *OR* ROLLS, HALVED LENGTHWISE
    CONDIMENTS (E.G. MUSTARD, GRILLED ONIONS, SAUERKRAUT)

Pour the beer into a heavy-duty foil pan and set over *Indirect Medium* heat. Grill the bratwurst over *Direct Medium* heat (on either side of the pan) until lightly browned, 6 to 8 minutes, turning once halfway through grilling time. Transfer the brats to the pan of beer, cover with foil, and grill for 25 minutes more. Serve the brats on the buns or rolls with your favorite condiments.

MAKES 5 SERVINGS

CLASSIC
BRATWURST
WITH THE WORKS

Bratwurst—famous sidekick of both grill and gridiron—is really a sausage for all seasons. We grill these first to get them nice and brown, then simmer them in beer, apples, sauerkraut, and onions for total sensory fulfillment. Inhale and be healed.

DIRECT/MEDIUM

10   FRESH BRATWURST

FOR THE SAUERKRAUT:

1   TEASPOON VEGETABLE OIL
1   MEDIUM YELLOW ONION, THINLY SLICED
2   BACON SLICES, CUT INTO 1-INCH PIECES
1   GRANNY SMITH APPLE, UNPEELED, CORED, AND CUT INTO 1/2-INCH CUBES
1   POUND FRESH SAUERKRAUT, RINSED AND FULLY DRAINED
1 1/2   TEASPOONS CARAWAY SEEDS
1/2   CUP BEER
    KOSHER SALT
    FRESHLY GROUND BLACK PEPPER

    PREPARED MUSTARD
10   HOT DOG BUNS *OR* ROLLS

Grill the bratwurst over *Direct Medium* heat until browned, 6 to 8 minutes, turning once halfway through grilling time.

To make the sauerkraut: In a large sauté pan over medium heat, warm the oil. Add the onion and bacon and cook for 5 minutes, stirring occasionally. Add the apple, sauerkraut, and caraway seeds and cook for 5 minutes more. Add the beer and grilled bratwurst. Cover and cook over low heat for 25 minutes. Stir and season with salt and pepper.

Spread a generous amount of the mustard on the inside of the buns or rolls. Add the bratwurst and top with the sauerkraut. Serve immediately.

MAKES 10 SERVINGS

BRATWURST WRAPS

Okay, here's something new for the tailgater: a cultural fusion dish that adds tortillas and Swiss cheese to the mix. Dare to wow them.

DIRECT/MEDIUM

- **4 FRESH BRATWURST**
- **1 CAN (12 OUNCES) BEER**

FOR THE SAUERKRAUT:
- **1 CUP CHOPPED ONION**
- **2 TABLESPOONS VEGETABLE OIL**
- **1 POUND FRESH SAUERKRAUT, RINSED AND FULLY DRAINED**
- **2 TABLESPOONS GRANULATED SUGAR**
- **1/2 TEASPOON KOSHER SALT**
- **1/4 TEASPOON CRUSHED RED PEPPER FLAKES**

- **4 FLOUR TORTILLAS (10 INCHES)**
- **4 TABLESPOONS HONEY-DIJON MUSTARD**
- **4 SLICES SMOKED SWISS CHEESE**

Place the bratwurst and beer in a medium saucepan and bring to a boil. Reduce heat to low, cover, and simmer for 25 minutes. Remove from the heat and allow the bratwurst to cool in the beer.

To make the sauerkraut: In a large sauté pan over medium heat, cook the onion in the vegetable oil, stirring occasionally, until browned, 8 to 10 minutes. Add the sauerkraut, sugar, salt, and red pepper flakes and mix well. Cook for 5 minutes more to blend the flavors. Set aside.

Remove the bratwurst from the beer and grill them over *Direct Medium* heat until browned, 6 to 8 minutes, turning once halfway through grilling time.

To assemble the wraps: Halve each bratwurst lengthwise. Place about a quarter of the sauerkraut down the center of each tortilla and lay two brat halves on top. Spread 1 tablespoon of the mustard on each bratwurst and add a slice of the cheese. Fold two sides of the tortilla over the cheese, then fold the top and bottom to close. Grill the wraps, flap side down, over *Direct Medium* heat until browned, 3 to 4 minutes, turning once halfway through grilling time. Serve immediately.

MAKES 4 SERVINGS

CHRISTINA'S GREEN CHILE

Our friend Christina's recipe for green chile is a traditional version found in southern Colorado and northern New Mexico. This dish is at its best when Anaheim peppers are fresh off the vine, just at the point of turning from green to red. Serve with warm tortillas or pan-roasted potatoes. Make plenty for leftovers—it's even better the next day.

DIRECT/MEDIUM

- **10 ANAHEIM CHILE PEPPERS (1 POUND)**
- **15 TOMATILLOS (1 POUND), HUSKED AND RINSED**

FOR THE CHILE:
- **1 BONELESS PORK SHOULDER, ABOUT 3 POUNDS, CUT INTO 1-INCH PIECES**
- **KOSHER SALT**
- **FRESHLY GROUND BLACK PEPPER**
- **1 TABLESPOON VEGETABLE OIL**
- **3/4 CUP FINELY CHOPPED WHITE ONION**
- **1 TABLESPOON MINCED GARLIC**
- **2 TABLESPOONS ALL-PURPOSE FLOUR**
- **2 CUPS LOW-SODIUM CHICKEN BROTH**

- **1/3 CUP FINELY CHOPPED FRESH CILANTRO**
- **1 TABLESPOON FINELY CHOPPED FRESH OREGANO**
- **FRESH LIME JUICE**

Grill the chile peppers and tomatillos over *Direct Medium* heat until charred evenly on all sides, turning every 5 minutes. Remove from the grill. Place the peppers in a paper bag; close tightly. Allow to stand for 10 to 15 minutes to steam off the skins. Remove the peppers from the bag and discard the skins, stems, and seeds. Place the peppers and tomatillos in a food processor. Pulse several times until coarsely chopped.

To make the chile: Season the pork with salt and pepper. In a large saucepan over medium-high heat, warm the vegetable oil. Add the pork and cook until nicely browned (you may need to cook in batches). Set the pork aside. Add the onion and garlic to the saucepan and cook for 4 to 5 minutes, stirring occasionally. Sprinkle the flour over the mixture. Stir and cook for 1 to 2 minutes more. Add the chicken broth and use a wooden spoon to scrape the bits off the bottom of the pan. Raise the heat to high and whisk the mixture as it comes to a boil. Lower the heat to a simmer. Return the pork to the saucepan. Stir in the chile peppers and tomatillos. Simmer, stirring occasionally, until the pork is tender, about 1 hour.

Just before serving, add the cilantro and oregano. Add the lime juice and salt to taste. Serve warm.

MAKES 6 SERVINGS

Pulled Pork Barbecue with Hot Pepper Vinegar Sauce

PULLED PORK BARBECUE
WITH HOT PEPPER VINEGAR SAUCE

A classic, this one smells so good as it cooks it'll drive you crazy. For the authentic touch, add hickory chips or chunks to the fire and a scoop of coleslaw to the sandwich.

INDIRECT/MEDIUM

FOR THE RUB:

- 1 TABLESPOON PAPRIKA
- 1 TABLESPOON FIRMLY PACKED LIGHT BROWN SUGAR
- 1 1/2 TEASPOONS CHILI POWDER
- 1 1/2 TEASPOONS GROUND CUMIN
- 1 TEASPOON COARSELY GROUND BLACK PEPPER
- 1 TEASPOON KOSHER SALT
- 1/2 TEASPOON CAYENNE

- 1 BONELESS PORK SHOULDER ROAST (BOSTON BUTT), 4 TO 5 POUNDS, ROLLED AND TIED

FOR THE SAUCE:

- 1 1/2 CUPS CIDER VINEGAR
- 2 TABLESPOONS GRANULATED SUGAR
- 1 TEASPOON TABASCO SAUCE
- 1/2 TEASPOON CRUSHED RED PEPPER FLAKES
- KOSHER SALT
- FRESHLY GROUND BLACK PEPPER

HAMBURGER BUNS

To make the rub: In a small bowl combine the rub ingredients. Coat the roast evenly with the rub. Allow to stand at room temperature for 30 minutes before grilling.

Grill the roast, fat side up, over *Indirect Medium* heat until the internal temperature reaches between 185°F and 190°F, 3 to 4 hours. The meat should be so tender it pulls apart easily. Remove from the grill, place on a platter, and loosely cover with foil. Allow to rest for about 20 minutes.

To make the sauce: In a medium saucepan combine the sauce ingredients, including salt and pepper to taste, and bring to a boil. Reduce heat to low and simmer for 10 minutes. Keep warm.

Thinly slice, chop, or "pull" the pork meat into shreds with your fingers or two forks, discarding any large bits of fat. Moisten the meat with some of the sauce and mix well in a bowl. Grill the buns over *Direct Medium* heat until lightly toasted, about 30 seconds. Serve the pulled pork warm on the buns with the remaining sauce on the side.

MAKES 12 TO 15 SERVINGS

PULLED PORK SANDWICHES
WITH WEST CAROLINA BARBECUE SAUCE

Here's strong evidence for North Carolina's claim to being America's "BBQ Capital." Along the eastern part of the state, residents prefer their 'cue (always pork) with a light vinegar-based sauce such as the one on the left. But folks in the western part of the state swear by a tomato-based sauce like the one below.

INDIRECT/MEDIUM

FOR THE SAUCE:

- 3 TABLESPOONS UNSALTED BUTTER
- 1/4 CUP MINCED YELLOW ONION
- 2 CUPS KETCHUP
- 2/3 CUP FIRMLY PACKED LIGHT BROWN SUGAR
- 1/2 CUP YELLOW MUSTARD
- 1/2 CUP CIDER VINEGAR
- 2 TEASPOONS WORCESTERSHIRE SAUCE
- 1 TEASPOON TABASCO SAUCE

- 1 BONELESS PORK SHOULDER ROAST (BOSTON BUTT), 4 TO 5 POUNDS, ROLLED AND TIED
- KOSHER SALT
- FRESHLY GROUND BLACK PEPPER

HAMBURGER BUNS

To make the sauce: In a small saucepan over medium-high heat, melt the butter and cook the onion, stirring occasionally, until translucent, 4 to 5 minutes. Add the rest of the sauce ingredients and bring to a boil. Reduce heat and simmer for 10 minutes more. Set aside and allow to cool to room temperature.

Allow the roast to stand at room temperature for 20 to 30 minutes before grilling. Season with salt and pepper. Grill the roast, fat side up, over *Indirect Medium* heat until the internal temperature reaches between 185°F and 190°F, 3 to 4 hours. The meat should be so tender it pulls apart easily. Remove from the grill, place on a platter, and loosely cover with foil. Allow to rest for about 20 minutes.

Thinly slice, chop, or "pull" the pork meat into shreds with your fingers or two forks, discarding any large bits of fat. Moisten the meat with some of the sauce and mix well in a bowl. Grill the buns over *Direct Medium* heat until lightly toasted, about 30 seconds. Serve the pulled pork warm on the buns with the remaining sauce on the side.

MAKES 12 TO 15 SERVINGS

SONORA-STYLE GREEN CHILE
PORK BURRITOS

This authentic rub turns a tender pork shoulder into something to shout about. Load up the tortillas with the chile-drenched pork, beans, and the classic Southwest condiments and serve it all up with a frosty, cold Mexican lager.

INDIRECT/MEDIUM

FOR THE RUB:

- 2 TABLESPOONS RED WINE VINEGAR
- 2 TABLESPOONS CHILI POWDER
- 1 TABLESPOON GRANULATED GARLIC
- 1 TABLESPOON CRACKED BLACK PEPPER
- 2 TEASPOONS GROUND CUMIN
- 2 TEASPOONS DRIED OREGANO
- 2 TEASPOONS DRIED MARJORAM
- 2 TEASPOONS KOSHER SALT

- 1 BONELESS PORK SHOULDER ROAST (BOSTON BUTT), ABOUT 2½ POUNDS, ROLLED AND TIED
  EXTRA-VIRGIN OLIVE OIL

FOR THE BURRITOS:

- 2 CUPS PREPARED GREEN CHILE SALSA
- 2 CANS (16 OUNCES EACH) REFRIED BEANS
- 1 TABLESPOON EXTRA-VIRGIN OLIVE OIL
- 6 FLOUR TORTILLAS (10 INCHES)
- 1 CUP GRATED MONTEREY JACK CHEESE
- 1 CUP SHREDDED LETTUCE
- 1 CUP SOUR CREAM

To make the rub: In a small bowl thoroughly mix together the rub ingredients.

Coat the roast thoroughly with the rub and lightly brush or spray with olive oil. Allow the roast to stand at room temperature for 20 to 30 minutes before grilling.

Grill the roast over *Indirect Medium* heat until the internal temperature reaches between 185°F and 190°F, 3 to 4 hours.

To make the burritos: Cut the roast into 3/4-inch chunks and place in a large saucepan with the salsa. Bring to a boil, reduce heat, and simmer for 10 minutes. In another pan, heat the refried beans with the olive oil.

Grill the tortillas over *Direct Medium* heat until warm, 15 to 20 seconds, turning once halfway through grilling time. Spread each tortilla with the refried beans, sprinkle on some cheese, and spoon a generous portion of the pork mixture on top. Top with some of the shredded lettuce and sour cream. Roll the tortillas into burritos and serve immediately.

MAKES 6 SERVINGS

JERK PORK
WITH TWO CHUTNEYS

Another great party dish, with two flavors to cover all the bases. Prepare the chutneys a day ahead to allow the flavors to blend. Definitely worth the effort. Or, for a short cut, you can always use your favorite bottled chutney. Try grilled okra on the side.

INDIRECT/MEDIUM

FOR THE GINGER-BANANA CHUTNEY:

- 2 TABLESPOONS VEGETABLE OIL
- 1 CUP MINCED RED ONION
- 3 SMALL RIPE BANANAS, PEELED AND CUT INTO SMALL PIECES
- 1 CUP PITTED DATES, COARSELY DICED
- ½ CUP CIDER VINEGAR
- 1 CUP PINEAPPLE JUICE
- ⅔ CUP RAISINS
- 2 TABLESPOONS FINELY CHOPPED CANDIED (CRYSTALLIZED) GINGER
- 1 TEASPOON MADRAS CURRY POWDER
- ½ TEASPOON KOSHER SALT

FOR THE PINEAPPLE CHUTNEY:

- 1 CAN (20 OUNCES) CRUSHED PINEAPPLE
- 1 CUP WHITE WINE VINEGAR
- 1 CUP LIGHT BROWN SUGAR, FIRMLY PACKED
- 1 CUP FINELY CHOPPED RED ONION
- 1 TABLESPOON MINCED FRESH GINGER
- ½ HABANERO *OR* 2 SERRANO CHILES, STEMMED, SEEDED, AND FINELY CHOPPED

FOR THE MARINADE:

- 1 CUP FINELY CHOPPED YELLOW ONION
- ¼ CUP EXTRA-VIRGIN OLIVE OIL
- 6 GREEN ONIONS (WHITE PART ONLY), FINELY SLICED
- 1 TABLESPOON MINCED GARLIC
- 2 TEASPOONS GROUND ALLSPICE
- 1 HABANERO *OR* OTHER HOT CHILE PEPPER, STEMMED, SEEDED, AND FINELY CHOPPED
- 1 TEASPOON FINELY CHOPPED FRESH THYME
- 1 TEASPOON CIDER *OR* WHITE VINEGAR
- 1 TEASPOON FIRMLY PACKED LIGHT BROWN SUGAR
- ½ TEASPOON GROUND CINNAMON
- ½ TEASPOON GROUND NUTMEG
- ½ TEASPOON KOSHER SALT
- ½ TEASPOON FRESHLY GROUND BLACK PEPPER

- 1 BONELESS PORK SHOULDER ROAST (BOSTON BUTT), 4 TO 5 POUNDS, ROLLED AND TIED

To make the ginger-banana chutney: In a large saucepan over medium-high heat, warm the oil and cook the onion, stirring occasionally, until softened and translucent, 4 to 5 minutes. Add the bananas, dates, and vinegar; mix well. Bring the mixture to a boil, reduce heat, and simmer for 15 minutes, stirring occasionally. Add the remaining chutney ingredients and cook 5 to 10 minutes more or until the mixture has the consistency of marmalade. Remove from the heat. Cover and refrigerate until ready to use, up to one week.

To make the pineapple chutney: In a 2-quart saucepan combine the pineapple chutney ingredients. Bring to a boil, reduce heat to medium-low, and simmer, uncovered, for 30 to 40 minutes or until the mixture thickens. If there is still liquid in the bottom of the pan, raise heat to medium-high and cook, stirring, until it evaporates. Remove from the heat. Cover and refrigerate until ready to use, up to one week.

To make the marinade: In a small bowl whisk together the marinade ingredients.

Place the roast in a large, resealable plastic bag and pour in the marinade, rubbing it into the meat. Press the air out of the bag and seal tightly. Turn the bag to distribute the marinade, place in a bowl, and refrigerate for 6 to 8 hours, turning occasionally.

Remove the roast from the bag and discard the marinade. Allow the roast to stand at room temperature for 20 to 30 minutes before grilling.

Grill the roast, fat side up, over *Indirect Medium* heat until the internal temperature reaches between 185°F and 190°F, 3 to 4 hours. The meat should be so tender it pulls apart easily. Remove from the grill, place on a platter, and loosely cover with foil. Allow to rest for about 20 minutes.

Thinly slice, chop, or "pull" the pork meat into shreds with your fingers or two forks, discarding any large bits of fat. Serve with the two chutneys.

MAKES 10 TO 12 SERVINGS

SOUTHWEST
HAM STEAKS

Easy. Tasty. Meaty. Grilled. What more could you want? Just be sure the steak's at least an inch thick so you get a nice, crispy surface without drying out the center. Excellent with all the standard barbecue sides, but you might even like it with hash browns and eggs for brunch.

DIRECT/MEDIUM

FOR THE RUB:

1 TABLESPOON CHILI POWDER

1 TEASPOON DRIED OREGANO

1 TEASPOON LIGHT BROWN SUGAR

1/2 TEASPOON CAYENNE

1/4 TEASPOON FRESHLY GROUND BLACK PEPPER

1 CENTER-CUT SMOKED HAM STEAK, 2 1/2 TO 3 POUNDS AND 1 TO 2 INCHES THICK

1 TABLESPOON UNSALTED BUTTER, MELTED

To make the rub: In a small bowl combine the rub ingredients. Brush both sides of the steak with the butter. Sprinkle the

rub evenly on both sides of the steak, pressing the spices into the meat. Grill over *Direct Medium* heat until nicely browned, 12 to 15 minutes, turning once halfway through grilling time. Serve warm or at room temperature.

MAKES 4 TO 6 SERVINGS

GRILLED HAM
WITH JACK DANIEL'S MOP

A no-miss crowd pleaser. Makes great sandwiches, too. Save the bone to simmer in baked beans or bean soup.

INDIRECT/LOW

FOR THE MOP:

1 CUP JACK DANIEL'S WHISKEY

1 CUP FIRMLY PACKED LIGHT BROWN SUGAR

1/4 CUP DIJON MUSTARD

1/4 CUP DARK CORN SYRUP

1 BONE-IN SMOKED HAM, 12 TO 14 POUNDS

2 TABLESPOONS CRUSHED BLACK PEPPERCORNS

2 TABLESPOONS CRUSHED MUSTARD SEEDS

To make the mop: In a medium bowl whisk together the mop ingredients.

Allow the ham to stand at room temperature for about 1 hour before grilling. Place the ham in a heavy-gauge foil baking pan. Score the ham in a diamond pattern by making shallow, diagonal cuts about 1 inch apart across the top surface. Rub the spices into the ham.

Grill the ham over *Indirect Low* heat until the internal temperature reaches 140°F, 3 to 4 hours. Baste with the mop during the last 20 minutes of grilling time. Remove from the grill and allow to rest for about 15 minutes before slicing. Serve warm or at room temperature.

MAKES 16 TO 20 SERVINGS

"And then there was pork."

— JOHN EGERTON

THINGS GOT OUT OF HAM

If you ever find yourself staring at a huge guest list, you might wonder how you'll ever pull off such an ambitious party. If you've already thrown one, you might wonder how you survived. And if you haven't tried one yet, you might just be inspired to host a major shindig after you read this. Witness how our friend Mike, with a quick and eager can-do attitude, got in over his head and emerged a hero.

Back in the 1970s, American banks enticed folks to open accounts by offering free toasters, transistor radios, eight-track tapes, and other irresistible treasures. Weber was a small company back then and I thought if we could convince banks to give away grills, we could grow our business fast. My first lead was a bank in St. Charles, Illinois, then a small, bucolic town along the Fox River. Today it's a western Chicago suburb regularly choked with traffic.

I managed to wrangle an appointment with none other than the president of the St. Charles National Bank, Mr. De Forest. Now, Mr. D was a rather intimidating pinstriped fellow—you know, the type who might glance over your loan application and negative net worth and, with an icy gaze over his half-glasses, unleash a resounding "No." Fortunately, I wasn't asking for a loan. I had almost made the sale when he asked, "And how do you plan to deliver customers, cash in hand, to the doorstep of my bank?"

To this day I don't know why I said, "We'll offer a free barbecued ham sandwich to anyone who comes by to meet the friendly staff." Mr. D loved the idea! We decided that Weber would do the grilling and the bank's executives would serve the sandwiches.

I had three weeks to wonder what had possessed me to make such a crazy offer and to come up with a plan. Meanwhile, newspaper ads broke and suddenly all the local media wanted to cover the event. I began to get nervous. If there was too little ham, we would have a mad mob. Too much ham would mean the bank's employees would be eating leftovers for weeks—not the best PR for Weber.

Well, on Sandwich Day I hauled eight of our 36-inch Ranch® kettles (which can cook five whole hams at a time), fifty 18-pound hams, and 500 pounds of charcoal to the bank. A local bakery, though they thought I was nuts, agreed to deliver a half-truckload of freshly baked rye bread.

I fired up the grills at 7:00 A.M. and showed the bank executives, decked out in aprons and chef hats, how to make sandwiches while pitching the services of their bank with a smile. The first sandwiches were to be served at 11:00 A.M.

I suspected we were in trouble when we had to call the St. Charles police for traffic control just after 9:00 A.M. We started furiously carving ham at 10:30 A.M.

172 PORK

As I pulled a cooked ham off a grill, I put another one in its place and loaded more charcoal into the grill. We carved as fast as we could. Bank tellers formed a conga line of platter bearers, and the bank executives became covered in mustard.

By noon the police were getting nervous. Parking was full for a mile radius around the town and they had never even witnessed, let alone handled, gridlock. I was nervous, too. A half-truck of rye and 900 pounds of ham were going fast!

But Mr. D was having a ball talking to customers, cutting up with the local disk jockey, and handing out account applications. By 1:00 P.M. (closing time back then), they had opened more than 300 accounts. Mr. D decided the bank would remain open until everyone received a sandwich. At my urging, he also sent some tellers to buy every ham they could find in St. Charles. We called the bakery for more rye bread. Reinforcements from the Weber factory showed up with more charcoal, sharp knives, and new cutting boards. For the first time that day, I began to believe there wouldn't be a riot.

The tellers came back with whole hams, rolled hams, and armloads of mustard jars, leaving empty grocery shelves in their wake. The second bread delivery made it through the police line just in time, and I kept stoking the kettles. By 3:00 P.M. the line was down to mere hundreds and the bank had opened 500 accounts. We kept carving and the exhausted, mustard-covered bankers kept dispensing sandwiches.

Shortly after 5:00 P.M., our team of shell-shocked grillers and servers gave away the last free sandwich, broke out some beer, and started tallying up the day's outcome. Some 1900 pounds of ham, 950 pounds of charcoal, one truckload of rye, and God knows how much mustard later, the bank had more than 650 new customers. I had hoped to sell 40 or 50 grills to the St. Charles National Bank, but the order came to almost three truckloads.

If you ever need a recipe and a shopping list for feeding a small town ham sandwiches, check out my recipe on the right. And if you're a bank executive and need some tips on pleasing customers, it's been my experience that people take much more kindly to mustard-speckled aprons and a smile than an icy, pinstriped gaze over half-glasses. A free lunch doesn't hurt, either.

GRILLED HAM SANDWICHES
TO FEED THE WHOLE TOWN

For a smaller crowd, say a wedding reception or family reunion, divide this recipe by five.

INDIRECT/MEDIUM

8	BARBECUE GRILLS, 36 INCHES IN DIAMETER EACH
1/2	TON HARDWOOD CHARCOAL BRIQUETS
105	WHOLE FULLY COOKED HAMS, ABOUT 18 POUNDS EACH
190	LOAVES OF FRESH RYE BREAD
6	GALLONS YELLOW MUSTARD
10	PEOPLE TO CARVE HAMS
10	PEOPLE TO SPREAD MUSTARD
10	PEOPLE TO BUILD SANDWICHES
8 TO 10	TRAFFIC COPS
	PLENTY OF PARKING

Pour 150 charcoal briquets into each grill; light briquets. Keep grill lids off until the briquets are lightly ashed over, 30 to 35 minutes. Place 75 briquets on opposite sides of each charcoal grate. Position cooking grates on grills so that hinges are above each pile of charcoal. Replenish charcoal every hour with 25 briquets per side.

Grill five hams on each grill over *Indirect Medium* heat until heated through to an internal temperature of 140°F, about 2 1/2 hours. Transfer from grills to cutting boards. Replace grilled hams with new ones. Repeat as necessary.

Carve the hams into thin slices. Reserve the bones for World's Biggest Pot of Ham and Bean Soup, if desired. Build sandwiches with about 2 ounces of ham and 1 tablespoon of mustard per sandwich. Keep the line moving. Dream about early retirement.

MAKES ABOUT 1500 SERVINGS

ROTISSERIE HAM
WITH SWEET GEORGIA CHUTNEY

Cider-glazed ham is a Southern classic and the slow turning of a rotisserie just helps spread the joy. If you don't have a rotisserie, place the ham, cut side down, in a large heavy-gauge foil pan and glaze as directed.

DIRECT/LOW

FOR THE CHUTNEY:

- 1/2 CUP LIGHT BROWN SUGAR
- 1/4 CUP CIDER VINEGAR
- 3 TABLESPOONS MINCED FRESH GINGER
- 2 TEASPOONS DRY MUSTARD
- 2 CINNAMON STICKS
- 1/2 TEASPOON CRUSHED RED PEPPER FLAKES
- 2 MEDIUM VIDALIA *OR* OTHER SWEET ONIONS, QUARTERED AND THINLY SLICED
- 6 MEDIUM RIPE PEACHES, PEELED AND COARSELY CHOPPED

FOR THE GLAZE:

- 1 CUP APPLE CIDER
- 1/4 CUP PEACH PRESERVES
- 1 TEASPOON PREPARED MUSTARD
- 1/2 TEASPOON GROUND CINNAMON

- 1 SMOKE-CURED BONELESS HAM, 6 TO 8 POUNDS

To make the chutney: In a medium saucepan combine the brown sugar, vinegar, ginger, dry mustard, cinnamon, and red pepper flakes. Bring to a boil. Add the onions and simmer over low heat until tender, about 10 minutes. Add the peaches and simmer over medium heat, stirring frequently, until the mixture is slightly thickened, about 20 minutes. Cool to room temperature. Remove the cinnamon sticks. Cover and refrigerate for several hours or up to 3 days.

To make the glaze: In a medium bowl whisk together the glaze ingredients.

Allow the ham to stand at room temperature for about 1 hour before grilling. Score the ham all over by making shallow cuts diagonally across the surface in a diamond pattern.

Follow the grill's instructions for using a rotisserie. Center the ham lengthwise on the spit and secure in place. Set the ham to rotate over *Direct Low* heat until the internal temperature reaches 140°F, 1 1/2 to 2 hours. (If you do not have a rotisserie, grill over *Indirect Low* heat for 1 1/2 to 2 hours.) During the last 20 minutes of grilling time, baste the ham generously with the glaze. Remove from the rotisserie and allow to rest for about 15 minutes before slicing. Serve warm or at room temperature with the chutney on the side.

MAKES 12 TO 16 SERVINGS

MESQUITE PORK STEAKS
WITH ANCHO CHILE BBQ SAUCE

The pork steaks used in this recipe are "Porterhouse" steaks, thick T-bones cut from the rib end of the loin. It's a common beef cut but you might have to special-order a pork version. Add a zesty rub, throw them on a mesquite fire, and you've just redefined "grilled steaks."

SEAR: HIGH, COOK: INDIRECT/MEDIUM

FOR THE SAUCE:

- 1 TABLESPOON EXTRA-VIRGIN OLIVE OIL
- 1/2 CUP FINELY CHOPPED RED ONION
- 1 TABLESPOON MINCED GARLIC
- 2 MEDIUM DRIED ANCHO CHILES, STEMMED, SEEDED, AND CUT INTO 1/4-INCH STRIPS
- 3/4 CUP DRY RED WINE
- 1/2 CUP FRESH ORANGE JUICE
- 1/4 CUP KETCHUP
- 2 TABLESPOONS BALSAMIC VINEGAR

FOR THE PASTE:

- 2 TABLESPOONS EXTRA-VIRGIN OLIVE OIL
- 2 TABLESPOONS WORCESTERSHIRE SAUCE
- 2 TEASPOONS CRACKED BLACK PEPPER
- 2 TEASPOONS CHILI POWDER
- 2 TEASPOONS GRANULATED GARLIC
- 2 TEASPOONS KOSHER SALT
- 1 TEASPOON GROUND CUMIN
- 1/2 TEASPOON GROUND CINNAMON

- 4 PORK LOIN PORTERHOUSE STEAKS, ABOUT 2 INCHES THICK

MESQUITE CHIPS SOAKED IN WATER FOR AT LEAST 30 MINUTES

To make the sauce: In a large saucepan over medium heat, warm the olive oil. Add the onion and garlic and cook until softened, about 3 minutes, stirring occasionally. Add the ancho chiles and cook for 2 to 3 minutes more, stirring occasionally. Pour in the red wine, orange juice, ketchup, and balsamic vinegar. Stir. Simmer for 15 minutes. Remove from the heat, cover, and allow to steep for 30 minutes. Pour into a blender and purée until smooth.

To make the paste: In a small bowl mix together the paste ingredients.

Allow the steaks to stand at room temperature for 20 to 30 minutes before grilling. Spread the paste evenly over the steaks. Follow the grill's instructions for using wood chips. Sear the steaks over *Direct High* heat for about 6 minutes, turning once halfway through searing time. Continue grilling over *Indirect Medium* heat until the juices run clear and the internal temperature reaches 160°F, 20 to 25 minutes. Remove from the grill, cover with foil, and allow to rest for about 5 minutes. Serve warm with the sauce.

MAKES 4 TO 6 SERVINGS

HERE ANCHO CHILE SAUCE RAISES THICK PORK STEAKS TO NEW CULINARY HEIGHTS.

Mesquite Pork Steaks with Ancho Chile BBQ Sauce

Adobo Pork Steaks with Peach Salsa

ADOBO PORK STEAKS
WITH PEACH SALSA

We start with a dip into a can of chipotles, take a spin on a spicy pork steak, then skid into a cool pile of fruit salsa. Use nectarines or mangoes if you're out of peaches—the main thing is to use something sweet to counter the heat. Dig in right away or pile it all into tortillas for excellent burritos.

DIRECT/MEDIUM

FOR THE MARINADE:

- 2 TABLESPOONS APPLE CIDER VINEGAR
- 1 CHIPOTLE CHILE IN ADOBO SAUCE, MINCED
- 1 TABLESPOON ADOBO SAUCE (FROM THE CANNED CHIPOTLE)
- 1 TEASPOON MINCED GARLIC
- 1 TEASPOON DRIED OREGANO
- 1 TEASPOON KOSHER SALT
- 1/4 TEASPOON FRESHLY GROUND BLACK PEPPER

- 2 BONE-IN PORK SHOULDER BLADE STEAKS (BOSTON BUTT), 3/4 TO 1 INCH THICK EACH

FOR THE SALSA:

- 2 1/2 CUPS PEACHES, PEELED AND DICED
- 2 PLUM TOMATOES, CORED, SEEDED, AND FINELY CHOPPED
- 2 GREEN ONIONS (WHITE PART ONLY), THINLY SLICED
- 1 JALAPEÑO PEPPER, STEMMED, SEEDED, AND FINELY CHOPPED
- 2 TABLESPOONS FINELY CHOPPED FRESH CILANTRO
- 2 TABLESPOONS FRESH LIME JUICE
- PINCH OF KOSHER SALT

To make the marinade: In a small bowl whisk together the marinade ingredients.

Brush the marinade on both sides of the steaks. Cover the steaks with plastic wrap and refrigerate for 4 to 8 hours.

To make the salsa: In a medium bowl mix together the salsa ingredients. Cover with plastic wrap and refrigerate until ready to serve.

Allow the steaks to stand at room temperature for 20 to 30 minutes before grilling. Grill over *Direct Medium* heat until the juices run clear, 10 to 12 minutes, turning once halfway though grilling time. Remove from the grill, loosely cover with foil, and allow to rest for 3 to 5 minutes. Slice the steaks across the grain into thin strips. Serve warm with the salsa.

MAKES 4 SERVINGS

DOUBLE-SHOT
BLADE STEAKS

Blade steaks (also called blade chops or arm chops) are great on the grill, where their generous marbling keeps them juicy and tender. These pack a double whammy from an aged bourbon marinade and a fiery rub.

DIRECT/HIGH

FOR THE MARINADE:

- 1 CUP AGED BOURBON
- 1/3 CUP WHOLE-GRAIN MUSTARD
- 1/4 CUP LIGHT BROWN SUGAR
- 2 TABLESPOONS MINCED SHALLOTS
- 1 TABLESPOON WORCESTERSHIRE SAUCE
- 1/2 TEASPOON TABASCO SAUCE

- 4 PORK SHOULDER BLADE STEAKS (BOSTON BUTT), ABOUT 1 1/4 INCHES THICK EACH, TRIMMED OF FAT

FOR THE RUB:

- 1 TABLESPOON CRACKED BLACK PEPPER
- 1 TABLESPOON GRANULATED GARLIC
- 1 TABLESPOON ONION POWDER
- 1 TABLESPOON KOSHER SALT
- 2 TEASPOONS DRIED THYME
- 2 TEASPOONS DRIED OREGANO
- 1 TEASPOON CAYENNE
- 1 TEASPOON PAPRIKA

- EXTRA-VIRGIN OLIVE OIL

To make the marinade: In a small bowl whisk together the marinade ingredients.

Place the steaks in a large, resealable plastic bag and pour in the marinade. Press the air out of the bag and seal tightly. Turn the bag to distribute the marinade, place in a bowl, and refrigerate for 2 to 4 hours, turning occasionally.

To make the rub: In a small bowl combine the rub ingredients.

Remove the steaks from the bag and discard the marinade. Pat the steaks with paper towels to remove excess marinade. Coat both sides of the steaks with the rub. Lightly brush or spray the steaks with olive oil. Allow to stand at room temperature for 20 to 30 minutes before grilling.

Grill the steaks over *Direct High* heat until the juices run clear and the internal temperature reaches 160°F, 12 to 14 minutes, turning once halfway through grilling time. Remove from the grill, loosely cover with foil, and allow to rest for 3 to 5 minutes before serving.

MAKES 4 SERVINGS

PORK ON THE GRILL

When "Tom, Tom, the piper's son/Stole a pig and away did run," he made off with more than a precursor to the football. He confiscated a veritable treasure trove since, when it comes to pigs, you can use "everything but the squeal." And if Tom was dashing home to a grill, he was all the more fortunate. On the grill, pork achieves peak flavor and optimal texture. Here are the best cuts for grilling:

ROASTS: You can buy **pork loin** in seemingly countless forms. The lean and meaty **center loin roast** is sold with or without the rib bones attached, and as a **double** or **single roast**. A single loin roast with the fat cap removed is called **Chef's Prime™**, (a marketing moniker that has nothing to do with a USDA rating). The short and narrow **tenderloin** (usually sold in pairs) weighs in at about a pound a piece, and is one of the easiest and most delicious cuts you can prepare on the grill. Tenderloin can actually be removed from the grill at 155°F if you cover it with foil and let it rest for three to five minutes before carving. Its finished temperature will be a safe 160°F.

- From the rib end of the loin section you have the fancy **crown roast**, which is two **loin back rib racks** tied together in a circle. The ever-popular **rib roast** does great on the grill whole and when cut into rib chops, steaks, and filets.
- At the shoulder end of the loin section, you find the sirloin, which is cut into **sirloin roasts**, **steaks**, and **chops**. These cuts are fattier than the center loin, and thus richer in flavor. All do marvelously well on the grill with just a rub or a dip in a marinade.
- **Pork shoulder** (also called **Boston butt**) is a great roast for the grill because of its structure and higher fat content. Several muscles come together at the joint; between each is a cushion of fat. Because it's a tougher cut, you can grill it to 185°F—very overdone for any other cut—but you need to slowly roast shoulder to a higher finishing temperature to break down its tough fibers. On the grill over Indirect Medium heat, pork shoulder turns to tender sections of flavorful meat you can then shred or chop for pulled pork sandwiches, green chile, and other dishes. You can cook shoulder roast on the bone, but it's easier to cut when boned, rolled, and tied. Because it varies in size from 2½ to 6 pounds and is relatively inexpensive, it's a good choice for a small family or a crowd.

CHOPS: We love chops on the grill—they're tasty, easy, and fast. Keep a stock pile in the deep freeze and see if your life doesn't get easier. Best of all, there's a chop for everyone (*see Meat Cuts, page 398*). Three-quarter-inch-thick chops over Direct Medium heat only take 8 to 10 minutes, so don't wander far from the grill. Chops at least 1 inch thick are best for grilling.

HAM: Ham is the happy brainchild of necessity and creativity. Imagine life before refrigerators, factor in the massive size of a fresh hog leg, and you can understand why earlier cooks around the globe were eager to figure out how to preserve these cuts. Luckily, they found many ways. Today we can sample rich prosciutto (an Italian-style unsmoked, dry-cured variety) and Westphalian ham (a German-style smoked, dry-cured version), to name just a few, alongside the artistry of a U.S. country ham. And we do mean artistry. The hams from Smithfield, Virginia, for example, are so prized for their flavor and texture that their name is a jealously guarded appellation.

- Grill **fully cooked hams** or **ham steaks** to an internal temperature of 140°F, just enough to warm them through. Add intrigue with a spice rub or a flavorful mop. **Fresh** or **partially cooked ham** must be cooked to an internal temperature of 160°F, like other raw pork cuts.

SAUSAGES: **Bratwurst** and **Italian** are the most popular choices for the grill, but any fresh pork-based sausage fares well on the grill. Try them this way and you'll never use a skillet again. Grill over Indirect Medium heat for about 25 minutes or until a meat thermometer inserted in the sausage's center registers 160°F, turning once halfway through grilling time.

REMOVING THE SILVER SKIN FROM PORK TENDERLOIN

Silver skin is a very thin membrane that runs the length of the tenderloin, connecting it to the loin. It's not only chewy when cooked, it can cause the meat to curl because it shrinks during cooking. Remove it with a sharp, short knife and discard it.

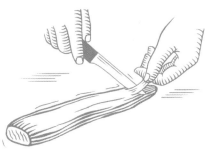

PULL THE MEMBRANE FROM THE MUSCLE

Depending on how closely the meat is trimmed, you might only see a streak of fat running the length of the tenderloin. Under that fat is the pearlescent silver skin. Start at the narrow end of the tenderloin. Pinch the meat to pull the membrane away from the muscle. Slide your knife under the membrane and slowly cut along the muscle toward the thick end of the meat in smooth sawing motions (above).

WORK ALONG THE GRAIN OF THE MEAT

Keep the knife blade close to the muscle, removing as little meat as possible. Because the silver skin attaches in different directions, you might find it helpful to start again from the thick end and work from that end as well. Some cooks remove the silver skin in strips. Just work along the grain of the meat lengthwise (above). Most importantly, be sure to always keep the knife blade angled away from you—raw meat can be more slippery than you think.

TIPS
FOR GREAT GRILLED PORK

Once you've decided on the cut, grilling pork to peak flavor is easy. Here are a few pointers to keep you on track:

Keep it juicy: *Pork is bred so lean today that its leanest cut, a boneless center-cut loin chop, has less fat than a boneless, skinless chicken breast. Great news for the dietician, but a challenge for the cook—so grill most pork only to 160°F to keep it from drying out (exceptions: see tenderloin, pork shoulder, and ham, far left). Brines and marinades are easy, effective ways to add moisture and flavor to leaner cuts. Rubs and pastes help create a flavorful crust on both small and larger cuts. For juicy kabobs, cut pork chunks into 1- to 1¼-inch cubes—anything smaller can dry out too quickly.*

To sear or not: *Chops benefit from a good searing. Six minutes per side over Direct High heat is sufficient to create a pleasing texture and give you tantalizing grill marks. Roasts also benefit from searing unless they're too fatty, in which case there's an increased risk of flare-ups. Hams are usually partially or fully cooked, so they don't need to be seared. And pork tenderloins, which cook quickly, need just the slightest outer crust to create the perfect counterpoint to their oh-so-tender centers, so they don't need to be seared. High heat also cooks tougher cuts such as ribs and shoulder so fast they don't have time to tenderize, so cook them over Indirect Medium or Low heat.*

Direct versus Indirect: *Remember foods that cook in less than 25 minutes (ham steaks, chops) can go over Direct heat. Use Indirect heat for roasts and ribs.*

CARIBBEAN TENDERLOIN
WITH BLACK BEAN SALSA

Pull out the wild tropical shirts and your flashiest shades. Here's another one you can make ahead for a no-hassle dinner party. Wear gloves when mincing the habaneros— they're extremely hot.

INDIRECT/MEDIUM

FOR THE MARINADE:

1/4 CUP FRESH LIME JUICE

1/4 CUP MAJOR GREY CHUTNEY

2 TABLESPOONS EXTRA-VIRGIN OLIVE OIL

2 TABLESPOONS MINCED ONION

1 TABLESPOON LIME ZEST

1 TABLESPOON GRATED FRESH GINGER

1 TABLESPOON MINCED GARLIC

1 HABANERO *OR* SCOTCH BONNET PEPPER, STEMMED, SEEDED, AND MINCED

2 PORK TENDERLOINS, ABOUT 1 POUND EACH

FOR THE RUB:

1 TABLESPOON KOSHER SALT

2 TEASPOONS CURRY POWDER

2 TEASPOONS GROUND CORIANDER

2 TEASPOONS GROUND ALLSPICE

1 TEASPOON FRESHLY GROUND BLACK PEPPER

1/2 TEASPOON GROUND NUTMEG

1/2 TEASPOON GROUND CUMIN

FOR THE SALSA:

1/4 CUP VEGETABLE OIL

3 TABLESPOONS FRESH LIME JUICE

2 TEASPOONS GROUND CUMIN

1 TEASPOON RED WINE VINEGAR

1 CAN (15 OUNCES) BLACK BEANS, RINSED AND DRAINED

1/2 CUP FINELY DICED YELLOW BELL PEPPER

1/2 CUP FINELY DICED RED ONION

1/2 CUP FINELY DICED TOMATOES

1/4 CUP FINELY CHOPPED GREEN ONIONS

1/2 HABANERO *OR* SCOTCH BONNET PEPPER, STEMMED, SEEDED, AND MINCED

2 TEASPOONS MINCED GARLIC

1 TABLESPOON FINELY CHOPPED FRESH BASIL

VEGETABLE OIL

To make the marinade: In a small bowl whisk together the marinade ingredients.

Trim excess fat and silver skin from the tenderloins (*see page 179*). Place in a large, resealable plastic bag and add the marinade. Press the air out of the bag and seal tightly. Turn the bag to distribute the marinade, place in a bowl, and refrigerate for 4 to 6 hours, turning occasionally.

To make the rub: In a small bowl combine the rub ingredients.

To make the salsa: In a medium bowl whisk together the vegetable oil, lime juice, cumin, vinegar, and 2 teaspoons of the rub. Add the remaining salsa ingredients. Mix, cover, and allow to stand at room temperature for about 2 hours.

Remove the tenderloins from the bag and discard the marinade. Pat the tenderloins dry with paper towels. Coat evenly with the remaining rub. Lightly brush or spray with oil. Allow to stand at room temperature for 20 to 30 minutes before grilling.

Grill over *Indirect Medium* heat until the centers are barely pink and the internal temperature reaches 155°F, 25 to 30 minutes, turning once halfway through grilling time. Remove from the grill and loosely cover with foil. Allow to rest for 3 to 5 minutes before slicing. Serve with the salsa.

MAKES 4 SERVINGS

DISAPPEARING TENDERLOIN
WITH PICO DE GALLO

After one bite you'll know how we came up with the name for this recipe.

INDIRECT/MEDIUM

FOR THE MARINADE:

1/3 CUP FRESH ORANGE JUICE

2 TABLESPOONS EXTRA-VIRGIN OLIVE OIL

2 TABLESPOONS WORCESTERSHIRE SAUCE

1 TABLESPOON MOLASSES

1 TABLESPOON MINCED GARLIC

2 PORK TENDERLOINS, ABOUT 1 POUND EACH

FOR THE RUB:

2 TEASPOONS CHILI POWDER

1 TEASPOON CRACKED BLACK PEPPER

1 TEASPOON KOSHER SALT

1/2 TEASPOON GROUND CUMIN

1/2 TEASPOON DRIED OREGANO

1/4 TEASPOON GRANULATED GARLIC

FOR THE PICO DE GALLO:

2 CUPS FINELY DICED RIPE TOMATO

1 CUP FINELY DICED RED ONION

3 TABLESPOONS FINELY CHOPPED FRESH CILANTRO

1 TABLESPOON FRESH LIME JUICE

1 TABLESPOON EXTRA-VIRGIN OLIVE OIL

1 TO 2 TEASPOONS MINCED SERRANO CHILES, INCLUDING SEEDS

1 TEASPOON KOSHER SALT

EXTRA-VIRGIN OLIVE OIL

To make the marinade: In a small bowl whisk together the marinade ingredients.

Trim any excess fat and silver skin from the tenderloins

(see page 179). Place the tenderloins in a large, resealable plastic bag and add the marinade. Press the air out of the bag and seal tightly. Turn the bag to distribute the marinade, place in a bowl, and refrigerate for 1 to 2 hours, turning occasionally.

To make the rub: In a small bowl combine the rub ingredients.

To make the pico de gallo: In a medium bowl combine the pico de gallo ingredients and mix thoroughly. Cover with plastic wrap and allow to stand at room temperature for about 1 hour to fully incorporate the flavors.

Remove the tenderloins from the bag and discard the marinade. Coat evenly with the rub and lightly brush or spray with olive oil. Allow to stand at room temperature for 20 to 30 minutes before grilling.

Grill over *Indirect Medium* heat until the centers are barely pink and the internal temperature reaches 155°F, 25 to 30 minutes, turning once halfway through grilling time. Remove from the grill, loosely cover with foil, and allow to rest for 3 to 5 minutes before cutting in thin slices on the bias. Serve warm with the pico de gallo.

MAKES 4 SERVINGS

TENDERLOIN
WRAPPED IN PANCETTA

Pancetta, a salt-cured Italian bacon, adds rich flavor here and, if crisped over Direct heat at the end, it creates a compelling contrast to the tenderloin.

INDIRECT/MEDIUM

FOR THE RUB:

1 TABLESPOON MINCED GARLIC

2 TEASPOONS MINCED FRESH ROSEMARY

2 TEASPOONS KOSHER SALT

1/4 TEASPOON FRESHLY GROUND BLACK PEPPER

2 PORK TENDERLOINS, ABOUT 1 POUND EACH

1/4 POUND THINLY SLICED PANCETTA

To make the rub: In a small bowl combine the rub ingredients.

Trim any excess fat and silver skin from the tenderloins *(see page 179)* and spread the rub evenly all over, pressing the spices into the meat. Cut six 12-inch pieces of cotton string, three for each tenderloin. Wrap the tenderloin with the slices of pancetta and secure the pancetta with the string. (The tenderloins do not need to be completely covered.) Allow to stand at room temperature for 20 to 30 minutes before grilling.

Grill the tenderloins over *Indirect Medium* heat until the centers are barely pink and the internal temperature reaches 155°F, 25 to 30 minutes, turning once halfway through grilling time. Move the tenderloins over *Direct Medium* heat for the last 3 minutes if you want to crisp the pancetta. Allow the tenderloins to rest for 3 to 5 minutes, then snip the strings with scissors and remove them. Cut the tenderloins in thin slices on the bias and serve warm.

MAKES 4 TO 6 SERVINGS

BUTTERFLIED TENDERLOIN
WITH RICE SALAD

Could delicious, lean pork get any easier? Or more flavorful? In a word, nope.

DIRECT/MEDIUM

FOR THE MARINADE:

2 TABLESPOONS HONEY

2 TABLESPOONS DIJON MUSTARD

2 TABLESPOONS ASIAN SESAME OIL

2 TABLESPOONS RICE VINEGAR

2 TABLESPOONS FINELY CHOPPED FRESH GINGER

1 TABLESPOON MINCED GARLIC

1 TABLESPOON SOY SAUCE

1/2 TEASPOON FRESHLY GROUND BLACK PEPPER

2 PORK TENDERLOINS, ABOUT 1 POUND EACH

FOR THE SALAD:

1 TABLESPOON FRESH LEMON JUICE

2 TEASPOONS DIJON MUSTARD

1/4 CUP PEANUT OIL

1 CUP PEELED, SEEDED, AND FINELY CHOPPED CUCUMBER

1/2 CUP FINELY CHOPPED CELERY

1/2 CUP FINELY CHOPPED FRESH MINT

3 CUPS COOKED WILD RICE (ABOUT 6 OUNCES UNCOOKED)

1/4 TEASPOON KOSHER SALT

1/4 TEASPOON FRESHLY GROUND BLACK PEPPER

PEANUT OIL

To make the marinade: In a large bowl whisk together the marinade ingredients.

Trim excess fat and silver skin from the tenderloins *(see page 179)*. Butterfly the tenderloins by cutting down the center lengthwise about three-quarters of the way through and opening them flat like a book. Place between sheets of plastic wrap and, using a mallet or heavy frying pan, lightly pound to a uniform thickness. Transfer the tenderloins to the marinade and coat evenly. Cover with plastic wrap and refrigerate for 2 to 4 hours, turning occasionally.

To make the salad: In a large bowl whisk together the lemon juice and mustard. Add the peanut oil and whisk until smooth. Add the cucumber, celery, mint, and cooked rice. Mix well and season with the salt and pepper. Set aside.

Remove the pork tenderloins from the marinade and discard the marinade. Lightly pat the tenderloins dry with paper towels and brush or spray with oil. Allow to stand for 20 to 30 minutes before grilling.

Grill over *Direct Medium* heat until the centers are barely pink, about 15 minutes, turning once halfway through grilling time. Allow to rest for 3 to 5 minutes before cutting in thin slices on the bias. Serve warm with the salad.

MAKES 4 SERVINGS

PACIFIC ISLAND
PORK KABOBS

Good news: Kabobs just got fun again. Yes, anyone can cube a pepper and a pineapple, but it's all about the marinade here. So easy, and sure to impress.

DIRECT/MEDIUM

FOR THE MARINADE:

1 CUP MANGO *OR* PEACH JUICE/NECTAR

2 TABLESPOONS FRESH LIME JUICE

2 TABLESPOONS SOY SAUCE

1 TABLESPOON CURRY POWDER

1 TEASPOON GROUND GINGER

1 TEASPOON CHILI POWDER

1 TEASPOON ASIAN SESAME OIL

2 POUNDS PORK LOIN, CUT INTO 1 1/4-INCH PIECES

10 GREEN ONIONS (WHITE PART ONLY),
CUT INTO 1-INCH PIECES

2 SMALL RED BELL PEPPERS, STEM, SEEDS,
AND RIBS REMOVED, CUT INTO 1 1/2-INCH CHUNKS

1 SMALL PINEAPPLE, PEELED, CORED,
AND CUT INTO 1 1/2-INCH CHUNKS
VEGETABLE OIL
KOSHER SALT

To make the marinade: In a large bowl whisk together the marinade ingredients.

Place the pork pieces in a large, resealable plastic bag and pour in the marinade. Press the air out of the bag and seal tightly. Turn the bag to distribute the marinade, place in a bowl, and refrigerate for 2 to 4 hours, turning occasionally.

Remove the pork from the bag, reserving the marinade. Pour the marinade into a small saucepan. Bring the marinade to a boil and boil for 1 full minute. Remove from the heat.

Skewer the pork, alternating with the onion, bell pepper, and pineapple. There should be four or five pieces of meat per skewer. Allow to stand at room temperature for 20 to 30 minutes before grilling.

Lightly brush or spray the kabobs with vegetable oil and season with salt. Grill over *Direct Medium* heat for 10 to 12 minutes, turning and basting with the reserved marinade once halfway through grilling time. The pork will be firm and the pineapple pieces will be lightly charred, juicy, and just beginning to slip off the skewers. Serve warm.

MAKES 6 SERVINGS

CEDAR-SMOKED
PORK LOIN
WITH PINEAPPLE SALSA

Fresh herbs, cedar smoke, and a sweet and kicky relish add loads of personality to this dream cut of pork. Be sure to use wood that's completely untreated. Many barbecue or cooking-supply stores carry food-safe cedar planks.

DIRECT/MEDIUM

1 UNTREATED CEDAR PLANK
(ABOUT 4 INCHES BY 12 INCHES)

FOR THE SALSA:

4 CUPS FINELY DICED PINEAPPLE

1/2 CUP GRANULATED SUGAR

1/4 CUP WHITE WINE VINEGAR

2 TABLESPOONS FRESH LIME JUICE

1 TEASPOON MINCED JALAPEÑO PEPPER

1/2 TEASPOON GROUND CUMIN

1/2 TEASPOON KOSHER SALT

1/8 TEASPOON FRESHLY GROUND BLACK PEPPER

4 GREEN ONIONS (WHITE PART ONLY),
FINELY SLICED

1/3 CUP FINELY CHOPPED FRESH BASIL
KOSHER SALT

FOR THE RUB:

1 TABLESPOON FINELY CHOPPED FRESH SAGE

2 TEASPOONS PAPRIKA

2 TEASPOONS FINELY CHOPPED FRESH THYME

1 TEASPOON KOSHER SALT

1/2 TEASPOON FRESHLY GROUND BLACK PEPPER

1 PORK LOIN ROAST, 3 TO 3 1/2 POUNDS

Immerse the untreated cedar plank in water; place a weight on it to keep it submerged. Soak for 4 to 24 hours.

To make the salsa: In a large sauté pan combine the pineapple, sugar, vinegar, lime juice, jalapeño, cumin, salt, and pepper. Bring to a boil and cook over medium-high heat until thickened, 7 to 10 minutes. (If there is still a lot of liquid left, use a slotted spoon to transfer the pineapple to a bowl and continue to cook the liquid over high heat for 5 minutes more, then pour the liquid over the pineapple.) Mix in the onions and basil. Season with salt, if desired.

To make the rub: In a small bowl combine the rub ingredients.

Trim any excess fat from the pork loin. Spread the rub over the roast and place on the cedar plank. Allow to stand at room temperature for 20 to 30 minutes before grilling.

Grill over *Direct Medium* heat until the internal temperature reaches 155°F, about 1 hour. Carefully remove the roast and plank from the grill and loosely cover the roast with foil. Allow to rest for 3 to 5 minutes before carving. Serve warm with the pineapple salsa.

MAKES 6 SERVINGS

Cedar-Smoked Pork Loin with Pineapple Salsa

Tuscan Pork Loin with White Bean Salad

TUSCAN PORK LOIN
WITH WHITE BEAN SALAD

Taste the best of earth, farm, and kitchen in this delicious example of Tuscan cuisine. Use the best extra-virgin olive oil you can afford and spring for a good loaf of crusty bread to sop up the dressing and juices.

SEAR: HIGH, COOK: INDIRECT/MEDIUM

FOR THE BEANS:

- 2 CUPS CANNELLINI BEANS (WHITE KIDNEY BEANS) *OR* NAVY BEANS
- 5 TO 6 CUPS CHICKEN BROTH
- 1 MEDIUM YELLOW ONION, QUARTERED
- 4 WHOLE CLOVES GARLIC, PEELED
- 1 RIB CELERY, CUT IN HALF
- 1 SPRIG FRESH ROSEMARY
- 1 BAY LEAF

- 1 EIGHT-BONE CENTER-CUT PORK LOIN, ABOUT 5 POUNDS
- 4 MEDIUM GARLIC CLOVES, CUT INTO 1/8-INCH SLIVERS

FOR THE MARINADE:

- 2 TABLESPOONS FINELY CHOPPED FRESH ROSEMARY
- 2 TABLESPOONS FRESH LEMON JUICE
- 2 TABLESPOONS EXTRA-VIRGIN OLIVE OIL
- 1 TABLESPOON CRACKED WHITE PEPPERCORNS
  KOSHER SALT

FOR THE SALAD:

- 2 TABLESPOONS WHITE WINE VINEGAR
- 2 TABLESPOONS FRESH LEMON JUICE
- 1/2 CUP EXTRA-VIRGIN OLIVE OIL
- 2 TEASPOONS MINCED GARLIC
- 1/2 CUP FINELY DICED YELLOW ONION
- 1/2 CUP FINELY DICED YELLOW BELL PEPPER
- 1/2 CUP FINELY DICED PLUM TOMATOES
- 3 TABLESPOONS FINELY CHOPPED FRESH BASIL
  KOSHER SALT
  FRESHLY GROUND BLACK PEPPER

To prepare the beans: In a large pot cover the beans with 2 quarts water and soak overnight. Drain the beans and return them to the pot. Add the remaining bean ingredients. Bring just to a boil, reduce heat, and allow to simmer very slowly for about 1 hour until the beans are tender but not mushy. Drain the beans into a colander. Remove and discard the vegetables, rosemary, and bay leaf.

Trim the pork loin of any excess fat. Using a thin, sharp knife, make 1/2-inch cuts in the meaty portion of the pork loin. Insert the garlic slivers into the incisions.

To make the marinade: In a small bowl whisk together the marinade ingredients, including salt to taste.

Rub the marinade into the pork loin, cover with plastic wrap, and refrigerate overnight or as long as 24 hours.

To make the salad: In a large bowl mix the hot beans with the vinegar, lemon juice, and olive oil. Add the garlic, onion, bell pepper, tomatoes, and basil. Season with salt and pepper, toss lightly, and cool to room temperature.

Allow the roast to stand at room temperature for 20 to 30 minutes before grilling. Season with salt. Sear the roast over *Direct High* heat for 6 minutes, turning once halfway through searing time. Continue grilling over *Indirect Medium* heat until the juices run clear and the internal temperature reaches 155°F, about 1 hour. Transfer to a serving platter, loosely cover with foil, and allow to rest for about 10 minutes before slicing between each bone. Serve warm with the salad.

MAKES 8 SERVINGS

MANGO TANGO
PORK CHOPS

Want something easy with a tropical flair? Ordinary chops take a big step up with this marinade. In a pinch, you can substitute apricot or orange juice for the mango juice. Serve with black beans and rice.

DIRECT/MEDIUM

FOR THE MARINADE:

- 1 CUP MANGO JUICE
- 1/4 CUP RICE VINEGAR
- 3 TABLESPOONS EXTRA-VIRGIN OLIVE OIL
- 2 TABLESPOONS SOY SAUCE
- 2 TABLESPOONS MINCED SHALLOTS
- 2 TEASPOONS MINCED GARLIC
- 2 TEASPOONS SRIRACHA (HOT CHILI-GARLIC SAUCE)
- 1 TEASPOON KOSHER SALT
- 1/2 TEASPOON GROUND CUMIN
- 1/2 TEASPOON FRESHLY GROUND BLACK PEPPER

- 6 BONE-IN PORK CHOPS, ABOUT 3/4 INCH THICK EACH

To make the marinade: In a medium bowl whisk together the marinade ingredients.

Place the pork chops in a large, resealable plastic bag and pour in the marinade. Press the air out of the bag and seal tightly. Turn the bag to distribute the marinade, place in a bowl, and refrigerate for 2 to 4 hours, turning occasionally.

Remove the chops from the bag, reserving the marinade. Allow the chops to stand at room temperature for 20 to 30 minutes before grilling. Pour the marinade into a small saucepan. Bring to a boil and boil 1 full minute. Remove from the heat.

Grill the chops over *Direct Medium* heat until the juices run clear and the meat is firm to the touch, 8 to 10 minutes, turning and basting with the marinade once halfway through grilling time. Serve warm.

MAKES 6 SERVINGS

PORK CHOPS
SMOTHERED IN RED GRAVY

In Creole cooking, tomato sauce is called "red gravy." Here we ladle it over sizzling pork chops seasoned with an authentic New Orleans–style rub.

SEAR: HIGH, COOK: INDIRECT/MEDIUM

FOR THE SAUCE:

- 1 TABLESPOON UNSALTED BUTTER
- 1/2 CUP FINELY CHOPPED YELLOW ONION
- 1/4 CUP FINELY CHOPPED GREEN BELL PEPPER
- 1/4 CUP FINELY CHOPPED CELERY
- 1 TEASPOON MINCED GARLIC
- 1/2 TEASPOON DRIED THYME
- 1/2 TEASPOON PAPRIKA
- 1/8 TEASPOON CAYENNE
- 1/8 TEASPOON FRESHLY GROUND BLACK PEPPER
- 1/4 CUP DRY RED WINE
- 1 CAN (14 1/2 OUNCES) CHOPPED TOMATOES
- 1/2 TEASPOON KOSHER SALT

FOR THE RUB:

- 1 TEASPOON PAPRIKA
- 1 TEASPOON DRIED THYME
- 1 TEASPOON GROUND OREGANO
- 1/2 TEASPOON GRANULATED ONION
- 1/2 TEASPOON GRANULATED GARLIC
- 1/2 TEASPOON KOSHER SALT
- 1/4 TEASPOON CAYENNE

- 4 BONE-IN, CENTER-CUT PORK CHOPS, ABOUT 1 INCH THICK EACH
- EXTRA-VIRGIN OLIVE OIL

To make the sauce: In a medium sauté pan over medium-high heat, melt the butter. Add the onion, bell pepper, celery, garlic, thyme, paprika, cayenne, and pepper. Stir occasionally until the vegetables are brown, 4 to 5 minutes. Add the red wine and cook until all the liquid has evaporated. Add the tomatoes and salt. Stir and simmer for about 5 minutes. Transfer to a food processor and purée. Return the mixture to the sauté pan and simmer until smooth. Set aside.

To make the rub: In a small bowl combine the rub ingredients.

Season the pork chops evenly with the rub. Lightly brush or spray with olive oil. Allow to stand at room temperature for 20 to 30 minutes before grilling.

Sear the pork chops over *Direct High* heat for 6 minutes, turning once halfway through searing time. Continue grilling over *Indirect Medium* heat until the juices run clear, 6 to 8 minutes. Meanwhile, warm the sauce over medium heat. Serve the pork chops warm with the sauce spooned on top.

MAKES 4 SERVINGS

HICKORY CHOPS
WITH RED-EYE BARBECUE SAUCE

In Tennessee they often fry ham steaks for breakfast, adding freshly brewed coffee to their juices for an eye-opening gravy. This barbecue sauce draws on that tradition, adding a kick to chops grilled over hickory.

SEAR: HIGH, COOK: INDIRECT/MEDIUM

FOR THE RUB:

- 1 1/2 TEASPOONS WHOLE BLACK PEPPERCORNS
- 1 1/2 TEASPOONS WHOLE MUSTARD SEEDS
- 1 TABLESPOON PAPRIKA
- 1 1/2 TEASPOONS BROWN SUGAR
- 1 1/2 TEASPOONS KOSHER SALT
- 1 TEASPOON GRANULATED GARLIC
- 1 TEASPOON ONION POWDER
- 1/2 TEASPOON GROUND CUMIN
- 1/4 TEASPOON CAYENNE
- 1/4 TEASPOON GROUND CLOVES

FOR THE SAUCE:

- 4 OUNCES COUNTRY HAM, DICED
- 1 CUP BREWED COFFEE
- 1/2 CUP KETCHUP
- 1 TABLESPOON WORCESTERSHIRE SAUCE
- 1 TABLESPOON PREPARED MUSTARD
- 1 TABLESPOON LIGHT BROWN SUGAR
- 2 TEASPOONS RED WINE VINEGAR
- 1/2 TEASPOON TABASCO SAUCE

- 4 BONELESS CENTER CUT PORK CHOPS, ABOUT 1 1/2 INCHES THICK EACH
- VEGETABLE OIL

HICKORY CHIPS *OR* CHUNKS SOAKED IN WATER FOR AT LEAST 30 MINUTES

To make the rub: Using a mortar and pestle or spice grinder, grind the peppercorns and mustard seeds. Combine with the remaining rub ingredients in a small bowl.

To make the sauce: Heat a sauté pan over high heat until smoking hot. Fry the country ham until dark brown and crusty, 5 to 6 minutes. Reduce heat and carefully add the coffee and 1/2 cup water. Whisk in the remaining sauce ingredients. Simmer until about 1 cup of liquid remains, about 30 minutes. Strain and reserve until ready to serve.

Coat the pork chops with the rub and lightly brush or spray with vegetable oil. Allow to stand at room temperature for 20 to 30 minutes before grilling.

Follow the grill's instructions for using wood chips. Sear the pork chops over *Direct High* heat for 6 minutes, turning once halfway through searing time. Continue grilling over *Indirect Medium* heat until the juices run clear, 6 to 8 minutes. Serve immediately with the warmed sauce.

MAKES 4 SERVINGS

MAPLE-GLAZED PORK CHOPS
WITH SUCCOTASH SALAD

A sweet glaze from the North meets a warm, dill-touched version of a Southern classic. The matchmaker? One tender pork cut: boneless loin chops. Succulent!

DIRECT/MEDIUM

FOR THE GLAZE:

- 2 TEASPOONS PURE MAPLE SYRUP
- 2 TEASPOONS DIJON MUSTARD
- 1 TEASPOON STEAK SAUCE

FOR THE SALAD:

- 2 CUPS FRESHLY COOKED CORN KERNELS (FROM ONE 10-OUNCE FROZEN PACKAGE)
- 2 CUPS FRESHLY COOKED LIMA BEANS (FROM ONE 10-OUNCE FROZEN PACKAGE)
- 1/4 CUP FINELY DICED CELERY
- 1/4 CUP FINELY CHOPPED WHITE ONION
- 1 TABLESPOON FINELY CHOPPED FRESH DILL
- 1/4 CUP VEGETABLE OIL
- 2 TABLESPOONS DIJON MUSTARD
- 2 TABLESPOONS WHITE WINE VINEGAR
- 2 TABLESPOONS GRANULATED SUGAR
- 1/2 TEASPOON KOSHER SALT
- 1/4 TEASPOON FRESHLY GROUND BLACK PEPPER

- 4 BONELESS PORK LOIN CHOPS, ABOUT 1 1/4 INCHES THICK EACH, TRIMMED OF EXCESS FAT
  VEGETABLE OIL
  KOSHER SALT
  FRESHLY GROUND BLACK PEPPER

To make the glaze: In a small bowl whisk together the glaze ingredients.

To make the salad: In a large bowl combine the corn, lima beans, celery, onion, and dill. In a small saucepan over medium heat, combine the vegetable oil, mustard, vinegar, sugar, salt, and pepper. Whisk and bring to a simmer. Pour over the corn and lima beans, toss well, and set aside.

Allow the pork chops to stand at room temperature for 20 to 30 minutes before grilling. Lightly brush or spray the chops with the oil, then brush with the glaze and season with salt and pepper.

Grill the chops over *Direct Medium* heat until the juices run clear, about 10 to 12 minutes, turning once halfway through grilling time. Serve warm with the salad.

MAKES 4 SERVINGS

ALL-AMERICAN PORK CHOPS
WITH HOMEMADE APPLESAUCE

You might not think you have time for homemade apple-sauce, but it's easier and more rewarding than you'd imagine. (Hint: You just can't get that great apple smell from a jar or can.) The dry rub makes the most of the pork taste, and the bone lends even more flavor.

SEAR: HIGH, COOK: INDIRECT/MEDIUM

FOR THE APPLESAUCE:

- 3 MEDIUM GRANNY SMITH APPLES, PEELED, CORED, AND CUT INTO WEDGES
- 2 TABLESPOONS UNSALTED BUTTER
- 1/4 CUP APPLE JUICE
- 1 TABLESPOON FRESH LEMON JUICE
- 2 TEASPOONS GRANULATED SUGAR
- 1/2 TEASPOON MUSTARD SEEDS
- 1/4 TEASPOON GROUND CINNAMON
- 1/4 TEASPOON GROUND GINGER

FOR THE RUB:

- 1 TEASPOON MUSTARD SEEDS
- 1 TEASPOON CELERY SEEDS
- 1 TEASPOON DRIED THYME
- 1/2 TEASPOON KOSHER SALT
- 1/4 TEASPOON FRESHLY GROUND BLACK PEPPER
- 1/4 TEASPOON CAYENNE

- 4 BONE-IN, RIB PORK CHOPS, ABOUT 1 INCH THICK EACH

To make the applesauce: In a medium sauté pan over medium-high heat, cook the apples with the butter, stirring occasionally, until the apples begin to brown, about 5 minutes. Add the remaining sauce ingredients, stir, lower heat to simmer, nd cook, covered, until the apples are very tender, about 5 minutes more. Transfer to a food processor and process until smooth. If the sauce seems too thin, return to the pan and simmer until thickened. Set aside.

To make the rub: In a small bowl combine the rub ingredients.

Season the pork chops evenly with the rub, pressing it into the meat. Allow to stand at room temperature for 20 to 30 minutes before grilling.

Sear the pork chops over *Direct High* heat for 6 minutes, turning once halfway through searing time. Continue grilling over *Indirect Medium* heat until the juices run clear, 6 to 8 minutes. Serve warm with the applesauce.

MAKES 4 SERVINGS

Pantry Pork Chops

PORK CHOPS

It's 5:30, you're starving, and you haven't a clue what to make. Don't worry, help is just on the other side of the pantry door. You'll be eating in less than an hour. Whew!

SEAR: HIGH, COOK: INDIRECT/MEDIUM

FOR THE MARINADE:

- 1/4 CUP PLUS 1 TABLESPOON FRESH LEMON JUICE
- 3 TABLESPOONS SOY SAUCE
- 1 TABLESPOON EXTRA-VIRGIN OLIVE OIL
- 1/2 TEASPOON LIGHT BROWN SUGAR
- 1/4 TEASPOON CHOPPED FRESH ROSEMARY
- 1/4 TEASPOON KOSHER SALT
- 1/4 TEASPOON FRESHLY GROUND BLACK PEPPER

- 4 PORK RIB CHOPS, ABOUT 1 1/4 INCHES THICK EACH

To make the marinade: In a medium bowl whisk together the marinade ingredients.

Place the chops in a large, resealable plastic bag and pour in the marinade. Press the air out of the bag and seal tightly. Turn the bag to distribute the marinade, place in a bowl, and refrigerate for 20 to 30 minutes.

Remove the chops from the bag and discard the marinade. Allow to stand at room temperature for 20 to 30 minutes before grilling.

Sear the chops over *Direct High* heat for 6 minutes, turning once halfway through searing time. Continue grilling over *Indirect Medium* heat until the juices run clear, 6 to 8 minutes. Season with salt and pepper. Serve warm.

MAKES 4 SERVINGS

Sooooo-Weee!
Swine in Latin is "sus"
or "suis." The latter form is
quite possibly the origin of the
hog call of pig farmers. These two
syllables may have earned swineherds
enviable titles such as Boss Hog or
Queen of the Hog Call....

PORK BURGERS
WITH GRILLED PINEAPPLE

Cross a pig with a turkey and what do you get? A tantalizing burger that will have the cows breathing a sigh of relief. The secret here is in the sauce. Of course, the juicy, grilled pineapple rings don't hurt either.

DIRECT/MEDIUM

FOR THE BURGERS:

- 3/4 POUND GROUND LEAN PORK
- 3/4 POUND GROUND TURKEY
- 1 TABLESPOON HERBES DE PROVENCE
- 1 TEASPOON KOSHER SALT
- 1/2 TEASPOON FRESHLY GROUND BLACK PEPPER

FOR THE SAUCE:

- 1/4 CUP DIJON MUSTARD
- 2 TABLESPOONS LIGHT BROWN SUGAR
- 2 TEASPOONS WORCESTERSHIRE SAUCE

- 4 FRESH PINEAPPLE RINGS, ABOUT 1/2 INCH THICK EACH, PEELED AND CORED

- 4 KAISER ROLLS, CUT IN HALF

To make the burgers: In a large bowl combine the burger ingredients, mixing gently with your hands. Form into four equal-sized patties, about 3/4 inch thick each.

To make the sauce: In a small bowl mix together the sauce ingredients.

Grill the patties over *Direct Medium* heat until fully cooked but still juicy and the internal temperature reaches 170°F, 12 to 15 minutes, turning once halfway through grilling time. Grill the pineapple slices over *Direct Medium* heat until well marked, about 5 minutes, turning once halfway through grilling time. During the last 2 to 3 minutes of grilling time, brush the patties and pineapple with the sauce for a nice tangy glaze. Grill the cut side of the rolls over *Direct Medium* heat until toasted, about 30 seconds.

Serve the patties warm on the toasted rolls with the grilled pineapple rings and the sauce.

MAKES 4 SERVINGS

There's certainly more than one meat with universal appeal, but none enjoys such careful attention to flavor as lamb. Because lamb's flavor can vary so much by the animal's age and diet, chefs around the world have devoted…oh, a few thousands years, give or take a century…to getting the seasonings and cooking techniques just right.

And what wondrous recipes they've concocted! From basic preparations involving garlic and lemon to the wilder side of cumin and curry blends, the rich texture and flavor of lamb has been manipulated to advantage in countless ways.

LAMB

Still, many American home cooks are just discovering this meat that's a staple in other nations. You may fondly remember Mom's oven-roasted leg of lamb with mint jelly, but have you ever cooked it yourself? Or do you only indulge when you find it on a restaurant menu? That's where most Americans have experienced delicious lamb. That dramatic presentation of rack of lamb can be quite a draw for the eyes as well as the taste buds—and all the more enjoyable if you don't know where to begin preparing it at home. And who wouldn't say yes to peppered lamb kabobs, spicy satays, or pesto-stuffed chops when all you have to do is order it, not figure out how to make it? Just the warm aroma of spice-infused lamb draped in a tangy dill-yogurt sauce is enough to embolden even the most timid diner.

If you've longed for great lamb on demand, we'll let you in on a secret: The lamb of your dreams is only as far away as your own backyard. That's right, nothing does more for lamb than the flame of the grill.

Whether you're a neophyte without a clue or a reformer set to kick the indoor oven habit, this chapter will help you master lamb at the grill.

Aside from price, America's stumbling block with lamb may be figuring out how best to prepare it and how many of those miniature cuts make up a serving. It's hard to believe that such a small animal could offer up so many confounding options, but if you can remember three things, you're on your way to great grilled lamb: preparation, cooking times, and accompaniments.

Preparation starts with choosing the right cut. Don't worry; in this chapter we've included a variety of those cuts best suited for the grill, as well as the best way to trim them and how many you'll need so no one leaves the table hungry. And what about seasonings? Gotcha covered. Between rubs, marinades, and dressings, we give you a sampling of "greatest hits," if you will, of different cuisines. To avoid too much of a good thing, just follow the marinating times and your lamb will stay firm and tasteful.

Most people prefer their lamb medium rare and we certainly fall into this camp. The USDA recommends for safety reasons that you cook lamb until it is medium rare as indicated by an internal temperature reading of 145°F. With smaller cuts like chops, where it's harder to get a temperature read, we've included a time range to shoot for. Just be sure to eat your lamb when it's hot off the grill—that's when it tastes best.

Finally, because we think contrast is the spice of life, many of these recipes include tantalizing accompaniments to make the most of lamb's tenderness and richness. From cool, crisp salads and slaws to sassy sauces and chutneys, the recipes here are guaranteed to please.

But even with all the tips on lamb we've included in this chapter, there is still one thing that even we don't understand: What's with the frilly hats? In the 1950s and '60s, it was *de rigueur* to crown the bones of lamb chops or a rack of lamb with little paper hats known as "cutlet frills." The effect was all the more impressive on a crown roast (two racks of lamb tied in a circle, with the bones curving outward) or the stately guard of honor (two racks interlocked back to back). Some restaurants and home cooks still use them. So we wonder: What's the attraction? Do the frills serve a practical purpose, such as hiding scorch marks or errant marrow? Maybe they keep that bony presentation from looking too much like something out of a Flintstones cartoon. Or maybe the flashy touch is the cook's reward for all the hard work. What do you think? Perhaps it will come to you as you're sampling these recipes....

IN THIS RECIPE, A MIX OF FRESH HERBS AND LEMON JUICE SERVES AS BOTH A DRESSING FOR THE SALAD AND A SAUCE FOR THE LAMB.

Butterflied Leg of Lamb

BUTTERFLIED
LEG OF LAMB

Since a butterflied leg of lamb is an uneven slab of meat, cut it into sections, separating the thicker areas from the thinner ones. Then you'll be able to get all parts to the same doneness by grilling the sections in succession, starting with the thicker ones.

DIRECT/MEDIUM

FOR THE MARINADE:

- 1/4 CUP EXTRA-VIRGIN OLIVE OIL
- 1 TABLESPOON FINELY CHOPPED FRESH ROSEMARY
- 1 TABLESPOON MINCED GARLIC
- 1 TEASPOON KOSHER SALT
- 1/2 TEASPOON COARSELY GROUND BLACK PEPPER

- 1 BUTTERFLIED BONELESS LEG OF LAMB, 3 TO 4 POUNDS, TRIMMED OF NEARLY ALL FAT, CUT INTO 3 OR 4 SECTIONS

FOR THE SALAD:

- 3/4 POUND SMALL ZUCCHINI, TRIMMED AND HALVED LENGTHWISE
- 1 SMALL RED ONION, CUT INTO 1/2-INCH SLICES
  EXTRA-VIRGIN OLIVE OIL
- 1/2 POUND RIPE CHERRY TOMATOES, HALVED VERTICALLY
- 2 TABLESPOONS PITTED, COARSELY CHOPPED KALAMATA OLIVES
- 2 TABLESPOONS FINELY CHOPPED SUN-DRIED TOMATOES (OIL-PACKED), DRAINED
- 2 TABLESPOONS FINELY CHOPPED FRESH MINT

FOR THE DRESSING:

- 6 TABLESPOONS EXTRA-VIRGIN OLIVE OIL
- 2 TABLESPOONS FRESH LEMON JUICE
- 2 TABLESPOONS FINELY CHOPPED FRESH ITALIAN PARSLEY
- 1/2 TEASPOON KOSHER SALT
- 1/4 TEASPOON FRESHLY GROUND BLACK PEPPER

To make the marinade: In a small bowl whisk together the marinade ingredients.

Place the lamb in a large, resealable plastic bag and pour in the marinade. Press the air out of the bag and seal tightly. Turn the bag to distribute the marinade, place the bag in a bowl, and refrigerate for 2 to 12 hours, turning occasionally.

To make the salad: Lightly brush or spray the zucchini and onion with the olive oil and grill over *Direct Medium* heat until barely tender, 5 to 7 minutes, turning once halfway through grilling time. When cool enough to handle, cut the zucchini on the bias into 1/2-inch slices and chop the onion. In a medium bowl combine the zucchini and onion with the cherry tomatoes, olives, sun-dried tomatoes, and mint.

To make the dressing: In a medium bowl whisk together the dressing ingredients with 2 tablespoons cold water. Taste and adjust the seasoning, if necessary. Spoon 3 tablespoons of the dressing over the salad. Toss to coat evenly.

Grill the lamb pieces over *Direct Medium* heat until the desired doneness, turning once halfway through grilling time. Pieces more than 2 inches thick will take 20 to 30 minutes to reach medium rare at 145°F; 1- to 2-inch-thick pieces will take 15 to 20 minutes. Allow the lamb to rest for about 5 minutes before carving. Cut the lamb across the grain into thin diagonal slices. Spoon the reserved dressing onto the meat. Serve hot with the salad.

MAKES 6 TO 8 SERVINGS

BRANDIED
LAMB POCKETS

Bathed in brandy and cumin, the grilled lamb morsels remain succulent while the iceberg slaw makes a crunchy contrast. Pack it all in pita and you're good to go.

DIRECT/HIGH

FOR THE MARINADE:

- 1/4 CUP BRANDY
- 2 TABLESPOONS EXTRA-VIRGIN OLIVE OIL
- 1 TEASPOON GROUND CUMIN
- 1 TEASPOON KOSHER SALT
- 1/2 TEASPOON FRESHLY GROUND BLACK PEPPER

- 1 1/2 POUNDS BONELESS LEG OF LAMB, TRIMMED OF NEARLY ALL FAT AND CUT INTO 1-INCH PIECES

FOR THE SLAW:

- 1/4 CUP MAYONNAISE
- 1 TABLESPOON DIJON MUSTARD
- 1 TEASPOON APPLE CIDER VINEGAR
- 1/2 TEASPOON CARAWAY SEEDS
- 1/4 TEASPOON FRESHLY GROUND BLACK PEPPER
- 4 CUPS SHREDDED ICEBERG LETTUCE

- 4 PITA BREAD POCKETS

To make the marinade: In a small bowl whisk together the marinade ingredients.

Place the lamb in a large, resealable plastic bag and pour in the marinade. Press the air out of the bag and seal tightly. Turn the bag to distribute the marinade, place the bag in a bowl, and refrigerate for 2 to 8 hours, turning occasionally.

Prepare the slaw just before grilling the lamb: In a medium bowl whisk together the mayonnaise, mustard, vinegar, caraway seeds, and pepper. Add the lettuce and toss to coat.

Thread the lamb on skewers, but don't crowd the meat. Grill over *Direct High* heat until the lamb is medium rare, 5 to 6 minutes, turning once halfway through grilling time. Remove the lamb from the skewers.

Grill the pita over *Direct High* heat until toasted, about 1 minute, turning once halfway through grilling time. Fill the pita pockets with the lamb and the slaw. Serve immediately.

MAKES 4 SERVINGS

LAMB KABOBS
WITH SAGE OIL MOP

Cook these kabobs just until the tomatoes begin to break open and their juices mingle with the lamb. Right about then the lamb pieces will be cooked through, if they're not crowded on the skewers.

DIRECT/HIGH

FOR THE MARINADE:

1 CUP DRY RED WINE

1/2 CUP MINCED RED ONION

2 TABLESPOONS FINELY CHOPPED FRESH SAGE

1 TEASPOON MINCED GARLIC

1 TEASPOON DRIED OREGANO

1/2 TEASPOON KOSHER SALT

1/4 TEASPOON FRESHLY GROUND BLACK PEPPER

1 BONELESS LEG OF LAMB, ABOUT 2 POUNDS, TRIMMED OF NEARLY ALL FAT, CUT INTO 1-INCH PIECES

FOR THE MOP:

1/3 CUP EXTRA-VIRGIN OLIVE OIL

1 TABLESPOON MINCED FRESH SAGE

1 TEASPOON MINCED GARLIC

1/4 TEASPOON KOSHER SALT

1/8 TEASPOON FRESHLY GROUND BLACK PEPPER

24 RIPE CHERRY TOMATOES

To make the marinade: In a medium bowl whisk together the marinade ingredients.

Place the lamb pieces in a large, resealable plastic bag and pour in the marinade. Press the air out of the bag and seal tightly. Turn the bag several times to distribute the marinade, place the bag in a bowl, and refrigerate for 8 to 12 hours, turning occasionally.

To make the mop: In a food processor blend together the mop ingredients until smooth. Set aside at room temperature for about 3 hours.

Remove the lamb pieces from the bag and discard the marinade. Thread the lamb and the tomatoes alternately on skewers, but don't crowd them; each skewer should have about six pieces of lamb and four tomatoes. Brush the lamb and tomatoes with the mop. Grill the kabobs over *Direct High* heat until the lamb is medium rare, 5 to 6 minutes, turning and basting with the mop once halfway through grilling time. Serve hot.

MAKES 4 TO 6 SERVINGS

SOUTHWEST
KABOBS

There's just enough fire here to cure the dinner blahs. The secret to the sauce is the chipotle, a dried, smoked jalapeño. This recipe uses the canned ones commonly found in the Mexican food section of most grocery stores.

DIRECT/HIGH

FOR THE PASTE:

1/4 CUP VEGETABLE OIL

2 TABLESPOONS CHILI POWDER

2 TABLESPOONS GROUND CUMIN

4 TEASPOONS KOSHER SALT

2 TEASPOONS GARLIC POWDER

2 TEASPOONS ONION POWDER

2 1/2 POUNDS BONELESS LEG OF LAMB, TRIMMED OF FAT AND SINEW, CUT INTO 1- TO 1 1/2-INCH CUBES

FOR THE SAUCE:

1 TABLESPOON VEGETABLE OIL

1/2 CUP FINELY CHOPPED YELLOW ONION

1/2 TEASPOON MINCED GARLIC

1/2 TEASPOON GROUND CUMIN

1/2 TEASPOON CHILI POWDER

1 CAN (14 1/2 OUNCES) CRUSHED TOMATOES WITH JUICES

1 TEASPOON GRANULATED SUGAR

1 TEASPOON TOMATO PASTE

1/2 CANNED CHIPOTLE CHILE (PACKED IN ADOBO SAUCE)

1/2 TEASPOON KOSHER SALT

1/4 TEASPOON DRIED THYME

1/4 TEASPOON DRIED OREGANO

To make the paste: In a large bowl mix together the paste ingredients.

Add the lamb cubes to the paste and stir to evenly coat the meat. Cover with plastic wrap and marinate at room temperature for 30 minutes or in the refrigerator for 1 hour.

To make the sauce: In a medium sauté pan over medium-high heat, warm the vegetable oil. Add the onion and cook, stirring occasionally, for 4 minutes. Add the garlic and cook, stirring occasionally, for 1 minute. Stir in the cumin and chili powder. Add the tomatoes and bring the mixture to a boil. Reduce heat to a simmer. Add the remaining sauce ingredients. Cook, stirring occasionally, until almost all of the liquid has evaporated, 10 to 15 minutes. Transfer the mixture to a food processor. Process until smooth. Return the sauce to the sauté pan. Set aside.

Thread the lamb on the skewers, but don't crowd the pieces. Grill over *Direct High* heat until the lamb is medium rare, 5 to 6 minutes, turning once halfway through grilling time. Meanwhile, reheat the sauce over low heat. Serve the lamb hot with the sauce.

MAKES 4 TO 6 SERVINGS

MADRAS-STYLE
MEATBALL KABOBS

Curry powder is a blend of numerous spices, most typically ground cumin, coriander, cinnamon, turmeric, black pepper, and chiles. Blends vary from region to region and even from cook to cook. This recipe uses a blend from Madras in the south of India. It has more heat than most and is widely available throughout North America.

DIRECT/HIGH

FOR THE SAUCE:

- 2 TABLESPOONS VEGETABLE OIL
- 1 CUP FINELY CHOPPED YELLOW ONION
- 1 TABLESPOON MINCED GARLIC
- 1 TABLESPOON MADRAS CURRY POWDER
- 1 TEASPOON GROUND CUMIN
- 1 TABLESPOON GRATED FRESH GINGER
- 1 CAN (28 OUNCES) PLUM TOMATOES WITH JUICES
- 1 TABLESPOON FIRMLY PACKED LIGHT BROWN SUGAR
- 1 TEASPOON KOSHER SALT
- 1/4 TEASPOON FRESHLY GROUND BLACK PEPPER

FOR THE MEATBALLS:

- 6 TABLESPOONS FINE DRY BREAD CRUMBS
- 2 LARGE EGGS
- 2 POUNDS GROUND LAMB
- 2 TABLESPOONS MINCED JALAPEÑO PEPPER
- 2 TEASPOONS KOSHER SALT
- 1/2 TEASPOON FRESHLY GROUND BLACK PEPPER

- 2 LARGE GREEN BELL PEPPERS, QUARTERED, STEMMED, AND SEEDED, CUT INTO 1-INCH PIECES
  VEGETABLE OIL

To make the sauce: In a medium sauté pan over medium heat, warm the vegetable oil. Add the onion and cook, stirring occasionally, until golden, about 5 minutes. Add the garlic and cook for 1 minute more. Stir in the curry powder and cumin. Cook for 30 seconds more. Stir in the ginger. Remove the pan from the heat. Remove half of the mixture from the pan and reserve it to blend with the lamb.

In a food processor purée the tomatoes and add to the onion mixture in the sauté pan. Add the brown sugar, salt, and pepper and bring to a boil over high heat. Reduce heat to a simmer and cook, stirring frequently, until the sauce is very thick and has reduced to about 1 1/2 cups, about 30 minutes. Set aside.

Meanwhile, make the meatballs: In a large bowl combine the bread crumbs with 1/2 cup cold water. Allow to stand for about 5 minutes. Stir in the eggs. Add the lamb, jalapeño, salt, pepper, and reserved onion mixture. Gently stir with

your fingers just until blended. Wet your hands with cold water and shape the meat into 40 balls, about 1 1/2 inches in diameter each. Be careful not to overwork the meat. Cover with plastic wrap and refrigerate for about 45 minutes or until very cold.

Thread the cold meatballs onto eight skewers, five per skewer, alternating with the bell pepper. Lightly brush the meatballs and bell pepper with the vegetable oil. Grill over *Direct High* heat until the meat is cooked to the center, 6 to 8 minutes, turning once halfway through grilling time. Meanwhile, reheat the sauce. Serve the kabobs hot with the sauce.

MAKES 6 TO 8 SERVINGS

PESTO-STUFFED
LOIN CHOPS

This recipe calls for only about a half cup of pesto—not really enough to make in a food processor or blender. Instead either chop it up on a cutting board or grind it in a mortar.

DIRECT/MEDIUM

FOR THE PESTO:

- 1 CUP LOOSELY PACKED FRESH BASIL LEAVES
- 1 SMALL GARLIC CLOVE, CRUSHED
- 1 TABLESPOON PINE NUTS
- 1/8 TEASPOON KOSHER SALT
- 1/4 CUP EXTRA-VIRGIN OLIVE OIL
- 1/4 CUP FRESHLY GRATED PARMIGIANO-REGGIANO CHEESE

- 8 DOUBLE-CUT LOIN LAMB CHOPS, ABOUT 1 1/4 INCHES THICK EACH
  FRESHLY GROUND BLACK PEPPER

To make the pesto: Put the basil leaves, garlic, pine nuts, and salt on a cutting board and chop very fine, or put them in a small mortar and grind with a pestle. Transfer to a small bowl and stir in the olive oil. Add the cheese and blend.

Trim the lamb chops of almost all fat. Use a small, sharp knife to cut a deep slash in the center of the meat of each chop on the side opposite the bone. Stuff each chop with about 1 teaspoon of the pesto. Season the outside of the chops with pepper. Grill over *Direct Medium* heat until the lamb is medium rare, about 10 minutes, turning once halfway through grilling time. Serve immediately.

MAKES 4 SERVINGS

Tuscan-Style Rib Chops with Panzanella

TUSCAN-STYLE RIB CHOPS
WITH PANZANELLA

Panzanella is a traditional Italian salad made with day-old bread moistened with tomatoes and a balsamic vinaigrette. Here we grill fresh bread and swap grilled eggplant for the traditional cucumbers. Paired with the lamb chops, it is a dish to devour.

DIRECT/HIGH

FOR THE DRESSING:

1/2 CUP EXTRA-VIRGIN OLIVE OIL

3 TABLESPOONS BALSAMIC VINEGAR

1 TEASPOON MINCED GARLIC

I TEASPOON DRIED OREGANO

1/2 TEASPOON KOSHER SALT

1/4 TEASPOON FRESHLY GROUND BLACK PEPPER

16 RIB LAMB CHOPS, ABOUT 3/4 INCH THICK EACH, TRIMMED OF NEARLY ALL FAT

FOR THE SALAD:

1 SMALL GLOBE EGGPLANT, CUT INTO 1/2-INCH SLICES

2 SLICES ITALIAN BREAD, ABOUT 1/2 INCH THICK EACH

2 LARGE RIPE TOMATOES, CORED AND CUT INTO 1/2-INCH PIECES

6 TO 8 LARGE BASIL LEAVES, CUT INTO STRIPS

KOSHER SALT

FRESHLY GROUND BLACK PEPPER

To make the dressing: In a small bowl whisk together the dressing ingredients.

Pour off 1/4 cup of the dressing to brush on the lamb chops and 2 tablespoons to dress the salad. Brush both sides of the chops with the 1/4 cup dressing, cover them with plastic wrap, and marinate at room temperature for 30 minutes or in the refrigerator for up to 2 hours. Discard any of this remaining dressing.

To make the salad: Brush both sides of the eggplant and bread slices with the remaining dressing in the bowl. Grill the eggplant over *Direct High* heat until tender, 4 to 6 minutes, turning once halfway through grilling time. Grill the bread over *Direct High* heat until lightly toasted, I to 2 minutes, turning once halfway through grilling time.

Cut the eggplant and bread into 1/2-inch cubes and place in a large bowl. Add the tomatoes, basil, and reserved 2 tablespoons of dressing, toss to blend, and season with salt and pepper.

Season the chops with pepper. Grill over *Direct High* heat until the lamb is medium rare, 3 to 5 minutes, turning once halfway through grilling time. Serve hot with the salad.

MAKES 4 SERVINGS

SPICE-GLAZED RIB CHOPS
WITH PEAR CHUTNEY

Warming the curry powder before adding the other ingredients allows its flavors to blossom, adding depth to the honey glaze. The tender chops get an extra lift from the chutney, where the smoky grilled flavors balance the sweetness. Serve it all with steamed jasmine rice.

DIRECT/MEDIUM

FOR THE GLAZE:

1 TABLESPOON CURRY POWDER

3 TABLESPOONS VEGETABLE OIL

3 TABLESPOONS CIDER VINEGAR

3 TABLESPOONS HONEY

1 1/2 TEASPOONS GARLIC POWDER

1 1/2 TEASPOONS KOSHER SALT

3/4 TEASPOON FRESHLY GROUND BLACK PEPPER

FOR THE CHUTNEY:

1 MEDIUM YELLOW ONION, CUT INTO 1/2-INCH SLICES

1 LARGE RIPE BOSC PEAR, QUARTERED AND CORED

VEGETABLE OIL

1/4 CUP RAISINS

KOSHER SALT

FRESHLY GROUND BLACK PEPPER

16 RIB LAMB CHOPS, ABOUT 3/4 INCH THICK EACH, TRIMMED OF NEARLY ALL FAT

To make the glaze: In a small sauté pan over medium heat, warm the curry powder just until fragrant, about 30 seconds. Whisk in the rest of the glaze ingredients and bring to a boil. Remove from the heat and set aside.

To make the chutney: Lightly brush or spray the onion slices and pear pieces on all sides with the vegetable oil. Grill the onion and pear over *Direct Medium* heat until barely tender, turning once halfway through grilling time. The onion will take 10 to 12 minutes and the pear will take 7 to 9 minutes. Allow to cool to room temperature, then cut into 1/2-inch pieces. In a medium sauté pan combine the onion and pear with the raisins and 1/4 cup of the glaze. Cook over high heat until the mixture starts to boil. Lower the heat and simmer, covered, stirring occasionally, until the onion and pear are soft, about 10 minutes. Adjust the seasoning with salt and pepper, if necessary. Keep warm over low heat.

Lightly brush or spray both sides of the lamb chops with the reserved glaze. Grill over *Direct Medium* heat until the lamb is medium rare, 5 to 8 minutes, turning once halfway through grilling time. Serve immediately with the warm chutney.

MAKES 4 SERVINGS

TERIYAKI
LAMB STEAKS

The marinade is really a homemade teriyaki sauce and it's about as good as it gets. You'll like the citrusy additions of fresh lemon and orange juice.

DIRECT/MEDIUM

FOR THE MARINADE:

- 1/2 CUP SOY SAUCE
- 1/2 CUP SAKE
- 1/2 CUP FRESH ORANGE JUICE
- 1/4 CUP FRESH LEMON JUICE
- 2 TABLESPOONS LIGHT BROWN SUGAR
- 1 TEASPOON FRESHLY GROUND BLACK PEPPER

- 4 LAMB ROUND BONE (SIRLOIN) STEAKS, ABOUT 3/4 INCH THICK EACH
- VEGETABLE OIL

To make the marinade: In a small saucepan whisk together the marinade ingredients. Bring the mixture to a boil, stirring to dissolve the sugar. Set aside to cool to room temperature.

Trim the lamb steaks of nearly all fat. Place the steaks in a large, resealable plastic bag and pour in the cooled marinade. Press the air out of the bag and seal tightly. Turn the bag several times to distribute the marinade, place the bag in a bowl, and refrigerate for 2 to 8 hours, turning occasionally.

Remove the steaks from the bag and discard the marinade. Pat the steaks dry with paper towels. Lightly brush or spray both sides of the steaks with the vegetable oil. Grill over *Direct Medium* heat until the lamb is medium rare, 5 to 7 minutes, turning once halfway through grilling time. Serve hot.

MAKES 4 SERVINGS

RACK OF LAMB
WITH ORANGE-CRANBERRY CHUTNEY

Lay the racks on their sides to get as much surface area on the cooking grate as possible. During grilling, the marinade forms an herb crust that underscores the sweetness of the lamb. The tangy chutney offers just enough bite to cut the meat's richness. Beautiful.

DIRECT/MEDIUM

FOR THE PASTE:

- 2 TABLESPOONS EXTRA-VIRGIN OLIVE OIL
- 2 TABLESPOONS FINELY CHOPPED FRESH ROSEMARY
- 1 TABLESPOON FINELY CHOPPED FRESH THYME
- 1 TABLESPOON MINCED SHALLOTS
- 1 TABLESPOON BALSAMIC VINEGAR
- 1 TABLESPOON WHOLE-GRAIN MUSTARD
- 1 TEASPOON MINCED GARLIC
- 1 TEASPOON KOSHER SALT
- 1 TEASPOON FRESHLY GROUND BLACK PEPPER

- 2 RACKS OF LAMB, 1 TO 1 1/2 POUNDS EACH, FRENCHED (SEE SIDEBAR, PAGE 201)

FOR THE CHUTNEY:

- 1 CUP SUN-DRIED CRANBERRIES
- 1/2 CUP CRANBERRY JUICE
- 1/4 CUP FRESH ORANGE JUICE
- 2 TABLESPOONS GRANULATED SUGAR
- 2 TABLESPOONS CRANBERRY JELLY
- 1/2 TABLESPOON BALSAMIC VINEGAR
- 1/4 TEASPOON KOSHER SALT
- 1/4 TEASPOON FRESHLY GROUND BLACK PEPPER
- PINCH GROUND CINNAMON

To make the paste: In a small bowl mix together the paste ingredients.

Spread the paste all over the lamb racks. Cover with plastic wrap and refrigerate for about 8 hours.

To make the chutney: In a medium saucepan combine the chutney ingredients. Bring the mixture to a boil, then reduce heat and simmer, stirring occasionally, until the cranberries are plump and juicy and the chutney has thickened, 10 to 15 minutes. Remove from the heat and allow to cool to room temperature.

Loosely cover the bones of the racks of lamb with aluminum foil to keep them from burning. Grill over *Direct Medium* heat until the internal temperature reaches 145°F and the lamb is medium rare, 20 to 30 minutes, turning once halfway through grilling time. Remove from the grill and allow to rest for 5 minutes before cutting into chops. Serve hot with the chutney.

MAKES 4 SERVINGS

LAMB ON THE GRILL

Lamb's appeal as a main course sets chefs a-twitter all over the globe. The French wax lyrical about cooking lamb, East Indian cooks have raised it to an art form, and New Zealanders are gladly outnumbered 20 to 1 by woolly citizens. While there are hundreds of ways to prepare lamb, the world agrees that the grill is by far the best way to cook most cuts. So tonight, whether you want lamb kabobs, chops, satay, burgers, or roast, the grill's the way to go. Read on.

CHOOSE LAMB that is light red and bones that are pinkish rather than white. Ask your butcher about the lamb's dietary history. The taste of lamb varies widely depending on age and diet. In the U.S., lamb is sold anywhere from three months to more than a year old (just this side of mutton). Younger lamb has whiter fat and is more tender and mildly flavored. Older lamb has grazed awhile, so the fat is slightly darker and the flavor more well-rounded.

LAMB IS NATURALLY FATTIER than most other meats you're probably used to buying, so trim it well before grilling to avoid flare-ups. Once it's cooked, discard the outer fat before eating the meat. It has already done its job flavoring the meat.

IS IT DONE YET? USDA recommends that ground lamb, like all ground meat, is safest when cooked to medium doneness, an internal temperature of 160°F. For other cuts, medium rare (145°F) is preferred by most people, so keep a close eye on the grill and use a timer and/or an instant meat thermometer to keep you on track.

A BONELESS LEG OF LAMB that is butterflied (meaning opened like a book) varies in thickness. If you grill it flat and whole, some parts end up well done while some are rare. We suggest that for more consistent results, you separate the sections by thickness and grill them in succession, starting with the thickest sections first.

WHEN YOU GRILL RACKS OF LAMB, cover the bones in foil to prevent them from burning and, for better flavor, lay the racks on their sides to get as much surface area on the cooking grate as possible.

LAMB FAT BECOMES LESS TASTY AS IT COOLS. Meat experts Bruce Aidells and Denis Kelly advise you to serve lamb hot (and to warm platters and plates) and to avoid serving ice water with the meal. Savvy tip!

FRENCHING A RACK OF LAMB

An undressed rack of lamb doesn't look anything like the fancy cut of meat you see gracing the pages of cooking magazines—you know, that juicy eye roast with slightly browned bones arcing out of it at perfectly spaced intervals. What you start with is a large "rib roast," containing seven or eight ribs. Here's how to clean it up like a pro:

CUT THROUGH FAT AND MEAT
Place the rack so the rib ends point downward. Halfway from the narrow end (2 to 3 inches), cut through the fat and meat across the bones.

CUT THE MEAT BETWEEN THE BONES
Turn the rack over and use a sharp, narrow knife to cut the meat between the bones along the same line.

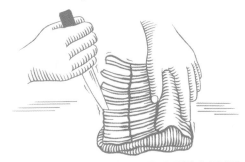

SCRAPE FROM CUT LINE
Using a boning knife, scrape away all the meat and fat from the cut line to the ends of the bones (above). Cut off the fat cap on the meaty portion, leaving a scant (⅛ inch) layer of fat. Revel in your butchering prowess. Once the rack is frenched, you can grill it whole, as in the recipe on page 200, or cut it into chops or double chops.

GREEK HOAGIES
WITH CREAMY FETA DRESSING

Feta cheese adds a refreshing tang to this classic mint–dill dressing. Layer it on toasted rolls and you've got the Greek sandwich you've been craving.

DIRECT/HIGH

FOR THE DRESSING:

- 2 OUNCES (ABOUT 1/4 CUP) FETA CHEESE
- 1/4 CUP LOOSELY PACKED FRESH MINT
- 1/4 CUP LOOSELY PACKED FRESH DILL
- 2 TABLESPOONS EXTRA-VIRGIN OLIVE OIL
- 1 SMALL CLOVE GARLIC, CRUSHED
- 1/2 TEASPOON KOSHER SALT
- 1/4 TEASPOON FRESHLY GROUND BLACK PEPPER

- 1 MEDIUM RED BELL PEPPER

- 4 SHOULDER BLADE LAMB CHOPS, ABOUT 5 OUNCES EACH AND 3/4 INCH THICK, TRIMMED OF NEARLY ALL FAT
- 1 SMALL YELLOW ONION, CUT INTO 1/2-INCH SLICES
- 1 SMALL EGGPLANT, CUT INTO 1/2-INCH SLICES
  EXTRA-VIRGIN OLIVE OIL
  KOSHER SALT
  FRESHLY GROUND BLACK PEPPER

- 4 CRUSTY ROLLS, HALVED

To make the dressing: In a blender combine the dressing ingredients and process until well mixed, scraping down the sides, if necessary. Place in a medium bowl and set aside.

Grill the bell pepper over *Direct High* heat until evenly charred on all sides, 10 to 12 minutes, turning every 3 to 5 minutes. Remove from the grill and place in a paper bag; close tightly. Allow to stand 10 to 15 minutes to steam off the skin. Remove the pepper from the bag and peel away the charred skin. Cut off the top and remove the seeds. Cut the pepper into 1/4-inch strips and place in the bowl with the dressing.

Lightly brush or spray the lamb, onion, and eggplant with the olive oil and season with salt and pepper. Grill the chops over *Direct High* heat until medium rare, 6 to 8 minutes, turning once halfway through grilling time. Grill the onions and eggplant over *Direct High* heat until well marked and tender, 8 to 10 minutes, turning once halfway through grilling time.

Slice the meat from the bones and cut into 1/4-inch strips. Cut the onion slices through the center to form strips. Cut the eggplant into 1/4-inch strips. Place the lamb, onions, and eggplant in the bowl with the dressing. Stir to evenly coat the lamb and vegetables.

Grill the rolls over *Direct High* heat until lightly toasted, about 30 seconds. Spoon the lamb and vegetables into the rolls. Serve immediately.

MAKES 4 SERVINGS

INDONESIAN LAMB SATAY
WITH SPICY PEANUT SAUCE

For a quick weekday dinner, make the marinade and sauce ahead and chill them. Add the lamb to the marinade when you're ready to start.

DIRECT/HIGH

FOR THE MARINADE:

- 1 LARGE CLOVE GARLIC, CRUSHED
- 1 STAR ANISE
- 2 TABLESPOONS VEGETABLE OIL
- 1 TABLESPOON FINELY CHOPPED FRESH GINGER
- 1 TABLESPOON FRESH LIME JUICE
- 1 TABLESPOON SOY SAUCE
- 1 TEASPOON CHILI POWDER

- 2 LAMB LOINS, ABOUT 1/2 POUND EACH

FOR THE SAUCE:

- 1 TABLESPOON VEGETABLE OIL
- 1 TEASPOON THAI RED CURRY PASTE
- 1 TEASPOON GROUND CUMIN
- 1 TEASPOON DRIED LEMONGRASS
- 1/2 CUP SMOOTH PEANUT BUTTER
- 1/2 CUP COCONUT MILK
- 1 TABLESPOON SOY SAUCE
- 1 TEASPOON FRESH LIME JUICE
- 1 TEASPOON GRANULATED SUGAR

To make the marinade: In a food processor or blender combine the marinade ingredients and process until smooth.

Trim the lamb of any excess fat or sinew. Cut the loins crosswise (against the grain) in 1/2-inch slices. Place the slices in a large, resealable plastic bag and pour in the marinade. Press the air out of the bag and seal tightly. Turn the bag several times to distribute the marinade, place the bag in a bowl, and marinate at room temperature for 30 minutes or in the refrigerator for 1 hour, turning occasionally.

To make the sauce: In a medium sauté pan over medium-high heat, warm the vegetable oil. Add the red curry paste, cumin, and lemongrass, stirring to release their fragrance, about 10 seconds. Add the peanut butter, coconut milk, and 1/2 cup water. Mix well. Add the soy sauce, lime juice, and sugar. Stir. Lower heat to a simmer and cook for 1 to 2 minutes. Set aside.

Remove the lamb from the bag and discard the marinade. Thread the lamb slices lengthwise on the skewers. Just before you grill the lamb, gently reheat the sauce; whisk in a little coconut milk or water, if needed, to thin it. Grill the lamb over *Direct High* heat for 3 to 4 minutes, turning once halfway through grilling time. Serve hot with the sauce.

MAKES 4 SERVINGS

SUPER-TENDER LAMB LOIN MAKES PERFECT INDONESIAN SATAY. IT COOKS QUICKLY, TOO, SO STAY NEAR THE GRILL.

Indonesian Lamb Satay with Spicy Peanut Sauce

Moroccan Lamb in Pita

MOROCCAN
LAMB IN PITA

Spiked with exotic spices and served with a cooling yogurt sauce, these lamb burgers make a festive lunch. And pita bread offers a welcome change from the standard burger bun. Try the seasoning mix on pork, beef, or chicken cuts.

DIRECT/MEDIUM

FOR THE SEASONING MIX:

- 1/2 TEASPOON KOSHER SALT
- 1/2 TEASPOON GROUND GINGER
- 1/4 TEASPOON GROUND CUMIN
- 1/4 TEASPOON TURMERIC
- 1/4 TEASPOON GROUND CINNAMON
- 1/4 TEASPOON GROUND ALLSPICE
- 1/4 TEASPOON COARSELY GROUND BLACK PEPPER
- 1/4 TEASPOON GROUND CARDAMOM
- 1/8 TEASPOON CRUMBLED SAFFRON THREADS

1 1/4 POUNDS GROUND LAMB

FOR THE SAUCE:

- 3/4 CUP PLAIN YOGURT
- 2 TABLESPOONS FINELY CHOPPED RED ONION
- 1 TABLESPOON FINELY CHOPPED FRESH DILL
- 1 TABLESPOON FINELY CHOPPED FRESH MINT
- 1 TABLESPOON FRESH LIME JUICE
- 1 TABLESPOON EXTRA-VIRGIN OLIVE OIL
- 1/2 TEASPOON FRESHLY GROUND BLACK PEPPER
- 1/4 TEASPOON KOSHER SALT

EXTRA-VIRGIN OLIVE OIL
- 4 PITA POCKETS
- 1 CUP TORN LETTUCE
- 1/2 CUP DICED FRESH TOMATO

To make the seasoning mix: In a small, dry, heavy sauté pan combine the seasoning mix ingredients and cook over medium heat, stirring, until fragrant, about 1 minute. Remove from the heat.

In a large bowl combine the lamb with the seasoning mix and 3 tablespoons cold water. Lightly mix with your hands; don't overwork the meat. With wet hands, lightly shape the meat into four equal-sized patties, about 3/4 inch thick each. Cover and refrigerate until ready to grill.

Just before grilling the patties, make the sauce: In a small bowl whisk together the sauce ingredients.

Lightly brush or spray the lamb patties with the olive oil. Grill over *Direct Medium* heat until the lamb is medium, 7 to 9 minutes, turning once halfway through grilling time. Grill the pita over *Direct Medium* heat until toasted, 30 to 60 seconds, turning once halfway through grilling time.

Slip the lamb patties inside the pita pockets along with a heaping spoonful of the yogurt sauce. Top with the lettuce and tomato. Serve immediately.

MAKES 4 SERVINGS

MEDITERRANEAN
LAMB BURGERS

Here the humble patty gets a flavor facelift as lamb replaces the old standby. Adding water is an old trick for keeping the meat moist while it cooks. Excellent with a sprinkling of feta on top.

DIRECT/MEDIUM

FOR THE SEASONING:

- 2 TABLESPOONS FINELY CHOPPED KALAMATA OLIVES
- 2 TABLESPOONS FINELY CHOPPED FRESH ITALIAN PARSLEY
- 2 TEASPOONS DIJON MUSTARD
- 2 TEASPOONS DRIED ROSEMARY, CRUSHED
- 1 TEASPOON MINCED GARLIC
- 1/2 TEASPOON KOSHER SALT
- 1/4 TEASPOON FRESHLY GROUND BLACK PEPPER

1 1/4 POUNDS GROUND LAMB
4 HAMBURGER BUNS

To make the seasoning: In a large bowl combine the seasoning ingredients with 2 tablespoons cold water.

Add the lamb and gently mix with the seasoning. Gently shape the meat into eight patties, about 3/4 inch thick each; don't overwork the meat.

Grill the patties over *Direct Medium* heat until the lamb is medium, 7 to 9 minutes, turning once halfway through grilling time. Grill the buns over *Direct Medium* heat until toasted, about 30 seconds. Serve the lamb hot on the toasted buns.

MAKES 4 SERVINGS

*The good supper
is known by its odor.*

— MOROCCAN PROVERB

Our friend Jim is a grouse hunter. He'll be the first to tell you that it's a sport taken a bit too seriously by some of its practitioners. It's ruffed grouse, not "ruffled," and certainly not the offending "partridge," as aficionados are quick to point out with a sniff. If you knew Jim, you'd find his involvement with this crowd kind of funny, as he is one of the most approachable guys you'll ever meet. He even tolerates our wisecracks on a regular basis. But don't get us wrong—he can lay it on pretty thick himself.

Once, after a hunting trip, he was talking up what a great time he had had out there in the woods with his dog and his buddies. You know, living the life, having all kinds of rugged fun, while the rest of us were

GAME

toiling away at work. He was practically begging for trouble. So we decided to give him some grief.

"Say, Jim," we said. "How much didya pay for that hunting dog of yours?"

"Six hundred bucks. Why?"

"And to train and board him?" We started scratching on a notepad.

"I dunno. Maybe $200. What're you getting at?"

And so it went. For food and vet bills, another $700 a year. Shotgun, one grand. Gas to his favorite hunting spot, another $100. We added on the cost of motels, food, and other incidentals, and let him simmer while we calculated.

"And one last thing, Jim. About how many birds do you bring home each time?"

"Heck. Two. Maybe three."

"Aaand," we said, pausing for effect, "if you were to buy grouse in a butcher shop, what would you shell out for that? Per bird."

"About 20 bucks," he said slowly. He knew what was coming, but he let us have our fun.

"Hmmm. Amortizing the cost of the dog and the gun, by our estimations…we'd say you're spending about $500 a bird—when you get one at all!"

He paused, scowling a bit in mock disgust. Then slowly, ever the calculator, he said, "Of course, if I had more time to hunt, the cost would go down considerably."

Which is why he's out there again and we're here writing this chapter introduction.

Now, aside from the hunter's pride, most people eat game meats because they offer intrigue and variety to their carnivorous spectrum. But even game fans will say in the same breath, "I like game—as long as it isn't too gamy."

Huh?

What sounds like a contradiction actually isn't. Let's face it, no one wants to eat meat that is too…pungent. Or chewy. But game meats can be amazingly tender and delicious—when you know how to cook them.

The secrets are in the preparation and grilling. Because game animals are naturally leaner than domesticated ones, they can start out tough and cook up dry if you're not careful. Enter marinades, brines, and bastes. They're your allies in tenderizing and moisturizing. And when you grill those meats, they remain tender and juicy. Plus, if you want to get philosophical about it (as many hunters do), cooking game on the grill fulfills that caveman imperative (without all that prehistoric mess and the elaborate rituals).

But the most compelling reason to hunt down game, whether literally or at the meat counter, is for the flavor. Take buffalo, for example. You like it for all the reasons you like beef. But buffalo is like…beef and a half. It's everything you like, but amplified—and healthier to boot.

Check out the tasty terrain we've laid out for you in this chapter. Most of these game meats are available in your supermarket, but for the best cuts and freshness, track down a good butcher. (You may need to special-order things such as buffalo steaks.) Just pay attention to the grilling times and the visual clues we offer to help you pull the meat off the grill at just the right time. You might discover that special entrée that becomes your signature dish. Or, if you're like Jim, you'll at least find an excuse to take a few days off work. Happy hunting!

FIVE-SPICE
GRILLED QUAIL

Chinese five-spice powder is a blend that typically contains Szechwan pepper, cinnamon, star anise, fennel seeds, and cloves. It may not have been invented for game birds, but it sure flies here.

INDIRECT/MEDIUM

FOR THE MARINADE:

1/3 CUP DRY SHERRY
1/4 CUP VEGETABLE OIL
2 TABLESPOONS SOY SAUCE
2 TABLESPOONS LIGHT BROWN SUGAR
1 1/2 TEASPOONS FIVE-SPICE POWDER

8 QUAIL, ABOUT 5 OUNCES EACH
VEGETABLE OIL

FOR THE SEASONING:

1 TEASPOON FIVE-SPICE POWDER
1/2 TEASPOON DRIED THYME
1/2 TEASPOON KOSHER SALT
1/2 TEASPOON FRESHLY GROUND BLACK PEPPER

To make the marinade: In a small bowl whisk together the marinade ingredients.

Place the quail in a large, resealable plastic bag and pour in the marinade. (If one bag isn't large enough, use two bags and divide the marinade.) Press the air out of the bag and seal tightly. Turn the bag to distribute the marinade, place in a bowl, and refrigerate 1 to 8 hours, turning occasionally.

Remove the quail from the bag and discard the marinade. Pat the quail dry with paper towels. Fold the quail legs up against the breast and tie with cotton string. Lightly brush the quail with the vegetable oil.

To make the seasoning: In a small bowl combine the seasoning ingredients.

Sprinkle the seasoning all over the quail. Grill, breast side down, over Indirect Medium heat until the juices are slightly pink, 15 to 20 minutes, turning once halfway through grilling time. Remove the string with kitchen scissors. Serve warm.

MAKES 4 SERVINGS

QUAIL WRAPPED
IN BACON AND GRAPE LEAVES

Seems fussy, but it's easier than it looks. Wrapping delicate quail in these savory packets is a fancy French technique that seals in moisture and flavor—so you'll not only look like a talented chef, you can actually play the part convincingly. Plus, you get to eat these beauties with your hands. Look for jarred grape leaves in the gourmet or olive section of your supermarket.

SEAR: MEDIUM, COOK: INDIRECT/MEDIUM

16 SLICES BACON

2 TEASPOONS KOSHER SALT
1 TEASPOON FRESHLY GROUND BLACK PEPPER
1 TEASPOON DRIED THYME
8 QUAIL, ABOUT 5 OUNCES EACH
8 TO 16 LARGE GRAPE LEAVES (WATER-PACKED)

In a large saucepan blanch the bacon slices in boiling water for 2 minutes. Drain, then rinse under cold water and pat dry with paper towels.

In a small bowl combine the salt, pepper, and thyme. Rub the outside of each quail with about 1/2 teaspoon of the mixture. Set each quail on the stem end of a grape leaf. Fold the legs up against the breast to make it more compact for wrapping. Then fold the outside edges of the leaf around the quail. (If the grape leaves are small, use two per quail.) Wrap two slices of bacon around each bird so they overlap at right angles, then secure the bacon by tying the birds snugly with cotton string. Don't worry about enclosing the quail perfectly; it's okay if small areas are exposed.

Sear over Direct Medium heat for 5 minutes, turning once halfway through searing time. Continue grilling over Indirect Medium heat until the bacon is well browned and the juices are slightly pink, 15 to 17 minutes more, turning occasionally. Remove from the grill and allow to rest for 5 minutes. Remove the string with kitchen scissors. Serve warm.

MAKES 4 SERVINGS

Quail Wrapped in Bacon and Grape Leaves

CIDER-GLAZED
WHOLE DUCK

Pricking a whole duck before grilling it allows the fat to drip away slowly and evenly, leaving the skin crisp and a beautiful mahogany color. Collect the fat in a foil pan set under the duck and use it to sauté foods that need extra flavor. If you're lucky enough to have any duck left over, slice and toss it with mixed greens, walnuts, and sliced pears for an easy luncheon salad.

INDIRECT/MEDIUM

FOR THE GLAZE:

- 4 CUPS FRESH APPLE CIDER (NOT FROM CONCENTRATE)
- 1 TEASPOON GRATED FRESH GINGER
- 1/2 TEASPOON GROUND CINNAMON
- 1/2 TEASPOON KOSHER SALT

- 1 MUSCOVY DUCK, 4 1/2 TO 5 POUNDS
  KOSHER SALT
  FRESHLY GROUND BLACK PEPPER
- 1 LEMON, QUARTERED
- 1 SMALL YELLOW ONION, QUARTERED

To make the glaze: In a medium saucepan combine the glaze ingredients and bring to a boil. Continue boiling until the mixture is reduced to 1/2 cup (but no more, or it will burn). Set the mixture aside and allow to cool to room temperature.

Remove and discard the neck, giblets, wings, and any excess fat from the duck. Rinse the duck under cold water and pat dry with paper towels. Prick the duck all over with a fork, especially along the sides under the breasts, to allow fat to escape during cooking. Season the duck, inside and out, with salt and pepper. Squeeze the lemon quarters into the cavity of the duck, then place them along with the onion into the cavity. Tie the legs together with cotton string.

Place the duck, breast side up, on a roasting rack set inside a 13- by 9-inch heavy-gauge foil pan. Grill over *Indirect Medium* heat until the internal temperature of the breast reaches 165°F, 1 1/2 to 2 hours. Start brushing the glaze over the duck about halfway through grilling time, then every 15 minutes until the juices are slightly pink and the duck is done. Remove from the grill and allow to rest for 15 to 20 minutes before carving. Serve warm or at room temperature.

MAKES 4 SERVINGS

SPICE-RUBBED
DUCK BREASTS
WITH PLUM SAUCE

This recipe is almost too easy. But you can keep that information to yourself—your guests will think you're a wizard. Crosshatching the skin and cooking the breasts over low heat gives a nice presentation and also reduces the risk of flare-ups.

DIRECT/LOW

FOR THE RUB:

- 1 TEASPOON DRIED THYME
- 1 TEASPOON MINCED GARLIC
- 1 TEASPOON KOSHER SALT
- 1/2 TEASPOON FRESHLY GROUND BLACK PEPPER
- 1/4 TEASPOON MACE

- 4 BONELESS MUSCOVY DUCK BREAST HALVES, 7 TO 8 OUNCES EACH AND ABOUT 1/2 INCH THICK

FOR THE PLUM SAUCE:

- 1 CUP PLUM JAM *OR* PLUM PRESERVES
- 2 TABLESPOONS CIDER VINEGAR
- 1 TABLESPOON SOY SAUCE
- 1 TABLESPOON GRATED FRESH GINGER
- 1/8 TEASPOON ASIAN SESAME OIL
  PINCH GROUND CLOVES

To make the rub: In a small bowl combine the rub ingredients.

Use a sharp knife to trim any excess fat from the duck breasts; if the skin is very fatty, trim it to a thickness of 1/4 inch. Score the skin in a diamond pattern (*see page 215*). Coat both sides of the breasts evenly with the rub, cover with plastic wrap, and marinate at room temperature for 30 minutes or in the refrigerator for up to several hours.

To make the plum sauce: In a small saucepan over medium heat, stir the plum jam until liquefied and bubbling, 3 to 4 minutes. Add the remaining sauce ingredients and cook, whisking frequently until smooth, about 2 minutes more. Allow the sauce to cool to room temperature before serving.

Grill the breasts, skin side down, over *Direct Low* heat, until the internal temperature reaches 160°F, 11 to 13 minutes, turning once halfway through grilling time. The juices should be slightly pink, the skin golden brown and crisp. Remove from the grill and allow to rest for 3 to 4 minutes. Slice thinly on the bias and serve warm with the sauce.

MAKES 4 SERVINGS

TANGERINE DUCK BREASTS
WITH TROPICAL FRUIT SAUCE

What a concept—start with a dozen tangerines and end up with a slice of paradise. The tangerine marinade flavors the duck, while the tangerine-juice sauce makes a wondrous glaze. Major Grey chutney, a mango-based variety available at most supermarkets, gives the sauce a major boost.

DIRECT/LOW

FOR THE MARINADE:

1/4 CUP FRESH TANGERINE JUICE
   (1 TO 2 TANGERINES)

2 TABLESPOONS SOY SAUCE

2 TABLESPOONS ASIAN SESAME OIL

2 TEASPOONS MINCED GARLIC

2 TEASPOONS GRATED FRESH GINGER

4 BONELESS MUSCOVY DUCK BREAST HALVES,
   7 TO 8 OUNCES EACH AND ABOUT 1/2 INCH THICK

FOR THE SAUCE:

2 TEASPOONS PEANUT OIL

1 TABLESPOON MINCED FRESH GINGER

2 TABLESPOONS RED WINE VINEGAR

1 1/2 CUPS FRESH TANGERINE JUICE
   (8 TO 10 TANGERINES)

1/4 CUP MAJOR GREY CHUTNEY

To make the marinade: In a small bowl whisk together the marinade ingredients.

Use a sharp knife to trim any excess fat from the duck breasts; if the skin is very fatty, trim it to a thickness of 1/4 inch. Score the skin in a diamond pattern *(see page 215)*.

Place the duck breasts in a large, resealable plastic bag and pour in the marinade. Press the air out of the bag and seal tightly. Turn the bag to distribute the marinade, place in a bowl, and refrigerate for 3 to 6 hours, turning occasionally.

To make the sauce: In a medium saucepan over high heat, warm the peanut oil. Add the ginger and cook, stirring often, for 1 minute. Add the vinegar and cook until almost all of the liquid has evaporated. Add the tangerine juice and cook until the liquid is reduced to 1/3 cup, 15 to 20 minutes. Whisk in the chutney. Simmer over low heat for 5 minutes. Set aside.

Remove the duck breasts from the bag and discard the marinade. Pat the breasts dry with paper towels. Grill, skin side down, over *Direct Low* heat, until the internal temperature reaches 160°F, 11 to 13 minutes, turning once halfway through grilling time. The juices should be slightly pink, the skin golden brown and crisp. Remove from the grill and allow to rest for 3 to 4 minutes. Slice thinly on the bias and serve warm with the sauce.

MAKES 4 SERVINGS

DUCK BREASTS
WITH BALSAMIC VINEGAR

Believe it or not, balsamic vinegar is made of white Trebbiano grape juice. After years of aging in wood barrels, it emerges a syrupy, black elixir prized by cooks for its intense flavor. Reducing it heightens its natural sweetness.

DIRECT/LOW

FOR THE BASTE:

1 CUP BALSAMIC VINEGAR

1 TABLESPOON HONEY

4 BONELESS MUSCOVY DUCK BREAST HALVES,
   8 TO 10 OUNCES EACH AND ABOUT 3/4 INCH THICK

FOR THE SEASONING:

4 TEASPOONS FINELY CHOPPED FRESH THYME

4 TEASPOONS FINELY CHOPPED FRESH MARJORAM

1 TEASPOON KOSHER SALT

1 TEASPOON FRESHLY GROUND BLACK PEPPER

To make the baste: In a small sauté pan combine the balsamic vinegar and honey. Bring to a boil and cook over high heat until reduced to 1/3 cup. Set aside.

Use a sharp knife to trim any excess fat from the duck breasts; if the skin is very fatty, trim it to a thickness of 1/4 inch. Score the skin in a diamond pattern *(see page 215)*.

To make the seasoning: In a small bowl combine the seasoning ingredients.

Sprinkle the breasts with the seasoning, then brush all over with the baste. Grill, skin side down, over *Direct Low* heat, until the internal temperature reaches 160°F, 12 to 14 minutes, basting and turning once halfway through grilling time. The juices should be slightly pink, the skin golden brown and crisp. Remove from the grill and allow to rest for 3 to 4 minutes. Slice thinly on the bias and serve warm.

MAKES 4 SERVINGS

"One can say everything best over a meal."

— GEORGE ELIOT

GAME ON THE GRILL

Game earns the praises of hunters and health advocates alike because it is high in protein yet lower in fat and cholesterol than domesticated animals. If game meats are new to you, you might wonder where to start. Turns out, your grill is the best way to greet them. Here are some pointers to get you acquainted:

A FEW WORDS ABOUT VENISON. Most people think venison = deer, but the truth is the term includes a broad range of large game animals: elk, moose, antelope, reindeer, caribou, and Yeti (just kidding about the Yeti). Ask your butcher about what's behind the label.

- Different types of venison can be cooked in the same way with the same cooking times. The best cuts are **loins** (also called back straps) and **roasts**. For **kabobs**, cubed loin is perfect.
- One cut you'll especially enjoy on the grill is **rack of venison**. It's trimmed much like a rack of lamb (see page 201 if you're going to french the rack yourself; otherwise have your butcher prepare the rack for you). Before grilling, cover the bones with foil to keep them from burning.
- Marinating venison tenderizes it, adds moisture, and mellows its flavor. Do it!
- Try adding cherry wood to the fire for a delicious smoked flavor similar to bacon.

A LITTLE SIZZLE GOES A LONG WAY. Duck and goose have a lot of fat in their skin (it's what keeps them afloat!), so here's how to minimize flare-ups:

- Muscovy duck is the best breed for the grill. It has less fat than Pekin duck and the breast is usually larger.
- When grilling whole birds, always place them on a roasting rack set inside a disposable pan.
- Prick whole ducks all over with a fork before grilling so fat escapes slowly as they cook.
- Trim fat off breasts by thinning the skin to 1/4 inch. Then, crosshatch the skin *(see page 215)*.
- You don't need to score goose flesh, but you will notice lots of fat accumulating in the roasting pan. Siphon it off frequently with a bulb baster during grilling, store it in the freezer, and treasure it. The fat will freeze to the consistency of ice cream and will be good for about 6 weeks. Scoop it out as needed, bring it to room temperature, and use it for making incredible biscuits or for sautéing potatoes, parsnips, or winter squash.
- As always, grill with the grill lid down: This will prevent flare-ups better than anything.

IS IT DONE YET? Grilling game meats to the right doneness can be a concern for the novice. After all, these cuts tend to cost more and who wants to eat mistakes? So, err on the side of safety. Just don't wait until it's burned to be sure it's ready; use a meat thermometer and/or the visual clues suggested in the recipes.

GAME BIRDS: The juices still run slightly pink even when game birds are thoroughly cooked. While this goes against our training on how to cook poultry—we know we're never to eat chicken or turkey with pink juices!—game birds are different. Duck breasts can be removed from the grill when the internal temperature reaches between 160°F and 165°F, a slightly lower temperature than for chicken. While whole duck is also safe when the breast reaches between 160°F and 165°F, whole goose should be pulled off the grill when the internal temperature of the breast reaches between 165°F and 170°F, and that of the thigh about 180°F. And let both whole duck and goose rest 15 to 20 minutes to allow for "carryover cooking." When cooking tiny quail and squab, it's almost impossible not to touch a bone with the thermometer (and thus get a misleadingly high reading), so just make sure the skin is crisp and follow the cooking times and visual clues in the recipes.

BUFFALO: Buffalo is much leaner than beef, so it cooks more quickly. Buffalo steaks are safe eaten medium rare but the USDA recommends that you grill buffalo burgers—like beef burgers—until they're medium and the internal temperature reaches 160°F.

RABBIT: Like chicken, rabbit should be cooked until it is no longer pink at the bone.

VENISON: One to watch closely. On bigger cuts, use a meat thermometer. They're done when the temperature reaches 145°F, medium rare. Look for a deep crimson color. For steaks and kabobs, follow the cooking times in the recipes.

AND A WORD TO THE WISE: If you shoot game or get game meats from a hunter friend, chew carefully. Buckshot and tooth enamel are not the best of friends.

FRUIT SAUCES FOR
GAME

A simple fruit sauce makes a great complement for grilled game. For a chutneylike flavor, try adding curry and ginger to the peaches, nectarines, or oranges.

- 1¼ **POUNDS FRESH FRUIT (E.G., PEACHES, NECTARINES, PLUMS, APRICOTS, BLUEBERRIES, BLACKBERRIES, ORANGES, CHERRIES, APPLES, OR PEARS)**
- ¼ **CUP GRANULATED SUGAR, PLUS MORE IF NEEDED**
- 1 **TABLESPOON CORNSTARCH**
- ¼ **CUP DRY VERMOUTH OR WHITE WINE**
- 3 **TABLESPOONS CIDER VINEGAR, PLUS MORE IF NEEDED**
- ⅛ **TEASPOON KOSHER SALT**
- ⅛ **TEASPOON GROUND CLOVES**
- 1 **TABLESPOON UNSALTED BUTTER**
- 1 **TEASPOON CURRY POWDER (OPTIONAL)**
- 1 **TABLESPOON GRATED FRESH GINGER (OPTIONAL)**

Wash and trim the fruit:

Peaches, nectarines, plums, and apricots: Halve and pit (it's not necessary to skin the fruit), then cut into chunks.

Blueberries and blackberries: Leave whole.

Oranges: Remove zest with a zester or fine grater and reserve zest; cut orange sections free of the membranes that divide them (*see page 119*); cut sections into chunks.

Cherries: Remove stems and pits.

Apples and pears: Peel, halve, and core; cut into chunks.

Purée the fruit in a food processor until fairly smooth and the consistency of applesauce. (Because the moisture content will vary depending on the fruit used, it may be necessary to adjust the consistency by adding water to thin it.)

Blackberries: Press blackberry purée through a fine sieve and discard the seeds.

Oranges: Add the reserved zest to the orange purée.

Apples and pears: Add ¼ cup water to the purée until almost smooth. Don't worry if the fruit discolors a little, it will not alter the flavor.

Transfer the purée to a medium saucepan, add the sugar, and stir to blend. In a small bowl stir the cornstarch and vermouth together until smooth. Add to the purée and whisk until blended. Whisking almost constantly, bring the purée to a boil over high heat, then reduce heat and boil gently for 1 minute. Remove from the heat, add the vinegar, salt, cloves, butter, and, if desired, curry and ginger. Whisk until blended. Adjust taste with more sugar or vinegar. Cool before serving. Store refrigerated in a tightly capped jar for up to a week.

MAKES ABOUT 2 CUPS

WHICH SAUCE FOR WHICH DISH?
DUCK, DUCK, GOOSE

Can't decide which fruit sauce to make for your particular entrée? The following suggestions should get you started, but don't be afraid to trust your own tastes.

peaches or nectarines:
duck or quail

plums:
duck, goose, or quail

apricots:
duck, goose, pheasant, or rabbit

blueberries or blackberries:
duck, quail, or buffalo

oranges:
duck, quail, or buffalo

cherries:
duck, buffalo, or venison

apples or pears:
duck, goose, pheasant, or quail

PREPARING DUCK BREASTS FOR THE GRILL

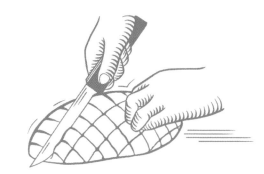

SCORE THE SKIN

To release the fat slowly during cooking and produce an attractive presentation, crosshatch the duck skin. Use a sharp knife and score the skin in a diamond pattern, cutting at ½-inch intervals. Be sure you don't cut into the meat.

RABBIT
WITH ROSEMARY-LIME BASTE

Some folks say rabbit tastes "just like chicken" but actually it has a meatier flavor and texture. Farm-raised rabbits are usually more robust and tender than wild ones, but the red wine in this marinade yields a fall-apart tenderness either way. The zesty basting sauce gives it a refreshing kick.

SEAR: HIGH, COOK: INDIRECT/MEDIUM

FOR THE MARINADE:

- 1 CUP DRY RED WINE
- 1/4 CUP EXTRA-VIRGIN OLIVE OIL
- 1/4 CUP FINELY CHOPPED YELLOW ONION
- 1 TABLESPOON FINELY CHOPPED FRESH ROSEMARY
- 1 TEASPOON MINCED GARLIC
- 1/2 TEASPOON KOSHER SALT
- 1/4 TEASPOON FRESHLY GROUND BLACK PEPPER

- 1 RABBIT, ABOUT 2 1/2 POUNDS, CUT INTO 6 PIECES

FOR THE BASTE:

- 2 TABLESPOONS EXTRA-VIRGIN OLIVE OIL
- 2 TABLESPOONS FRESH LIME JUICE
- 1 TABLESPOON FINELY CHOPPED FRESH ROSEMARY
- 2 TEASPOONS GRATED LIME ZEST
- 1/4 TEASPOON KOSHER SALT

To make the marinade: In a medium bowl whisk together the marinade ingredients.

Place the rabbit pieces in a large, resealable plastic bag and pour in the marinade. Press the air out of the bag and seal tightly. Turn the bag to distribute the marinade, place in a bowl, and refrigerate 2 to 12 hours, turning occasionally.

Just before grilling, make the baste: In a small bowl whisk together the baste ingredients.

Remove the rabbit pieces from the bag and discard the marinade. Wipe off most of the marinade from the rabbit with paper towels. Sear over *Direct High* heat for 5 minutes, turning once halfway through searing time. Continue grilling over *Indirect Medium* heat until the meat is no longer pink at the bone: 15 to 20 minutes more for the larger pieces, 10 to 12 minutes more for the smaller pieces. During the last 5 minutes of grilling, brush the rabbit pieces with the baste. Serve warm or at room temperature.

MAKES 3 TO 4 SERVINGS

GOOSE
WITH APPLE-CRAN STUFFING

Goose is a dark-meat bird, rich and full of flavor. This fruit stuffing is just tart enough to cut the richness without diminishing its appeal. To make the bread crumbs, toast several slices of bread for 5 to 10 minutes on the rack of an oven preheated to 350°F. Remove, cool to room temperature, and crumble in a food processor.

INDIRECT/MEDIUM

FOR THE STUFFING:

- 1/3 CUP UNSALTED BUTTER
- 1 1/2 CUPS FINELY CHOPPED YELLOW ONION
- 1 CUP FINELY CHOPPED CELERY
- 3 GOLDEN DELICIOUS APPLES, PEELED, CORED, AND FINELY CHOPPED (ABOUT 4 CUPS)
- 1 CUP DRIED CRANBERRIES
- 1 TEASPOON DRIED SAGE
- 1 TEASPOON DRIED THYME
- 1/4 TEASPOON CINNAMON
- 1/2 TEASPOON KOSHER SALT
- 1/4 TEASPOON FRESHLY GROUND BLACK PEPPER
- 4 CUPS WHITE BREAD CRUMBS

- 1 GOOSE, 10 TO 12 POUNDS
  KOSHER SALT
  FRESHLY GROUND BLACK PEPPER

To make the stuffing: In a large sauté pan melt the butter over medium heat. Add the onion, celery, apples, and cranberries and cook, stirring frequently, until the onion and apples soften, 10 to 12 minutes. Add the sage, thyme, cinnamon, salt, and pepper, then transfer to a large bowl. Add the bread crumbs and stir the stuffing to distribute the ingredients evenly. Allow to cool before stuffing the goose.

Rinse the goose, inside and out, under cold water and pat dry with paper towels. Season the goose, inside and out, with salt and pepper. Spoon the cooled stuffing into the chest cavity, being careful not to stuff the goose too tightly. Then, truss the goose (*see page 233*) and place it, breast side up, on a roasting rack set in a 13- by 9-inch heavy-gauge foil pan.

Grill the goose over *Indirect Medium* heat until the internal temperature of both the breast and the stuffing reaches 165°F, about 3 hours. Every 20 minutes, use a bulb baster to extract the accumulated fat from the roasting pan and transfer it to a container. Remove the roasting pan from the grill and allow the goose to rest about 15 minutes before carving. Serve warm.

MAKES 6 SERVINGS

BOURBON-MUSTARD
SQUAB

A squab is a small, remarkably tender bird with dark, rich meat and a more robust flavor than quail, pheasant, or Cornish game hen. Butterflied or whole, it is well suited to the grill, where it picks up smoky flavors. Try this recipe with earthy vegetables such as grilled winter squash or sautéed cabbage.

INDIRECT/MEDIUM

FOR THE MARINADE:

1/4 CUP BOURBON

1/4 CUP VEGETABLE OIL

2 TABLESPOONS FRESH LEMON JUICE

1 TABLESPOON FINELY CHOPPED FRESH THYME

2 TEASPOONS GRATED LEMON ZEST

1/2 TEASPOON KOSHER SALT

1/4 TEASPOON FRESHLY GROUND BLACK PEPPER

4 SQUABS, ABOUT 1 POUND EACH, BUTTERFLIED *(SEE PAGE 243)*

FOR THE BASTE:

1/4 CUP MAPLE SYRUP *OR* HONEY

2 TABLESPOONS BOURBON

2 TABLESPOONS DIJON MUSTARD

VEGETABLE OIL

To make the marinade: In a small bowl whisk together the marinade ingredients.

Place the squabs in a large, resealable plastic bag and pour in the marinade. (If one bag isn't big enough, use two and divide the marinade.) Press the air out of the bag and seal tightly. Turn the bag to distribute the marinade, place in a bowl, and refrigerate 2 to 12 hours, turning occasionally.

Just before grilling, make the baste: In a small bowl whisk together the baste ingredients. Set aside.

Remove the squabs from the bag and discard the marinade. Pat the squabs dry with paper towels and lightly brush with the vegetable oil. Grill the squabs, skin side down, over *Indirect Medium* heat until the skin is golden brown and the juices are still slightly pink, 35 to 45 minutes, turning once halfway through grilling time. During the last 10 minutes of grilling, brush on the baste. Serve warm.

MAKES 4 SERVINGS

BRINED SQUAB
WITH SWEET SPICES

A spicy brine is a great way to lock in moisture while enhancing the flavor of rich squab. The salt in the water draws water into the bird, so you end up with succulent grilled meat that slides right off the bone. An elegant but simple dish to prepare for guests—and it's easy to double for a dinner party.

INDIRECT/MEDIUM

FOR THE BRINE:

1/3 CUP KOSHER SALT

1/4 CUP GRANULATED SUGAR

2 MEDIUM GARLIC CLOVES, PEELED AND CRUSHED

4 WHOLE ALLSPICE, CRUSHED

4 WHOLE CLOVES, CRUSHED

1 BAY LEAF, BROKEN IN HALF

1 TEASPOON DRIED MARJORAM

4 SQUABS, ABOUT 1 POUND EACH

2 TABLESPOONS UNSALTED BUTTER, SOFTENED

1/2 TEASPOON FRESHLY GROUND BLACK PEPPER

To make the brine: In a large bowl combine 6 cups cold water with the salt and sugar and stir until they have dissolved, about 1 minute. Add the remaining brine ingredients.

With a sharp knife, remove the necks from the squabs. Rinse the squabs under cold water and add them to the brine; if necessary, use a weight to keep them submerged. Refrigerate for 2 to 4 hours.

Remove the squabs from the bowl and discard the brine. Drain the squabs and pat them dry with paper towels. Rub each squab with some of the butter and sprinkle on the pepper. Grill the squabs, breast side down, over *Indirect Medium* heat, until the skin is golden brown and the juices are still slightly pink, 35 to 45 minutes, turning once halfway through grilling time. Serve warm.

MAKES 4 SERVINGS

BUFFALO BURGERS
WITH CHIPOTLE MAYONNAISE

Chipotle chile peppers are dried, smoked jalapeños used to season Mexican adobo sauces and other dishes. Here their piquancy highlights the richness of buffalo. Work the patties lightly to avoid a compressed, tough texture.

DIRECT/MEDIUM

FOR THE SEASONING MIX:

1   TEASPOON KOSHER SALT

1/2   TEASPOON FRESHLY GROUND BLACK PEPPER

1/2   TEASPOON DRY MUSTARD

1/2   TEASPOON CHILI POWDER

1   POUND FRESHLY GROUND BUFFALO MEAT

FOR THE CHIPOTLE MAYONNAISE:

1/4   CUP MAYONNAISE

1/2   TEASPOON MINCED CANNED CHIPOTLE CHILE PEPPERS

1   YELLOW ONION, CUT INTO FOUR 1/3-INCH-THICK SLICES

EXTRA-VIRGIN OLIVE OIL

4   HAMBURGER BUNS

To make the seasoning mix: In a small bowl combine the seasoning ingredients.

Sprinkle the seasoning mix over the buffalo meat and gently distribute the spices throughout with your fingers. Gently shape the meat into four patties, about 3/4 inch thick each.

To make the chipotle mayonnaise: In a small bowl combine the mayonnaise and chile peppers.

Lightly brush or spray the onion slices on both sides with the olive oil and grill over *Direct Medium* heat until tender and well marked, about 8 minutes, turning once halfway through grilling time. Grill the buffalo patties over *Direct Medium* heat until the internal temperature reaches 160°F for medium, 7 to 9 minutes, turning once halfway through grilling time.

Spread the inside of the hamburger buns with the chipotle mayonnaise. Place the buffalo patties on the buns and top with the grilled onions. Serve immediately.

MAKES 4 SERVINGS

BUFFALO STRIP STEAKS
WITH LUSTY RED WINE SAUCE

This is definitely a dish for chest-pounders. But watch these hunks carefully—buffalo steaks have less marbling than beef, so it's easy to overcook them.

DIRECT/HIGH

FOR THE SAUCE:

2   TABLESPOONS EXTRA-VIRGIN OLIVE OIL

2   CUPS COARSELY CHOPPED YELLOW ONION

1   CUP COARSELY CHOPPED CARROTS

1   CUP COARSELY CHOPPED CELERY

5   MEDIUM GARLIC CLOVES, COARSELY CHOPPED

2   TABLESPOONS TOMATO PASTE

3   CUPS BEEF BROTH

2   CUPS DRY RED WINE

1/2   CUP BALSAMIC VINEGAR

1   TEASPOON DRIED THYME

2   BAY LEAVES

1/2   TEASPOON FRESHLY GROUND BLACK PEPPER

KOSHER SALT

4   BUFFALO STRIP STEAKS, ABOUT 1 INCH THICK EACH

EXTRA-VIRGIN OLIVE OIL

FRESHLY GROUND BLACK PEPPER

To make the sauce: In a large saucepan over high heat, warm the olive oil. Add the onion, carrots, and celery and cook, stirring occasionally, until the vegetables are browned, 6 to 8 minutes. Add the garlic and cook, stirring occasionally, for about 2 minutes more. Reduce heat to medium, add the tomato paste, and cook, stirring often, for about 2 minutes more. Add the broth, wine, vinegar, thyme, bay leaves, and pepper. Simmer, uncovered, for 45 minutes. Strain the sauce through a fine sieve into a medium saucepan, pressing down on the solids with the back of a spoon. Continue to simmer until about 1/2 cup liquid remains, about 45 minutes more. Season with salt and pepper to taste. Remove from the heat.

Brush or spray both sides of the steaks with the olive oil and season with salt and pepper. Grill over *Direct High* heat until the steaks are medium rare, 6 to 7 minutes, turning once halfway through grilling time. Remove from the grill and allow to rest for 1 to 2 minutes before slicing. Serve warm with the sauce.

MAKES 4 SERVINGS

A RICH,
FULL-BODIED
WINE SAUCE
UNDERSCORES
THE RED-
MEATINESS
OF THESE
BUFFALO
STRIP
STEAKS.

Buffalo Strip Steaks with Lusty Red Wine Sauce

Rack of Venison with Cran–Currant Sauce

RACK
OF VENISON
WITH CRAN-CURRANT SAUCE

Rack of venison resembles rack of lamb, but checks in at twice the fully trimmed weight. See page 201 to learn how to french the rack, or have the butcher do it instead. To crush juniper berries, wrap them in a dish towel, then whack them a few times with the bottom of a heavy pan. (Don't try this on a tile countertop unless you want an extra weekend remodeling project.)

INDIRECT/MEDIUM

FOR THE MARINADE:

1/2 CUP GIN

1/2 CUP APPLE JUICE

1/4 CUP VEGETABLE OIL

2 TEASPOONS JUNIPER BERRIES, CRUSHED

1/2 TEASPOON KOSHER SALT

1/2 TEASPOON FRESHLY GROUND BLACK PEPPER

1 RACK OF VENISON, 2 1/2 TO 3 POUNDS, FRENCHED

FOR THE SAUCE:

2 1/2 CUPS FRESH CRANBERRIES

3/4 CUP DRIED CURRANTS

2/3 CUP GRANULATED SUGAR

1 TABLESPOON GRATED ORANGE ZEST
   OR 2 TEASPOONS GRATED LIME ZEST

VEGETABLE OIL

To make the marinade: In a medium bowl whisk together the marinade ingredients.

Place the venison in a large, resealable plastic bag and pour in the marinade. Press the air out of the bag and seal tightly. Turn the bag to distribute the marinade, place in a bowl, and refrigerate 6 hours to 2 days, turning occasionally.

To make the sauce: In a medium saucepan combine the cranberries, currants, and sugar with 2/3 cup water. Bring to a boil over high heat, stirring occasionally, then reduce heat and simmer, stirring occasionally, until the cranberries stop popping and the sauce thickens slightly, 3 to 4 minutes. Remove from the heat and stir in the orange zest. Allow to cool to room temperature before serving.

Remove the venison from the bag and discard the marinade. Wipe off most of the marinade from the meat with paper towels. Lightly brush with the vegetable oil. Loosely cover the tips of the bones with foil to keep them from charring.

Grill the venison, bone side down, over *Indirect Medium* heat, until the internal temperature reaches 145°F for medium rare, about 45 minutes, turning once halfway through grilling time. Remove from the grill and allow to rest for 5 minutes. Cut the rack between the rib bones into individual chops. Serve warm with the cran-currant sauce.

MAKES 4 SERVINGS

VENISON AND
MUSHROOM
KABOBS

The perfect (easy) dish for those prized back straps you've been saving. The meaty, tender, and full-flavored venison cubes are paired with moist and chunky cubes of portabello mushroom. Add the red pepper and you've got a complete meal on a stick. Look for a vibrant crimson center to indicate that the meat is done to perfection.

DIRECT/MEDIUM

FOR THE MARINADE:

1/4 CUP EXTRA-VIRGIN OLIVE OIL

2 TABLESPOONS SHERRY VINEGAR

1 TABLESPOON MINCED GARLIC

1 TABLESPOON FINELY CHOPPED FRESH THYME

2 TEASPOONS WHOLE-GRAIN MUSTARD

1/2 TEASPOON KOSHER SALT

1/4 TEASPOON FRESHLY GROUND BLACK PEPPER

1 1/4 POUNDS VENISON LOIN, CUT INTO
   1-INCH CHUNKS

2 MEDIUM PORTABELLO MUSHROOM CAPS,
   CUT INTO 1-INCH PIECES

2 MEDIUM RED BELL PEPPERS, STEMS AND
   SEEDS REMOVED, CUT INTO 1-INCH PIECES

To make the marinade: In a large bowl whisk together the marinade ingredients.

Place the venison chunks, mushrooms, and peppers in a large, resealable plastic bag and pour in the marinade. Press the air out of the bag and seal tightly. Turn the bag to distribute the marinade, place in a bowl, and refrigerate 6 to 8 hours, turning occasionally.

Remove the venison and vegetables from the bag and discard the marinade. Thread the meat and the vegetables alternately onto skewers. Grill the kabobs over *Direct Medium* heat until the venison is medium rare, about 8 minutes, turning once halfway through grilling time.

MAKES 4 SERVINGS

Admittedly, for the majority of people, poultry isn't the most fascinating topic. We, however, feel differently. Just think of the personalities involved.

Consider, if you will, the lowly chicken. Let's face it, chicken can't get no respect. In the vernacular, a comparison to a chicken is an insult of pure dismissal. And rather than being esteemed by the masses it sustains, chicken is relegated to the mundane. If you don't quite know how to describe another food, what do you say? "It tastes just like chicken."

But no meat works harder at pleasing the palate. Chicken is, above all, selfless. It gladly takes on

POUL

whatever flavor you care to achieve (or simply resort to). You can dress it up or down, stuff it with exotic mushrooms, or just slather it with barbecue sauce.

Is it fair, then, that turkey gets so much fanfare and attention? Once or twice a year the vainglorious turkey struts across the table and, for whatever reason (perhaps its impressive size or its Mayflower connections), everyone makes a fuss. Oooo, it's tuuurkey! Maybe the fact that it doesn't show up as often is why we appreciate it more. We look for ways to add it to our repertoire—a cutlet here, a ground pound there. *Please, please,* the nation cries, *more turkey!*

And then there's the precocious debutante of the poultry world, the Cornish game hen, which nowadays is neither Cornish nor game. But that doesn't stop these farm-raised local beauties from being invited to dinner parties and special gatherings, usually escorted by a handsome rice pilaf or a charming stuffing. They may be petite, but they deliver the flavor with an almost masculine gusto. Real party gals, if you ask us.

But whether your taste buds, your budget, or the occasion drives you, you can do no wrong preparing any of these birds on the grill. The only thing you need to remember is to let the grill do the work.

Now, we know a lot of folks have been led to believe that they need to fuss with their food to make it a legitimate grilling experience. The way some people flip those poor chicken pieces left, then right, then chase them around the grill, you'd think they were going for the Stanley Cup! But please, if you're a full-contact griller (and you know who you are), play with the fire, not your food. Get the Scout stuff out of your system building a charcoal pyre and setting up the coals, and leave the food alone! One flip should do it. Every additional time you lift the lid to poke or prod, you'll have to increase your grilling time to compensate for the heat loss (if you don't think you're losing heat, check your grill thermome-

ter). If you're just the nervous type, keep a yoyo by your grill or practice synchronized tong twirling. Your dinner will thank you for it. Especially if you're dining on poultry.

Oh, we know people only pester poultry because they have a legitimate fear of undercooking it (a health hazard) or overcooking it (which you end up doing when you fuss so much that you finally give up and just let it sit there...a bit too long). But the fact is, poultry seems to thrive on independence. Whole turkey, for example, should be checked hourly and no more. That's about how often you need to check for even browning and replenish charcoal, if you're not gas grilling. But as for turkey breasts, whole chickens, and game hens, the general rule is to leave them be for the cooking time. If you want to crisp up the skin, you can do so over *Direct* heat during the last 5 to 10 minutes of grilling. If you don't flip out (literally), your poultry will come out juicy and moist.

This chapter has lots of clues and tips on how to get the upper wing on poultry on the grill. The recipes feature a wide range of flavors and techniques that celebrate the diversity of the birds and the cuisines that feature them. And there's enough material here to make dinner tasty and fun for any crowd, big or small. Let your imagination take flight!

STEAMING BEER KEEPS A WHOLE CHICKEN MOIST WHILE THE HIGH HEAT CRISPS THE SKIN FOR A PERFECT BIRD EVERY TIME.

Beer Can Chicken

BEER CAN
CHICKEN

Here's a technique that delivers great-tasting chicken and makes a lively conversation starter as well. We've used one of our special rubs, but you can sub in 2 to 3 tablespoons of your favorite one. Bottoms up!

INDIRECT/MEDIUM

FOR THE RUB:

1 TEASPOON DRY MUSTARD

1 TEASPOON GRANULATED ONION

1 TEASPOON PAPRIKA

1 TEASPOON KOSHER SALT

1/2 TEASPOON GRANULATED GARLIC

1/2 TEASPOON GROUND CORIANDER

1/2 TEASPOON GROUND CUMIN

1/2 TEASPOON FRESHLY GROUND BLACK PEPPER

1 WHOLE CHICKEN, 4 TO 5 POUNDS

2 TEASPOONS VEGETABLE OIL

1 CAN (16 OUNCES) BEER (TALL BOY)

To make the rub: In a small bowl combine the rub ingredients.

Remove and discard the neck, giblets, and any excess fat from the chicken. Rinse the chicken, inside and out, under cold water and pat dry with paper towels. Lightly spray or brush all over with the vegetable oil and season, inside and out, with the rub.

Open the beer can and pour off half of the beer. Set the half-full can on a flat surface and slide the chicken over the top so the can fits inside the cavity. Transfer the bird to the grill, keeping the can upright. Carefully balance the bird on its two legs and the can. Grill over *Indirect Medium* heat until the juices run clear and the internal temperature reaches 170°F in the breast and 180°F in the thickest part of the thigh, 1 1/4 to 1 1/2 hours. Wearing barbecue mitts, carefully remove the chicken and the can from the grill, being careful not to spill the beer—it will be hot. Let the chicken rest for about 10 minutes before lifting it from the can. Discard the beer. Cut the chicken into serving pieces. Serve warm.

MAKES 4 TO 6 SERVINGS

ACHIOTE
ROAST CHICKEN

If you're not familiar with achiote—a powder made from red annatto seeds that's used to color butter, cheddar cheese, and other foods—you're about to become a fan. Found in Latino and East Indian grocery stores, achiote paste comes in a small brick seasoned with herbs and spices. Mellow in flavor, it adds a wonderful bronze color to roasted chicken or turkey.

INDIRECT/MEDIUM

FOR THE PASTE:

3 TABLESPOONS ACHIOTE PASTE (ABOUT 2 OUNCES)

2 TABLESPOONS FRESH LEMON JUICE

2 TABLESPOONS VEGETABLE OIL

1 TABLESPOON MINCED GARLIC

2 TEASPOONS DRIED OREGANO

1 TEASPOON KOSHER SALT

1/2 TEASPOON CAYENNE

1/2 TEASPOON FRESHLY GROUND BLACK PEPPER

1 WHOLE CHICKEN, 4 TO 5 POUNDS

To make the paste: In a small bowl whisk together the paste ingredients.

Remove and discard the neck, giblets, and any excess fat from the chicken. Rinse the chicken, inside and out, under cold water and pat dry with paper towels. Loosen the chicken skin gently with your fingers and spread some of the paste under the skin on the breast and legs (*see page 229*). Brush the remaining paste over the outside of the skin and on the inside of the cavity. Tuck the wing tips behind the wing joints and tie the legs together. Place the chicken on a plate, cover, and refrigerate for 2 to 4 hours.

Grill the chicken, breast side up, over *Indirect Medium* heat until the juices run clear and the internal temperature reaches 170°F in the breast and 180°F in the thickest part of the thigh, 1 1/4 to 1 1/2 hours. Check after 45 minutes; if the chicken is browning too quickly, cover with a piece of aluminum foil and finish grilling. Transfer to a platter, loosely cover with foil, and allow to rest for about 10 minutes before carving. Serve warm.

MAKES 4 TO 6 SERVINGS

POULTRY ON THE GRILL

For this chapter, we've narrowed "poultry" to three different types of domesticated birds: game hens, chicken, and turkey. Before you cry "fowl!", please note that we have recipes for duck and goose in our Game chapter. Here are a few things to keep in mind when you're taking these fine feathered creatures to the grill:

KEEP IT CLEAN! Hey, paranoia may be overrated, but when it comes to working with poultry, you can't be too careful. Always wash your hands with plenty of soap and warm water before and after handling poultry. Also wash all utensils, cutting boards, work surfaces, and sponges that come into contact with raw poultry with hot soapy water and rinse well.

USE IT OR LOSE IT. Poultry has a very short shelf life, so be sure to keep it refrigerated and cook it or freeze it by the "use by" date on the label. Frozen poultry will keep for up to two months. Always thaw and/or marinate poultry in the refrigerator.

IS IT DONE YET? Poultry is thoroughly cooked when the juices run clear and the meat is no longer pink at the bone. It's hard to take a temperature reading on a game hen without touching the bone, so follow the times and visual clues set down in the recipes for doneness. On a whole chicken or a turkey (or on their bone-in parts), however, you're best to use an instant-read thermometer to check for doneness. The thermometer should read 180°F when inserted into the meatiest part of the thigh on a whole bird or bone-in thighs and legs. Just make sure the thermometer tip isn't touching bone or fat. Chicken and turkey breasts are thoroughly cooked at 170°F. According to the USDA, ground chicken or turkey is fully cooked at 165°F.

TRY A ROTISSERIE. If you're fond of rotisserie-grilled meats, a rotisserie can be a great grill accessory. It slowly turns the meat on a spit above the surface of the cooking grate for slow, even browning (the food has to be well balanced on the spit, of course). Now, a well-engineered grill also gives you even browning, but the rotisserie offers a special benefit. The meat juices roll around the outside of the meat as it turns, rather than dripping onto the flames. The result is a juicy, flavorful bird or roast. There are just a few tricks to remember when you're using a rotisserie for poultry:

- Consider the height of the bird. You lose a few inches of clearance when you lift the bird off the grate (a charcoal grill rotisserie should come with a collar that adds a few inches of height to the entire grill), so you may be limited on the size of turkey that will fit. Always make sure you'll have at least an inch of headroom between the bird and the lid before you put the bird on the spit. If you can't fit it, you can always cook it on the cooking grate.
- Know your temperature settings. For rotisserie cooking, use Indirect High heat for game hens and other small birds, Direct Medium for chickens and medium-sized birds, and Indirect Medium for turkeys.
- Convert a rotisserie recipe to a regular grilling recipe by cooking the bird over Indirect Medium heat. Consult the Grilling Guide on page 398 for cooking times. Use an instant-read thermometer to ensure the bird is fully cooked to the bone, where the juices should run clear.

JUST BAG IT. Resealable plastic bags are convenient for marinating poultry in the refrigerator because you can toss them when you're done, as opposed to scouring a bowl. One-gallon bags are big enough for a whole chicken or two game hens. Larger sizes are also available in just about any grocery store. Always place the bag(s) in a bowl in case they leak.

BOIL THAT MARINADE! If you want to use your poultry marinade for a baste, boil it first. Pour it into a small saucepan and bring it to a full boil over high heat. Continue to boil vigorously for 1 full minute.

BOOSTING THE FLAVOR
BEFORE YOU GRILL

Whether you're preparing game hens, chickens, or turkeys, another great way to add flavor and moisture is to "stuff" the bird under the skin with a paste made of seasonings blended with butter. Try your favorite blend of poultry seasonings, fresh or dried herbs and spices, and salt and pepper. Blend with enough softened butter to make a spreadable paste—1/4 cup butter should make enough paste for a medium-sized turkey, two chickens, or four game hens.

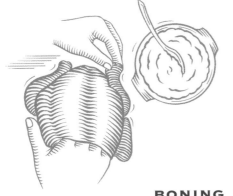

STUFF THE SKIN

Loosen the skin by working your fingers up between the skin and flesh, from breast to leg. Be careful not to tear the skin. Then, take a clump of paste in your fingers and work it up beneath the skin, spreading it evenly over the meat as far as your fingers can reach.

BONING A WHOLE
CHICKEN OR A TURKEY LEG

Boning a chicken or a turkey leg is not as difficult as it sounds. The bones come out quite easily after being cut away with a sharp knife.

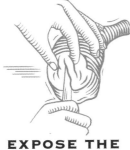

EXPOSE THE
THIGH BONE

Place the whole leg, skin side down, on a cutting board. Using a sharp boning knife, make an incision through the meat along the length of the thigh bone.

FREE THE
THIGH BONE

Cut through the muscle around the thigh bone to free it, scraping away the meat (above). Cut through the joint connecting the thigh to the drumstick. Do not cut through the skin. Remove the thigh bone.

REMOVE THE
DRUMSTICK

Cut the meat from around the drumstick bone. Scrape down the bone to within 1 inch of the end of the leg. Push the meat down to expose the bone. With a heavy knife or cleaver, cut through the bone (above). Do not cut through the skin.

RE-FORM
THE DRUMSTICK

Feel for any remaining bone chips and remove any tendons. Push the short end of the drumstick bone back through to the end and re-form the leg into its original form (above). If you plan to stuff the cavity, wait until you're just about to grill before doing so, then close the cavity with a metal or bamboo skewer through the meat and skin.

OKTOBERFEST
BRINED CHICKEN

This chicken grills up extra crispy, brown, and juicy. A nice addition to an Oktoberfest menu, but you'll want it year-round, guaranteed.

INDIRECT/MEDIUM

1/2 CUP PICKLING SPICES
1/2 CUP KOSHER SALT

1 WHOLE CHICKEN, 3 1/2 TO 4 POUNDS

3 TABLESPOONS UNSALTED BUTTER, MELTED

In a Dutch oven or stockpot combine the pickling spices and salt with 1 gallon water. Bring to a boil over high heat. Remove from the heat and allow to cool to room temperature, about 2 hours.

Remove and discard the neck, giblets, and any excess fat from the chicken. Rinse the chicken, inside and out, under cold water, drain, and submerge in the cooled pickling marinade. Cover and refrigerate for 8 to 12 hours.

Remove the chicken from the Dutch oven and discard the brine. Pat the chicken dry with paper towels. Truss the chicken with cotton string *(see page 233)*. Grill, breast side up, over *Indirect Medium* heat until the juices run clear and the internal temperature reaches 170°F in the breast and 180°F in the thickest part of the thigh, 1 to 1 1/4 hours. Brush occasionally with the butter. Remove the chicken from the grill and allow to rest for about 10 minutes before removing the string and cutting into serving pieces. Serve warm.

MAKES 4 SERVINGS

*If the spit is right,
then the meat is right.*

— INDIAN PROVERB

SAFFRON-ORANGE
ROTISSERIE CHICKEN

The Spanish Mission influence is evident throughout California, where monks planted vineyards and olive and orange groves. Their peasant style of cooking lives on in recipes like this one. So good, you'll want to double it.

INDIRECT/MEDIUM

FOR THE MARINADE:

1/4 CUP EXTRA-VIRGIN OLIVE OIL
1 TABLESPOON COARSELY GROUND WHITE PEPPERCORNS
GRATED ZEST FROM 2 ORANGES
2 TEASPOONS MINCED GARLIC
1 TEASPOON FINELY CHOPPED FRESH ROSEMARY
1 TEASPOON FINELY CHOPPED FRESH THYME
1/4 TEASPOON SAFFRON THREADS

1 WHOLE CHICKEN, 4 TO 5 POUNDS
1 WHOLE ORANGE, WASHED
1 BAY LEAF
JUICE FROM 2 ORANGES

KOSHER SALT

To make the marinade: In a small bowl whisk together the marinade ingredients.

Remove and discard the neck, giblets, wing tips, and any excess fat from the chicken. Rinse the chicken, inside and out, under cold water and pat dry with paper towels. Rub the marinade all over the inside and outside of the chicken. Place the whole orange and bay leaf in the chicken cavity and truss the chicken with cotton string *(see page 233)*. Place the chicken in a large, resealable plastic bag and pour in the orange juice. Press the air out of the bag and seal tightly. Turn the bag to distribute the juice, place in a bowl, and refrigerate for 8 to 24 hours, turning occasionally.

Remove the chicken from the bag and discard the juice. Season the chicken with salt. Center lengthwise on the spit, running the skewer through the orange, and let the chicken rotate over *Indirect Medium* heat until the juices run clear and the internal temperature reaches 170°F in the breast and 180°F in the thickest part of the thigh, 1 1/4 to 1 1/2 hours.

Turn off the rotisserie and, using barbecue mitts, remove the spit from the grill. Slide the chicken from the spit onto a cutting board. Loosely cover with aluminum foil and allow to rest for about 10 minutes. Remove the string, orange, and bay leaf. Cut the chicken into serving pieces and serve warm.

MAKES 4 TO 6 SERVINGS

Saffron-Orange Rotisserie Chicken

IT'S ALL ABOUT THE MARINADE, AND THIS ONE TAKES A PAGE FROM CALIFORNIA'S SPANISH MISSION HISTORY: ZESTY AND AROMATIC.

Three-Lemon Chicken

THREE-LEMON CHICKEN

Bright lemon and roasted garlic make this chicken a wonderful start to a summer picnic or the perfect ending to a relaxing weekend.

INDIRECT/MEDIUM

1 HEAD OF GARLIC
1 TEASPOON EXTRA-VIRGIN OLIVE OIL

FOR THE PASTE:
   LEMON ZEST FROM 2 LEMONS
2 TABLESPOONS FRESH LEMON JUICE, DIVIDED
1 1/2 TEASPOONS FINELY CHOPPED FRESH ROSEMARY
1 TEASPOON KOSHER SALT
1/2 TEASPOON FRESHLY GROUND BLACK PEPPER

1 WHOLE CHICKEN, 4 TO 5 POUNDS
   KOSHER SALT
   FRESHLY GROUND BLACK PEPPER
4 SPRIGS FRESH ROSEMARY
1/4 CUP DRY WHITE WINE

1 WHOLE LEMON, THINLY SLICED (OPTIONAL)

Remove the loose, papery outer skin from the head of garlic. Cut about 1/2 inch off the top to expose the cloves. Place on a large square of aluminum foil. Drizzle the olive oil over the cloves. Fold up the foil sides and seal to make a packet, leaving a little room for the expansion of steam. Grill over *Indirect Medium* heat until the cloves are soft, 30 to 45 minutes. Remove the garlic from the grill and allow to cool. Squeeze the garlic from the individual cloves into a small bowl.

To make the paste: In the bowl with the garlic, combine the lemon zest, 1 tablespoon of the lemon juice, rosemary, salt, and pepper. Mix well.

Remove and discard the neck, giblets, and any excess fat from the chicken. Rinse the chicken, inside and out, under cold water and pat dry with paper towels. Loosen the chicken skin gently with your fingers and spread half of the paste under the skin on the breast *(see page 229)*. Season the inside of the chicken cavity with salt and pepper and add the rosemary sprigs. Truss the chicken with cotton string *(see sidebar, right)*. Pour the remaining 1 tablespoon of lemon juice and the wine into the cavity. Coat the outside surface of the chicken with the other half of the paste, pressing it into the skin.

Grill the chicken, breast side up, over *Indirect Medium* heat until the juices run clear and the internal temperature reaches 170°F in the breast and 180°F in the thickest part of the thigh, 1 1/4 to 1 1/2 hours. Halfway through grilling, slide three lemon slices under the string on top of the breasts.

Transfer the chicken to a platter, loosely cover with aluminum foil, and allow to rest for about 10 minutes before removing the string and carving. Serve warm.

MAKES 4 TO 6 SERVINGS

TRUSSING

Trussing is simply tying a bird, large or small, into a more compact shape for cooking so the breast doesn't become overcooked. Some fancy methods involve a 4- to 10-inch trussing needle to run cotton string through the bird at various junctures. Here's the easy way to do it. For an average-sized chicken (3 1/2 to 4 pounds), use a piece of cotton string about 3 feet long. If you're trussing a turkey or small game bird, adjust the length of the string accordingly.

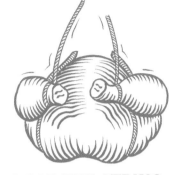

LOOP THE STRING
Set the bird on its back. Slip the string under the rear end of the bird. Loop the string around the end of each drumstick.

CROSS THE STRING
Cross the string over the center of the breast (above). Turn the bird over on its breast.

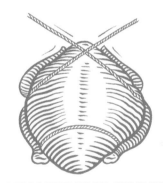

SECURE THE WINGS
Pass the string under and around the wings to keep them flat against the body, crossing it over the back.

TIE THE STRING
Turn the bird back over on its back. Pull the string together firmly and tie a bow or a knot (above). Trim the ends of the string.

MESQUITE-ROASTED
CHICKEN

In West Texas, mesquite trees grow wild, so it's no surprise they make their way into the fire more often than not. Few things are better for smoking a well-seasoned chicken. Add a high-octane barbecue sauce and you can almost hear the coyotes.

INDIRECT/MEDIUM

FOR THE RUB:

2   TABLESPOONS PAPRIKA

2   TABLESPOONS LIGHT BROWN SUGAR

1   TABLESPOON CHILI POWDER

1   TABLESPOON KOSHER SALT

1   TABLESPOON CRACKED BLACK PEPPERCORNS

2   TEASPOONS GRANULATED GARLIC

2   TEASPOONS GRANULATED ONION

1   TEASPOON GROUND CUMIN

2   WHOLE CHICKENS, 3¹/2 TO 4 POUNDS EACH

FOR THE SAUCE:

1   CUP KETCHUP

1   TABLESPOON MOLASSES

1   TABLESPOON RED WINE VINEGAR

1   TABLESPOON WORCESTERSHIRE SAUCE

2   TEASPOONS CHILI POWDER

2   TEASPOONS GRANULATED ONION

2   TEASPOONS FRESHLY GROUND BLACK PEPPER

1   TEASPOON GROUND CUMIN

MESQUITE CHUNKS *OR* CHIPS SOAKED IN WATER FOR AT LEAST 30 MINUTES

To make the rub: In a small bowl combine the rub ingredients.

Remove and discard the neck, giblets, and any excess fat from the chickens. Rinse the chickens, inside and out, under cold water and pat dry with paper towels. Remove the backbones and cut in half *(see page 243)*. Coat each chicken half thoroughly with the rub, cover with plastic wrap, and refrigerate for 2 to 4 hours.

To make the sauce: In a small bowl whisk together the sauce ingredients along with ¹/2 cup water.

Follow the grill's instructions for using wood chunks. Grill the chicken halves, skin side up, over *Indirect Medium* heat until the juices run clear and the internal temperature reaches 170°F in the breast and 180°F in the thickest part of the thigh, about 1¹/4 hours. Remove from the grill and loosely cover with aluminum foil. Allow to rest for about 5 minutes before cutting the halves in two. Serve warm with the sauce on the side.

MAKES 8 SERVINGS

CHICKEN
UNDER BRICKS

Here's a cool way to cook everyone's favorite bird. The meat cooks evenly and quickly, and the skin comes out so crispy, even the Colonel will be jealous. Just a word of caution: The baking sheet loaded with bricks slides off the chicken easily, so handle with care.

INDIRECT/HIGH

FOR THE PASTE:

2   TABLESPOONS MINCED GARLIC

2   TABLESPOONS WHOLE-GRAIN MUSTARD

2   TABLESPOONS FINELY CHOPPED FRESH THYME

2   TABLESPOONS FINELY CHOPPED FRESH ROSEMARY

2   TABLESPOONS COARSELY GROUND WHITE PEPPER

2   TABLESPOONS FRESH LEMON JUICE

2   TABLESPOONS EXTRA-VIRGIN OLIVE OIL

2   WHOLE CHICKENS, ABOUT 4 POUNDS EACH
    EXTRA-VIRGIN OLIVE OIL
    KOSHER SALT

To make the paste: In a small bowl mix together the paste ingredients.

Remove and discard the neck, giblets, and any excess fat from the chickens. Rinse the chickens, inside and out, under cold water and pat dry with paper towels. Remove the backbones and cut in half *(see page 243)*. Coat each chicken half thoroughly with the paste. Place the chicken halves in a large, resealable plastic bag (if one bag isn't large enough, use two). Press the air out of the bag, seal tightly, and refrigerate for 8 to 24 hours.

Lightly brush or spray the chicken halves with olive oil. Season with salt. Place the chicken, skin side down, over *Indirect High* heat. Lightly coat the bottom of a baking sheet with oil. Wrap three bricks in aluminum foil. Place the baking sheet on top of the chicken halves and weight the sheet down with the bricks. Grill the chickens until the skin is crispy and the juices run clear, 30 to 40 minutes. Using barbecue mitts, carefully remove the bricks and baking sheet. Turn the chickens and continue to grill for 2 to 3 minutes to crisp the underside. Transfer from the grill to a platter, loosely cover with foil, and allow to rest for about 5 minutes before cutting the halves in two. Serve warm.

MAKES 8 SERVINGS

Chicken Under Bricks

Chicken on the grill—what does it mean to you? Maybe a juicy kabob or satay with a carefully prepared sauce on the side. Perhaps nothing less than a deliciously browned, whole grill-roasted bird will do. Or maybe you like things simple—chicken pieces slathered with barbecue sauce. Whatever effect you're going for, here are some tips to make your chicken trip easy as can be:

TRIM THE FAT. Chicken fat tends to render out very quickly, so when you're cooking chicken pieces over Direct heat, trim any excess fat or skin to minimize flare-ups. (Flare-ups, while rare on a well-designed grill, are more likely over charcoal than gas.) If you have a flare-up, it takes just a moment to move the chicken pieces to Indirect heat until the flames die, then move the chicken back over Direct heat.

TO FLIP OR NOT TO FLIP? That is the question many grillers struggle with, so here's the scoop: The only time it's really necessary is when you're cooking boneless chicken pieces, kabobs, or burgers over Direct heat. That's because your cooking time is so short (less than 25 minutes) that you need to expose both sides to the heat for even browning, grill marks, and thorough cooking. One flip halfway through grilling time will do it. Bone-in pieces, on the other hand, should generally be grilled bone side down (skin side up) over Indirect heat and do not need to be turned. The exceptions are recipes that have you sear the chicken first, to achieve a desired texture. You don't need to turn bone-in pieces or whole chickens cooked only over Indirect heat because they brown evenly over a longer grilling time (more than 25 minutes). Depending on their size, individual bone-in thighs and legs grilled over Indirect Medium heat will take 40 to 50 minutes each. Wings and bone-in breasts take 30 to 40 minutes. If you want crispier skin, however, do feel free to finish bone-in pieces, skin side down, over *Direct* heat during the last 5 minutes of grilling time.

PARTS IS PARTS—or are they? Many of our chicken recipes call for a whole chicken cut into eight pieces (*see sidebar, page 237*). This seems like an extra step when you can buy chicken parts in assortment packs, but it's an important one. If you cut up one chicken, the parts will be proportionate. Those handy assortment packs include parts from lots of different chickens, so you may get tiny drumsticks and oversized breast halves or vice versa. Cooking times between these different-sized pieces may vary greatly. When the parts come from one chicken, however, they're more likely to cook up evenly and within about 10 minutes of each other. Which brings us to timing: If you want all the pieces to be done at the same time, place the thighs and legs on the grill first, then the breast halves and wings about 10 minutes later.

Small chickens ranging from 2 ¹/₂ to 3 pounds can be cut into six reasonable-sized serving pieces, typically two breast halves (with wings attached), two thighs, and two drumsticks. Larger chickens, between 3 and 5 pounds, can be cut into eight serving pieces, such as are shown below. Wing tips can be cut off and reserved for stock; same with the backbone. Before cutting the bird into pieces, remove and discard the neck, giblets, and any excess fat.

REMOVE THE LEG

Using poultry shears or a sharp, sturdy butcher knife, cut through the skin between the leg and breast. Twist the leg outward to break the joint. Sever the leg from the body by cutting down between the ball and socket of the joint (left). Then, separate the drumstick from the thigh by cutting down firmly through the joint (right). Repeat with the leg on the other side.

REMOVE
THE WING

Press the wing up against the body of the bird so that the flesh bunches at the joint. Using a sharp knife, make a starting incision at the joint between the ball and socket. Then, cut through the joint (above). Cut any skin still holding the wing to the body. Repeat with the wing on the other side.

REMOVE
THE BACKBONE

Pull the backbone from the breast; it will come away fairly easily. Then, cut between the rib cage and shoulder joints. Split the breast in half lengthwise by cutting along one side of the breastbone as shown on page 243. There, you'll also find another way of removing the backbone.

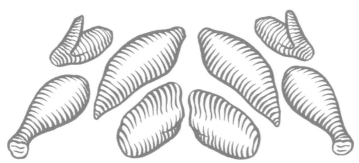

EIGHT SERVING PIECES

HALVED CHICKEN
WITH MUSTARD MARINADE

An exciting mix of ingredients with Southern roots.

INDIRECT/HIGH

FOR THE MARINADE:

- 1/4 CUP **CREOLE MUSTARD** *OR* **SPICY BROWN MUSTARD**
- 1/4 CUP RED WINE VINEGAR
- 1/4 CUP EXTRA-VIRGIN OLIVE OIL
- 2 TABLESPOONS GRANULATED GARLIC
- 2 TABLESPOONS DRIED THYME
- 2 TABLESPOONS WORCESTERSHIRE SAUCE
- 1 TEASPOON KOSHER SALT
- 1 TEASPOON FRESHLY GROUND BLACK PEPPER

- 2 WHOLE CHICKENS, 3 1/2 TO 4 POUNDS EACH

To make the marinade: In a small bowl whisk together the marinade ingredients.

Remove and discard the neck, giblets, and any excess fat from the chickens. Rinse the chickens, inside and out, under cold water and pat dry with paper towels. Remove and discard the backbones and cut the chickens in half *(see page 243)*.

Place the chicken halves in a large, resealable plastic bag and pour in the marinade. (If one bag isn't large enough, use two and divide the marinade.) Press the air out of the bag and seal tightly. Turn the bag to distribute the marinade, place in a bowl, and refrigerate for 24 hours, turning occasionally.

Remove the chicken halves from the bag and discard the marinade. Grill, skin side up, over *Indirect High* heat until the juices run clear and the internal temperature reaches 170°F in the breast and 180°F in the thickest part of the thigh, 45 minutes to 1 hour. Remove the chicken from the grill and allow to rest for about 5 minutes before cutting into serving pieces. Serve warm.

MAKES 8 SERVINGS

GREEK
GARLIC CHICKEN

A tapenade is a thick paste typically made from olives, anchovies, capers, garlic, lemon juice, olive oil, and seasonings. Here it adds deep flavor to the chicken. Look for it in stores with a good olive selection—or try our tapenade recipe on page 245.

INDIRECT/MEDIUM

FOR THE MARINADE:

- 1/2 CUP FINELY CHOPPED FRESH ITALIAN PARSLEY
- 1/4 CUP DRY WHITE WINE
- 1/4 CUP EXTRA-VIRGIN OLIVE OIL
- 2 TABLESPOONS FRESH LEMON JUICE
- 1 TABLESPOON MINCED GARLIC
- 1 TABLESPOON BLACK OLIVE TAPENADE
- 1 TEASPOON DRIED OREGANO
- 1 TEASPOON PAPRIKA
- 1/2 TEASPOON KOSHER SALT
- 1/4 TEASPOON FRESHLY GROUND BLACK PEPPER

- 1 WHOLE CHICKEN, 3 1/2 TO 4 POUNDS, CUT INTO 8 SERVING PIECES *(SEE PAGE 237)*

To make the marinade: In a medium bowl whisk together the marinade ingredients.

Rinse the chicken pieces under cold water and pat dry with paper towels. Place in a large, resealable plastic bag and pour in the marinade. Press the air out of the bag and seal tightly. Turn the bag to distribute the marinade, place in a bowl, and refrigerate for 4 to 6 hours, turning occasionally.

Remove the chicken from the bag, reserving the marinade. Pour the marinade into a small saucepan, bring to a boil, and boil for 1 full minute. Set aside.

Grill the chicken, skin side up, over *Indirect Medium* heat until the juices run clear and the internal temperature reaches 180°F in the thickest part of the thighs and 170°F in the breasts. The leg and thigh pieces will take 40 to 50 minutes and the breast and wing pieces will take 30 to 40 minutes. Baste with the marinade during the last 10 to 20 minutes of grilling time. Remove from the grill and serve warm.

MAKES 4 SERVINGS

ANOTHER RECIPE THAT'S EASY TO DOUBLE FOR A PARTY. SERVE WITH ORZO, A GREEK SALAD, AND PITA BREAD.

Greek Garlic Chicken

Kingston Jerk Chicken

KINGSTON
JERK CHICKEN

This spicy style of grilling comes from Jamaica, where native wild chiles and spices were traditionally used to preserve meat. When working with fresh chiles, such as the very hot habanero, wear rubber gloves to protect your skin and keep your hands away from your eyes.

INDIRECT/MEDIUM

FOR THE PASTE:

4   GREEN ONIONS (WHITE PART ONLY), COARSELY CHOPPED

1   HABANERO CHILE, STEMMED, SEEDED, AND COARSELY CHOPPED

3   TABLESPOONS CANOLA OIL

2   TABLESPOONS FRESH LIME JUICE

1   TABLESPOON GRANULATED GARLIC

2   TEASPOONS DRIED THYME

2   TEASPOONS GROUND ALLSPICE

1   TEASPOON GRANULATED SUGAR

1   TEASPOON KOSHER SALT

1/2 TEASPOON FRESHLY GROUND BLACK PEPPER

1   WHOLE CHICKEN, 3 1/2 TO 4 POUNDS, CUT INTO 8 SERVING PIECES *(SEE PAGE 237)*

To make the paste: In a food processor combine the paste ingredients and process until smooth.

Rinse the chicken pieces under cold water and pat dry with paper towels. Rub the paste all over, cover with plastic wrap, and refrigerate for 6 to 12 hours.

Grill the chicken pieces, skin side up, over *Indirect Medium* heat until the juices run clear and the internal temperature reaches 180°F in the thickest part of the thighs and 170°F in the breasts. The leg and thigh pieces will take 40 to 50 minutes and the breast and wing pieces will take 30 to 40 minutes. For crispier skin, grill the chicken, skin side down, over *Direct Medium* heat during the last 5 to 10 minutes of grilling time. Serve warm.

MAKES 4 SERVINGS

"Men like to barbecue. Men like to cook only if danger is involved."

— RITA RUDNER

TANDOORI-STYLE
CHICKEN

Tandoori cooking gets its name from the clay oven, or tandoor, in which the food is cooked. Meat is marinated, placed on long skewers, and cooked quickly at very high temperatures. We admit that the authentic version is the best, but how many of us have a real tandoor in our backyard? Like other tandoori dishes, this one uses yogurt to tenderize the chicken and just the right blend of spices to make it mouth-watering.

INDIRECT/MEDIUM

FOR THE MARINADE:

1   CUP PLAIN YOGURT

1   TABLESPOON GRATED FRESH GINGER

2   TEASPOONS MINCED GARLIC

2   TEASPOONS PAPRIKA

1   TEASPOON GROUND CINNAMON

1   TEASPOON GROUND CUMIN

1   TEASPOON GROUND CORIANDER

1   TEASPOON KOSHER SALT

1/2 TEASPOON FRESHLY GROUND BLACK PEPPER

1/4 TEASPOON GROUND CLOVES

1   WHOLE CHICKEN, 3 1/2 TO 4 POUNDS, CUT INTO 8 SERVING PIECES *(SEE PAGE 237)*

EXTRA-VIRGIN OLIVE OIL

To make the marinade: In a medium bowl whisk together the marinade ingredients.

Rinse the chicken pieces under cold water and pat dry with paper towels. Place in a large, resealable plastic bag and pour in the marinade. Press the air out of the bag and seal tightly. Turn the bag to distribute the marinade, place in a bowl, and refrigerate for 6 to 8 hours, turning occasionally.

Remove the chicken from the bag and discard the marinade. Wipe the marinade off the chicken with paper towels. Lightly brush or spray each piece with olive oil. Grill the chicken, skin side up, over *Indirect Medium* heat until the juices run clear and the internal temperature reaches 180°F in the thickest part of the thighs and 170°F in the breasts. The leg and thigh pieces will take 40 to 50 minutes and the breast and wing pieces will take 30 to 40 minutes. For crispier skin, grill the chicken, skin side down, over *Direct Medium* heat during the last 5 to 10 minutes of grilling time. Serve warm.

MAKES 4 SERVINGS

CAROLINA PULLED
BARBECUE CHICKEN

This updated, leaner version of the classic pulled pork sandwich satisfies like the real thing. It's that tangy Carolina-style barbecue sauce that keeps folks comin' back for more—but don't skip the rub.

INDIRECT/MEDIUM

FOR THE COLESLAW:

- 3 CUPS SHREDDED GREEN CABBAGE (ABOUT 3/4 POUND)
- 1 CUP COARSELY GRATED CARROT
- 1/2 SMALL WHITE ONION, THINLY SLICED
- 1/2 CUP MAYONNAISE
- 1 TABLESPOON DIJON MUSTARD
- 1 TABLESPOON GRANULATED SUGAR
- 2 TEASPOONS WHITE WINE VINEGAR
- 1/2 TEASPOON CELERY SEEDS
- 1/4 TEASPOON KOSHER SALT
- 1/8 TEASPOON CAYENNE

FOR THE RUB:

- 1 TABLESPOON PAPRIKA
- 1 1/2 TEASPOONS HOT MUSTARD POWDER
- 1 1/2 TEASPOONS LIGHT BROWN SUGAR
- 1 1/2 TEASPOONS KOSHER SALT
- 1 TEASPOON GRANULATED GARLIC
- 1 TEASPOON GRANULATED ONION
- 1/2 TEASPOON GROUND CUMIN
- 1/4 TEASPOON CAYENNE
- 1/4 TEASPOON GROUND CLOVES

- 1 WHOLE CHICKEN, 4 TO 5 POUNDS
  VEGETABLE OIL

  HICKORY CHUNKS *OR* CHIPS SOAKED IN WATER FOR AT LEAST 30 MINUTES

FOR THE SAUCE:

- 1 CUP KETCHUP
- 1/2 CUP PINEAPPLE JUICE
- 2 TABLESPOONS DIJON MUSTARD
- 1 1/2 TABLESPOONS CIDER VINEGAR
- 1 1/2 TABLESPOONS LIGHT BROWN SUGAR
- 1 TEASPOON TABASCO SAUCE
  KOSHER SALT

- 8 HAMBURGER BUNS *OR* POTATO ROLLS

To make the slaw: In a large bowl combine the cabbage, carrot, and onion. In a small bowl whisk together the remaining slaw ingredients. Pour the dressing over the vegetables and mix thoroughly. Refrigerate until ready to serve.

To make the rub: In a small bowl combine the rub ingredients.

Remove and discard the neck, giblets, and any excess fat from the chicken. Rinse the chicken, inside and out, under cold water and pat dry with paper towels. Coat the chicken, inside and out, with the rub, then brush or spray with vegetable oil.

Follow the grill's instructions for using wood chunks. Grill the chicken, breast side up, over *Indirect Medium* heat until the internal temperature reaches 170°F in the breast and 180°F in the thickest part of the thigh, 1 1/4 to 1 1/2 hours. Remove the chicken from the grill and allow to rest. When cool enough to handle, tear the chicken into bite-sized pieces, discarding the skin and bones.

Meanwhile, make the sauce: In a small mixing bowl whisk together the sauce ingredients, including salt to taste.

To serve, pile the shredded chicken on buns, and top with a generous spoonful of the sauce and coleslaw.

MAKES 8 SERVINGS

TIPSY
CHICKEN

A splash of bourbon, a drizzle of maple syrup, and you're good to grill. So juicy, they'll never guess how easy it is.

INDIRECT/MEDIUM

FOR THE MARINADE:

- 1/3 CUP BOURBON
- 2 TABLESPOONS MAPLE SYRUP
- 1 TABLESPOON COUNTRY-STYLE DIJON MUSTARD
- 1 TABLESPOON MINCED GARLIC

- 1 ROASTER CHICKEN, 6 TO 7 POUNDS

- 2 TABLESPOONS EXTRA-VIRGIN OLIVE OIL
- 2 TEASPOONS KOSHER SALT
- 1/2 TEASPOON COARSELY GROUND BLACK PEPPER

To make the marinade: In a small bowl whisk together the marinade ingredients.

Remove and discard the neck, giblets, and any excess fat from the chicken. Rinse the chicken, inside and out, under cold water and pat dry with paper towels. Butterfly the chicken by removing its backbone and flattening it *(see sidebar, page 243)*. Place the chicken in a large, resealable plastic bag and pour in the marinade. Press the air out of the bag and seal tightly. Turn the bag to distribute the marinade, place in a bowl, and refrigerate for at least 2 hours, turning occasionally.

Remove the chicken from the bag and discard the marinade. Wipe the marinade off the chicken with paper towels. To keep it flat for even cooking, skewer the chicken with two metal skewers *(see sidebar, page 243)*. Lightly spray or brush with olive oil and season with salt and pepper.

Grill the chicken, skin side up, over *Indirect Medium* heat until the internal temperature registers 170°F in the breast and 180°F in the thickest part of the thigh, 1 1/2 to 2 hours. Remove from the grill, loosely cover with aluminum foil, and allow to rest for about 10 minutes before carving.

MAKES 6 SERVINGS

CUTTING POULTRY FOR THE GRILL

If you don't have poultry shears, now's the time to get some. They're specially designed to cut through poultry bones and flesh with minimal slippage and effort. Alternatively, use a sharp, sturdy butcher knife and extra caution. Once you've halved or butterflied a bird or two, you'll be hooked—they cook faster than whole birds, get exposed to more seasonings, are easier to carve up and serve, and still look elegant. The techniques shown here are even easier when applied to small birds such as Cornish game hens.

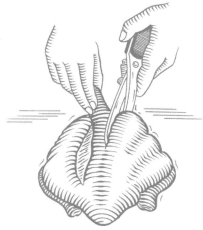

REMOVE THE BACKBONE

If using poultry shears, place the bird on a cutting board, breast side down, and cut along both sides of the backbone (above). If using a sharp knife, position the chicken breast side up on the cutting board. Then, start at the tail end and cut through the ribs to the board.

HALVE

If you're going to halve the bird, first remove the backbone (left). Then, turn the bird over and cut along one side of the breastbone (above).

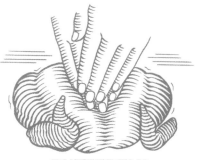

BUTTERFLY

If you're going to butterfly the bird, remove the backbone (top). Then, turn the bird over, breast side up. Pull the body open and press down firmly, cracking the rib bones slightly, until the bird lies relatively flat.

SKEWER

Once you've butterflied the bird (left), use two sturdy, metal skewers to help keep the bird flat for even cooking. Thread one skewer crosswise through the middle of the large wing joints and the breasts, perpendicular to the thigh bones. Thread the second one through the meat of the legs.

POLLO DIABLO

An Italian favorite that rewards the griller for remarkably little effort. The crushed red pepper flakes are what make it devilishly hot.

INDIRECT/HIGH

FOR THE MARINADE:

3 TABLESPOONS EXTRA-VIRGIN OLIVE OIL

3 TABLESPOONS FRESH ORANGE JUICE

3 TABLESPOONS FRESH LEMON JUICE

2 TABLESPOONS FINELY CHOPPED FRESH ROSEMARY

1 TABLESPOON MINCED GARLIC

1 TABLESPOON CRUSHED RED PEPPER FLAKES

2 TEASPOONS KOSHER SALT

1 WHOLE CHICKEN, 3 1/2 TO 4 POUNDS

To make the marinade: In a medium bowl whisk together the marinade ingredients.

Remove and discard the neck, giblets, and any excess fat from the chicken. Rinse the chicken, inside and out, under cold water and pat dry with paper towels. Butterfly the chicken by removing the backbone and flattening it *(see page 243)*.

Place the chicken in a large, resealable plastic bag and pour in the marinade. Press the air out of the bag and seal tightly. Turn the bag to distribute the marinade, place in a bowl, and refrigerate for 4 to 6 hours, turning occasionally.

Remove the chicken from the bag and discard the marinade. Grill, skin side up, over *Indirect High* heat until the internal temperature reaches 170°F in the breast and 180°F in the thickest part of the thigh, 45 minutes to 1 hour. The juices should run clear and the meat should no longer be pink at the bone. Remove from the grill and allow to rest for about 5 minutes before cutting into serving pieces. Serve warm.

MAKES 4 SERVINGS

BUTTERFLIED THAI CHICKEN

Butterflying the bird exposes more meat to the lively paste. Look for fish sauce—a salty, fermented condiment widely used in Southeast Asian cuisine—in the Asian cuisine section of your grocery store. It's called "nam pla" in Thai or "nuoc nam" in Vietnamese.

INDIRECT/HIGH

FOR THE PASTE:

6 LARGE GARLIC CLOVES, COARSELY CHOPPED

1/4 CUP THINLY SLICED GREEN ONIONS (WHITE PART ONLY)

2 TEASPOONS GRATED FRESH GINGER

1/2 TEASPOON GROUND CORIANDER

1/2 TEASPOON FRESHLY GROUND BLACK PEPPER

1 TO 2 TABLESPOONS FISH SAUCE

1 WHOLE CHICKEN, 3 1/2 TO 4 POUNDS
  VEGETABLE OIL

To make the paste: With a mortar and pestle, grind together the garlic, onions, ginger, coriander, and pepper. Transfer to a small bowl and add the fish sauce to form a coarse paste.

Remove and discard the neck, giblets, and any excess fat from the chicken. Rinse the chicken, inside and out, under cold water and pat dry with paper towels. Butterfly the chicken by removing the backbone and flattening it *(see page 243)*. Rub the paste all over the chicken. Cover with plastic wrap and refrigerate for 6 to 8 hours.

Lightly brush or spray the chicken with vegetable oil. Grill, skin side up, over *Indirect High* heat until the juices run clear and the internal temperature reaches 170°F in the breast and 180°F in the thickest part of the thigh, 45 minutes to 1 hour. Remove from the grill and loosely cover with aluminum foil. Allow to rest for about 5 minutes before cutting into serving pieces. Serve warm.

MAKES 4 SERVINGS

CLASSIC BARBECUED
CHICKEN BREASTS

Just like you remember, only better.

INDIRECT/MEDIUM

FOR THE MARINADE:

1/4 CUP KETCHUP

2 TABLESPOONS DIJON MUSTARD

2 TABLESPOONS HONEY

2 TABLESPOONS CIDER VINEGAR

2 TABLESPOONS CANOLA OIL

1 TABLESPOON DARK BROWN SUGAR

2 TEASPOONS WORCESTERSHIRE SAUCE

2 TEASPOONS DRY MUSTARD

1 TEASPOON PAPRIKA

1 TEASPOON GRANULATED GARLIC

1 TEASPOON GRANULATED ONION

1/2 TEASPOON KOSHER SALT

1/4 TEASPOON CAYENNE

4 CHICKEN BREAST HALVES (WITH BONE AND
SKIN), 10 TO 12 OUNCES EACH

To make the marinade: In a medium bowl whisk together the marinade ingredients.

Rinse the chicken breasts under cold water and pat dry with paper towels. Place in a large, resealable plastic bag and pour in the marinade. Press the air out of the bag and seal tightly. Turn the bag to distribute the marinade, place in a bowl, and refrigerate for 4 to 6 hours, turning occasionally.

Remove the breasts from the bag and discard the marinade. Grill, bone side down, over *Indirect Medium* heat until the juices run clear and the meat is no longer pink at the bone, 30 to 40 minutes. For crispier skin, grill the breasts, skin side down, over *Direct Medium* heat during the last 5 minutes of grilling time. Serve warm.

MAKES 4 SERVINGS

CHICKEN BREASTS
WITH TAPENADE

You'll want to earmark this homemade tapenade recipe. It not only works wonders on the chicken—you'll want to make some up to spread on crusty bread next time you're in the snacking mood.

SEAR: MEDIUM, COOK: INDIRECT/MEDIUM

FOR THE TAPENADE:

3/4 CUP PITTED KALAMATA OLIVES

2 ANCHOVY FILLETS

2 TABLESPOONS COARSELY CHOPPED SHALLOTS

2 TABLESPOONS EXTRA-VIRGIN OLIVE OIL

1 TABLESPOON FRESH LEMON JUICE

1 TABLESPOON CAPERS, DRAINED

1 TEASPOON MINCED GARLIC

1/4 TEASPOON FRESHLY GROUND BLACK PEPPER

FOR THE MARINADE:

1/4 CUP DRY WHITE WINE

3 TABLESPOONS EXTRA-VIRGIN OLIVE OIL

4 CHICKEN BREAST HALVES (WITH BONE AND
SKIN), ABOUT 8 OUNCES EACH

To make the tapenade: In a food processor combine the tapenade ingredients and process to make a spreadable paste. Place 1/4 cup of the tapenade in a medium bowl (for the marinade) and reserve the remaining tapenade.

To make the marinade: Add the wine and olive oil to the tapenade reserved for the marinade. Whisk to combine.

Rinse the chicken breasts under cold water and pat dry with paper towels. Place in a large, resealable plastic bag and pour in the marinade. Press the air out of the bag and seal tightly. Turn the bag to distribute the marinade, place in a bowl, and refrigerate for 4 to 6 hours, turning occasionally.

Remove the breasts from the bag and discard the marinade. Sear the breasts, skin side down, over *Direct Medium* heat for 4 minutes, turning once halfway through searing time. Continue grilling over *Indirect Medium* heat until the juices run clear and the meat is no longer pink at the bone, 20 to 30 minutes more. Serve with the reserved tapenade on the side.

MAKES 4 SERVINGS

Citrus–Avocado Chicken Breasts

CITRUS-AVOCADO
CHICKEN BREASTS

In a word, refreshing. As a way to dress up your everyday chicken breast, ingenious. See page 119 for an easy way to section citrus.

DIRECT/MEDIUM

FOR THE SALSA:

- 2 LIMES
- 2 ORANGES
- 1 MEDIUM GRAPEFRUIT
- 1/3 CUP RED CURRANTS
- 1 SERRANO CHILE, STEMMED, SEEDED, AND MINCED
- 1 GREEN ONION (WHITE PART ONLY), MINCED
- 1 TABLESPOON FINELY CHOPPED FRESH BASIL
- 1 TABLESPOON FINELY CHOPPED FRESH CILANTRO
- 1 TABLESPOON HONEY
- 1 TEASPOON MINCED ANAHEIM CHILE PEPPER

FOR THE MARINADE:

- 2 TABLESPOONS CITRUS ZEST, RESERVED FROM THE SALSA
- 1/2 CUP CITRUS JUICE, RESERVED FROM THE SALSA
- 2 TABLESPOONS HONEY
- 1 TABLESPOON EXTRA-VIRGIN OLIVE OIL
- 1 TEASPOON MINCED GARLIC
- 1 SERRANO CHILE, STEMMED, SEEDED, AND MINCED
- 1 TABLESPOON FINELY CHOPPED FRESH BASIL
- 1 TABLESPOON FINELY CHOPPED FRESH CILANTRO
- 1/2 TEASPOON GROUND CUMIN

- 4 BONELESS, SKINLESS CHICKEN BREAST HALVES, ABOUT 6 OUNCES EACH

- 2 FIRM RIPE AVOCADOS
  KOSHER SALT

  EXTRA-VIRGIN OLIVE OIL

To make the salsa: Wash and dry the limes, oranges, and grapefruit. Grate their zests and set the zests aside for use in the marinade. With a sharp paring knife, peel and section the citrus fruit *(see page 119)*, reserving the membranes. Squeeze the juice from the membranes (you should have about 1/2 cup) and reserve the juice for the marinade. Discard the membranes. Cut each citrus segment into three or four pieces and place in a large, stainless steel mixing bowl with the remaining salsa ingredients. Mix thoroughly, cover, and refrigerate until 1 hour before serving.

To make the marinade: In a small bowl whisk the reserved citrus zests and juices with the remaining marinade ingredients.

Rinse the chicken breasts under cold water and pat dry with paper towels. Place in a large, resealable plastic bag and pour in the marinade. Press the air out of the bag and seal tightly. Turn the bag to distribute the marinade, place in a bowl, and refrigerate for 4 to 8 hours, turning occasionally.

Cut the avocados in half and remove the pits. Peel and discard the skin and cut the avocado into chunks. Lightly mix into the salsa and season with salt. Let the salsa stand at room temperature for up to 1 hour to blend the flavors fully.

Remove the breasts from the bag and discard the marinade. Season with salt and lightly brush or spray with olive oil. Grill over *Direct Medium* heat until the juices run clear and the meat is no longer pink in the center, 8 to 12 minutes, turning once halfway through grilling time. Serve warm with the salsa.

MAKES 4 SERVINGS

MARGARITA
CHICKEN BREASTS

We knew the title would catch your eye. And yes, it uses many of the same ingredients that the drink does. Now just heat up some black beans and toss up a jicama salad—party time!

DIRECT/MEDIUM

FOR THE MARINADE:

- 1/4 CUP FRESH LIME JUICE
- 1/4 CUP EXTRA-VIRGIN OLIVE OIL
- 2 TABLESPOONS TEQUILA
- 1 TEASPOON KOSHER SALT
- 1 TEASPOON GRATED LIME ZEST
- 1/8 TEASPOON CAYENNE

- 4 BONELESS CHICKEN BREAST HALVES (WITH SKIN), ABOUT 6 OUNCES EACH

To make the marinade: In a medium bowl whisk together the marinade ingredients.

Rinse the chicken breasts under cold water and pat dry with paper towels. Place in a large, resealable plastic bag and pour in the marinade. Press the air out of the bag and seal tightly. Turn the bag to distribute the marinade, place in a bowl, and refrigerate for about 1 hour.

Remove the breasts from the bag and reserve the marinade. Pour the marinade into a small saucepan, bring to a boil, and boil for 1 full minute.

Grill the breasts, skin side down, over *Direct Medium* heat until the juices run clear and the meat is no longer pink in the center, 8 to 12 minutes, turning and basting with the marinade once halfway through grilling time. Serve warm.

MAKES 4 SERVINGS

THE ULTIMATE SUMMER
SANDWICH

Homemade pesto, seasoned grilled chicken, crisp arugula, and creamy goat cheese all spread on a baguette... what are you waiting for? Grab a knife!

DIRECT/MEDIUM

FOR THE PESTO:

- 1 SMALL CLOVE OF GARLIC, CRUSHED
- 1 CUP LOOSELY PACKED FRESH BASIL LEAVES
- 3 TABLESPOONS EXTRA-VIRGIN OLIVE OIL
- 3 TABLESPOONS COARSELY CHOPPED SUN-DRIED TOMATOES (OIL-PACKED)
- 1 TABLESPOON PINE NUTS
- 1/4 TEASPOON FRESHLY GROUND BLACK PEPPER
- 1/4 CUP FRESHLY GRATED PARMIGIANO-REGGIANO CHEESE

FOR THE RUB:

- 2 TABLESPOONS LIGHT BROWN SUGAR
- 1 TEASPOON KOSHER SALT
- 1/8 TEASPOON CAYENNE

- 2 BONELESS, SKINLESS CHICKEN BREAST HALVES, ABOUT 6 OUNCES EACH
  EXTRA-VIRGIN OLIVE OIL

- 1 FRENCH BAGUETTE
- 2 TO 3 OUNCES FRESH GOAT CHEESE
- 2 CUPS LIGHTLY PACKED TRIMMED ARUGULA
- 1/2 RED ONION, THINLY SLICED

To make the pesto: In a food processor with the motor running, drop in the garlic clove and process. Scrape down the sides of the bowl and add the basil, olive oil, sun-dried tomatoes, pine nuts, and pepper and process to form a loose paste. Transfer to a small bowl. Stir in the cheese and set aside. (Pesto can be refrigerated, covered, for as long as 24 hours. Bring to room temperature before serving.)

To make the rub: In a small bowl mix together the rub ingredients. Spread the rub over both sides of the chicken breasts. Cover with plastic wrap and refrigerate for 4 to 6 hours.

Wipe most of the rub off the breasts with paper towels. Lightly brush or spray with olive oil. Grill over *Direct Medium* heat until the meat is firm and the juices run clear, 8 to 12 minutes, turning once halfway through grilling time. Remove from the grill. Slice on the bias into 1/2-inch strips.

Cut the baguette lengthwise down the middle. Spread one half of the baguette with the pesto and the other half with the goat cheese, and layer the chicken, arugula, and red onion in between. Cut the baguette into four equal sections. Serve at room temperature.

MAKES 4 SERVINGS

CHICKEN
PENNE

Talk about flavor! The intense basil marinade is enlivened by the heat of the grill and the bold flavors of the red-wine tomato sauce are enhanced with a secret ingredient: minced anchovies. Be prepared to be hit up for the recipe for this one.

DIRECT/MEDIUM

FOR THE MARINADE:

- 1/3 CUP TIGHTLY PACKED FRESH BASIL LEAVES
- 3 MEDIUM CLOVES GARLIC, COARSELY CHOPPED
- 3 TABLESPOONS EXTRA-VIRGIN OLIVE OIL
- 1 TABLESPOON WHITE WINE VINEGAR
- 1/4 TEASPOON KOSHER SALT
- 1/4 TEASPOON FRESHLY GROUND BLACK PEPPER

- 4 BONELESS, SKINLESS CHICKEN BREAST HALVES, ABOUT 6 OUNCES EACH

FOR THE SAUCE:

- 3 TABLESPOONS EXTRA-VIRGIN OLIVE OIL
- 1/2 TEASPOON FRESHLY GROUND BLACK PEPPER
- 1/4 TEASPOON CRUSHED RED PEPPER FLAKES
- 1 MEDIUM YELLOW ONION, FINELY DICED
- 2 TEASPOONS MINCED GARLIC
- 2 TEASPOONS MINCED ANCHOVIES
- 1/2 CUP DRY RED WINE
- 2 CUPS CANNED CHOPPED TOMATOES
- 1/4 TEASPOON KOSHER SALT

- 1/2 POUND PENNE PASTA

- 1/4 CUP FINELY CHOPPED FRESH BASIL

- 1/4 CUP FRESHLY GRATED PARMIGIANO-REGGIANO CHEESE

To make the marinade: In a food processor purée the marinade ingredients.

Rinse the chicken breasts under cold water and pat dry with paper towels. Place in a large, resealable plastic bag and pour in the marinade. Press the air out of the bag and seal tightly. Turn the bag to distribute the marinade, place in a bowl, and refrigerate for 4 to 6 hours, turning occasionally.

To make the sauce: In a large saucepan over medium-high heat, warm the olive oil. Add the pepper and red pepper flakes. Add the onion and cook, stirring occasionally, until soft and translucent, 4 to 5 minutes. Add the garlic and anchovies and cook for 2 minutes more, stirring occasionally. Add the red wine, tomatoes, and salt and simmer for 15 minutes. Remove from the heat and set aside.

Remove the chicken breasts from the bag and discard the marinade. Grill over *Direct Medium* heat until the meat is firm and the juices run clear, 8 to 12 minutes, turning once halfway through grilling time. Remove the chicken from the grill and cut into 1/2-inch slices.

In a large pot of boiling salted water, cook the pasta until al dente. Reserve 2/3 cup pasta water and drain the cooked pasta into a colander. Add the pasta and reserved pasta water to the sauce and bring to a boil over medium-high heat. Add the chicken and fresh basil and cook until the chicken is heated through, 2 to 3 minutes. Spoon the pasta into heated bowls and serve immediately. Garnish with the cheese.

MAKES 4 TO 6 SERVINGS

LEMONGRASS
CHICKEN BREASTS

You love this one in Thai restaurants—now you can enjoy it without having to angle for reservations.

DIRECT/MEDIUM

FOR THE MARINADE:

3 TABLESPOONS MINCED FRESH LEMONGRASS

2 TABLESPOONS VEGETABLE OIL

2 TABLESPOONS FRESH LIME JUICE

1 TABLESPOON GROUND CORIANDER

1 TABLESPOON FISH SAUCE

2 TEASPOONS GRATED FRESH GINGER

1 TEASPOON GROUND CUMIN

1 TEASPOON FRESHLY GROUND BLACK PEPPER

1 TEASPOON KOSHER SALT

1 TEASPOON GRANULATED SUGAR

6 BONELESS CHICKEN BREAST HALVES (WITH SKIN), ABOUT 6 OUNCES EACH

To make the marinade: In a medium bowl whisk together the marinade ingredients.

Rinse the chicken breasts under cold water and pat dry with paper towels. Place the breasts in a large, resealable plastic bag and pour in the marinade. Press the air out of the bag and seal tightly. Turn the bag to distribute the marinade, place in a bowl, and refrigerate for 3 to 4 hours.

Remove the chicken breasts from the bag and reserve the marinade. Pour the marinade into a small saucepan, bring to a boil, and boil for 1 full minute.

Grill the breasts, skin side down, over *Direct Medium* heat until the meat is firm and the juices run clear, 8 to 12 minutes, turning and basting with the marinade once halfway through grilling time. Serve warm.

MAKES 6 SERVINGS

HONEY-MUSTARD
CHICKEN BREASTS

You might be surprised to see mint here, but you'll like how it plays off the honey-mustard combination. A good recipe for when you're rushed—especially if you grow mint in your garden.

DIRECT/MEDIUM

FOR THE MARINADE:

1/3 CUP COARSELY CHOPPED FRESH MINT

1/4 CUP EXTRA-VIRGIN OLIVE OIL

1/4 CUP FRESH LEMON JUICE

1 TABLESPOON COARSELY CHOPPED GARLIC

1 TEASPOON KOSHER SALT

1/2 TEASPOON FRESHLY GROUND BLACK PEPPER

4 BONELESS, SKINLESS CHICKEN BREAST HALVES, ABOUT 6 OUNCES EACH

FOR THE SAUCE:

2 TABLESPOONS EXTRA-VIRGIN OLIVE OIL

2 TABLESPOONS UNSALTED BUTTER

1/3 CUP FINELY CHOPPED YELLOW ONION

1 TEASPOON MINCED JALAPEÑO PEPPER, WITHOUT SEEDS

1/4 CUP DIJON MUSTARD

2 TABLESPOONS HONEY

To make the marinade: In a medium bowl whisk together the marinade ingredients.

Rinse the chicken breasts under cold water and pat dry with paper towels. Place the breasts in a large, resealable plastic bag and pour in the marinade. Press the air out of the bag and seal tightly. Turn the bag to distribute the marinade, place in a bowl, and refrigerate for about 1 hour.

To make the sauce: In a medium sauté pan over medium-high heat, warm the olive oil and melt the butter. Add the onion and jalapeño and cook until the onion is translucent, 4 to 5 minutes. Remove from the heat. Whisk in the mustard and honey. Set aside.

Remove the chicken breasts from the bag and discard the marinade. Grill over *Direct Medium* heat until the meat is firm and the juices run clear, 8 to 12 minutes, turning once halfway through grilling time. Baste with the sauce during the last 5 minutes of grilling time. Serve warm.

MAKES 4 SERVINGS

TEQUILA-ORANGE
CHICKEN BREASTS

These skin-on chicken breasts are twice baptized in a spicy-sweet brew that will really wake up your taste buds.

DIRECT/MEDIUM

FOR THE MARINADE:

- 1/2 CUP TIGHTLY PACKED FRESH MINT LEAVES
- 1/2 CUP TIGHTLY PACKED FRESH ITALIAN PARSLEY LEAVES WITH SOME STEMS
- 1/2 CUP FRESH ORANGE JUICE
- 2 TABLESPOONS TEQUILA
- 2 TABLESPOONS EXTRA-VIRGIN OLIVE OIL
- 2 MEDIUM GARLIC CLOVES, CRUSHED
- 2 TEASPOONS MINCED JALAPEÑO PEPPER, WITHOUT SEEDS
- 1 1/2 TEASPOONS KOSHER SALT
- 1/2 TEASPOON GROUND CUMIN
- 1/2 TEASPOON GROUND CHILI POWDER
- 1/4 TEASPOON FRESHLY GROUND BLACK PEPPER

- 4 BONELESS CHICKEN BREAST HALVES (WITH SKIN), ABOUT 6 OUNCES EACH

To make the marinade: In a food processor combine the marinade ingredients and process until smooth.

Rinse the chicken breasts under cold water and pat dry with paper towels. Place in a large, resealable plastic bag and pour in the marinade. Press the air out of the bag and seal tightly. Turn the bag to distribute the marinade, place in a bowl, and refrigerate for 2 to 4 hours, turning occasionally.

Remove the chicken breasts from the bag and reserve the marinade. Pour the marinade into a small saucepan, bring to a boil over high heat, and boil for 1 full minute.

Grill the breasts, skin side down, over *Direct Medium* heat until the meat is firm and the juices run clear, 8 to 12 minutes, turning and basting with the marinade once halfway through grilling time. Serve warm.

MAKES 4 SERVINGS

ARTICHOKE-STUFFED
CHICKEN BREASTS

A tasty departure from the ordinary. If flare-ups occur, finish these breasts over Indirect Medium heat.

DIRECT/MEDIUM

FOR THE STUFFING:

- 2 TABLESPOONS EXTRA-VIRGIN OLIVE OIL
- 1 TEASPOON DRIED THYME
- 1/4 TEASPOON CRUSHED RED PEPPER FLAKES
- 1 JAR (7 OUNCES) ARTICHOKE HEARTS
- 2 TEASPOONS MINCED GARLIC
- 1/4 TEASPOON KOSHER SALT
- 1/4 TEASPOON FRESHLY GROUND BLACK PEPPER
- 3 OUNCES FRESH GOAT CHEESE, CRUMBLED
- 3 TABLESPOONS MINCED SUN-DRIED TOMATOES (OIL-PACKED)
- 2 TABLESPOONS FINELY CHOPPED FRESH BASIL

- 4 LARGE BONELESS CHICKEN BREAST HALVES (WITH SKIN), ABOUT 8 OUNCES EACH
  EXTRA-VIRGIN OLIVE OIL
  KOSHER SALT
  FRESHLY GROUND BLACK PEPPER

To make the stuffing: In a medium sauté pan combine the olive oil, thyme, and red pepper flakes. Set the pan over medium-high heat to warm the mixture for 1 to 2 minutes. Drain, rinse, and coarsely chop the artichokes and add along with the garlic, salt, and pepper. Cook for 3 to 4 minutes, stirring occasionally. Remove from the heat. Add the goat cheese, sun-dried tomatoes, and basil. Mix to evenly distribute the ingredients and allow to cool.

Rinse the chicken breasts under cold water and pat dry with paper towels. Place each breast between two sheets of plastic wrap and, with a meat mallet or the back of small pan, pound to flatten to a thickness of about 1/4 inch. Place the breasts, skin side down, and spread each one with a quarter of the stuffing. Fold the breasts in half over the stuffing and use toothpicks to skewer the sides closed. Brush or spray both sides with olive oil and season with salt and pepper.

Grill the breasts over *Direct Medium* heat until the meat juices run clear and the cheese is melted, 8 to 12 minutes, turning once halfway through grilling time. Remove from the grill and carefully remove the toothpicks. Serve warm.

MAKES 4 SERVINGS

MELTED GOAT CHEESE, ARTICHOKE HEARTS, AND SUN-DRIED TOMATOES, ALL SANDWICHED BETWEEN GRILLED CHICKEN. DOES IT GET ANY BETTER?

Artichoke–Stuffed Chicken Breasts

SHIITAKE
CHICKEN BOWL

Comfort food, Japanese style. Grilling mushrooms concentrates their flavor and a generous coating of oil keeps them moist. Grill them cap side up first, then finish with the gills up to capture their juices to add to the sauce. Serve the steaming mixture ladled over warm rice.

DIRECT/MEDIUM

FOR THE PASTE:

1 TEASPOON DRIED LEMONGRASS

1 TEASPOON CHILI POWDER

1 TEASPOON GRANULATED GARLIC

1/2 TEASPOON FRESHLY GROUND BLACK PEPPER

2 TABLESPOONS VEGETABLE OIL

2 BONELESS, SKINLESS CHICKEN BREAST HALVES, ABOUT 6 OUNCES EACH

FOR THE SAUCE:

1/4 CUP LOW-SODIUM SOY SAUCE

1/4 CUP MIRIN (SWEET RICE WINE)

1/2 TEASPOON GRATED FRESH GINGER

1/4 TEASPOON ASIAN SESAME OIL

1/4 TEASPOON FRESHLY GROUND BLACK PEPPER

1 TABLESPOON CORNSTARCH DISSOLVED IN 1 TABLESPOON COLD WATER

3/4 POUND SHIITAKE MUSHROOMS, 3 TO 4 INCHES IN DIAMETER EACH

10 GREEN ONIONS, TRIMMED AT BOTH ENDS
VEGETABLE OIL

4 CUPS STEAMED WHITE RICE, WARM

To make the paste: In a small bowl combine the lemongrass, chili powder, garlic, and pepper. Whisk in the vegetable oil.

Rinse the chicken breasts under cold water and pat dry with paper towels. Coat evenly with the paste. Cover with plastic wrap and refrigerate for 1 to 2 hours.

To make the sauce: In a medium saucepan combine the soy sauce, mirin, ginger, sesame oil, and pepper along with 1 cup water. Bring to a boil. Whisk in the cornstarch mixture and cook until thickened slightly. Remove from the heat and set aside.

Remove the stems from the shiitake mushrooms and discard. Wipe the mushrooms clean with a damp paper towel. Brush or spray the mushrooms and green onions generously with vegetable oil. Grill the mushrooms over *Direct Medium* heat until tender, 8 to 12 minutes, turning once halfway through grilling time. Grill the onions over *Direct Medium* heat until barely tender, 3 to 4 minutes, turning once halfway through grilling time. Remove the mushrooms and onions from the grill and cut into bite-sized pieces.

Grill the chicken breasts over *Direct Medium* heat until the meat is firm and the juices run clear, 8 to 12 minutes, turning once halfway through grilling time. Remove the breasts from the grill and cut into bite-sized pieces.

Transfer the mushrooms, onions, and chicken to the sauce and simmer until heated through, 2 to 3 minutes. Spoon the rice into individual serving bowls and spoon the chicken and sauce on top. Serve warm.

MAKES 4 SERVINGS

ITALIAN
CHICKEN KABOBS

A taste of Italy on a stick.

DIRECT/MEDIUM

FOR THE MARINADE:

1/2 CUP EXTRA-VIRGIN OLIVE OIL

2 TABLESPOONS WHITE WINE

2 TABLESPOONS FINELY CHOPPED FRESH THYME

1 TABLESPOON MINCED GARLIC

1 TEASPOON KOSHER SALT

1 TEASPOON FRESHLY GROUND BLACK PEPPER

2 POUNDS BONELESS, SKINLESS CHICKEN THIGHS

1 SMALL ZUCCHINI

1 GREEN BELL PEPPER

20 LARGE CHERRY TOMATOES

To make the marinade: In a small bowl whisk together the marinade ingredients.

Cut the chicken into 1-inch chunks, the zucchini into 1/2-inch coins, and the bell pepper into 1-inch squares. Place the chicken, zucchini, bell pepper, and cherry tomatoes in a large, resealable plastic bag and pour in the marinade. Press the air out of the bag and seal tightly. Turn the bag to distribute the marinade, place in a bowl, and refrigerate for 30 minutes to 2 hours, turning occasionally.

Remove the chicken and vegetables from the bag and discard the marinade. Thread the chicken chunks alternately with the zucchini coins, bell pepper squares, and cherry tomatoes onto skewers. Grill the kabobs over *Direct Medium* heat until the vegetables are tender, the chicken is firm to the touch, and the meat juices run clear, 8 to 10 minutes, turning once halfway through grilling time. Serve warm.

MAKES 6 SERVINGS

MIKE'S
CHICKEN KABOBS

We wrangled this one out of our friend Mike, whose stories are scattered throughout this book. He says to go for fresh pineapple—canned pineapple chunks are too small for kabobs and they're usually packed in sweetened juice, which can make the pineapple burn.

DIRECT/MEDIUM

FOR THE MARINADE:

- 1/2 CUP DRY WHITE WINE
- 1/3 CUP LOW-SODIUM SOY SAUCE
- 2 TABLESPOONS FINELY CHOPPED ORANGE ZEST
- 2 TABLESPOONS PEANUT OIL
- 1 TABLESPOON ASIAN SESAME OIL
- 2 TEASPOONS CURRY POWDER

- 4 BONELESS, SKINLESS CHICKEN BREAST HALVES, 6 TO 8 OUNCES EACH
- 2 LARGE RED BELL PEPPERS

- 1/2 MEDIUM FRESH PINEAPPLE

  PEANUT OIL

To make the marinade: In a small bowl whisk together the marinade ingredients.

Rinse the chicken breasts under cold water and pat dry with paper towels. Cut into 1 1/2-inch chunks. Remove the stem, ribs, and seeds from the bell peppers and cut into 1-inch squares. Place the chicken and bell peppers in a large, resealable plastic bag and pour in the marinade. Press the air out of the bag and seal tightly. Turn the bag to distribute the marinade, place in a bowl, and refrigerate for 4 to 6 hours.

Just before assembling the kabobs, cut the fresh pineapple into 1-inch dice. Remove the chicken and bell peppers from the bag and discard the marinade. Thread the chicken chunks alternately with the bell pepper and pineapple onto skewers. Lightly spray or brush the kabobs with peanut oil.

Grill the kabobs over *Direct Medium* heat until the chicken is firm and the bell pepper and pineapple are tender, 8 to 10 minutes, turning once halfway through grilling time. Serve warm.

MAKES 6 SERVINGS

CHICKEN ON A STICK
WITH AN ASIAN DIP

The paste in this recipe does amazing things for chicken, giving it complexity in a matter of minutes. The dipping sauce brings it all together and adds a splash of moisture. A must for the well-rounded griller, an instant favorite among kabob fans.

DIRECT/MEDIUM

FOR THE PASTE:

- 1 TEASPOON GRANULATED GARLIC
- 1 TEASPOON GRANULATED ONION
- 1 TEASPOON PAPRIKA
- 1/2 TEASPOON CUMIN
- 1/2 TEASPOON DRIED LEMONGRASS
- 1/2 TEASPOON DRIED BASIL
- 1/2 TEASPOON DRIED THYME
- 1/2 TEASPOON KOSHER SALT
- 1/4 TEASPOON FRESHLY GROUND BLACK PEPPER
- 1/8 TEASPOON CAYENNE
- 1/4 CUP CANOLA OIL

- 4 BONELESS, SKINLESS CHICKEN BREAST HALVES, ABOUT 6 OUNCES EACH

FOR THE DIPPING SAUCE:

- 1/2 CUP SOY SAUCE
- 2 TABLESPOONS FRESH LEMON JUICE
- 2 TABLESPOONS RICE VINEGAR
- 1 TABLESPOON MINCED GREEN ONION (WHITE PART ONLY)
- 1/4 TEASPOON CRUSHED RED PEPPER FLAKES

To make the paste: In a medium bowl combine the garlic, onion, paprika, cumin, lemongrass, basil, thyme, salt, pepper, and cayenne. Whisk in the canola oil.

Rinse the chicken breasts under cold water and pat dry with paper towels. Cut into 1-inch chunks and add to the paste. Toss to coat evenly. Cover with plastic wrap and refrigerate for 30 to 60 minutes.

To make the dipping sauce: In a small bowl whisk together the sauce ingredients with 2 tablespoons water. Pour the sauce into individual serving bowls.

Thread the chicken chunks onto skewers. Grill over *Direct Medium* heat until the meat is firm and the juices run clear, 8 to 10 minutes, turning once halfway through grilling time. Serve warm with the dipping sauce.

MAKES 4 SERVINGS

ORANGE-PINE NUT
CHICKEN BREASTS

A nice change of taste you can whip up in a hurry. The pine nuts add a nice crunch and a buttery richness that will inspire you to toss them into more dishes. Just toast them on a low setting in a heavy skillet, stirring often and watching them closely—pine nuts burn easily. Grilled asparagus is a great side for this dish.

DIRECT/MEDIUM

FOR THE MARINADE:

- 1/4 CUP FRESH ORANGE JUICE
- 1/4 CUP DRY WHITE WINE
- 1 TABLESPOON EXTRA-VIRGIN OLIVE OIL
- 1 TABLESPOON FINELY CHOPPED FRESH ITALIAN PARSLEY
- 1 TEASPOON MINCED GARLIC
- 1 TEASPOON GRATED ORANGE ZEST
- 1 TEASPOON DRIED THYME LEAVES
- 1/2 TEASPOON KOSHER SALT

- 4 BONELESS, SKINLESS CHICKEN BREAST HALVES, ABOUT 6 OUNCES EACH
  EXTRA-VIRGIN OLIVE OIL

FOR THE SAUCE:

- 1 TABLESPOON HONEY
- 1/3 CUP TOASTED PINE NUTS

To make the marinade: In a medium bowl whisk together the marinade ingredients.

Rinse the chicken breasts under cold water and pat dry with paper towels. Place in a large, resealable plastic bag and pour in the marinade. Press the air out of the bag and seal tightly. Turn the bag to distribute the marinade, place in a bowl, and refrigerate for about 1 hour, turning once.

Remove the chicken breasts from the bag, reserving the marinade. Pat the chicken dry with paper towels and brush or spray both sides of the breasts with olive oil. Grill over *Direct Medium* heat until firm and the juices run clear, 8 to 12 minutes, turning once halfway through grilling time.

Meanwhile, prepare the sauce: In a small sauté pan combine the reserved marinade, honey, and toasted pine nuts. Bring to a boil and boil for 1 full minute. Spoon the sauce over the grilled chicken. Serve warm.

MAKES 4 SERVINGS

YAKITORI CHICKEN

Yakitori literally means "grilled fowl" in Japanese and it's very popular. When you see how tasty and easy the chicken is, you'll understand why. Serve with steamed white rice.

DIRECT /MEDIUM

FOR THE MARINADE:

- 3/4 CUP SOY SAUCE
- 1/2 CUP MIRIN (SWEET RICE WINE)
- 1/4 CUP KETCHUP
- 2 TABLESPOONS RICE VINEGAR
- 2 TEASPOONS MINCED GARLIC
- 1 TEASPOON ASIAN SESAME OIL

- 2 POUNDS BONELESS, SKINLESS CHICKEN BREAST OR THIGH MEAT
- 2 MEDIUM RED BELL PEPPERS
- 6 PEARL ONIONS
  VEGETABLE OIL

To make the marinade: In a small bowl whisk together the marinade ingredients.

Rinse the chicken under cold water and pat dry with paper towels. Cut into 1 1/2-inch chunks. Remove the stem, ribs, and seeds from the bell peppers and cut into 1-inch chunks. Cut the pearl onions in half.

Place the chicken, bell peppers, and pearl onions in a large, resealable plastic bag and pour in the marinade. Press the air out of the bag and seal tightly. Turn the bag to distribute the marinade, place in a bowl, and refrigerate for 30 minutes to 2 hours, turning occasionally.

Remove the chicken, bell peppers, and pearl onions from the bag and reserve the marinade. Pour the marinade into a small saucepan, bring to a boil, and boil for 1 full minute. Remove from the heat and set aside.

Thread the chicken, bell peppers, and pearl onions onto skewers. Lightly brush or spray with vegetable oil. Grill over *Direct Medium* heat until the meat is firm and the vegetables are tender, 8 to 10 minutes, turning and basting with the marinade once halfway through grilling time. Serve warm.

MAKES 4 TO 6 SERVINGS

Yakitori Chicken

GRILLED
CHICKEN
TACOS

Using chicken thighs instead of breasts is a smart approach to this popular taco variation. The dark meat lends a richer flavor and juicier texture. And because they're boned and skinned before you start, you'll be sitting down to eat even faster.

DIRECT/MEDIUM

FOR THE MARINADE:

2 TABLESPOONS EXTRA-VIRGIN OLIVE OIL

2 TABLESPOONS FRESH LIME JUICE

1 TEASPOON CHILI POWDER

1/2 TEASPOON KOSHER SALT

1/4 TEASPOON FRESHLY GROUND BLACK PEPPER

6 BONELESS, SKINLESS CHICKEN THIGHS, ABOUT 4 OUNCES EACH

FOR THE SALSA:

1 1/2 CUPS COARSELY CHOPPED RIPE TOMATOES

1 LARGE RIPE AVOCADO, PEELED AND DICED

4 TO 5 GREEN ONIONS (WHITE PART ONLY), FINELY CHOPPED

1/4 CUP FINELY CHOPPED FRESH CILANTRO

1 TABLESPOON MINCED JALAPEÑO PEPPER, WITHOUT SEEDS

1 TABLESPOON FRESH LIME JUICE

KOSHER SALT

FRESHLY GROUND BLACK PEPPER

1 CUP GRATED MONTEREY JACK CHEESE

3 TO 4 CUPS SHREDDED ROMAINE *OR* ICEBERG LETTUCE

1 CUP SOUR CREAM THINNED WITH 2 TABLESPOONS MILK (OPTIONAL)

1 CAN (15 OUNCES) BLACK BEANS

10 FLOUR TORTILLAS (6 INCHES)

To make the marinade: In a small bowl whisk together the marinade ingredients.

Rinse the chicken thighs under cold water and pat dry with paper towels. Place the thighs in a large, resealable plastic bag and pour in the marinade. Press the air out of the bag and seal tightly. Turn the bag to distribute the marinade, place in a bowl, and refrigerate for about 1 hour.

To make the salsa: In a medium bowl combine the salsa ingredients, including salt and pepper to taste. Transfer to a serving bowl.

Remove the chicken thighs from the bag and discard the marinade. Grill over *Direct Medium* heat until the meat is firm and the juices run clear, 8 to 10 minutes, turning once halfway through grilling time. Remove from the grill, cut into 1/4-inch slices, and place in a serving bowl.

Meanwhile, grate the cheese, shred the lettuce, and prepare the sour cream. Place each in serving bowls. In a small saucepan heat the black beans in their liquid. Just before serving, drain the beans and place in a serving bowl, too.

Wrap five tortillas in each of two foil packets. Grill over *Direct Medium* heat for 2 to 4 minutes to warm and soften.

To serve, give each person a warm tortilla and pass around the chicken and fillings so everyone can assemble their own tacos.

MAKES 4 TO 6 SERVINGS

WEST AFRICAN
CHICKEN
THIGHS

These everyday spices are probably all in your cupboard. The West African influence is in the quantities used. The paprika aids in browning and the other ingredients add a spicy jolt. Try the paste on other meats and fish as well.

SEAR: MEDIUM, COOK: INDIRECT/MEDIUM

FOR THE PASTE:

1 TABLESPOON PAPRIKA

2 TEASPOONS GRANULATED GARLIC

1 TEASPOON GRANULATED ONION

1 TEASPOON KOSHER SALT

1 TEASPOON FRESHLY GROUND BLACK PEPPER

1/4 TEASPOON CAYENNE

2 TABLESPOONS CANOLA OIL

8 CHICKEN THIGHS (WITH BONE AND SKIN), ABOUT 4 OUNCES EACH

To make the paste: In a small bowl combine the paprika, garlic, onion, salt, pepper, and cayenne. Whisk in the canola oil.

Trim the chicken thighs of any excess skin and fat. Rinse under cold water and pat dry with paper towels. Coat with the paste. Cover with plastic wrap and refrigerate for 4 to 8 hours.

Sear the chicken thighs, skin side down, over *Direct Medium* heat for 4 minutes, turning once halfway through searing time. Continue grilling over *Indirect Medium* heat until the juices run clear and the meat is no longer pink at the bone, 30 to 40 minutes more. Serve warm.

MAKES 4 SERVINGS

BUTTERMILK HERBED
CHICKEN THIGHS

Buttermilk makes an exceptional marinade, adding lots of moisture as it tenderizes. The herb mixture here adds a pleasant homey flavor, reminiscent of lazy Sundays in the country. Serve with marinated tomatoes and a pasta salad for a quick picnic or light outdoor dinner.

SEAR: MEDIUM, COOK: INDIRECT/MEDIUM

FOR THE MARINADE:

1 CUP BUTTERMILK

1 TABLESPOON DIJON MUSTARD

1 TABLESPOON HONEY

1 TABLESPOON FINELY CHOPPED FRESH ROSEMARY

1 TEASPOON KOSHER SALT

1/2 TEASPOON DRIED THYME

1/2 TEASPOON DRIED SAGE

1/2 TEASPOON DRIED MARJORAM

1/2 TEASPOON FRESHLY GROUND BLACK PEPPER

8 CHICKEN THIGHS (WITH BONE AND SKIN), ABOUT 4 OUNCES EACH

EXTRA-VIRGIN OLIVE OIL

To make the marinade: In a medium bowl whisk together the marinade ingredients.

Trim the chicken thighs of any excess skin and fat. Rinse under cold water. Place in a large, resealable plastic bag and pour in the marinade. Press the air out of the bag and seal tightly. Turn the bag to distribute the marinade, place in a bowl, and refrigerate for 6 to 8 hours, turning occasionally.

Remove the thighs from the bag and discard the marinade. Wipe the marinade off the thighs with paper towels. Lightly brush or spray with olive oil.

Sear the thighs, skin side down, over *Direct Medium* heat for 4 minutes, turning once halfway through searing time. Continue grilling over *Indirect Medium* heat until the juices run clear and the meat is no longer pink at the bone, 30 to 40 minutes more. Serve warm.

MAKES 4 SERVINGS

CAJUN
CHICKEN THIGHS

Rich dark meat coated with a peppery rub, then roasted on the grill...a good excuse for an impromptu barbecue!

DIRECT/MEDIUM

FOR THE RUB:

1 TABLESPOON LIGHT BROWN SUGAR

1 TABLESPOON GRANULATED GARLIC

1 TABLESPOON GRANULATED ONION

1 TABLESPOON PAPRIKA

2 TEASPOONS DRIED THYME

2 TEASPOONS DRIED OREGANO

2 TEASPOONS COARSELY GROUND BLACK PEPPER

2 TEASPOONS KOSHER SALT

16 BONELESS, SKINLESS CHICKEN THIGHS, ABOUT 4 OUNCES EACH

EXTRA-VIRGIN OLIVE OIL

To make the rub: In a small bowl combine the rub ingredients.

Rinse the chicken thighs under cold water and pat dry with paper towels. Coat with the rub, then brush or spray with olive oil.

Grill the thighs over *Direct Medium* heat until the meat is firm and the juices run clear, 8 to 10 minutes, turning once halfway through grilling time. Serve warm.

MAKES 8 SERVINGS

PACIFIC RIM
CHICKEN THIGHS

Lots of flavor is your reward for a quick bout of whisking. Just what we all want in a marinade.

SEAR: MEDIUM, COOK: INDIRECT/*MEDIUM*

FOR THE MARINADE:

1/4 CUP KETCHUP

1/4 CUP HOISIN SAUCE

2 TABLESPOONS RICE VINEGAR

2 TABLESPOONS SOY SAUCE

4 TEASPOONS CURRY POWDER

4 TEASPOONS ASIAN SESAME OIL

1/4 TEASPOON TABASCO SAUCE

8 CHICKEN THIGHS (WITH BONE AND SKIN), ABOUT 4 OUNCES EACH

To make the marinade: In a small bowl whisk together the marinade ingredients.

Trim the chicken thighs of any excess skin and fat. Rinse under cold water and pat dry with paper towels. Place in a large, resealable plastic bag and pour in the marinade. Press the air out of the bag and seal tightly. Turn the bag to distribute the marinade, place in a bowl, and refrigerate for 2 to 6 hours, turning occasionally.

Remove the thighs from the bag and discard the marinade. Sear the thighs, skin side down, over *Direct Medium* heat for 4 minutes, turning once halfway through searing time. Continue grilling over *Indirect Medium* heat until the meat is firm and the juices run clear, 30 to 40 minutes more. Serve warm.

MAKES 4 SERVINGS

FAR EASTERN
CHICKEN LEGS

Fresh cilantro, green onions, fish sauce ("nuoc nam"), and ginger are widely used in Vietnamese cooking. Here they get an extra boost from hot bean paste, a popular condiment in Chinese cooking.

SEAR: MEDIUM, COOK: INDIRECT/*MEDIUM*

FOR THE MARINADE:

1/2 CUP CHOPPED FRESH CILANTRO

1/4 CUP VEGETABLE OIL

1/4 CUP FINELY SLICED GREEN ONIONS (WHITE PART ONLY)

3 TABLESPOONS FRESH LIME JUICE

1 TABLESPOON FISH SAUCE

1 TABLESPOON GRANULATED SUGAR

2 TEASPOONS MINCED GARLIC

2 TEASPOONS MINCED FRESH GINGER

1 TEASPOON HOT BEAN PASTE

1/2 TEASPOON KOSHER SALT

6 WHOLE CHICKEN LEGS, 8 TO 10 OUNCES EACH
VEGETABLE OIL

To make the marinade: In a medium bowl combine the marinade ingredients.

Trim the chicken legs of any excess skin and fat. Rinse under cold water. Place in a large, resealable plastic bag and pour in the marinade. Press the air out of the bag and seal tightly. Turn the bag to distribute the marinade, place in a bowl, and refrigerate for 2 to 4 hours, turning occasionally.

Remove the chicken legs from the bag and discard the marinade. Lightly brush or spray with vegetable oil. Sear, skin side down, over *Direct Medium* heat for 10 minutes, turning once halfway through searing time. Continue grilling over *Indirect Medium* heat until the juices run clear and the internal temperature reaches 180°F in the thickest part of the thigh, 40 to 50 minutes more. Serve warm.

MAKES 6 SERVINGS

"What is sauce for the goose may be sauce for the gander, but it is not necessarily sauce for the chicken, the duck, the turkey or the Guinea hen."

— ALICE B. TOKLAS

SAKE-MARINATED
CHICKEN LEGS

If you don't have a bottle of sake sitting in your cupboard, it's time to invest. The heart of this marinade, sake also makes a nice sip to go with the finished dish. (Serve it the traditional way: gently warmed and in porcelain cups.)

SEAR: MEDIUM, COOK: INDIRECT/MEDIUM

FOR THE MARINADE:

- 1/2 CUP SAKE *OR* DRY SHERRY
- 2 TABLESPOONS SOY SAUCE
- 1 TABLESPOON ASIAN SESAME OIL

- 4 WHOLE CHICKEN LEGS, 8 TO 10 OUNCES EACH

FOR THE SAUCE:

- 1/2 CUP SESAME SEEDS
- 3 TABLESPOONS VEGETABLE OIL
- 2 TABLESPOONS FRESH LEMON JUICE
- 2 TABLESPOONS SOY SAUCE
- 1 TABLESPOON GRATED FRESH GINGER
- 1 TABLESPOON BROWN SUGAR
- 1 TEASPOON MINCED GARLIC
- 1/8 TEASPOON CAYENNE

VEGETABLE OIL

KOSHER SALT

To make the marinade: In a small bowl whisk together the marinade ingredients.

Trim the chicken legs of any excess skin and fat. Rinse under cold water. Place in a large, resealable plastic bag and pour in the marinade. Press the air out of the bag and seal tightly. Turn the bag to distribute the marinade, place in a bowl, and refrigerate for 1 to 2 hours, turning occasionally.

To make the sauce: In a medium sauté pan over medium heat, toast the sesame seeds until golden, about 5 minutes, shaking the pan often. (Watch carefully as the seeds brown very quickly.) Transfer to a blender, add the remaining sauce ingredients and 1/4 cup water, and process until a smooth paste forms.

Remove the chicken legs from the bag, reserving the marinade. Pour the marinade into a small saucepan, bring to a boil, and boil for 1 full minute.

Lightly brush or spray the legs with vegetable oil and season with salt. Sear, skin side down, over *Direct Medium* heat for 10 minutes, turning once halfway through searing time. Continue grilling over *Indirect Medium* heat until the juices run clear and the internal temperature reaches 180°F in the thickest part of the thigh, 40 to 50 minutes more. Baste with the marinade during the last 10 to 20 minutes of grilling time. Serve warm with the sauce.

MAKES 4 SERVINGS

WILD MUSHROOM–STUFFED
CHICKEN LEGS

Filling whole (boned) chicken legs with a rich mushroom stuffing makes this dish a gastronomic treasure hunt. If you don't want to remove the bones yourself, you can always have them done—just be sure to tell the butcher you're planning to stuff them.

INDIRECT/MEDIUM

FOR THE STUFFING:

- 1/2 OUNCE DRIED PORCINI MUSHROOMS
- 1/2 CUP DRY RED WINE
- 1 TABLESPOON UNSALTED BUTTER
- 1 TABLESPOON EXTRA-VIRGIN OLIVE OIL
- 1/4 CUP FINELY CHOPPED SHALLOTS
- 1/2 TABLESPOON MINCED GARLIC
- 3/4 POUND FRESH, MIXED WILD *OR* DOMESTIC MUSHROOMS SUCH AS CHANTERELLES, OYSTER, SHIITAKE, BUTTON, CUT INTO 1/2-INCH DICE
- 2 CUPS COARSELY CHOPPED FRESH SPINACH LEAVES
- 2 TEASPOONS FINELY CHOPPED FRESH THYME
- 1/2 CUP FRESHLY GRATED PARMIGIANO-REGGIANO CHEESE

KOSHER SALT

FRESHLY GROUND BLACK PEPPER

- 4 WHOLE CHICKEN LEGS, 8 TO 10 OUNCES EACH

EXTRA-VIRGIN OLIVE OIL

To make the stuffing: Soak the porcini mushrooms in the red wine for 15 to 30 minutes. Remove the mushrooms and strain the wine through a coffee filter to remove any grit. Set the wine aside. Coarsely chop the porcini mushrooms. In a very large sauté pan over medium-high heat, melt the butter with the olive oil. Add the shallots and cook, stirring occasionally, until softened, 1 to 2 minutes. Add the porcini mushrooms, garlic, and fresh mushrooms. Cook over medium-high heat, stirring occasionally, until the mushrooms are tender, about 10 minutes. Add the reserved filtered wine and cook until the liquid has evaporated. Add the spinach and cook until wilted, about 30 seconds. Let cool. Stir in the thyme and cheese. Season with salt and pepper.

Bone the chicken legs *(see page 229)*, then rinse under cold water and pat dry with paper towels. Season the leg cavities with salt and pepper, then stuff with the mushroom mixture. Sew the cavities closed with metal or bamboo skewers. Brush or spray the legs all over with olive oil.

Grill the stuffed chicken legs over *Indirect Medium* heat until the meat is firm and the juices run clear, 30 to 40 minutes, turning once halfway through grilling time. For crispier skin, grill over *Direct Medium* heat during the last 5 to 10 minutes of grilling time. Serve warm.

MAKES 4 SERVINGS

MARIACHI
CHICKEN LEGS

The name's so cheesy, you won't need to grate any Cheddar for this one. For the marinade we use prepared salsa—hey, some days you need to cheat. Serve with a fruit salad and warm tortillas. Leftovers are great, too.

SEAR: MEDIUM, COOK: INDIRECT/MEDIUM

FOR THE MARINADE:

1 CUP PREPARED SALSA (MEDIUM *OR* HOT)

1/4 CUP FRESH ORANGE JUICE

1 TABLESPOON FRESH LIME JUICE

1 TABLESPOON FINELY CHOPPED FRESH ITALIAN PARSLEY

1 TABLESPOON LIGHT BROWN SUGAR

1 TABLESPOON EXTRA-VIRGIN OLIVE OIL

1 TEASPOON GRATED ORANGE ZEST

1 TEASPOON DRIED OREGANO

1/4 TEASPOON GROUND CUMIN

KOSHER SALT

FRESHLY GROUND BLACK PEPPER

4 WHOLE CHICKEN LEGS, 8 TO 10 OUNCES EACH

EXTRA-VIRGIN OLIVE OIL

To make the marinade: In a food processor combine the marinade ingredients, including salt and pepper to taste. Pulse several times until the mixture is fairly smooth.

Trim the chicken legs of any excess skin and fat. Rinse under cold water. Place in a shallow glass baking dish and pour in the marinade. Cover and refrigerate for 3 to 4 hours, turning occasionally to distribute the marinade.

Remove the chicken legs from the baking dish, reserving the marinade. Pour the marinade into a small saucepan, bring to a boil, and boil for 1 full minute.

Lightly brush or spray the chicken legs with olive oil. Sear, skin side down, over *Direct Medium* heat for 10 minutes, turning once halfway through searing time. Continue grilling over *Indirect Medium* heat until the juices run clear and the internal temperature reaches 180°F in the thickest part of the thigh, 40 to 50 minutes more. Baste with the reserved marinade during the last 10 to 20 minutes of grilling time. Serve warm.

MAKES 4 SERVINGS

TERIYAKI
CHICKEN BURGERS

Take your taste buds for a joy ride with this spin on the classic American burger. Try them with grilled onions or pineapple. Ground chicken is widely available in most urban areas, but if you have trouble finding it, you can always ask your butcher to grind some up for you.

DIRECT/MEDIUM

FOR THE BURGERS:

1 POUND FRESHLY GROUND CHICKEN

1 1/2 CUPS FRESH BREAD CRUMBS

1/4 CUP MINCED GREEN ONIONS

1/4 CUP FINELY CHOPPED FRESH ITALIAN PARSLEY

1 LARGE EGG, LIGHTLY BEATEN

3 TABLESPOONS TERIYAKI SAUCE

2 TEASPOONS DIJON MUSTARD

1 TEASPOON ASIAN SESAME OIL

1/2 TEASPOON KOSHER SALT

1/2 TEASPOON FRESHLY GROUND BLACK PEPPER

EXTRA-VIRGIN OLIVE OIL

4 HAMBURGER BUNS

MAYONNAISE

To make the burgers: In a large bowl combine the burger ingredients. Mix gently with your hands, being careful not to overwork the meat. Moisten your hands with water and shape the meat into four burgers, about 4 inches in diameter each. Cover with plastic wrap and refrigerate for about 1 hour.

Lightly brush or spray the burgers with olive oil. Grill over *Direct Medium* heat until well done and the internal temperature reaches 165°F, 10 to 12 minutes, turning once halfway through grilling time.

Lightly toast the buns over *Direct Medium* heat for about 30 seconds just before serving. Brush with mayonnaise to taste, add the burgers, and serve warm.

MAKES 4 SERVINGS

CHICKEN STICKS

CORNISH GAME HENS

Don't let the long ingredient list intimidate you: This recipe is easier than you think. And it shows how great Vietnamese food is made.

A splash of brandy adds to the allure of these game hens. Serve them for dinner or cut them into serving pieces and you have a fun nibble to accompany cocktails.

DIRECT/MEDIUM

FOR THE CHICKEN STICKS:

- 4 GREEN ONIONS (WHITE PART ONLY), FINELY CHOPPED
- 2 TABLESPOONS FRESH LIME JUICE
- 2 TABLESPOONS SOY SAUCE
- 1 TABLESPOON MINCED GARLIC
- 1 TABLESPOON HOT CHILI OIL
- 1 TABLESPOON VEGETABLE OIL
- 2 TEASPOONS GRATED FRESH GINGER
- 1 TEASPOON GRANULATED SUGAR
- 1/2 TEASPOON KOSHER SALT
- 1/4 TEASPOON FRESHLY GROUND BLACK PEPPER
- 2 POUNDS FRESHLY GROUND CHICKEN

FOR THE SAUCE:

- 1/3 CUP LOW-SODIUM SOY SAUCE
- 3 TABLESPOONS FRESH LEMON JUICE
- 2 TEASPOONS GRANULATED SUGAR
- 1 TEASPOON MINCED GARLIC
- 1 TEASPOON GRATED FRESH GINGER
- 1 TEASPOON FISH SAUCE
- 1/4 TEASPOON SRIRACHA (HOT CHILI-GARLIC SAUCE)

VEGETABLE OIL

- 24 BUTTER LETTUCE LEAVES
- 1/2 CUP COARSELY CHOPPED FRESH MINT
- 1/2 CUP COARSELY CHOPPED FRESH CILANTRO
- 1/2 CUP COARSELY CHOPPED WATER CHESTNUTS *OR* PEANUTS
- 1/3 CUP MINCED GREEN ONIONS

To make the chicken sticks: In a large bowl whisk together the first 10 chicken stick ingredients, then add the ground chicken. Mix gently with your hands, being careful not to overwork the meat. Moisten your hands with water and shape the meat into 3-inch cylinder-shaped sticks, using about 3 tablespoons of the mixture for each one. Cover with plastic wrap and refrigerate for at least 2 hours.

To make the sauce: In a medium bowl whisk together the sauce ingredients.

Generously brush or spray the chicken sticks all over with vegetable oil. Grill over *Direct Medium* heat until just cooked through, 8 to 10 minutes, turning once halfway through grilling time. Serve the sticks in the lettuce leaves and topped with the mint, cilantro, nuts, and green onions, as desired. Provide your guests with individual bowls of sauce for dipping the rolls.

MAKES 6 TO 8 SERVINGS

INDIRECT/MEDIUM

FOR THE MARINADE:

- 1/2 CUP FRESH ORANGE JUICE
- 1/3 CUP BRANDY
- 1/4 CUP VEGETABLE OIL
- 1 TEASPOON GRATED ORANGE ZEST
- 1/2 TEASPOON KOSHER SALT
- 1/4 TEASPOON FRESHLY GROUND BLACK PEPPER

- 4 CORNISH GAME HENS, 1 1/2 TO 2 POUNDS EACH

FOR THE BASTING SAUCE:

- 1/2 CUP ORANGE MARMALADE
- 2 TABLESPOONS GRATED FRESH GINGER
- 1/4 TEASPOON KOSHER SALT
- 1/4 TEASPOON FRESHLY GROUND BLACK PEPPER

VEGETABLE OIL

To make the marinade: In a medium bowl whisk together the marinade ingredients.

Remove the giblets from the hens and discard. Rinse the hens, inside and out, under cold water and pat dry with paper towels. Remove the backbones and cut in half *(see page 243)*. Place in a large, resealable plastic bag and pour in the marinade. (If one bag isn't big enough, use two bags and divide the marinade.) Press the air out of the bag and seal tightly. Turn the bag to distribute the marinade, place in a bowl, and refrigerate for 2 to 12 hours, turning occasionally.

To make the basting sauce: In a small bowl whisk together the basting sauce ingredients.

Remove the hen halves from the bag and discard the marinade. Wipe the marinade off the hens with paper towels and lightly brush or spray with vegetable oil.

Grill the hen halves, bone side down, over *Indirect Medium* heat for 30 to 45 minutes. During the last 10 minutes of grilling, baste with the sauce. For crispier skin, grill, skin side down, over *Direct Medium* heat during the last 5 minutes of grilling time. Serve warm.

MAKES 6 TO 8 SERVINGS

Game Hens with Sage-Rice Stuffing

ROTISSERIE GAME HENS
WITH NECTARINE CHUTNEY

Here the curry in the marinade beckons to the ginger in the chutney. Sort of like Nelson Eddy wooing Jeanette MacDonald in the song "Indian Love Call."

INDIRECT/HIGH

FOR THE PASTE:

- 1 TABLESPOON FINELY CHOPPED FRESH THYME
- 1 TABLESPOON FINELY CHOPPED FRESH ROSEMARY
- 1 TABLESPOON MINCED SHALLOTS
- 1 TABLESPOON CURRY POWDER
- 1 TABLESPOON COARSELY GROUND WHITE PEPPER
- 1 TABLESPOON DIJON MUSTARD
- 1 TABLESPOON VEGETABLE OIL

- 2 CORNISH GAME HENS, 1 1/2 TO 2 POUNDS EACH

FOR THE CHUTNEY:

- 3 FIRM RIPE NECTARINES, PEELED AND CHOPPED (ABOUT 1 1/2 CUPS)
- 1/2 CUP FRESH ORANGE JUICE
- 1/4 CUP ORANGE MARMALADE
- 2 TABLESPOONS GRANULATED SUGAR
- 1 TABLESPOON CIDER VINEGAR
- 1 TABLESPOON MINCED FRESH GINGER
- 1 RED CHILE PEPPER, STEMMED, SEEDED, AND MINCED

- KOSHER SALT

To make the paste: In a small bowl mix together the paste ingredients.

Remove the giblets from the hens and discard. Rinse the hens, inside and out, under cold water and pat dry with paper towels. Rub the paste all over, inside and out. Place in a large, resealable plastic bag. Press the air out of the bag, seal tightly, and refrigerate for 8 to 24 hours.

To make the chutney: In a medium, heavy saucepan combine the chutney ingredients. Bring to a boil, then simmer over moderate heat, stirring frequently, until the mixture is reduced and slightly thickened, 20 to 30 minutes. Cool to room temperature. Cover and refrigerate for several hours or up to 3 days. Divide into two bowls. Allow to come to room temperature before serving.

Remove the hens from the bag. Truss with cotton string *(see page 233)* and season with salt. Center lengthwise on the spit and adjust on the rotisserie. Let the hens rotate over *Indirect High* heat until the juices run clear and the meat is no longer pink at the bone, 45 minutes to 1 hour. For a succulent glaze, baste with the chutney from one of the bowls during the last 10 minutes of grilling time; discard any that remains.

Turn off the rotisserie. Using barbecue mitts, remove the spit from the rotisserie and slide the hens from the spit onto a cutting board. Loosely cover with aluminum foil and allow to rest for 5 to 10 minutes. Using poultry shears or a sharp knife, remove the string and split each hen in half. Serve warm with the reserved bowl of chutney.

MAKES 2 TO 4 SERVINGS

GAME HENS
WITH SAGE-RICE STUFFING

Roasting these little birds over Indirect heat on a covered grill is the secret to keeping them moist.

INDIRECT/MEDIUM

FOR THE STUFFING:

- 1/4 CUP UNSALTED BUTTER
- 1 CUP FINELY CHOPPED YELLOW ONION
- 1/2 CUP FINELY CHOPPED CELERY
- 2 CUPS COOKED, COOLED WHITE RICE
- 1/2 CUP RAISINS
- 2 TABLESPOONS CHOPPED FRESH SAGE
- 1/2 TEASPOON KOSHER SALT
- 1/4 TEASPOON FRESHLY GROUND BLACK PEPPER

- 4 CORNISH GAME HENS, 1 1/2 TO 2 POUNDS EACH
  KOSHER SALT
  FRESHLY GROUND BLACK PEPPER

- 2 TABLESPOONS UNSALTED BUTTER, MELTED

To make the stuffing: In a large sauté pan over medium heat, melt the butter. Add the onion and celery and cook, stirring frequently, until softened, 5 to 7 minutes. Stir in the remaining stuffing ingredients and cook, stirring two or three times, until the rice is heated through, about 5 minutes. Remove from the heat and set aside to cool.

Remove the giblets from the hens and discard. Rinse the hens, inside and out, under cold water and pat dry with paper towels. Season, inside and out, with salt and pepper. Loosely fill the cavity of each bird with about 1/2 cup of the stuffing, then truss with cotton string *(see page 233)*.

Brush the hens with the melted butter and grill, breast side down, over *Indirect Medium* heat until the stuffing reaches 165°F in the center, the juices run clear, and the meat is no longer pink at the bone, 40 to 50 minutes. Remove the string and serve warm.

MAKES 4 TO 6 SERVINGS

HONEY-LIME GLAZED
CORNISH GAME HENS

An easy dinner that's elegant enough for guests.

INDIRECT/MEDIUM

FOR THE MARINADE:

1/4 CUP FRESH LIME JUICE

3 TABLESPOONS VEGETABLE OIL

2 TABLESPOONS HONEY

2 TEASPOONS FINELY CHOPPED FRESH THYME

2 TEASPOONS FINELY CHOPPED FRESH ROSEMARY

1 TEASPOON MINCED GARLIC

1 TEASPOON KOSHER SALT

1/2 TEASPOON PAPRIKA

1/2 TEASPOON FRESHLY GROUND BLACK PEPPER

2 CORNISH GAME HENS, 1 1/2 TO 2 POUNDS EACH

To make the marinade: In a medium bowl whisk together the marinade ingredients.

Remove the giblets from the hens and discard. Rinse the hens, inside and out, under cold water and pat dry with paper towels. With poultry shears or a sharp knife, remove the backbones and cut in half *(see page 243)*.

Place the hen halves in a large, resealable plastic bag and pour in the marinade. Press the air out of the bag and seal tightly. Turn the bag to distribute the marinade, place in a bowl, and refrigerate for 2 to 3 hours, turning occasionally.

Remove the hen halves from the bag and discard the marinade. Grill the hens, bone side down, over *Indirect Medium* heat until the juices run clear and the meat is no longer pink at the bone, 30 to 40 minutes. Serve warm.

MAKES 2 TO 4 SERVINGS

SAGE, ORANGE, AND CLOVE
ROTISSERIE TURKEY

One whiff of the orange, clove, and sage in this recipe is guaranteed to drive the neighbors wild. If you don't have a rotisserie, grill this 12- to 14-pound turkey over Indirect Medium heat for 2 1/4 to 2 1/2 hours.

INDIRECT/MEDIUM

FOR THE RUB:

2 TABLESPOONS GRANULATED ORANGE PEEL

1 TABLESPOON DRIED SAGE

1 TABLESPOON KOSHER SALT

1/2 TEASPOON FRESHLY GROUND BLACK PEPPER

1 TABLESPOON VEGETABLE OIL

1 TURKEY, 12 TO 14 POUNDS

2 SMALL ORANGES, WASHED AND DRIED

12 WHOLE CLOVES

6 MEDIUM GARLIC CLOVES, CRUSHED

1 BUNCH FRESH SAGE, TIED WITH COTTON STRING

To make the rub: In a small bowl combine the rub ingredients. Set aside.

Remove the pop-up timer, as well as the neck, giblets, and any excess fat from the turkey and discard. Rinse the turkey, inside and out, under cold water and pat dry with paper towels.

Pierce the oranges several times with a knife and insert six whole cloves into each of them. Put the clove-studded oranges, garlic, and sage into the turkey cavity. Truss the turkey with cotton string *(see page 233)*. Pin the neck skin flap to the body with two or three small trussing needles.

Skewer the turkey lengthwise through the oranges and center on the spit. Rub the entire exterior with the rub mixture, pressing it into the skin. Set the spit on the rotisserie and let the turkey rotate over *Indirect Medium* heat until the internal temperature reaches 170°F in the breast and 180°F in the thickest part of the thigh, 2 1/4 to 2 1/2 hours.

Turn off the rotisserie. Wearing barbecue mitts, carefully remove the spit from the rotisserie and place it on a cutting board. Loosely cover the turkey with aluminum foil and allow to rest for at least 20 minutes. Remove the spit and discard the oranges, garlic, and sage. Carve the turkey into serving pieces *(see page 269)*. Serve warm.

MAKES 12 TO 14 SERVINGS

Sage, Orange,
and Clove Rotisserie Turkey

TURKEY ON THE GRILL

So, Aunt Clara's still the grand champion of roasted holiday turkey, and this year it's your turn to host the big shindig? The pressure's on! If you want to succeed—and quite possibly become the new hero of family feasts—roast that bird on your grill. Try it once and you'll never go back to the oven. The skin crisps up beautifully, the meat remains moist and juicy, and you get a more intense turkey flavor. (You can console Aunt Clara by loudly declaring her pies the best in the league, bar none.) Here's all you need to know to pull it off:

WEIGHT: Weight is not an issue as long as the turkey fits your grill with the lid down. So think structure: A broad, flat bird will fit better than one with a high breastbone. At least 1 inch clearance between the turkey and the lid is ideal.

THAWING: A turkey should be completely defrosted in the refrigerator before grilling. Never thaw poultry at room temperature. Place the frozen turkey in its original wrapping on a tray in the refrigerator and allow 24 hours of thawing time for every 4 pounds of turkey.

FRESH TURKEY: Grill fresh turkey just as you would a completely defrosted one. Since fresh turkey is highly perishable, check the "sell by" date before you buy. Buy the turkey 1 to 2 days before you plan to cook it and keep it refrigerated.

DONENESS: When it comes to poultry, don't trust your eyes, use a meat thermometer. It should register 170°F in the breast and 180°F in the thickest part of the thigh. Remember that a smoke-cooked turkey may appear a little pink, even when it is thoroughly cooked.

STRATEGIC FOILING: After the first 45 minutes to 1 hour of cooking, check the turkey for even browning. The wings and drumsticks are likely to brown first. Loosely covering them in foil will keep them from browning too much. Continue checking the turkey every hour and cover the breast once it reaches a deep golden hue.

TO STUFF OR NOT TO STUFF: Bread stuffing (*see page 268*) is as much a part of a turkey dinner as the gravy. You can grill the stuffing in a heavy-duty aluminum pan or, if you're one who likes the smokey flavor acquired by the stuffing in a grilled bird, you can stuff the bird itself. Just follow these guidelines:

- Stuff right before you put the turkey on the grill.
- Don't stuff the bird too tightly.
- Grill the bird until the stuffing reaches 165°F in the center to be sure any food-borne bacteria is destroyed. (Keep in mind that getting the stuffing up to the safe temperature may mean overcooking the meat itself—a good reason to roast bird and stuffing separately.)

TURNING AND BASTING: The best part about grilling your bird is that you don't have to turn or baste it. Simply set up the grill for Indirect grilling, place the turkey on the cooking grate, and close the lid. Add charcoal according to the chart on page 25 or be sure you have an adequately full tank for your gas grill before you start.

BRINING: Brining is a great way to add flavor and moisture to turkey, but what do you put that big bird in? Use a deep, narrow container to keep the bird submerged. A large stock pot will hold a small to medium turkey. For large birds, try a clean 5-gallon paint bucket, available at home centers, or a deeper 6-gallon beer fermentation bucket, available at home-brewing supply stores. Line the bucket with two clean plastic trash bags, one set inside the other. Place the turkey in the inner bag and pour in the brine. Gather the plastic around the turkey so it's completely covered with the brine and tie the bags shut. Place the container in the fridge (be prepared to remove a shelf or two). If it just won't fit and it's cold enough outside, you can place the bucket outside in snow and monitor its temperature hourly to make sure it's not getting too warm or starting to freeze. You must keep the brine at 40°F or colder. As soon as you remove the bird, discard the marinade and wash the bucket with hot soapy water and dry thoroughly. Reserve the bucket for brining use only.

CLASSIC GRILLED
TURKEY

Okay, you're ready to take the big leap and leave the oven behind. Good for you! This basic recipe gets great results every time—you get the compliments. Count on 1 pound of bird per person.

INDIRECT/MEDIUM

1 **THAWED OR FRESH TURKEY**
  VEGETABLE OIL
  KOSHER SALT
  FRESHLY GROUND BLACK PEPPER
  HERBS, RUB, OR OTHER SEASONINGS
  BREAD STUFFING *(PAGE 268)*

Remove the pop-up timer, as well as the neck, giblets, and any excess fat from the turkey and discard. Rinse the turkey, inside and out, under cold water and pat dry with paper towels. Brush generously with vegetable oil. Season with salt and pepper and herbs, rub, or other seasonings, inside and out.

Place the turkey, breast side up, on a roast holder set inside a large heavy-gauge aluminum foil pan. If stuffing the turkey *(see page 268)*, spoon the stuffing in now, being careful not to pack too tightly.

Grill the turkey over *Indirect Medium* heat for 11 to 13 minutes per pound to an internal temperature of 180°F in the thickest part of the thigh, 170°F in the breast, and 165°F in the stuffing. Remove from the grill and allow to rest for about 20 minutes before carving *(see page 269)*.

NOTE: To make gravy, pour a little water into the foil pan and replenish as needed during grilling to keep drippings from burning. Remove the pan from under the turkey about 30 minutes before the bird should be done and make the gravy *(see page 269)*. Continue cooking the turkey over *Indirect Medium* heat until done.

FLAVOR
ENHANCERS

Ay, there's the rub! *After brushing the turkey with oil or butter, rub it inside and out with your favorite poultry rub or improvise with a blend of equal parts dried sage, thyme, rosemary, and tarragon. If you opt for fresh, finely chopped herbs, you'll need twice as much as dried herbs. For peak flavor, blend the rub with about ¼ cup softened butter and spread it under the skin (see page 229).*

Add some smoking woods *to the fire or smoker box. Try hickory or mesquite for a traditional taste, apple or cherry for a slightly sweet and fruity flavor, or maple for a mild, slightly sweet accent. Wine barrel chips (available at gourmet shops) will add a sultry, wine-smoked flavor, while grape vines add a fruity and aromatic element. Soak wood chunks and grape vines for 1 hour, chips for 30 minutes. Shake off excess water; place chunks on the coals or chips in the smoker box. Add a handful (more or less to taste) every 1 to 2 hours.*

Tip: *Go easy on the wood until you find the right amount for your taste. Test on a chicken or two before the Big Day to see how much smoke flavor your family likes.*

COOKING TIMES
FOR WHOLE TURKEYS

Turkey is thoroughly cooked when a meat thermometer registers 180°F when inserted in the thickest part of the thigh (be sure it's not touching bone) or 170°F when inserted in the breast. Remove the turkey from the grill and allow to rest about 20 minutes before carving. If you're grilling on charcoal, don't forget to stoke the fire every hour (see "How Much Charcoal?" page 25). If you're using a gas grill, be sure you have enough gas before you start. A full 20-pound tank will provide about 17 hours of grilling time.

Turkey Size	Grilling Time
10-11 lbs	1¾ to 2½ hrs
12-14 lbs	2¼ to 3 hrs
15-17 lbs	2¾ to 3¾ hrs
18-22 lbs	3½ to 4 hrs
23-24 lbs	4 to 4½ hrs

Note: *Above cooking times are approximate. Allow more time on cold or windy days or at high altitudes.*

For a safe feast, *do not rely on a "pop-up" timer. When the recommended cooking time has elapsed, use an instant-read meat thermometer. If you stuffed the bird, be sure to check the temperature of the stuffing, too. It should register at least 165°F.*

PERFECT PARTNER
BREAD STUFFING

You can adapt this recipe to go with a roasted bird or pig. For your favorite poultry, make it with cranberries, mushrooms, and sage; for pork, substitute pineapple and macadamia nuts. This recipe will make enough stuffing to accompany a 12- to 15-pound turkey or suckling pig. For smaller pieces of meat, reduce accordingly. And if you have extra, who will complain?

FOR THE BASIC STUFFING:

4 CUPS 1/4-INCH-CUBED SOFT WHITE BREAD (ABOUT 8 SLICES)

3 CUPS CRUMBLED CORNBREAD

1/2 CUP UNSALTED BUTTER

1/2 CUP COARSELY CHOPPED ONION

1/2 CUP FINELY DICED CELERY

2 EGGS, BEATEN

1 TEASPOON KOSHER SALT

1/4 TEASPOON FRESHLY GROUND BLACK PEPPER

FOR TURKEY (OR OTHER POULTRY) STUFFING, ADD:

1/2 CUP DRIED CRANBERRIES

2 TABLESPOONS UNSALTED BUTTER

1/2 POUND MUSHROOMS (ANY KIND YOU LIKE)

1 TABLESPOON CHOPPED FRESH SAGE

1 TABLESPOON CHOPPED FRESH THYME

1 1/2 TEASPOONS CHOPPED FRESH ROSEMARY

FOR PORK STUFFING, ADD:

1 CUP WELL-DRAINED CANNED CRUSHED PINEAPPLE

1/2 CUP CHOPPED MACADAMIA NUTS

To make the basic stuffing: In a large bowl combine the bread crumbs and cornbread. Set aside. In a large sauté pan over medium-high heat, melt the butter. Add the onion and celery and cook, stirring occasionally, until the onion is translucent, 4 to 5 minutes. Add to the bread mixture and toss lightly. Add the eggs, salt, and pepper. Toss until well mixed. Set aside.

For poultry: Place the cranberries in a small bowl with enough hot water to cover them. Let sit for at least 15 minutes to rehydrate. Meanwhile, warm the butter in a medium sauté pan and cook the mushrooms in it for about 10 minutes, stirring occasionally. Drain the cranberries. Add the cranberries, sautéed mushrooms, sage, thyme, and rosemary to the bread mixture.

For pork: Add the pineapple and macadamia nuts to the basic stuffing.

To prevent bacterial growth, don't pack stuffing into the bird or pig too tightly, and only stuff the meat just before placing it on the grill. The stuffing is done when an instant-read meat thermometer inserted into the center registers 165°F.

Alternatively, put the stuffing in a heavy-duty aluminum baking pan. Cover with aluminum foil and grill over *Indirect Medium* heat (or in the oven at 350°F) for 30 to 35 minutes until the internal temperature reaches 165°F in the center. Note: For a crispy top, take off the foil and grill or bake for 10 minutes more.

CRANBERRY-ORANGE BRINED
SMOKED TURKEY

The brine, with its cranberry and orange juices, will remind you of a holiday punch. The hickory smoke just adds to that cozy feeling. This one could easily become a family tradition.

INDIRECT/MEDIUM

FOR THE BRINE:

2 QUARTS CRANBERRY JUICE

2 QUARTS ORANGE JUICE

2 SMALL GARLIC HEADS, CLOVES CRUSHED BUT NOT PEELED

1 CUP KOSHER SALT

1/4 CUP CRUSHED RED PEPPER FLAKES

1/4 CUP WHOLE FENNEL SEEDS

4 OUNCES FRESH GINGER, THINLY SLICED

6 BAY LEAVES

1 TURKEY, 12 TO 14 POUNDS

  CANOLA OIL

HICKORY CHUNKS *OR* CHIPS SOAKED IN WATER FOR AT LEAST 30 MINUTES

To make the brine: In a large saucepan or stockpot, combine the brine ingredients and bring to a boil over high heat. Boil for about 1 minute, then remove from the heat. Add about 4 cups ice cubes and allow the brine to cool to room temperature, about 1 1/2 hours.

Remove the pop-up timer, as well as the neck, giblets, and any excess fat from the turkey and discard. Rinse the turkey, inside and out, under cold water, drain, and place in a 5-gallon bucket or other container large enough to hold it easily *(see page 266)*. Pour the cooled brine over the turkey. If necessary, place a heavy weight on the turkey to keep it completely submerged. Cover the container with plastic wrap and refrigerate for about 24 hours.

Remove the turkey from the brine and pat dry with paper towels. Discard the brine. Truss the turkey with cotton string *(see page 233)*. Pin the neck skin flap to the body with two or three small trussing needles. Place the turkey on a roast holder set inside a heavy-gauge aluminum foil pan and lightly brush or spray with canola oil.

Follow the grill's instructions for using wood chunks. Grill the turkey over *Indirect Medium* heat until the internal temperature reaches 170°F in the breast and 180°F in the thickest part of the thigh, 2 1/4 to 3 hours. After about 45 minutes, when the wings and drumsticks are golden brown, wrap them with aluminum foil to prevent them from burning. When the breast is golden brown, loosely cover it with foil. When fully cooked, transfer the turkey to a cutting board or platter, loosely cover the whole bird with foil, and allow to rest for about 20 minutes before carving.

MAKES 12 TO 14 SERVINGS

SERVING UP TURKEY

Okay, you've managed to pull that gorgeous bird off the grill without a hitch. Now what? While it's resting under its foil tent, make the gravy. Don't worry, our recipe will keep you on course. Just smile as you whisk and you're home free. Next up, the ultimate test of your hosting skills: carving the turkey. Again, don't sweat. Just follow our step-by-steps and lose that terrified look on your face. See, that was easy.

CARVING A ROAST TURKEY

Before carving, remove any trussing string. As you carve, arrange the carved meat on a warmed serving platter, the sliced breast meat at one end and the dark meat of the thigh and drumstick at the other.

REMOVE THE WHOLE LEG

Steadying the turkey with the carving fork, cut down between the thigh and the body (above). Pull the thigh away from the bird to locate the hip joint and cut through the joint.

SEPARATE DRUM-STICK FROM THIGH

Locate the joint between the drumstick and the thigh with the knife and cut down firmly, severing the leg into two pieces.

CARVE DRUMSTICK AND THIGH

Holding the knife parallel and close to the bone, cut a thick slice of meat from the drumstick (above, left). Roll the drumstick over halfway and cut another slice. Repeat for the other two sides. Cut the slices to the desired thickness. Carve the thigh into four or more slices (above, right), depending on the size of the thigh.

REMOVE THE WING

Cut through the corner of the breast toward the wing. Pull the wing outward to find the joint; cut through the joint (above). Repeat with the other wing. A turkey wing generally amounts to one serving.

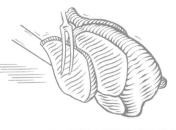

CARVE THE BREAST

Carve equal-width slices from one side of the breast (above). Transfer each slice to the warmed serving platter. Repeat on the other side.

DELICIOUS
TURKEY GRAVY

It's not a turkey dinner until it's covered with piping hot gravy. Never made it? Don't worry. Here's the basic technique Mom always used:

Remove all but $\frac{1}{4}$ cup of the fat from the drippings in the roasting pan. Set the pan over medium heat and gradually add 6 tablespoons of flour, whisking until smooth.

Slowly add 4 cups of liquid (broth, cooking water from the boiled giblets, or milk), whisking constantly. Bring to a boil, whisking constantly, then reduce heat and simmer for about 20 minutes, during which time the gravy will thicken and the flour taste will be cooked out. Loosen the bits of cooked turkey from the bottom of the pan as the gravy simmers (very important for peak flavor). Season with salt and pepper. Serve warm.

TURKEY KABOBS
WITH GREEK SALAD

Bet you never thought you could get to Greece on a turkey. Blend lemon, olive oil, oregano, and mint, add a little orzo salad on the side, and you're there.

DIRECT/HIGH

FOR THE MARINADE:

- 1/4 CUP FRESH LEMON JUICE
- 1/4 CUP EXTRA-VIRGIN OLIVE OIL
- 2 TABLESPOONS CHOPPED FRESH OREGANO
- 2 TABLESPOONS CHOPPED FRESH MINT
- 1 TABLESPOON MINCED GARLIC
- 1 TABLESPOON LEMON-PEPPER

- 1 BONELESS, SKINLESS TURKEY BREAST, ABOUT 2 POUNDS

FOR THE SALAD:

- 8 OUNCES ORZO, COOKED ACCORDING TO PACKAGE DIRECTIONS, WARM
- 1/4 CUP EXTRA-VIRGIN OLIVE OIL
- 2 TABLESPOONS FRESH LEMON JUICE
- 1 CUP FINELY CHOPPED RIPE TOMATOES
- 1 CUP FINELY DICED BABY SUMMER SQUASH
- 1/2 CUP CHOPPED GREEN ONIONS (WHITE PART ONLY)
- 2 TABLESPOONS FINELY CHOPPED FRESH MINT
- 2 TABLESPOONS FINELY CHOPPED FRESH ITALIAN PARSLEY
- 2 TEASPOONS FINELY CHOPPED FRESH OREGANO
- 2 TEASPOONS MINCED GARLIC
- 1/4 TEASPOON CRUSHED RED PEPPER FLAKES
- KOSHER SALT

- 2 MEDIUM WHITE ONIONS
- 2 LARGE BELL PEPPERS
- EXTRA-VIRGIN OLIVE OIL

To make the marinade: In a small bowl whisk together the marinade ingredients.

Rinse the turkey breast under cold water and pat dry with paper towels. Cut into 1 1/2-inch chunks. Place in a large, resealable plastic bag and add the marinade. Press the air out of the bag and seal tightly. Turn the bag to distribute the marinade, place in a bowl, and refrigerate for 4 to 6 hours, turning occasionally.

To make the salad: In a serving bowl toss the warm orzo with the olive oil and lemon juice. Add the remaining salad ingredients and mix well. Set aside at room temperature.

Cut the onions and bell peppers into 1 1/2-inch chunks. Remove the meat from the bag and discard the marinade. Thread the turkey and vegetables onto skewers. Lightly brush or spray with olive oil. Season with salt. Grill over *Direct High* heat until the meat is firm and the vegetables are tender, 6 to 8 minutes, turning once halfway through grilling time. Remove from the skewers and serve with the salad.

MAKES 6 TO 8 SERVINGS

JALAPEÑO-PEACH
TURKEY BREAST

For crispier skin, grill the breast, skin side down, over Direct Medium heat during the last 5 to 10 minutes.

INDIRECT/MEDIUM

FOR THE PASTE:

- 1 TABLESPOON BLACK PEPPERCORNS
- 1 TABLESPOON CUMIN SEEDS
- 1 TABLESPOON CHILI POWDER
- 1 TABLESPOON DRIED OREGANO
- 1 TABLESPOON DRIED SAGE
- 1 TEASPOON GRANULATED GARLIC
- 1/4 CUP FRESH LIME JUICE
- 2 TABLESPOONS EXTRA-VIRGIN OLIVE OIL

- 1 TURKEY BREAST (WITH BONE), 4 TO 5 POUNDS, SPLIT IN HALF

FOR THE JAM:

- 6 FIRM RIPE PEACHES, PEELED AND FINELY CHOPPED (ABOUT 4 CUPS)
- 1 CUP PEACH PRESERVES
- 2/3 CUP PEACH JUICE
- 1/4 CUP GRANULATED SUGAR
- 2 TABLESPOONS CIDER VINEGAR
- 4 JALAPEÑO PEPPERS, STEMMED, SEEDED, AND MINCED
- 1 TABLESPOON CHOPPED FRESH CILANTRO

- MESQUITE CHUNKS *OR* CHIPS SOAKED IN WATER FOR AT LEAST 30 MINUTES

- VEGETABLE OIL
- KOSHER SALT

To make the paste: Crush the peppercorns and cumin seeds, then combine with the remaining paste ingredients.

Rinse the turkey under cold water and pat dry with paper towels. Coat with the paste. Place in a large, resealable plastic bag, press the air out of the bag, and seal tightly. Refrigerate for 8 to 24 hours.

To make the jam: In a heavy-bottomed saucepan combine the peaches, preserves, juice, sugar, and vinegar. Bring to a boil, then reduce heat to medium-low and continue cooking, stirring often, until the peaches are cooked and the liquid has thickened, 30 to 40 minutes. Allow to cool for 10 minutes, then pour into a food processor and process until smooth. Add the jalapeños and cilantro. Cool to room temperature, cover, and refrigerate. (The jam may be made up to 3 days in advance. Bring to room temperature before serving.)

Follow the grill's instructions for using wood chunks. Lightly brush or spray the turkey with vegetable oil and season with salt. Grill, skin side up, over *Indirect Medium* heat until the internal temperature reaches 170°F, 1 to 1 1/2 hours. Allow to cool for 20 minutes before slicing. Serve warm with the jam.

MAKES 6 TO 8 SERVINGS

Jalapeño-Peach Turkey Breast

Turkey Pot Pie

TURKEY
POT PIE

Best thing ever to happen to turkey leftovers. And this homemade version is simply over the top.

INDIRECT/MEDIUM

FOR THE VEGETABLES:

- 2 TABLESPOONS UNSALTED BUTTER, DIVIDED
- 1 MEDIUM YELLOW ONION, CUT INTO 1/2-INCH DICE
- 3 MEDIUM CARROTS, PEELED AND CUT INTO 1/2-INCH DICE
- 2 CELERY STALKS, CUT INTO 1/2-INCH DICE
- 1/2 POUND BUTTON MUSHROOMS, THINLY SLICED
- 1 TEASPOON DRIED THYME
- 1/2 TEASPOON DRIED OREGANO

FOR THE SAUCE:

- 3 TABLESPOONS UNSALTED BUTTER
- 2 TEASPOONS MADRAS CURRY POWDER
- 1/4 CUP ALL-PURPOSE FLOUR
- 1 1/2 CUPS CHICKEN BROTH

- 3 CUPS DICED GRILLED TURKEY
- 1/4 CUP FINELY CHOPPED FRESH ITALIAN PARSLEY
- 2 TABLESPOONS FRESH LEMON JUICE
- 1/2 TEASPOON KOSHER SALT
- 1/4 TEASPOON FRESHLY GROUND BLACK PEPPER

- 1 SHEET (9- BY 10-INCH) FROZEN PUFF PASTRY, THAWED
- 1 LARGE EGG

To prepare the vegetables: In a medium sauté pan over medium-high heat, melt 1 tablespoon of the butter and cook the onion and carrots, stirring occasionally, until the onion is translucent, 6 to 8 minutes. Transfer the onion-carrot mixture to a large bowl. Melt the remaining 1 tablespoon of butter in the sauté pan over medium-high heat. Add the celery, mushrooms, thyme, and oregano. Cook, stirring occasionally, until the juices from the mushrooms have evaporated, 6 to 8 minutes. Add the celery-mushroom mixture to the other vegetables.

To make the sauce: In a large saucepan over low heat, melt the butter. Add the curry powder and cook for 1 minute to bring out the flavor. Add the flour and cook for 1 minute, stirring constantly. Whisk in the chicken broth and simmer until the sauce thickens.

Add the cooked vegetables, turkey, parsley, lemon juice, salt, and pepper to the sauce. Stir and simmer for 1 minute. Transfer the mixture to an ovenproof 10-inch skillet or deep 10-inch pie pan.

On a lightly floured surface roll out the puff pastry to 1/8-inch thickness. Lay the pastry over the skillet, trimming any excess with a knife. Cut three or four slashes in the pastry to allow steam to escape. Beat the egg with 2 teaspoons water; lightly brush the entire surface of the pastry with the egg mixture.

Place the skillet on a small baking sheet and place on the cooking grate. Grill over *Indirect Medium* heat until the filling is bubbling and the pastry is golden brown, 40 to 50 minutes. Carefully remove the hot pan from the grill. Allow the pie to cool for about 10 minutes before serving.

MAKES 6 TO 8 SERVINGS

TURKEY PAILLARDS
WITH SUMMER FRUIT SALSA

Paillard (pronounced "pie-YAR") is a term for a thin cut of boneless meat that's pounded thin and cooked quickly. Here we use a lean turkey breast and pair it with a colorful fruit salsa.

DIRECT/HIGH

FOR THE SALSA:

- 1 CUP 1/4-INCH-DICED PEACHES
- 1 CUP 1/4-INCH-DICED NECTARINES
- 1 CUP 1/4-INCH-DICED PLUMS
- 1/2 CUP 1/4-INCH-DICED RED ONIONS
- 1/2 CUP PITTED CHERRIES, QUARTERED
- 1 SERRANO CHILE, STEMMED, SEEDED, AND MINCED
- 3 TABLESPOONS FRESH LIME JUICE, DIVIDED

- 1 BONELESS, SKINLESS TURKEY HALF-BREAST, ABOUT 1 POUND

VEGETABLE OIL

KOSHER SALT

To make the salsa: In a medium bowl combine the peaches, nectarines, plums, onion, cherries, chile, and 1 tablespoon of the lime juice.

Rinse the turkey breast under cold water and pat dry with paper towels. With a sharp knife and slicing on the diagonal, cut the breast into four equal-sized slices, about 3/4 inch thick each. Place the slices between two sheets of plastic wrap on a cutting board. Using a meat mallet or the bottom of a small, heavy pan, pound the slices into 1/4-inch-thick paillards.

Brush the paillards with the remaining 2 tablespoons of lime juice, then lightly brush or spray with vegetable oil and season with salt. Grill over *Direct High* heat for 3 to 4 minutes, turning once halfway through grilling time. Serve warm with the salsa.

MAKES 4 SERVINGS

A FIREHOUSE TURKEY TALE

What do a grill-roasted turkey and a house full of firefighters have in common? Both can be great ways to share the joy of grilling. See, firefighters spend a lot of time between alarms at the firehouse, where a designated cook keeps the troops fed. Firehouse food is often less than tantalizing, so when our friend Mike was recruiting grill peddlers back in the 1970s, these hungry heroes made attentive candidates.

In my early Weber days, my job was to set up grilling demonstrations in retail stores across the nation. Our demos had gotten so popular that I often found myself scrambling for part-timers who could make a sales pitch while demonstrating our grills. Equipped with my trusty Weber kettle, I came up with an unusual but highly effective way to recruit people with a good grip on barbecue basics, including fire safety.

At the time, firefighters typically worked long shifts for 10 straight days, then had several days off. In this downtime, many picked up odd jobs to supplement their income. So I would drive up to a firehouse, remove a shiny, fire-engine red Weber charcoal kettle grill from my car, wheel it up to the firehouse, and go find whoever was in charge (if they hadn't already appeared to chase me off the property). After finding the usually suspicious watch commander, I would volunteer to cook a turkey for the crew and leave the grill

behind for their use. I was generally regarded as insane, but the prospect of a tasty meal usually earned me the green light. After all, if there were any unintended pyrotechnics, they could handle it.

As I lit the charcoal, I'd tell the firefighters stories about folks who didn't follow lighting instructions and some of the crazy things that could happen. I'd invariably hear about someone in their district who had used gasoline or another forbidden fire starter and unintentionally torched a lawn or deck. While we discussed ways of teaching fire safety, I could easily identify the natural storytellers and those comfortable speaking with a stranger—two important qualities for a grill demonstrator.

While the briquets were ashing over, I'd prepare the turkey, usually placing a stick of butter in the cavity along with a bay leaf or two and some poultry seasoning. As the turkey roasted to a golden brown, I'd baste the outside of it with peanut oil.

While the turkey was cooking, someone would ask why Weber had sent me out to cook a turkey and give away a grill. I'd explain that we needed demonstrators who could set up a Weber charcoal grill for Indirect cooking, safely light a fire, prepare a turkey for roasting, and then talk about the grill while the turkey was cooking. Since they had just witnessed a guy show up from nowhere and do all of this, they knew it was pretty much a no-brainer. When I explained that they could earn a daily fee doing it, three or four fire-fighters usually applied for the job right on the spot.

The only thing that ever sidelined my recruiting efforts was a fire alarm. One such time I was in Des Moines, Iowa, chatting up a firefighter who was a natural for the job. He could tell a story, he was the firehouse cook, and he need-ed some culinary help with his job. His name was Stewart Leathers, but his nickname was Shoe-Leather, obviously a jab at his firehouse steaks, which he cooked in a cast-iron skillet on the stove. I was just at the point of recruiting Stu when bells went off and the men—Stu included—scrambled into their gear, jumped onto fire trucks, and roared off.

About two hours later, they returned, grinning and...mischievous. Evidently they had just answered a call at a burning horse barn. Fortunately, no one was injured, but one of the firefighters had picked up a horribly scorched saddle as a trophy. Now, after washing off the smoke, they assembled near my grill to present it to Shoe-Leather. There was a raucous speech about the saddle being more edible than Stu's firehouse cuisine and every-one laughed. But it lit a fire under poor Stu.

The turkey was ready just as the "ceremony" ended. Everyone raved about how juicy and flavorful it was, and quickly reduced the bird to bones. No one asked more questions about how to grill a turkey than Stu. Before my firehouse visit ended, Stu and two other firefighters had signed up to demonstrate our grills.

Over the next three months I spoke to Stu by phone sever-al times, instructing him on grilling steaks, hamburgers, chicken pieces, pork chops, and even fish fillets on the kettle grill I'd left behind. When I returned to Des Moines for the official demonstrator training session, Stu was there learning how to sell grills. After the session, he invited me back to the firehouse, where I was greeted with several air-horn blasts from the now happily fed company. Stu's former nickname of Shoe-Leather had been changed to Stupendous Griller.

If your cooking doesn't inspire the company around your house, maybe it's time to fire up the grill. You may never get to jump on a fire truck and put out a fire, but you just may earn yourself a nickname you'll be proud to add to an apron.

FIREHOUSE
TURKEY

Does regular oven-roasted turkey leave you a little cold? Try grilling that bird! When it comes to flavor, this spicy number's a three-alarmer. Rubbing the spices under the skin lets the flavor sink in, while the butter keeps the meat moist and juicy.

INDIRECT/MEDIUM

FOR THE PASTE:

3 TABLESPOONS CRACKED BLACK PEPPERCORNS

2 TABLESPOONS GARLIC SALT

1 TABLESPOON DRY MUSTARD

1 TABLESPOON PAPRIKA

3/4 TEASPOON CAYENNE

4 TABLESPOONS UNSALTED BUTTER, SOFTENED

1 TURKEY, 12 TO 14 POUNDS

EXTRA-VIRGIN OLIVE OIL

To make the paste: In a small bowl mix together the pepper, garlic salt, mustard, paprika, and cayenne. Add the butter and mash with a fork until all the spices are blended with the butter, forming a thick paste.

Remove the pop-up timer, as well as the neck, giblets, and any excess fat from the turkey and discard. Rinse the turkey, inside and out, under cold water and pat dry with paper towels. Spread the paste under the skin (*see page 229*) and inside the entire cavity. Generously brush or spray the turkey with olive oil.

Place the turkey, breast side up, in a roast holder set inside a large heavy-gauge foil pan. Grill over *Indirect Medium* heat until the internal temperature reaches 170°F in the breast and 180°F in the thickest part of the thigh. When the wings and drumsticks are golden brown, after about 1 hour, wrap them with aluminum foil to prevent them from burning. Remove from the grill and allow to rest for about 20 minutes before carving. Serve warm.

MAKES 12 TO 14 SERVINGS

TURKEY
MARSALA

We've found chicken cordon bleu's rich cousin, and guess what? It's Italian. Tender turkey breast cutlets are stuffed with fontina cheese and prosciutto, then draped in a regal marsala wine sauce.

DIRECT/HIGH

FOR THE TURKEY:

- 8 TURKEY BREAST CUTLETS, ABOUT 3 OUNCES EACH
- KOSHER SALT
- FRESHLY GROUND BLACK PEPPER
- 4 PAPER-THIN SLICES PROSCIUTTO
- 1/2 CUP COARSELY SHREDDED FONTINA CHEESE (ABOUT 2 OUNCES)
- 6 FRESH SAGE LEAVES, FINELY CHOPPED

- EXTRA-VIRGIN OLIVE OIL

FOR THE SAUCE:

- 1 CUP LOW-SODIUM CHICKEN BROTH
- 1 TABLESPOON MINCED SHALLOTS
- 1 TABLESPOON FRESH LEMON JUICE
- 1/4 CUP DRY MARSALA WINE
- 2 TEASPOONS TOMATO PASTE
- 3 TABLESPOONS COLD, UNSALTED BUTTER, CUT INTO 3 PIECES
- KOSHER SALT
- FRESHLY GROUND BLACK PEPPER

To prepare the turkey: Lightly pound the turkey cutlets to a uniform thickness, about 3- by 6-inches each. Season four cutlets with salt and pepper and place a prosciutto slice on each one, folding the prosciutto to make it the same size as the cutlet. Distribute the cheese over the prosciutto slices and sprinkle with the chopped sage. Lay the other four cutlets on top of the first cutlets, pressing down firmly around the edges to seal. Skewer the cutlet packages along each edge with toothpicks to hold them together. Place on a plate lightly coated with olive oil. Cover with plastic wrap and refrigerate until ready to grill.

To make the sauce: In a small saucepan combine the chicken broth, shallots, and lemon juice. Bring to a boil over high heat and cook until the mixture is reduced to 1/2 cup. Add the marsala wine and tomato paste and continue cooking until again reduced to 1/2 cup. Just before serving, heat the sauce over low heat and whisk in the butter, one piece at a time. Cook until the butter is incorporated and the sauce thickens slightly. Season with salt and pepper. Set aside.

Lightly brush or spray both sides of the cutlet packages with oil. Grill over *Direct High* heat until the meat is lightly browned and firm to the touch, 5 to 6 minutes, turning once halfway through grilling time. Remove from the grill and pull out the toothpicks. Place a cutlet package on each serving plate and top with 1 to 2 tablespoons of the sauce. Serve warm.

MAKES 4 SERVINGS

HICKORY-SMOKED
TURKEY LEGS

Here rich, dark meat is enhanced with crisp apples, warming spices, and the scent of hickory wood.

INDIRECT/MEDIUM

FOR THE SAUCE:

- 1 TART APPLE (SUCH AS GRANNY SMITH), PEELED, CORED, AND THINLY SLICED
- 1 CUP FINELY CHOPPED WHITE ONION
- 1 CUP APPLE CIDER
- 1/2 CUP KETCHUP
- 1/4 CUP DARK BROWN SUGAR
- 1 TABLESPOON CIDER VINEGAR
- 1 TABLESPOON WORCESTERSHIRE SAUCE
- 1 TABLESPOON DIJON MUSTARD
- 1 CINNAMON STICK

FOR THE RUB:

- 1 TABLESPOON PAPRIKA
- 1 TABLESPOON DARK BROWN SUGAR
- 2 TEASPOONS KOSHER SALT
- 1 TEASPOON GRANULATED GARLIC
- 1 TEASPOON GRANULATED ONION
- 1/4 TEASPOON GROUND CINNAMON
- 1/4 TEASPOON CAYENNE
- 1/4 TEASPOON GROUND CLOVES

- 4 TURKEY DRUMSTICKS, ABOUT 1/2 POUND EACH
- VEGETABLE OIL

- HICKORY CHUNKS *OR* CHIPS SOAKED IN WATER FOR AT LEAST 30 MINUTES

To make the sauce: In a small saucepan whisk together the sauce ingredients. Bring to a boil, reduce heat to medium-low, and simmer until the apples are fully cooked and the sauce is thickened, about 20 minutes. Discard the cinnamon stick. Allow to cool for 5 minutes, then pour into a food processor and purée. Divide the sauce into two bowls.

To make the rub: In a bowl combine the rub ingredients.

Rinse the turkey drumsticks under cold water and pat dry with paper towels. Coat with the rub mixture and allow to stand at room temperature for 20 minutes before grilling. Lightly brush or spray with vegetable oil.

Follow the grill's instructions for using wood chunks. Grill the turkey over *Indirect Medium* heat until the internal temperature reaches 180° F in the thickest part of the meat, about 1 hour, basting occasionally from one bowl of the baste.

Remove the turkey legs from the grill. Discard any remaining baste. Serve the turkey legs warm or at room temperature with the reserved sauce.

MAKES 4 SERVINGS

HERE'S ONE FOR THE PICNIC BASKET: SPICE-COATED TURKEY LEGS, GRILLED AND SMOKED OVER HICKORY CHUNKS.

Hickory–Smoked Turkey Legs

When the first humans to stand upright gazed into the nearest pool of water, something amazing happened. Those early hominids saw fascinating creatures swimming beneath the surface and, being evolutionarily mobile bipeds, decided they should eat them. Thus began the timeless tradition of big people chasing little scaled critters with sticks, hooks, and rocks.

Despite technological advances that have since spawned entire fishing empires, when it comes to the lone rod-and-reel fisher versus an unseen population of fish, not much has changed. When you're standing streamside or lakeside in the great outdoors, you can feel a primal connection to the timeless

FISH & S

pursuit of dinner. And when you're matching wits with a creature with a brain the size of a pea, you can feel pretty silly gazing at an empty creel.

It's this very uncertainty of the quest that makes you either love fishing or hate it. When you think about it, dangling a tiny, random hook in a large or swiftly moving body of water is a very inefficient way to go about feeding yourself. And who really understands how fish think? We like to believe we can second-guess their appetites, cruising speeds, vectors, and relative intelligence when it comes to taking the bait. And every fisherman has tried something wild—such as lacing a fly with anise oil or loading a hook with a Cheeto®—and then landed a lunker and declared himself or herself the "Fishing God." But the truth is, it's a wild gamble most days. In fact, there are times when you might as well be casting your

bait between the stars. Who knows where those critters are lurking? As you run up and down the river bank trying to get that lure unstuck without losing it, you can almost hear the fish sing, "Na na na na na!" as they swim by unscathed.

But then that aggravating wait while the mosquitoes have their way with you is finally rewarded with a strong tug on the other end of the line.

Suddenly it's all worthwhile. The caveperson within awakens with a roar. Who cares if it's a throwback? At least something happened! If you're real lucky, it's a keeper.

And that's why we love fishing. Few things are as satisfying as catching, cooking, and eating your own dinner.

Grilling also fulfills an ancient urge. But for some reason, few people are as confident grilling their catch as they are casting out that first line. This chapter should fix that. Next time you come home with a cooler full of actual fish, not just stories, don't stash them in the freezer and forget about them.

Show them off on the grill and have the ultimate human experience. And even if you prefer to pick up your catch at the wharf or angle for it at the grocery store counter, you can still experience the thrill of a perfectly grilled fillet or shrimp kabob.

Oh sure, you can poach, bake, bread, and fry—and smother this and that with a rich cream sauce when you feel like it. But for a truly satisfying fish texture, nothing beats direct contact with the hot grate and the flame. You can always add that cream sauce later. First, get the important stuff done right. This chapter's easy recipes and masterful techniques will help you to do just that.

The most important rule is to be attentive at the grill. Since fish and seafood are very high in water, they grill up quickly. If you stray, you will pay. But it doesn't take long to become an expert either. Plus, it's lots of fun to practice (and you won't have the smell of cooked fish in your house for the next three days). If you're a nervous novice, start with a fish that's very forgiving on the grill: sea bass or swordfish. Or practice on small items you can grill one at a time, such as shrimp or scallops. Pretty soon you'll be pulling whole stuffed salmons or delicate calamari off the grill with a flourish. The recipes here have all the clues you need to succeed. Release the archetypal fisher within!

FISH FAJITAS REQUIRE JUST THE RIGHT SEASONINGS AND FULLY RIPE VEGETABLES TO ALLOW THE DELICATE FLAVORS TO STEP FORWARD. THAT'S WHAT'S GOOD ABOUT THIS RECIPE— IT HITS THAT SWEET SPOT.

Red Snapper Fajitas with Black Bean Salsa

RED SNAPPER FAJITAS
WITH BLACK BEAN SALSA

Limit the fish's marinating time to 30 minutes. Any more and the natural acid in the lime juice will make the red snapper mushy.

DIRECT/HIGH

FOR THE MARINADE:

3　TABLESPOONS FRESH LIME JUICE

2　TABLESPOONS VEGETABLE OIL

1　TABLESPOON MINCED GARLIC

1　TEASPOON GROUND CUMIN

1　TEASPOON KOSHER SALT

1/4　TEASPOON CRUSHED RED PEPPER FLAKES

4　SKINLESS RED SNAPPER FILLETS,
　　ABOUT 6 OUNCES EACH

FOR THE SALSA:

1　POUND PLUM TOMATOES, CORED AND DICED

1　MEDIUM AVOCADO, FINELY DICED

1/2　CUP CANNED BLACK BEANS, RINSED AND
　　FULLY DRAINED

1/4　CUP FINELY DICED RED ONION

1/4　CUP FINELY CHOPPED FRESH CILANTRO

2　TABLESPOONS FRESH LIME JUICE

1　TABLESPOON VEGETABLE OIL

1　TABLESPOON MINCED JALAPEÑO PEPPER,
　　WITH SEEDS

1　TEASPOON MINCED GARLIC

1/2　TEASPOON KOSHER SALT

　　VEGETABLE OIL

8　TO 10 FLOUR TORTILLAS (10 INCHES)

1/2　HEAD ROMAINE LETTUCE

To make the marinade: In a medium bowl whisk together the marinade ingredients.

Place the fillets in a large, resealable plastic bag and pour in the marinade. Press the air out of the bag and seal tightly. Turn the bag to distribute the marinade and refrigerate for 30 minutes.

To make the salsa: In a medium bowl combine the salsa ingredients. Season with more salt and lime juice, if desired.

Remove the fillets from the bag and discard the marinade. Lightly brush or spray both sides with vegetable oil. Grill over *Direct High* heat until the fish begins to flake, 3 to 4 minutes, turning once halfway through grilling time. Remove from the grill. Separate into large flakes with two forks.

Heat the tortillas over *Direct High* heat for about 1 minute without turning. Wrap in a kitchen towel to keep warm. Clean, core, and cut the lettuce into thin, crosswise slices. Let your guests assemble their own fajitas, piling the lettuce and fish on the warm tortillas and topping with the salsa.

MAKES 4 SERVINGS

MEXICAN
RED SNAPPER

This Mexico-inspired dish is perfect for a picnic at the beach. When the fish is fresh and the local vegetables are ripe, it's as easy as stuff, tie, drizzle. In the end, you have a rustic entrée or a super filling for a fish taco. Serve with tortilla chips and beans. (Suitable substitutes: halibut, striped bass.)

INDIRECT/MEDIUM

FOR THE VINAIGRETTE:

3　TABLESPOONS EXTRA-VIRGIN OLIVE OIL

1　TABLESPOON FRESH LIME JUICE

1　TABLESPOON FINELY CHOPPED FRESH CILANTRO

1　TEASPOON MINCED GARLIC

1/4　TEASPOON DRIED OREGANO

1/4　TEASPOON GROUND CUMIN

1/4　TEASPOON KOSHER SALT

1/8　TEASPOON CAYENNE

1/2　CUP THINLY SLICED RED ONION

1/2　CUP THINLY SLICED ANAHEIM CHILES

1/2　CUP THINLY SLICED RIPE TOMATOES

1　WHOLE RED SNAPPER, 2 TO 2 1/2 POUNDS,
　　SCALED AND GUTTED

To make the vinaigrette: In a medium bowl whisk together the vinaigrette ingredients.

In another medium bowl combine the onion, chiles, and tomatoes. Add half the vinaigrette, reserving the other half. Toss the vegetables to coat evenly.

With a sharp knife, extend the cut in the belly of the fish from the head to the tail. Open the fish and make a second cut inside the cavity running along one side of the backbone and cutting the rib bones, without slicing through the skin on the other side. Fill the cavity of the fish with the dressed vegetables. Wind a piece of cotton string around the fish three or four times to close the cavity and tie it.

Brush both sides of the fish with the reserved vinaigrette. Grill over *Indirect Medium* heat until the fish is opaque in the thickest part, 20 to 30 minutes. Brush the fish occasionally with the reserved vinaigrette during the last 5 minutes of grilling time. Carefully transfer the fish on a long spatula from the grill to a work surface. Cut off the head and tail with a sharp knife. Remove the string. Carefully make a cut lengthwise through the skin along the length of the backbone and slide the fillets off the bones. Add some vegetables to each serving. Serve warm.

MAKES 2 SERVINGS

STREAMSIDE DINNER

A traditional fish fry is always tasty, but bring that fresh-ly caught trout to the grill and you'll never go back. This recipe is great for camping—the foil packets seal in the butter, herbs, and capers in a use-and-dispose "skillet."

DIRECT/HIGH

FOR THE BUTTER MIXTURE:

1/2 CUP UNSALTED BUTTER

2 TABLESPOONS MINCED SHALLOTS

2 TABLESPOONS FRESH LEMON JUICE

2 TABLESPOONS FINELY CHOPPED ITALIAN PARSLEY

2 TABLESPOONS FINELY CHOPPED FRESH DILL

2 TABLESPOONS CAPERS, DRAINED

1 TEASPOON GRATED LEMON ZEST

1/2 TEASPOON KOSHER SALT

1/2 TEASPOON FRESHLY GROUND BLACK PEPPER

4 BROOK TROUT, 10 TO 12 OUNCES EACH, GUTTED AND CLEANED, WITH HEADS REMOVED

To make the butter mixture: In a medium sauté pan over medium-high heat, melt the butter. Add the shallots and cook for 2 to 3 minutes. Add the rest of the butter mixture ingredients. Cook for about 10 seconds, stirring constantly.

Cut four sheets of heavy-duty aluminum foil slightly longer than the trout and at least twice as wide. Place a trout on each sheet. Evenly distribute the butter mixture inside each trout and over the top. Fold over the ends of each foil sheet and crimp them to completely enclose each trout.

Grill the trout packets over *Direct High* heat for 6 minutes, turning once halfway through grilling time. Remove from the grill and carefully open each packet with scissors and peel back the foil. Serve warm.

MAKES 4 SERVINGS

"There's a fine line between fishing and just standing on the shore like an idiot."

— STEVEN WRIGHT

SMOKED TROUT
WITH FRENCH LENTIL SALAD

This fancy but easy recipe may be just the excuse you need to get you going on your next skeeter-slappin', bait-danglin' fishing trip. Cut the grilling time by a few min-utes for boned trout.

INDIRECT/MEDIUM

FOR THE MARINADE/DRESSING:

6 TABLESPOONS EXTRA-VIRGIN OLIVE OIL

2 TABLESPOONS BALSAMIC VINEGAR

2 TEASPOONS DIJON MUSTARD

1 TEASPOON FINELY CHOPPED GARLIC

1 TEASPOON KOSHER SALT

1/2 TEASPOON FRESHLY GROUND BLACK PEPPER

4 BROOK TROUT, 10 TO 12 OUNCES EACH, GUTTED AND CLEANED, WITH HEADS REMOVED

FOR THE SALAD:

1/2 CUP FRENCH GREEN LENTILS

1/2 TEASPOON KOSHER SALT

1/4 CUP FINELY CHOPPED CELERY

1/4 CUP FINELY CHOPPED RED ONION

1/4 CUP FINELY CHOPPED RED BELL PEPPER

2 TABLESPOONS FINELY CHOPPED FRESH ITALIAN PARSLEY

APPLE WOOD CHIPS SOAKED IN WATER FOR AT LEAST 30 MINUTES

KOSHER SALT

LEMON WEDGES

To make the marinade/dressing: In a medium bowl whisk together the marinade/dressing ingredients.

Place the trout in a large, resealable plastic bag and pour in all but 2 tablespoons of the marinade/dressing (reserve the 2 tablespoons in the bowl). Press the air out of the bag and seal tightly. Turn the bag to distribute the marinade, place in a bowl, and refrigerate for 30 minutes to 1 hour.

To make the salad: Rinse the lentils under cold running water, then put them in a small saucepan with 2 cups water and the salt. Bring to a boil, then simmer until the lentils are tender, 25 to 30 minutes. Drain and add the lentils to the reserved marinade/dressing. Add the remaining salad ingredients. Stir and adjust the seasonings, if necessary.

Follow the grill's instructions for using wood chips. Remove the trout from the bag and discard the marinade. Grill the trout over *Indirect Medium* heat until cooked through, about 15 minutes. Do not turn. Remove from the grill. Cut through the skin and flesh along the backbone and carefully peel off the skin on both sides. Use the knife blade to slide the flesh away from the backbone, leaving the rib bones behind. Remove any bones sticking to the flesh. Season with salt, garnish with lemon wedges, and serve warm or at room temperature with the salad.

MAKES 4 SERVINGS

FABULOUS FISH CAKES
WITH LEMON AÏOLI

Moist and succulent, these unusual and satisfying cakes get more than good looks from the grape leaves—they add a delicate layer of seasoning as well. A super sharp knife will help you to dice the fish to the requisite size. (Suitable substitutes: sole, flounder.)

DIRECT/MEDIUM

FOR THE AÏOLI:

- ¾ CUP MAYONNAISE
- 2 TABLESPOONS FRESH LEMON JUICE
- 1 TABLESPOON MINCED GARLIC
- 1 TEASPOON GRATED LEMON ZEST
- 1 TEASPOON DIJON MUSTARD

FOR THE FISH CAKES:

- ½ POUND FRESH SALMON FILLET *OR* STEAK
- ½ POUND FRESH HALIBUT FILLET *OR* STEAK
- ½ CUP BREAD CRUMBS
- 3 GREEN ONIONS (WHITE PART ONLY), FINELY CHOPPED
- 2 TABLESPOONS MAYONNAISE
- 1 TABLESPOON FINELY CHOPPED FRESH ITALIAN PARSLEY
- 1 TEASPOON DIJON MUSTARD
- ½ TEASPOON DRIED THYME
- ½ TEASPOON KOSHER SALT
- ¼ TEASPOON FRESHLY GROUND PEPPER

- 8 TO 12 GRAPE LEAVES
  EXTRA-VIRGIN OLIVE OIL

To make the aïoli: In a small bowl whisk together the aïoli ingredients. Cover with plastic wrap and refrigerate until a few minutes before serving.

To make the fish cakes: Cut the fish fillets into ¼-inch dice. Place in a medium bowl and add the rest of the fish cake ingredients. Gently mix with a fork, then refrigerate for 1 hour for easier handling. Remove from the refrigerator and shape into four cakes, about 3½ inches in diameter each.

Place a large grape leaf, shiny side down, on a plate. Position a fish cake in the center of the leaf and fold the leaf up around it. Place a second grape leaf on top and fold the edges down to enclose the cake. (If the grape leaves are small, a third leaf may be needed.) Wrap the remaining cakes the same way. Lightly oil the packets.

Grill the packets over *Direct Medium* heat until the grape leaves are well marked and the fish cakes are firm to the touch, about 10 minutes, turning once halfway through grilling time. Before serving, cut an X in the top leaf of each packet and turn back the edges. The grape leaves are edible, if desired. Serve warm with the aïoli.

MAKES 4 SERVINGS

FISHY CHOICES
FRESH OR FROZEN?

Well, we've all been taught that "fresh is better," right? Not necessarily so when it comes to seafood. If the label says "fresh-frozen," chances are that seafood was frozen on the ship just after being caught, which may actually make it fresher than the "fresh" seafood in your store. And ask if the fresh stuff you see in the case was previously frozen; the flesh tends to deteriorate with subsequent freezings. More tips on preserving flavor:

Storage: Consume fresh fish and seafood within a day of purchase. As for fresh-frozen, most household freezers don't get cold enough to hold seafood's peak flavor for more than a week or two. If you're not going to eat it by then, place it in a deep freezer that can get down to -10°F to -20°F to maintain that just-caught flavor longer.

Scallops: Available both fresh and fresh-frozen. Fresh scallops should smell sweet and glisten. Refrigerate immediately and prepare within a day. Fresh-frozen are the next best thing—just don't buy too far in advance. Color should range from light beige to pale pink.

Squid: Fresh-frozen is probably your best bet for peak flavor. Thaw only in your refrigerator, never at room temperature.

Whole fish: Scaled and gutted fish are usually sold fresh. Look for clear eyes (exception: the cloudy-eyed walleye) that are nicely rounded. And note how the fish is stored. Whole fish should be placed belly side down on a sloped bed of fresh ice so that any melting ice drains away. Look for firm and shiny flesh, and avoid fish with darkening edges or any discoloration. Gills should be bright red and free of...uh, slime (ugly word, but we have to tell it like it is).

Fresh fillets: Look for compact flesh with tight layers and bright color. When poked firmly with a finger, the flesh should spring back. (If it's in a case, have the person behind the counter do it. They should be glad to oblige. If they're not, move on.) Give it a whiff. If it smells fishy or like ammonia, it's starting to deteriorate.

Frozen fillets: These are hardest to judge because you have to rely on your eyes. Again, compact layers and good color are key (although a certain amount of dulling occurs with freezing). The FDA advises you to avoid packages that are torn, crushed, or stored above the frost line of the store's freezer. Once you've thawed them at home, make sure frozen fillets pass the tests for fresh ones.

Finally, to avoid cross-contamination, don't buy any cooked seafood that's been stored with raw fish.

OPAH
WITH CREAMY ROASTED RED PEPPER SAUCE

The taste of this pink-fleshed fish is so mouth-filling it might not surprise you that an opah can weigh in at a whopping 200 pounds. Cut into generous steaks, it does wonderfully well on the grill. Most of the opah (or "moonfish") you'll find in the store comes from Hawaii. Make the sauce ahead of time so the flavors have time to blend. (Suitable substitutes: swordfish, tuna.)

DIRECT/HIGH

FOR THE SAUCE:

- 1 LARGE RED BELL PEPPER
- 1 TEASPOON MINCED GARLIC
- 2 TEASPOONS BALSAMIC VINEGAR
- 1/4 TEASPOON KOSHER SALT
- 1 TABLESPOON FINELY CHOPPED FRESH DILL
- 1/3 CUP SOUR CREAM
- 1/4 CUP MAYONNAISE

- 4 OPAH FILLETS, 7 TO 8 OUNCES EACH AND ABOUT 1 INCH THICK
- EXTRA-VIRGIN OLIVE OIL
- KOSHER SALT
- FRESHLY GROUND BLACK PEPPER

To make the sauce: Grill the pepper over *Direct Medium* heat until the skin is black and blistered on all sides, 10 to 12 minutes, turning every 3 to 5 minutes. Remove the pepper from the grill and place in a paper bag; close tightly. Let stand for 10 to 15 minutes to steam off the skin. Peel away the charred skin. Cut off the top and remove the seeds. Cut the pepper into small dice. Place in a food processor along with the remaining sauce ingredients. Process until smooth. Transfer to a serving bowl, cover with plastic wrap, and refrigerate for several hours.

Brush both sides of the opah fillets with olive oil and season with salt and pepper. Grill over *Direct High* heat until just cooked, 6 to 8 minutes, turning once halfway through grilling time. Remove from the grill and serve warm with the sauce.

MAKES 4 SERVINGS

CAROLINA WAHOO
WITH BLACK-EYED PEA SALAD

In North Carolina, wahoo (a type of mackerel) is prized by anglers for its fighting resolve. In Hawaii it's called ono, which means "delicious." Firm, meaty wahoo steaks are similar to swordfish—slather them with a sweet and smoky sauce for this recipe, which includes an authentic black-eyed pea salad. If you want the full effect, toss some hickory chips on the fire. (Suitable substitutes: tuna, swordfish.)

DIRECT/MEDIUM

FOR THE SALAD:

- 2 TABLESPOONS VEGETABLE OIL
- 1/2 CUP FINELY DICED SMOKED HAM
- 1/2 CUP FINELY DICED YELLOW ONION
- 1/2 CUP FINELY DICED CELERY
- 1/2 CUP FINELY DICED RED BELL PEPPER
- 1 CAN (15 OUNCES) COOKED BLACK-EYED PEAS, RINSED AND DRAINED
- 1 TABLESPOON GRANULATED SUGAR
- 1 TABLESPOON CIDER VINEGAR
- FRESHLY GROUND BLACK PEPPER

- 4 WAHOO STEAKS, 6 TO 8 OUNCES EACH AND ABOUT 1 INCH THICK
- VEGETABLE OIL
- KOSHER SALT
- 1/2 CUP BARBECUE SAUCE

To make the salad: In a medium sauté pan over medium-high heat, warm the vegetable oil. Add the ham and cook for 2 to 3 minutes, stirring occasionally. Add the onion and cook, stirring occasionally, until translucent, 4 to 5 minutes. Add the celery and bell pepper and cook for a 3 to 4 minutes more, stirring occasionally. Add the black-eyed peas, sugar, and vinegar. Simmer for 2 to 3 minutes. Season with pepper and set aside to cool.

Lightly brush or spray both sides of the fish steaks with vegetable oil and season with salt and pepper. Brush the steaks with the barbecue sauce. Grill over *Direct Medium* heat until opaque throughout but still moist, 8 to 10 minutes, turning once halfway through grilling time. Brush with additional sauce after turning. Remove from the grill and serve warm with the salad.

MAKES 4 SERVINGS

SOUTHWEST SWORDFISH
WITH FRESH TOMATO SALSA

Swordfish is very popular in North America, probably because it's mild and firm, and it's easy to turn on the grill. Add a zippy marinade and homemade salsa, and you're a genius.

DIRECT/MEDIUM

FOR THE MARINADE:

- 2 TABLESPOONS FRESH LEMON JUICE
- 1 TABLESPOON EXTRA-VIRGIN OLIVE OIL
- 1/2 TEASPOON CHILI POWDER
- 1/2 TEASPOON PAPRIKA
- 1/2 TEASPOON KOSHER SALT
- 1/2 TEASPOON GROUND CUMIN

- 4 SWORDFISH FILLETS, ABOUT 6 OUNCES EACH AND 1 INCH THICK

FOR THE SALSA:

- 2 MEDIUM RIPE TOMATOES, FINELY CHOPPED
- 1/2 CUP FINELY CHOPPED WHITE ONION
- 1/4 CUP FINELY CHOPPED GREEN BELL PEPPER
- 2 TABLESPOONS FINELY CHOPPED FRESH CILANTRO
- 1 TABLESPOON FRESH LIME JUICE
- 1 TO 2 TEASPOONS MINCED JALAPEÑO PEPPER, WITH SEEDS
- 1/4 TEASPOON GROUND CUMIN
- 1/4 TEASPOON KOSHER SALT
- 1/4 TEASPOON FRESHLY GROUND BLACK PEPPER

To make the marinade: In a small bowl whisk together the marinade ingredients.

Place the fillets in a large, resealable plastic bag and pour in the marinade. Press the air out of the bag and seal tightly. Turn the bag to distribute the marinade, place on a plate, and refrigerate for 20 to 30 minutes.

To make the salsa: In a serving bowl combine the salsa ingredients and mix well. Allow to stand for about 10 minutes to blend flavors. Salsa tastes best served fresh and at room temperature.

Remove the swordfish from the bag and discard the marinade. Grill over *Direct Medium* heat until the fillets are opaque in the center, 8 to 10 minutes, turning once halfway through grilling time. Remove from the grill and serve warm with the salsa.

MAKES 4 SERVINGS

SWORDFISH STEAKS
WITH PUTTANESCA SAUCE

Puttanesca sauce should be part of every good cook's repertoire. It's excellent on pasta and especially good over firm fish like swordfish. We won't tell you the origin of the sauce's name because we run a clean-cut operation here, but look it up in a food dictionary—it might make for interesting chatter at your next dinner party. (Suitable substitute: salmon.)

DIRECT/MEDIUM

FOR THE SAUCE:

- 2 TABLESPOONS EXTRA-VIRGIN OLIVE OIL
- 1/4 CUP FINELY DICED RED ONION
- 1 TEASPOON MINCED GARLIC
- 1 CUP COARSELY CHOPPED TOMATOES
- 2 TEASPOONS BALSAMIC VINEGAR
- 1 TEASPOON MINCED ANCHOVIES PACKED IN OIL
- 1/4 TEASPOON CRUSHED RED PEPPER FLAKES
- 2 TABLESPOONS PITTED AND SLICED KALAMATA OLIVES
- 2 TEASPOONS FINELY CHOPPED FRESH THYME

- 4 SWORDFISH FILLETS, ABOUT 6 OUNCES EACH AND 1 INCH THICK
  EXTRA-VIRGIN OLIVE OIL
  KOSHER SALT
  FRESHLY GROUND BLACK PEPPER

To make the sauce: In a small sauté pan over low heat, warm the olive oil. Add the onion and garlic and cook, stirring occasionally, just until the garlic begins to brown, 3 to 5 minutes. Add the tomatoes, vinegar, anchovies, and red pepper flakes. Bring the mixture to a simmer and cook for 2 to 3 minutes, stirring occasionally. Add the olives and thyme. Stir and set aside.

Lightly brush or spray both sides of the fillets with olive oil and season with salt and pepper. Grill over *Direct Medium* heat until the fillets are opaque in the center, 8 to 10 minutes, turning once halfway through grilling time. Meanwhile, warm the sauce over high heat. Remove the fillets from the grill and serve warm with the sauce.

MAKES 4 SERVINGS

Sicilian Stuffed Swordfish Rolls

SICILIAN STUFFED
SWORDFISH ROLLS

Rolled stuffed swordfish is a classic Sicilian preparation, particularly when dried currants are in the filling. This presentation leads to a delicacy and lightness you'll love. Use the flat side of a meat mallet to pound the steaks. Everything but the grilling can be done hours ahead. If desired, serve with broccoli raab (also known as rapini) sautéed in olive oil with a little garlic.

DIRECT/HIGH

FOR THE STUFFING:

- 1 SMALL PLUM TOMATO, SEEDED AND FINELY CHOPPED
- 1/4 CUP FRESH BREAD CRUMBS
- 1 TABLESPOON DRIED CURRANTS
- 1 TABLESPOON FINELY CHOPPED FRESH ITALIAN PARSLEY
- 1 TABLESPOON FINELY CHOPPED FRESH MINT
- 1 TEASPOON FINELY CHOPPED FRESH OREGANO
- 1 TEASPOON GRATED LEMON ZEST
- 1 TEASPOON FINELY CHOPPED GARLIC
- 1/2 TEASPOON KOSHER SALT
- 1/4 TEASPOON FRESHLY GROUND BLACK PEPPER

- 4 SKINLESS SWORDFISH STEAKS, 5 TO 6 OUNCES EACH AND ABOUT 1/2 INCH THICK
  KOSHER SALT
  FRESHLY GROUND BLACK PEPPER

  EXTRA-VIRGIN OLIVE OIL

- 4 LEMON WEDGES

To make the stuffing: In a small bowl mix together the stuffing ingredients.

Place the swordfish steaks between two sheets of waxed paper and gently pound to a 1/4-inch thickness. Season with salt and pepper. Place about 2 tablespoons of the stuffing at one end of each steak and roll it up. Secure each roll with a toothpick or cotton string.

Lightly brush or spray the swordfish rolls with olive oil. Grill over *Direct High* heat until the fish is opaque throughout but still moist, 8 to 10 minutes, turning once halfway through grilling time. Remove the toothpicks or string. Serve warm with the lemon wedges.

MAKES 4 SERVINGS

SWORDFISH KABOBS
WITH PASTA PROVENÇAL

Here's one for a weekday when you want something simple. Make the marinade early in the day, then marinate the fish and cook it up in the evening. The tomato-garlic sauce is delicious!

DIRECT/MEDIUM

FOR THE MARINADE:

- 6 TABLESPOONS EXTRA-VIRGIN OLIVE OIL
- 1/4 CUP FRESH LEMON JUICE
- 2 TEASPOONS MINCED GARLIC
- 1/2 TEASPOON CRUSHED RED PEPPER FLAKES
- 1/2 TEASPOON KOSHER SALT

- 2 POUNDS SWORDFISH
- 1 SMALL RED ONION

FOR THE PASTA:

- 1/4 CUP EXTRA-VIRGIN OLIVE OIL
- 1/4 CUP FINELY DICED YELLOW ONION
- 1 TABLESPOON MINCED GARLIC
- 1/2 TEASPOON CRUSHED RED PEPPER FLAKES
- 1/4 CUP DRY WHITE WINE
- 2 CUPS COARSELY CHOPPED TOMATOES
- 8 OUNCES ANGEL HAIR PASTA
- 1/4 CUP FINELY CHOPPED FRESH BASIL
  KOSHER SALT
  FRESHLY GROUND BLACK PEPPER

To make the marinade: In a small bowl whisk together the marinade ingredients.

Cut the swordfish into 1-inch cubes. Quarter the onion and separate it into leaves. Place the fish and onion in a large, resealable plastic bag and pour in the marinade. Press the air out of the bag and seal tightly. Turn the bag to distribute the marinade, place in a bowl, and refrigerate for 30 minutes.

To make the pasta: In a large sauté pan over medium-high heat, warm the oil and cook the onion until translucent, 2 to 3 minutes. Add the garlic and pepper flakes and cook for 1 to 2 minutes more. Add the wine and tomatoes; bring to a boil, then reduce heat to a simmer. Keep warm over low heat.

In a large pot of boiling salted water cook the pasta according to the package directions until al dente. Drain and pour into the sauté pan. Toss to combine. Add the basil and season with salt and pepper. Set aside over very low heat.

Remove the swordfish and onion from the bag and discard the marinade. Thread the pieces alternately onto skewers. Grill over *Direct Medium* heat until the swordfish is cooked through but still moist, 6 to 8 minutes, turning once halfway through grilling time. Remove from the grill and serve warm with the pasta.

MAKES 4 SERVINGS

FISH ON THE GRILL

If you've been sticking to the comfort zone of steaks and burgers and haven't tried fish on the grill yet, you're not alone. Even those bold enough to throw a prime rib on the grill might sweat a bit thinking about how they're going to get that beautiful—and no doubt pricey—fillet off the grate without a major disaster. Friends, it's time to conquer your fear of fins-over-flames! Here are some pointers to guide you:

IS IT DONE YET? The old rule of thumb that "fish is thoroughly cooked when it flakes easily with a fork" is still true—too true, in fact. Chefs as far inland as Oklahoma have recently figured out that flaky fish is overcooked fish. (If you don't believe it, take a bite: mmmm, dry and chewy!) Truth is, fish is adequately cooked when it is just opaque throughout. You'll still need a knife to test it (a knife is less destructive than a fork), but now you're trying to save the fish, not shred it. Carefully slide a sharp paring knife between the layers of the fish meat, then turn it slightly to get a good look inside. (Remember, you don't need to make a gaping hole.) If the meat still looks translucent in the middle, give it another minute or two.

That's the foolproof way to test for doneness. But if you don't want to mar the fish with a knife, there is a more advanced way. It takes some practice, but once you master this method, you'll impress friends and family with your ability to angle the fish off the grill at just the right time: Fish firms up much like meat does as it cooks. Next time you grill your favorite fish, use the knife test above to test for doneness. Once it's done, press on it with your finger and make a mental note of how firm it is. That's the firmness you want to achieve next time. After grilling the same cut a few times, you'll know when to pull it off the grill without having to peek first. But still use a timer as a guardrail—no one will be the wiser.

Opacity is also the rule for properly cooked shellfish, such as shrimp. As soon as they're opaque throughout, they're done. Just cut one open to test (a good excuse to throw on a couple of extras just for the chef!).

ALWAYS USE OIL: Of course, you don't want to leave any fish stuck to the grill where it won't do anybody any good, so oil the fish just before you grill it. We're not talking about a major bath here, but a good coating of oil spray or a hearty stroke of the basting brush will do the trick. If you've used a marinade with oil in it, you may not need to add more oil. But the thinner the cut, the better it is to play it safe with an extra spray. We've included specific instructions in each recipe. Also, if your grill is new or you've recently done a major cleaning of the grates, your grill won't be fully seasoned, so reach for the oil. (Remember, oil the food, not the grill.)

FORGET THE FOIL: Now, Mom might have taught you to wrap your fish in foil before grilling, but we're here to tell you that you can save the shiny stuff for more important things (such as wrapping up grilled leftovers). In most cases, a coating of oil will do the trick—remember, the whole point of grilling is to get the benefit of exposure to the flame. We know even the thickest fillets taper off at the edges, but if you notice a big discrepancy, just fold the thin ends over so the fillet will cook evenly.

Of course, every rule has its exception. In this case, it's very thin fillets such as sole. You can cook sole or dory or flounder on the grill, but you will need to use foil packets. We make up for it, though, with a nice simmering sauce. See page 309 for a sample recipe suitable for thin white fish fillets.

THE SKINNY ON
SKINNING A FILLET

It's easy to skin the entire side of a fish or fillet for grilling. The critical tool here is a very sharp knife: the sharper the knife, the easier the work. Make sure the blade is longer than the fillet is wide. It's also important to keep the flat side of the knife blade slightly angled toward the the cutting board. If the fish tail is still attached, the technique is a little easier because there's more to hold on to.

SLIDE THE BLADE
BETWEEN FLESH AND SKIN

Place the fillet, flesh side up, on a cutting board. Holding the tail end of the fillet with one hand, slide the blade of a sharp knife between the flesh and skin, using a steady sawing motion. Begin at the tail end and keep the fillet lying as flat as possible.

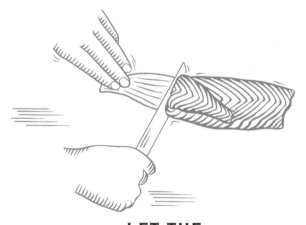

LET THE
SKIN DO THE WORK

Once the blade has detached about 2 inches of skin, take hold of the skin firmly. Now you're ready to work the secret to this technique: You are going to let the skin, not the knife, do the work. Keeping the knife blade stationary and slightly angled toward the cutting board (and as close as possible to the skin), pull the skin out from under the blade, sliding it gently from side to side to ease the cutting. The flesh will slide off parallel to the skin. (Think of a magician whisking the tablecloth out from under the dishes. Here the skin is the tablecloth and you are working the magic by keeping a firm, steady grasp of the blade.) Now, you have a beautiful skinless fillet and minimal waste. Good going!

> *"Many go fishing all their lives without knowing that it is not fish they are after."*
>
> — HENRY DAVID THOREAU

FROM FLATFISH TO SHELLFISH
GRILLING TIPS

To make you a grilling expert on some favorite sea creatures, here are a few more pointers:

Halibut: *Halibut's mild flavor offers a fine canvas for all kinds of marinades and sauces. The challenge is that halibut quickly goes from done to overdone, so pay close attention to cooking times and pull it from the grill as soon as it turns opaque in the center.*

Shrimp: *When it comes to grilling shrimp, large and jumbo sizes are the only ones to use. We're partial to jumbos in entrées because you're less likely to overcook them. Plus, they're too big to fall through the cooking grates, so you can forego the skewers.*

Shrimp is thoroughly cooked when it's opaque in the center, about the same time it turns reddish pink on both sides. Over Direct High heat, that's about 2 to 4 minutes for jumbo shrimp. Over Indirect High heat (best if there's a lot of marinade dripping down), they take 6 to 7 minutes. For breaded shrimp, we recommend Direct Medium heat to give the crumbs a good toasting—which will take 4 to 6 minutes. Again, slice one in half to test (especially important when bread crumbs make it hard to see if the color has changed).

Mussels, clams, oysters, scallops: *On the grill, fresh bivalves gently pop open when they're done. Be sure to discard any that don't—they can be harmful. Also, remember to "debeard" mussels before grilling, i.e. remove the silky filaments they use to attach themselves to hard surfaces. Scrub them with a stiff-bristled brush under cold running water.*

ROCKFISH
WITH ROASTED RED PEPPER AND GARLIC SAUCE

On the West Coast there are about 60 members of the rockfish variety. Some are called rock cod and Pacific red snapper, though they are neither cods nor snappers. The one we recommend here has a reddish tone and firm flesh. The garlicky condiment adds the right touch. Just don't overdo it with the Tabasco—it's there to accent, not take over. Note: The pepper for the sauce is grilled over Direct Medium heat and the rockfish over Direct High heat. (Suitable substitutes: halibut, sea bass.)

DIRECT/MEDIUM

FOR THE SAUCE:

- 1 RED BELL PEPPER
- ¼ CUP MAYONNAISE
- 1 TEASPOON MINCED GARLIC
- 1 TEASPOON HERBES DE PROVENCE
- 1 TEASPOON RICE VINEGAR
- 1 TO 2 SHAKES TABASCO SAUCE

- 4 ROCKFISH (ROCK COD) FILLETS, ABOUT 6 OUNCES EACH AND ½ INCH THICK
  EXTRA-VIRGIN OLIVE OIL
- 2 TABLESPOONS FINELY CHOPPED FRESH DILL
  KOSHER SALT
  FRESHLY GROUND BLACK PEPPER

To make the sauce: Grill the pepper over *Direct Medium* heat until the skin is black and blistered on all sides, 10 to 12 minutes, turning every 3 to 5 minutes. Remove the pepper from the grill and place in a paper bag; close tightly. Let stand for 10 to 15 minutes to steam off the skin. Peel away the charred skin. Cut off the top, remove the seeds, and coarsely chop. Place in a food processor and add the rest of the sauce ingredients. Process until smooth. Transfer to a bowl, cover with plastic wrap, and refrigerate until ready to serve.

Generously brush or spray the fish fillets with olive oil. Season with the dill, salt, and pepper. Grill over *Direct High* heat until the fish is opaque throughout, 2 to 3 minutes, turning once halfway through grilling time. Remove from the grill and serve warm with the sauce.

MAKES 4 SERVINGS

TERIYAKI MAHI MAHI
WITH MANGO SALSA

Mahi mahi (the fish so good they named it twice!) is great on the grill because it's firm and moist with a low-fat flesh that has an endearing sweetness. This simple marinade turns to a nice glaze as it cooks—just oil the fillets well before grilling so the glaze doesn't stick to the grate. If you like a hotter salsa, add more jalapeño. (Suitable substitute: sea bass.)

DIRECT/HIGH

FOR THE SALSA:

- 1 LARGE RIPE MANGO
- ¼ CUP FINELY CHOPPED RED ONION
- 1 TABLESPOON VEGETABLE OIL
- 1 TABLESPOON FRESH LIME JUICE
- 1 TABLESPOON FINELY CHOPPED FRESH MINT
- 1 TEASPOON MINCED JALAPEÑO PEPPER, WITH SEEDS
- ¼ TEASPOON KOSHER SALT

FOR THE MARINADE:

- ¼ CUP SOY SAUCE
- ¼ CUP SWEET SAKE
- 1 TABLESPOON VEGETABLE OIL
- 1 TABLESPOON LIGHT BROWN SUGAR
- 1 TEASPOON GRATED FRESH GINGER
- 1 TEASPOON MINCED GARLIC

- 4 MAHI MAHI FILLETS, ABOUT 6 OUNCES EACH AND 1 INCH THICK
  VEGETABLE OIL

To make salsa: Peel the mango and cut into 1/4-inch dice. Place in a small bowl along with the remaining salsa ingredients. Stir to blend. Cover with plastic wrap and refrigerate until ready to serve.

To make the marinade: In a small bowl whisk together the marinade ingredients.

Place the mahi mahi fillets in a large, resealable plastic bag and pour in the marinade. Press the air out of the bag and seal tightly. Turn the bag to distribute the marinade, place in a bowl, and refrigerate for 20 to 30 minutes.

Remove the fillets from the bag and discard the marinade. Brush or spray both sides of the fillets with vegetable oil. Grill over *Direct High* heat until the fish is opaque throughout, 8 to 10 minutes, turning once halfway through grilling time. Remove from the grill and serve warm with the salsa.

MAKES 4 SERVINGS

Teriyaki Mahi Mahi with Mango Salsa

SALMON ON THE GRILL
TIMING IS EVERYTHING

The sight of beautiful, silvery fresh salmon is enough to bring out the grizzly bear in any fish eater. And salmon is a year-round grilling favorite for two simple reasons: Its firm texture holds up well on the grill, and the higher fat content keeps the flesh moist and flavorful over the flame. The only tricky part is knowing when to turn it. And here's the answer to that mystery:

Make sure the fillet is well oiled and place the fillet flesh side down first. As soon as you lay it on the cooking grate, it will begin to cling, and it will cling tighter and tighter until it has cooked enough to conveniently release its grip entirely. This is the time to turn it. Now, lots of cookbooks will tell you to grill 1-inch-thick salmon fillets for about 5 minutes on each side. Well, 5 minutes is usually not enough time for the salmon to surrender its hold. If you extend the grilling time when the flesh side is on the grate to 7 or 8 minutes, the fillet will come off the hot grill easily.

To pinpoint the ideal turning time, check the salmon after about 7 minutes by very lightly gripping the fillet with metal tongs. Turn your wrist gently to lift one edge off the grate. If it is sticking, wait a minute and try again. If it pulls away easily, slip a spatula underneath and make the turn. You can then finish cooking the salmon with the second (skin) side on the grate for a mere 2 or 3 minutes. Then simply slide a spatula between the flesh and skin, leave the skin on the cooking grate, and deliver your masterpiece.

Besides avoiding the hassle of stuck fish, this method, which is sometimes called "the 70/30 rule," produces deep mahogany grill marks on the flesh side, a nice presentation on the plate (no unsightly skins left there after dinner), and a proud chef. Enjoy!

WHOLE STUFFED SALMON

Slide the stuffed, oiled salmon onto your grill set up for Indirect cooking and it will roast magnificently—no turning, no burning. When it's done, use two long spatulas to carefully lift it from the grill, then have a trusty assistant slide a platter underneath.

INDIRECT/MEDIUM

FOR THE STUFFING:

3 SLICES BACON, CUT INTO 1/2-INCH DICE
1 1/2 CUPS FINELY CHOPPED YELLOW ONION
1 TABLESPOON MINCED GARLIC
2 TABLESPOONS FINELY CHOPPED FRESH ITALIAN PARSLEY
1 TABLESPOON FINELY CHOPPED FRESH SAGE
1 TEASPOON DRIED OREGANO
1/2 TEASPOON FENNEL SEEDS
1/4 TEASPOON KOSHER SALT
1/4 TEASPOON FRESHLY GROUND BLACK PEPPER

1 WHOLE SALMON, 4 TO 5 POUNDS, SCALED, BUTTERFLIED, AND BONED (INCLUDING PIN BONES)
1/2 TEASPOON KOSHER SALT
1/4 TEASPOON FRESHLY GROUND BLACK PEPPER
EXTRA-VIRGIN OLIVE OIL

LEMON WEDGES

To make the stuffing: In a sauté pan over medium heat, fry the bacon for 6 minutes, stirring occasionally. Add the onion and garlic and cook, stirring occasionally, until the onion begins to brown, about 10 minutes. Add the rest of the stuffing ingredients. Stir. Set aside to cool to room temperature.

Lay the salmon, skin side down, on an oiled work surface. Season with salt and pepper. Spread the stuffing on one side of the salmon and fold the other side over on top. Tie the salmon closed with cotton string and brush the exterior with olive oil. Cover the tail with foil.

Grill the salmon over Indirect Medium heat until the flesh is opaque throughout and the internal temperature reaches 135°F, 40 to 50 minutes. Remove from the grill, take off the string, and carefully peel away the skin. Allow to stand for 5 to 10 minutes before cutting crosswise into slices. Serve warm with the lemon wedges.

MAKES 8 TO 10 SERVINGS

GRILLED SALMON
WITH SUMMER SALAD

Check out the advice on how to grill salmon (see sidebar, page 294) and give it a go. Topped with this zesty salad, it makes a perfect meal for dining al fresco.

DIRECT/MEDIUM

FOR THE SALAD:

- 1 TABLESPOON MINCED SHALLOTS
- 2 TEASPOONS SHERRY VINEGAR
- 1/2 TEASPOON DIJON MUSTARD
- 1/2 TEASPOON KOSHER SALT
- 1/4 TEASPOON FRESHLY GROUND BLACK PEPPER
- 2 TABLESPOONS EXTRA-VIRGIN OLIVE OIL
- 2 EARS SWEET CORN, HUSKED
- 1/2 CUP QUARTERED CHERRY TOMATOES
- 1/4 CUP FINELY CHOPPED FRESH BASIL

- 4 SALMON FILLETS (WITH SKIN), 6 TO 8 OUNCES EACH AND ABOUT 1 INCH THICK
  KOSHER SALT
  FRESHLY GROUND BLACK PEPPER
  EXTRA-VIRGIN OLIVE OIL

To make the salad: In a medium bowl whisk together the shallots, vinegar, mustard, salt, and pepper. Slowly whisk in the olive oil to make a smooth vinaigrette.

Place the corn in a large pot of boiling salted water. Turn off the heat, cover, and allow to cook until barely tender, 4 to 5 minutes. Remove the corn from the water. When cooled, cut the kernels off the cobs and add to the vinaigrette along with the tomatoes and basil. Stir and set aside.

Season the flesh side of the salmon fillets with salt and pepper. Generously brush or spray with olive oil. Grill, flesh side down, over *Direct Medium* heat until you can lift the fillets with tongs without them sticking to the grate, 7 to 8 minutes. Turn, skin side down, and finish cooking for 2 to 3 minutes more. Slide a spatula between the skin and flesh and transfer the fillets to serving plates. Spoon the salad over the fillets and serve immediately.

MAKES 4 SERVINGS

OAK-GRILLED SALMON

This salmon gets marinated just long enough to incorporate the flavor of the dill and then it's grilled over oak chips for a light smokehouse fragrance (make sure the smoke is really going good before you place the fillet on the grill). The flavors are so rich, you really don't need a sauce—but if you can't resist, we suggest a good mustard.

INDIRECT/MEDIUM

FOR THE RUB:

- 1/2 CUP FINELY CHOPPED FRESH DILL
- 1/3 CUP FINELY CHOPPED SHALLOTS
- 1/4 CUP GRANULATED SUGAR
- 2 TABLESPOONS KOSHER SALT
- 1 TABLESPOON CRACKED WHITE PEPPERCORNS

- 6 SALMON FILLETS (WITH SKIN), ABOUT 6 OUNCES EACH AND 1 INCH THICK
  VEGETABLE OIL

  OAK CHIPS SOAKED IN WATER FOR AT LEAST 30 MINUTES

To make the rub: In a small bowl combine the rub ingredients.

Coat the salmon fillets thoroughly with the rub. Cover with plastic wrap and refrigerate for 8 to 12 hours.

Remove the fillets from the refrigerator and scrape off any excess rub. Blot the fillets with paper towels and brush generously with vegetable oil.

Follow the grill's instructions for using wood chips. Grill the salmon, skin side down, over *Indirect Medium* heat for 10 to 12 minutes without turning. Slide a spatula between the skin and flesh and transfer the fillets to serving plates. Serve warm.

MAKES 6 SERVINGS

A BOUT WITH A TROUT

For whatever reason, many folks who are otherwise dedicated grillers shy away from grilling fish and seafood. We suspect it's the delicate nature of water-born critters that intimidates them. But even the most hesitant fin flipper can quickly gain the expertise needed to slap any size fish or crustacean on the grill with confidence. How do we know? Well, consider this story from our friend Mike, born and raised in Kansas City, where beef steaks and barbecue reign supreme and the bounty of coastal waters couldn't be any farther away, geographically or otherwise.

I grew up in a big Catholic family, and when I was a kid, fish on Fridays was obligatory. My mother was an okay cook, but she didn't have a clue about preparing seafood. Now, if your whole experience with seafood consists of oily, overcooked fish sticks and sandpaper-dry tuna casseroles, you're probably not going to be real gung-ho about preparing fish on your own. But sometimes you end up learning things through "trial by fire," as they say.

In the 1970s I moved to Chicago as a young, ambitious salesman for Weber. To get hardware stores to carry Weber grills, we sales guys would invite the owners to a humdinger of a grilling demonstration/cocktail party after trade shows. One year, I remember, we were at the Twin Cities trade show. We had reserved "The Top of the MAC" (the rooftop dining room of the Minneapolis Athletic Club) for the party. It promised to be quite a draw because, from the lofty eighth story, revelers would be able to enjoy a sparkling cityscape while sipping cocktails and eating grilled delicacies, all at Weber's expense.

On the last day of the trade show, my boss, Art, took off to "check out the competition" (or as we say in plain English, "play golf"). Just after he left, the president of a major hardware distributorship came by our booth. In the exchange of small talk, he boasted of the 16-pound trout he'd just caught on Lake Superior. Having once seen Art demonstrate how to grill lake trout, he asked if we would grill and serve the fish at our party that evening. Although I couldn't recall having ever seen a lake trout up close and personal, I immediately volunteered (and hoped that Art would be back in time to grill it).

That afternoon as we prepared for the party, the president's son dropped off the trophy trout (I smiled hugely to hide my nervousness). Art was still checking out the competition and I had to get grilling. I unwrapped the fish. It had been cleaned, thank God, but it was clearly much too long to fit on any of our grills. Terror struck.

Fortunately, one of the chefs at the MAC had prepared lake trout before. He offered a recipe for stuffing the darn thing, but wisely withdrew from helping me possibly ruin it on my grill. I wished for the same wisdom sometime in the future.

With the clock ticking, I jumped into the deep end. I cut off the tail and the head, leaving the meaty center of the fish in one piece. I prepared two grills for Indirect cooking and placed the head and tail on one, the stuffed center on the other. My plan was to reassemble the fish parts on a large platter and add garnishes to hide the wounds.

About an hour into grilling, I actually started to relax as the aroma from the stuffing made my mouth water. But then I discovered a new problem. The head and tail were cooking much faster than the center. They would be grilled to a crisp before the meatier center was done! I wrapped the head and tail in aluminum foil to keep them from burning, closed the grill's top and bottom dampers, and crossed my fingers.

An hour later the chef came out to witness what he was sure would be a disaster. He found my colleagues chatting up the early arrivals, but I had ducked into the alley to avoid a very public embarrassment.

But the grilling gods were kind to me that day. The fish center had cooked faster than expected and the head and tail were cooked to the same degree. Once the chef and I performed the final touches of cosmetic surgery, covering the cuts with sautéed lemon slices and lots of parsley, the fish parts actually looked like they all came from the same species.

Just as we finished, Art arrived, placed the chef's toque on his own head, grabbed a spatula, and marched out for the presentation. I followed with the president's trout beautifully displayed on the platter. The president beamed with pride and thanked Art for cooking it to perfection. Raising his glass in a toast, Art proclaimed he couldn't have done it without the help of his Weber grill. I bit my tongue, the chef winked knowingly at me, and the president announced that he had never tasted a better lake trout.

And that's how I overcame my fear of grilling fish. With the recipes in this chapter, you'll surely have a much gentler learning curve. But if you're ever so inclined, here's my recipe for how to handle the big one that didn't get away.

HOW TO GRILL
A MONSTER FISH

INDIRECT/MEDIUM

1 WHOLE FISH, ABOUT 15 POUNDS, SCALED, GUTTED, AND CLEANED

FOR THE STUFFING:

2 TO 5 CUPS CHOPPED FRESH BASIL

10 TO 12 GARLIC CLOVES, SLIVERED

VEGETABLE OIL

12 TO 15 THIN LEMON SLICES

2 CUPS ALMOND SLIVERS

2 STICKS UNSALTED BUTTER

2 BUNCHES FRESH ITALIAN PARSLEY

Set up one or two grills for *Indirect* cooking.

To make the stuffing: In a large bowl thoroughly mix the stuffing ingredients.

If the fish is too long to fit flat across the surface of your cooking grate, carefully cut off the head just below the gills and the tail and set aside. Brush or spray a large tray with a generous coating of vegetable oil and gently place the fish on its side on the tray. Scoop the stuffing into the cavity, gently patting it down until it all fits inside. Wrap cotton string around the fish at even intervals and tie shut. Generously spray the top of the fish with oil.

Carefully place the fish on the cooking grate and grill over *Indirect Medium* heat for 12 to 15 minutes per inch of thickness at the thickest part of the fish. If the head and tail are detached, grill them over *Indirect Medium* heat until just cooked through, then wrap in aluminum foil and keep warm; if still attached, wrap in foil as soon as almost cooked through.

When the center portion is opaque but the flesh is still moist and just beginning to flake, carefully remove the fish from the grill using two long spatulas. You'll need an assistant to slide the platter under the fish once you raise it off the cooking grate. Reassemble the fish if you removed the head and tail. Garnish with the lemon slices and almond slivers sautéed in butter, and fresh parsley sprigs. Serve warm.

Note: Unless your job depends on it, don't let anyone else take credit for your work!

MAKES 1 SERVING PER POUND

SIMPLE
SALMON

In a rush? Relax. This flavor kick is a lifesaver on hectic weekdays—but don't be surprised if you find yourself serving it up to friends on the weekend, too.

INDIRECT/HIGH

FOR THE MARINADE:

- 1/4 CUP EXTRA-VIRGIN OLIVE OIL
- 1/4 CUP SOY SAUCE
- 1/4 CUP DIJON MUSTARD
- 3 TABLESPOONS PREPARED HORSERADISH
- 2 TABLESPOONS LIGHT BROWN SUGAR
- 1 TEASPOON RICE VINEGAR

- 6 SALMON FILLETS (WITH SKIN), ABOUT 6 OUNCES EACH AND 1 INCH THICK

To make the marinade: In a medium bowl whisk the marinade ingredients until smooth.

Place the salmon fillets in a large, resealable plastic bag and pour in all but 1/3 cup of the marinade. Press the air out of the bag and seal tightly. Turn the bag to distribute the marinade, place in a bowl, and refrigerate for 15 to 30 minutes.

Remove the fillets from the bag and discard the marinade. Grill the fillets, skin side down, over *Indirect High* heat until opaque throughout, 10 to 12 minutes. During the last 2 minutes of grilling time, brush the fillets with the 1/3 cup reserved marinade. Slide a spatula between the skin and flesh and transfer the fillets to serving plates. Serve warm.

MAKES 6 SERVINGS

Give a man a fish and you feed him for a day. Teach a man to fish and you feed him for life. Teach him how to grill that fish and you give him reason to live!

TEQUILA
SALMON

In this rousing dish, bright citrus and classic seasonings do a hat dance with tequila around firm marinated salmon.

DIRECT/MEDIUM

FOR THE MARINADE:

- 1/3 CUP FRESH ORANGE JUICE
- 3 TABLESPOONS EXTRA-VIRGIN OLIVE OIL
- 3 TABLESPOONS TEQUILA
- 1 TABLESPOON CHOPPED FRESH CILANTRO
- 1 TABLESPOON MINCED JALAPEÑO PEPPER, WITH SEEDS
- 1 TEASPOON GRANULATED GARLIC
- 1 TEASPOON KOSHER SALT
- 1 TEASPOON GROUND CUMIN

- 4 SALMON FILLETS (WITH SKIN), ABOUT 6 OUNCES EACH AND 1 INCH THICK

FOR THE DRESSING:

- 3 TABLESPOONS EXTRA-VIRGIN OLIVE OIL
- 1 TABLESPOON FRESH LIME JUICE
- 1/2 TEASPOON CHILI POWDER
- 1/2 TEASPOON KOSHER SALT
- 1/4 TEASPOON FRESHLY GROUND BLACK PEPPER

- 4 HANDFULS MIXED SALAD GREENS (3 TO 4 OUNCES)
- 1 CUP CHERRY TOMATOES, HALVED
- 1/2 CUP FRESH CILANTRO LEAVES, DIVIDED

To make the marinade: In a small bowl whisk together the marinade ingredients.

Place the salmon fillets in a large, resealable plastic bag and pour in the marinade. Press the air out of the bag and seal tightly. Turn the bag to distribute the marinade, place in a bowl, and refrigerate for 30 to 45 minutes.

To make the dressing: In a large bowl whisk together the dressing ingredients. Set aside until ready to serve.

Remove the fillets from the bag and discard the marinade. Grill the salmon, flesh side down, over *Direct Medium* heat until you can lift the fillets with tongs without them sticking to the grate, 7 to 8 minutes. Turn, skin side down, and finish cooking for 2 to 3 minutes more. Slide a spatula between the skin and flesh and transfer the fillets to serving plates.

Toss the salad greens, tomatoes, and half of the cilantro in the dressing. Divide the greens among the serving plates, garnish the fillets with the remaining cilantro, and serve.

MAKES 4 SERVINGS

Tequila Salmon

ADVANCED TECHNIQUE
MAKING SALMON ROLL-UPS

The technique for forming a disk from a salmon steak may seem a bit tricky, but you'll quickly master it. Here's how:

TRIM THE ENDS

Trim about 1½ inches from the two narrow ends of the salmon steak. Then trim about 1 inch of skin from the tip of one end of the steak.

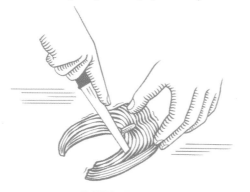

CUT AWAY THE BACKBONE

Run a sharp knife along both sides of the steak's backbone. Be careful not to cut through the skin at the wide end. Continue to cut along the ribs on the inside edge of the narrow ends, removing the whitish flesh and any bones. Carefully cut away and discard the large backbone and the ribs.

ROLL THE STEAK INTO A DISK

Fold the narrow end without skin in toward the center of the steak. Then fold the other end over so it overlaps a bit. Secure the steak with toothpicks or cotton string.

PESTO SALMON ROLL-UPS

Hot off the grill and gleaming with a final brush of pesto, these salmon disks practically beg to be eaten.

INDIRECT/HIGH

FOR THE PESTO:

1 CUP LOOSELY PACKED FRESH BASIL

1 SMALL GARLIC CLOVE, CRUSHED

1 TABLESPOON PINE NUTS

⅛ TEASPOON KOSHER SALT

¼ TEASPOON FRESHLY GROUND BLACK PEPPER

¼ CUP EXTRA-VIRGIN OLIVE OIL

¼ CUP FRESHLY GRATED PARMIGIANO-REGGIANO CHEESE

4 BONE-IN SALMON STEAKS, 8 TO 10 OUNCES EACH AND ABOUT 1 INCH THICK

To make the pesto: Place the basil leaves, garlic, pine nuts, salt, and pepper on a cutting board and chop very finely, or put the ingredients in a mortar and grind with a pestle. Transfer to a bowl and stir in the olive oil. Add the cheese and blend. Divide the pesto in half and place in separate bowls.

Make the salmon disks *(see sidebar, left)*. Brush both sides of the disks with one half of the pesto. Reserve the rest to use as a sauce. Grill the disks over *Indirect High* heat until the flesh is firm to the touch, 10 to 12 minutes. Transfer to a cutting board. Carefully remove the toothpicks or cotton string from each disk, then remove the skin. Serve warm with the reserved pesto.

MAKES 4 SERVINGS

SALMON-ASPARAGUS PENNE

The luscious cream sauce is a nice backdrop, but the real stars are the grilled salmon and asparagus pieces. If they weren't sporting those grill marks and that marvelous fire-induced texture, this would be just another pasta dish. We assure you it isn't.

DIRECT/MEDIUM

FOR THE SAUCE:

2 TABLESPOONS UNSALTED BUTTER
2 TABLESPOONS MINCED SHALLOTS
1/2 CUP DRY WHITE WINE
3/4 CUP LOW-SODIUM CHICKEN BROTH
3/4 CUP HEAVY CREAM
1/4 TEASPOON KOSHER SALT
1/4 TEASPOON FRESHLY GROUND BLACK PEPPER
1 TABLESPOON DIJON MUSTARD
1 TABLESPOON FINELY CHOPPED FRESH CHIVES
1 TABLESPOON FINELY CHOPPED FRESH TARRAGON

1/2 POUND PENNE PASTA

3 SALMON FILLETS (WITH SKIN), ABOUT 6 OUNCES EACH AND 1 INCH THICK
1 POUND ASPARAGUS SPEARS, TOUGH ENDS REMOVED
EXTRA-VIRGIN OLIVE OIL
KOSHER SALT
FRESHLY GROUND BLACK PEPPER
1 TABLESPOON FRESH LEMON JUICE

To make the sauce: In a medium sauté pan over medium-high heat, melt the butter and cook the shallots for about 2 minutes (do not brown), stirring occasionally. Add the wine and simmer until all but 3 to 4 tablespoons have evaporated, about 5 minutes. Add the chicken broth, cream, salt, and pepper. Whisk and simmer until about 1 cup of liquid remains and the sauce coats the back of a spoon, 15 to 20 minutes. Add the mustard, chives, and tarragon. Whisk and set aside.

Cook the penne in a large pot of boiling salted water until al dente. Strain and set aside in a large bowl. Reheat the sauce (if necessary) but do not boil it. Pour the sauce over the pasta and toss. Cover and set aside.

Lightly brush or spray the salmon fillets and asparagus with olive oil. Season with salt and pepper. Grill the salmon, flesh side down, over *Direct Medium* heat until you can lift the fillets with tongs without them sticking to the grate, 7 to 8 minutes. Turn, skin side down, and finish cooking for 2 to 3 minutes more. Slide a spatula between the skin and flesh and transfer the fillets to a cutting board. Cut into bite-sized pieces. Grill the asparagus over *Direct Medium* heat until tender, 6 to 8 min-utes, turning occasionally. Transfer to a cutting board and cut into 1-inch pieces. Add the salmon and asparagus to the cooked pasta, add the lemon juice, and season with salt and pepper. Stir gently. Serve warm.

MAKES 4 SERVINGS

SEA BASS
WITH INDIAN SPICES

Now here's a fish everyone can love. Succulent sea bass really takes to the grill, retaining its moisture and flavor while cooking to an appealing texture. And the marinade's spice blend offers great flavor with little effort. Put this recipe on your list of weekday slam-dunks. (Suitable substitutes: red snapper, striped bass.)

DIRECT/HIGH

FOR THE MARINADE:

2 TABLESPOONS EXTRA-VIRGIN OLIVE OIL
2 TEASPOONS FRESH LEMON JUICE
1 TEASPOON GRATED FRESH GINGER
1/2 TEASPOON MINCED GARLIC
1/2 TEASPOON TURMERIC
1/2 TEASPOON CHILI POWDER
1/2 TEASPOON GROUND CUMIN
1/2 TEASPOON KOSHER SALT
1/4 TEASPOON FRESHLY GROUND BLACK PEPPER
1/4 TEASPOON CAYENNE

4 SKINLESS CHILEAN SEA BASS FILLETS, ABOUT 6 OUNCES EACH AND 1 INCH THICK
EXTRA-VIRGIN OLIVE OIL
CILANTRO SPRIGS (OPTIONAL)
LIME WEDGES (OPTIONAL)

To make the marinade: In a small bowl whisk together the marinade ingredients.

Brush the bass fillets all over with the marinade. Cover with plastic wrap and refrigerate for 30 minutes to 1 hour.

Remove the fillets from the marinade. Lightly brush or spray with olive oil. Grill over *Direct High* heat until the flesh is opaque throughout, 5 to 7 minutes, turning once halfway through grilling time. Remove from the grill and serve warm, garnished with cilantro sprigs and lime wedges, with jasmine rice, if desired.

MAKES 4 SERVINGS

Mediterranean Sea Bass

MEDITERRANEAN SEA BASS

*This recipe is all about Provence, and these are the ingre-
dients that make the region's food sing. Keep it simple and
enjoy. (Suitable substitutes: red snapper, striped bass.)*

DIRECT/HIGH

FOR THE PASTE:

3 TABLESPOONS EXTRA-VIRGIN OLIVE OIL
1 TABLESPOON FINELY CHOPPED FRESH BASIL
1 TABLESPOON FINELY CHOPPED FRESH THYME
2 TEASPOONS DRIED LAVENDER
1 TEASPOON MINCED GARLIC
1/2 TEASPOON KOSHER SALT
1/4 TEASPOON FRESHLY GROUND BLACK PEPPER

4 SKINLESS CHILEAN SEA BASS FILLETS,
   ABOUT 6 OUNCES EACH AND 1 INCH THICK
   LEMON WEDGES (OPTIONAL)

To make the paste: In a small bowl whisk together the paste
ingredients.

Spread the paste evenly on both sides of the fish fillets.
Grill over *Direct High* heat until the flesh is opaque throughout
and starting to flake, 5 to 7 minutes, turning once halfway
through grilling time. Serve warm and garnish with lemon
wedges, if desired.

MAKES 4 SERVINGS

*"The two best times
to fish are when
it's rainin' and
when it ain't."*

— PATRICK F. MCMANUS

CURRIED SEA BASS
WITH TROPICAL FRUIT SALSA

*Sea bass seems made for the grill. It has a firm texture and
a mild taste, and it slides off the grate effortlessly. The
flesh divides into silky layers when it's done, all buttery
and moist. Add a little seasoning and you're in business.
(Suitable substitutes: red snapper, striped bass.)*

DIRECT/HIGH

FOR THE SALSA:

1 CUP DICED PINEAPPLE
1/2 CUP DICED MANGO
1/2 CUP DICED PAPAYA
1/3 CUP DICED RED ONION
2 TABLESPOONS FRESH LIME JUICE
2 TO 3 TEASPOONS MINCED JALAPEÑO PEPPER,
   WITH SEEDS
1/2 TEASPOON GRATED FRESH GINGER
1/4 TEASPOON KOSHER SALT
1/4 TEASPOON FRESHLY GROUND BLACK PEPPER

4 SKINLESS CHILEAN SEA BASS FILLETS,
   ABOUT 6 OUNCES EACH AND 1 INCH THICK
   VEGETABLE OIL
1 TEASPOON CURRY POWDER
   KOSHER SALT
   FRESHLY GROUND BLACK PEPPER

To make the salsa: In a large glass or stainless steel mixing
bowl combine the salsa ingredients. Mix well and allow to
stand at room temperature until ready to serve.

Brush or spray both sides of the fillets with vegetable oil.
Sprinkle the curry powder evenly over the fish and season
with salt and pepper. Grill over *Direct High* heat until the fish
is opaque and starting to flake, 5 to 7 minutes, turning once
halfway through grilling time. Serve warm with the salsa.

MAKES 4 SERVINGS

THE EXCEPTION
TO THE CARDINAL RULE
SEARED AHI

We think there should be a badge for outdoor chefs who master ahi on the grill, but the final product is really the best reward. Ahi (also called yellowfin) is a firm, dark red tuna that makes wonderful steaks for grilling because it's rich with oils. But ahi's delicate flavor—and rich texture—quickly deteriorate when overcooked. So the secret to great ahi is to merely sear the outside and leave the middle raw.

Only buy the best: That's why it's imperative that you use sushi-quality ahi, the highest grade. It's so fresh and so carefully handled that you can eat it raw. To protect that freshness, make the fish counter your last stop at the store, double check that it's sushi-grade ahi, and take the steaks straight home to the refrigerator. Remove the ahi steaks from the store wrappings and seal them in a plastic bag. Place the bag in a colander full of ice set in a large bowl and refrigerate (the colander ensures the melting ice drains away from the fish). If you're using frozen ahi steaks, thaw them in the refrigerator. Eat the thawed steaks within 24 hours.

How to grill perfect ahi: This is the ONLY exception to the Weber mantra "Keep a lid on it!" Ahi that's been cooked through becomes dry and flaky, so use Direct High heat and leave the lid open. Closing the lid creates a roasting effect that will cook the center too quickly. Sear ahi for a couple of minutes on each side and the outside will be beige and the inside will be red. It will slice like butter and taste even better.

Note: Remember, only the highest quality ahi should be used (eating raw or rare fish carries certain risks) and pregnant women shouldn't eat raw or rare fish at all.

HONEY-SOY AHI
WITH CRISP CUCUMBER SALAD

Grilling the perfect ahi is a high art (see sidebar, left). The grill must be super-hot when you start because you're just going to sear the steaks. In this recipe, the delicate flavor of the fish is drawn out by the sweet-salty marinade and the crisp, cool salad makes the perfect contrast. For the full experience, serve with pickled ginger and plenty of wasabi.

DIRECT/HIGH

FOR THE MARINADE:

- 1/4 CUP SOY SAUCE
- 2 TABLESPOONS HONEY
- 1 TABLESPOON ASIAN SESAME OIL
- 1 TABLESPOON GRATED FRESH GINGER
- 1/2 TEASPOON FRESHLY GROUND BLACK PEPPER

- 4 SUSHI-QUALITY AHI TUNA STEAKS, ABOUT 6 OUNCES EACH AND 1 1/2 INCHES THICK

FOR THE SALAD:

- 1/2 CUP RICE VINEGAR
- 1 TEASPOON GRANULATED SUGAR
- 1/2 TEASPOON KOSHER SALT
- 1 SEEDLESS CUCUMBER (ABOUT 1 POUND), PEELED AND THINLY SLICED
- 1 SMALL RED ONION, THINLY SLICED
- 1 TABLESPOON FINELY CHOPPED FRESH MINT

To make the marinade: In a small bowl whisk together the marinade ingredients.

Place the tuna steaks in a large, resealable plastic bag and add the marinade. Press the air out of the bag and seal tightly. Turn the bag to distribute the marinade, place in a bowl, and refrigerate for about 30 minutes.

Meanwhile, make the salad: In a medium bowl whisk together the vinegar, sugar, and salt until the sugar and salt are dissolved. Add the remaining salad ingredients. Toss, cover with plastic wrap, and refrigerate until ready to serve.

To make the ahi: Remove the steaks from the bag and discard the marinade. Grill the steaks over Direct High heat (with the grill lid open) just until the surface is well marked and the center is still red, 3 to 4 minutes, turning once halfway through grilling time. Remove from the grill.

Drain the excess liquid from the cucumber salad and serve with the tuna.

MAKES 4 SERVINGS

SEARED AHI
WITH THAI DIPPING SAUCE

Here we use toasted sesame seeds and white peppercorns to make a pungent crust for the extremely fresh tuna. Grill just until the outside is seared and the inside is still red. The dipping sauce delivers the final note. Take a bow.

DIRECT/HIGH

FOR THE DIPPING SAUCE:

1/3 CUP FRESH LIME JUICE

3 TABLESPOONS SOY SAUCE

1 TABLESPOON FISH SAUCE

2 TEASPOONS GRANULATED SUGAR

1 TEASPOON MINCED JALAPEÑO PEPPER, WITH SEEDS

FOR THE RUB:

1 TABLESPOON CRACKED WHITE PEPPERCORNS

1 TABLESPOON SESAME SEEDS

1 TEASPOON KOSHER SALT

4 SUSHI-QUALITY AHI TUNA STEAKS, ABOUT 6 OUNCES EACH AND 1 1/2 INCHES THICK
VEGETABLE OIL

To make the dipping sauce: In a small bowl whisk together the sauce ingredients. Divide the sauce into four small, individual serving bowls.

To make the rub: In a sauté pan over medium heat, combine the white peppercorns, sesame seeds, and salt. Cook, stirring occasionally, until the sesame seeds are lightly toasted, about 5 minutes.

Lightly brush both sides of the tuna steaks with vegetable oil. Sprinkle on the rub, gently pressing the spices into the flesh.

Grill the steaks over *Direct High* heat (with the grill lid open) just until the surface is well marked and the center is still red, 3 to 4 minutes, turning once halfway through grilling time. Remove from the grill and serve immediately with the dipping sauce.

MAKES 4 SERVINGS

THAI ALBACORE
WITH SOY-GINGER BUTTER

Albacore tuna is a smaller, paler, and leaner fish than the dark-meat ahi tuna. Chefs across the country are now discovering its amazing compatibility with the grill. Try it with this intense curry marinade and silky butter sauce, and you'll fall for it, too.

DIRECT/MEDIUM

FOR THE MARINADE:

1 TABLESPOON FISH SAUCE

1 TABLESPOON FRESH LIME JUICE

1 TABLESPOON GRANULATED SUGAR

1 TEASPOON RED THAI CURRY PASTE

1/4 TEASPOON ASIAN SESAME OIL

4 ALBACORE TUNA STEAKS, ABOUT 6 OUNCES EACH AND 1 INCH THICK
VEGETABLE OIL

FOR THE BUTTER:

4 TABLESPOONS UNSALTED BUTTER

1/2 TEASPOON GRATED FRESH GINGER

1 TEASPOON SOY SAUCE

To make the marinade: In a small bowl whisk together the marinade ingredients.

Place the tuna steaks on a plate and coat both sides with the marinade. Cover with plastic wrap and refrigerate for 15 to 30 minutes.

Lightly brush or spray both sides of the steaks with vegetable oil. Grill over *Direct Medium* heat until opaque throughout and firm to the touch, 8 to 10 minutes, turning once halfway through grilling time.

Meanwhile, make the butter: In a small sauté pan over medium-high heat, melt the butter. Add the ginger and soy sauce. Stir to blend. Cook for 20 to 30 seconds.

Remove the steaks from the grill. Serve warm with the sauce.

MAKES 4 SERVINGS

HALIBUT CASABLANCA

Stay cool and eat light with this easy recipe spiked with Moroccan spices. You can rub this marinade on any firm white fish, shrimp, or scallops—even chicken. Best of all, it's ready to go in the time it takes to heat the grill. Serve with a salad of marinated summer vegetables.

DIRECT/HIGH

FOR THE MARINADE:
- 1/2 CUP FRESH ITALIAN PARSLEY LEAVES
- 1/4 CUP FRESH MINT LEAVES
- 1/4 CUP EXTRA-VIRGIN OLIVE OIL
- 2 TABLESPOONS SHERRY VINEGAR
- 2 TEASPOONS MINCED GARLIC
- 1 TEASPOON PAPRIKA
- 1/2 TEASPOON KOSHER SALT
- 1/4 TEASPOON FRESHLY GROUND BLACK PEPPER
- 1 TO 2 DASHES TABASCO SAUCE

- 4 HALIBUT FILLETS, 7 TO 8 OUNCES EACH AND ABOUT 1 INCH THICK

To make the marinade: In a food processor combine the marinade ingredients and process until smooth.

Place the halibut fillets on a platter and pour the marinade on top. Turn to coat evenly. Cover with plastic wrap and refrigerate for 10 to 15 minutes.

Remove the fillets from the marinade. Grill over *Direct High* heat until the fish is just opaque at the center and slightly firm to the touch, 8 to 10 minutes, turning once halfway through grilling time. Remove from the grill. Serve warm.

MAKES 4 SERVINGS

LEMON HALIBUT
WITH CAPER SAUCE

Pull these steaks off the grill as soon as they become opaque—use a knife to test one. A cold glass of Sauvignon Blanc is a fitting complement. (Suitable substitutes: flounder, turbot.)

DIRECT/HIGH

FOR THE PASTE:
- 2 TABLESPOONS EXTRA-VIRGIN OLIVE OIL
- 1 TABLESPOON FINELY CHOPPED FRESH ITALIAN PARSLEY
- 1 TEASPOON GRATED LEMON ZEST
- 1/4 TEASPOON KOSHER SALT
- 1/4 TEASPOON FRESHLY GROUND BLACK PEPPER

- 4 HALIBUT FILLETS, ABOUT 6 OUNCES EACH AND 1 1/4 INCHES THICK

FOR THE SAUCE:
- 2 TABLESPOONS EXTRA-VIRGIN OLIVE OIL
- 2 TABLESPOONS FRESH LEMON JUICE
- 2 TABLESPOONS FINELY CHOPPED OIL-PACKED SUN-DRIED TOMATOES
- 2 TABLESPOONS CAPERS
- 1 TABLESPOON FINELY CHOPPED FRESH ITALIAN PARSLEY
- 1/2 TEASPOON GRANULATED SUGAR
- 1/4 TEASPOON CRUSHED RED PEPPER FLAKES
- 1/4 TEASPOON KOSHER SALT

To make the paste: In a small bowl whisk together the paste ingredients.

Rub the halibut fillets on all sides with the paste. Cover with plastic wrap and refrigerate until ready to grill.

To make the sauce: In a small bowl whisk together the sauce ingredients. Set aside at room temperature.

Grill the fillets over *Direct High* heat until the fish is just opaque at the center and slightly firm to the touch, 8 to 10 minutes, turning once halfway through grilling time. Remove from the grill and serve warm with the sauce spooned on top.

MAKES 4 SERVINGS

Lemon Halibut with Caper Sauce

LITTLE GRAINS OF WONDER
GRANULATED GARLIC

Along the barbecue circuit, there's one little spice jar that really gets around: granulated garlic. Not to be confused with its pulverized cousin, garlic powder, granulated garlic is a totally different seasoning: dried garlic bits crushed or ground into tiny granules. Garlic powder is so fine that it blends in completely with other spices and dissolves in liquids. Granulated garlic, on the other hand, retains its autonomy. Its bigger size makes it great for rubs because it sits on the outside of the meat or fish where it will hit the taste buds first. Granulated garlic is not as big as garlic flakes, which can be over-powering on more delicate cuts. That's probably why granulated garlic is a hit in sauces, too—it retains some structural integrity and makes its presence a bit more pronounced without being obnoxious.

Granulated garlic is particularly useful when raw garlic might be too harsh. That's important for fish, which cooks quickly. Raw garlic crusted on the outside of delicately flavored fish might not have enough cooking time to mellow out. And because texture is such an important part of cooked fish, granulated garlic adds a nice dimension that's hard to beat. So if your spice cupboard is lacking, get cracking. It could be the jar that takes you from okay to gourmet.

SPICE-RUBBED HALIBUT
WITH GRILLED VEGETABLE RATATOUILLE

Ratatouille is just another great way to get you to eat your vegetables, which you'll do with gusto once you taste this grilled version. (Suitable substitutes: flounder, turbot.)

DIRECT/MEDIUM

FOR THE RATATOUILLE:

1 MEDIUM YELLOW ONION

1 MEDIUM JAPANESE EGGPLANT

1 MEDIUM ZUCCHINI SQUASH

2 SMALL RIPE TOMATOES

1 LARGE RED BELL PEPPER

1 TABLESPOON EXTRA-VIRGIN OLIVE OIL, PLUS MORE FOR BRUSHING THE VEGETABLES

   KOSHER SALT

   FRESHLY GROUND BLACK PEPPER

2 TEASPOONS MINCED GARLIC

2 TABLESPOONS FINELY CHOPPED FRESH BASIL

2 TEASPOONS BALSAMIC VINEGAR

FOR THE RUB:

2 TEASPOONS FINELY CHOPPED FRESH THYME

1 TEASPOON FRESHLY GROUND BLACK PEPPER

1 TEASPOON GRANULATED GARLIC

1 TEASPOON PAPRIKA

1/2 TEASPOON KOSHER SALT

1/4 TEASPOON CAYENNE

4 HALIBUT FILLETS, ABOUT 6 OUNCES EACH AND 1 INCH THICK

   EXTRA-VIRGIN OLIVE OIL

2 LEMONS, CUT IN HALF

To make the ratatouille: Cut the onion crosswise into 1/2-inch slices; cut the eggplant and zucchini lengthwise into 1/2-inch slices; core the tomatoes, halve them crosswise, and seed them; quarter and seed the bell pepper. Brush the vegetables all over with the olive oil and season with salt and pepper. Grill over *Direct Medium* heat until tender, turning once halfway through grilling time. The onion will take 10 to 12 minutes, the eggplant 8 to 10 minutes, and the zucchini, tomatoes, and bell pepper 6 to 8 minutes. Allow to cool, then chop into 1/2-inch pieces.

In a medium sauté pan over medium-high heat, warm 1 tablespoon of the olive oil. Add the garlic and cook for 1 to 2 minutes, stirring occasionally. Add the grilled vegetables, basil, and vinegar. Season with salt and pepper. Stir, reduce heat to low, and keep warm while you grill the fish.

To make the rub: In a small bowl combine the rub ingredients and mix well.

Lightly brush or spray both sides of the halibut fillets with olive oil and season evenly with the rub. Grill over *Direct Medium* heat until the fish is just opaque and slightly firm to the touch, 8 to 10 minutes, turning once halfway through grilling time. Remove from the grill, squeeze the lemons on top, and serve immediately with the ratatouille.

MAKES 4 SERVINGS

SOULFUL SOLE

As fish go, sole, with its super-thin fillets and delicate taste, doesn't have the boldest personality. Until now. Heap on a tomato and herb salad, seal in a foil packet, and you'll be surprised at how this wallflower blossoms. (Suitable substitutes: red snapper, trout.)

DIRECT/MEDIUM

FOR THE SALAD:

2 MEDIUM RIPE TOMATOES

2 TABLESPOONS EXTRA-VIRGIN OLIVE OIL

2 TABLESPOONS FINELY CHOPPED FRESH MINT

2 TABLESPOONS FINELY CHOPPED FRESH DILL

1 TABLESPOON FRESH LIME JUICE

1 TEASPOON MINCED GARLIC

1/2 TEASPOON KOSHER SALT

1/4 TEASPOON FRESHLY GROUND BLACK PEPPER

4 SOLE FILLETS, 5 TO 6 OUNCES EACH

3 GREEN ONIONS (WHITE PART ONLY), THINLY SLICED CROSSWISE

To make the salad: Core the tomatoes, cut in half lengthwise, and cut into 1/2-inch wedges. Remove the seeds. In a medium bowl combine with the remaining salad ingredients.

Cut four sheets of heavy-duty aluminum foil slightly longer than the fillets and at least twice as wide. Place a fillet in the center of each sheet. Spoon one quarter of the salad on top of each fillet. Drizzle with the juices left in the bowl. Fold over the ends of each foil sheet and crimp them to completely enclose each fillet.

Grill the fish packets over *Direct Medium* heat for 5 minutes. Remove from the grill and carefully open each packet with scissors and peel back the foil. Transfer the fillets with the salad to rimmed plates or shallow bowls. Garnish with the onion, drizzle on the cooking juices, and serve warm.

MAKES 4 SERVINGS

ORANGE-MARINATED ESCOLAR
WITH RED PEPPER RELISH

Escolar produces firm, oil-rich steaks that are ideal for the grill. Similar in size and shape to tuna, escolar swims the Gulf of Mexico and the Pacific. The spectacle-like rings around its golden eyes earned it its name, which is Spanish for "student." Note: The bell pepper is grilled over Direct Medium heat and the escolar over Direct High heat. (Suitable substitute: tuna.)

DIRECT/MEDIUM

FOR THE MARINADE:

1/2 CUP FRESH ORANGE JUICE

1/4 CUP FINELY CHOPPED FRESH BASIL

2 TABLESPOONS EXTRA-VIRGIN OLIVE OIL

2 TABLESPOONS FRESH LEMON JUICE

1 TABLESPOON SOY SAUCE

1 TABLESPOON MINCED GARLIC

1/2 TEASPOON KOSHER SALT

1/4 TEASPOON FRESHLY GROUND BLACK PEPPER

4 ESCOLAR STEAKS, ABOUT 6 OUNCES EACH AND 1 INCH THICK

FOR THE RELISH:

1 RED BELL PEPPER

12 PITTED AND COARSELY CHOPPED KALAMATA OLIVES

1/4 CUP FINELY CHOPPED SWEET WHITE ONION

1/4 CUP FINELY CHOPPED FRESH BASIL

2 TABLESPOONS EXTRA-VIRGIN OLIVE OIL

1 TABLESPOON SHERRY VINEGAR

1/4 TEASPOON FRESHLY GROUND BLACK PEPPER

To make the marinade: In a small bowl whisk together the marinade ingredients.

Place the escolar steaks in a large, resealable plastic bag and pour in the marinade. Press the air out of the bag and seal tightly. Turn the bag to distribute the marinade, place in a bowl, and refrigerate for 1 to 2 hours.

To make the relish: Grill the pepper over *Direct Medium* heat until the skin is black and blistered on all sides, 10 to 12 minutes, turning every 3 to 5 minutes. Remove the pepper from the grill and place in a paper bag; close tightly. Let stand for 10 to 15 minutes to steam off the skin. Peel away the charred skin. Cut off the top, remove the seeds, and coarsely chop. Place in a bowl and add the remaining relish ingredients. Stir to blend. Set aside at room temperature.

Remove the steaks from the bag and discard the marinade. Grill over *Direct High* heat until the fish is opaque in the center, 8 to 10 minutes, turning once halfway through grilling time. Remove from the grill and serve warm with the relish.

MAKES 4 SERVINGS

ESCOLAR
WITH GRILLED VEGETABLE SALAD

Escolar is one of the sweetest, juiciest fish in the seafood case. You can use any firm white fish in this recipe, but as always, leave it moist in the middle. The vegetables work here as a sort of Mediterranean salsa. Finely diced and dressed in complementary flavors, they round out the range of tastes in this dish.

DIRECT/HIGH

FOR THE VEGETABLES:

1   LARGE FENNEL BULB, STALKS REMOVED
1   LARGE JAPANESE EGGPLANT
    EXTRA-VIRGIN OLIVE OIL
    KOSHER SALT
    FRESHLY GROUND BLACK PEPPER
1   CUP FINELY CHOPPED RIPE TOMATO

FOR THE DRESSING:

2   TABLESPOONS EXTRA-VIRGIN OLIVE OIL
1   TABLESPOON FRESH ORANGE JUICE
1   TABLESPOON BALSAMIC VINEGAR
1   TABLESPOON FINELY CHOPPED FRESH MINT
1/2 TEASPOON KOSHER SALT
1/4 TEASPOON GRATED FRESH GINGER
1/4 TEASPOON FRESHLY GROUND BLACK PEPPER

4   ESCOLAR FILLETS, ABOUT 6 OUNCES EACH
    AND 1 INCH THICK

To prepare the vegetables: Cut the fennel bulb lengthwise into 1/2-inch slices, leaving the root end intact so it holds the slices together. Cut the eggplant crosswise into 1/2-inch coins. Brush or spray the fennel and eggplant with olive oil. Season with salt and pepper. Grill over *Direct High* heat until lightly charred on each side, turning once halfway through grilling time. The fennel will take 8 to 10 minutes. The eggplant will take 4 to 6 minutes. Transfer the fennel and eggplant to a cutting board and cut into 1/2-inch dice, removing and discarding the tough root end of the fennel. Place in a medium bowl and add the chopped tomato.

To make the dressing: In a small bowl whisk together the dressing ingredients.

Pour the dressing over the grilled vegetables. Stir and set aside at room temperature while you grill the fish.

Brush or spray both sides of the escolar fillets with olive oil. Season with salt and pepper. Grill over *Direct High* heat until the fish is opaque in the center, 8 to 10 minutes, turning once halfway through grilling time. Remove from the grill and serve warm with the vegetable mixture spooned on top.

MAKES 4 SERVINGS

JUMBO SHRIMP
WITH COCONUT MILK CURRY

Tamarind pulp adds a nice zip to this coconut curry sauce. If you can't find it in the Asian section of your grocery store (look for pulp that's free of any seeds and fibers), substitute an equal amount of lime juice.

DIRECT/HIGH

FOR THE SAUCE:

2   TABLESPOONS VEGETABLE OIL
2   TABLESPOONS MINCED SHALLOTS
2   TEASPOONS MINCED LEMONGRASS
      (WHITE PART ONLY)
1   TEASPOON MINCED GARLIC
1   TABLESPOON CURRY POWDER
1   CUP COCONUT MILK
1 1/2 TEASPOONS GRANULATED SUGAR
1   TEASPOON FISH SAUCE
1   TEASPOON LIME JUICE
1   TEASPOON TAMARIND PULP
1/2   TEASPOON KOSHER SALT
1/4   TEASPOON FRESHLY GROUND BLACK PEPPER
1   PINCH CLOVES

16   TO 20 JUMBO SHRIMP (1 1/2 TO 2 POUNDS),
      PEELED AND DEVEINED
      VEGETABLE OIL
      KOSHER SALT
      FRESHLY GROUND BLACK PEPPER

2   TABLESPOONS COARSELY CHOPPED FRESH BASIL

To make the sauce: In a medium saucepan over medium-high heat, warm the vegetable oil. Add the shallots, lemongrass, and garlic. Cook for 2 to 3 minutes, stirring occasionally. Add the curry powder and cook for 1 minute more, stirring occasionally. Add the remaining sauce ingredients. Bring to a boil, then lower heat to a simmer. Cook for about 5 minutes. Strain through a fine-mesh sieve. Set aside.

Lightly brush or spray the shrimp with vegetable oil. Season with salt and pepper. Grill over *Direct High* heat until the shrimp are just opaque in the center and firm to the touch, 2 to 4 minutes, turning once halfway through grilling time. Remove from the grill and serve warm with the sauce and jasmine rice, if desired. Sprinkle with the fresh basil.

MAKES 4 SERVINGS

HULA
SHRIMP

Easy to fix and quick-cooking, wrapped shrimp served with this jazzy pineapple salsa will quickly become a favorite. A very nice salty-sweet combination.

DIRECT/HIGH

FOR THE SALSA:

- **1 CUP FRESH OR CANNED AND DRAINED PINEAPPLE**
- **2 TABLESPOONS MINCED GREEN ONIONS (WHITE PART ONLY)**
- **2 TEASPOONS RICE VINEGAR**
- **1 TEASPOON SOY SAUCE**
- **1 TEASPOON VEGETABLE OIL**
- **1/2 TEASPOON GRATED FRESH GINGER**
- **1/4 TEASPOON FRESHLY GROUND BLACK PEPPER**

- **8 PAPER-THIN SLICES PROSCIUTTO**
- **16 TO 20 JUMBO SHRIMP (1 1/2 TO 2 POUNDS), PEELED AND DEVEINED**
  VEGETABLE OIL
  FRESHLY GROUND BLACK PEPPER

To make the salsa: Cut the pineapple into 1/4-inch dice and place in a small bowl. Add the remaining salsa ingredients and stir to blend. Cover with plastic wrap and set aside until ready to serve.

Cut each prosciutto slice lengthwise into two equal-sized strips and wrap a strip around each shrimp. Brush or spray the shrimp with vegetable oil. Season with pepper.

Grill the shrimp over *Direct High* heat until they are just opaque in the center and firm to the touch, 2 to 4 minutes, turning once halfway through grilling time. Remove from the grill and serve warm with the salsa.

MAKES 4 SERVINGS

SHRIMP AND ONIONS
WITH COCKTAIL SAUCE

Want to make it look like you worked hard? Grill fresh shrimp to perfection and serve with your own cocktail sauce made from scratch (trust us, it's easy). Are they impressed? Oh, yes.

DIRECT/HIGH

FOR THE SAUCE:

- **1 CUP BOTTLED MILD CHILI SAUCE**
- **2 TABLESPOONS FRESH LEMON JUICE**
- **2 TEASPOONS PREPARED HORSERADISH**
- **2 TEASPOONS WORCESTERSHIRE SAUCE**
- **4 TO 5 DROPS TABASCO SAUCE**

- **1 MEDIUM YELLOW ONION**
- **16 TO 20 JUMBO SHRIMP (1 1/2 TO 2 POUNDS), PEELED AND DEVEINED**
  VEGETABLE OIL
  KOSHER SALT
  FRESHLY GROUND BLACK PEPPER

To make the sauce: In a medium bowl combine the sauce ingredients. Cover with plastic wrap and refrigerate until ready to use.

Quarter the onion, separate the leaves, and cut into 3/4-inch pieces, if necessary. Place the onion and shrimp in a large bowl. Add enough vegetable oil to lightly coat. Season with salt and pepper. Stir to evenly distribute the oil and seasonings.

Thread the shrimp and onion pieces alternately onto skewers. Grill over *Direct High* heat until the shrimp are just opaque in the center and firm to the touch, 2 to 4 minutes, turning once halfway through grilling time. Remove from the grill. Serve warm or at room temperature with the sauce.

MAKES 4 SERVINGS

TEQUILA
SHRIMP

A perfect appetizer for a Mexican grilled dinner. Add cornbread and black beans, you've got an entrée. Call some friends, break out the Corona®, and a fiesta is born.

DIRECT/HIGH

FOR THE MARINADE:

- 1/3 CUP TEQUILA
- 2 TABLESPOONS EXTRA-VIRGIN OLIVE OIL
- 2 TABLESPOONS FRESH LIME JUICE
- 1 TABLESPOON MINCED GARLIC
- 1 TABLESPOON MINCED JALAPEÑO PEPPER, WITH SEEDS
- 1 TEASPOON GROUND CORIANDER
- 1/2 TEASPOON FRESHLY GROUND BLACK PEPPER

- 32 LARGE SHRIMP (ABOUT 1 1/2 POUNDS), PEELED AND DEVEINED
  KOSHER SALT
- 2 FRESH LIMES, CUT INTO WEDGES

For the marinade: In a small bowl whisk together the marinade ingredients.

Place the shrimp in a large, resealable plastic bag and pour in the marinade. Press the air out of the bag and seal tightly. Turn the bag to distribute the marinade, place in a bowl, and refrigerate for 30 to 45 minutes.

Remove the shrimp from the bag and discard the marinade. Thread the shrimp onto skewers and season with salt. Grill over *Direct High* heat until the shrimp are just opaque in the center and firm to the touch, 2 to 4 minutes, turning once halfway through grilling time. Remove from the grill and serve warm with the lime wedges.

MAKES 4 SERVINGS

N'AWLINS BARBECUE
SHRIMP

The herbs and spices of this peel-and-eat shrimp taste great on a bed of rice pilaf. And you can forget about being dainty—this one's a finger-lickin' feast!

DIRECT/HIGH

FOR THE MARINADE:

- 6 TABLESPOONS UNSALTED BUTTER
- 2 TEASPOONS MINCED GARLIC
- 1 TABLESPOON FRESH LEMON JUICE
- 2 TEASPOONS FINELY CHOPPED FRESH THYME
- 2 TEASPOONS PAPRIKA
- 1/2 TEASPOON KOSHER SALT
- 1/4 TEASPOON CAYENNE
- 1/4 TEASPOON TURMERIC

- 32 LARGE SHRIMP (ABOUT 1 1/2 POUNDS), IN THEIR SHELLS

To make the marinade: In a small sauté pan over medium heat, melt the butter. Add the garlic and cook, stirring occasionally, until soft, 2 to 3 minutes. Remove from the heat and add the remaining marinade ingredients. Stir and allow to cool to room temperature.

Using a sharp knife, split open the back of each shrimp and devein it. Place the shrimp in a large, resealable plastic bag and pour in the marinade. Press the air out of the bag and seal tightly. Turn the bag to distribute the marinade, place in a bowl and refrigerate for 20 to 30 minutes.

Remove the shrimp from the bag and discard the marinade. Grill over *Direct High* heat until the shrimp are just opaque in the center and firm to the touch, 2 to 4 minutes, turning once halfway through grilling time. Remove from the grill and serve warm or at room temperature with rice, if desired.

MAKES 4 SERVINGS

"Kissing don't last: cookery do!"

— GEORGE MEREDITH

N'Awlins Barbecue Shrimp

SPANISH SCAMPI
WITH GAZPACHO SALAD

True scampi are the deep, red-shelled prawns found throughout the Mediterranean. These large succulent cousins to our native shrimp are perfect for grilling and right at home with this festive salad. If you can't find scampi, substitute jumbo shrimp.

DIRECT/HIGH

FOR THE MARINADE:

1/4 CUP EXTRA-VIRGIN OLIVE OIL

2 TABLESPOONS FRESH LEMON JUICE

2 TABLESPOONS CHOPPED FRESH BASIL

1 TEASPOON GRANULATED GARLIC

1 TEASPOON CRUSHED RED PEPPER FLAKES

16 TO 20 LARGE RED SPANISH SCAMPI *OR* JUMBO SHRIMP (1 1/2 TO 2 POUNDS), PEELED, DEVEINED, AND RINSED

FOR THE SALAD:

2 TABLESPOONS EXTRA-VIRGIN OLIVE OIL

1/2 CUP FINELY DICED YELLOW ONION

1 TEASPOON MINCED GARLIC

1/2 CUP FINELY DICED RIPE TOMATOES

1/4 CUP FINELY DICED ZUCCHINI

1/4 CUP FINELY DICED CUCUMBER

1/4 CUP FINELY DICED RED BELL PEPPER

2 TEASPOONS BALSAMIC VINEGAR

1 TABLESPOON FINELY CHOPPED FRESH DILL
KOSHER SALT
FRESHLY GROUND BLACK PEPPER

To make the marinade: In a small bowl whisk together the marinade ingredients.

Place the scampi in a large, resealable plastic bag and pour in the marinade. Press the air out of the bag and seal tightly. Turn the bag to distribute the marinade, place in a bowl, and refrigerate for 30 minutes to 1 hour.

To make the salad: In a medium sauté pan over medium-high heat, warm the olive oil. Add the onion and cook, stirring occasionally, until translucent, 4 to 5 minutes. Add the garlic and cook for 1 minute more, stirring occasionally. Add the tomatoes, zucchini, cucumber, and bell pepper. Stir to combine and cook until the vegetables are heated through, about 1 minute. Remove from the heat. Add the vinegar and dill. Season with salt and pepper. Give the mixture a final stir. Set aside at room temperature.

Remove the scampi from the bag and discard the marinade. Season with salt. Grill over *Direct High* heat until the scampi are just opaque in the center and firm to the touch, 3 to 5 minutes, turning once halfway through grilling time. Remove from the grill and serve warm with the salad.

MAKES 4 SERVINGS

PARMESAN BREADED SCALLOPS
WITH LEMON GARNISH

Clean, refreshing flavors just meant for a balmy summer evening. A simple recipe like this gets its strength from the quality of the ingredients, so use the real thing: Parmigiano-Reggiano from Parma, Italy.

DIRECT/HIGH

FOR THE COATING:

1/2 CUP FINE DRY PLAIN BREAD CRUMBS

1/4 CUP FRESHLY GRATED PARMIGIANO-REGGIANO CHEESE

1/2 TEASPOON KOSHER SALT

1/2 TEASPOON FRESHLY GROUND BLACK PEPPER

20 LARGE SEA SCALLOPS (ABOUT 1 1/4 POUNDS)

2 TABLESPOONS EXTRA-VIRGIN OLIVE OIL

FOR THE GARNISH:

1/2 CUP LOOSELY PACKED FRESH ITALIAN PARSLEY LEAVES

2 TABLESPOONS LEMON ZEST

1 TABLESPOON EXTRA-VIRGIN OLIVE OIL

1 TEASPOON LEMON JUICE

EXTRA-VIRGIN OLIVE OIL

To make the coating: Combine the coating ingredients on a plate and mix with your fingers.

Wash the scallops and remove the small, tough side muscle *(see sidebar, page 316)*. Pat the scallops dry with paper towels and place in a small bowl. Add the olive oil and mix to coat. Dip the scallops in the coating, turning to cover evenly. Gently press the crumbs onto the scallops. Place the scallops in a single layer on a clean plate. Cover with plastic wrap and refrigerate for 30 minutes to set the crumbs.

To make the garnish: Finely chop the garnish ingredients and mix together.

Brush or spray the scallops with olive oil. Place on the grate 1 to 2 inches apart and grill over *Direct High* heat until just opaque in the center, 4 to 6 minutes, turning once halfway through grilling time. Remove from the grill, sprinkle with the garnish, and serve warm.

MAKES 4 SERVINGS

Parmesan Breaded Scallops with Lemon Garnish

GRILLING SCALLOPS

We get very excited about grilling tender, succulent scallops. No other cooking method gives them such a nice texture. The slight crispiness they get from the grill marks—enhanced by an exterior caramelized by marinades or crusted with a rub—makes all the difference in the world. Here's how to grill them like a master:

Don't use skewers—they can tear through the scallops when you lift them to turn. Instead, place large scallops (they won't fall through the grate) on the grill individually. Start timing them when you place the first one down. Work quickly to place them all on the grate, an inch or two apart. Close the lid. Halfway through the grilling time, turn them. Scallops are ready to turn when you can easily lift them from the cooking grate with a pair of tongs. Grip the scallop gently, and slightly turn your wrist. If it releases easily, it's done on that side. If it clings, move on to another that's ready, or close the lid and count to 10. Turn the smaller ones first, judging their doneness one by one. Finish cooking them with the lid down, and remove them, again smallest to largest. A perfectly grilled scallop will be firm to the touch but not rubbery. If you've never done them before, start with just one or two at a time until you get the hang of it. Pretty soon it'll be like second nature.

As always, there are exceptions to the rule: Two recipes in this chapter do call for skewers—we use them for our Scallop and Zucchini Kabobs (page 317) and to keep scallops wrapped in prosciutto in Honey-Glazed Sea Scallops (page 318). There's a trick to turning them so they don't tear. Slide a long spatula under the length of the skewer, then gently lift the whole skewer, and flip it. If you meet resistance along the way, close the lid and count to 10...you get the picture.

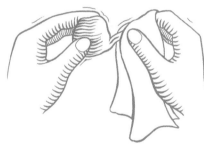

REMOVE THE SIDE MUSCLE

Another secret to tender scallops is to remove and discard the flat muscle on the side that helps them open and close their shells. It's the same color as the rest of the scallop, so it's easier to find by feel—it may stick up a bit, too. Since raw scallops are a bit slippery, try gripping the muscle with a clean paper towel and give a firm tug. It will tear off easily. You're good to go!

SEA SCALLOPS
WITH YELLOW PEPPER SAUCE

If you haven't tried scallops laced with orange juice, you're in for a treat. The citrus gives these delicate creatures a boost of confidence and the vibrant pepper sauce makes them almost sassy. Note: The peppers are grilled over Direct Medium heat and the scallops over Direct High heat.

DIRECT/MEDIUM

FOR THE MARINADE:
- ¼ CUP FRESH ORANGE JUICE
- 2 TABLESPOONS EXTRA-VIRGIN OLIVE OIL
- ½ TEASPOON DRIED THYME
- ½ TEASPOON KOSHER SALT
- ½ TEASPOON FRESHLY GROUND BLACK PEPPER

20 LARGE SEA SCALLOPS (ABOUT 1¼ POUNDS)

FOR THE SAUCE:
- 2 MEDIUM YELLOW BELL PEPPERS
- 2 TABLESPOONS EXTRA-VIRGIN OLIVE OIL
- ½ CUP ROUGHLY DICED YELLOW ONION
- 2 TEASPOONS MINCED GARLIC
- 1 TEASPOON WHITE WINE VINEGAR
- ¼ TEASPOON TABASCO GREEN PEPPER SAUCE
- ½ TEASPOON KOSHER SALT

To make the marinade: In a medium bowl whisk together the marinade ingredients.

Wash the scallops and remove the small, tough side muscle *(see sidebar, left)*. Add the scallops to the marinade and stir to coat. Cover with plastic wrap and refrigerate for 30 minutes to 1 hour.

To make the sauce: Grill the peppers over *Direct Medium* heat until the skin is black and blistered on all sides, 10 to 12 minutes, turning every 3 to 5 minutes. Remove the peppers from the grill and place in a paper bag; close tightly. Let stand for 10 to 15 minutes to steam off the skins. Peel away the charred skins. Cut off the tops, remove the seeds, and finely chop.

In a small sauté pan over medium-high heat, warm the olive oil. Add the onion and cook for 3 to 4 minutes, stirring occasionally. Add the garlic and peppers and cook for 3 to 4 minutes more, stirring occasionally. Add the vinegar, green pepper sauce, and salt. Purée in a food processor until the consistency of ketchup. If the sauce seems too thick, add a bit of water. If it seems too thin, simmer for a few minutes more to reduce it. Set aside.

Remove the scallops from the bowl and discard the marinade. Place the scallops on the grate 1 to 2 inches apart. Grill over *Direct High* heat until just opaque in the center, 4 to 6 minutes, turning once halfway through grilling time. Meanwhile, reheat the sauce. Remove the scallops from the grill and serve warm with the sauce drizzled on top.

MAKES 4 SERVINGS

GRILLED SCALLOPS
WITH CHILI DIPPING SAUCE

Carrots may seem like an unlikely base for a dipping sauce, but when blended with sriracha, soy, and other seasonings, they contribute a brilliant orange color and flirty sweetness.

DIRECT/HIGH

FOR THE SAUCE:

- 1 MEDIUM CARROT
- 2 TEASPOONS SOY SAUCE
- 1 TEASPOON SRIRACHA (HOT CHILI-GARLIC SAUCE)
- 1/4 TEASPOON GROUND CUMIN
- 1 TABLESPOON RICE VINEGAR
- 1 TABLESPOON EXTRA-VIRGIN OLIVE OIL
- 1 TEASPOON FINELY CHOPPED FRESH MINT

- 20 LARGE SEA SCALLOPS (ABOUT 1 1/4 POUNDS)
  EXTRA-VIRGIN OLIVE OIL
  KOSHER SALT
  FRESHLY GROUND BLACK PEPPER

To make the sauce: Cut the carrot into 1/4-inch slices. Place in a small saucepan along with 1 cup water, the soy sauce, sriracha, and cumin. Bring the mixture to a boil. Lower the heat to a simmer and cook until the carrots are just tender, about 15 minutes. Purée the mixture in a food processor, adding the vinegar, olive oil, and mint as the motor is running. The sauce should have the consistency of ketchup. If the sauce seems too thick, add a bit of water. If it seems too thin, simmer the sauce for a few more minutes to reduce it. Set aside.

Wash the scallops and remove the small, tough side muscle *(see sidebar, page 316)*. Place in a medium bowl. Add enough olive oil to lightly coat. Season with salt and pepper.

Place the scallops on the grate 1 to 2 inches apart. Grill over *Direct High* heat until just opaque in the center, 4 to 6 minutes, turning once halfway through grilling time. Remove from the grill and serve warm with the sauce drizzled on top or serve the sauce in small, individual dipping bowls.

MAKES 4 SERVINGS

SCALLOP AND ZUCCHINI
KABOBS

If you've got an herb garden, you're going to love this one. Blending fresh herbs with lime adds layers of flavor to delicate scallops and crisp zucchini (substitute mushrooms or onions, if you prefer).

DIRECT/HIGH

FOR THE MARINADE:

- 3 TABLESPOONS VEGETABLE OIL
- 1 TABLESPOON FRESH LIME JUICE
- 1 TABLESPOON FINELY CHOPPED FRESH BASIL
- 1 TABLESPOON FINELY CHOPPED FRESH ROSEMARY
- 1 TABLESPOON FINELY CHOPPED FRESH PARSLEY
- 2 TEASPOONS WORCESTERSHIRE SAUCE
- 1/4 TEASPOON GRATED LIME ZEST
- 1/4 TEASPOON KOSHER SALT
- 1/4 TEASPOON FRESHLY GROUND BLACK PEPPER
- 2 TO 3 DROPS TABASCO SAUCE

- 24 LARGE SEA SCALLOPS (ABOUT 1 1/2 POUNDS)
- 2 MEDIUM ZUCCHINI

To make the marinade: In a large bowl whisk together the marinade ingredients.

Wash the scallops and remove the small, tough side muscle *(see sidebar, page 316)*. Trim and cut the zucchini into 1/4-inch slices. Add the scallops and zucchini to the marinade and stir to coat. Cover with plastic wrap and refrigerate for 20 to 30 minutes.

Remove the scallops and zucchini from the bowl, reserving the marinade. Thread the scallops and zucchini alternately onto skewers; do not crowd them. Thread the scallops through their sides so they lie flat; thread the zucchini slices through the center so they stand perpendicular to the grill. Brush the skewers with the reserved marinade.

Grill the kabobs over *Direct High* heat until the scallops are just opaque in the center and the zucchini slices are barely tender, 4 to 6 minutes, turning once halfway through grilling time. Remove from the grill and serve warm.

MAKES 4 SERVINGS

HONEY-GLAZED SEA SCALLOPS
WITH APPLE RINGS

This departure from our no-skewer rule is a sure cure for the same-old-dinner routine. The sweet-salty contrast of the scallops and prosciutto get an extra boost from crisp apple rings. The honey glaze, added just at the end, ties it all together. Anything but boring.

DIRECT/MEDIUM

- **16 LARGE SEA SCALLOPS (ABOUT 1 POUND)**
- **1 TABLESPOON EXTRA-VIRGIN OLIVE OIL**
- **1 TABLESPOON FINELY CHOPPED FRESH THYME**
- **1/4 TEASPOON KOSHER SALT**
- **1/4 TEASPOON FRESHLY GROUND BLACK PEPPER**
- **8 PAPER-THIN SLICES PROSCIUTTO**

FOR THE GLAZE:

- **3 TABLESPOONS HONEY**
- **1 TABLESPOON FRESH LEMON JUICE**
- **1/4 TEASPOON KOSHER SALT**

- **2 LARGE GOLDEN DELICIOUS APPLES**

Wash the scallops and remove the small, tough side muscle (*see sidebar, page 316*). Place the scallops in a medium bowl. Add the olive oil, thyme, salt, and pepper. Stir to coat. Cut each prosciutto slice lengthwise into two equal-sized strips and wrap a strip around each scallop. Thread the scallops through their sides onto skewers, four scallops per skewer. Place the skewers on a plate. Cover with plastic wrap and refrigerate for 30 minutes to 1 hour.

Meanwhile, make the glaze: In a small bowl whisk together the glaze ingredients.

Peel and core the apples, then cut crosswise into 1/2-inch-thick rings. Grill the apple rings over *Direct Medium* heat until golden and tender, 4 to 6 minutes, turning once halfway through grilling time. Brush both sides of the apple rings with the glaze and grill for 2 minutes more, turning once halfway through grilling time.

Grill the scallops over *Direct Medium* heat until just opaque in the center, 4 to 6 minutes, turning once half way through grilling time. Brush with the glaze during the last 1 to 2 minutes of grilling time. Remove the scallops from the grill and serve warm with the apple rings.

MAKES 4 SERVINGS

LOBSTER TAILS
WITH CHAMPAGNE VANILLA SAUCE

We call this one "rapture on a fork." For special occasions, this is a winner. When done, the lobster shells will be a rich reddish brown and the meat will be firm, juicy, and coral-white.

DIRECT/MEDIUM

FOR THE SAUCE:

- **1 VANILLA BEAN (ABOUT 4 INCHES LONG)**
- **1 SMALL SPRIG FRESH THYME**
- **1 TABLESPOON MINCED SHALLOTS**
- **1 CUP BRUT CHAMPAGNE**
- **1/2 CUP UNSALTED BUTTER, COLD**
  KOSHER SALT
  FRESHLY GROUND BLACK PEPPER

- **4 LOBSTER TAILS (UNCOOKED), ABOUT 7 OUNCES EACH**
- **1/2 CUP UNSALTED BUTTER, SOFTENED**
- **2 TEASPOONS LEMON JUICE**
- **1 TEASPOON SNIPPED FRESH CHIVES**
- **1/4 TEASPOON KOSHER SALT**

To make the sauce: Cut the vanilla bean in half and split lengthwise. Place in a small saucepan with the thyme, shallots, and champagne. Bring just to a boil, reduce the heat, and simmer until reduced to 1/4 cup. The reduction will be a clear golden color.

Remove from the heat and strain the reduction through a sieve. Reserve the vanilla bean. Rinse the saucepan and return the reduction to the pan. Using a sharp paring knife, scrape the seeds from the vanilla bean into the reduction.

Bring the reduction to a simmer and whisk in the butter, 1 tablespoon at a time to fully incorporate, until glistening and smooth. Adjust the seasoning with salt and pepper, if necessary. Remove from the heat and set aside until the lobsters are ready. Keep warm.

Place the tails, shell-side down, on a cutting board. Split the tails lengthwise to expose the meat. In a small bowl mash the butter with the lemon juice, chives, and salt using the back of a fork. Spread the butter over the lobster meat and between the shell and the meat. Grill the tails, shell side down, over *Direct Medium* heat, until opaque throughout, 8 to 10 minutes. Remove the meat from the shells and serve immediately with the warm sauce.

MAKES 4 SERVINGS

THE RICH CHAMPAGNE BUTTER SAUCE FOR THESE LOBSTER TAILS GOES BEYOND MEMORABLE TO ALMOST INCREDIBLE.

Lobster Tails with Champagne Vanilla Sauce

MAINE LOBSTER
WITH TARRAGON-MUSTARD AÏOLI

Lobsters from the deep, cold crags off the coast of Maine are unsurpassed for their sweet-rich flavor. Grilled with a touch of tarragon and dressed with this garlicky aïoli, this could become another favorite.

DIRECT/MEDIUM

FOR THE AÏOLI:

- 1 LARGE GARLIC CLOVE
- ¹/4 CUP MAYONNAISE
- 2 TEASPOONS FINELY CHOPPED FRESH TARRAGON
- 1 TEASPOON DIJON MUSTARD
- 1 TEASPOON FRESH LEMON JUICE

FOR THE BUTTER:

- ¹/2 CUP UNSALTED BUTTER, MELTED
- 2 TABLESPOONS FRESH LEMON JUICE
- 1 TABLESPOON FINELY CHOPPED FRESH TARRAGON
- 1 TABLESPOON MINCED GREEN ONIONS (WHITE PART ONLY)

- 2 LIVE MAINE LOBSTERS, ABOUT 1¹/2 POUNDS EACH

To make the aïoli: In a small saucepan blanch the garlic in boiling water for 5 minutes to soften it and take away the sharp bite. Mince the garlic and combine in a small bowl with the remaining aïoli ingredients. Use within 30 minutes or cover and refrigerate until ready to serve.

To prepare the butter: In a small bowl combine the melted butter with the remaining butter ingredients and set aside.

Place one lobster, shell side up and with the head pointing toward you, on a cutting board. Place the tip of a sharp knife at the point where the tail section meets the top section. Swiftly split the top section in half lengthwise, being careful not to cut the claws. Then split the tail in half lengthwise. Spread open the split shell; remove and discard the head sac from both halves. Remove and discard the intestine from one of the halves. If desired, scoop out and remove any tomalley with a spoon. Rinse the lobster under cold running water. Twist and pull off the claws and crack their shells with the back of a heavy knife or a nutcracker. Prepare the other lobster the same way. Generously brush the lobster meat with the seasoned butter.

Grill the lobster pieces, shell side down, over *Direct Medium* heat until opaque throughout, 8 to 10 minutes, brushing occasionally with the seasoned butter. Remove from the grill and serve warm with the aïoli on the side.

MAKES 2 SERVINGS

LOBSTER ON THE GRILL
WITH FLAVORED BUTTERS

The delectable flavor of lobster on the grill is unmatched. If you want to eat the tomalley (and roe, if the lobster is a female), leave it in and cook it with the rest of the lobster. Here we couldn't resist and included two decadent dipping butters.

DIRECT/HIGH

FOR THE CUMIN BUTTER:

- 1 TEASPOON GROUND CUMIN
- ¹/2 CUP UNSALTED BUTTER
- 2 TEASPOONS MINCED JALAPEÑO PEPPER, WITHOUT SEEDS
- ¹/4 TEASPOON KOSHER SALT

FOR THE LEMON-AND-GARLIC BUTTER:

- ¹/2 CUP UNSALTED BUTTER
- 1 TEASPOON FINELY CHOPPED GARLIC
- 1 TEASPOON GRATED LEMON ZEST
- 1 TEASPOON FINELY CHOPPED FRESH THYME LEAVES

- 4 LIVE LOBSTERS, 1¹/2 TO 2 POUNDS EACH

To make the cumin butter: In a small sauté pan over medium heat, sprinkle the cumin and warm just until fragrant, about 1 minute. Add the butter, jalapeño, and salt. Cook over low heat until the butter has melted. Keep warm until ready to serve.

To make the lemon-and-garlic butter: In a small sauté pan over medium heat, melt the butter. Add the garlic and heat until sizzling. Stir in the lemon zest and thyme. Remove from the heat. Keep warm until ready to serve.

Heat a large pot of heavily salted water to a boil. Plunge one of the lobsters headfirst into the boiling water. Cover and cook over high heat for 3 minutes (the lobster will not be fully cooked). Lift from the water to a large platter. Repeat with the remaining lobsters.

When cool enough to handle, place one of the lobsters on a work surface, shell side down. Remove rubber bands or pegs from the claws. Split the lobster in half from head to tail using a large heavy knife, cleaver, or poultry shears. Remove and discard the head sac from both halves. Remove and discard the intestine from one of the halves. If desired, scoop out and remove any tomalley with a spoon. Rinse the lobster under cold running water. Twist and pull off the claws and crack their shells with the back of a heavy knife or a nutcracker. Prepare the other lobsters the same way.

Grill the claws and tails, shell side down, over *Direct High* heat until opaque throughout, 6 to 8 minutes, without turning. Brush the lobster meat occasionally with a little of one of the prepared butters. Remove from the grill and serve warm with small dishes of the butters on the side.

MAKES 4 SERVINGS

GINGER-CHILE CRAB

A simple and impressive meal that will score you big points if served by candlelight. Choose live crabs that seem heavy for their size—they pack the most meat—and only partially precook them so they can finish up on the grill. The marinade makes the most of their delicate flavor.

DIRECT/HIGH

FOR THE MARINADE:

- 1/4 CUP SOY SAUCE
- 3 TABLESPOONS VEGETABLE OIL
- 2 TABLESPOONS RICE VINEGAR
- 1 TEASPOON GRATED FRESH GINGER
- 1 TEASPOON SRIRACHA (HOT CHILI-GARLIC SAUCE)
- 1/2 TEASPOON ASIAN SESAME OIL

- 2 LIVE DUNGENESS CRABS, ABOUT 2 POUNDS EACH

To make the marinade: In a small bowl whisk together the marinade ingredients with 2 tablespoons water.

Place the crabs in a large pot of cold water. The water should cover them by 1 to 2 inches. Cover the pot with a heavy lid and place on the stovetop. Turn the heat to high. Just before the water comes to a simmer (and just as the edges of the shells are turning red), use tongs to lift the crabs from the water (the crabs will not be fully cooked). Stop the cooking by running them under cold water.

Lay one crab on its back on a work surface and prepare it for the grill: Pull off and discard the triangular belly tab, then carefully lift and discard the spines underneath. Turn the crab over and lift off the top shell from the rear and discard. Also discard the gills on both sides of the body, the jaws at the front, and the soft material in the center of the back. Rinse the body well until only meat and shell remain. Drain. Split the crab in half from front to rear, leaving the legs and claws attached. Gently crack each leg and claw with a mallet. Prepare the other crab the same way. Then, place each crab in a large, resealable plastic bag. Pour half of the marinade into each bag. Press the air out of the bags and seal tightly. Turn the bags to distribute the marinade, place in a large bowl, and refrigerate for 2 to 3 hours.

Remove the crabs from the marinade, reserving the marinade. Pour the marinade into a small saucepan, bring to a boil, and boil for 1 full minute. Set aside.

Grill the crabs over *Direct High* heat until the shells are bright red and the meat in the claws is opaque, 5 to 7 minutes, turning and basting with the marinade once halfway through grilling time. Remove from the grill and serve warm.

MAKES 2 SERVINGS

GRILLED CALAMARI
WITH TOMATO-BASIL VINAIGRETTE

Grilling is an excellent way to prepare squid because the quick cooking keeps it tender. Still, it's easy to overdo it and end up with a chewy texture, so stick to 3 or 4 minutes total. Dressed with this simple vinaigrette, the squid takes on a refreshing flavor that will take you right to the coast of Italy in summer.

DIRECT/HIGH

FOR THE MARINADE:

- 1/4 CUP EXTRA-VIRGIN OLIVE OIL
- 1/4 CUP FRESH LEMON JUICE
- 2 TEASPOONS MINCED GARLIC
- 1 TEASPOON FRESHLY GROUND BLACK PEPPER
- 1/2 TEASPOON CRUSHED RED PEPPER FLAKES

- 2 POUNDS CLEANED MEDIUM SQUID (ABOUT 4 POUNDS UNCLEANED)

FOR THE VINAIGRETTE:

- 1 MEDIUM TOMATO, COARSELY CHOPPED
- 1/2 CUP TIGHTLY PACKED FRESH BASIL LEAVES
- 1 TABLESPOON BALSAMIC VINEGAR
- 1 TEASPOON MINCED GARLIC
- 1/2 TEASPOON FRESHLY GROUND BLACK PEPPER
- 1/4 TEASPOON KOSHER SALT
- 1/4 CUP EXTRA-VIRGIN OLIVE OIL

KOSHER SALT

To make the marinade: In a small bowl whisk together the marinade ingredients.

Place the cleaned squid in a large, resealable plastic bag and pour in the marinade. Press the air out of the bag and seal tightly. Turn the bag to distribute the marinade, place in a bowl, and refrigerate for 1 to 2 hours.

To make the vinaigrette: In a food processor combine the tomato, basil, vinegar, garlic, pepper, and salt and process until smooth. With the motor running, slowly pour in the olive oil and process until fully incorporated.

Remove the squid from the bag and discard the marinade. Season with salt. Grill over *Direct High* heat until just cooked, 3 to 4 minutes, turning once halfway through grilling time. Remove from the grill and cut into 1/4-inch strips. Place in a medium bowl and add as much of the vinaigrette as desired. Toss to coat the squid evenly. Serve warm.

MAKES 4 SERVINGS

Clams Provençal (top) and Gingered Mussels (bottom)

CLAMS
PROVENÇAL

Try this one on a cold day and see if the world doesn't take on a warm, rosy hue. Steamed in a zesty tomato base infused with saffron, white wine, fresh rosemary, and garlic, these clams will cure whatever ails you. Serve in bowls with crusty bread to sop up every bit of the broth.

DIRECT/HIGH

- 1 LARGE RIPE TOMATO
- 1/4 TEASPOON SAFFRON THREADS
- 1 1/2 CUPS DRY WHITE WINE
- 1 TABLESPOON MINCED GARLIC
- 2 TABLESPOONS EXTRA-VIRGIN OLIVE OIL
- 1 STRIP (1/2 INCH BY 2 INCHES) ORANGE ZEST, CUT IN SLIVERS
- 1 TEASPOON FINELY CHOPPED FRESH ROSEMARY
- 1 TEASPOON FINELY CHOPPED FRESH THYME
- 1 TABLESPOON FINELY CHOPPED FRESH ITALIAN PARSLEY
- 1/2 TEASPOON KOSHER SALT
- FRESHLY GROUND BLACK PEPPER

- 4 TO 5 POUNDS MANILLA *OR* OTHER SMALL CLAMS (ABOUT 4 DOZEN), SCRUBBED AND RINSED

- FRESH BASIL, CHOPPED (OPTIONAL)

Core and seed the tomato, then cut into 1/4-inch dice. In a medium sauté pan over medium-low heat, toast the saffron threads for 30 seconds. Add the wine and garlic, bring to a boil, and cook for 2 minutes. Remove from the heat. Add the diced tomato, olive oil, orange zest, rosemary, thyme, parsley, salt, and a grinding of pepper. Stir well.

Spread the clams in a single layer in a 13- by 9-inch heavy-duty aluminum foil pan. Spoon the hot tomato mixture over the top of the clams. Cover the pan with aluminum foil.

Grill the clams over *Direct High* heat until they are opened, 8 to 10 minutes. Transfer to individual soup bowls, discarding any clams that are still unopened. Spoon the juices over the top and garnish with the chopped fresh basil, if desired. Serve warm.

MAKES 4 SERVINGS

GINGERED
MUSSELS

Simple, healthful—and delicious! For the purest ginger flavor, use knobs of fresh ginger heavy with juice. Peel and cut into paper-thin slivers. Serve the cooking juices as a dipping sauce for the mussels.

DIRECT/HIGH

- 2 POUNDS FRESH MUSSELS, BLACK AND NEW ZEALAND GREEN LIP (ABOUT 4 DOZEN)

- FOR THE SAUCE:
- 1/4 CUP SOY SAUCE
- 1/4 CUP RICE VINEGAR
- 4 TEASPOONS ASIAN SESAME OIL
- 1 TEASPOON GRANULATED SUGAR

- 1 PIECE FRESH GINGER, ABOUT 1 INCH LONG
- 2 GREEN ONIONS

Scrub and rinse the mussels, then remove the beards. Spread the mussels in a single layer in a 13- by 9-inch heavy-duty aluminum foil pan.

To make the sauce: In a small bowl whisk together the sauce ingredients and pour over the mussels.

Peel the ginger and cut into slivers. Trim the onions and chop finely. Scatter the ginger and onions over the mussels. Cover the pan with aluminum foil.

Grill the mussels over *Direct High* heat until they are opened, 5 to 6 minutes. Transfer immediately to individual soup bowls, discarding any mussels that are still unopened. Spoon the sauce over the top and serve warm.

MAKES 4 SERVINGS

For generations, mothers and grandmothers alike have extolled the virtues of vegetables. More recently, health experts have practically gone hoarse reminding us that we need our A, C, E, and B12. Antioxidants are the superheroes of the moment. And yet very few of us manage to choke down our "five a day for better health." What gives?

We suspect it's not *all* our fault. So where does it start? At the grocery store, we argue. Countless polls confirm how bored we've become with the shopping process. Most of us make do with a pit stop after work, or fly in to grab a couple of things on a Saturday morning. Just enough to get us by. Why?

VEGET

Of course, we're all time-pressed. But maybe our taste buds are just a little bored with the same old routine. Face it, once you've steamed one asparagus spear, you've steamed them all.

America, isn't it time we gave vegetables another chance? Imagine, instead of trolling the produce aisle, going through the motions, we could put some fun back in the courtship! We might start looking forward to that chance encounter with a perfectly ripe tomato or significant moment with a handsome acorn squash. We might find unimagined fulfillment with an artichoke.

Of course, if you're wise enough to grow a vegetable garden, you don't have to look any farther than your own backyard for veggie bliss. There's nothing better than homegrown sweet corn or a vine-ripened tomato. But what about those of us who don't have a garden?

First, it helps to learn the season for each vegetable and then eat it when Nature meant it to be eaten. (This seems totally obvious, but it's easy to be misled when just about everything is available all year round.) We know tomatoes in winter are just never going to taste like summer's. August's asparagus can't hold a candle to April's. And trying winter squash in June is just setting yourself up for a letdown. Still, it's hard to resist when special offers beckon from the food section of the local paper.

And it's so easy to be seduced by looks. (We've all fallen for the gorgeous but tasteless type, no?) Much of today's grocery produce is bred for uniformity, color, and the ability to survive a long haul on a truck. Sadly, most is picked too early to reach its full potential in smell and taste, then left to "ripen" under the glare of artificial lights. The cure? Shop whenever you can at a farmer's market, where you'll find food grown for the table (not the produce bin) and that has had a chance to ripen in the field.

Small farmers have the advantage of being closer to their retail outlets, so they can wait to pick the

produce when it's ripe. Since this produce is grown as food and not necessarily beauty-pageant material, you'll often find odd-shaped specimens. These quirky profiles just add charm to the pursuit. You could love a zucchini with a crooked nose, couldn't you, if it was sweet and tender?

But wherever you find your vegetables, you'll do right by them if you put them on the grill. The grill does something to vegetables that makes us all a little weak in the knees. It draws out their natural sugars and caramelizes them on the surface right where you can taste them. Add that little hint of smoke and they become downright irresistible. And because the grill cooks them quickly, it heightens their color and appearance, too. All those veggies need is a light coating of olive oil to prevent them from sticking to the grate and to keep them nice and moist. That, and a dash of salt and pepper.

We have plenty of recipes in this chapter that feature vegetables as the main course, as well as side dishes that round out a great grilled meal. Once you're hooked on grilled veggies, you'll discover their amazing versatility. Grilling vegetable ingredients before you add them to a dish can make an ordinary meal spectacular. Soon you'll be grilling up extra asparagus, peppers, and onions for tomorrow's omelette, sandwiches, soup, or pasta dish. And more importantly, you'll be eating your veggies because you want to. Mom would be proud.

SUMMER VEGETABLES
WITH ROMESCO SAUCE

This rich tomato sauce is from Catalonia, Spain. We've substituted dried ancho chile—known as poblano chile when fresh—for the red bell pepper that is typically used. This sauce is great on grilled chicken and seafood, too. It's thick enough to spread on bread and eat straight up, either warm or at room temperature.

DIRECT/MEDIUM

FOR THE SAUCE:

- 1   LARGE RIPE TOMATO, COARSELY CHOPPED
- 1   MEDIUM DRIED ANCHO CHILE, SEEDED AND SOAKED IN WARM WATER FOR ABOUT 20 MINUTES, THEN COARSELY CHOPPED
- 1   SLICE WHITE TOAST, TORN INTO PIECES
- 1/3 CUP SLIVERED ALMONDS, TOASTED
- 1/4 CUP TIGHTLY PACKED FRESH ITALIAN PARSLEY
- 1   SMALL GARLIC CLOVE, CRUSHED
- 2   TABLESPOONS EXTRA-VIRGIN OLIVE OIL
- 2   TEASPOONS RED WINE VINEGAR

     KOSHER SALT
     FRESHLY GROUND BLACK PEPPER

- 2   LARGE YELLOW ONIONS
- 1   LARGE FENNEL BULB
- 1   LARGE BELL PEPPER, RED, YELLOW, *OR* GREEN
- 1   MEDIUM ZUCCHINI
     EXTRA-VIRGIN OLIVE OIL

- 2   PITA POCKETS

To make the sauce: In a food processor, combine the sauce ingredients. Pulse until coarsely chopped. Season with salt and pepper. Transfer to a serving bowl.

Cut the onions crosswise into 1/2-inch slices. Cut off and discard the fennel stalks, remove the wilted outer leaves, and cut the bulb lengthwise into 1/4-inch slices. Halve the bell pepper lengthwise. Stem, core, and seed the pepper, then flatten it with the palm of your hand. Trim the zucchini ends and cut on the bias into 1/2-inch slices.

Brush or spray both sides of the vegetables with the olive oil. Season with salt and pepper. Grill over *Direct Medium* heat until tender but not limp, turning once halfway through grilling time. The onion and fennel will take 10 to 12 minutes. The bell pepper and zucchini will take 6 to 8 minutes. Grill the pita pockets over *Direct Medium* heat until toasted, about 1 minute, turning once halfway through grilling time. Cut the pockets into wedges. Cut the vegetables into bite-sized pieces. Serve with the sauce and pita.

MAKES 4 SERVINGS

MIDDLE EASTERN PITA
WITH TZATZIKI SAUCE

In this recipe, the refreshing tastes of mint and cucumber mingle with the deeper flavors of yellow squash, eggplant, and—yes—lettuce. Lettuce, not a veggie usually associated with grilling, adds a nice nutty taste.

DIRECT/MEDIUM

FOR THE SAUCE:

- 1/2 CUP PLAIN YOGURT
- 1/4 CUP PEELED, FINELY CHOPPED, SEEDLESS CUCUMBER
- 1   TABLESPOON FINELY CHOPPED FRESH MINT
- 1   TABLESPOON MINCED RED ONION
- 2   TEASPOONS EXTRA-VIRGIN OLIVE OIL
- 1   TEASPOON MINCED GARLIC
- 1/2 TEASPOON KOSHER SALT
- 1/4 TEASPOON FRESHLY GROUND BLACK PEPPER

- 1   LARGE GLOBE EGGPLANT, PEELED AND CUT CROSSWISE INTO 1/2-INCH SLICES
- 2   MEDIUM YELLOW SQUASHES, CUT LENGTHWISE INTO 1/2-INCH SLICES
- 1   HEART OF ROMAINE LETTUCE, CUT IN HALF LENGTHWISE
- 1/4 CUP EXTRA-VIRGIN OLIVE OIL
     KOSHER SALT
     FRESHLY GROUND BLACK PEPPER

- 4   WHOLE-WHEAT PITA POCKETS

To make the sauce: In a small bowl whisk together the sauce ingredients.

Brush or spray the eggplant, squash, and lettuce with the olive oil. Grill over *Direct Medium* heat, turning once halfway through grilling time. The eggplant will take 8 to 10 minutes and the squash will take 6 to 8 minutes. The lettuce will take 3 to 5 minutes; grill it just until wilted. Season the vegetables with salt and pepper as you remove them from the grill. Coarsely chop the vegetables, place them in a bowl, and stir to combine.

Grill the pita pockets over *Direct Medium* heat until lightly toasted, about 30 seconds, turning once halfway through grilling time. Fill the pockets with the vegetables, spooning a little sauce on top. Serve warm.

MAKES 4 SERVINGS

PORTABELLO BURGERS
WITH ROASTED PEPPERS

Try these juicy 'shroom burgers and you may never go back to meat patties. The portabellos are why: They have a firm texture that rivals steak.

DIRECT/MEDIUM

FOR THE TAPENADE:

- 1 MEDIUM SHALLOT, COARSELY CHOPPED
- 1 MEDIUM GARLIC CLOVE, COARSELY CHOPPED
- 3/4 CUP PITTED KALAMATA OLIVES
- 1 TABLESPOON CAPERS, DRAINED
- 1 TO 2 ANCHOVY FILLETS (OIL-PACKED), DRAINED
- 2 TO 3 TABLESPOONS EXTRA-VIRGIN OLIVE OIL
- 1 TO 2 TABLESPOONS FRESH LEMON JUICE
  FRESHLY GROUND BLACK PEPPER

- 4 MEDIUM RED BELL PEPPERS

- 4 LARGE PORTABELLO MUSHROOMS, STEMS REMOVED, GILLS SCRAPED OUT, AND CAPS WIPED
  EXTRA-VIRGIN OLIVE OIL
  KOSHER SALT

- 4 LARGE HAMBURGER BUNS
- 4 LEAVES FRESH LETTUCE

To make the tapenade: In a food processor finely chop the shallot and garlic. Scrape down the sides of the bowl. Add the olives, capers, and anchovies and process until uniformly chopped. Add the remaining tapenade ingredients. Pulse and adjust quantities to make a spreadable paste.

Grill the bell peppers whole over *Direct Medium* heat until evenly charred on all sides, 10 to 12 minutes, turning every 3 to 5 minutes. Remove the peppers from the grill and place in a paper bag; close tightly. Let stand 10 to 15 minutes to steam off the skins. Remove the peppers from the bag and peel away the charred skins. Cut off the tops and remove the seeds. Cut each pepper into two or three same-sized pieces.

Lightly brush or spray the mushrooms on both sides with olive oil and season with salt and pepper. Grill, smooth side up first, over *Direct Medium* heat until tender, 12 to 15 minutes, turning and basting with the oil once halfway through grilling time.

Grill the hamburger buns over *Direct Medium* heat until toasted, about 30 seconds. Spread the tapenade on the buns, then add the mushrooms, red peppers, and lettuce. Serve warm or at room temperature.

MAKES 4 SERVINGS

HOT LITTLE NUMBERS
GRILL-ROASTED PEPPERS

Classic roasted bell peppers play countless roles in great cooking. Use them in sauces or to top a burger (such as the portabello burgers at left) or a sandwich. Toss pepper strips with any sort of salad or just drizzle them with olive oil and balsamic vinegar for a light snack. You can prepare a bunch at a time and keep extras on hand in the refrigerator for up to a week if you pack them in a vinaigrette (3 parts olive oil to 1 part vinegar). Here's how to grill them:

> *Place whole red, yellow, or orange bell peppers over Direct Medium heat. Grill until evenly charred on all sides, 10 to 12 minutes, turning every 3 to 5 minutes. Remove the peppers from the grill and place in a paper bag; close tightly. Let stand 10 to 15 minutes to steam off the skins. Remove the peppers from the bag and peel away the charred skins. Cut off the tops and remove the seeds. Slice, chop, or use as desired.*

You can use the same grill-roasting and skinning method for large chile peppers, such as Anaheims and poblanos, or even the smaller jalapeño. Just grill them until charred all over, turning as needed. (Be careful not to rub your eyes while working with these hot ones; you may even want to wear rubber gloves.) Meaty chiles are particularly impressionable when it comes to taking on smoky undertones from the grill. Try them whole in stuffed pepper recipes (such as the poblano rellenos on page 344), puréed in sauces, diced in salsas, or as a garnish.

VEGETABLES ON THE GRILL

The dance of the grilling novice is a curious series of sprints between the grill and the kitchen. While the meat sizzles outside, the vegetable side dishes are boiled, steamed, or microwaved indoors. Maybe you've been there? Then, one day you discover that both can be done on the grill. Hooray! Now you can leave your workouts for the gym and, vegetable platter in hand, step up to the grill with confidence. Or can you? To spot you on your form, we've jotted down some pointers:

MOST VEGETABLES CAN BE GRILLED. The trick is in how you cut them. The chart at right suggests the best cuts and approximate grilling times to guide your efforts. Grilling times may vary slightly depending on moisture content—today's zucchini might be moister than yesterday's and thus take a little longer. We're not talking vast differences here, but with practice you'll be able to identify the outliers and adjust.

VEGETABLES NEED A LITTLE OIL before grilling so they don't stick to the cooking grate or dry out. A spray or mister will leave a nice, light, even coat; alternatively, use a basting brush. Let excess oil drip off before you place the veggies on the grate—and never spray oil onto a hot grill! Try flavored or seasoned oils *(see page 361)* or a dip in a marinade (look in the index under "Marinades" for a variety of recipes to choose from) to add moisture and intrigue.

TO MINIMIZE MOISTURE LOSS during preparation, cut vegetables just before grilling. Vegetables with a low moisture content, such as mushrooms, may also need an extra brush of oil before turning.

ADD A DRIZZLE OF OIL or a pat of butter to veggies before you foil-wrap them—for example, whole artichokes or cabbages. Fold the edges of the foil over to create a tight seal, but leave a little room for steam expansion. When done, open packets carefully to avoid steam burns. But don't stuff your veggies into foil packets unless you really have to; why miss out on the benefit of the exposure to the open flame? Instead, skewer the little devils—new potatoes, button mushrooms, and cherry tomatoes are great candidates for this method. Run two skewers side-by-side through the veggies and they won't spin around when you turn them.

SELECT VEGETABLES OF SIMILAR SIZE and structure or cut them into more uniform pieces. And for fire-roasting, choose bell and chile peppers that are as flat-sided as possible. A square pepper will blister more evenly than a round or dimpled one, and its skin will slip right off. Whole peppers do not need a coat of oil before grilling.

VEGETABLE GRILLING CHART

VEGETABLE		PREPARATION	METHOD/GRILL TIME	SPECIAL INSTRUCTIONS
Artichokes	Whole	Drizzle with melted butter or oil, then foil-wrap	Indirect High/30 to 45 min	Remove tough outer leaves and trim stems before grilling
Asparagus	Whole	Toss with melted butter or oil	Direct Medium/6 to 8 min	Snap off tough ends before preparing
Beets	Whole	Oil	Direct Medium/1 to 1½ hr, until tender	Remove tops before grilling, but leave root ends intact; turn 3 or 4 times
Bell Peppers	Whole Halved or quartered	 Flatten and oil	Direct Medium/10 to 12 min Direct Medium/6 to 8 min	See page 329 Turn once
Cabbage	Whole or quartered	Butter or oil, then foil-wrap	Indirect Medium/1½ to 2 hr	Add 30 min to grilling time if foil pack left open, as in recipe on page 347
Chiles Anaheim or Poblano	 Whole		 Direct Medium/7 to 9 min	 See page 329
Corn	In husks Husked	Leave plain or butter Butter	Direct Medium/25 to 30 min Direct Medium/10 to 12 min	See page 346 See page 346
Eggplant Globe Japanese	 ½-inch slices Halved lengthwise	 Oil Oil	 Direct Medium/8 to 10 min Direct Medium/12 to 15 min	
Fennel	¼-inch slices	Oil	Direct Medium/10 to 12 min	
Garlic	Whole	Drizzle with oil then foil-wrap	Indirect Medium/45 to 60 min	See page 335
Green Beans		Toss with melted butter or oil	Direct Medium/8 to 10 min	
Mushrooms Portabello Shiitake or Button	 Whole Whole	 Marinate, butter, or oil Marinate, butter, or oil	 Direct Medium/12 to 15 min Direct Medium/8 to 10 min	Grilling times depend on thickness and moisture content; baste with oil as needed to prevent drying
Onions White, Yellow, or Red Green	 ½-inch slices Whole or trimmed	 Oil Oil	 Direct Medium/10 to 12 min Direct Medium/3 to 4 min	Grill onion slices until tender; baste with oil as needed
Potatoes Russet, Yukon Gold, or Red New or Small	 Whole ½-inch wedges ½-inch slices Halved or quartered	 Butter or oil Toss with melted butter or oil Toss with melted butter or oil Toss with melted butter or oil	 Indirect Medium/45 to 60 min Direct Medium/10 to 12 min Direct Medium/14 to 16 min Direct Medium/20 to 25 min	 Skewer for easy turning
Squashes, Summer Yellow or Zucchini	 ½-inch slices	 Oil	 Direct Medium/6 to 8 min	
Squashes, Winter Acorn, Buttercup, Butternut, Golden Nugget, Hubbard, or Spaghetti Pumpkin	 Halved Hollowed, with top on	 Brush open halves with butter or oil Brush interior with butter or oil	Indirect Medium/ 1-lb 40 to 45 min 2-lb 50 to 55 min 3-lb spaghetti 1¼ to 1½ hr Indirect Medium/ 3-lb 1½ to 2 hr	Scrape out seeds and strings from halves. Grill, cut side down first; turn once. Squash is done when you can pierce the flesh easily with a fork Grill, right side up, with top on; no need to turn
Sweet Potatoes	Whole	Butter or oil	Indirect Medium/About 50 min to 1 hr, until tender	Turn 3 or 4 times
Tomatoes Plum Beefsteak Cherry	 Whole Halved lengthwise ½-inch slices Halved Whole		 Direct Medium/8 to 10 min Direct Medium/6 to 8 min Direct Medium/2 to 4 min Direct Medium/6 to 8 min Direct Medium/2 to 4 min	Tomatoes become quite tender on the grill, so use care to gently remove them; cooking time varies according to ripeness and moisture content Skewer for easy turning

ROASTED ARTICHOKES

Here we season artichokes with generous amounts of garlic and roast them in foil packets. With such flavorful treatment, they don't need any more embellishment. The best artichokes are available in spring and fall; buy them when they're deep green and their spiky outer leaves are tightly closed and unblemished.

INDIRECT/HIGH

4 MEDIUM ARTICHOKES
  JUICE OF 2 LEMONS

4 TEASPOONS MINCED GARLIC
  KOSHER SALT
4 TABLESPOONS EXTRA-VIRGIN OLIVE OIL

Cut off the stems of the artichokes so they can stand upright. Pull off the tough exterior leaves, exposing the tender, pale green leaves underneath. If the remaining leaves are thorny, snip off their ends with scissors. Submerge the artichokes in a large bowl of cold water mixed with the lemon juice for at least 5 minutes or up to 3 hours; if necessary, use a weight to keep them submerged.

Tear off four sheets of heavy-duty aluminum foil, about 12 inches long each. Put 1/2 teaspoon of the minced garlic in the center of one of the sheets and place the base of an artichoke on top. Distribute a second 1/2 teaspoon of garlic evenly between the artichoke's leaves. Season with salt and drizzle 1 tablespoon of the olive oil on top. Pull up the corners of the foil around the artichoke, twist them together at the top to leave a little room for the expansion of steam, and seal any gaps. Repeat with the other artichokes.

Grill the artichokes over *Indirect High* heat until tender, 30 to 45 minutes. To test for doneness, insert a knife into the artichoke base; it should slide in and out easily, without resistance. Allow the artichokes to cool slightly before unwrapping them. Serve warm, at room temperature, or chilled.

MAKES 4 SERVINGS

ARTICHOKES
WITH LEMON-DILL MAYONNAISE

These artichokes are just the ticket for entertaining since the steaming and sauce can be done ahead. "Shocking" the artichokes in ice water after steaming fixes their green color; the technique also works with other vegetables such as green beans.

DIRECT/MEDIUM

FOR THE MAYONNAISE:
1 CUP MAYONNAISE
2 TABLESPOONS FINELY CHOPPED FRESH DILL
2 TEASPOONS FRESH LEMON JUICE
2 TEASPOONS FRESH LIME JUICE
1 TEASPOON KOSHER SALT

4 MEDIUM ARTICHOKES
  EXTRA-VIRGIN OLIVE OIL

To make the mayonnaise: In a medium bowl whisk together the mayonnaise ingredients. Cover and refrigerate until ready to use.

Trim the stems of the artichokes, leaving about 1/2 inch of stem attached. Pull off the tough exterior leaves, exposing the tender, pale green leaves underneath. If the remaining leaves are thorny, snip off their ends with scissors. Level the tops of the artichokes by cutting them off about 1/2 inch from the end.

Place a steaming rack in a large saucepan and add water up to the base of the rack. Bring the water to a boil and put in the artichokes, upside down. Cover the saucepan and steam the artichokes until tender, 20 to 25 minutes; check to make sure the water doesn't boil away and add more if necessary. To test for doneness, insert a knife into the artichoke base; it should slide in and out easily, without resistance.

As soon as the artichokes are done, transfer them to a large bowl of ice water to stop the cooking. Drain well and place on a plate with the stem ends up. Cover and refrigerate for at least 1/2 hour.

Halve the artichokes lengthwise, through the stem. Using a spoon or small knife, scrape the purple leaves and fuzzy choke out of each one. Brush or spray the artichokes all over with olive oil. Grill over *Direct Medium* heat until marked on the outside and warm throughout, 8 to 12 minutes, turning once or twice during grilling time. Serve warm, at room temperature, or chilled, with the mayonnaise.

MAKES 4 SERVINGS

Artichokes with Lemon–Dill Mayonnaise (left) and Cajun Corn with Louisiana Butter (page 334)

CAJUN CORN
WITH LOUISIANA BUTTER

Another easy recipe to multiply. Serve these ears of corn at your next barbecue and you'll wake up more than your taste buds!

DIRECT/MEDIUM

4 EARS FRESH SWEET CORN IN THEIR HUSKS

FOR THE BUTTER:

1 TEASPOON HUNGARIAN PAPRIKA
1/2 TEASPOON ONION POWDER
1/2 TEASPOON KOSHER SALT
1/4 TEASPOON DRIED THYME
1/4 TEASPOON DRIED OREGANO
1/8 TEASPOON CAYENNE
4 TABLESPOONS UNSALTED BUTTER, SOFTENED

Soak the ears of corn in cold water for at least 30 minutes. If necessary, use a weight to keep the ears submerged. Drain.

Meanwhile, make the butter: In a small bowl mix together the paprika, onion powder, salt, thyme, oregano, and cayenne. Add the butter and mash it with the back of a fork, then stir to distribute the seasonings throughout.

Pull back the husks on each ear of corn, leaving them attached at the stem. Remove and discard the corn silk. Spread about 1 tablespoon of the seasoned butter evenly over the kernels of each ear. Fold the husks back over the kernels and use string or a thin strip of husk to tie them at the top.

Grill the corn over *Direct Medium* heat until the kernels are tender, 25 to 30 minutes, turning three or four times during grilling time. Don't worry if the husks brown or burn. Remove from the grill. When cool enough to handle, carefully pull the husks back and cut them off with a knife. Serve warm.

MAKES 4 SERVINGS

CORN ON THE COB
ITALIAN-STYLE

Sweet summer corn is a treat all by itself—when seasoned with butter and Parmesan cheese, it's over the top. Be sure to give these ears a good long soak before placing them on the grill. The husks will end up beautifully dappled with grill marks, the kernels moist and tender.

DIRECT/MEDIUM

4 EARS FRESH SWEET CORN IN THEIR HUSKS

4 TABLESPOONS UNSALTED BUTTER, SOFTENED
2 TABLESPOONS FINELY CHOPPED ITALIAN PARSLEY

1/4 CUP FRESHLY GRATED PARMIGIANO-REGGIANO CHEESE

Soak the ears of corn in cold water for at least 30 minutes. If necessary, use a weight to keep the ears submerged. Drain.

In a small bowl mix together the butter and parsley with the back of a fork.

Pull back the husks on each ear of corn, leaving them attached at the stem. Remove and discard the corn silk. Spread about 1 tablespoon of the butter evenly over the kernels of each ear. Fold the husks back over the kernels and use string or a thin strip of husk to tie them at the top.

Grill the corn over *Direct Medium* heat until the kernels are tender, 25 to 30 minutes, turning three or four times during grilling time. Don't worry if the husks brown or burn. Remove from the grill. When cool enough to handle, carefully pull the husks back and cut them off with a knife. Sprinkle the corn kernels with the cheese. Serve warm.

MAKES 4 SERVINGS

PROVENÇAL SANDWICHES
WITH ROASTED GARLIC PASTE

Something wonderful happens to garlic when it's roasted: The flavor deepens and mellows, losing the pungency that gives garlic lovers a bad rep on a crowded bus. Here it transforms sandwiches of grilled vegetables and goat cheese into something purely Provençal. Bon appétit!

INDIRECT/MEDIUM

FOR THE PASTE:

1   **MEDIUM HEAD GARLIC**

1   **TEASPOON EXTRA-VIRGIN OLIVE OIL**

2   **LARGE RIPE PLUM TOMATOES, CUT IN HALF LENGTHWISE, SEEDED, AND COARSELY CHOPPED**

1   **TEASPOON BALSAMIC VINEGAR**

12   **FRESH BASIL LEAVES**

2   **ANCHOVY FILLETS (OIL-PACKED), DRAINED**

1/4   **TEASPOON FRESHLY GROUND BLACK PEPPER**

1   **SMALL GLOBE EGGPLANT**

1   **MEDIUM RED BELL PEPPER**

1   **MEDIUM YELLOW BELL PEPPER**

    EXTRA-VIRGIN OLIVE OIL

    KOSHER SALT

    FRESHLY GROUND BLACK PEPPER

4   **FRENCH ROLLS**

4   **RED-LEAF LETTUCE LEAVES**

3   **OUNCES FRESH GOAT CHEESE, SLICED**

To make the paste: Prepare and wrap the garlic in aluminum foil as described at right. Grill over *Indirect Medium* heat until the cloves are soft, 45 minutes to 1 hour. Remove the garlic from the grill and allow to cool. Squeeze the garlic pulp into a food processor. Add the remaining paste ingredients and process until smooth.

Cut the eggplant crosswise into 1/2-inch slices. Halve the bell peppers lengthwise. Stem, core, and seed the peppers, then flatten them with the palm of your hand. Lightly brush or spray the eggplant and bell peppers with the olive oil. Season with salt and pepper. Grill over *Direct Medium* heat until tender but not limp, turning once halfway through grilling time. The eggplant will take 8 to 10 minutes and the bell peppers will take 6 to 8 minutes.

Just before serving, split the rolls and grill them, cut side down, over *Direct Medium* heat until toasted, about 30 seconds. Brush the inside of the rolls with the garlic paste and layer with the grilled vegetables, lettuce, and goat cheese. Serve warm or at room temperature.

MAKES 4 SERVINGS

MOM'S OWN COMFORT FOOD

GREAT GRILLED GARLIC

Is there any comfort food more near and dear to the heart than mashed potatoes? Whether you're cold or lonely, hungry or depressed, nothing mends the soul like a hot mountain of this creamy cure-all topped with a lake of melted butter. Mommy!

Mashed potatoes are only one food roasted garlic elevates to the celestial. That's why we always keep some on hand. Just throw a couple of garlic heads on the grill whenever dinner's cooking. Here's how:

> *Remove the loose, papery outer skin from a head of garlic and cut off the head to expose the cloves. Drizzle a teaspoon of olive oil over the cloves. Place the garlic on a large square of aluminum foil. Fold up the sides and seal to make a packet, leaving a little room for the expansion of steam. Grill over Indirect Medium heat until the cloves are soft, 45 minutes to 1 hour. Remove the garlic from the grill and allow to cool. Unwrap the foil and squeeze out the cloves into a small bowl.*

While the garlic is still warm, spread it on toasted baguette slices as an irresistible appetizer. It won't leave any lingering odors or aftertaste, so slather it on. Use roasted garlic in pasta sauces. Mash it into some soft butter with a fork to top a sizzling hot steak. For those comforting potatoes, add the garlic during mashing. And for a real mind-blower, add chopped fresh rosemary leaves that have been fried in butter.

Arugula Pizza

ARUGULA PIZZA

The peppery taste of pesto made with arugula hits the on-button with this delicious pizza. Be sure to rotate the pizza occasionally for a nice, evenly browned crust.

DIRECT/MEDIUM

1 PIZZA DOUGH RECIPE (SEE PAGE 339)

FOR THE PESTO:

2 CUPS ARUGULA

1 LARGE CLOVE GARLIC, CRUSHED

2 TABLESPOONS PINE NUTS

1/4 TEASPOON FRESHLY GROUND BLACK PEPPER

1/2 CUP EXTRA-VIRGIN OLIVE OIL

1/2 CUP FRESHLY GRATED PARMIGIANO-REGGIANO CHEESE

FOR THE TOPPING:

3 MEDIUM BELL PEPPERS, RED AND/OR YELLOW

1 1/2 POUNDS FRESH SHIITAKE MUSHROOMS, STEMS REMOVED

EXTRA-VIRGIN OLIVE OIL

KOSHER SALT

FRESHLY GROUND BLACK PEPPER

1 CUP CHOPPED ARUGULA

1 TOMATO, CHOPPED

1/2 CUP FRESHLY SHAVED PARMIGIANO-REGGIANO CHEESE

JUICE OF 1 LEMON

Make the pizza dough and prepare the four crusts as described on page 339.

To make the pesto: In a food processor finely chop the arugula, garlic, and pine nuts. Add the pepper. With the motor running, slowly pour in the olive oil. Transfer the mixture to a bowl and stir in the cheese.

To prepare the topping: Grill the bell peppers over *Direct Medium* heat until evenly charred on all sides, 10 to 12 minutes, turning every 3 to 5 minutes. Remove the peppers from the grill and place in a paper bag; close tightly. Let stand 10 to 15 minutes to steam off the skins. Remove the peppers from the bag and peel away the charred skins. Cut off the tops and remove the seeds. Cut each pepper into thin strips.

Brush or spray both sides of the mushroom caps with olive oil. Season with salt and pepper. Grill over *Direct Medium* heat until tender, 8 to 10 minutes, turning and basting with the oil as needed to keep them moist. Remove from the grill and cut into 1/2-inch slices.

Grill one side of the pizza crusts over *Direct Medium* heat until toasted, about 1 to 3 minutes. Spread the pesto on the toasted side of the crusts. Distribute the mushrooms and peppers on top.

Grill the pizzas over *Direct Medium* heat until the crusts are crisp, 4 to 6 minutes. Remove from the grill. Top with the arugula, tomato, cheese, and lemon juice. Cut into wedges and serve warm.

MAKES 4 SERVINGS

PIZZA MARGHERITA

Legend has it that the original Pizza Margherita was created in 1889 to honor the visit of Queen Margherita, consort of King Umberto I, to his fair city of Naples. The three colors of the topping—red (tomatoes), white (mozzarella), and green (basil)—represent the colors of the Italian flag. Use only fresh tomatoes and tear the basil leaves into pieces; cutting them with a knife will turn them black along the edges.

DIRECT/MEDIUM

1 PIZZA DOUGH RECIPE (SEE PAGE 339)

FOR THE TOPPING:

8 TO 10 RIPE PLUM TOMATOES, CORED AND FINELY CHOPPED

2 TABLESPOONS EXTRA-VIRGIN OLIVE OIL

1 TEASPOON MINCED GARLIC

1/2 CUP TIGHTLY PACKED BASIL LEAVES, TORN INTO SMALL PIECES

1/2 TEASPOON KOSHER SALT

1/4 TEASPOON FRESHLY GROUND BLACK PEPPER

8 OUNCES SHREDDED MOZZARELLA CHEESE (ABOUT 2 CUPS)

Make the pizza dough and prepare the four crusts as described on page 339.

To prepare the topping: In a large bowl combine the topping ingredients. Stir to blend.

Grill one side of the pizza crusts over *Direct Medium* heat until toasted, about 1 to 3 minutes. Distribute about 1 cup of the topping on the toasted side of each crust, leaving any liquid in the bowl. Top each pizza with about 1/2 cup of the cheese, leaving a 1/2-inch border around the edges.

Grill the pizzas over *Direct Medium* heat until the crusts are crisp and the cheese has melted, 4 to 6 minutes. Remove from the grill. Cut into wedges and serve warm.

MAKES 4 SERVINGS

HOW TO GRILL FOR A VEGETARIAN

If you're of the carnivorous persuasion, it may seem simple enough to make dinner for any vegetarian guests: Pass them a bowl of crudités and try not to make any remarks about their strange ways with nutrition while you serve all the "normal" people their burgers and brats. Oh, but there's so much more to a vegetarian's diet than the omission of meat.

First of all, people have many different reasons for avoiding meat in their diets: religious, ethical, political, and other personal beliefs. All are valid reasons and certainly the dinner hour is no time to challenge or debate them. Second, it's important to know what kind of vegetarian your guest is. Yes, there are different kinds.

"Vegetarians": Why the quotation marks? Certainly not purists, these folks have issues with and avoid certain meats, but eat others. ("I'm vegetarian, but I eat chicken.") They may have legitimate concerns about certain food groups or they may just be picky eaters. But we're less concerned with the "why" than the "what," right?

Lacto-ovo vegetarians: Eat no animal meat or stocks, but do consume milk and egg products.

Vegans: Don't eat anything derived from animals. Plant-only diet. 100%. No exceptions.

It helps to think a bit about the ingredients of your ingredients, too. Marshmallows, for example, a staple of backyard grill-fests, are made of gelatin, which is derived from beef marrow. Then there's fish. Some people who consider themselves rather strict vegetarians will eat fish and seafood, while others are mortified at the mere suggestion. So ask. Then, there are many ways to proceed.

GO WITH THE FLOW. If the thought of a dual menu stresses you out, just pick one of the many vegetable-based entrées in this chapter and be done worrying. These recipes are so rich in flavors and textures that you won't even miss the meat—in fact, you'll probably be really glad you skipped it to discover something new and wonderful.

PURIFY THE GRILL. You're used to doing a burn-off of cooking residues after each time you use the grill. When you preheat the grill for dinner, you purify the grates again by fire. For most vegetarians, this is adequate for removing any lingering bits of meatiness from the cooking surface. But to be courteous, just ask. Some people prefer the use of a totally separate cooking surface. If you have a second grill, offer to use it for the meal. But such people are probably sensitive to the potential inconvenience to their host and may be willing to make other arrangements out of respect for you.

REMEMBER THE SPLATTER FACTOR. Once the cooking grate is cleaned, you may want to prepare the vegetarian meal first so that meat juices from the rest of the meal don't splatter onto their food. Good news is that most veggie-based dishes grill up fast so you don't have to keep your other guests waiting.

RELAX. If you have vegetarian friends or family members, they will most certainly appreciate any effort to make them feel more at home. And then you can all get on with the real business at hand: enjoying a great meal in the company of loved ones.

"One farmer says to me, 'you cannot live on vegetable food solely, for it furnishes nothing to make bones with;'...walking all the while he talks behind his oxen, which, with vegetable-made bones, jerk him and his lumbering plow along in spite of every obstacle."

— HENRY DAVID THOREAU, *Walden*

VEGETABLES

338

PIZZA DOUGH
ON THE GRILL

Here's a pizza dough that works like a dream on the grill. Check out the vegetarian pizza recipes on page 337 or make up your own.

DIRECT/MEDIUM

- 1 ENVELOPE ACTIVE DRY YEAST
- 1/2 TEASPOON GRANULATED SUGAR
- 2/3 CUP WARM WATER (105°F TO 115°F)
- 2 CUPS ALL-PURPOSE FLOUR, PLUS MORE FOR ROLLING OUT DOUGH
- 1 TEASPOON KOSHER SALT
- 1/2 TEASPOON FRESHLY GROUND BLACK PEPPER
- 2 TABLESPOONS EXTRA-VIRGIN OLIVE OIL, PLUS MORE FOR BRUSHING CRUSTS

To make the dough: In a medium bowl combine the yeast, sugar, and water. Stir briefly and let stand until foamy, 5 to 10 minutes. Add the 2 cups flour, salt, pepper, and 2 tablespoons olive oil. Stir until the dough holds together. Transfer to a lightly floured work surface and knead until smooth, 5 to 10 minutes. Shape into a ball and place in a lightly oiled bowl. Turn the ball to coat the surface with oil. Cover the bowl with plastic wrap and set aside in a warm place until the dough doubles in size, 1 to 1 1/2 hours.

To make the crusts: Punch down the dough in the bowl. Transfer to a lightly floured work surface and cut into four equal pieces. Roll out each piece into an 8-inch round about 1/8 inch thick. Use a rolling pin dusted with flour to keep the dough from sticking. Lightly brush both sides of each round with olive oil and place the rounds on the back of two baking sheets. Gently slide the crusts from the baking sheets onto the cooking grate and grill over *Direct Medium* heat until the undersides are marked, 1 to 3 minutes. Don't worry if the crusts bubble in spots; they will deflate when turned over. Transfer the crusts back to the baking sheets, grilled side up.

To assemble the pizzas: Add the desired sauces and toppings to the toasted side of the crusts. Transfer to the cooking grate and grill over *Direct Medium* heat until the crusts are crisp, 4 to 6 minutes. Remove from the grill. Add any extra toppings called for in your recipe. Cut into wedges and serve warm.

MAKES 4 CRUSTS

QUICK & EASY
MEAT SUBSTITUTES

For steak or burgers, try big, fat portabello mushroom caps marinated in oil, red wine or vinegar, rosemary, salt, and pepper. Grill over Direct Medium heat and top with grilled onions, goat or blue cheese crumbles, or grill-roasted peppers. The texture of these brown beauties is so similar to beef it's uncanny. Polenta squares, brushed with olive oil, grilled over Direct High heat, and topped with sauces and grilled veggies also offer a wonderful change of texture and taste. And of course there are countless soy and veggie burger products on the market.

For chicken or veal, season thick slices of eggplant just as you would the meat and grill over Direct Medium heat. Made all the more wonderful by the grill.

For meat chunks in kabobs, consider chunks of texturized vegetable protein ("TVP" in veggie-speak), which are available at health food stores and some grocers. They have a wonderfully dense, meatlike texture. Marinate 'em, skewer 'em, grill 'em over Direct Medium heat, devour 'em.

And of course, tofu (firm). Drain it, slice it, marinate it, grill it over Direct Medium heat, top it, layer it...you get the picture. Tofu's most endearing quality is that it takes on flavors easily without a fight. Season away!

GRILLED VEGETABLES STIRRED INTO A RISOTTO MAKE THIS ITALIAN CLASSIC A MIDSUMMER FAVORITE.

Summer Vegetable Risotto

SUMMER VEGETABLE
RISOTTO

The secrets to creamy and al dente risotto are attention and patience. Add the cheese at the end and go for the real thing: Parmigiano-Reggiano, and lots of it.

DIRECT/MEDIUM

- **2 EARS FRESH SWEET CORN IN THEIR HUSKS**
- **1 LARGE RED BELL PEPPER**
- **2 RIPE PLUM TOMATOES**
- **1 MEDIUM ZUCCHINI**
- **1 MEDIUM YELLOW SQUASH**
- **1 SMALL GLOBE EGGPLANT**

- **EXTRA-VIRGIN OLIVE OIL**
- **KOSHER SALT**
- **FRESHLY GROUND BLACK PEPPER**

FOR THE RISOTTO:

- **5 TO 6 CUPS VEGETABLE OR LOW-SODIUM CHICKEN BROTH, PLUS WATER IF NEEDED**
- **2 TABLESPOONS EXTRA-VIRGIN OLIVE OIL**
- **1/2 CUP FINELY CHOPPED YELLOW ONION**
- **1 1/2 CUPS ARBORIO RICE**
- **1 TEASPOON MINCED GARLIC**
- **1/2 CUP DRY WHITE WINE**
- **1/2 CUP FRESHLY GRATED PARMIGIANO-REGGIANO CHEESE**
- **6 TO 8 BASIL LEAVES, TORN INTO SMALL PIECES**

Soak the ears of corn in cold water for at least 30 minutes; if necessary, use a weight to keep them submerged. Drain. Pull back the husks on each ear of corn, leaving them attached at the stem. Remove and discard the corn silk. Fold the husks back over the kernels and use string or a thin strip of husk to tie them at the top. Grill the corn over *Direct Medium* heat until the kernels are tender, 25 to 30 minutes, turning three or four times during grilling time. Don't worry if the husks brown or burn. Remove from the grill. When cool enough to handle, carefully pull the husks back and cut the kernels from the cob. Set the kernels aside.

Halve the bell pepper lengthwise. Stem, core, and seed the pepper, then flatten it with the palm of your hand. Core the tomatoes. Trim the ends from the zucchini and yellow squash and halve them lengthwise. Peel the eggplant and cut into 1/2-inch coins.

Lightly brush or spray the bell pepper, tomatoes, zucchini, squash, and eggplant with olive oil. Grill over *Direct Medium* heat until lightly browned and tender, turning once halfway through grilling time. The tomatoes, zucchini, squash, and eggplant will take 8 to 10 minutes. The pepper will take 6 to 8 minutes. Transfer the vegetables as they are cooked to a plate and loosely cover with aluminum foil.

When cool enough to handle, peel the loosened skins from the bell pepper and tomatoes and discard. Chop the vegetables into 1/2-inch pieces and place them in a medium bowl along with any accumulated juices. Add the reserved corn kernels, salt to taste, and a generous grinding of pepper. Toss and set aside until ready to use.

To make the risotto: Heat the broth in a saucepan to boiling; reduce heat to low and keep the broth hot.

In a large, broad saucepan or a deep sauté pan over medium heat, warm the olive oil. Add the onion and sauté until translucent, about 5 minutes. Add the rice and garlic and stir until the rice is coated with oil. Add the wine and cook, stirring, until the wine is absorbed. Add the hot broth to the rice 1/2 cup at a time, stirring until the broth is absorbed before adding another 1/2 cup. Keep stirring and adding the broth 1/2 cup at a time, cooking over medium heat for about 18 minutes. Taste a grain of rice. It should be barely cooked through, but not mushy. Add all the vegetables and continue cooking and adding broth 3 minutes more or until the risotto is creamy and the vegetables are warm. Stir in the cheese and the basil. Serve immediately.

MAKES 4 SERVINGS

GRILLED
ASPARAGUS
WITH TARRAGON BUTTER

One bite and you'll say, Why didn't I try this before?! Look for stalks with tightly formed spear heads.

DIRECT/MEDIUM

FOR THE BUTTER:

- **1/3 CUP UNSALTED BUTTER, SOFTENED**
- **2 TEASPOONS FINELY CHOPPED FRESH TARRAGON**
- **1/4 TEASPOON ONION POWDER**
- **1/4 TEASPOON KOSHER SALT**
- **1/4 TEASPOON FRESHLY GROUND BLACK PEPPER**

- **1 1/2 POUNDS ASPARAGUS SPEARS, TOUGH ENDS REMOVED**

To make the butter: In a large bowl combine the butter ingredients. Stir with a fork to evenly distribute the seasonings. In a small sauté pan melt 2 tablespoons of the butter mixture.

Brush the melted butter mixture all over the asparagus spears. Grill over *Direct Medium* heat until the spears are marked and tender, 6 to 8 minutes depending on their thickness, turning once halfway through grilling time. Transfer the asparagus to the bowl with the reserved butter mixture. Toss the spears to melt and evenly distribute the butter mixture. Serve warm.

MAKES 4 SERVINGS

CAULIFLOWER AND RED ONION
CURRY

This simple curry sauce accents the flavor of the grilled vegetables. The apple juice and raisins serve as a sweet counterpoint to the cauliflower, while the cream pulls the whole thing together.

DIRECT/MEDIUM

- **1 1/4 POUNDS CAULIFLOWER FLORETS, ABOUT 1 INCH IN DIAMETER EACH**
- **1 LARGE RED ONION, CUT CROSSWISE INTO 1/2-INCH SLICES**
- **VEGETABLE OIL**

FOR THE SAUCE:

- **2 TABLESPOONS UNSALTED BUTTER**
- **2 TABLESPOONS ALL-PURPOSE FLOUR**
- **1 TABLESPOON CURRY POWDER**
- **2 TEASPOONS MINCED GARLIC**
- **2 TEASPOONS MINCED FRESH GINGER**
- **2 TEASPOONS GROUND CUMIN**
- **1/2 TEASPOON KOSHER SALT**
- **1/4 TEASPOON FRESHLY GROUND BLACK PEPPER**
- **1 CUP APPLE JUICE**
- **1 TABLESPOON FRESH LEMON JUICE**
- **1/3 CUP RAISINS**
- **1/4 CUP HEAVY CREAM**

- **KOSHER SALT**
- **FRESHLY GROUND BLACK PEPPER**

Brush or spray the cauliflower and onion with vegetable oil. Grill the cauliflower over *Direct Medium* heat until evenly browned, 12 to 16 minutes, turning three times during grilling time. Grill the onion over *Direct Medium* heat until tender, 10 to 12 minutes, turning once halfway through grilling time. Cut the vegetables into bite-sized pieces. Set aside.

To make the sauce: In a large saucepan combine the butter, flour, curry powder, garlic, ginger, cumin, salt, and pepper. Blend well and cook over medium heat for 2 minutes. Add the apple juice and lemon juice. Raise heat to high and whisk the mixture as it comes to a boil. Lower heat and simmer for 3 to 4 minutes. Add the cauliflower, onions, raisins, and cream. Cook over medium heat, stirring occasionally, until the cauliflower is tender, 3 to 5 minutes. Season with salt and pepper. Serve warm.

MAKES 4 SERVINGS

SWEET POTATOES
WITH CINNAMON BUTTER

The best sweet potatoes are available in late fall through late winter. Look for ones that are firm, unblemished, and heavy for their size. For this recipe, it helps if they're relatively even-shaped so the crosswise slices are about the same in diameter. Because of their sugar content, the slices get caramelized grill marks pretty easily: Check them every few minutes and turn them when they are nicely browned. Serve with pork or duck.

DIRECT/MEDIUM

- **2 LARGE SWEET POTATOES**

- **1/3 CUP UNSALTED BUTTER**
- **2 TABLESPOONS FINELY CHOPPED ITALIAN PARSLEY**
- **1 TABLESPOON LIGHT BROWN SUGAR**
- **1/4 TEASPOON CINNAMON**
- **1/4 TEASPOON KOSHER SALT**
- **1/4 TEASPOON FRESHLY GROUND BLACK PEPPER**

Trim the tapered ends from the sweet potatoes. Grill over *Direct Medium* heat until tender but not falling apart, about 30 minutes, turning three times during grilling time. Remove the sweet potatoes from the grill and allow to cool. Peel and cut crosswise into 1/2-inch slices.

Meanwhile, in a small sauté pan melt the butter. Remove from the heat and immediately add the remaining ingredients. Stir to dissolve the sugar.

Brush both sides of the sweet potato slices generously with some of the butter mixture. Grill the slices over *Direct Medium* heat until they are well marked and tender, about 6 minutes, turning and basting with the reserved butter mixture once halfway through grilling time. Serve warm.

MAKES 4 SERVINGS

YUKON GOLD POTATOES
AND BUTTON MUSHROOMS

Serve this comfort food with grilled leg of lamb or whole roasted chicken, or devour it all by itself.

DIRECT/MEDIUM

- 1/3 CUP UNSALTED BUTTER
- 1/3 CUP FINELY CHOPPED FRESH THYME
- 1/2 TEASPOON KOSHER SALT
- 1/2 TEASPOON GARLIC POWDER
- 1/4 TEASPOON PAPRIKA
- 1/4 TEASPOON FRESHLY GROUND BLACK PEPPER

- 5 SMALL YUKON GOLD POTATOES, CUT INTO 1/2-INCH SLICES
- 3/4 POUND BUTTON MUSHROOMS, STEMS TRIMMED AND CAPS WIPED

In a large sauté pan over medium-high heat, melt the butter. Remove from the heat and add the thyme, salt, garlic powder, paprika, and pepper. Stir to combine.

Place the potatoes and mushrooms in a medium bowl and pour the butter mixture on top. Stir to coat evenly.

Grill the potatoes and mushrooms over *Direct Medium* heat until tender and golden brown, turning once halfway through grilling time. The potatoes will take 14 to 16 minutes and the mushrooms will take 8 to 10 minutes. Transfer the vegetables to a serving bowl and gently mix together. Serve warm.

MAKES 4 SERVINGS

*"Time ripens all things.
No man is born wise."*

— MIGUEL CERVANTES

GRILLED VEGETABLE
PASTA SALAD

Sherry vinegar is the basis of a unifying dressing that is first used to baste the veggies, then added to the pasta. The dish tastes delicious warm, but also makes top-notch leftovers when served at room temperature.

DIRECT/MEDIUM

FOR THE DRESSING:
- 1/4 CUP EXTRA-VIRGIN OLIVE OIL
- 3 TABLESPOONS SHERRY VINEGAR
- 2 TABLESPOONS FINELY CHOPPED FRESH BASIL
- 2 TEASPOONS MINCED GARLIC
- 1 TEASPOON DIJON MUSTARD
- 1/2 TEASPOON KOSHER SALT
- 1/4 TEASPOON FRESHLY GROUND BLACK PEPPER

- 1 MEDIUM JAPANESE EGGPLANT
- 1 LARGE RED ONION
- 2 LARGE BELL PEPPERS
- 4 MEDIUM RIPE TOMATOES

- 8 OUNCES FUSILLI (CORKSCREW-SHAPED) PASTA

- 3 TABLESPOONS PINE NUTS, LIGHTLY TOASTED
- 1/3 CUP FRESHLY GRATED PARMIGIANO-REGGIANO CHEESE
- 1/4 CUP FINELY CHOPPED FRESH BASIL
  KOSHER SALT
  FRESHLY GROUND BLACK PEPPER

To make the dressing: In a large bowl whisk together the dressing ingredients.

Trim the ends from the eggplant and halve it lengthwise. Cut the onion crosswise into 1/2-inch slices. Halve the bell peppers lengthwise. Remove the stems, cores, and seeds from the bell peppers, then flatten them with the palm of your hand. Core the tomatoes, halve them crosswise, and seed them.

Brush the vegetables on all sides with some of the dressing, leaving the rest in the bowl. Grill the vegetables over *Direct Medium* heat until tender and lightly charred, turning once halfway through grilling time. The eggplant will take 12 to 15 minutes, the onion 10 to 12 minutes, and the peppers and tomatoes 6 to 8 minutes. Cut all the vegetables into 1/2-inch pieces. Set aside.

Cook the pasta according to package directions. Drain and add to the bowl with the reserved dressing. Stir to combine. Add the vegetables and toss to mix thoroughly. Allow to stand about 10 minutes for the flavors to meld. Stir in the pine nuts, cheese, and basil. Taste and adjust seasoning with salt and pepper, if necessary. Serve warm.

MAKES 4 TO 6 SERVINGS

POBLANO
RELLENOS

Here's a vegetable main dish that's all about bold flavors: goat cheese in the stuffing and chipotle chiles in the tomato-based sauce. Instead of dipping the chile rellenos in batter and deep-frying them, we rely on the grill to get the taste we want. Note: You will start grilling over Direct Medium, then switch to Indirect Medium.

DIRECT/MEDIUM

4 LARGE STURDY POBLANO CHILES

FOR THE SAUCE:

4 LARGE RIPE PLUM TOMATOES

1 SMALL CANNED CHIPOTLE CHILE (PACKED IN ADOBO SAUCE)

1/2 TEASPOON KOSHER SALT

FRESHLY GROUND BLACK PEPPER

FOR THE STUFFING:

2 TABLESPOONS EXTRA-VIRGIN OLIVE OIL

1/2 CUP FINELY CHOPPED WHITE ONION

I CUP COOKED WHITE RICE, AT ROOM TEMPERATURE

4 OUNCES FRESH GOAT CHEESE, AT ROOM TEMPERATURE

1/4 CUP RAISINS, PLUMPED IN HOT WATER AND DRAINED

Grill the poblano chiles over *Direct Medium* heat until the skin is blistered in spots but the chiles still hold their shape, 7 to 9 minutes, turning as needed. When the chiles are cool enough to handle, peel off the loosened skin. With a small, sharp knife, make a lengthwise slit in each chile. Leave the stems intact, remove the seeds, and cut away most—but not all—of the ribs; leave enough to keep the chiles' structure.

To make the sauce: Grill the tomatoes over *Direct Medium* heat until the skins are blistered and loosened on all sides, 8 to 10 minutes, turning occasionally. Set aside. When the tomatoes are cool enough to handle, peel off the skins, cut out the cores, and place in a food processor. Add the chipotle chile and process until smooth. Transfer the mixture to a medium saucepan and simmer over medium heat until it thickens, about 10 minutes. Add the salt and season with the pepper. Set aside.

To make the stuffing: In a medium sauté pan over medium heat, warm the olive oil. Add the onion and cook, stirring occasionally, until golden brown, 6 to 8 minutes. Place the onion in a medium bowl and allow to cool for 5 minutes. Add the rice, goat cheese, and raisins and mix well. Stuff the chiles, but don't overfill them.

Grill the chiles, open side up, over *Indirect Medium* heat until the stuffing is warm, 8 to 10 minutes. Warm the sauce. Transfer the chiles to a platter and spoon the sauce on top. Serve immediately.

MAKES 4 SERVINGS

RUSTIC WHITE BEAN
SOUP

This satisfying bean soup is rich with the intense flavors of grilled plum tomatoes and onions. Like the best of Italian cooking, it takes only a few ingredients and is simple to make. Add a loaf of crusty Italian bread and a bottle of Chianti and you've got a hearty meal.

DIRECT/HIGH

1 LARGE YELLOW ONION, CUT INTO 1/2-INCH SLICES

8 LARGE RIPE PLUM TOMATOES, CORED

2 TABLESPOONS EXTRA-VIRGIN OLIVE OIL, PLUS MORE FOR BRUSHING ONIONS AND TOMATOES

1 TEASPOON MINCED GARLIC

2 CANS (15 OUNCES EACH) CANNELLINI BEANS (WHITE KIDNEY BEANS)

1/2 CUP COARSELY CHOPPED FRESH BASIL

KOSHER SALT

FRESHLY GROUND BLACK PEPPER

2 TEASPOONS BALSAMIC VINEGAR

Lightly spray or brush the onion slices and tomatoes with olive oil. Grill the onion over *Direct High* heat until lightly charred on both sides, 10 to 12 minutes, turning once halfway through grilling time. Grill the tomatoes over *Direct High* heat until the skins are loosened and lightly charred on all sides, 3 to 5 minutes, turning occasionally. Set aside.

Peel and discard the loosened skins from the tomatoes. Roughly chop the tomatoes and onions. In a large saucepan over medium-high heat, warm the 2 tablespoons olive oil. Add the garlic and grilled onions and cook for 2 minutes, stirring occasionally. Add the grilled tomatoes, cannellini beans (with liquid), and basil. Season with salt and pepper. Bring to a boil, then simmer for 10 minutes, stirring occasionally. Season again with salt and pepper, if necessary. Add the balsamic vinegar, give the soup a final stir, and serve.

MAKES 4 SERVINGS

Rustic White Bean Soup

YEAR-ROUND HEROES
CORN & SQUASH

Nothing makes you a backyard hero faster than serving perfectly grilled sweet corn. Unless it's waltzing in from the cold with a steaming platter of winter squash glistening with spiced butter. Here's how to succeed at both:

Corn: *Start with the freshest ears possible. Pick or purchase them no more than two to three days before grilling. Keep them chilled. Look for ears with fresh-looking (not dried) cuts at their stems. The brown silk should be slightly sticky and the kernels should shine. Pop a kernel with your thumbnail; the liquid should be milky and plentiful.*

Soak ears in the husk in cold water for 30 minutes or more before grilling. Give them a good shake, trim any silk off the top, and grill. For extra flavor, peel back the husks, remove the silk, and brush the kernels with plain or seasoned butter, about 1 tablespoon per ear. Fold the husks back up, tie with wet string, and grill over Direct Medium heat for 25 to 30 minutes, turning three or four times during grilling.

For tantalizing grill marks, you can grill husked ears, too. Husk them, brush them with seasoned butter, and grill them over Direct Medium heat for 10 to 12 minutes, turning every few minutes.

Winter Squash: *Grilled squash spiked with warming spices can melt a snowman's heart. Try it with miniature or pie pumpkins (4 to 9 inches across are best for grilling), acorn, buttercup, butternut, or golden nugget.*

Cut a lid for a small pumpkin as you would for a jack-o'-lantern. For other squash, cut the squash in half vertically. Careful! The rind can be tough. Scoop out the seeds and strings. Brush with butter and season to taste.

Put the lids back on pumpkins and grill them, right side up, over Indirect Medium heat; there's no need to turn them. Grill other squash, cut side down first, over Indirect Medium heat until grill marks appear, then turn and brush with a seasoned or sweetened butter—which will pool temptingly in the hollowed middle. (For a sweetened butter, blend softened butter with brown sugar, maple syrup, or honey and cinnamon, nutmeg, mace, or pumpkin pie spice.) Grill until flesh is tender (see the chart on page 331). Top with toasted pecans, if desired.

FRITTATA PRIMAVERA
WITH ASIAGO CHEESE

A frittata is an Italian omelet that is cooked slowly until it sets. When cooking it on the grill, keep the lid of the grill down as much as possible. If you want to improvise, use the spring vegetables of your choice—just grill them until they're tender (but not mushy!) before mixing them with the eggs. Don't be surprised if this becomes part of your standard brunch menu—it's that good.

DIRECT/MEDIUM

- 1/2 **POUND YUKON GOLD POTATOES, CUT CROSSWISE INTO 1/2-INCH SLICES**
- 2 **SMALL PORTABELLO MUSHROOMS, STEMS REMOVED**
- 2 **SLICES RED ONION, 1/2 INCH THICK EACH**
- 6 **TO 8 MEDIUM ASPARAGUS SPEARS, TOUGH ENDS REMOVED**
- 1/2 **MEDIUM RED BELL PEPPER, SEEDS, RIBS, AND CORE REMOVED, THEN FLATTENED WITH YOUR HAND**
  EXTRA-VIRGIN OLIVE OIL
  KOSHER SALT
  FRESHLY GROUND BLACK PEPPER

FOR THE FRITTATA:

- 8 **EGGS**
- 2 **TABLESPOONS FINELY CHOPPED FRESH THYME**
- 1 **TABLESPOON EXTRA-VIRGIN OLIVE OIL**
- 1/2 **CUP SHREDDED ASIAGO CHEESE**

Lightly brush or spray the vegetables on all sides with olive oil. Season with salt and pepper. Grill over *Direct Medium* heat until tender, turning once halfway through grilling time. The potatoes will take 14 to 16 minutes, the mushrooms 12 to 15 minutes—baste them with more oil when you turn them to prevent them from drying out—the onions 10 to 12 minutes, the asparagus and bell pepper 6 to 8 minutes. Transfer the vegetables to a cutting board and cut them into 1/2-inch pieces.

To make the frittata: In a medium bowl whisk the eggs and thyme together. Season with salt and pepper. In a 10-inch, nonstick sauté pan with a fireproof handle over *Direct Medium* heat, warm the olive oil for 2 to 3 minutes. Add the vegetables and sauté for 2 to 3 minutes. Stir, pour in the eggs, and stir again to distribute the ingredients. Cook for 2 minutes more. Sprinkle the cheese on top. Move the pan over *Direct Low* heat and cook until the frittata center is barely firm, 12 to 15 minutes. Remove and allow to rest for 5 to 10 minutes. Cut the frittata into wedges with a spatula and serve warm straight from the pan.

MAKES 4 TO 6 SERVINGS

SPRING VEGETABLE
PLATTER

This is a dish Epicurus himself would have lauded. Add good conversation, a crusty baguette, and a nice white wine, and you have the perfect excuse to while away the hours "à table."

DIRECT/MEDIUM

- **4 MEDIUM BEETS, TOPS TRIMMED AND ROOT ENDS INTACT**

- **2 TABLESPOONS EXTRA-VIRGIN OLIVE OIL**
- **1 TEASPOON MINCED GARLIC**
  KOSHER SALT
  FRESHLY GROUND BLACK PEPPER
- **10 SMALL NEW RED POTATOES, HALVED**
- **1/2 POUND GREEN BEANS, TRIMMED**
- **8 TO 10 MEDIUM ASPARAGUS SPEARS, TOUGH ENDS REMOVED**

FOR THE DRESSING:

- **3 TABLESPOONS EXTRA-VIRGIN OLIVE OIL**
- **2 TABLESPOONS THINLY SLICED GREEN ONION (WHITE PART ONLY)**
- **1 TABLESPOON FRESH LEMON JUICE**
- **1 TABLESPOON FINELY CHOPPED FRESH DILL**
- **1 TABLESPOON FINELY CHOPPED FRESH ITALIAN PARSLEY**
- **1 TABLESPOON MINCED SUN-DRIED TOMATOES (PACKED IN OIL), DRAINED**
- **1 TEASPOON GRATED ORANGE ZEST**
- **1/2 TEASPOON KOSHER SALT**
- **1/8 TEASPOON FRESHLY GROUND BLACK PEPPER**

- **4 HARD-COOKED EGGS, PEELED AND CUT LENGTHWISE INTO QUARTERS**
- **6 OUNCES FRESH GOAT CHEESE, CRUMBLED**
- **12 KALAMATA OLIVES, PITTED**

Grill the beets over *Direct Medium* heat until tender when pierced with a knife, 1 to 1 1/2 hours, turning three or four times during grilling time. Allow to cool thoroughly, then cut off the roots, peel off the skins, and quarter. Place in a small bowl and set aside.

While the beets are grilling, prepare the other vegetables: In a medium bowl combine the olive oil and garlic. Season with salt and pepper. Add the potatoes, green beans, and asparagus and mix to coat evenly.

Grill the vegetables over *Direct Medium* heat until tender, turning once halfway through grilling time. The potatoes will take 20 to 25 minutes, the green beans 8 to 10 minutes, the asparagus 6 to 8 minutes. Transfer the vegetables from the grill to a large bowl.

To make the dressing: In a medium bowl whisk together the dressing ingredients. Add 1 tablespoon of the dressing to the bowl with the beets and toss to coat. Add as much of the remaining dressing as you would like to the bowl with the mixed vegetables and toss to coat.

Arrange the beets, mixed vegetables, and egg quarters on plates or a large platter. Top with the goat cheese and olives. Drizzle with any remaining dressing and season with salt and pepper. Serve at room temperature.

MAKES 4 SERVINGS

BARBECUED
CABBAGE

Tired of coleslaw? Here's a way of grilling cabbage that raises this pedestrian veggie to new heights. The leaves melt with the butter and spices, and the barbecue sauce gives it a nice kick. Next time you're cooking up some ribs, plop one of these over Indirect heat and let it go.

INDIRECT/MEDIUM

FOR THE SEASONING MIX:

- **1 TEASPOON KOSHER SALT**
- **1/2 TEASPOON ONION POWDER**
- **1/2 TEASPOON CELERY SEED**
- **1/4 TEASPOON FRESHLY GROUND BLACK PEPPER**

- **1 MEDIUM WHOLE GREEN CABBAGE, ABOUT 2 POUNDS**
- **4 TABLESPOONS UNSALTED BUTTER**
- **1/2 CUP BARBECUE SAUCE**

To make the seasoning mix: In a small bowl combine the seasoning mix ingredients.

Using a sharp paring knife, remove the core of the cabbage, leaving a cavity about 3 inches deep. Gently pry the cabbage leaves open with your fingertips. Spread the butter in the cavity and between the leaves, and season inside and out with the seasoning mix. Wrap the cabbage in heavy-duty aluminum foil so that all but the cavity end is covered.

Grill the cabbage, cavity end facing up, over *Indirect Medium* heat until the leaves are tender, 2 to 2 1/2 hours, basting occasionally with the barbecue sauce to prevent the exposed leaves from drying out. Set aside until cool enough to handle. Remove the foil. Cut into wedges and serve warm.

MAKES 4 TO 6 SERVINGS

Dinner without side dishes may fulfill a basic need, but it's less than thrilling. You might as well eat standing at the sink (if you aren't already). Side dishes add balance, dimension, and even identity to an entrée. Not to mention the health benefits of tapping into another strata of the food pyramid. Throw a salad in there, too, and you're really living right.

When we talk about preparing side dishes, however, we don't just mean reaching for the bag of frozen green beans. While a side dish can add color to your plate, there's more to it than that. Adding vegetables and grains to your diet doesn't have to be boring and predictable. While side dishes certainly

SIDES &

don't have to be elaborate, a little effort can generate a great payback. Figuring out what to serve up alongside the entrée can be broken into a few easy steps.

First of all, think of how you'd like to contrast or complement the entrée by temperature, color, texture, and flavor. A cool, crisp green salad topped with crunchy toasted nuts will counterpoint the warm tenderloin's yielding nature quite nicely. Creamy mashed sweet potatoes will snuggle up to the richness of a grilled turkey breast, while a fresh fruit salad will cool off that spicy jerk chicken. You can also go for contrasts *within* the side dish. How about a drizzle of balsamic vinegar on your grilled sweet peppers? Add a sprinkle of bread crumbs or a splash of a flavored oil to your veggies and you take them a notch higher.

Then, think dimension. Would fluffy light buttermilk biscuits add lift to your grill-roasted chicken or pork ribs? If you're going for a special theme, such as a classic barbecue or an Asian dinner, side dishes make the whole scene. Imagine a backyard barbecue without baked beans, cornbread, or coleslaw. In some parts of this great land, such an omission could be considered borderline sacrilege. After all, entire songs have been written in honor of such venerated accompaniments! And while a classic Japanese spread without a crisp cucumber salad is no crime, it's certainly a sad oversight. Sort of like a carnival without the cotton candy.

Another thing to consider is timing. Do you want something you can make ahead so all you do is pull it out of the refrigerator or oven as you set the table? Or do you want to grill something alongside your entrée and take it all off the cooking grate at the same time? Grilled vegetables are a great way to go

if that's your aim. Getting all the food done to the proper temperature at the same time is an art. Master that and you're a backyard hero.

Having a salad waiting in the wings is another wise move that sounds obvious, but the difference is in how imaginative your salads are. Time to exorcise those "grated carrots and unripe tomatoes on romaine" demons! In this chapter, we give you lots of help on expanding your green salad horizons, and offer deliciously innovative lettuce-free salads as well. Lentil, quinoa, or brown rice salads add healthy legumes and grains to your daily intake in a most alluring way. We've also got salads that could easily make a meal. Toss a grilled seasoned chicken breast on a Caesar salad, for instance, or stuff a chicken-and-snow-pea salad into a pita, and you've got a hearty lunch or light dinner. The secret, of course, is in the sauce. We dress these classics to the nines with fresh ingredients balanced for "more, please!" flavor.

Lastly, we must admit that we feel the same way about sides and salads as we do about starters. If you like what you see, pick two or more and make a meal of them!

Twice-Grilled Potatoes

TWICE-GRILLED
POTATOES

A new take on an old steak house standard. This version ups the ante with Gruyère cheese and Dijon mustard.

DIRECT/MEDIUM

4　RUSSET POTATOES (ABOUT 2½ POUNDS), SCRUBBED AND HALVED LENGTHWISE
　VEGETABLE OIL

　FOR THE STUFFING:
¾　CUP SOUR CREAM
½　CUP WHOLE MILK
½　CUP MINCED COOKED HAM
1½　CUPS GRATED GRUYÈRE CHEESE, DIVIDED
2　TEASPOONS DIJON MUSTARD
　KOSHER SALT
　FRESHLY GROUND BLACK PEPPER

Brush or spray the potato halves with vegetable oil. Grill over *Direct Medium* heat until tender when pierced with a fork, 30 to 35 minutes, turning three or four times during grilling time. Remove from the grill and allow to cool slightly.

When cool enough to handle, use a small sharp knife to cut around the cut side of the potato to within ¼ inch of the skin. Using a teaspoon or melon baller, scoop out the interior of the potato, leaving a ¼-inch-thick shell attached to the skin. Place the potato pulp in a large bowl. Set the potato shells aside while preparing the stuffing.

To make the stuffing: Using a potato masher or pastry blender, mash the potato pulp. Add the sour cream and milk and mix well. Stir in the ham and half of the cheese. Add the mustard and season with salt and pepper. Mix well. Adjust the seasoning with more mustard, if desired. Divide the stuffing evenly among the skins so the stuffing mounds slightly. Sprinkle the remaining cheese over the stuffing.

Grill the stuffed potatoes over *Direct Medium* heat until the cheese is melted and the potatoes are heated through, about 10 minutes. Serve immediately.

MAKES 8 SERVINGS

MASHED SWEET
POTATOES
WITH GRILLED ONIONS

How sweet it is! This easy recipe uses the grill to reinvent a traditional holiday side dish. Choose similar-sized potatoes for even cooking. Note: The sweet potatoes are grilled over Indirect Medium heat and the onion slices over Direct Medium heat.

INDIRECT/MEDIUM

4　POUNDS SWEET POTATOES, SCRUBBED

1　LARGE YELLOW ONION, CUT INTO ½-INCH SLICES
　EXTRA-VIRGIN OLIVE OIL
　KOSHER SALT
　FRESHLY GROUND BLACK PEPPER

¾　CUP UNSALTED BUTTER, SOFTENED

Grill the sweet potatoes over *Indirect Medium* heat until tender when pierced with a fork, about 1 hour, turning three or four times during grilling time. Remove from the grill and allow to cool slightly.

When cool enough to handle, cut the potatoes in half lengthwise. Remove and discard the skins. Place the potatoes in a medium bowl and cover with aluminum foil.

Brush or spray the onion slices with olive oil and season with salt and pepper. Grill over *Direct Medium* heat for 10 to 12 minutes, turning once halfway through grilling time. Remove from the grill and allow to cool, then cut into ¼-inch dice.

Using a heavy-duty mixer or potato masher, mash the potatoes with the butter until smooth. Add the diced onions and mix well. Season with more salt and pepper, if desired. Serve warm.

MAKES 8 TO 10 SERVINGS

"I have made a lot of mistakes falling in love, and regretted most of them, but never the potatoes that went with them."

— NORA EPHRON,
Heartburn

The onion is the hardest working vegetable in the world. Selflessly, it adds flavor, body, and texture to sauces, entrées, soups, and more. And yet...no other food has caused more tears to be shed when called into service.

Well, that's just a matter of sulfurous compounds released when an onion is sliced. Many throughout the years have tried to figure out how to crack the code on cutting onions without getting weepy—with little or no success. While you may not be able to completely stop those tears from falling, you can at least shorten your cutting time by using a simple wagon wheel—shaped device called an apple corer-slicer (a.k.a. wedger). Center the ring of the corer-slicer over the root end and push down. You'll end up with nested wedges. Cut them in half crosswise, separate the leaves, and you have perfect kabob-sized pieces. Or keep cutting to get the dice size you want.

Onions come in white, red, yellow, and green varieties. White onions can be harsh, so they're best in stews and soups, where the liquid dilutes their punch. Red onions are so mild and sweet they can be enjoyed raw when thinly sliced—in salads, on burgers, with lox, or simply marinated. (But if left too long in the bin or refrigerator, even red onions can become quite pungent.) Yellow and Spanish onions are milder varieties. The delicate yellow Vidalia (named after the city in east-central Georgia that originally cultivated them) is actually rather sweet. Same with Maui onions, which get their trademark sweetness from the rich volcanic soil of their home island. Spanish onions have a mild yellow flesh and can weigh a pound or more. Hollowed and stuffed with cooked sausage and bread crumbs and grilled over Indirect heat, they can make a nice starter.

Grilled onions are one of life's simple pleasures. Because the sugars caramelize on the surface as the onion flesh becomes tender and milder, grilled onions add special flavor to mashed potatoes, soups, stews, fajitas, burgers, sandwiches—anywhere you want a slightly sweet effect. There is a simple art to getting them right:

To grill bulb onions, slice them crosswise ½ inch thick. Oil and salt them, and place them over Direct Medium heat. Grill the slices for 10 to 12 minutes, turning them once halfway through grilling time. For the most tender grilled onions, rotate them a half-turn a couple of minutes before and after flipping them. (In drier climates, you may need to brush them again with oil at this point.)

Note: Before grilling, some cooks like to run a skewer crosswise through the slices to keep them from falling apart during turning, but if you use a wide spatula and a deft wrist, you can forego the hassle.

Green onions, or scallions, are young plants harvested before the bulb is formed. Use these slender beauties thinly sliced as garnishes or whole on relish trays. They're mild enough to eat raw with a pinch of salt. Grilled, they make a delicious addition to grilled steak or a vegetable platter.

To grill green onions, trim both ends, peel off the outermost layer, and rinse well to remove any dirt. Oil and salt them, then place them over Direct Medium heat for 3 to 4 minutes, turning once halfway through grilling time. Perfect!

NEW
POTATO SALAD

These grilled potatoes and onions are studded with crunchy scallions and fresh herbs. Leave plenty of room on your plate for a hearty serving—or just plan to circle back for seconds.

DIRECT/MEDIUM

FOR THE POTATOES:

- 3 TABLESPOONS EXTRA-VIRGIN OLIVE OIL
- 1/2 TEASPOON KOSHER SALT
- 1/2 TEASPOON FRESHLY GROUND BLACK PEPPER
- 2 1/2 POUNDS NEW POTATOES, ABOUT 1 1/2 INCHES IN DIAMETER EACH, WASHED AND CUT IN HALF

- 1/2 POUND THICK-CUT BACON, CUT INTO 1/4-INCH DICE

- 3 MEDIUM VIDALIA, MAUI, *OR* OTHER SWEET ONIONS, CUT CROSSWISE INTO 1/2-INCH SLICES
  KOSHER SALT
  FRESHLY GROUND BLACK PEPPER
- 6 GREEN ONIONS (WHITE PART ONLY), THINLY SLICED CROSSWISE
- 3 TABLESPOONS FINELY CHOPPED FRESH ITALIAN PARSLEY
- 1 TABLESPOON FINELY CHOPPED FRESH THYME

FOR THE DRESSING:

- 1/3 CUP EXTRA-VIRGIN OLIVE OIL
- 3 TABLESPOONS SHERRY VINEGAR
- 3 TABLESPOONS CHICKEN BROTH *OR* WATER
- 1/4 TEASPOON KOSHER SALT
- 1/4 TEASPOON FRESHLY GROUND BLACK PEPPER

To prepare the potatoes: In a large bowl combine the olive oil, salt, and pepper. Add the potatoes and toss to coat evenly. Grill over *Direct Medium* heat until easily pierced with a skewer and golden brown, 20 to 25 minutes, turning once halfway through grilling time. Remove the potatoes from the grill and allow to cool for a few minutes. When cool enough to handle, cut each potato half into two pieces and place in a large bowl. Cover and set aside at room temperature.

In a large sauté pan over medium heat, fry the bacon, stirring occasionally, until crisp, 10 to 12 minutes. With a slotted spoon transfer the bacon to the bowl of potatoes; reserve the bacon fat.

Brush the sweet onion slices with some of the reserved bacon fat and season with salt and pepper. Grill over *Direct Medium* heat until lightly browned and tender, 10 to 12 minutes, turning and basting with the reserved bacon fat once halfway through grilling time. Remove from the grill and cut each slice into quarters. Add to the potatoes along with the green onions, parsley, and thyme.

To make the dressing: In a medium bowl whisk together the dressing ingredients.

Pour the dressing over the potatoes and toss gently. Cover and allow to stand at room temperature for about 1 hour before serving.

MAKES 10 TO 12 SERVINGS

GOLD RUSH
POTATO SALAD

Grilled red onions and Yukon gold potatoes kick-start this classic. It's best hot off the grill. Mix all the ingredients together while the potatoes are still warm.

DIRECT/MEDIUM

FOR THE DRESSING:

- 1/3 CUP MAYONNAISE
- 3 TABLESPOONS FINELY CHOPPED ITALIAN PARSLEY
- 2 TABLESPOONS RED WINE VINEGAR
- 1 TEASPOON GRANULATED GARLIC
- 1 TEASPOON DIJON MUSTARD

- 2 POUNDS YUKON GOLD POTATOES, CUT INTO 1-INCH CHUNKS
  EXTRA-VIRGIN OLIVE OIL
  KOSHER SALT
  FRESHLY GROUND BLACK PEPPER
- 1 LARGE RED ONION, CUT CROSSWISE INTO 1/2-INCH SLICES
- 3 TO 4 CELERY STALKS, DICED

To make the dressing: In a small bowl whisk together the dressing ingredients.

Place the potato chunks in a medium bowl. Add enough olive oil to lightly coat. Season with salt and pepper and toss lightly. Brush or spray both sides of the onion slices with oil; season with salt and pepper.

Grill the potatoes and onion slices over *Direct Medium* heat until the potatoes are browned and the onion slices are tender, turning once halfway through grilling time. The potatoes will take 15 to 20 minutes and the onion slices will take 10 to 12 minutes. Transfer the potatoes to a large bowl. Transfer the onion slices to a cutting board and chop coarsely. Add the onion and celery to the potatoes.

Pour the dressing over the vegetables and toss gently. Adjust seasoning with salt and pepper, if necessary. Serve warm.

MAKES 4 TO 6 SERVINGS

Sausage Salad with Arugula

SAUSAGE SALAD
WITH ARUGULA

Grilled corn, fresh tomatoes, sweet peppers, and warm, spicy andouille sausage spooned over crisp arugula. Serve with crusty French bread and call it dinner.

DIRECT/MEDIUM

- **3 EARS FRESH SWEET CORN, IN THEIR HUSKS**

- **3 TABLESPOONS EXTRA-VIRGIN OLIVE OIL**
- **1/3 POUND ANDOUILLE SAUSAGE, CUT CROSSWISE INTO 1/8-INCH SLICES**
- **1/2 CUP FINELY CHOPPED YELLOW ONION**
- **3/4 CUP FINELY CHOPPED RED *OR* YELLOW BELL PEPPER**
- **2 TEASPOONS MINCED GARLIC**

- **3/4 CUP SEEDED, FINELY CHOPPED RIPE TOMATO**
- **1/4 CUP WHITE WINE VINEGAR**
- **1/4 CUP CHICKEN BROTH, HOT**
- **1/2 TEASPOON KOSHER SALT**
- **1/4 TEASPOON FRESHLY GROUND BLACK PEPPER**
- **1/4 CUP LOOSELY PACKED FRESH BASIL LEAVES, CUT INTO RIBBONS**

- **1 1/2 CUPS TIGHTLY PACKED ARUGULA LEAVES**

Soak the corn in cold water for 30 minutes or more. If necessary, use a weight to keep the ears submerged. Drain.

In a medium sauté pan over medium heat, warm the olive oil. Add the sausage and cook for 5 minutes, turning occasionally. Add the onion, bell pepper, and garlic, and cook, stirring occasionally, until the pepper is tender, 7 to 8 minutes. Remove from the heat and set aside.

Grill the corn over *Direct Medium* heat for 20 to 25 minutes, turning three or four times during grilling time. Remove from the grill and allow to cool slightly. When cool enough to handle, carefully pull back the husks and remove the silk. With a sharp knife, cut the kernels from the cobs. Add the kernels to the sausage mixture.

Just before serving, add the tomatoes, vinegar, chicken broth, salt, pepper, and basil to the andouille mixture. Stir gently to mix.

Arrange the arugula on a platter, spoon the warm salad on top, and serve immediately.

MAKES 4 TO 6 SERVINGS

SHRIMP SALAD

Almost every kitchen has a stash of potatoes in the cupboard, a couple of onions on the counter, and some celery in the refrigerator. Add some grilled shrimp and a quick vinaigrette and you're in business.

DIRECT/HIGH

FOR THE DRESSING:
- **3 TABLESPOONS EXTRA-VIRGIN OLIVE OIL**
- **1 TABLESPOON SHERRY VINEGAR**
- **1 TABLESPOON FRESH LEMON JUICE**
- **1 TABLESPOON FINELY CHOPPED FRESH THYME**
- **1 TEASPOON WHOLE-GRAIN DIJON MUSTARD**
- **1/2 TEASPOON KOSHER SALT**
- **1/4 TEASPOON FRESHLY GROUND BLACK PEPPER**

- **1 POUND YUKON GOLD POTATOES, ABOUT 2 INCHES IN DIAMETER EACH, SCRUBBED**

- **1 POUND LARGE SHRIMP, SHELLED AND DEVEINED**
  EXTRA-VIRGIN OLIVE OIL
  KOSHER SALT
  FRESHLY GROUND BLACK PEPPER
- **3 TO 4 STALKS CELERY, CUT ON THE BIAS IN 1/3-INCH SLICES**
- **1/2 SMALL RED ONION, CUT INTO SLIVERS**

To make the dressing: In a small bowl whisk together the dressing ingredients.

In a medium saucepan cook the potatoes in boiling salted water until tender when pierced with a skewer, 15 to 20 minutes. Drain. When cool enough to handle, quarter each potato and place in a large bowl. While the potatoes are still warm, toss with 2 to 3 tablespoons of the dressing.

Brush or spray the shrimp with olive oil and season with salt and pepper. Grill over *Direct High* heat until just opaque in the center and firm to the touch, 2 to 4 minutes, turning once halfway through grilling time. Add the shrimp and the remaining ingredients to the potatoes. Pour the remaining dressing over the salad and gently toss to coat. Serve warm or at room temperature.

MAKES 4 TO 6 SERVINGS

CONFETTI
SALAD

If you want to make this salad ahead, prepare all the ingredients except the lettuce and keep them refrigerated. Then, just before serving, chop the lettuce and toss everything with the dressing. It's good with or without the ricotta salata—a salted ricotta that's firm and crumbles well—but the cheese makes it a little heartier.

FOR THE SALAD:
- 3 CUPS LIGHTLY PACKED CHOPPED CURLY LETTUCE
- 1 CUP FINELY CHOPPED RADICCHIO
- 1 CUP FINELY DICED RED BELL PEPPER
- 1 CUP FINELY DICED GREEN BELL PEPPER
- 1 CUP FINELY DICED FENNEL BULB
- 1 CUP FINELY DICED CARROTS
- 1 CUP FINELY DICED CELERY
- 1 CUP FINELY DICED SEEDLESS CUCUMBER
- 1/2 CUP FINELY DICED RED ONION
- 1/4 CUP FINELY CHOPPED FRESH DILL, DIVIDED
- 2 TABLESPOONS FINELY CHOPPED FRESH MINT, DIVIDED

FOR THE DRESSING:
- 6 TABLESPOONS EXTRA-VIRGIN OLIVE OIL
- 1/4 CUP FRESH LEMON JUICE
- 1 TEASPOON KOSHER SALT
- 1/2 TEASPOON MINCED GARLIC
- 1/4 TEASPOON FRESHLY GROUND BLACK PEPPER

- 4 OUNCES RICOTTA SALATA, CRUMBLED

To make the salad: In a large bowl combine the salad ingredients, including half of the dill and half of the mint.

To make the dressing: In a small bowl whisk together the dressing ingredients, along with the remaining dill and mint.

Pour the dressing over the salad and toss to combine. Spoon onto a deep platter, top with the crumbled cheese, and serve immediately.

MAKES 8 TO 10 SERVINGS

STEAK AND TOMATO
SALAD

A good steak salad is usually the first thing to go at the buffet table, whether it's intended as a first course or a main dish. Lesson learned? Make plenty.

DIRECT/MEDIUM

FOR THE DRESSING:
- 1/2 CUP EXTRA-VIRGIN OLIVE OIL
- 1/4 CUP BALSAMIC VINEGAR
- 1 TEASPOON FINELY CHOPPED FRESH OREGANO
  KOSHER SALT
  FRESHLY GROUND BLACK PEPPER

- 1 FLANK STEAK, 1 1/2 TO 2 POUNDS AND 3/4 INCH THICK

- 6 PLUM TOMATOES, CUT IN HALF AND SEEDS REMOVED
- 4 TABLESPOONS EXTRA-VIRGIN OLIVE OIL
- 1 TEASPOON KOSHER SALT
- 1/2 TEASPOON FRESHLY GROUND BLACK PEPPER

- 2 CANS (14 OUNCES EACH) HEARTS OF PALM, RINSED AND DRAINED
- 3 HEADS ROMAINE LETTUCE HEARTS, CUT OR TORN INTO BITE-SIZED PIECES (ABOUT 8 CUPS)
- 2 TABLESPOONS CAPERS, DRAINED
- 2 TABLESPOONS CHOPPED FRESH CHIVES
- 1 TABLESPOON FINELY SLICED FRESH BASIL

To make the dressing: In a small bowl whisk together the dressing ingredients, including salt and pepper to taste.

Trim the flank steak of surface fat. Place on a platter and pour a little of the dressing over both sides. Allow to marinate at room temperature for 20 to 30 minutes.

Grill the steak over *Direct Medium* heat until the internal temperature reaches 145°F for medium rare, 8 to 10 minutes, turning once halfway through grilling time. Transfer to a cutting board, loosely cover with aluminum foil, and allow to cool for about 20 minutes. Cut across the grain into thin diagonal slices, then cut each slice into two or three bite-sized pieces. Drizzle with a little more of the dressing.

Lightly brush or spray the tomato halves with the olive oil and season with the salt and pepper. Grill over *Direct Medium* heat until lightly charred, 6 to 8 minutes, turning once halfway through grilling time. Remove from the grill and cut each tomato half into sixths.

Cut the hearts of palm into 1/4-inch pieces. In a large shallow bowl combine the lettuce with the hearts of palm and capers. Add the remaining dressing. Toss to combine. Arrange the tomatoes and steak pieces over the lettuce, sprinkle on the chives and basil, and serve.

MAKES 6 SERVINGS

CUCUMBER SALAD
WITH TOASTED SESAME SEEDS

Cooling cucumbers provide a first-rate match to many grilled foods. This salad goes particularly well with Asian-inspired dishes.

- 2 TEASPOONS SESAME SEEDS

FOR THE DRESSING:
- 2 TABLESPOONS RICE VINEGAR
- 1 TABLESPOON HONEY
- 1 1/2 TEASPOONS ASIAN SESAME OIL
- 1 1/2 TEASPOONS SOY SAUCE
- 1 TEASPOON FRESHLY GRATED GINGER
- 1/4 TEASPOON FRESHLY GROUND BLACK PEPPER

- 1 SEEDLESS CUCUMBER, ABOUT 12 INCHES LONG
- 1 MEDIUM RED ONION

In a small sauté pan over medium heat, toast the sesame seeds, stirring occasionally, until golden brown, about 5 minutes.

To make the dressing: In a small bowl whisk together the dressing ingredients.

Cut the cucumber in half lengthwise, then cut each half crosswise as thinly as possible. Place in a medium bowl. Cut the red onion in half through the root end. Trim the root end off the halves, then slice the halves as thinly as possible. Add the onion slices to the cucumbers. When ready to serve, pour the dressing over the vegetables. Sprinkle with the sesame seeds. Toss to coat evenly. Serve at room temperature.

MAKES 4 SERVINGS

> "Lettuce is like conversation:
> It must be fresh and crisp,
> and so sparkling
> that you scarcely notice
> the bitter in it."
>
> — CHARLES DUDLEY
> WARNER

BLUE CHEESE,
APPLE, AND HONEYED WALNUT SALAD

If you want, you can toast this recipe's sweet and spicy nuts right on the grill. Just place the baking pan over Indirect Medium heat and keep the grill at about 350°F. They're excellent on just about any salad—you might even want to make a double batch to keep some on hand just for noshing.

FOR THE WALNUTS:
- VEGETABLE OIL
- 1 CUP WALNUT HALVES
- 1 TABLESPOON HONEY
- CAYENNE
- KOSHER SALT

FOR THE DRESSING:
- 1/4 CUP MAYONNAISE
- 2 TABLESPOONS FRESH LEMON JUICE
- 2 TABLESPOONS HONEY
- 1/2 TEASPOON KOSHER SALT

FOR THE SALAD:
- 2 APPLES, QUARTERED, CORED, AND CUT CROSSWISE INTO THIN SLICES
- 3 TO 4 CELERY RIBS, CUT INTO THIN DIAGONAL SLICES
- 1/2 CUP SLIVERED RED ONION
- 3 OUNCES BLUE CHEESE (ROQUEFORT, DANISH BLUE, *OR* GORGONZOLA), CRUMBLED

To prepare the walnuts: Preheat oven to 350°F. Line a baking pan or cookie sheet with aluminum foil and lightly oil the foil. Spread the walnuts in the prepared pan and drizzle with the honey. Bake until dark golden brown, 20 to 25 minutes, stirring every 5 minutes to coat the nuts evenly with the honey. While the walnuts are still hot, sprinkle with cayenne and salt to taste. Immediately transfer to a small bowl and set aside.

To make the dressing: In a small bowl whisk together the dressing ingredients.

To make the salad: In a large bowl combine the apples, celery, and onion. Drizzle with the dressing, then toss well. Transfer to a serving platter and top with the blue cheese crumbles and honeyed walnuts. Serve at room temperature.

MAKES 4 SERVINGS

KNOW YOUR GREENS...
AND REDS AND WHITES

Remember when "salad" only meant iceberg lettuce with a few chopped veggies? Today we have so many tasty and nutritious variations on salad, it's like the Garden of Eden joined an international farmers' co-op. Great news, but the choices can cause confusion. What if instead of reaching for a pre-fab "salad in a bag," you want to create your own mix? Here are some best uses for these versatile greens:

HEAD LETTUCES make the best salad base. Use mature or baby greens. For mature heads, look for vibrant color and firm structure. Separate the leaves, rinse them under cold water, roll loosely in damp paper towels, and refrigerate in a plastic bag until you're ready to use them. They'll stay crisp and fresh for several days. Baby greens come in individual leaves; store in a plastic bag and use within 2 days. Rinse in cold water just before using.

- **Red or green leaf**: Both have ruffled leaves. Red leaf is more tender and frail; eat within a few days.
- **Romaine**: The king of crisp, in green or red, with long, strong spears. Chop or tear into bite-sized pieces for salad, or slice the head lengthwise through the root end and grill. What, lettuce on the grill? Sure! A minute on the grill can add a slightly nutty taste to very firm greens. Lightly brush romaine spears with a vinaigrette, shake off the excess, and place over Direct Medium heat for 1 to 2 minutes to wilt and warm them, turning once halfway through grilling time. Add to a sandwich or garnish with grated cheese for a side dish.
- **Butter lettuce (a.k.a. Boston or Bibb)**: This tender, pale green sweetie has a buttery texture. Leaves pale to yellow-green near the center. Their cuplike shape is also great for garnishes and for wrapping around chicken salads and egg rolls.
- **Spinach**: Iron-rich; comes in bunches. Rinse well to get the sand out and snap off stems about 1 inch from the leaf. Also great sautéed with garlic in olive oil just to wilting.

SPECIALTY GREENS, harvested as individual leaves, are sometimes difficult to find. Include as accents to take your salad to a higher level. Eat within a couple days of purchase; rinse just before using.

- **Arugula**: A treasure to perk up any salad or sandwich. Also called rocket, this peppery number is best eaten right away.
- **Red oak**: This fluttery leaf is sweet, soft, and downright flirtatious. Great for color.
- **Dandelion leaves**: That's right, the same guys you try to kill in your lawn make great salad pals. But don't harvest your own; these sweet specimens are specially grown and harvested young for tenderness.
- **Others**: Beet tops (tender and small only) and mizuna add color and intrigue.

BITTER GREENS can be white, green, or purple and last up to a week in the fridge. In salads, use sparingly for balance.

- **Frisée or curly endive**: The frizzy little leaves spring from thin, firm stems. If you buy a whole head, use the tender, inner leaves. Their pale green to white color and slightly bitter taste make them a good choice for contrast and texture. Keep bite-sized.
- **Radicchio**: The most common species of this softball-sized globe is purple and white variegated. Discard browned outer leaves. Adds color to salads, or quarter and core the head for grilling. A minute or two on the grill will tenderize it and mellow its bite; serve with blue cheese crumbles, walnuts, and grilled pears.
- **Belgian endive**: Torpedo-shaped and white with pale green tips, these crisp, small (about 4 inches long) heads are tightly nested long spears. Use whole spears for garnish, slice them to add crunch and a slight bitterness to salads, or slice lengthwise and dip in dressing before grilling for a couple minutes over Direct Medium heat.
- **Escarole**: Broad stem, ruffled green leaf, and very firm. Can also be braised or grilled to accompany grilled meats.
- **Others**: For sautéing or braising, try kale; mustard or collard greens; bok choy; and red, green, or Swiss chard.

FRESH HERBS add interest and flavor. Toss in a little dill, cilantro, mint, parsley, or sorrel. Just be sure to pick herbs that work with your dressing.

OILS AND VINEGARS

Oils and vinegars not only enrich marinades, sauces, and side dishes, they're the heart and soul of a good salad. If you don't have several to choose from in your pantry, consider your options for matchmaking.

Olive oil: The most important for salad aficionados. Here's how to decode the label. One day after harvesting, fresh olives are crushed by giant stone wheels. The resulting mash is pressed, and oil and water are released. The water contains the olives' natural bitterness and so is discarded. The oil is rated. If it has superior taste, color, aroma, and less than 1% acidity, it is labeled extra virgin. "Extra" means premium and "virgin" means it's pure, unrefined, and unprocessed—"first cold pressed" is another way to put it. If the oil doesn't make the "extra" cut, it's further processed with heat or chemicals, quality virgin oil is added for flavor, and it's labeled "pure olive oil" (sometimes "classic" is on there, too). "Light" olive oil is not light in calories but rather in flavor; it's further refined and fortified with just a little virgin oil. The color of an olive oil is not an indication of its flavor, but rather of the type of olive used. Most olive oils are blends of olive types, but the better oils use a higher concentrate of one olive. Choose an olive oil that suits your tastes—experimenting is half the fun.

General-purpose oils: Neutral-flavored canola (or rapeseed) oil is a darling of the health-conscious because it's lower in saturated fat and high in monounsaturated fat. Use it where strongly flavored oils would upset your flavor balance. Colorless, flavorless safflower oil is valued for salad dressings because it doesn't solidify when chilled. Like safflower oil, corn oil has a high smoking point, which makes it good for frying. Odorless and virtually tasteless, it's also often used in salad dressings.

Specialty oils: Walnut and hazelnut oils are heavy with the flavor and fragrance of these nuts. They're also strong, so blend them with a less flavorful oil (such as canola) to add a boost of nuttiness to salads or sides such as sautéed spinach. Peanut oil is lighter in flavor but higher in saturated fats. Its neutral flavor and high smoking point make it a top choice for deep-frying and stir-frying, but it's also used in salad dressings, especially those with an Asian bent. The very mildly flavored grapeseed oil (yes, it's made from grape seeds) is perhaps the least known or used; try it in salads or for sautéing.

Flavored oils: Add dimension to salads and sauces, and are good just drizzled over grilled vegetables or meats. Chili, basil, garlic, lemon, and rosemary flavored oils are fairly easy to find. Truffle oil—extra-virgin olive oil infused with white or black truffles—is harder to come by; be prepared to hand over some serious cash for this gourmet treat.

Vinegars: Also come in a variety of types and flavors. Their bases vary: red, white, or rice wine; sherry; champagne; and apple cider vinegars all start out as their namesakes. The liquid is exposed to air and airborne organisms, then left to ferment, usually in wooden barrels. As the liquid evaporates, acidity and flavor are concentrated. Rice vinegar is made from fermented rice. Simple vinegars can be infused with other flavors, e.g. raspberry, tarragon, blackberry, fig, and thyme. Flavored vinaigrettes are great on salads and even on sweeter meats such as game or pork.

Balsamic vinegar: Made from the must—that is, the pulp and skins of crushed grapes—of the white Trebbiano grape, balsamic vinegar is aged in wood until it turns inky black (although white balsamic vinegar is also available). The quality (and price) of balsamic vinegar can run the gamut from tabletop condiment to work of art. The original balsamic vinegar is called "aceto balsamico traditionale di Modena." Modena, Italy, is the birthplace of authentic balsamico, which is aged for years in ever smaller wooden barrels as it evaporates. The woods used add complexity and nuance. Some balsamico has been aged up to 100 years and is consumed literally drop by precious drop. You can pay up to $300 for a tiny bottle of the oldest. The balsamic vinegar you find in your grocery store is not authentic, but it's what we use in this cookbook. Usually aged a mere 6 months, these Yankee cousins do achieve balsamic vinegar's characteristic sweetness and thus do the trick. Buy the best you can afford, but don't go nuts. Do avoid any with caramel flavoring or color added.

HAIL CAESAR! SALAD

This take on the classic Caesar salad uses toasted whole wheat croutons and anchovy fillets, but skips the raw egg. A good whirl in the blender makes the dressing ingredients thick and creamy, even without it. But don't skimp on the anchovy. It adds a nice salty edge and richness without imparting a fishy taste.

FOR THE CROUTONS:

1 TABLESPOON EXTRA-VIRGIN OLIVE OIL

1 TEASPOON MINCED GARLIC

2 CUPS CUBED (1/2-INCH) DAY-OLD WHOLE WHEAT ITALIAN *OR* OTHER FIRM WHOLE-GRAIN BREAD

1/2 TEASPOON KOSHER SALT

2 HEARTS ROMAINE LETTUCE

FOR THE DRESSING:

1/3 CUP EXTRA-VIRGIN OLIVE OIL

2 TABLESPOONS FRESH LEMON JUICE

2 ANCHOVY FILLETS (OIL-PACKED), DRAINED AND BLOTTED DRY

2 TEASPOONS RED WINE VINEGAR

1 TEASPOON DIJON MUSTARD

1/2 TEASPOON MINCED GARLIC

1/4 CUP FRESHLY GRATED PARMIGIANO-REGGIANO CHEESE, DIVIDED

FRESHLY GROUND BLACK PEPPER

To make the croutons: Preheat oven to 350°F. In a medium bowl combine the olive oil and garlic. Add the bread cubes, toss to coat, and season with the salt. Spread on a baking sheet and bake until lightly toasted, about 15 minutes, turning once halfway through cooking time. Set aside to cool.

Trim the stem end of the romaine hearts. Rinse the leaves, drain, and pat dry. Wrap in a clean towel and refrigerate until ready to use.

To make the dressing: In a food processor combine the dressing ingredients and purée until creamy.

Tear the lettuce into bite-sized pieces. In a large bowl combine the lettuce pieces and dressing, then add the croutons and half of the cheese. Toss to evenly coat the lettuce. Divide among four large dinner plates and sprinkle with the remaining cheese. Season with a generous grinding of pepper. Serve immediately.

MAKES 4 SERVINGS

CHICKEN AND SNOW PEA SALAD
WITH SPICY PEANUT DRESSING

A crunchy, satisfying little number. Go for fresh snow peas—if they aren't available, substitute sugar snaps or, in a pinch, fresh green beans.

FOR THE SALAD:

1/2 POUND SNOW PEAS, TRIMMED AND CUT INTO 1/2-INCH DIAGONAL SLICES

3 CUPS COOKED CHICKEN, PULLED FROM THE BONES IN STRIPS, SKIN DISCARDED

4 GREEN ONIONS, TRIMMED AND CUT INTO 1/4-INCH DIAGONAL SLICES

1/2 SEEDLESS CUCUMBER, TRIMMED, PEELED, HALVED LENGTHWISE, AND CUT INTO 1/8-INCH SLICES

1/2 RED BELL PEPPER, RIBS AND SEEDS REMOVED, CUT INTO 1/8- BY 1-INCH PIECES

FOR THE DRESSING:

1/2 CUP CREAMY PEANUT BUTTER

3 TABLESPOONS SOY SAUCE

2 TABLESPOONS CHINESE BLACK VINEGAR *OR* RED WINE VINEGAR

2 TEASPOONS ASIAN SESAME OIL

1 TEASPOON GRATED FRESH GINGER

1 TEASPOON MINCED GARLIC

1/2 TEASPOON CHILI OIL

1/4 CUP CHICKEN BROTH

KOSHER SALT

FRESHLY GROUND BLACK PEPPER

2 TABLESPOONS SESAME SEEDS

1/4 CUP FRESH CILANTRO LEAVES

To make the salad: In a small saucepan heat about 2 cups salted water to boiling. Add the snow peas and blanch until crisp-tender, about 1 minute. Drain and plunge into ice water to crisp. When cold, drain well and pat dry with paper towels. In a large bowl combine the snow peas with the remaining salad ingredients.

To make the dressing: In a food processor combine the first seven dressing ingredients and process until well blended. With the processor running slowly, add the broth to thin the dressing to a pouring consistency. Season with salt and pepper.

In a small sauté pan over medium heat, toast the sesame seeds, stirring occasionally, until golden brown, about 5 minutes.

Pour the dressing over the chicken and vegetables and gently fold to coat. Just before serving, sprinkle the salad with the sesame seeds and garnish with the cilantro leaves. Serve cool or at room temperature.

MAKES 4 SERVINGS

CHILLED CANTALOUPE SALAD
WITH RASPBERRY VINAIGRETTE

This salad is only as good as the cantaloupe, so be choosy. Hunt for a firm, heavy, ripe melon. If melons aren't in season, buy one a day or two ahead and let it ripen in a dark place at room temperature.

FOR THE SALAD:

1   **MEDIUM RED ONION**

1   **SMALL RIPE CANTALOUPE (1 1/2 TO 2 POUNDS)**

1   **TO 2 HEARTS OF ROMAINE LETTUCE, TRIMMED AND CUT CROSSWISE INTO 1/4-INCH STRIPS**

1/2   **CUP TORN FRESH BASIL LEAVES, DIVIDED**

2   **TABLESPOONS TORN FRESH MINT LEAVES, DIVIDED**

FOR THE VINAIGRETTE:

1/4   **CUP EXTRA-VIRGIN OLIVE OIL**

2   **TABLESPOONS RASPBERRY VINEGAR**

1   **TEASPOON BALSAMIC VINEGAR**

1/2   **TEASPOON KOSHER SALT**

FRESHLY GROUND BLACK PEPPER

To make the salad: Cut the onion in half through the root end, then cut into 1/2-inch wedges. Cut off the core from each wedge and discard. Separate the onion wedges into individual leaves. Place in a bowl, cover with cold water, and add a handful of ice cubes. Allow to stand for 20 minutes.

Cut the melon in half, scoop out the seeds, and cut into 1-inch wedges. With a small sharp knife, remove the rind from the melon flesh and cut each wedge crosswise into 1/2-inch pieces. Place the melon pieces in a large bowl; add the lettuce, along with half of the basil and half of the mint. Cover with plastic wrap and refrigerate until ready to serve.

To make the vinaigrette: In a food processor combine the remaining basil and mint with the other vinaigrette ingredients. Process until well blended.

When ready to serve, drain the onions and pat dry with a paper towel. Add the onions to the cantaloupe mixture. Add the dressing and toss to combine. Season with a grinding of black pepper. Serve chilled.

MAKES 4 SERVINGS

HOW TO MAKE
A GREAT SALAD

1. Start with a good base of greens such as 2 parts head or baby lettuces, 1 part specialty greens, and 1 part bitter greens (see page 360).

2. Select your oil or oil blend to match the other flavors in the menu. If you're having a light fish entrée, pick a lighter-flavored oil such as canola or peanut. A hearty beef dish can take a salad with a splash of, say, walnut oil. And if the salad is the entrée, follow your cravings.

3. Pick a vinegar to complement the oil. Balsamic and fruit-flavored vinegars are generally less acidic, so they're good with lighter oils. Start with a basic proportion of 3 parts oil to 1 part vinegar. You can adjust this to 4:1 or 2:1, but wait until after you've added the seasonings.

4. Add herbs to taste. Try thyme, basil, tarragon, oregano, dill, chives, chervil, or fresh minced lemongrass. We prefer fresh herbs in vinaigrettes, both for flavor and because dried herbs are better in recipes with longer cooking times, when they can soften. For body, consider yogurt or buttermilk. For flavor, try roasted garlic, minced chipotles, grated ginger, mustard, honey, minced garlic or shallots, tapenade, anchovies (minced or paste), citrus zest, toasted seeds (sesame, cumin, poppy), crushed red pepper flakes, or dried fruits (currants, cranberries, sour cherries, raspberries). Remember, the key is balance, so be selective. Shake it all up and add salt and pepper to taste.

5. Dip a lettuce leaf in your creation to taste it. If it's too acidic, add more oil or even water, a little at a time. Keep tasting as you go. Take notes so when you hit the perfect balance you can re-create your masterpiece. If you make a big batch, taste it the next day, as the flavors may have shifted as they blended.

6. Finally, add special effects to the greens before tossing with the vinaigrette: Think pine nuts, toasted or sugared nuts, orange sections or other fresh fruit bits, jicama, diced veggies, cheese, etc. Choose colors and flavors with discretion, but let your wild imagination lead you!

Warm Beet and Onion Salad

WARM BEET AND ONION
SALAD

The grill intensifies the sweetness and flavor of beets for a result you just can't get from a can. If the beet tops are tender and unblemished, use them as part of the greens in the salad. Otherwise, use three romaine hearts. If you can't find golden beets, all red beets will do. Great served as a light lunch or a first course to a special dinner.

INDIRECT/MEDIUM

2   MEDIUM GOLDEN BEETS WITH LEAFY TOPS,
    ABOUT 2¹/2 INCHES IN DIAMETER EACH

2   MEDIUM RED BEETS WITH LEAFY TOPS,
    ABOUT 2¹/2 INCHES IN DIAMETER EACH

    EXTRA-VIRGIN OLIVE OIL

FOR THE DRESSING:

1   MEDIUM ORANGE

¹/3 CUP EXTRA-VIRGIN OLIVE OIL

2   TABLESPOONS RED WINE VINEGAR

1   TABLESPOON FINELY SLICED FRESH BASIL

1   TEASPOON MINCED GARLIC

¹/2 TEASPOON KOSHER SALT

    FRESHLY GROUND BLACK PEPPER

1   LARGE RED ONION, CUT INTO
    FOUR ¹/2-INCH SLICES

2   HEARTS ROMAINE LETTUCE

Trim the leafy tops from the beets, leaving about ¹/2 inch attached; reserve the tops. Leave the root ends intact. Scrub the beets under cold water. Lightly spray or brush with olive oil. Grill over *Indirect Medium* heat until tender when pierced with the tip of a knife, I to I¹/2 hours depending on size, turning once halfway through grilling time. Remove from the grill and allow to stand until cool enough to handle. Trim the ends from the beets and discard. Rub off the skins. Cut the beets into ¹/4- to ¹/2-inch slices and place the red beets and the golden beets in separate bowls (to keep the red beets from dying the golden beets red).

To make the dressing: Wash and dry the orange. With a zester, scrape off I tablespoon of zest. Alternatively, use a vegetable peeler to remove enough strips of zest to total I tablespoon when finely chopped. Reserve the zest.

Cut the remaining skin and white pith from the orange and, working over a separate medium bowl, separate the orange into sections, letting the sections and any juice fall into the bowl *(see page 119)*. Add the reserved zest and the remaining dressing ingredients to the orange sections, including pepper to taste. Gently stir to combine.

Lightly brush the onion slices with some of the dressing and grill over *Direct Medium* heat until tender, 10 to 12 minutes, turning once halfway through grilling time. Remove from the grill and allow to cool slightly, then separate into rings.

Rinse the reserved leafy tops of the beets under cold water. Select the smallest, most tender leaves and place with the romaine lettuce in a large bowl. Add half of the dressing and toss. Divide the lettuce mixture among four salad plates. Top with the beets and the onion rings and drizzle on the remaining dressing. Serve warm or at room temperature.

MAKES 4 SERVINGS

FRENCH GREEN LENTIL SALAD
WITH MUSTARD VINAIGRETTE

Either brown or green lentils can be used in this salad, but we're partial to green—they have a firmer texture and are a little more handsome. But whichever you use, don't overcook them. Since cooking times can vary, you'll have to taste them often during cooking time.

FOR THE DRESSING:

¹/3 CUP EXTRA-VIRGIN OLIVE OIL

¹/4 CUP RED WINE VINEGAR

1   TABLESPOON DIJON MUSTARD

¹/2 TEASPOON MINCED GARLIC

FOR THE LENTILS:

1   SPRIG FRESH ITALIAN PARSLEY

1   GARLIC CLOVE, CRUSHED

1   BAY LEAF

1   CINNAMON STICK

1   TEASPOON KOSHER SALT

2   CUPS FRENCH GREEN LENTILS,
    SORTED AND RINSED

¹/2 CUP MINCED RED ONION

    KOSHER SALT

    FRESHLY GROUND BLACK PEPPER

¹/4 CUP FINELY CHOPPED FRESH ITALIAN PARSLEY

To make the dressing: In a large bowl whisk together the dressing ingredients.

To prepare the lentils: In a large saucepan combine 2 quarts water with the parsley, garlic, bay leaf, cinnamon stick, and salt. Bring the water to a boil over high heat. Stir in the lentils and cook, uncovered, in gently boiling water until tender, 15 to 30 minutes. Drain the lentils. Pick out the seasonings and discard.

Whisk the dressing again. Add the cooked lentils and red onion. Fold to combine. Season with salt and pepper. Just before serving, sprinkle with the parsley. Serve warm or at room temperature.

MAKES 6 SERVINGS

SIX-STORY
SALAD

This layered salad looks great on the table; toss it just before serving so the ingredients are more evenly distributed. Quinoa (pronounced "KEEN-wa") is a small round grain about the size of a sesame seed. It has long been cultivated in the Andes. As it cooks, the seed expands and becomes springy. It's important to rinse quinoa before using, so don't be tempted to skip that step. Zest the lime before you juice it.

DIRECT/MEDIUM

FOR THE QUINOA:

- 1 CUP QUINOA
- 1 TABLESPOON VEGETABLE OIL
- 1 TEASPOON MINCED GARLIC
- 1/2 TEASPOON KOSHER SALT

FOR THE DRESSING:

- 1 TEASPOON GROUND CUMIN
- 6 TABLESPOONS VEGETABLE OIL
- 3 TABLESPOONS FRESH LIME JUICE
- 1 TABLESPOON MINCED JALAPEÑO PEPPER, WITH SEEDS
- 1 TABLESPOON FINELY CHOPPED FRESH CILANTRO
- 1 TEASPOON MINCED GARLIC
- 1/2 TEASPOON GRATED LIME ZEST
- 1/2 TEASPOON HONEY
- 1/2 TEASPOON KOSHER SALT

FOR THE SALAD:

- 2 EARS FRESH SWEET CORN, HUSKED
- VEGETABLE OIL
- KOSHER SALT
- FRESHLY GROUND BLACK PEPPER
- 1 CAN (15 OUNCES) BLACK BEANS
- 3 LARGE RIPE TOMATOES, CORED, SEEDED, AND DICED
- 2 GREEN ONIONS (WHITE PART ONLY), TRIMMED AND THINLY SLICED CROSSWISE
- 1/4 CUP COARSELY CHOPPED FRESH CILANTRO LEAVES, DIVIDED

- 2 CUPS CHOPPED ROMAINE *OR* CURLY LEAF LETTUCE

- 1 AVOCADO, HALVED, PITTED, PEELED, AND DICED

To prepare the quinoa: Rinse the quinoa in several changes of water and drain well. In a large deep saucepan over low heat, heat the vegetable oil and garlic until the garlic sizzles. Add the quinoa and cook, stirring occasionally, until the grains are separate and golden, about 5 minutes. Add 2 cups water and the salt. Bring the liquid to a boil over high heat, then reduce heat to low and cook, covered, until the liquid is absorbed, about 15 minutes. Uncover and allow to cool at room temperature. Fluff with a spoon.

To make the dressing: In a small sauté pan over low heat, toast the cumin until fragrant, about 1 minute. Transfer to a small bowl and whisk in the remaining dressing ingredients.

To make the salad: Brush or spray the corn with vegetable oil and season with salt and pepper. Grill over *Direct Medium* heat until browned in spots and tender, 10 to 12 minutes, turning three or four times during grilling time. Remove from the grill. When the corn is cool enough to handle, use a small sharp knife to cut the kernels from the cob. Place in a small bowl and set aside.

Rinse the beans with cold water; drain well. In a small bowl combine with 1 tablespoon of the dressing and set aside.

In a separate bowl combine the tomatoes, green onions, half of the cilantro, and 2 tablespoons of the dressing. Stir to blend. Set aside. In a separate bowl combine the cooked quinoa with the remaining dressing. Stir to blend. Set aside.

Select a 3-quart serving bowl, preferably glass so you can see the layers of the salad through the sides. Spread the lettuce on the bottom of the bowl and layer on the other ingredients, beginning with half of the tomato mixture, then all the black beans, then all the corn, and then all the quinoa. Sprinkle the remaining tomato mixture on top and garnish with the diced avocado and the remaining cilantro leaves. Cover and refrigerate for at least 20 minutes before serving. Toss at the table just before serving.

MAKES 8 SERVINGS

*"It takes four men
to dress a salad:
a wise man for the salt,
a madman for the pepper,
a miser for the vinegar, and
a spendthrift for the oil."*

— ANONYMOUS

SIDES & SALADS

OLD-FASHIONED
CREAMY COLESLAW

A backyard barbecue just isn't the same without a good 'slaw on the side. This one is just the ticket.

FOR THE DRESSING:

1 CUP MAYONNAISE

1/2 CUP SOUR CREAM

1 TABLESPOON FRESH LEMON JUICE

1 TABLESPOON CIDER VINEGAR

1 TEASPOON CELERY SEEDS

KOSHER SALT

FRESHLY GROUND BLACK PEPPER

1 HEAD GREEN CABBAGE (ABOUT 2 POUNDS), TRIMMED, QUARTERED, CORED, AND SLICED VERY THIN

1 CUP COARSELY SHREDDED CARROT

To make the dressing: In a large bowl whisk together the dressing ingredients, including salt and pepper to taste.

Add the cabbage and carrot to the dressing and mix well. Cover with plastic wrap and refrigerate for 1 to 24 hours. Serve cold or at room temperature.

MAKES 8 SERVINGS

RED AND GREEN
CABBAGE SLAW

A perky twist on ordinary coleslaw, this recipe calls for red and green cabbage tossed with a creamy but light but- termilk dressing. The lemon gives it a little zip. Nice.

FOR THE DRESSING:

1/3 CUP BUTTERMILK

1/3 CUP MAYONNAISE

2 TABLESPOONS FINELY CHOPPED FRESH DILL

2 TABLESPOONS FRESH LEMON JUICE

2 TEASPOONS GRANULATED SUGAR

2 TEASPOONS DIJON MUSTARD

1/2 TEASPOON FINELY GRATED LEMON ZEST

1/4 HEAD RED CABBAGE, CORED AND CUT INTO THIN SLICES (ABOUT 3 CUPS)

1/4 HEAD GREEN CABBAGE, CORED AND CUT INTO THIN SLICES (ABOUT 3 CUPS)

KOSHER SALT

FRESHLY GROUND BLACK PEPPER

To make the dressing: In a small bowl whisk together the dressing ingredients.

In a medium bowl mix together the cabbage slices. Pour the dressing over the cabbage and mix thoroughly. Season with salt and pepper. Cover with plastic wrap and refrigerate for 1 to 24 hours. Serve cold or at room temperature.

MAKES 4 SERVINGS

TOMATO, CUCUMBER, AND ONION
SALAD

The simplest of salads for the height of summer, when tomatoes are their juiciest and most flavorful.

FOR THE SALAD:

3 LARGE RIPE TOMATOES, CORED AND CUT INTO 1/2-INCH SLICES

1 SEEDLESS CUCUMBER, PEELED AND CUT INTO 1/8-INCH DIAGONAL SLICES

1 LARGE RED ONION, CUT CROSSWISE INTO 1/8-INCH SLICES

1/4 CUP TORN FRESH BASIL LEAVES

2 TABLESPOONS TORN FRESH MINT LEAVES

KOSHER SALT

FRESHLY GROUND BLACK PEPPER

FOR THE DRESSING:

1/2 CUP PLAIN YOGURT

2 TABLESPOONS EXTRA-VIRGIN OLIVE OIL

1/2 TEASPOON MINCED GARLIC

WHOLE BASIL LEAVES (OPTIONAL)

BLACK OLIVES (OPTIONAL)

To make the salad: On a large platter arrange the tomato, cucumber, and onion slices in overlapping concentric circles. Sprinkle with the basil and mint and season with salt and pepper.

To make the dressing: In a small bowl whisk together the dressing ingredients.

Drizzle the dressing over the salad. Garnish with the basil leaves and a few black olives, if desired. Serve immediately.

MAKES 4 SERVINGS

LONG NOODLE
AND BEAN SPROUT SALAD

Spaghetti isn't exactly the noodle of choice in Beijing or Bangkok, but it works so well picking up the flavors of the dressing that we put it to work here. It's even better served cold the next day, so make it ahead.

FOR THE DRESSING:

- 1/4 CUP CREAMY PEANUT BUTTER
- 2 TABLESPOONS ASIAN SESAME OIL
- 2 TABLESPOONS RICE VINEGAR
- 1 TABLESPOON GRATED FRESH GINGER
- 1 TABLESPOON DARK BROWN SUGAR
- 1 TABLESPOON FISH SAUCE
- 1 TABLESPOON SOY SAUCE
- 1 TABLESPOON OYSTER SAUCE
- 2 TEASPOONS SRIRACHA
  (HOT CHILI-GARLIC SAUCE)

- 1/2 POUND SPAGHETTI

- 2 CUPS BEAN SPROUTS
- 2 CUPS SHREDDED NAPA CABBAGE
- 1 CUP GRATED CARROTS
- 4 GREEN ONIONS, TRIMMED AND THINLY SLICED CROSSWISE
- 1/4 CUP FINELY CHOPPED FRESH CILANTRO

To make the dressing: In a large bowl combine the dressing ingredients and whisk until smooth. The dressing will look curdled for a little while, but keep whisking until smooth.

In a large pot of boiling salted water cook the spaghetti according to package directions until al dente. Drain and transfer to the bowl with the dressing.

Add the remaining ingredients to the spaghetti. Stir until evenly mixed. Serve warm, at room temperature, or cold.

MAKES 4 TO 6 SERVINGS

MACARONI SALAD
WITH A HORSERADISH KICK

A tangy, sweet, and creamy version of one of America's favorite side dishes.

- 3 LARGE EGGS
- 2 CUPS SMALL ELBOW MACARONI

FOR THE DRESSING:

- 1/2 CUP MAYONNAISE
- 1/2 CUP FINELY DICED SWEET PICKLES
- 1/3 CUP FINELY CHOPPED FRESH ITALIAN PARSLEY
- 4 GREEN ONIONS (WHITE PART ONLY), FINELY CHOPPED
- 2 TABLESPOONS SWEET PICKLE JUICE
- 1 TABLESPOON FRESH LEMON JUICE
- 2 TEASPOONS DIJON MUSTARD
- 1 TEASPOON PREPARED HORSERADISH
- 1/2 TEASPOON KOSHER SALT
- 1/4 TEASPOON FRESHLY GROUND BLACK PEPPER

Fill a medium saucepan two-thirds full with water. Bring to a gentle boil over high heat. Using a spoon or ladle, carefully lower the eggs one at a time into the water. Cook for 12 minutes. Drain the eggs in a colander and rinse under cold water to stop the cooking. Peel the eggs and roughly chop.

Cook the macaroni according to package directions. Drain well and allow to cool to room temperature.

To make the dressing: In a large bowl combine the dressing ingredients and stir to blend.

Add the eggs and macaroni to the dressing and gently fold to combine. Cover with plastic wrap and refrigerate until ready to serve.

MAKES 4 TO 6 SERVINGS

> "To make a good salad is to be a brilliant diplomatist— the problem is entirely the same in both cases. To know exactly how much oil one must put with one's vinegar."
>
> — OSCAR WILDE

BLACK RICE AND SNOW PEA
SALAD

Black rice, imported from China under the name "Forbidden Rice," is available in health food and other specialty stores. Worth the hunt, but if you can't find it, you can substitute short- or long-grain brown rice, or long-grain white rice.

FOR THE DRESSING:

- 1/4 CUP VEGETABLE OIL
- 2 TABLESPOONS FRESH LIME JUICE
- 2 TABLESPOONS RICE VINEGAR
- 1 TABLESPOON SOY SAUCE
- 1 TABLESPOON ASIAN SESAME OIL
- 1/2 TEASPOON GRATED FRESH GINGER
- 1/2 TEASPOON MINCED GARLIC

FOR THE SALAD:

- 1 CUP BLACK RICE
- 1/4 POUND SNOW PEAS
- 2 MEDIUM CARROTS, TRIMMED, PEELED, AND GRATED
- 4 GREEN ONIONS, TRIMMED AND THINLY SLICED CROSSWISE
- 1/4 CUP FINELY DICED RED BELL PEPPER

To make the dressing: In a large bowl whisk together the dressing ingredients.

To make the salad: Rinse the rice and drain well. Cook in plenty of boiling salted water until the grains are soft to the bite, 30 to 35 minutes. Drain well. Allow to cool for about 10 minutes, then add to the dressing. Mix well.

In a small saucepan bring about 2 cups salted water to a boil. Add the snow peas and blanch until crisp-tender, about 1 minute. Drain and plunge into ice water to crisp. When cold, drain well and pat dry with paper towels. Stack and cut into 1/4-inch diagonal slices.

When the rice has cooled to room temperature, add the snow peas, carrots, green onions, and bell pepper and toss to combine. Serve at room temperature.

MAKES 4 TO 6 SERVINGS

BROWN RICE SALAD
WITH LIME DRESSING

This combo—nutty brown rice, dry roasted peanuts, and toasted sesame oil—is borderline irresistible. Add the dressing to the rice while it's still warm.

- 1 1/2 CUPS SHORT- *OR* MEDIUM-GRAIN BROWN RICE

FOR THE DRESSING:

- 1/4 CUP VEGETABLE OIL
- 2 TABLESPOONS RICE VINEGAR
- 2 TABLESPOONS FRESH LIME JUICE
- 1 TEASPOON ASIAN SESAME OIL
- 1 TEASPOON MINCED GARLIC
- 1/2 TEASPOON KOSHER SALT
- 1/4 TEASPOON FRESHLY GROUND BLACK PEPPER

- 1 LARGE CARROT, PEELED AND GRATED *OR* FINELY CHOPPED
- 3 GREEN ONIONS, TRIMMED AND THINLY SLICED CROSSWISE
- 3 TABLESPOONS FINELY CHOPPED FRESH CILANTRO
- 1/2 CUP CHOPPED UNSALTED DRY-ROASTED PEANUTS

Cook the rice in plenty of boiling salted water until tender, about 45 minutes (see package directions for exact times). Drain, rinse with cold water, and shake off excess moisture.

To make the dressing: In a large bowl whisk together the dressing ingredients.

Add the cooked rice, carrot, green onions, and cilantro to the dressing. Toss to blend. Sprinkle on the peanuts. Serve warm or at room temperature.

MAKES 4 TO 6 SERVINGS

RAISIN-PINE NUT
COUSCOUS

Couscous, delicate granules of semolina that can be cooked up quickly and served either warm or at room temperature, is a staple in North Africa. This dish takes advantage of the affinities between orange juice, raisins, ginger, and pine nuts. A handful of fresh mint animates the whole mixture.

1/2 CUP PINE NUTS

1 CUP FRESH ORANGE JUICE
1/3 CUP RAISINS
2 TABLESPOONS UNSALTED BUTTER
1 TABLESPOON FRESH LIME JUICE
1 TEASPOON GRATED FRESH GINGER
1 TEASPOON KOSHER SALT
1/2 TEASPOON FRESHLY GROUND BLACK PEPPER
1 CUP QUICK-COOKING COUSCOUS
1/3 CUP FINELY CHOPPED FRESH MINT

In a small sauté pan over medium heat, toast the pine nuts, stirring occasionally, until golden brown, about 5 minutes. Set aside.

In a medium saucepan combine the orange juice, raisins, butter, lime juice, ginger, salt, and pepper along with 1/2 cup water. Bring to a boil over high heat. Add the couscous, stir briefly, cover, and remove from the heat. Allow the couscous to absorb the liquid for 5 to 10 minutes. Fluff the couscous with a fork and transfer to a serving dish. Add the toasted pine nuts and chopped mint. Stir gently. Serve warm or at room temperature.

MAKES 4 SERVINGS

COUSCOUS-STUFFED
TOMATOES

Ripe tomato meets hot grill. The chemistry is a little heady. Fill the tomatoes with couscous seasoned with feta, black olives, fresh herbs, and garlic—and things start to get really intense.

DIRECT/MEDIUM

4 MEDIUM RIPE TOMATOES

FOR THE STUFFING:
1/4 CUP QUICK-COOKING COUSCOUS
1/2 CUP CRUMBLED FETA CHEESE
6 KALAMATA OLIVES, PITTED AND FINELY CHOPPED
1 TABLESPOON EXTRA-VIRGIN OLIVE OIL
1 TABLESPOON FINELY CHOPPED FRESH DILL
1 TABLESPOON FINELY CHOPPED FRESH BASIL
1/4 TEASPOON MINCED GARLIC
KOSHER SALT
FRESHLY GROUND BLACK PEPPER

Cut a 1/2-inch slice off the top of each tomato; reserve the tops. With a small knife cut around the inside of the fleshy part of the tomato (do not cut through the bottom of the tomato) to within 1/2 inch of the skin. With a teaspoon, scoop out the tomato flesh, leaving about 1/2 inch of flesh attached to the skin. Discard the juice and seeds to make room for the stuffing. Turn the tomatoes, cut side down, on a plate lined with paper towels to drain while you prepare the stuffing.

To make the stuffing: In a small saucepan bring 1/3 cup water to a boil and add the couscous. Stir to combine. Cover and remove from the heat. Allow the couscous to absorb the liquid for about 5 minutes. Fluff the couscous with a fork and transfer to a medium bowl. Add the remaining stuffing ingredients, including salt and pepper to taste, and stir to blend. Spoon the stuffing into the tomatoes. Replace the tops.

Grill the stuffed tomatoes over *Direct Medium* heat until the tomatoes are blistered and the cheese is melted, about 5 minutes. Carefully remove from the grill with a wide spatula. Serve warm.

MAKES 4 SERVINGS

SERVE THESE YUMMY GRILLED TOMATOES AS A SIDE DISH WITH GRILLED LAMB OR FISH, OR AS A MAIN COURSE WITH GARLIC BREAD AND A GREEN SALAD.

Couscous-Stuffed Tomatoes

Grilled Asparagus with Prosciutto and Orange Mayonnaise

GRILLED ASPARAGUS
WITH PROSCIUTTO AND ORANGE MAYONNAISE

A great recipe for Sunday brunch!

DIRECT/MEDIUM

FOR THE MAYONNAISE:

- 1/3 CUP MAYONNAISE
- 1 TABLESPOON FRESH ORANGE JUICE
- 1 TEASPOON FRESH LEMON JUICE
- 1/2 TEASPOON FINELY GRATED ORANGE ZEST
- PINCH CAYENNE

- 1 POUND LARGE ASPARAGUS, TOUGH ENDS REMOVED
- 1 1/2 TABLESPOONS EXTRA-VIRGIN OLIVE OIL
- 1/4 TEASPOON KOSHER SALT
- 1/8 TEASPOON FRESHLY GROUND BLACK PEPPER

- 1/4 POUND THINLY SLICED PROSCIUTTO

To make the mayonnaise: In a small bowl whisk together the mayonnaise ingredients.

Place the asparagus on a plate or platter. Drizzle the olive oil over the spears and turn to coat evenly. Season with the salt and pepper.

Grill the asparagus over *Direct Medium* heat until browned and tender, 6 to 8 minutes, turning once halfway through grilling time. Remove from the grill and keep warm.

Grill the prosciutto slices over *Direct Medium* heat just until crisp, 2 to 3 minutes, turning once halfway through grilling time. Remove from the grill and cut each slice into pieces about 2 inches across.

Arrange the prosciutto and asparagus on four plates and spoon the mayonnaise over the top. Serve immediately.

MAKES 4 SERVINGS

STUFFED ZUCCHINI

Savory little zucchini boats filled with a simple bread and mozzarella cheese mixture. These go well as part of a medley of dishes set out as a main meal or as a side to a main dish of grilled meat or fish.

DIRECT/MEDIUM

FOR THE STUFFING:

- 1 TABLESPOON EXTRA-VIRGIN OLIVE OIL
- 2 TABLESPOONS FINELY CHOPPED RED ONION
- 1/4 TEASPOON MINCED GARLIC
- 1/2 CUP DRIED BREAD CRUMBS
- 1/2 CUP GRATED MOZZARELLA CHEESE
- 1 TABLESPOON FINELY CHOPPED FRESH MINT
- 1/2 TEASPOON KOSHER SALT

- 4 MEDIUM ZUCCHINI, TRIMMED AND CUT IN HALF LENGTHWISE
- EXTRA-VIRGIN OLIVE OIL

- 1/4 CUP FRESHLY GRATED PARMIGIANO-REGGIANO CHEESE

To make the stuffing: In a medium sauté pan over medium-high heat, warm the olive oil and cook the onion, stirring occasionally, until tender, 4 to 5 minutes. Add the garlic and cook for 1 minute more, stirring occasionally. Add the bread crumbs and continue to cook, stirring occasionally, until light golden brown, about 2 minutes. Transfer to a medium bowl. Add the remaining stuffing ingredients and mix well.

Lightly brush or spray the zucchini all over with olive oil. Grill, skin side down, over *Direct Medium* heat for 6 minutes, turning once halfway through grilling time. Remove from the grill and allow to cool slightly.

Using the tip of a teaspoon, scoop out the partially cooked centers of the zucchini to within 1/4 inch of the skin. Finely chop the zucchini centers. Mix the chopped zucchini with the stuffing ingredients. Carefully spoon the stuffing into the zucchini shells, mounding slightly. Sprinkle the tops lightly with the cheese.

Grill the stuffed zucchini, skin side down, over *Direct Medium* heat until the stuffing is heated through, about 3 minutes. Serve warm.

MAKES 4 TO 6 SERVINGS

SPICY MAPLE
BAKED BEANS

Barbecue comfort food. The chili powder gives the beans a nice zing, but the sweetness of the maple syrup smooths out the flavors. A natural with grilled franks or ribs.

INDIRECT/MEDIUM

- 1 **TABLESPOON VEGETABLE OIL**
- 1 **MEDIUM YELLOW ONION, FINELY CHOPPED**
- 3/4 **POUND HAM STEAK, TRIMMED AND FINELY DICED**
- 1 **TABLESPOON MINCED GARLIC**
- 3/4 **CUP MAPLE SYRUP**
- 2 **TABLESPOONS TOMATO PASTE**
- 1 **TABLESPOON WORCESTERSHIRE SAUCE**
- 1 **TABLESPOON CHILI POWDER**
- 1/4 **TEASPOON CAYENNE**
- 3 **CANS (15 OUNCES EACH) PORK AND BEANS, DRAINED**

- 1 **TABLESPOON YELLOW MUSTARD**
  KOSHER SALT
  FRESHLY GROUND BLACK PEPPER

In a fireproof Dutch oven or heavy saucepan over medium-low heat, warm the vegetable oil and cook the onion, stirring occasionally, until soft, 8 to 10 minutes. Add the ham and garlic and cook for 2 minutes more, stirring occasionally. Add the maple syrup, tomato paste, Worcestershire sauce, chili powder, cayenne, and pork and beans. Bring to a boil over high heat.

Remove from the stove and place on the grill over *Indirect Medium* heat. Cook, uncovered, for about 45 minutes, stirring once or twice. Just before serving, add the mustard and season with salt and pepper. Serve warm.

MAKES 8 SERVINGS

GRILLED GARLIC
BREAD

Finely minced garlic is the key to making mouth-watering but not eye-watering garlic bread. For best results, flatten the peeled garlic on a cutting board with the side of a large knife. Then chop the garlic until it is almost a paste.

INDIRECT/HIGH

- 1 **LOAF ITALIAN *OR* FRENCH BREAD**

- 1 **STICK UNSALTED BUTTER, SOFTENED**
- 1 **TABLESPOON MINCED GARLIC**
- 1 **TABLESPOON FINELY CHOPPED FRESH ITALIAN PARSLEY**
- 1/2 **TEASPOON KOSHER SALT**
- 1/2 **TEASPOON PAPRIKA**

Cut the loaf crosswise into 3/4-inch slices but do not cut through the bottom of the loaf; keep all the slices attached. Place the cut bread on a piece of heavy-duty aluminum foil slightly more than twice as long and twice as wide as the loaf.

In a medium bowl combine the remaining ingredients and mash them together with the back of a fork. Spread the butter mixture evenly over one side of each slice of bread. Wrap the loaf completely in the foil.

Grill the loaf over *Indirect High* heat until the butter is melted and the outside of the bread is crispy, about 10 minutes. Carefully unwrap the loaf and serve the bread warm.

MAKES 6 TO 8 SERVINGS

BACON
CORNBREAD

A meaty slab of ribs and a cool, crisp coleslaw practically beg for cornbread straight from the grill. This one is extra-delicious with the inclusion of a little bacon. Use a cast iron skillet that's well seasoned so you can easily invert the bread whole onto a plate or a cutting board.

INDIRECT/MEDIUM

- 4 SLICES BACON, CUT INTO 1/2-INCH PIECES
- 1 CUP FINELY CHOPPED YELLOW ONION

FOR THE BATTER:
- 1 CUP YELLOW CORNMEAL
- 1/2 CUP ALL-PURPOSE FLOUR
- 1 1/2 TABLESPOONS BAKING POWDER
- 1 TABLESPOON GRANULATED SUGAR
- 1/2 TEASPOON BAKING SODA
- 1/2 TEASPOON KOSHER SALT
- 1 1/2 CUPS BUTTERMILK
- 2 LARGE EGGS
- 1/4 TEASPOON TABASCO SAUCE

In a 9- or 10-inch iron skillet over medium heat, fry the bacon, stirring occasionally, until the fat is rendered and the bacon is crisp, 10 to 12 minutes. With a slotted spoon transfer the bacon bits to a small bowl. Add the onion to the bacon fat and cook over low heat, stirring occasionally, until browned, about 10 minutes. With a slotted spoon, transfer the onion to the bowl with the bacon. Tilt the skillet to coat the bottom and sides evenly with any remaining bacon fat. Keep the skillet warm over very low heat.

To make the batter: In a large bowl whisk together the cornmeal, flour, baking powder, sugar, baking soda, and salt. In a separate medium bowl whisk the buttermilk, eggs, and Tabasco sauce until thoroughly blended. Pour the buttermilk mixture over the cornmeal mixture and stir just until blended. Add the bacon-and-onion mixture and stir once or twice to blend. Pour the batter into the warm skillet.

Grill the cornbread over *Indirect Medium* heat, keeping the grill's temperature near 350°F, until the top is golden brown around the edges and a toothpick inserted in the center comes out clean, 20 to 30 minutes. Invert the cornbread onto a plate or cutting board, cut into wedges, and serve immediately.

MAKES 8 SERVINGS

BUTTERMILK
BISCUITS

The secret to light biscuits is to handle them as little as possible. The damp, sticky batter should be pressed together ever so gently with lightly floured hands. Go easy on them—at least until they're out of the oven!

- 2 CUPS ALL-PURPOSE FLOUR
- 2 TEASPOONS BAKING POWDER
- 1/2 TEASPOON BAKING SODA
- 1/2 TEASPOON KOSHER SALT
- 1/3 CUP UNSALTED BUTTER, COLD, CUT INTO 10 TO 12 PIECES
- 3/4 TO 1 CUP BUTTERMILK

Preheat oven to 450°F.

In a food processor mix the flour, baking powder, baking soda, and salt. Add the butter and pulse several times until blended. Add 3/4 cup of the buttermilk and process just until the mixture forms a ball. The ball should be a little sticky. If it feels too dry, add 2 to 4 tablespoons more buttermilk and process briefly.

Transfer the ball onto a lightly floured work surface and lightly press and flatten into a disk about 8 inches in diameter and 1/2 inch thick. Use a floured biscuit cutter or inverted glass to cut 3-inch rounds. Press the remaining dough together and cut into more rounds. Transfer the biscuits to an ungreased baking pan.

Bake the biscuits until golden brown, 12 to 15 minutes. Serve warm.

MAKES 8 BISCUITS

When it comes to dessert, there are three kinds of eaters. The Gotta-Haves never pass up an opportunity to indulge their sweet tooth. For them, dinner ends when the dessert forks are safely tucked into the dishwasher. The Why-Nots will eat dessert when it's offered, but will only occasionally venture into the kitchen to concoct something special. In restaurants, however, they might gamely beckon the dessert cart. And then there are the Not-for-Mes. They rarely if ever partake, whether driven by guilt or lack of interest in the sweet stuff. Frankly, we find this last group a bit puzzling. After all, when it comes to expanding your gastronomic horizons, dessert is sweet country indeed. Explore it and live a little!

DESSE

A casual outdoor gathering is a great place to start. Maybe the best thing about a post-barbecue dessert is that here simple can reign supreme. It just has to be sweet and satisfying, not a work of art. Witness the incredible magnetism of a chilled watermelon. And let's face it. While we all admire pastry chefs—those dessert-makers of the highest order—we rarely emulate them because petits fours and caramel cages are not the stuff of cookouts.

But there will be times when a carton of Häagen Dazs® and a plate of chocolate chip cookies just won't do. When that hankering for something sweet demands something fresh, exciting, different. Or even—and maybe especially—a classic ending done exactly right.

That's where this chapter comes in. Imagine sinking your teeth into sweet vanilla pastry cream as flakes of delicate pie crust shower your chin. Feel the ripe berries bursting between your teeth, their juices gushing into your mouth. Or take a walk on the comfy side. How about a chewy bite of mocha-tinged brownie, crowned with a dollop of vanilla ice cream and rich chocolate sauce? These, and more, are all within easy reach of even the humblest abilities. And you'd be surprised at how many desserts you can prepare on the grill.

Dessert on the grill? You bet your sweet molasses. With fruit-based treats ranging from grilled bananas and strawberries to cakes and puddings baked right on the grill, you can keep the fire going and wow them one more time with your outdoor cooking wizardry. Or, if your perfect reward for a dinner well done is a dessert you just have to retrieve from indoors, we've got some make-ahead finales, too. And if it's nostalgia you crave, we've also got some stunning takes on childhood classics such as ice cream sandwiches, S'mores, and the sweetheart of summer, the frozen fruit pop.

Anything you choose will be well received when you serve it up with panache. Believe it or not, there is an art to that. Start by considering your audience. Are the kids going to be impressed with homemade pie crust, or will they be just as happy with a bag of marshmallows and a couple of sticks? If you can get off easy, why slave away?

Which brings up another point: Know your limitations. If you're whipping up a grilled dinner for twelve, the make-ahead route could be your best bet. And don't be afraid to cheat. Take the easy route and serve up Dovebars®, a fancy box of chocolates, or a big bowl of mixed candy. Sometimes an easy or wacky dessert will do more to enliven the conversation than an elaborate cake and coffee.

Lastly, go for contrast. If dinner was heavy—say, ribs and beans—lighten up at dessert with grilled pineapple drizzled with honey. If dinner was light—such as grilled fish and salad—you can lean toward the rich with a chocolate cupcake smothered in peanut butter frosting. Or some such wonder.

Most of all, remember that we all have the right to enjoy a sweet indulgence every now and then. Exercise your right to dessert!

Apples Grilled in Parchment Paper

APPLES
GRILLED IN
PARCHMENT PAPER

A grown-up treat from the grill that even kids will devour. Simple. Sublime.

DIRECT/MEDIUM

2 GRANNY SMITH APPLES
¹/₂ CUP DRIED CRANBERRIES
¹/₄ CUP PURE MAPLE SYRUP
2 TEASPOONS LIGHT BROWN SUGAR
¹/₂ TEASPOON GROUND CINNAMON

2 TABLESPOONS UNSALTED BUTTER, DIVIDED

Quarter the apples through the core. Remove and discard the core, then cut each quarter into thin slices. Place the slices in a medium bowl. Add the cranberries, maple syrup, sugar, and cinnamon. Stir to combine.

To make the packets: Cut four pieces of baking parchment paper, about 12 by 15 inches each. Spoon one-quarter of the apple mixture into the center of each piece of paper and dot with one-quarter of the butter. Bring the two long ends of each paper together and fold them over several times to seal the top of the packet. Twist the other two ends of the papers in opposite directions to close the packets.

Grill the packets over *Direct Medium* heat for about 10 minutes. Serve in packets or pour the apple mixture from each packet into a separate bowl. Either way, serve warm with ice cream, if desired.

MAKES 4 SERVINGS

GRILLED PEARS
WITH POUND CAKE
AND CARAMEL SAUCE

The sumptuous flavor of grilled pears is made all the more irresistible with this to-die-for caramel sauce. Good enough for Christmas dinner, garnished with whipped cream, if desired.

DIRECT/MEDIUM

FOR THE SAUCE:
¹/₂ CUP GRANULATED SUGAR
¹/₂ CUP HEAVY CREAM
¹/₄ CUP UNSALTED BUTTER
1 TEASPOON ALMOND EXTRACT

4 PEARS, FIRM BUT RIPE
4 SLICES POUND CAKE, ABOUT ¹/₂ INCH THICK EACH
CONFECTIONERS' SUGAR

To make the sauce: Place the sugar in a small, heavy-bottomed saucepan and set over medium heat. Without touching the sugar, allow it to melt and turn dark brown, occasionally swirling the pan by its handle to be sure all the sugar turns to clear liquid, 8 to 12 minutes.

In another pan bring the cream and butter to a simmer. Carefully add the mixture to the sugar (it will bubble up). The sugar will stiffen, so simmer the mixture for a few minutes while you whisk it to melt the sugar again and smooth out the sauce. Remove the sauce from the heat. Whisk in the almond extract. Set the sauce aside (if it gets too stiff, reheat and whisk it over low heat).

Quarter the pears vertically and core them. Lightly dust the pears and the pound cake all over with the confectioners' sugar (tap off any excess). Grill the pears over *Direct Medium* heat until tender, 5 to 7 minutes, turning once halfway through grilling time. Grill the pound cake over *Direct Medium* heat until the slices are well marked and warm, about 1 minute, turning once halfway through grilling time.

Arrange the pears and cake slices on serving dishes. Drizzle with the caramel sauce and serve warm.

MAKES 4 SERVINGS

DESSERT ON THE GRILL

Okay, here's your chance to wow them once more with your skill at the grill. Since few folks are hip to the fact that you can make dessert on the grill, it shouldn't be hard to impress them. Especially with these few pointers under your belt:

YES, YOU CAN BAKE ON THE GRILL. A thick, heavy-gauge baking pan will provide even heating. Go for cast iron, a stainless steel pan lined with aluminum, or a disposable, heavy-gauge aluminum baking pan. If you're baking pastries, place the baking sheet atop an inverted jelly roll pan (a cookie sheet with a 1-inch lip) on the cooking grate for an extra cushion of air to help prevent burning. And never use glass baking dishes on a grill—they can shatter. "Ovenproof" and "fireproof" are two different things. All of the recipes for baking on the grill in this chapter call for the temperature of the grill to be kept at 350°F, or as close to that as possible. So, be sure to monitor your temperature gauge and adjust the heat accordingly.

MAKE THE SWITCH. All of the recipes for baking on the grill in this chapter can be adapted to baking in the oven: Follow the same instructions and timing, just set the oven at 350°F. If you'd like to adapt your favorite dessert recipe for the grill, set your grill up for Indirect Medium heat for recipes that are baked between 325°F and 375°F. Use a thermometer to check the internal temperature of the grill before you place the dessert on the cooking grate. For best results, monitor the grill's temperature throughout cooking time. (About the only thing you can't convert to baking on the grill is a soufflé, which requires a more airtight environment to rise properly. What, you don't think you'd even try it? We know of at least one wacky chef who has!) It may take a little practice to get this conversion thing down to a routine, but isn't your favorite recipe worth the effort?

BURN OFF DINNER. Once you've taken dinner off the grill, calculate how long you'll need to enjoy it and how long it will take for dessert to cook. Factor in a meandering conversation under the stars. In between you should do a burn-off and, if you're grilling on charcoal, that means adding more briquets and allowing them to ash over.

CHARCOAL GRILLERS: Remove dinner from the grill. Remove the cooking grate and place on a fireproof surface. If you've been using smoking woods, remove any remaining chunks or chips and place them in a metal bucket full of water. Add another layer of briquets and, after 5 minutes, replace the cooking grate and grill lid, keeping all vents open. Once the residue burns off the cooking grate and the smoking stops, brush the cooking grate thoroughly with a brass grill brush. If you're going to change cooking methods (i.e. from Direct to Indirect), arrange the briquets now. Important: Give the coals a few more minutes to get a decent ash coating—it will prevent any charcoal flavor from permeating your dessert.

GAS GRILLERS: Remove dinner from the grill. If you've been using smoking woods, remove any remaining chunks or chips from the smoker and place them in a metal bucket full of water. Turn all burners to High. Once the residue burns off the cooking grate and the smoking stops, brush the cooking grate thoroughly with a brass grill brush and adjust the burners for the temperature and cooking method in the dessert recipe.

DON'T WANT TO USE A RECIPE? Just drizzle grilled fruit with honey or top a bowl of ice cream with hot grilled fruit chunks.

STRAWBERRIES
BALSAMICO

Here's a great recipe for serving a crowd—simply make it all ahead of time. You'll love what the balsamic adds to the berries-and-cream combo. Strawberries that are red to the core are the best.

DIRECT/MEDIUM

2 **POUNDS FRESH STRAWBERRIES, HULLED, DIVIDED**

¼ **CUP GRANULATED SUGAR**

¼ **CUP BALSAMIC VINEGAR**

1 **TEASPOON GRATED ORANGE ZEST**

1 **TEASPOON ORANGE-FLAVORED LIQUEUR (OPTIONAL)**

8 **SCOOPS VANILLA ICE CREAM**

Place half of the strawberries in a medium bowl.

In a small bowl, whisk together the sugar, vinegar, orange zest, and liqueur. Pour the liquid over the strawberries in the bowl, turning them to coat evenly. Allow to stand for 15 minutes. Strain, reserving the liquid.

Thread the coated strawberries onto skewers. Grill over *Direct Medium* heat until lightly marked, 4 to 5 minutes, turning once halfway through grilling time. Allow to cool slightly. Purée the grilled strawberries along with the reserved liquid in a food processor.

Slice the remaining strawberries. Add the purée to the sliced berries. Pour the strawberry mixture over the ice cream and serve.

MAKES 8 SERVINGS

"I generally avoid temptation unless I can't resist it."

— MAE WEST

STRAWBERRIES, PEACHES, AND PEARS, OH MY!
FRUIT ON THE GRILL

Grilling fruit? Use Direct Medium heat unless the recipe instructs otherwise. The key to your success is the fruit's ripeness:

Strawberries: *Pick large, red, firm berries. Double-skewer them to keep them from spinning around when you turn them. Use a wide spatula to loosen them from the grate before turning.*

Peaches and nectarines: *Barely ripened fruit is best—make sure the peaches are of the freestone variety.*

Pears and apples: *Ripe but firm pears are best—Bartlett pears get too soft. Bosc, Anjou, and other fall-to-winter varieties are great. Same with the traditional baking apples (e.g. Granny Smith, Golden Delicious, Pippin, Gravenstein, Fuji). Grill Granny Smith apples in halves—when they're done, the skins pop right off.*

Pineapples: *We love grilled fresh pineapple for lots of reasons. The grill marks add a nice textural contrast to the juicy fruit. And whether you're grilling rings or wedges or chunks, you can enjoy the results in a dessert or as a great complement to pork, chicken, or seafood. But first, be sure you're selecting one that's ripe enough. Color isn't a good indicator because ripe pineapple can vary from gold to green. Some folks contend that if you can easily pluck its center leaves, the pineapple is ripe. But the best ripeness indicator is a sweet pineapple fragrance at the bottom of the fruit. Take your time choosing: Pineapples don't ripen further once picked.*

Bananas: *Select firm unblemished bananas with a touch of green at the ends. If they somewhat resist being peeled, they'll stand up better to the heat and tongs.*

Figs: *Firm, barely ripe figs are best. If they're too soft, they can stick to the grate.*

TROPICAL FRUIT
CRISP

Don't let the oatmeal topping fool you—this one has all the decadence you want in a dessert. But what a great way to work in those daily fruit servings.

INDIRECT/MEDIUM

FOR THE TOPPING:

1 1/2 CUPS FIRMLY PACKED LIGHT BROWN SUGAR

1 1/2 CUPS ALL-PURPOSE FLOUR

1 1/2 CUPS REGULAR *OR* QUICK-COOKING OATMEAL (*NOT* INSTANT)

3/4 CUP UNSALTED BUTTER, SOFTENED, CUT INTO 10 TO 12 PIECES

1/3 CUP COARSELY CHOPPED PISTACHIOS

1/2 TEASPOON KOSHER SALT

1 LARGE RIPE PINEAPPLE

1 TO 2 LARGE RIPE PAPAYAS

1 TO 2 RIPE MANGOES

4 KIWIS

1/3 CUP GRANULATED SUGAR

1 TABLESPOON QUICK-COOKING TAPIOCA

1 TEASPOON GROUND CINNAMON

To make the topping: In a large bowl combine the topping ingredients. Work in the butter until the mixture resembles large, coarse bread crumbs. Set aside while you prepare the fruit.

Cut the top and bottom from the pineapple, then stand it upright. With a sharp knife, slice off the skin all around, cutting deeply enough to remove all the brown "eyes." Quarter the pineapple lengthwise, then cut the fibrous core from each wedge. Cut each wedge in half lengthwise. Cut crosswise into 1/2-inch pieces.

Peel the papayas and halve them, then scoop out and discard the seeds. Cut into 1-inch chunks.

Peel the mangoes, then slice the fruit from the fibrous pit.

Peel the kiwis. Cut the mangoes and kiwis into 1-inch chunks. Mix all the fruit together in a large bowl along with the sugar, tapioca, and cinnamon. Toss to combine evenly.

Spread the fruit in a greased 9- by 13-inch heavy-gauge metal baking pan or 3-quart metal casserole. Sprinkle the oatmeal topping in a thick layer on top. Grill over *Indirect Medium* heat until the topping has browned and the juices are bubbling, 50 to 60 minutes. Keep the grill's temperature as close to 350°F as possible. Remove from the grill and cool at least 1 hour before serving. Serve with ice cream, if desired.

MAKES 10 TO 12 SERVINGS

PEACHES
WITH RASPBERRY SAUCE AND LEMON CREAM

Raspberry sauce makes a seductive topping for these peaches, but a dollop of lemon-flavored whipped cream is the "pièce de résistance." A flavor combination you could call triumphant.

DIRECT/MEDIUM

FOR THE RASPBERRY SAUCE:

3 CUPS FRESH RASPBERRIES *OR* 1 BAG (12 OUNCES) FROZEN RASPBERRIES, THAWED

1 TABLESPOON FRESH LEMON JUICE

1 TABLESPOON TEQUILA *OR* RASPBERRY LIQUEUR (OPTIONAL)

2 TO 4 TABLESPOONS GRANULATED SUGAR

FOR THE LEMON CREAM:

1 CUP HEAVY CREAM, COLD

1 TABLESPOON SUPERFINE INSTANT DISSOLVING SUGAR

1 TABLESPOON FRESH LEMON JUICE

2 TEASPOONS FINELY GRATED LEMON ZEST

6 LARGE PEACHES, FIRM BUT RIPE

6 TABLESPOONS UNSALTED BUTTER

1/4 CUP GRANULATED SUGAR

To make the raspberry sauce: In a food processor purée the raspberries with 1/3 cup water. Strain through a fine-mesh sieve into a bowl, pressing on the pulp to extract the liquid. (A few seeds may pass through the sieve and remain in the sauce.) Add the lemon juice, tequila, and sugar to taste. (Fresh raspberries will likely need the full amount of sugar; sweetened frozen berries will require less.) Stir or whisk until the sugar dissolves. Refrigerate until ready to serve.

To make the lemon cream: In a mixing bowl mix together the cream and sugar. Whip at high speed until soft peaks form. Add the lemon juice and grated lemon zest and continue whipping at high speed until stiff peaks form. Set aside in the refrigerator while you prepare the peaches.

Halve and pit the peaches; set aside. In a small saucepan over low heat, melt the butter, then add the sugar and stir until the sugar is dissolved. Remove from the heat. Brush the peach halves all over with the butter mixture. Grill over *Direct Medium* heat until browned in spots and warm throughout, 8 to 10 minutes, turning every 2 or 3 minutes. Serve the peaches warm with the raspberry sauce and lemon cream.

MAKES 6 SERVINGS

PEACHES
WARMED
ON THE
GRILL
BECOME
BEAUTIFULLY
CARAMELIZED.

Peaches with Raspberry Sauce and Lemon Cream

RASPBERRY-LIME
MERINGUE PIE

Here we top a fluffy meringue shell with a luscious lime custard, sprinkle on fresh red raspberries, and crown the whole thing with whipped cream. And you didn't leave room for dessert? Think again.

FOR THE SHELL:
- 1/2 CUP EGG WHITES (FROM 4 LARGE EGGS)
- 1/2 TEASPOON CREAM OF TARTAR
- 1/4 TEASPOON KOSHER SALT
- 1 TEASPOON PURE VANILLA EXTRACT
- 1 CUP GRANULATED SUGAR

FOR THE FILLING:
- 3 LIMES
- 4 LARGE EGG YOLKS
- 1/2 CUP GRANULATED SUGAR
- 1/4 TEASPOON KOSHER SALT
- 1/2 CUP HEAVY CREAM

- 2 1/2 CUPS FRESH RASPBERRIES, DIVIDED
- 1 CUP HEAVY CREAM
- 2 TABLESPOONS GRANULATED SUGAR

Preheat oven to 275°F. Place a piece of baking parchment paper on a cookie sheet. With a pencil, trace a circle, 9 inches in diameter, on the paper. Turn the paper over.

To make the shell: In a large bowl combine the egg whites, cream of tartar, and salt. Using an electric mixer, beat the whites at medium speed until foamy, about 30 seconds. Add the vanilla. Continue beating as you pour in the sugar in a thin stream, then beat at high speed until the whites become stiff and satiny and peaks form when the mixer is lifted, at least 3 minutes.

Spread the meringue on the parchment paper, filling in the traced circle, then build up the sides to form a 2-inch-high rim, about 1 inch thick. The shape should resemble a shallow bowl with a flat bottom. Bake until the meringue is firm and dry to the touch, 60 to 70 minutes. Turn off the oven and let the meringue cool in the oven for at least several hours or overnight. (The meringue will crack a bit as it cools.) Carefully transfer the meringue shell to a serving plate.

To make the filling: Zest the limes, finely chop the zest, then cut the limes in half and juice them. Place the chopped zest and juice in a heavy-bottomed saucepan together with the egg yolks, sugar, and salt. Whisk vigorously for about 30 seconds. Place over medium heat and cook, whisking constantly, until the mixture is foamy, opaque, and as thick as melted ice cream, about 4 to 6 minutes. Do not allow the mixture to come to a boil. Remove from the heat and immediately pour into a large bowl. Let cool to room temperature, stirring occasionally. Meanwhile, whip the heavy cream until stiff peaks form, then fold into the cooled custard. Spread the filling into the meringue shell and chill for 3 to 8 hours.

Before serving, spread half the raspberries over the custard. Whip the cream with the sugar until stiff peaks form, then spread over the berries. Top with the remaining raspberries. After cutting the pie into pieces, use a wide spatula or pie server to transfer them to plates since they will be fragile.

MAKES 6 TO 8 SERVINGS

BREAD PUDDING
WITH DRIED CHERRIES

A classic dessert that makes a seamless transition to the grill. Let it bake while you're eating dinner. We gave the traditional recipe a twist by adding sweet dried cherries in place of raisins. Serve warm with ice cream and a honey glaze drizzled over top.

INDIRECT/MEDIUM
- 3 LARGE EGGS
- 1 CUP GRANULATED SUGAR
- 2 TEASPOONS PURE VANILLA EXTRACT
- 1 TEASPOON GROUND CINNAMON
- 1/8 TEASPOON FRESHLY GRATED NUTMEG
- 2 TABLESPOONS UNSALTED BUTTER, MELTED
- 2 CUPS WHOLE MILK
- 1 CUP DRIED CHERRIES *OR* OTHER DRIED FRUIT
- 1 TEASPOON GRATED LEMON ZEST
- 5 CUPS 1-INCH CUBED DAY-OLD FRENCH BREAD

In a mixing bowl beat the eggs until frothy, 1 to 2 minutes. Add the sugar, vanilla, cinnamon, nutmeg, and melted butter. Beat until well blended. Add the milk, then stir in the dried cherries and lemon zest. Add the bread cubes and toss until mixed well. Cover and refrigerate for about 45 minutes, stirring occasionally and pushing the bread cubes down into the liquid.

Using a slotted spoon, transfer the bread cubes into a greased 8- by 8-inch heavy-gauge metal baking pan. Pour the liquid over the top, evenly distributing the cherries. Press the bread cubes down so the liquid rises about halfway up them.

Grill over *Indirect Medium* heat until the pudding is puffed and brown and a toothpick inserted in the center comes out clean, 50 to 60 minutes. Keep the grill's temperature as close to 350°F as possible. Serve warm.

MAKES 6 SERVINGS

BLUEBERRY
TART

This could be the epitome of good summertime eating. A flaky pie crust filled with vanilla pastry cream and topped with fresh blueberries is a slice of Americana that leans toward the rapturous without getting corny. Even if you cheat and buy a decent pre-fab crust at the grocery store, you'll still be golden.

FOR THE CRUST:

1 1/4 CUPS ALL-PURPOSE FLOUR
  2 TABLESPOONS GRANULATED SUGAR
1/2 TEASPOON KOSHER SALT
1/2 CUP UNSALTED BUTTER, COLD

FOR THE PASTRY CREAM:

  3 LARGE EGG YOLKS
    PINCH KOSHER SALT
1/3 CUP GRANULATED SUGAR, DIVIDED
  2 TABLESPOONS ALL-PURPOSE FLOUR
  1 CUP WHOLE MILK
  2 TEASPOONS PURE VANILLA EXTRACT

  1 PINT FRESH BLUEBERRIES

To make the crust: In a medium bowl stir together the flour, sugar, and salt. Cut the butter into 1/2-inch dice, then, using a pastry blender or the back of a fork, cut in the butter until the mixture has the consistency of coarse cornmeal with some pea-sized pieces. Add 3 tablespoons ice water and stir with a fork until the dough begins to hold together. If it seems too dry, add another tablespoon ice water. Gather the dough into a ball, flatten into a disk, wrap in plastic wrap, and refrigerate for at least 2 hours.

Remove the dough from the plastic wrap. On a lightly floured surface, roll it out into a circle about 1/8 inch thick. Fold the dough in half and, slipping both hands underneath, transfer it to a 10-inch tart pan with removable bottom. Unfold the dough and center it in the pan, gently pressing it in place. Using a small knife, trim the dough flush to the edges of the rim. Gently press the dough against the rim. Cover with plastic wrap and refrigerate for 2 to 24 hours.

To make the pastry cream: In a medium bowl whisk together the egg yolks, salt, and half of the sugar until the sugar dissolves. Whisk in the flour.

In a medium saucepan combine the milk, vanilla, and remaining sugar. Bring to a boil over high heat. Slowly pour half of the hot milk mixture into the egg mixture, whisking constantly. Set the milk mixture back on the stove and reduce the heat to medium. Pour the egg-and-milk mixture back into the saucepan, whisking constantly. Continue whisking until the mixture comes to a boil and thickens, 1 to 2 minutes. Pour and scrape the mixture into a medium bowl. Cover with plastic wrap, pressing the wrap directly onto the surface to prevent a skin from forming. Refrigerate for at least 1 hour.

Preheat oven to 350°F.

Remove the plastic wrap from the dough. Using the tines of a fork, pierce the bottom of the dough at 1/2-inch intervals. Cover the dough with a piece of baking parchment paper slightly larger than the pan. Fill the pan with 2 cups dried beans or pie weights (available in gourmet shops) to weigh down the crust and prevent shrinkage during baking.

Bake the weighted dough until the edges look dry and are barely golden brown, 20 to 25 minutes. Remove the paper and the weights (you can reserve the beans to use again for the same purpose). Bake the uncovered dough until lightly golden brown all over, 15 to 25 minutes, watching that the crust does not burn. Remove from the oven, remove the tart pan's rim, and allow the crust to cool on a rack.

Spread the pastry cream evenly over the bottom of the crust. Distribute the blueberries on top, pressing them down a bit. Serve at room temperature.

MAKES 8 SERVINGS

GRILLED FIGS
AND GOAT CHEESE
DRIZZLED WITH HONEY

They've yet to uncover any archeological evidence, but we suspect they dined on this stuff on Mount Olympus. Truly food for the gods.

DIRECT/HIGH

16 RIPE FIGS, ABOUT 1 OUNCE EACH, STEMS REMOVED
    EXTRA-VIRGIN OLIVE OIL

  4 OUNCES FRESH GOAT CHEESE, CUT INTO 1/4-INCH SLICES
  2 TABLESPOONS HONEY
  4 LEMON WEDGES

Thread four figs lengthwise (through the stem end) onto skewers and lightly brush or spray with olive oil. Grill over *Direct High* heat until soft and warm, 3 to 5 minutes, turning once halfway through grilling time.

Slide the figs onto individual serving plates. Arrange the cheese slices beside the figs. Drizzle the honey all over. Garnish each plate with a lemon wedge. Serve while the figs are warm.

MAKES 4 SERVINGS

BANANAS
CALYPSO

This has all the ingredients for a great dessert—a little show with the flaming rum and a little decadence with the buttery sauce. Serve it with a little modesty, if you can.

DIRECT/MEDIUM

- ¼ CUP UNSALTED BUTTER
- ⅓ CUP GRANULATED SUGAR
- 2 TABLESPOONS FRESH LIME JUICE
- 1 TEASPOON GROUND CINNAMON

- 4 BANANAS, FIRM BUT RIPE, PEELED

- ¼ CUP DARK RUM
- 4 SCOOPS VANILLA ICE CREAM

In a medium saucepan with a fireproof handle over *Direct Medium* heat, melt the butter. Add the sugar, lime juice, and cinnamon. Stir to dissolve the sugar. Remove from the grill.

Brush the bananas with about ¼ cup of the butter mixture, leaving the rest in the pan. Grill the bananas over *Direct Medium* heat until well marked, 2 to 4 minutes, turning once halfway through grilling time.

Transfer the bananas to a work surface, slice on the bias, and add to the remaining butter mixture in the saucepan. Grill over *Direct Medium* heat, stirring gently, until the bananas are hot, 4 to 5 minutes. Remove from the grill.

Immediately add the rum and carefully light it with a long kitchen match. After the flames die out, serve the warm grilled bananas with rum sauce over the ice cream.

MAKES 4 SERVINGS

PARADISE
GRILLED

Pepper on pineapple? Yes! It adds an exciting burst of flavor to the juicy fruit. The quality/freshness of the pineapple is all-important.

INDIRECT/MEDIUM

FOR THE GLAZE:

- ¾ CUP FRESH ORANGE JUICE
- 1 TABLESPOON HONEY
- 1 TABLESPOON FRESH LIME JUICE
- 2 TEASPOONS CORNSTARCH

- 4 SLICES FRESH PINEAPPLE, ABOUT ½ INCH THICK EACH
- 1 TEASPOON CRACKED DRIED GREEN PEPPERCORNS *OR* CRACKED BLACK PEPPERCORNS

- 4 SCOOPS VANILLA ICE CREAM

To make the glaze: In a small saucepan combine the glaze ingredients and whisk until smooth. Bring to a boil over medium-high heat and cook until thickened, 1 to 2 minutes. Keep the glaze warm or reheat when ready to serve.

Season both sides of the pineapple slices with the peppercorns. Grill over *Indirect Medium* heat until well marked, 6 to 8 minutes, turning once halfway through grilling time. Serve each pineapple slice with a scoop of ice cream and some of the glaze drizzled over the top.

MAKES 4 SERVINGS

PINEAPPLE LOVES THE GRILL. HERE IT'S SERVED WITH ICE CREAM, BUT YOU CAN SERVE IT AS PART OF A MAIN DISH, TOO, ESPECIALLY GRILLED PORK.

Paradise Grilled

GINGERBREAD STOUT CAKE

Beer in a dessert—who'da thunk! You might be surprised by this one, but Guinness® fans won't be. They've got a staggering number of uses for the creamy brew. Warning: You will fall hard for this jazzed up classic.

INDIRECT/MEDIUM

- 2½ CUPS ALL-PURPOSE FLOUR
- 3 TABLESPOONS GROUND GINGER
- 1 TABLESPOON BAKING SODA
- 2 TEASPOONS GROUND CINNAMON
- ½ TEASPOON GROUND CLOVES
- ½ TEASPOON KOSHER SALT
- 1 CUP UNSALTED BUTTER, SOFTENED
- 1½ CUPS FIRMLY PACKED DARK BROWN SUGAR
- 2 LARGE EGGS
- 1 CUP MOLASSES
- ¾ CUP GUINNESS® STOUT, FLAT, AT ROOM TEMPERATURE

CONFECTIONERS' SUGAR

In a large bowl sift together the flour, ginger, baking soda, cinnamon, cloves, and salt.

In mixing bowl, using an electric mixer on high speed, beat the butter and sugar until light and fluffy, 2 to 3 minutes. Lower the speed to medium and beat in the eggs one at a time. Beat in the molasses and stout (the batter may look curdled at this point; don't worry). Beat in the flour mixture one-third at a time. Scrape the batter into a greased and floured 9- by 13-inch heavy-gauge metal baking pan and smooth the top with a spatula.

Grill over *Indirect Medium* heat until a toothpick inserted in the center comes out clean, 40 to 50 minutes. Keep the grill's temperature as close to 350°F as possible. Remove the cake from the grill and let it sit in the pan for about 10 minutes. Invert the pan to release the cake and let the cake cool on a rack. Dust with confectioners' sugar and serve warm or at room temperature.

MAKES 12 TO 15 SERVINGS

CHOCOLATE CAKE
ON THE GRILL

You can mix up this moist wonder by hand in about 5 minutes, then bake it right on the grill. Great flavor for little effort. You can even skip the whipped cream and cocoa topping and simply dust it with powdered sugar (or add a scoop of ice cream—we won't tell).

INDIRECT/MEDIUM

FOR THE CAKE:
- 1½ CUPS ALL-PURPOSE FLOUR
- 1 CUP GRANULATED SUGAR
- ⅓ CUP UNSWEETENED COCOA
- 1 TEASPOON BAKING SODA
- ½ TEASPOON KOSHER SALT
- 2 LARGE EGGS
- ⅓ CUP VEGETABLE OIL
- 1 TABLESPOON PURE VANILLA EXTRACT
- 1 TABLESPOON CIDER VINEGAR

FOR THE TOPPING:
- 1½ CUPS HEAVY CREAM, COLD
- 2 TABLESPOONS CONFECTIONERS' SUGAR

UNSWEETENED COCOA

To make the cake: In a large bowl combine the flour, sugar, cocoa, baking soda, and salt. Sift the ingredients together into another large bowl.

In a small bowl whisk together 1 cup water (at room temperature) with the eggs, vegetable oil, vanilla, and vinegar. Pour over the dry ingredients and stir briskly just until the batter is smooth, about 30 seconds. Pour into a greased 8- by 8-inch heavy-gauge metal baking pan.

Grill over *Indirect Medium* heat until a toothpick inserted in the center of the cake comes out clean, 35 to 40 minutes. Keep the grill's temperature as close to 350°F as possible. Remove from the grill and allow to cool in the pan on a rack for at least 15 minutes before serving.

To make the topping: In a medium bowl whip the cream with the confectioners' sugar until soft peaks form.

Serve the cake in pieces with a generous spoonful of the topping and a light dusting of unsweetened cocoa.

MAKES 8 SERVINGS

WARM CHERRY PUDDING
WITH CHERRY JUICE SAUCE

This English-style pudding has a firm but light texture similar to a soft cake. It tastes great served warm from the grill and even gently reheated the next day. Drizzle on the sauce and dig in. Top with whipped cream or ice cream, if desired.

INDIRECT/MEDIUM

FOR THE PUDDING:

4 LARGE EGGS

1/4 CUP GRANULATED SUGAR

2 TABLESPOONS DARK RUM

2 TEASPOONS VANILLA EXTRACT

PINCH KOSHER SALT

1 3/4 CUPS MILK

1 1/2 CUPS ALL-PURPOSE FLOUR

2 CANS (16 1/2 OUNCES EACH) BING CHERRIES IN JUICE

FOR THE SAUCE:

1/4 CUP GRANULATED SUGAR

2 TABLESPOONS DARK RUM

2 TABLESPOONS CORNSTARCH

To make the pudding: In a large bowl beat the eggs and sugar until smooth. Add the rum, vanilla, and salt and beat well. Add the milk and flour; mix until the flour is fully incorporated.

Strain the cherries, reserving the juice.

To make the sauce: In a small saucepan combine the reserved cherry juice, sugar, and rum. Bring to a boil. Meanwhile, dissolve the cornstarch in 2 tablespoons cold water, stirring until smooth. Whisk the cornstarch mixture into the hot cherry juice mixture. Return to a boil. Boil for 1 full minute, whisking constantly, to thicken. Remove from the heat.

Pour one-third of the batter into a greased 4-quart heavy-gauge metal baking dish. Cover the batter with the cherries. Pour the remaining batter over the cherries. Grill over *Indirect Medium* heat until a toothpick inserted in the center of the pudding comes out clean, 40 to 45 minutes. Keep the grill's temperature as close to 350°F as possible. Serve warm with the sauce.

MAKES 8 SERVINGS

You cannot satisfy hunger by drawing a cake.

— CHINESE PROVERB

SWEET NOSTALGIA
GOURMET S'MORES

Is there any backyard bash finale more American, more sugar-rushing than the classic campfire dessert called S'mores? When's the last time you indulged? Keep the tradition going and check out these exotic variations.

Start with the basic recipe of a toasted large marshmallow and a piece of your favorite chocolate bar (splurge on the good stuff) sandwiched between two graham cracker halves—then experiment. Make a tray with the following ingredients for a self-serve "S'mores Bar" everyone will love.

Viennese S'mores: *Substitute cinnamon-sugar graham crackers for plain ones.*

S'mores à la Menthe: *Slip a freshly picked mint leaf or two under the chocolate.*

S'mores Italiano: *A fresh basil leaf under the chocolate adds an interesting twist.*

S'mores à Go-Go: *For a real adventure, try adding a fresh nasturtium blossom for a sweet, peppery kick to the chocolate!*

Euro-S'mores: *For a rich torte flavor, spread one cracker with jam: raspberry, peach, apricot—even orange marmalade.*

Tin Roof S'Mores: *Spread crunchy peanut butter on one cracker.*

Mocha S'Mores: *Add a pinch of your favorite instant coffee powder to the chocolate bar just before adding the hot marshmallow. Make it a grande!*

German Chocolate S'Mores: *Sprinkle sweetened coconut flakes over the chocolate.*

Snap-Crackle-S'mores: *Roll the hot marshmallow in Rice Krispies® before you add it to the sandwich.*

Uptown S'mores: *Top the chocolate with strips of candied orange or lemon.*

Santa S'Mores: *Roll the hot marshmallow in crushed peppermint candies.*

Frozen Fruit Pops

FROZEN FRUIT POPS

These fruit pops take several hours to freeze solid, so plan ahead. If you skip the plastic molds and sticks and opt for paper cups and plastic spoons, you'll send nostalgic shivers down everyone's spine. There's simple joy in authenticity, no?

- **1 POUND RIPE STRAWBERRIES** *OR* **PEACHES** *OR* **1 1/2 POUNDS RIPE RASPBERRIES** *OR* **BLACKBERRIES**
- **2/3 CUP WATER** *OR* **ORANGE JUICE**
- **2/3 CUP GRANULATED SUGAR**
- **1/2 CUP NONFAT PLAIN YOGURT**
- **1/4 CUP RUM, FRUIT JUICE,** *OR* **ADDITIONAL WATER**
  PINCH KOSHER SALT

If using strawberries, hull them. If using peaches, peel, halve, and pit them. In a food processor, blend the fruit until smooth. If using raspberries or blackberries, force the purée through a fine-meshed sieve to remove the seeds. You should have about 1 1/2 cups of purée.

Add the remaining ingredients to the purée and process a few seconds more until the sugar is dissolved and the mixture is well blended.

Divide the purée among eight 5-ounce paper cups, filling each cup about three-quarters full. Place in the freezer until partially frozen, 1 to 1 1/2 hours. Remove from the freezer and insert a small plastic spoon, handle up, into the center of each pop. Return to the freezer for at least 6 hours. When frozen, the fruit pops can be stored together in tightly sealed plastic bags. To unmold, peel away the paper cups.

MAKES 8 SERVINGS

OATMEAL MOLASSES COOKIES

A little chewy, a little crispy, and just sweet enough, these cookies are easy to make at home or even on a camping trip.

INDIRECT/MEDIUM

- **1 CUP QUICK-COOKING OATS, UNCOOKED**
- **1 CUP GRATED COCONUT**
- **1 CUP ALL-PURPOSE FLOUR**
- **1 CUP GRANULATED SUGAR**
- **1/2 TEASPOON KOSHER SALT**
- **1/4 CUP UNSALTED BUTTER, MELTED**
- **2 TABLESPOONS UNSULPHERED DARK MOLASSES**
- **1 TEASPOON BAKING SODA**

In a large bowl thoroughly mix the oats, coconut, flour, sugar, and salt with your fingers.

In a small saucepan combine the butter, molasses, and baking soda along with 1/3 cup very hot water. Stir and bring the mixture to a boil. Remove from the heat and pour into the bowl with the dry ingredients. Using a fork, mix the hot liquid with the dry ingredients just until everything is evenly distributed. The dough will be sticky.

Using one spoon to scoop up the dough and one spoon to shape it into little mounds, arrange the dough by tablespoonfuls, about 2 inches apart, on two greased cookie sheets. Place one cookie sheet at a time on the grill and grill over *Indirect Medium* heat until the cookies have flattened and turned dark brown on top, 10 to 15 minutes. Keep the grill's temperature as close to 350°F as possible. Remove from the grill and let the cookies cool on the cookie sheets until they are easy to remove with a spatula, 2 to 3 minutes. Transfer to a cooling rack and allow to cool completely.

MAKES ABOUT 24 COOKIES

ICE CREAM
SANDWICHES

What can we say about this summertime classic? This homemade version stands head and shoulders above store-bought ones. And the cookies retain their fudgy chewiness even when frozen.

- **2 CUPS ALL-PURPOSE FLOUR**
- **3/4 CUP UNSWEETENED COCOA**
- **1 TEASPOON BAKING SODA**
- **1/2 TEASPOON KOSHER SALT**
- **1 1/4 CUPS UNSALTED BUTTER, SOFTENED**
- **2 CUPS GRANULATED SUGAR**
- **2 TEASPOONS PURE VANILLA EXTRACT**
- **2 LARGE EGGS**

- **2 QUARTS VANILLA ICE CREAM**

In a medium bowl combine the flour, cocoa, baking soda, and salt. Stir to blend, then sift together onto a piece of waxed paper.

In a large bowl beat the butter, sugar, and vanilla until evenly blended. Add the eggs one at a time, beating thoroughly after each addition. (It's okay if the mixture looks curdled at this point.) Add the sifted dry ingredients and stir vigorously until completely mixed. Cover the bowl with plastic wrap and refrigerate for about 1 hour.

Place the dough on a work surface and divide it in half. Roll each half into a log 1 1/2 to 2 inches in diameter. Use the dough right away or wrap in plastic wrap and refrigerate for up to 1 week. For longer storage, freeze up to 1 month, then thaw overnight in the refrigerator before baking.

Preheat oven to 350°F. Grease cookie sheets or line with baking parchment paper. Using a sharp knife, cut the chilled dough into 1/3-inch rounds; you will get 18 to 20 slices from each log. Place the rounds about 2 inches apart on the cookie sheets. Bake 10 to 11 minutes; the cookies will spread and puff as they bake, then flatten as they cool. Allow to cool 1 to 2 minutes before transferring to racks to cool completely.

Meanwhile, place the ice cream in the refrigerator for 10 to 20 minutes so it softens slightly.

Place a scoop (1/3 to 1/2 cup) of ice cream in the middle of a cookie. Top with another cookie and gently press down just until the ice cream oozes to the cookie's edges. Sandwich the other cookies and ice cream in the same way. Place the sandwiches in a single layer on a baking sheet and set in the freezer for about 1 hour. Once frozen, wrap individually in plastic wrap and return to the freezer until ready to serve.

MAKES 18 TO 20 SERVINGS

CHOCOLATE CUPCAKES
WITH PEANUT BUTTER FROSTING

What is it about peanut butter that brings out the kid in all of us? About the only thing better is a warm chocolate cupcake. Get the best of both worlds here. You can bake these cupcakes on the grill over Indirect Medium heat.

FOR THE CUPCAKES:
- **1/3 CUP UNSALTED BUTTER, SOFTENED**
- **1 1/2 CUPS GRANULATED SUGAR**
- **3 OUNCES UNSWEETENED CHOCOLATE, FINELY CHOPPED**
- **2 TEASPOONS PURE VANILLA EXTRACT**
- **2 1/4 CUPS ALL-PURPOSE FLOUR**
- **1 TEASPOON BAKING POWDER**
- **1 TEASPOON BAKING SODA**
- **1/2 TEASPOON KOSHER SALT**
- **2 LARGE EGGS, SLIGHTLY BEATEN**
- **3/4 CUP SOUR CREAM**

FOR THE FROSTING:
- **1/4 CUP UNSALTED BUTTER, SOFTENED**
- **2/3 CUP CREAMY PEANUT BUTTER**
- **1/4 TEASPOON KOSHER SALT**
- **1 TEASPOON PURE VANILLA EXTRACT**
- **1 CUP CONFECTIONERS' SUGAR**
- **2 TO 4 TABLESPOONS HEAVY CREAM**

To make the cupcakes: Preheat oven to 350°F. Line muffin pans with fluted paper baking cups. Place the butter in a large bowl with the sugar and chocolate. Add 3/4 cup boiling water and whisk until smooth. (It's okay if a few small lumps of butter remain.) Stir in the vanilla.

Combine the flour, baking powder, baking soda, and salt and sift together onto a sheet of waxed paper. Add to the chocolate mixture and stir until smooth. Add the eggs and sour cream and beat until the batter is blended and creamy.

Spoon the batter into the prepared muffin pans, filling each cup about three-quarters full. Bake until a toothpick inserted in the center of the cupcakes comes out clean, 20 to 25 minutes. Remove from the oven and allow to cool completely before frosting.

To make the frosting: Cut the butter into 6 to 8 pieces and place in a large bowl with the peanut butter, salt, and vanilla. Beat until smooth. Add the confectioners' sugar and beat briskly until incorporated. Beat in as much cream as necessary to create a frosting consistency. Spread the top of each cooled cupcake with frosting.

MAKES 18 TO 20 SERVINGS

BUTTERMILK SPICE CAKE
WITH COCONUT-RAISIN FROSTING

A rich cake with a sweet Southern drawl. Apricot jam is the secret to its moistness. It's even better a day or two after baking (if it lasts that long!). You can also bake this one on the grill over Indirect Medium heat if the temperature is kept at (or very near) 350°F.

FOR THE CAKE:

- 3/4 CUP VEGETABLE SHORTENING
- 1 CUP FIRMLY PACKED DARK BROWN SUGAR
- 3 LARGE EGGS
- 1 CUP APRICOT JAM
- 2 CUPS ALL-PURPOSE FLOUR
- 1 1/2 TEASPOONS BAKING SODA
- 1 TEASPOON GROUND CINNAMON
- 1/2 TEASPOON GROUND CLOVES
- 1/2 TEASPOON GROUND ALLSPICE
- 1/2 TEASPOON KOSHER SALT
- 2/3 CUP BUTTERMILK
- 1 CUP RAISINS

FOR THE FROSTING:

- 5 LARGE EGG YOLKS
- 1/4 CUP UNSALTED BUTTER, CUT INTO 4 OR 5 PIECES
- 1/2 TEASPOON KOSHER SALT
- 1 CUP FIRMLY PACKED DARK BROWN SUGAR
- 1/2 CUP WHOLE RAISINS
- 1/4 CUP BUTTERMILK
- 1 CUP SHREDDED COCONUT
- 2 TABLESPOONS RUM
- 2 TEASPOONS PURE VANILLA EXTRACT

To make the cake: Preheat oven to 350°F. In a large bowl using an electric mixer, cream the shortening and sugar together until smooth. Add the eggs one at a time, beating well after each addition. Beat in the apricot jam.

In another large bowl combine the flour, baking soda, cinnamon, cloves, allspice, and salt, then sift together onto a sheet of waxed paper. Add to the jam mixture, then pour in the buttermilk and beat until the batter is blended and smooth. Stir in the raisins. Spread the batter evenly in a greased and floured 9- by 13-inch baking pan.

Bake until a toothpick inserted in the center comes out clean, 35 to 45 minutes. Remove from the oven and let sit in the pan for about 10 minutes. Invert the pan to release the cake and allow to cool completely on a rack before frosting.

To make the frosting: In a medium saucepan whisk the egg yolks vigorously for about 30 seconds. Add the butter along with the salt, sugar, raisins, and buttermilk. Stir to combine. Cook over medium heat, stirring frequently, until the mix-

ture comes to a boil, then continue to cook for 1 full minute, stirring constantly. Remove from the heat, add the remaining ingredients, and stir vigorously until thoroughly mixed. Spread the warm frosting evenly over the cake. Serve slightly warm or at room temperature.

MAKES 12 TO 15 SERVINGS

MOCHA BROWNIE SUNDAES

A timeless cookout favorite gets a nice upgrade with the addition of coffee flavor. No complaints here! If you like your brownies chewy and fudgy (the best kind for sundaes), these are your brownies. You can even eat them frozen, if you're lucky enough to have leftovers.

- 1/2 CUP UNSALTED BUTTER, CUT INTO 6 TO 8 PIECES
- 2 SQUARES (2 OUNCES) UNSWEETENED CHOCOLATE, CUT INTO 5 TO 6 PIECES
- 1 1/2 TABLESPOONS INSTANT COFFEE GRANULES
- 1 CUP GRANULATED SUGAR
- 1 TEASPOON PURE VANILLA EXTRACT
- 1/2 TEASPOON KOSHER SALT
- 2 LARGE EGGS
- 1/4 CUP ALL-PURPOSE FLOUR

- 8 SCOOPS VANILLA ICE CREAM
- CHOCOLATE SAUCE

Preheat oven to 325°F. In a medium saucepan over low heat, blend the butter, chocolate, and coffee. Stir frequently until the chocolate is melted and the mixture is smooth, about 5 minutes. Remove from the heat and stir in the sugar, vanilla, and salt. Add the eggs and beat until smooth, then add the flour and stir until evenly mixed.

Spread the batter evenly in a greased and floured 9-inch round pie pan. Bake until the top is dry and has puffed slightly, 35 to 40 minutes. Remove from the oven and allow to cool completely; the top will sink a bit as it cools. The brownies are easier to remove from the pan if they are allowed to cool for an hour or so first. Cut the brownies into wedges and serve each one with a scoop of ice cream and a dollop of chocolate sauce.

MAKES 8 SERVINGS

APPENDIX

WEIGHTS AND MEASURES

BASIC EQUIVALENTS

U.S.	METRIC
1 ounce	28.4 grams
1 pound	454 grams
1 teaspoon	5 milliliters
2 teaspoons	10 milliliters
3 teaspoons (1 tablespoon)	15 milliliters
2 tablespoons	30 milliliters
3 tablespoons	45 milliliters
4 tablespoons (1/4 cup)	60 milliliters
1/3 cup	75 milliliters
1/2 cup	125 milliliters
2/3 cup	150 milliliters
3/4 cup	175 milliliters
1 cup	250 milliliters
1 1/2 cups	375 milliliters
2 cups	500 milliliters
3 cups	750 milliliters
4 cups (1 quart)	1 scant liter
1 gallon	3 3/4 liters

HANDY SUBSTITUTES

1 pinch	less than 1/8 teaspoon
1 dash	3 drops (no more than 1/8 teaspoon)
1/2 teaspoon	30 drops
1 teaspoon	1/3 tablespoon or 60 drops
3 teaspoons	1 tablespoon or 1/2 fluid ounce
2 tablespoons	1/8 cup or 1 fluid ounce
3 tablespoons	1 1/2 fluid ounces or 1 jigger
4 tablespoons	2 fluid ounces or 1/4 cup
8 tablespoons	4 fluid ounces or 1/2 cup
12 tablespoons	3/4 cup or 6 fluid ounces
16 tablespoons	1 cup or 8 fluid ounces or 1/2 pint

TEMPERATURE CONVERSIONS

300°F	149°C
325°F	163°C
350°F	177°C
375°F	191°C
400°F	204°C
425°F	218°C
450°F	232°C
475°F	246°C
500°F	260°C

CONVERTING TO METRIC

FROM	MULTIPLY BY	TO GET
teaspoons	4.93	milliliters
tablespoons	14.79	milliliters
fluid ounces	29.57	milliliters
cups	236.59	milliliters
cups	0.237	liters
pints	473.18	milliliters
pints	0.473	liters
quarts	946.36	milliliters
quarts	0.946	liters
gallons	3.79	liters
ounces	28.35	grams
pounds	0.454	kilograms
inches	2.54	centimeters
Fahrenheit	subtract 32, multiply by 5, divide by 9	Celsius

MEAT CUTS

You don't realize how big the world is until you ask two different butchers how they cut up a hog or a side of beef. Regional and training differences affect cuts as well as their names. No grilling enthusiast should underestimate the value of a strong relationship with a knowledgeable butcher (same goes for fish retailers). Pick one whose cutting style you like and make friends.

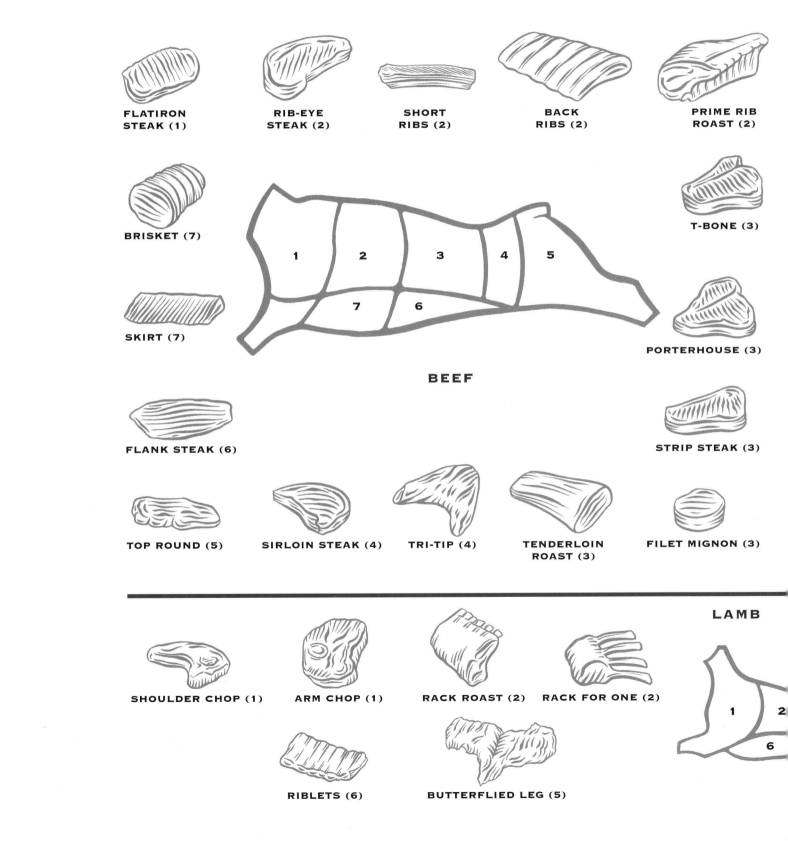

FLATIRON STEAK (1)

RIB-EYE STEAK (2)

SHORT RIBS (2)

BACK RIBS (2)

PRIME RIB ROAST (2)

BRISKET (7)

T-BONE (3)

SKIRT (7)

PORTERHOUSE (3)

BEEF

FLANK STEAK (6)

STRIP STEAK (3)

TOP ROUND (5)

SIRLOIN STEAK (4)

TRI-TIP (4)

TENDERLOIN ROAST (3)

FILET MIGNON (3)

LAMB

SHOULDER CHOP (1)

ARM CHOP (1)

RACK ROAST (2)

RACK FOR ONE (2)

RIBLETS (6)

BUTTERFLIED LEG (5)

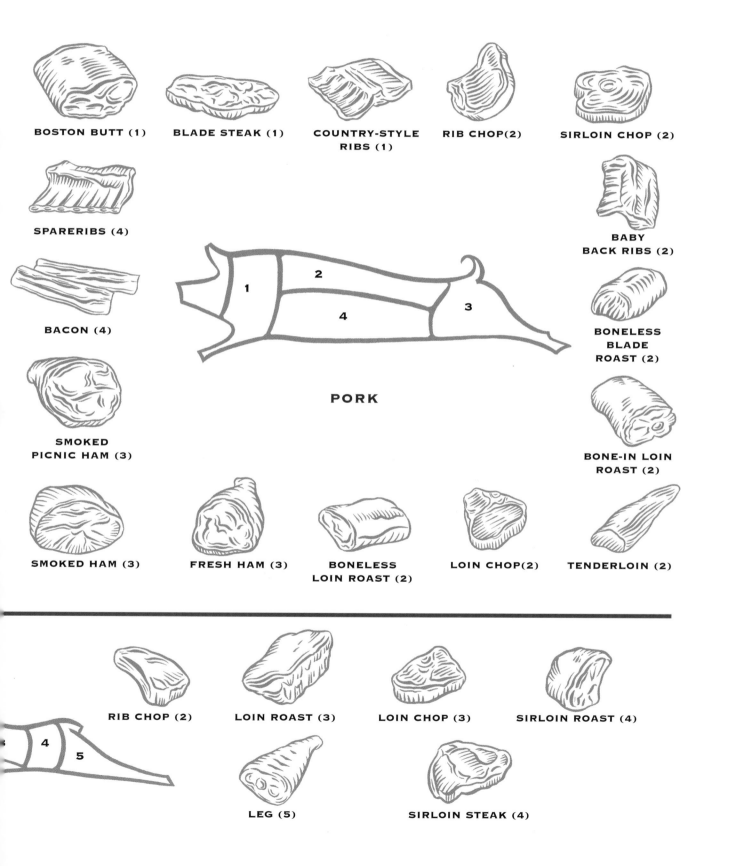

BOSTON BUTT (1) BLADE STEAK (1) COUNTRY-STYLE
RIBS (1) RIB CHOP(2) SIRLOIN CHOP (2)

SPARERIBS (4)

BABY
BACK RIBS (2)

BACON (4)

BONELESS
BLADE
ROAST (2)

PORK

SMOKED
PICNIC HAM (3)

BONE-IN LOIN
ROAST (2)

SMOKED HAM (3) FRESH HAM (3) BONELESS
LOIN ROAST (2) LOIN CHOP(2) TENDERLOIN (2)

RIB CHOP (2) LOIN ROAST (3) LOIN CHOP (3) SIRLOIN ROAST (4)

LEG (5) SIRLOIN STEAK (4)

GRILLING GUIDE

The following cuts, thicknesses, weights, and grilling times are meant to be guidelines rather than hard and fast rules. Cooking times are affected by such factors as altitude, wind, outside temperature, and desired doneness. Two rules of thumb: Grill steaks, fish fillets, boneless chicken pieces, and vegetables using the Direct Method for the time given on the chart or to the desired doneness, turning once halfway through grilling time. Grill roasts, whole poultry, bone-in poultry pieces, whole fish, and thicker cuts using the Indirect Method for the time given on the chart or until an instant-read thermometer reaches the desired internal temperature. Cooking times for beef and lamb are for the USDA's definition of medium doneness unless otherwise noted. Let roasts, larger cuts of meat, and thick chops and steaks rest for 5 to 10 minutes before carving. The internal temperature of the meat will rise by 5 to 10 degrees during this time.

BEEF

CUT	THICKNESS AND/OR WEIGHT	APPROXIMATE GRILLING TIME
Steak: New York, porterhouse, rib-eye, T-bone, or tenderloin	3/4 inch thick	8 to 10 minutes Direct Medium
	1 inch thick	10 to 12 minutes Direct Medium
	1 1/4 inches thick	14 to 16 minutes; sear 10 minutes Direct High, grill 4 to 6 minutes Indirect Medium
	1 1/2 inches thick	16 to 18 minutes; sear 10 minutes Direct High, grill 6 to 8 minutes Indirect Medium
	2 inches thick	20 to 24 minutes; sear 10 minutes Direct High, grill 10 to 14 minutes Indirect Medium
Skirt steak	1/4 to 1/2 inch thick	5 to 7 minutes Direct High
Flank steak	1 1/2 to 2 pounds, 3/4 inch thick	12 to 15 minutes Direct Medium
Kabob	1 to 1 1/2 inch cubes	10 to 12 minutes Direct Medium
Tenderloin, whole	3 1/2 to 4 pounds	35 to 50 minutes (medium rare); sear 20 minutes Direct Medium, grill 15 to 30 minutes Indirect Medium
Ground beef patty	3/4 inch thick	8 to 10 minutes Direct Medium
Rib-eye roast, boneless	5 to 6 pounds	1 1/2 to 2 hours Indirect Medium
Tri-tip roast	2 to 2 1/2 pounds	30 to 40 minutes; sear 10 minutes Direct High, grill 20 to 30 minutes Indirect Medium
Rib roast	12 to 14 pounds	2 1/2 to 2 3/4 hours Indirect Medium
Veal loin chop	1 inch thick	10 to 12 minutes Direct Medium

LAMB

CUT	THICKNESS OR WEIGHT	APPROXIMATE GRILLING TIME
Chop: loin, rib, shoulder, or sirloin	3/4 to 1 1/4 inches thick	8 to 12 minutes Direct Medium
Leg of lamb, semi-boneless, rolled	6 to 7 pounds	2 1/2 hours Indirect Medium
Rib crown roast	3 to 4 pounds	1 to 1 1/4 hours Indirect Medium
Ground lamb patty	3/4 inch thick	10 minutes Direct Medium
Rack of lamb	1 to 1 1/2 pounds	25 to 35 minutes Direct Medium

GAME

TYPE	THICKNESS OR WEIGHT	APPROXIMATE GRILLING TIME
Ground buffalo patty	3/4 inch thick	7 to 9 minutes (medium) Direct Medium
Buffalo strip steak	1 inch thick	6 to 7 minutes (medium rare) Direct High
Quail, whole	5 ounces	15 to 20 minutes Indirect Medium
Squab, whole or butterflied	1 pound	35 to 45 minutes Indirect Medium
Duck, whole	4 to 6 pounds	1 1/2 to 2 hours Indirect Medium
Duck breast, boneless	7 to 8 ounces	10 to 15 minutes Direct Low
Goose, whole	10 to 12 pounds	3 hours Indirect Medium
Rack of venison	2 1/2 to 3 pounds	45 minutes (medium rare) Indirect Medium

PORK

CUT	THICKNESS OR WEIGHT	APPROXIMATE GRILLING TIME
Chop: rib, loin, or shoulder	3/4 to 1 inch thick	10 to 15 minutes Direct Medium
	1 1/4 to 1 1/2 inches thick	14 to 18 minutes; sear 8 minutes Direct High, grill 6 to 10 minutes Indirect Medium
Loin chop, boneless	3/4 to 1 inch thick	10 to 12 minutes Direct Medium
Loin roast: blade, sirloin, or center rib	3 to 5 pounds	1 1/4 to 1 3/4 hours Indirect Medium
Rib crown roast	4 to 6 pounds	1 1/2 to 2 hours Indirect Medium
Ribs: country-style, baby back, or spareribs	3 to 4 pounds	1 1/2 to 2 hours Indirect Medium
Tenderloin, whole	3/4 to 1 pound	25 to 30 minutes Indirect Medium
Bratwurst		25 to 30 minutes Indirect Medium

POULTRY

TYPE	WEIGHT	APPROXIMATE GRILLING TIME
Chicken breast, boneless, skinless	6 ounces	8 to 12 minutes Direct Medium
Chicken thigh, boneless, skinless	4 ounces	8 to 10 minutes Direct Medium
Chicken, half	1 1/4 to 1 1/2 pounds	1 to 1 1/4 hours Indirect Medium
Chicken pieces, bone-in breast/wing		30 to 40 minutes Indirect Medium
Chicken pieces, bone-in leg/thigh		40 to 50 minutes Indirect Medium
Chicken, whole	3 1/2 to 5 pounds	1 to 1 1/2 hours Indirect Medium
Cornish game hen	1 1/2 to 2 pounds	30 to 45 minutes Indirect Medium
Turkey, whole, unstuffed	10 to 11 pounds	1 3/4 to 2 1/2 hours Indirect Medium
	12 to 14 pounds	2 1/4 to 3 hours Indirect Medium
	15 to 17 pounds	2 3/4 to 3 3/4 hours Indirect Medium
	18 to 22 pounds	3 1/2 to 4 hours Indirect Medium
	23 to 24 pounds	4 to 4 1/2 hours Indirect Medium
Turkey drumstick	1/2 to 1 1/2 pounds	3/4 to 1 1/4 hours Indirect Medium
Turkey breast, bone-in	4 to 5 pounds	1 to 1 1/2 hours Indirect Medium

FISH & SEAFOOD

TYPE	THICKNESS OR WEIGHT	APPROXIMATE GRILLING TIME*
Fish, fillet or steak	1/4 to 1/2 inch thick	3 to 5 minutes Direct High
	1/2 to 1 inch thick	5 to 10 minutes Direct High
	1 to 1 1/4 inches thick	10 to 12 minutes Direct High
Fish, whole	1 pound	15 to 20 minutes Indirect Medium
	2 to 2 1/2 pounds	20 to 30 minutes Indirect Medium
	3 pounds	30 to 45 minutes Indirect Medium
Shrimp		2 to 5 minutes Direct High
Scallop		3 to 6 minutes Direct High
Mussel		5 to 6 minutes Direct High (discard any that do not open)
Clam		8 to 10 minutes Direct High (discard any that do not open)
Oyster		3 to 5 minutes Direct High

*Note: General rule for grilling fish: 4 to 5 minutes per 1/2-inch thickness; 8 to 10 minutes per 1-inch thickness.

FRUIT

TYPE	APPROXIMATE GRILLING TIME**
Apple, whole Apple, 1/2-inch-thick rounds	35 to 40 minutes Indirect Medium 4 to 6 minutes Direct Medium
Apricot, halved, pit removed	6 to 8 minutes Direct Medium
Banana, halved lengthwise	6 to 8 minutes Direct Medium
Cantaloupe, wedges	6 to 8 minutes Direct Medium
Nectarine, halved lengthwise, pit removed	8 to 10 minutes Direct Medium
Peach, halved lengthwise, pit removed	8 to 10 minutes Direct Medium
Pear, halved lengthwise	10 to 12 minutes Direct Medium
Pineapple, peeled and cored, 1/2-inch rings or 1-inch wedges	5 to 10 minutes Direct Medium
Strawberry	4 to 5 minutes Direct Medium

**Note: Grilling times for fruit will depend on ripeness.

VEGETABLES

TYPE	WEIGHT	APPROXIMATE GRILLING TIME
Artichoke, whole		Steam 20 to 25 minutes; cut in half and grill 8 to 10 minutes Direct Medium
Asparagus		6 to 8 minutes Direct Medium
Beet		1 to 1 1/2 hours Indirect Medium
Bell pepper, whole Bell pepper, halved or quartered		10 to 12 minutes Direct Medium 6 to 8 minutes Direct Medium
Cabbage, whole		2 to 2 1/2 hours Indirect Medium
Chile		7 to 9 minutes Direct Medium
Corn, husked Corn, in husk		10 to 12 minutes Direct Medium 25 to 30 minutes Direct Medium
Eggplant, 1/2-inch slices Eggplant, halved		8 to 10 minutes Direct Medium 12 to 15 minutes Direct Medium
Fennel, 1/4-inch slices		10 to 12 minutes Direct Medium
Garlic, whole		45 to 60 minutes Indirect Medium
Green bean, whole		8 to 10 minutes Direct Medium
Green onion, whole		3 to 4 minutes Direct Medium
Leek		14 to 16 minutes Direct Medium
Mushroom: shiitake or button		8 to 10 minutes Direct Medium
Mushroom: portabello		12 to 15 minutes Direct Medium
Onion, whole (leave paper leaves on—do not peel) Onion, halved Onion, 1/2-inch slices		45 to 50 minutes Indirect Medium 35 to 40 minutes Indirect Medium 8 to 12 minutes Direct Medium
Potato, whole Potato, 1/2-inch slices		45 to 60 minutes Indirect Medium 14 to 16 minutes Direct Medium
Potato: new, halved		20 to 25 minutes Direct Medium
Pumpkin	3 pounds	1 1/2 to 2 hours Indirect Medium
Squash: acorn	1 pound	40 to 45 minutes Indirect Medium
Squash: buttercup or butternut	2 pounds	50 to 55 minutes Indirect Medium
Squash: pattypan		10 to 12 minutes Direct Medium
Squash: spaghetti	3 pounds	1 1/4 to 1 1/2 hours Indirect Medium
Squash: yellow, 1/2-inch slices Squash: yellow, halved		6 to 8 minutes Direct Medium 6 to 10 minutes Direct Medium
Sweet potato, whole Sweet potato, 1/4-inch slices		50 to 60 minutes Indirect Medium 8 to 10 minutes Direct Medium
Tomatillo		6 to 8 minutes Direct Medium
Tomato: cherry, whole		2 to 4 minutes Direct Medium
Tomato: garden, 1/2-inch slices Tomato: garden, halved		2 to 4 minutes Direct Medium 6 to 8 minutes Direct Medium
Tomato: plum, halved Tomato: plum, whole		6 to 8 minutes Direct Medium 8 to 10 minutes Direct Medium
Zucchini, 1/2-inch slices Zucchini, halved		6 to 8 minutes Direct Medium 6 to 10 minutes Direct Medium

SPICES AND HERBS

Master the secrets of seasoning with this handy spice and herb chart. On the following three pages, we've alphabetically listed descriptions and uses for 50 seasonings. Where applicable, we've also included helpful tips on storage and substitution. For flavor, nothing beats fresh herbs, but they may not always be available (and you may not always have the time to clean and cut them). Dried herbs work well as substitutes provided you use less of them. In general, you can use 1 teaspoon of dried herbs for every 1 tablespoon of fresh herbs. When using highly flavorful herbs such as sage or dillweed, however, go with 1/2 teaspoon of dried for every tablespoon of fresh. Crush the herbs between your fingertips to make them the same size and to release their flavors.

ALLSPICE
(also called pimento or Jamaican pepper)

Description: Dried, nearly ripe berries from the Jamaican myrtle tree; sweet and savory flavor. Smells and tastes like combination of nutmeg, cinnamon, and clove. Available whole or ground.

Uses: A key ingredient in "jerk" seasoning, but also added to pickling spice mixtures, mincemeat, pot roast and stews, sausage and cured meats, ham, gravies, ketchup, poultry marinades, and fish. Also good on vegetables such as beets, carrots, sweet potatoes, pumpkin, and winter squash. Sprinkle on rice, puddings, cakes, and pies.

ANISE

Description: Mediterranean herb of parsley family with a warm, licorice taste. Yields the spice Anise seed—available whole, ground, or as an extract—when seeds are dried.

Uses: Soups, veal stews, curries (including vegetable curry), fish and shellfish (add a handful of anise leaves when you boil shrimp), cookies, and cakes. Leaves are less flavorful than seeds, but make a nice garnish.

BASIL

Description: The spicy sweet "tomato herb." Available fresh or dried in leaf or ground form. Even comes in scented varieties—cinnamon, anise, and lemon.

Uses: Mediterranean and Italian cuisine; pesto; tomato and minestrone soups; spiced-meat dishes such as meatballs, chicken, and lamb; potato salad; vegetables (especially zucchini); and fish and seafood. Charcoal grill users: Throw some basil on the coals after your meat is cooked and the mosquitoes will stay away while you feast!

BAY LEAVES

Description: Dried, Mediterranean herb of the bay laurel (dried leaves are more flavorful than fresh ones). Watch out for ornamental plants bearing the laurel name; some are poisonous.

Uses: Beef, hearty soups, stews, pot roast, marinades for chicken, and spaghetti sauce. Releases oil over a long time. When poaching fish or boiling potatoes for salad, drop a leaf in the water. Remove bay leaves from the dish you're serving; they're too tough to eat and could cause someone to choke. A leaf in your flour canister will keep bugs out.

BOUQUET GARNI

Description: Marjoram, parsley (or chervil), thyme, and bay leaf—may also contain other herbs.

Uses: Bundle herbs together with string or in a cheesecloth pouch/sachet and add to dish while it's cooking, then remove before serving. Use with beef or fish, or in soups.

CARAWAY

Description: Tangy flavor, similar to dill. Entire plant is edible, but generally used in whole seed form, occasionally ground.

Uses: Hungarian goulash, sauerkraut, chicken paprikash, pork sausage, pork or veal stew, and split pea soup. Also: potatoes, cabbage, carrots, breads, cookies, and cakes.

CARDAMOM

Description: Spice related to ginger. Available as whole seed pods, whole seeds, or ground. Lightly crush entire pod; shell disintegrates as it cooks.

Uses: Most common uses: Scandinavian baked goods and Middle Eastern coffee. Try in pork marinades, on cabbage or carrots, or in citrus fruit salad. Note: Cardamom loses flavor when exposed to air.

CAYENNE
(also called red pepper)

Description: Dried, ground red chile peppers. This spice can be very hot! To cool your mouth after a potent dose, drink milk or beer, or eat yogurt, ice cream, or a banana. Water doesn't help because the hot part of the chile is an oil, which the water can't dissolve and will usually spread.

Uses: Commonly found in Mexican cuisine and Indian curries. Add a dash to ground beef for hamburgers or casseroles, sprinkle some in meat loaf, or add to dips and spreads for some bite.

CELERY SEED

Description: Dried fruit of an herb of the parsley family—the celery. Three types: white, green, and turnip rooted, all slightly bitter.

Uses: Flavors fish, stews, winter vegetable salads, egg dishes, pickles, ketchup, and tomato juice.

CHERVIL

Description: Herb used like parsley, but with a delicate anise flavor.

Uses: Most popular in egg dishes, but good on veal, chicken, and fish; in soups and sauces; in chicken, egg, and potato salads; and with carrots, corn, and peas. Add near the end of cooking.

CHILE PEPPER
(see also Cayenne and Paprika)

Description: Fresh green or red hot pepper pods (small ones tend to be the hottest), whole dried red peppers (range from medium to hot), or dried pepper flakes (hot, found in your grocer's spice rack and in shakers at pizza joints).

Uses: Adds fire to: chili con carne, seafood bisque and cocktail sauces, Italian tomato sauce, stewed tomatoes, and tomato salad dressing. Wear gloves when cooking with fresh chiles, wash hands thoroughly after handling, and keep your fingers out of your eyes. The hottest parts of a chile pepper are the seeds and membranes.

CHILI POWDER

Description: Ground chile pepper, ground cumin, ground oregano, and powdered garlic. Some brands also include salt, cloves, or chocolate.

Uses: Use for beef, chili con carne, pork, shellfish (add to cooking water), cocktail sauce, steak marinades, Spanish rice, cauliflower, carrots, corn, and cream soups (tomato, pea, or potato). Store in refrigerator to preserve freshness.

CHINESE ANISE
(see Star Anise)

CHINESE PARSLEY
(see Cilantro)

CHIVES

Description: Herb of the onion family with a mild flavor (also comes in a garlic variety).

Uses: Flavors chicken, fish and seafood, potatoes, cream soups, eggs, carrots, and cauliflower. Add near end of cooking. Dried chives have very little flavor, so use fresh or frozen when you can.

CILANTRO
(also called Chinese parsley)

Description: The same plant as coriander, but refers to the leaves rather than the seeds. Spicy, peppery taste.

Uses: Mostly Mexican and Oriental cuisine: salsas, stews, soups, sauces, dips, curries, and vegetables.

CINNAMON

Description: Most popular sweet spice, made from the dried bark of the evergreen tree. Available in whole sticks or as ground powder.

Uses: Central and South American and Middle Eastern meat dishes (Greek lamb stew), pies, cakes, sweet rolls, fruit, and hot drinks.

CLOVES

Description: Dried flower buds of fragrant evergreen clove tree. Member of the "Big Four," which includes cinnamon, nutmeg, and pepper. Available whole or ground.

Uses: Whole cloves flavor pot roast, pork roast and ham, pickles, stews, and mulled cider. Use ground to flavor mincemeat, beets, sweet potatoes, onions, or winter squash; also, baked goods and chocolate desserts, fruit dishes, juices, syrups, and preserves.

CORIANDER

Description: The same plant as cilantro, but refers to the seeds rather than the leaves. Available whole or ground. Simultaneously sweet and tart.

Uses: Adds rich flavor to meat loaf, spicy meat mixtures, sausage, stews, ham or pork roast, poultry stuffing, and cooked beets. Common ingredient in gingerbread, sweets and breads, baked apples, and fruit salad.

CUMIN

Description: Strongly flavored spice. Comes in whole or ground seeds.

Uses: Ingredient in curry and chili con carne. Add to beef, roast pork, chicken marinades, vegetable salads, cabbage dishes and sauerkraut, black beans, and sugar cookies. Flavor doesn't blend well with other flavors; use sparingly.

CURRY POWDER

Description: East Indian blend of coriander, turmeric, fenugreek, cinnamon, cumin, cardamom, ginger, black pepper, cloves, cayenne, allspice, and mustard seed.

Uses: Use in sauces to flavor beef, chicken, lamb, pork, seafood, and vegetables.

DILL

Description: Available as a seed (whole or ground) and in a milder leaf form (called dill weed).

Uses: More than just pickles! Use with meat stews, veal, chicken, lamb chops, and fish and shellfish such as salmon or herring. Try it with these vegetables: cucumber, cabbage, carrots, turnips, winter squash, and cauliflower. Add a touch to potato salad, egg salad, coleslaw, cottage cheese, and hot buttered popcorn. Knead into herb bread dough.

FAGARA
(see Szechwan Pepper)

FENNEL

Description: Spice comes in seed form, fresh and whole, or dried and ground, and tastes like licorice. Also available as a vegetable in bulbous form similar to celery stalks.

Uses: Great for fish; in fact, it's called the "fish herb." If you have a whole plant, throw the long stalks on the charcoal when grilling fish. Dip bases of fresh stalks in olive oil for a snack. Also good in meatballs, roast pork, and spaghetti sauce. Seeds are also used in lentil dishes, cabbage, celery, potatoes, and sauerkraut; to top breads and rolls; or sweeten apple pie, cookies, and cakes.

FENUGREEK

Description: This seed (available whole or ground), a member of the legume family, is considered a food by vegetarians. Flavor is bitter and maplelike.

Uses: Curry and Indian cuisine, pickling spice, and imitation maple. Use in beef casserole, black bean soup, and vegetable stew.

FILÉ GUMBO

Description: Dried sassafras leaves and thyme.

Uses: Use as a thickener for meat, poultry, fish sauces; stews; soups; and gumbo.

FINES HERBES

Description: Finely chopped chervil, chives, parsley, and tarragon. May also include marjoram, savory, or watercress.

Uses: Add to a cooked mixture shortly before serving. Do not remove.

FIVE-SPICE POWDER

Description: Different brands vary, but this blend includes a combination of five of the following spices: star anise, Szechwan pepper (fagara) cassia or cinnamon, fennel, clove, ginger, and licorice root.

Uses: Use in Chinese and Southeast Asian cooking on beef, chicken, pork, fish and seafood, and vegetables.

GARLIC

Description: Member of the onion family with strong odor and taste; bulbs break into cloves. Available in white, pink, and purple varieties. Comes fresh or powdered.

Uses: Widely used in Italian, Mediterranean, and Mexican cuisine. Garlic powder accents beef, pork, lamb, and game. Of course, garlic bread is a dinnertime staple.

GINGER

Description: Spicy-sweet spice from ginger root; available fresh, dried, powdered, preserved in syrup or crystalized (candied), and even pickled.

Uses: Use fresh, powdered, or pickled form with steak, meat loaf, chicken, and fish and seafood. Refrigerate fresh ginger root for up to 1 week or store covered with dry sherry in a jar. Use ginger as needed; use the ginger-flavored sherry in other recipes.

Use powdered form in cakes, cookies, puddings, and sweet breads. A key ingredient in many Asian cuisines.

HERBES DE PROVENCE

Description: Mediterranean blend of oregano, savory, rosemary, thyme, and marjoram. May also contain lavender, basil, or fennel seeds.

Uses: Use to season kabobs, chicken, pork, stews, tomato dishes, and pizza.

ITALIAN SEASONING

Description: Blend of marjoram, basil, oregano, thyme, and rosemary. May also contain savory or sage.

Uses: Great with dips, herb breads, and tomato dishes. Mix with olive oil to create a quick and easy rub for chicken. Crumble over pizza sauce before layering on toppings.

MACE

Description: Comes from same tree as nutmeg; mace comes from outer covering of the seed. Cinnamon and pepper flavor, stronger than nutmeg. Available in whole blades (dried filaments) or ground.

Uses: Practically speaking, mace and nutmeg are interchangeable. Mace is sweeter and lighter colored. Use in light-colored cookies and cakes, puddings, and doughnuts. Also good in chicken pie, cream vegetable sauces, and cream-based or clear soups such as oyster stew.

MARJORAM

Description: Herb similar to oregano, but milder and sweeter.

Uses: Hamburgers, meat loaf, stews, chicken pot pie, fish dishes and sauces, and poultry stuffing. Try it with cabbage, carrots, peas, carrots, beans, and summer squash.

MINT

Description: Comes in several hundred varieties, but most common are peppermint and spearmint. Available dried (for tea) and fresh.

Uses: Everything from roast lamb to fruit salad, including potatoes, carrots, peas, zucchini, beans, cookies, and cakes. Also as a flavoring and garnish for drinks.

MUSTARD

Description: Whole or ground seeds in white (milder and used to make prepared yellow mustard), brown (for spicy, sweet, or beer mustard), and black varieties.

Uses: Use ground mustard for ham, pork pâté, barbecue and cocktail sauces (for seafood), salad dressings, chowders and bisques, and on baked beans, beets, and succotash. Seeds go well in pickling brines, relishes, and chutneys. Add seeds to the cooking water when cooking cabbage, sauerkraut, and beets. Can be used instead of caraway or dill seeds on cooked vegetables, but toast the seeds first.

NUTMEG

Description: Whole or ground nutmeg comes from same tree as mace and has a cinnamon, nutty flavor.

Uses: Veal, beef, chicken, lamb, and vegetable stew. Common in sweet, spicy dishes. Add to fruit breads, desserts, sauces, milk-or cream-based custards, white sauces, and eggnog. Also good for squash or candied yams; green, leafy vegetables such as spinach; tomatoes; green beans; corn; eggplant; onions; and mashed potatoes.

OREGANO

Description: Herb related to marjoram, but stronger flavor.

Uses: Most famous in spaghetti sauce and pizza. Break from tradition and try it in chili con carne, hamburgers, meat loaf, bean or lentil soup, poultry stuffing, squash, eggplant, beans, breads, or with fish and seafood.

PAPRIKA

Description: Dried, powdered fruit of a red sweet pepper; also known as "pimiento." Comes in a few varieties, mainly Hungarian (strong and rich) and Spanish (mild); none are hot.

Uses: Flavoring and as a garnish. Ingredient in goulash and paprikash. Sprinkle over poultry, stews, eggs, and vegetables. Loses its punch quickly, so store away from heat and light.

PARSLEY

Description: Curly parsley (the famous garnish!) and Italian, or flat-leaf, parsley, which has a richer, spicier taste. Available fresh (which freezes well) or dried.

Uses: Soups, stews, sauces; herb butter for bread, fish, and poultry; salads, potatoes, and omelets. Parsley brings out the flavor of other herbs. Dried parsley is not nearly as flavorful as fresh or fresh-frozen.

PEPPERCORNS

Description: Black pepper is made from dried peppercorn berries harvested while green and immature. It has a strong flavor and aroma, and is one of the world's oldest known spices. White pepper is made from fully-ripened berries soaked in water to loosen the red skin, and has a milder flavor.

Uses: Use it when you don't want black flecks to show up in your food. Fresh-tasting green peppercorns are picked green off the vine, not dried conventionally, and have a slightly different flavor. Finally, pink peppercorns, although unrelated to the others, have a peppery taste and are a decorative addition to your pepper grinder. Available whole (for maximum freshness) and ground (coarse or fine).

Uses: Just about anything! But do yourself a favor: Invest a few dollars in a small pepper grinder; whole peppercorns keep their flavor indefinitely, while ground pepper loses it quickly.

PIMENTO
(see Allspice)

POPPY SEED

Description: Crunchy, slightly sweet seeds from the same plant that produces opium, but don't worry—the narcotic alkaloids are removed during processing.

Uses: Common in baked goods and salad dressings. Try on buttered noodles; mashed potatoes; steamed veggies such as cabbage, spinach, carrots, onions, and zucchini; and in macaroni salad or coleslaw. Toast lightly in a dry skillet to crisp and bring out full nutty flavor.

RED PEPPER
(see Cayenne)

ROSEMARY

Description: Robustly flavored spice with needlelike leaves and a taste reminiscent of pine trees.

Uses: Roast meats, especially chicken, lamb, and pork; carrots, winter squash, beans, cauliflower, and potatoes. Often used with pasta dishes as a spice and garnish. Not a dessert spice, but goes with breads and yogurt dips.

SAFFRON

Description: Dried stigmas from inside the flower of the saffron crocus. This yellow spice comes whole and powdered. Very difficult to grow and harvest, it is the most expensive spice in the world (1 ounce can cost more than $150). Fortunately, one or two threads is enough to flavor most dishes.

Uses: Combines well with garlic; use with chicken, fish and shellfish, and rice dishes. Also: breads, cakes, and cookies. Flavoring in both bouillabaisse and paella. Tip: Don't use wooden utensils; wood will absorb it.

SAGE

Description: A "mint" spice. Leaves contain a pungent oil, giving sage a sweet taste and herbal scent. Comes whole, rubbed (crushed), or ground.

Uses: Veal, beef stew, hamburgers, turkey and chicken, pork, stuffing, fish chowder, cornbread, stewed tomatoes, cheese spreads, vegetables, and breads.

SAVORY

Description: A mint relative with a spicy, peppery taste. Winter (darker green and smaller) and summer (milder) varieties, but for all practical purposes can be used interchangeably. Available fresh or dried.

Uses: Beef, country sausage, chicken, lamb, and vegetable soup. Top herb for beans, but also use with brussels sprouts, turnips, cabbage, green beans, peas, potatoes, and tomatoes. Tip: Rub savory leaves on bee stings to instantly relieve the pain!

SESAME

Description: Very nutritious seeds (lots of protein). Oil from seeds, used to make sesame oil, is high in vitamin E, cholesterol-free, and high in polyunsaturates.

Uses: Widely used in Japanese, Chinese, and Middle Eastern cuisine. Also used as a topping for breads and rolls or mixed into cakes and cookies. Used to make a "sesame butter" called tahini, a paste made from ground-up seeds. Lightly toast in a dry skillet before use to release nutty flavor. Sprinkle on tomatoes, baked potatoes, cream cheese, vegetable or fruit salads, and tossed salads. Go nuts!

STAR ANISE
(also called Chinese Anise)

Description: Chinese spice from the dried star-shaped fruit of a small evergreen native to southern China and Vietnam. Comes whole or ground. No relation to anise, but yields a similar, but stronger, licorice taste.

Uses: Chinese duck and pork dishes and Vietnamese beef-noodle soup. Used whole, it adds beauty and elegance, but don't try to eat it. You can choke on those little stars (and they burn extra hot!).

SZECHWAN PEPPER
(also called Fagara)

Description: Dried berry of a prickly ash tree with a spicy-woody aroma.

Uses: Ingredient in five-spice blend. Flavors pork and poultry and is a key ingredient in Szechwan crispy duck.

TARRAGON

Description: Rich, sweet herb with slight licorice taste. An essential herb in French cuisine.

Uses: Chicken and fish, mild vegetables, cucumber salad, potato salad, and salad dressing. It's strong, so use near the end of cooking.

THYME

Description: Another mint family herb; has a strong flavor. Its many varieties include lemon thyme.

Uses: Meat loaf, pot roast, hamburgers, lamb, game, fish dishes, New England clam chowder, hearty soups and stews, poultry stuffing, and most vegetables. Great with slow-cooked dishes.

TURMERIC

Description: Spice in the ginger family that comes from the root of the turmeric plant. Available powdered and you can sometimes find whole fresh or dried pieces of the root in stores that sell Asian foods.

Uses: Curried lamb, chutney, legumes, and zucchini. Can use as a substitute for saffron, but expect the taste to differ.

VANILLA

Description: Full-sized fruit of an orchid, harvested while still green, then fermented and cured. Gets its flavor from the chemical compound vanillin. Available as whole beans or an extract. Choose beans that look moist and are flexible, not stiff, and keep both beans and extract away from heat or light.

Uses: Drinks or sweet dishes, including chocolate. Tip: Store whole beans in sugar. In a couple of weeks, the sugar will take on the vanilla flavor, making it great for baking use, and the beans will last this way for years.

MAINTENANCE TIPS

If you enjoy outdoor cooking, keeping your grill in tip-top shape just makes sense. With simple, routine maintenance, it'll perform better and last longer. The general guidelines below will apply to most grills. Refer to your owner's manual for maintenance information specific to your model.

CHARCOAL GRILLS

Cooking grates. After each use, remove debris using a brass-bristle brush. As needed, remove from the grill and wash with warm, soapy water or a soap-embedded steel wool pad.

Inside lid. Periodically, while the lid is warm but not hot, wipe with a paper towel. You may use a mild soap and water solution. With extreme build-up, gently use a soap-embedded steel wool pad. Don't use oven cleaner—those fumes can be dangerous and are highly flammable.

Outside surfaces. Periodically wash with warm, soapy water. To return some of the shine, nontoxic glass cleaner may also be used.

Vents and ash catcher. Periodically clean with a mild soap and water solution. With extreme buildup, a soap-embedded steel wool pad may be used. For the ash catcher, first dump out cold ashes into the trash.

Smoke stains on the lid. Smoke stains may appear at the edges of the lid or around the vents. These stains are black or reddish brown and may look like rust. A soapy scrub pad used very gently on the porcelain should remove the stains.

GAS GRILLS

Flavorizer® bars (or burner tents) and cooking grates. Periodically remove debris using a brass-bristle brush. If necessary, remove from the grill and wash with warm, soapy water. Avoid using any cleaning products with chemicals!

Bottom tray. Periodically remove excess grease that might have accumulated in the bottom tray (to prevent grease fires) and replace the catch pan liner. Use a putty knife to carefully scrape off excess accumulation, then wash the bottom tray with warm, soapy water. A brass-bristle brush can be used for easier cleaning.

Inside cooking box. Periodically use a putty knife and a steel-bristle brush to remove excess grease. Wash the inside of the cooking box with warm, soapy water.

Inside lid. While the lid is warm but not hot, clean with a paper towel, soapy scrub pad, or brass-bristle brush.

Outside surfaces. Periodically wash with warm, soapy water.

Worktables and accessory trays. To clean wooden or plastic tables after use, wipe with warm water using a rag or sponge. If the barbecue is older and needs refinishing, sand it down with fine sandpaper and restain it with a water-based stain. Once it is dry, seal it with a water-based sealant.

Check for gas leaks. Check for gas leaks every time you disconnect and reconnect a gas fitting. Do not use an open flame to check for gas leaks. Use a soap and water solution. Be sure there are no sparks or open flames in the area. Perform a gas leak check even if your grill was dealer- or store-assembled. Check the hose for nicks, cracking, abrasions, and cuts.

Always store the LP tank outdoors. Do not store a spare or disconnected LP tank under or near the grill. The gas must be turned off at the LP tank when the grill is not in use. If the grill is stored indoors, the gas supply must be disconnected and LP tanks must be stored outdoors.

INDEX

Page numbers in *italics* refer to photographs.

From the quiz on page 29. Add up your points to determine your grilling personality.

1. a=2; b=3; c=3; d=1

2. a=1; b=3; c=1

3. a=3; b=1; c=1

4. a=1; b=3; c=2

5. a=1; b=3; c=2

6. a=1; b=3; c=2

7. a=1; b=3; c=2

8. a=1; b=3; c=3

8–10 points: Die-Hard Charcoal Fan. You sneer at the "convenience" of gas grilling. You are beyond Scout and heading toward Caveperson. At parties, you're the boisterous voice in the corner. Everyone secretly admires your sense of humor and, believe us, they want your recipe for ribs more than they're letting on. Make them beg for it.

11–18 points: Crossover Artist. A delightfully flexible person, you're the center of attention at parties, usually surrounded by admirers. Your backyard is filled with grills, both gas and charcoal. You sparkle when you entertain, even though underneath it all you may be a bundle of nerves. Your grace is your ace up your sleeve. Your friends love you because you are so considerate.

19–24 points: Gas or Bust. For you there simply is no choice. Give you a controlled flame and great marinade and you won't bother anyone. Quick, decisive, in command. You approach the cutting board with confidence and people are always angling for a dinner invitation at your house. You ask yourself if it is you or your grill.

ACKNOWLEDGMENTS

The authors would like to offer special thanks: To the entire Stephen family. Trust is a great thing—thanks for believing in this project. We hope we've done you proud. To Christina Schroeder, whose vision and passion fueled the fire. To Betty Hughes, Weber's true grilling guru, who started it all and has shared her invaluable expertise with us down through the years. To Susan Maruyama for planting the seed for this book and setting us on the road to make it a reality. To all of those who helped in the development and testing of the recipes, especially John Carroll, Russell Cronkhite, Marie Simmons, and Bob and Coleen Simmons. To Marsha Capen, who painstakingly edited every recipe in her unwavering commitment to make each one perfect. To David Wojdyla and the creative team at the advertising agency & Wojdyla—great save! To Tim Turner, Lynn Gagné, and Rod LaFleur for your stellar work, and for lending us your culinary experience to make this book that much better. To Bob Aufuldish for turning the cover on a dime. To Bill LeBlond, Jason Mitchell, and all the amazing folks at Chronicle Books whose skill at the art of bookmaking is inspirational. And finally, to Mike Kempster, Sr.: Weber wouldn't be Weber without you. We're all blessed to know you and work with you.

Personal thanks to Fran Purviance for giving thoughtful opinions and being a tremendous support throughout the whole process. To Joe and Sarah Sajbel for their loving support and incredible patience—you are a blessing and a joy!—and to Nana McRae for babysitting and more. To all the folks at St. Remy Media, especially Elizabeth Lewis, our most devoted and infinitely patient editor/counselor; Michelle Turbide, the most diplomatic deadline enforcer ever to crack a whip; and Solange Laberge, tireless juggler of layout revisions.

Special thanks to the following authors, whose work has contributed greatly to our own edification: Sharon Tyler Herbst for *The New Food Lover's Companion*, James Trager for *The Food Chronology*, and Bruce Aidells and Denis Kelly for *The Complete Meat Cookbook*. Thanks also to the fine folks at Sunshine Foods in St. Helena, Calif., who always made time to answer our questions.

St. Remy Media would like to thank the following for their contributions: Philippe Arnoldi, Jessica Braun, Lorraine Doré, Sergio Evangelista, Peter Fedun, Dominique Gagné, Pascale Hueber, Patrick Jougla, Rob Lutes, Alexander Ostrofsky, Reuben Ostrofsky, Odette Sévigny, and Roxanne Tremblay.